Making History Now and Then

Making History
Now and Then

Discoveries, Controversies and Explorations

DAVID CANNADINE

Softcover reprint of the hardcover 1st edition 2008 978-0-230-21889-5

First published 2008 by
PALGRAVE MACMILLAN
Houndmills, Basingstoke, Hampshire RG21 6XS and
175 Fifth Avenue, New York, N.Y. 10010
Companies and representatives throughout the world

PALGRAVE MACMILLAN is the global academic imprint of the Palgrave Macmillan division of St. Martin's Press, LLC and of Palgrave Macmillan Ltd. Macmillan® is a registered trademark in the United States, United Kingdom and other countries. Palgrave is a registered trademark in the European Union and other countries.

ISBN 978-1-349-30470-7   ISBN 978-0-230-59426-5 (eBook)
DOI 10.1057/9780230594265

This book is printed on paper suitable for recycling and made from fully managed and sustained forest sources. Logging, pulping and manufacturing processes are expected to conform to the environmental regulations of the country of origin.

A catalogue record for this book is available from the British Library.

A catalog record for this book is available from the Library of Congress.

10   9   8   7   6   5   4   3   2
17   16   15   14   13   12   11   10   09

*To
the
Staff,
Members,
Friends
and
Benefactors
of the
Institute of Historical Research,
1998–2008
in
Gratitude,
Admiration
and
Affection*

Any society that is alive is a society
with a history.

Vaclav Havel
Open Letters: Selected Prose, 1965–1990
(London, 1991), p. 73

Contents

Preface   ix

Prologue: Making History, Now!   1

1. Perspectives: One Hundred Years of History in Britain   19
2. Monarchy: Crowns and Contexts, Thrones and Dominations   39
3. Parliament: Past History, Present History, Future History   59
4. Economy: The Growth and Fluctuations of the Industrial
   Revolution   83
5. Heritage: The Historic Environment in Historical Perspective   112
6. Tradition: Inventing and Re-Inventing the 'Last Night of
   the Proms'   135
7. Nation: British Politics, British History and British-ness   171
8. Dominion: Britain's Imperial Past in Canada's Imperial Past   196
9. Empire: Some Anglo-American Ironies and Challenges   214
10. Recessional: Two Historians, the Sixties and Beyond   235

Epilogue: Making History, Then?   274

Appendix: On Reviewing and Being Reviewed   298

Acknowledgements   307
Notes   308
Index   380

Preface

There are two good reasons why I have called this book *Making History Now and Then*. The first is that it conflates and amalgamates the titles of the inaugural and valedictory lectures with which I began and ended my ten-year association (initially as Director, subsequently as Queen Elizabeth the Queen Mother Professor of British History) with the Institute of Historical Research, located in the Senate House of the University of London, which intrudes itself between Malet Street and Russell Square, and is just a few minutes' walk from the British Museum in one direction, and from the British Library in another. These hello-goodbye opinion pieces are printed here as the prologue and epilogue to a book which is very much the product of these London years and of these London locations, and which they thus appropriately frame. Taken together, as both a manifesto and as a retrospective, they give some indication of what I was appointed to do, of what I set out to do, and of what I was able to accomplish at the IHR between 1998 and 2008, in terms of academic leadership and administration, fund-raising and development, entrepreneurship and outreach, research and writing, public service and cultural engagement. As these two lectures record, there are many ways of making history, in terms of promoting it, writing it and (in a minor way) actually becoming part of it, even (perhaps especially) for an academic based in Bloomsbury, where the scholarly and the public worlds so often encounter each other and where (best of all) they merge and meld and morph into one another.

During my decade at the IHR, I was constantly reminded that its reach and its remit were national and international as well as local and metropolitan, and in furtherance of this agenda, I was myself as willing to get out of London as I was happy to be there. Moreover, there was ample opportunity to go away, as I regularly received invitations to speak elsewhere in the United Kingdom, and also in the United States, on such matters as the current condition of the discipline of history, on the ways in which it had evolved across the twentieth century (and also evolved across the Atlantic), and on changing attitudes to such new-old subjects as monarchy and parliament, heritage and tradition, nation and empire.

Some of these were topics with which I was already familiar, about which I had written before, and about which I discovered I still had things left to say; others were entirely new to me, which rendered them, if anything, even more challenging and appealing. Either way, they seemed to me to be subjects that transcended mere ephemeral interest, I greatly enjoyed the opportunities to research, think and speak about them, and I invariably learned a lot in the ensuing discussions. Although these lectures and addresses were one-off occasions for my hosts and for my audiences, it soon became clear to me that they were inter-linked and inter-connected pieces, and I resolved to bring them together as a book when they reached a critical mass and when the time was ripe.

That mass and that time are now, respectively, reached and ripe; so here is the resulting harvest from this decade of doing and making history, both here in London and beyond. In preparing them for publication, I have extensively modified, re-written, extended and developed the original lecture-texts, I have brought them into closer and more direct relation with one another, and in this, their final form, they constitute the substance of the pages that follow. As it happens, three of these ten chapters had been written before I took up my jobs at the IHR, but they were already addressing very similar issues, and I have substantively revised and updated them for inclusion here, since they formed a kind of retrospective starting-point for the new work of this kind that I began to undertake in London from 1998 onwards. Together, they are unified by a concern to explore some of the ways in which history is being made (meaning written and practised) in the present and in which history has been made (again meaning written and practised) in the past; and as such they furnish the second and greater reason for launching this book with the title that it bears. For the study of history, as E.H. Carr once famously observed, is an unending dialogue between the past and the present, between the then and the now, and this book eavesdrops on some snatches of that conversation – a conversation which is not only eternal, but also essential. For as the epigraph to this book makes plain, I wholeheartedly share Vaclav Havel's belief that in any society which claims to be alive and well, sane and flourishing, and open and democratic, such past-and-present dialogues are not an optional extra, but are a vital component of individual self-awareness and of collective well-being.

I have recorded particular thanks as they are due in the chapters which follow, but there are also some more general debts which I incurred during the ten years that I worked in the Senate House, and it is a pleasure to acknowledge them here: to three Vice-Chancellors of the University of London (Graeme Davies, the late Andrew Rutherford, and Graham Zellick); to three senior administrators (Tony Bell, John Davidson, and John Morgan); to three Deans of the School of Advanced Study (Terence Daintith, Roderick Floud, and Nicholas Mann); and to two Directors of sister institutes (James Dunkerley and Gary MacDowell). At the IHR itself, I owe much to four Chairs of its Advisory Council (Martin Daunton, Peter Marshall, Jinty Nelson, and Rick Trainor); to my predecessors and successors in the Director's chair (F.M.L. Thompson, Patrick O'Brien, and David Bates); to the senior staff (John Beckett, Helen Cornish, Matthew Davies, Diana Greenway, Joyce Horn, Clyve Jones, Michael Kandiah, Derek Keene, Elisabeth Kehoe, Robert Lyons, Olwen Myhill, Mel Porter, Virginia Preston, Dick Roberts, Bridget Taylor, Alan Thacker, Pat Thane, Caroline Underwood, Elaine Walters, Michelle Waterman, Elizabeth Williamson, and Jane Winters); and to my former assistants (Charlotte Alston, Debra Birch, Samantha Jordan, and Cathy Pearson). I am also deeply grateful to the Linbury Trust (John and Anya Sainsbury, Patricia Morison, and Philip Lawford), to the Andrew W. Mellon Foundation of New York (Bill Bowen, Harriet Zuckerman, and Joseph Meisel), and to two anonymous benefactors, for generously financing the Queen Elizabeth the Queen Mother Professorship during my tenure of that chair.

In preparing this book for publication, it is a pleasure to acknowledge the help and assistance of Helen McCarthy, and of my agents Gill Coleridge (in London) and Michael Carlisle (in New York). It has been an equal delight to work with the staff of Palgrave Macmillan, especially my editor Michael Strang, and I am also grateful to Oliver Howard for copy-editing the text, to Tracey Day for her work on the proofs, to Sue Carlton for compiling the index, and to Ray Addicott of Chase Publishing Services for seeing the book through the press. While working at the IHR, I have become more than ever convinced that history is as much about engaging with the present as it is about the study of the past, and for providing both inspiration and reassurance, I thank Andrew Adonis, the late Noel Annan, Timothy Garton Ash, Melvyn Bragg, Gordon Brown, Richard Carrick, John Chilcott, Kevin Clancy, Patrick Cormack, Neil Cossons, Mark Damazer, Mark Fisher, Christopher Frayling, the late Ian Gilmour, Gareth Griffiths, Nicholas Henderson, Peter Hennessy, Eric Hobsbawm, Jennifer Jenkins, the late Roy Jenkins, Simon Jenkins, Nicholas Kenyon,

Mervyn King, Nomi Levy-Carrick, Mark Lewisohn, Oscar Lewisohn, Neil
MacGregor, Claus Moser, Sandy Nairne, Elaine Paintin, Jill Pellew, David
Reynolds, Peter Riddell, Emma Rothschild, Jacob Rothschild, John Sainty,
Paul Seaward, John Shakeshaft, Keith Simpson, Charles Saumarez Smith,
Simon Thurley, John Tusa, Giles Waterfield, Merlin Waterson, Stewart
Wood, the late Giles Worsley, Tony Wright, and the late Hugo Young.
But once again, my best and most loving thanks go Linda Colley, who has
herself made history, now and then.

David Cannadine
Institute of Historical Research,
Senate House,
University of London
1 July 2008

Prologue:
Making History, Now!

On the afternoon of 12 November 1940, Winston Churchill rose to address the assembled House of Commons, and delivered his parliamentary tribute to Neville Chamberlain, the man whom he had succeeded as Prime Minister, and who had died earlier that month.[1] It was a spacious and eloquent speech, noteworthy for its breadth of vision, for its generosity of feeling, for its ready appreciation of the transience of public esteem and renown, and for its imaginative sympathy with the cruel disillusion of disappointed hopes. For historians of the twentieth-century Conservative Party, no less than for students of Churchillian rhetoric, it is an oration which merits careful analysis and close attention.[2] But my interest in it today centres on some remarks which come early in the speech, and which might have been composed with the imperatives of inaugural-lecture-giving very much in mind. 'History', Churchill observed, 'with its flickering lamp, stumbles along the trail of the past, trying to reconstruct its scenes, to revive its echoes, and kindle with pale gleams the passions of former days.' And he went on to pose a question which historians should ask themselves every day throughout their working lives, and which I welcome the opportunity to reflect on this afternoon. 'What', Churchill inquired, 'is the worth of all this?'[3]

Oddly enough, this is rarely a question addressed by those professors of history in British universities who have recently risked inaugurating themselves in this very exposed and public manner.[4] Understandably, most of them believe that the worth of history can be taken for granted, and that they have more important and original things to be talking about: in some cases by presenting the fruits of their own research, which highlight the importance and liveliness of their chosen branch of study; in others by reviewing their own field, by affirming its general significance, and by saying something that is both synthetic and provocative; or just occasionally by trying to put forward and develop one single, 'big idea'.[5] But Churchill's naggingly insistent inquiry remains one which it is essential to ask and to answer – especially here in the Senate House, in the very

1

heart of London, where cloistered academe and bustling public affairs inevitably and fruitfully intermingle, where it is impossible to ignore the 'world at large' which it is the historian's duty to reach and enlighten, and where the Institute of Historical Research has flourished for more than three quarters of a century as a local, national and international centre of scholarly excellence and educational outreach.[6]

It is, then, by turns both exciting and challenging to stand here this afternoon in a direct line of directorial descent from A.F. Pollard, who established the Institute of Historical Research in London in 1921, as a 'world centre' for the study of the past and for the dissemination of scholarly learning about it, and who spent much of his subsequent career developing it, protecting it, and raising money for it.[7] Yet these were only a part of his creative accomplishments, as an enabler and as an academic. For Pollard was the most outstanding Tudor historian of his day, and the primacy of London University in sixteenth-century studies, which lasted well into the 1950s, was largely owning to his example, his inspiration and his research students.[8] He was also Professor of Constitutional History at University College, London, where he did more than anyone to make history an important subject of undergraduate education in this university. He was an assistant editor of the *Dictionary of National Biography*, the founder of the Historical Association, the saviour and editor of its journal *History*, and a staunch supporter of the *Victoria County History*, which he helped bring to the IHR in 1934.[9] And he was eventually drawn into public work: during the 1930s, he advised the government about the League of Nations, and he vigorously supported the scheme for a *History of Parliament* initiated by his friend Colonel Josiah Wedgwood.[10]

To follow in the footsteps of someone who excelled with equal energy and distinction in the realms of scholarship and administration, fund-raising and outreach, entrepreneurship and public service, and who possessed an unrivalled capacity to 'make things happen', is simultaneously humbling and exhilarating.[11] But I only recently discovered just how humbling it was, when I came across a letter from Pollard to Wedgwood, written in 1936. 'I am', he admitted, 'hopelessly tied to the IHR.... I don't know what will happen when I cease to be Honorary Director. They will probably offer £1,200.00 a year to someone – and then fail to get a competent person.'[12] Since Pollard was eventually followed by V.H. Galbraith, en route from a chair at Edinburgh University to the Regius Professorship in Oxford, his successor's competence could scarcely have been in doubt. I, on the other hand, come to the Senate House by way of Columbia University, New York (where, by agreeable coincidence, Pollard was once himself a visiting professor), and this must be both my excuse and my justification for sketching out an answer to Churchill's question which may seem transatlantically brash, broad and bold. How, to reformulate his inquiry in more specific and immediate terms, do the profession and practice of history in Britain look to someone who has returned to them after ten years away? What is happening to history in this country, what is going to happen to history, and what ought to be happening? And what part does – and should – the Institute of Historical Research play in these unfolding developments?[13]

I

The good news must surely be that in the Britain of the late 1990s, history seems to matter a great deal. Take the case – our case – of higher education. One of the many things the IHR does is to generate data about historians actively working in British universities: in January 1980, there were 1,999 of them; in January this year there were 2,896. Of course, these figures are inflated by the enhancement in status of former polytechnics in the middle of this decade: but that is not a sufficient explanation for the 50 per cent increase during that time. The *Annual Bibliographies of British History* published by the Royal Historical Society reveal a similar upward trend: in 1989, 3,222 authors published 1,116 books and 2,561 articles; in 1997 the figures were, respectively, 6,064, 2,016 and 4,748.[14] Again, there are difficulties of interpretation: books on British history are written by overseas scholars and by those not employed in universities; and many British-based university historians write about countries other than their own. But it seems highly unlikely that these caveats would substantially modify the general picture: a near-doubling in numbers of authors, books and articles. And here, in further corroboration of this optimistic view of things, is one final statistic; in the Research Assessment Exercise of 1992, only five departments of history out of 83 were awarded the highest ranking (at that time a grade five); but by 1996, 27 departments out of 107 were rated five or five star.[15]

The provisional conclusion to be drawn from these statistics might be that everything in Clio's mansion is fine. Since the end of the Second World War returned scholars from Bletchley to their books, and from fighting Germans to teaching Britons, two full generations of university-based historians have been unprecedentedly abundant in their numbers, unprecedentedly productive in their output, and unprecedentedly distinguished in their quality. And these impressive and encouraging trends have merely intensified in the 1990s: the best decade for history in Britain so far. There are more university-based historians teaching and researching and writing here today than ever before; they are producing more scholarly work here today than ever before; and so it is scarcely surprising that the general standard of history departments in this country is rising. Under these circumstances, it is difficult not to smile at those gloom-mongers who claimed, in the early 1990s, that our subject was in a terminal crisis: in part because post-modern critics doubted history's claims and historians' capacities to tell the truth about anything; in part because it had become over-specialized to the point of complete incoherence; and in part because the triumph of liberal-democratic, free-market capitalism meant that history itself had now come to an end.[16]

How wrong, in retrospect, these paranoiacs and pessimists were! For history in Britain today seems more vital and vigorous than it has ever been: stimulated and enriched by the insights of post-modernism, rather than overwhelmed and undermined by them; and with its claims that it seeks and finds something of the truth of what really happened in the past both vindicated and reasserted. Nor, as we look around the world today, does it seem remotely plausible to argue that the historical discipline ran out of subject matter somewhere about the year 1990, and that history had indeed come to a full stop.[17] Still less has history vanished from the broader public culture and public consciousness of which it has always been a part. Senior politicians from Roy Jenkins via Ian Gilmour to Alan Clark write hugely popular histories and biographies. There are more knighted and ennobled historians today than at any earlier time. The Chancellor of the Exchequer, Gordon Brown, has a Ph.D. in history.[18] The former editor of *History Today*, Gordon Marsden, is an MP and (a much more exclusive distinction, this!) he is also a member of the Advisory Council of the IHR. In recent years there has been a clutch of best-selling history books, from such writers as John Keegan, Orlando Figes, Richard Overy and Niall Ferguson. And who can doubt that Simon Schama's forthcoming television history of Britain will hold hundreds of thousands of people agog and enthralled at the millennium?[19]

Thus regarded, history is indeed flourishing in Britain as never before, and so, too, are its principal – and abiding – justifications. For history is above all a *humane* subject, providing the quintessential 'liberal education', which does much more than research and record and teach about particular episodes and periods in the past. At a deeper level, history makes plain the complexity and contingency of human affairs and the range and variety of human experience; it enjoins suspicion of simplistic analysis, simplistic explanation, and simplistic prescription; it teaches proportion, perspective, reflectiveness, breadth of view, tolerance of differing opinions, and thus a greater sense of self-knowledge.[20] By enabling us to know about other centuries and other cultures, it provides, along with the collections housed in our great museums and galleries, the best antidote to the temporal parochialism which assumes that the only time is *now*, and the geographical parochialism which assumes that the only place is *here*. There is not only here and now; there is there; and there is then. And the best guide to there and then, and thus also the best guide to here and now, is history: in part because it helps us understand how our world got to be the way it is; in part because it helps us understand how other worlds got to be the way they were – and the way they are. History has always been rightly justified in these terms, and they still provide the most convincing answer to Churchill's question.[21]

All this is right and true and good. But only as far as it goes; and it does not go very far: certainly not as far as it ought, and not as far as it once did. It may, for example, be true that there are more historians working in British universities than ever before, but this does not necessarily mean that all is well. Far from being (as some post-modernist critics claim) an entrenched and intolerant power elite, ruthlessly controlling knowledge and foisting a dominant bourgeois ideology on powerless and malleable students, teachers of history in British universities seem almost without exception to be underpaid and overworked, to feel insufficiently respected or rewarded, and to be suffering from extremely low morale.[22] They discourage their brightest students from following in their footsteps, on the (highly responsible) grounds that their prospects would be bleak; and many of them, once they reach their forties, are waiting and longing for early retirement. It may be objected that this is merely anecdotal evidence, and that ever since the days of Kingsley Amis's Jim Dixon, historians have always been alienated, depressed and complaining. But when A.H. Halsey wrote about British academics in 1992, he found these characteristics to be widespread across the whole profession, and there seems no evidence that things have improved in the intervening period. There is, then, something to be said for John Vincent's view that 'Historians today are not the holders of power.... They live among the foothills of society, where they engage anxiously in downward social mobility.'[23]

This may be an exaggeration; but not, I suspect, by all that much. For academics in general, and historians in particular, have in recent decades undergone the dismal experience of becoming proletarianized: losing income, status, facilities, prospects, autonomy and security. Yet at the same time, this large and depressed professoriate has been producing a superabundance of material, with all the frenzied energy of battery chickens on overtime, laying for their lives.[24] Two thousand books and nearly five thousand articles is a prodigious quantity of specialized information about the past to produce – and all this in only one country in only one year! Indeed, it is not only prodigious: it is, in a sense, preposterous. For who, apart from the History Panel of the Research Assessment Exercise, is actually reading all this stuff? Certainly not the general public or undergraduates: they confine themselves, respectively, to the few history books that get wide coverage in the broadsheets and to prescribed lists of recommended reading. And certainly not professional historians: for so great is the information overload from which we are suffering that no scholar today, however eager, however energetic, however curious, can keep up in his (or her) own field, even narrowly defined (say one country across a hundred years), let alone hope to read more broadly.[25] The result is that much of this vast published output is read by so small an audience that it is tempting to wonder, in a pessimistic re-formulation of Churchill's question: what is the point of writing it or of publishing it? To which, in many cases, the only answer is the compelling need to meet the demands and the dictates of the RAE.

But this is not the only damaging effect which the Research Assessment Exercise is having on history and on historians, for in addition to inflating the quantity of output, it is deflating the quality. Indeed, it is widely believed that the RAE is obsessed with quantity, and largely indifferent to quality. The imperatives for regular and rapid production are now so great and so insistent that the overall standard of published output in history is generally thought to be declining, and it is easy to see why. What might, in an earlier era, have been one big, important, provocative, ground-breaking article is now salami-sliced into three, to give more impressive evidence of quantity of output.[26] What might, in the 1960s or 1970s, have been a lengthily researched and deeply pondered book – say J.H. Plumb's *The Growth of Political Stability in England, 1675–1725* (London, 1967), or Robinson and Gallagher's *Africa and the Victorians* (London, 1961), or E.P. Thompson's *The Making of the English Working Class* (London, 1963), or Keith Thomas's *Religion and the Decline of Magic* (London, 1971) – becomes instead a prematurely published survey, with inadequate documentation and insufficiently thought-through argument, or an arid and lifeless monograph selling fewer than two or three hundred copies, which scarcely anyone reads. The obsession with output and performance requires visible and measurable products. But a culture of *productivity* is not only different from, it is inimical to, a culture of *creativity* – a point to which I shall return.[27]

These developments are not only intrinsically regrettable: they also carry with them extremely worrying public consequences. For as historians are compelled to grind out their specified quota of specialized articles and inaccessible monographs, which are at best read only by a handful of professional colleagues, and are at worst almost completely ignored, this makes them less and less able to fulfil that essential public function which remains their real and abiding justification: satisfying the interest and furthering the comprehension of that broader, non-professional audience memorably described by Hugh Trevor-Roper as 'the laity'.[28] Yet in a world ever more burdened by an infinite amount of information, instantly available, the need to provide a humane and historical perspective on people and events becomes more urgent, not less. For it seems generally agreed that we live in a society which is increasingly amnesiac and ahistorical: where many politicians (and many think-tanks) seem to believe the world began on 1 May 1997;[29] where historians of my generation wield far less cultural authority than those of an earlier era;[30] where the media coverage of events is increasingly devoid of any temporal dimension; and where the Millennium will be marked by a Dome from which history has been conspicuously and unconscionably excluded.[31]

Please do not misunderstand what I am saying. I do not deny that our universities, being in receipt of substantial sums of government money, should be accountable to our paymasters for the way that it is spent, and should recognize their obligations to try to explain what they do to the general public.[32] I have no time for those historians who spend their lives storing up vast mounds of esoteric erudition, but who can scarcely bring

themselves to write an article, let alone a book, and who are condescend-
ingly remembered and euphemistically obituarized as good teachers and
sound college chaps. I accept absolutely, and I recognize with appreciation
and delight, that some work is still being published by professional,
university-based historians, which is either of a high quality, or reaches a
broad audience, or both. My concern is that there is a growing discrepancy
between the figures, produced in the name of accountability, which suggest
that everything is fine and getting better, and the reality, which is in truth
much more complex and much more sombre. In producing more and more
goods, on which a diminishing value is placed, while the customer looks
elsewhere for novelty and excitement, late twentieth-century historians are
increasingly coming to resemble another sad, demoralized and proletarianized fraternity: the handloom weavers of the early nineteenth century.[33]
This is, no doubt, an over-theatrical comparison; and it is also, perhaps,
a rather parochial parallel. For having looked at British historians as a
collective group, I should now like to turn to take a rather broader view
of things, which means, inevitably and unapologetically, encompassing
both a national and a transatlantic perspective.

II

The case for such a broader approach should scarcely need making, yet
perhaps it does. Historians are supposed to advocate and exemplify viewing
people and processes and problems in perspective and in proportion.
They are also supposed to be the fearless champions of the pursuit of
truth (however inconvenient, uncomfortable and unpalatable), and of the
right to follow their evidence and their argument wheresoever they might
lead. How, then, do we historians look today if we apply these precepts
and practices to ourselves? Like all working academics who are based in
universities, British historians live and move and have their being in two
separate but interconnected worlds: one is the national university system
which employs us to teach, to research, to write and (increasingly) to
administer and sit on committees; the other is the international republic of
letters which constitutes a cosmopolitan fellowship of like-minded scholars,
working on similar subjects and dealing with similar problems, and which
also functions as a global job market for academic talent. How do the
anxieties (and the accomplishments) of British historians working and

writing today look when set in these broader national and international contexts?

Let me begin by making some international comparisons, the first of which gives grounds for comfort, the second of which does not. Compared with most university systems in western Europe (to say nothing of those in eastern Europe or Asia or Africa), British universities are in relatively good shape. Here in Britain, student numbers are generally smaller, staff–student ratios are generally better, and degree courses are generally more rigorous and more serious enterprises, than they are on the continent. Our funding is also more stable and more secure, and British academics are certainly not hired and fired at the behest of the state, or expected to ply their trade in conformity with the current party ideology of whoever happens to be in power. These are privileges and benefits of enormous importance, which we here in Britain are inclined to take too easily for granted.[34] But in France and Germany and Italy, universities are less well resourced and more over-subscribed than they are here, while in the former Communist bloc, it is going to take years to construct a viable, independent university system, emancipated from the thralldom of Marxist dogma and thought control, and from decades of inadequate funding. It may be that with abundant and imaginative assistance from the European Union, continental universities will be revived and reinvigorated; but at present that prospect still seems some way off.[35]

But if we turn our perspective westwards, the comparison is much less to the advantage of British universities – and this in two very serious ways. To begin with, even the richest British universities are chronically under-funded and under-endowed compared to their American counterparts. Consider the facts. In the summer of 1998, the market value of the endowments of Columbia, Stanford, Princeton, Yale and Harvard Universities was, respectively, $3.4, $4.5, $5.5, $6.6 and $13 billion; and in the months since then, the buoyant stock market means these endowments have increased still further. These are prodigious accumulations of academic wealth, by comparison with which even the riches of Oxford and Cambridge (so often pilloried and criticized in the press) pale into relative insignificance.[36] And it is this superabundance of material resources which in turn makes so much else possible in the world of American higher education – not just the higher professorial salaries (true and important though those undoubtedly are), but the broader and deeper back-up of support in teaching and research, and the fostering of a buoyant, optimistic environment where these activities are seen and supported, promoted and valued, as the whole point and purpose of university life – and of life beyond, in the wider national public culture.[37]

Moreover, it is not just that even the richest British universities are chronically under-funded and under-endowed by comparison with American universities, with all the disadvantages and limitations that that entails: it is also that they are no less chronically over-bureaucratized. Of course, American universities have to be administered, and they, too, have their hierarchies of committees. But they are more concerned with spending money than (as in Britain) with worrying about how little of it there will be, and how to second guess the aims and actions of the funding councils; and there is still in the United States a widespread insistence that professors should be given as much freedom as possible to get on with the things they are expert at and employed to do, namely research and teaching. Indeed, those professors who show particular distinction are rewarded with promotions which give them extra time to teach and write, by protecting them from the distracting demands of administration. In Britain, the position is the exact reverse – and it is getting worse. In part this is because the more eminent and the more promoted British academics become, the more administration they are expected to undertake; and in part this is because the insistent and growing demands from the government for accountability bring with them ever more committees and meetings.[38]

It is this debilitating combination of inadequate resources and excessive bureaucracy which has brought about the proletarianization of British academic life, the increasingly pervasive culture of accountability and productivity, and the consequent (and very serious) loss of academic freedom. These developments are not only regrettable in themselves: they are also inimical to any serious culture of creativity.[39] For most hard-pressed academics, lacking adequate time and resources, research and writing are now relegated to a low-level, residual activity, to be fitted in to those few hours or days when there are no more pressing obligations. This may still allow for the grinding out of routine pieces of research and writing, but it is not an environment in which serious or sustained or original or wide-ranging creative labour can be carried on, which will open up a whole new subject, or treat an old problem in an entirely new way, or capture the imagination and interest of the general public. Here is one account of such endeavour, which ought to be a model for us all. In 1908, the young George Macaulay Trevelyan declined an invitation to become Director of the fledgling London School of Economics. His chief reason was that he was 'in the middle of another job', by which he meant the writing of his Garibaldi books. It required, he explained, 'a complete devotion of all my faculties; I work up to breaking point as it is'. He was bursting with 'masses of specialised knowledge and thought': 'the whole thing is in me, and I must pour it out or it will cool'. 'History to me', he went on, 'is both science and an art; science and art are severally the most exacting things in the world.' 'So you see', he concluded, 'I can't break off this job, and slow off the pace.'[40]

Most of us today cannot hope to rival Trevelyan's prodigious gifts of head and heart, mind and spirit. We lack his dynastic pride, his personal confidence, his abundant energies, his imaginative sweep, his passion for poetry no less than for prose. But as historians, we should never lose sight of the fact that this is precisely the sort of intense, original, brain-fatiguing, time-consuming labour to which all of us should aspire – or, at least, to which all of us should try to aspire. And we should never cease to deplore those developments in higher education which not only make such aspirations as unrealistic as they are unrealizable, but which are also the result of decisions taken, and policies implemented, by people who seem to have no comprehension of what those creative activities and aspirations are, or mean, or why they matter. And behold the result: at all levels of the historical profession, most British academics today are less free and confident and creative and imaginative than their American counterparts. I do not mean this as a criticism of them, any more than I am criticizing hard-pressed vice-chancellors, battle-scarred administrators, and stressed-out heads of department, for whose heroic labours my admiration is boundless. But no amount of fudging and fixing by them can summon up those material resources and personal freedoms from government interference without which a culture of creativity can neither exist nor thrive.[41]

This is, to put it at its most understated, a very serious matter: in part because senior administrators lack the time, the funds and the confidence to get their universities out of a predicament into which they have been forced by circumstances beyond their control; in part because the broader implications have not been fully spelt out, adequately discussed, or properly thought through. It remains the belief of some in Britain, reinforced by the many five and five star ratings so liberally given out in the 'fever of enhancement' that characterized the 1996 Research Assessment Exercise, that our best universities and university departments are successfully competing with the best universities and departments in the world – which means, of course, with those in North America.[42] But on the basis of such transatlantic experiences I have had, and of such transatlantic comparisons as I and others have been able to make, I have to report that that view is at best nostalgic delusion, at worst mistaken fact. For as even the richest and most privileged of British universities become, by comparison with the richest and most privileged of American universities, relatively less rich, relatively more bureaucratized, relatively less creative, and relatively more un-free, this means the capacity of Cambridge, or Oxford, or the colleges of London University to compete on equal terms with Harvard, or Yale, or Princeton or Stanford or Chicago dwindles and diminishes by the day.[43]

Perhaps this is inevitable and unavoidable: for in the long run, universities, like nations, tend to rise and fall. Indeed, they tend to rise and fall together, since great powers are generally rich powers, and rich nations can better afford world-class universities than poor nations. In an earlier era, Bologna and Prague and Heidelberg and Paris were the pre-eminent universities of the world; that supremacy passed to Edinburgh and Glasgow and Cambridge and Oxford and London; now it is passing to Harvard and Yale and Princeton and Stanford and Chicago.[44] Perhaps we should resign ourselves to the inevitable, and recognize that in higher education, as in everything else, there is an international division of labour, and accept that in this world league, as in so many others, from cars to cricket, Britain is no longer a serious competitor at the very highest level. I am not myself sure we should give up so easily: and we should certainly not give up before the matter has been properly aired and debated and discussed. But if we do not wish to give up, then we have to address, and to address very soon as a matter of urgent national importance, a question which no one in high places is even prepared to admit needs to be posed: does Britain want to make the effort to continue to maintain even a handful of world-class universities in this country on into the next century? And if it does, then what, in terms of massively increased endowments and funding, and no less massively reduced intrusion and bureaucracy, is it prepared to do about it?[45]

As Noel Annan has recently and rightly written, the life blood of any university with serious claims to distinction is 'outstanding and productive scholars, devoted and stimulating teachers, men and women of originality and imagination, open-hearted and magnanimous'.[46] There are many people working in British universities today who embody and exemplify these admirable, indeed essential, qualities: but everywhere, from Oxford to Luton, Cambridge to Huddersfield, Edinburgh to Bath, they are held back, kept down, hemmed in, by a system which, through no fault of their own, hinders and harasses them, instead of encouraging and liberating them. Under these circumstances – by turn dispiriting and depressing, but still with the hope, indeed the necessity, of action and response – I am reminded of Marshal Foch's defiant words at the Battle of the Marne, which well sum up the present, shell-shocked state of British academe, and which will also provide the theme for the final part of my lecture: 'Hard pressed on my right', Foch observed. 'My centre is yielding. Impossible to manoeuvre. Situation excellent. I shall attack.'[47]

III

But how? It may seem to be journeying a long way from these general (and rather gloomy) considerations, to turn to the Institute of Historical Research, which it has been both my responsibility and my delight to have been directing for almost exactly twelve months. Yet I would want to insist that this is not so. From one perspective, the IHR partakes of the generally depressed character of contemporary British academe; from another, it holds out the hope and the possibility of escaping from it. For as I have already suggested, it is at once the burden and the opportunity of history that it is both a demanding academic discipline and an integral part of contemporary public culture, and from its prime location here in London, the Institute of Historical Research is ideally positioned to bear those burdens and rise to those challenges. For more than 75 years since Pollard first founded it, it has been a unique place and a unique resource – for scholars living and working within the orbit of the M25, for historians throughout the length and breadth of the United Kingdom, for academics from around the world for whom it is their first and last port of call in Britain, and for all those who care about the past, and regard it as an essential element in public consciousness, cultural enrichment and civilized living.

There is much about what the IHR has achieved and now does that gives cause for pride and satisfaction. Its library, amounting to 160,000 volumes, is the best open-access collection for historical research in Britain. Its seminars are among the most important in the English-speaking world, and they have been lead by many of the most famous and distinguished historians of their day, including Arnold Toynbee, Sir Lewis Namier, Sir John Neale, and Eric Hobsbawm. Its conferences are unrivalled in their range and frequency, and draw participants from around the globe, especially the Anglo-American Conference of Historians held here every July. Its publications are essential scholarly reading, and for more than a decade the IHR has pioneered the application of the new technology to the study and dissemination of information about the past. As befits its name, the IHR also accommodates three great collective enterprises of scholarly research and public education: the *Victoria County History*, the Centre for Metropolitan History, and (since last summer) the Institute for Contemporary British History.[48] And we are also collaborating with many of the great galleries and cultural institutions of London on research projects, conferences and exhibitions.

This wide and expanding range of services and activities, which reaches an audience across Britain, in Europe and around the world, is sustained by a devoted staff – and by inadequate funding. The Vice-Chancellor on behalf of the University of London, and the British Friends of the Institute, have between them recently provided £250,000 to refurbish parts of our building. But the IHR urgently needs to raise money which would enable it to secure and extend its mission to support the study and dissemination of history – to undergraduates, research students and professional historians; to schools, local history societies and non-academic historians; and to play a more active and engaged part in the cultural life of this city and our nation. At present the IHR enjoys an annual income of £1.5 million, mostly derived from government funding and research grants. This is insufficient for the things it does – and for the things it urgently wants – and is wanted – to do. We need additional funds to support our publications, conferences and seminars; to allow us to put on public lectures and develop our educational outreach programme; and to enable us to appoint more library, administrative and research staff. We need to refurbish parts of the library and expand its holdings, to upgrade our computer training room, to provide a lecture theatre and seminar rooms, and to create office space for an enlarged community of resident historians. We intend to make this space and this support available to junior research fellows completing their first publications; to visiting fellows and visiting professors from Britain and from overseas; and to a number of full-time research professors, who will provide academic leadership within the IHR, and who will raise its public profile in London, across Britain, in Europe, and around the world.

Our aim, then, is to make the IHR the place that Pollard dreamed it would be, but for our time rather than his – a place of welcome and excitement for all those who care about the past, and where historians will work together in a confident and creative environment; and from this secure base we shall reach out and respond to a wider world and larger audience. In short, we seek to renew the IHR as a centre where history is practised and brought alive, and where historians may work freed from many of the shackles which constrain and hold back so much of British academe today; and thus to reaffirm, by our activities, our example and our leadership, the essential importance of history in the scholarly life of our universities, and in the public life of our nation. But to accomplish all of this we need to raise a sum of not less than £20 million, and it is for contributions to that target that I am appealing to you tonight.

This is, in all conscience, a demanding enough endeavour, both in terms of what we are hoping and planning to do at the IHR, and in terms of the time it will take and the money we shall need to do it. But there is something about working in this monumental 1930s building – which, it is rumoured, would have been Hitler's headquarters had he successfully invaded England in 1940 – that encourages even more wide-ranging speculations bordering, perhaps, on megalomaniac fantasies, one of which I should like to sketch out in the remaining minutes of this lecture. My starting point is to remind you that the Institute of Historical Research is a constituent part of the School of Advanced Study of the University of London.[49] As such, it is one institute among eleven, the remainder being concerned with the law, the classics, the Commonwealth, the United States, Latin America, romance languages, Germanic Studies, English Studies, philosophy, and the influence of the classical tradition on art. Individually, these Institutes are as important for *their* subjects – locally, nationally and internationally – as the IHR is for history; and collectively, they ought to form one of the most exciting places for the advanced study of the humanities anywhere in the world – partly because of the range of subjects represented, partly because of the distinction of their staff and students, and partly because of their unrivalled location, equidistant between the British Library and the British Museum.

That is, as it were, the positive side of things, and it is a side I would very much want to emphasize. But there is a negative side as well: for the School of Advanced Study, like the individual member institutes which comprise it, is chronically under-funded, under-staffed and under-resourced. Its income for the academic year 1997–98 was less than £8 million, and its endowment is less than £5.5 million.[50] To try to run what should be a great, world-class centre for the humanities – the equivalent in London of, say, the Woodrow Wilson Center in Washington, or the Institute for Advanced Study in Princeton – on resources as limited as this is, it pains me to say, at best unrealistic, at worst impossible. Yet who can doubt that the scholarly and cultural life of London, and of the nation as whole, would be greatly enriched and enhanced by the creation, in the very heart of this world-city, of the sort of well-funded, well-endowed, highly-profiled centre that I have suggested – building on the Institutes that are already here, but consolidating and developing them into an international powerhouse of advanced learning that would draw scholars and students from all round the globe? This, I would like to suggest, ought to be the splendid and exciting future of the School of Advanced Study and of the Institutes which comprise it. The only problem? It would need an endowment substantially in excess of £100 million to make it happen. And where, in the Britain of the late 1990s, is that sum to be found?[51]

It is at this point, with speculation in full, abundant, and perhaps delirious flow, that I recall a saying of George Bernard Shaw's, which was much popularized during the 1960s by John F. Kennedy and his brother Robert Kennedy: 'Other people see things [as they are] and... say: "why?".... But I dream things that never were – and I say: "why not?"'[52] In these post-Camelot days, GBS may be a little over the top, so let me also quote A.F. Pollard once again, and in the same vein: 'It is often made a reproach to young people that they dream dreams and see visions. But if it is commonly a reproach, it becomes once again a privilege; for a vision may be one of the future, and a dream does sometimes come true.'[53] Uniquely among the historians of his day, Pollard dreamed dreams which he worked to make come true; and if he accomplished such things in his generation, then why should we shy away from trying to accomplish similar things in ours?

IV

It may be objected that these grandiloquent speculations about the form and future of higher education in London take me too far from my proper area of directorial responsibility, namely the researching and writing and teaching of history here at the IHR in the Senate House; but I would want to insist that they do no such thing. For insofar as I *have* felt compelled, on this occasion, to address these broader issues in higher education, as they impinge on our own world here in London, and as they resonate in the wider nation beyond, I have done so because the future of history in this country is inevitably and inextricably linked with the general state and health of the university system in which that writing and teaching about the past are now preponderantly carried on. But that system of higher education, as at present funded and structured, operated and audited, is incapable of delivering or nurturing those very things which universities, to be worthy of the name, should exist to sustain and promote, not just in history, but in every subject: freedom and opportunity, confidence and optimism, talent and excellence, curiosity and creativity, insight and imagination, bright ideas and big books of lasting value.

And why does this matter? Why is this how things ought to be, and need to be? Because, and once again I turn back to A.F. Pollard, 'a university should be a focus of national intellect, and a source of national inspiration; and it fulfils its function badly if it does not help to expand the national mind'.[54] This remains a fine and noble vision for higher education in this country, albeit one that is less confidently articulated and proclaimed than it was in Pollard's day. But here at the IHR, we firmly believe in our founder's vision, and proudly hold to it, and with your help and your support, your goodwill and your gifts, I hope it may be possible for us to turn the tide, and to do bold and exciting and creative and imaginative things, in the University of London, for the School of Advanced Study, and above all in the Institute of Historical Research itself. In only one way would I seek to alter Pollard's words and adjust his vision, and that is by extension of them, rather than modification. For as his successor V.H. Galbraith once explained, what was most remarkable about the IHR was that it promoted 'the study of the past', not only as a London University activity, and 'as an activity common to all British universities', but also 'as a vital international enterprise, which offers a great hope for the future'.[55] So it did, and so it does, and in recognizing the essential truth of Pollard's words, we should never lose sight of that broader vision and larger hope.

I began this lecture by quoting one great man, who never doubted that history mattered, and it is not just in the interests of symmetry and sentiment (though they have their place) that I shall conclude by quoting another great man, of similar views. They are familiar words, rich in allusion and association. But they bear repeating, because they still provide, over half a century after they were originally uttered, the best brief answer to that Churchillian interrogative which was my original starting point. And they also serve to exhort us and to remind us: about the sort of creative historians that we should try to be, about the sort of imaginative history that we should try to write and teach, and about the sort of creative and imaginative history that universities should strive to encourage, and that the Institute of Historical Research exists to cherish. Here is G.M. Trevelyan, delivering his inaugural lecture, as Regius Professor of Modern History, at the University of Cambridge in 1927:

> The poetry of history does not consist of imagination roaming at large, but of imagination pursuing the fact and fastening upon it. That which compels the historian to scorn delights and live laborious days is the ardour of his own curiosity to know what really happened long ago in that land of mystery which we call the past. To peer into that magic mirror and see fresh figures there every day is a burning desire that consumes and satisfies him all his life, and carries him each morning, eager as a lover, to the library and the muniment room.... The dead were and are not. Their place knows them no more and is ours today. Yet they were once as real as we, and we shall tomorrow be shadows like them.[56]

So, indeed, they were; so, indeed, they are; and so, indeed, we shall ourselves assuredly one day be. But meanwhile, there is life to be lived, there is work to be done, there is history to be written, and (who knows?) there may even in some small way be history to be made. We have a great deal to be getting on with. It is high time we made a start.

1

Perspectives:
One Hundred Years of History in Britain[1]

Shortly before the outbreak of the First World War, James Bryce delivered his presidential address to the British Academy, an organization which he had helped to establish in 1902 for 'the promotion of historical, philosophical and philological studies'.[2] In the course of his long, varied and distinguished career, Viscount Bryce (he was ennobled in 1907) was a lawyer, journalist, historian, explorer, Liberal MP, cabinet minister, British Ambassador to the United States, chairman of Royal Commissions, and holder of the Order of Merit. In the language of our own time, he was a fully paid-up and card-carrying member of the 'great and the good', and like many of those who belonged to the Liberal intelligentsia, he regarded history as both a demanding academic discipline and also as an essential component of the national culture.[3] Their age, Bryce told his audience, with evident approval, had seen 'an immense expansion' in historical studies and an unprecedented specialization in 'the various branches of historical inquiry': so much so, indeed, that all 'the main lines of human activity' were now recognized as coming within the bounds of those scholarly endeavours being directed towards the past. 'This widening of our field', Bryce went on, 'may be primarily due to a larger conception of history, which we have now come to regard as a record of every form of human effort and achievement' – efforts and achievements which he insisted were no longer exclusively restricted to the political activities of a privileged elite, but encompassed the deeds and doings of ordinary people.[4] In a subsequent lecture, Bryce would reaffirm this view, asserting that traditional political history was but 'a comparatively small' part of what contemporaries now understood as 'the past', and that more time was being spent studying the history of religion, industry, culture, nature, scientific discovery and the human mind.[5]

In calling for, and celebrating, such a wide-ranging and accessible approach to the study of the past, Bryce was not alone. Indeed, the first book defining and advocating something called the 'new' history had been published in America in 1912, edited by J.H. Robinson, scarcely a year before Bryce delivered his own presidential address. Yet such claims to innovation and expansiveness were at best programmatic, at worst premature: for on neither side of the Atlantic were there sufficient historians working, researching and writing, in universities or beyond academe, to realize the ambitious and broad-ranging agenda that Bryce and Robinson had sketched out for their subject. Not surprisingly, then, many later scholars, preoccupied with what they saw as the exciting and belated creation of their own version of the 'new' history in the buoyant and heady decades following the end of the Second World War, persisted in regarding the first half of the twentieth century as a dark age, and paid scant attention to what their predecessors hoped to achieve, or realistically might have expected to accomplish.[6] Such exaggerations are a salutary reminder that we should give careful and sceptical attention to the statements that practising historians often make – about themselves, their work, and their subject. For many of them make assertions concerning the novelty or importance of their own type of history which are at best over-stated, at worst incorrect; and we should assess their claims and manifestos about history with that same sort of critical acumen, contextual scrutiny and long-term perspective that we bring to bear on other forms of evidence from and about the past.[7]

In any case, such assertions of originality and significance are not the only avowals that historians make about themselves and their sub-fields which should be treated with healthy scepticism. Consider the very different view, which is widespread in many quarters, that the practice and profession of history has for some time been in a crisis so deep and so divisive that it may prove terminal.[8] According to Gertrude Himmelfarb, it has been ruined twice-over, by the sixties generation in thrall to Marx and the social sciences, and by the post-modernists no less in thrall to Foucault and Derrida: but this is little more than ignorant and paranoid ranting, not least because political history remains indestructibly alive and well. According to Peter Novick, 'the discipline of history' as 'a community of scholars, united by common aims, common standards, and common purposes' has 'ceased to exist': but this exaggerates both an earlier (and largely mythical) golden age of consent and consensus, and also the true extent of present day divisions and discontents.[9] According to Francis Fukuyama, history had come to an end with the global triumph of liberalism and democracy: but even before 9/11 in 2001, this was an implausibly parochial and naively optimistic view of human nature and world affairs. And according to Christopher Andrew, 'no period in recorded history has been so persuaded of the irrelevance of the past experience of the human race': but this is a generalization of such cosmic scope that it is impossible to see how it could be either verified or disproven.[10]

Indeed, it would be fair to say that during virtually every decade of the last one hundred years, some historians have been urging that history must be made completely anew, while others have insisted that what they regard as such modish and ephemeral fashionability threatens everything that is good and noble and decent and traditional about the discipline. But it should scarcely be a surprise that both these progressive and paranoid modes have persisted, for in scholarship, as in politics, they feed off each other: one historian's great leap forward is another historian's terminal crisis, and what is presented as an improvement and enhancement by some is regarded as a threat and a disaster by others.[11] Depending on which scholars you read, history now (as throughout the whole of the twentieth century) is either doing (and being done) very badly – or, alternatively, it is doing (and being done) very well. Paradoxically but appropriately, the only antidote to such Manichean attitudes and over-simplified perspectives is to turn back to history itself. For the way in which the study of the past evolved in Britain during the last one hundred years tells us more about what history has been – and about what history is now – than we are generally inclined to allow.[12] More precisely, much discussion of history during that period was indeed structured around deep and often bitter polarities, which turn out on close investigation to be at best exaggerated and at worst fundamentally misleading. Indeed, it is only by getting a clear picture of the practice of history and the polemics of historians during the twentieth century that we can obtain a surer and steadier perspective on the tasks which face historians today, and on the challenges which will face historians tomorrow.

I

At the beginning of the twentieth century, the past occupied a very equivocal niche in British life and British culture. There was a powerful Victorian legacy of great writers such as Lord Macaulay, J.A. Froude, Thomas Carlyle, J.R. Green and S.R. Gardiner, who wrote national, narrative histories, which reached a wide and general audience; and that reading public became yet broader after W.E. Forster's Education Act of 1870, and the expansion in public schools and grammar schools during the last quarter of the nineteenth century, which ensured that the study of the past became an essential part of what we would now call the national curriculum. At the same time, degree courses in the subject had recently been established at Oxford and Cambridge, in the Scottish universities, and on the new civic campuses of Leeds, Liverpool, Manchester, Birmingham and Sheffield.[13] Here was a new, young, mass audience for history, avidly devouring the new, multi-authored series of text books published by Methuen, Longmans and Macmillan; and here also was a new professional activity, exemplified by the setting up of the Royal Historical Society and the *English Historical Review*, and by the presence of Stubbs and Freeman in Oxford, and Seeley and Acton in Cambridge. The result was that, by the early twentieth century, knowledge of the past was deemed to be essential, not only for exercising British citizenship, but also for practising British statesmanship.[14]

In all these ways, and at all these levels, history was an institutionalized element in Britain's post-Victorian national culture to a greater extent than had been true before, and there was also widespread popular engagement with the past as evidenced by (among other things) the proliferation of historical pageants, the expansion of historical tourism and the popularity of historical novels.[15] But this was only one side of the picture: for in other ways, Britain in the 1900s was seen by many to be a worryingly ahistorical nation, with little deeply-rooted or seriously-developed or widely-shared sense of the past at all. According to Professor C.H. Firth, the teaching of history in primary schools was carried on by staff with virtually no training in the subject, while at secondary level, instruction was 'neither thorough nor systematic' – anxieties and criticisms which, across a hundred-year chasm, still retain a curiously contemporary resonance.[16] This, in turn, meant that as the twentieth century opened, many Britons seemed indifferent to the past, and it was in a (largely vain) effort to counter this pervasive ignorance of history that a whole variety of preservationist societies and proselytizing enterprises were established, most of them within a decade, either side, of 1900. Among them were the National Trust, the *Victoria County History*, the *Survey of London*, the Royal Commission on Historical Monuments, and the Historical Association. Here were some first, faltering steps towards the promotion and practice of what we would now call public history: but they were undertaken with limited membership and precarious finances, and they were not so much a sign that history was flourishing in Britain, but rather an indication that it needed all the help it could get – and it was not getting all that much.[17]

Nor was serious, academic, university-based history exactly thriving. In 1900, only two hundred graduates from Oxford and Cambridge had taken their degrees in the subject, and the total number of graduating historians in Britain can barely have been in four figures. Across the whole of the national university system, there were scarcely one hundred people teaching history, and most of them were lowly tutors and instructors, with no first-hand experience of research, scholarship or writing. (Indeed, the main reason why the same handful of names keep cropping up at this time – Tout, Firth, Stubbs, Maitland – is that there were so few scholars of any real distinction.)[18] How, indeed, could it have been otherwise, given that there was very little systematic training available in historical research? There was Tout in Manchester, Pollard in London, and there were pockets of activity in Oxbridge. But there was no national research culture or structure: of seminars, of training in source criticism, of graduate programmes or research degrees. Compared to the position in France, in Germany, or on the eastern seaboard of the United States, professional history, as those contemporaries understood it, scarcely existed in Britain. Accordingly, when Lord Bryce urged that the whole of past human experience was a fit subject for historical inquiry, he was more expressing a hope than describing a reality. For in practice, there were insufficient trained and university-based scholars to carry out so broadly-defined and labour-intensive an agenda. Indeed, when some British historians urged that their subject must be recognized as a branch of scientific inquiry, they were seeking to gain an academic recognition and professional legitimacy which at that time it conspicuously lacked.[19]

Thus history in Britain in the years from the turn of the century to the outbreak of the First World War: compared with what had gone before, it might seem unprecedentedly flourishing; compared with what would come after, it was not, in retrospect, doing especially well.[20] How, then, do we move from history as practised and perceived in Britain in 1900 to history as it is practised and perceived in Britain in our own time, a century further on? These days, historians are very wary of their capacity to explain anything, but on any hierarchy of causation, the expansion of higher education must surely be given pride of place, resulting from unprecedented commitment by successive governments to supporting a national, university-based intellectual class in both the sciences and the humanities – something that had never happened before, in the long history of this country (or, indeed, in the long history of anywhere else). One sign of this has been the successful establishment of graduate research in history, the absence of which was so much lamented before 1914. Most universities, beginning with Oxford, Cambridge and London, introduced the Ph.D. dissertation and degree between the wars, and the foundation of the Institute of Historical Research in 1921 gave a further fillip to such scholarly endeavours; but even in 1940, there were scarcely three hundred graduate students registered for research degrees in history at all levels. Since then, the number of research students in history has shot up: to 1,200 in 1960, to 2,400 in 1970, and to 3,000 in 1975 where, with slight variations, it has since remained.[21]

Here, then, was an extraordinary transformation, which could not have been foreseen in 1900, or even in 1945: the appearance during the last four decades of the twentieth century of *thousands* of qualified history Ph.D.s, and thus of potential authors and university teachers, where scarcely any had existed before. Tout and Firth and their few contemporaries would surely have been delighted, not only at this development which they had so devoutly desired (though little expected), but also at the corresponding rise in the number of learned articles and academic monographs which these young professional historians produced, thereby further (and fundamentally) transforming the academic landscape after 1945. Part cause, part consequence of this increase in the numbers of scholarly people and in the number of scholarly publications at a junior level has been a corresponding (and a correspondingly recent) explosion in the numbers of historians paid and employed to teach the subject in British universities. Even as late as 1949 there were only 548 of them, but thereafter, an expansion began which has been virtually exponential: in 1960, 800; in 1970, 1,500; in 1980, 2,000; in 1990, 2,100; in 2000, 3,000. Never have there been so many academics teaching history in universities in this country: indeed, the number in post now may be greater than the sum total of all their predecessors put together, and it cannot be too strongly emphasized just how recent and how extraordinary this change has been.[22]

It has also been transformative for history in many ways beyond the merely numerical. To begin with, it has resulted in the full-scale professionalization of the subject, following closely the model already established by the experimental sciences: with a career ladder going from post-doctoral fellow via lecturer and reader to professor; with journals, meetings, conferences and specialist societies; and with major grants, funding councils and large-scale collective research projects. A second sign of change has been the growing diversity, in the sociological sense, of those studying and teaching history in British universities: initially their backgrounds were overwhelmingly public school and Oxbridge (as recounted by Noel Annan in *Our Age*); they were followed, after the Butler Education Act of 1944, by the 'scholarship boys' who won places at Oxford, Cambridge and London (and it is that generation, which is my generation, which is now in charge); and we in turn are training and recruiting a yet more diverse cohort, many of whom have been educated at comprehensive schools and at universities far beyond the golden triangle (and of whom an unprecedented number are women and from those who are termed ethnic minorities).[23] Moreover, the combined effects of increased numbers, growing professionalism, and widening access help explain why history in practice has evolved and expanded into the wider and more varied subject that Bryce and his contemporaries had (in retrospect) prematurely anticipated; and also why, since the 1960s, there has been in existence a ready and growing market for books explaining and justifying academic history, of which those by E.H. Carr and G.R. Elton were the first and remain the most famous.[24]

These are some of the broader consequences of the numerical expansion and institutional growth of history in British universities during the twentieth century, and especially since the Second World War. But we should also see that efflorescence in terms of generational dynamics and shifts in fashion, as successive age-bands and cohorts of historians, often influenced by contemporary events, and with their own intellectual (and political?) agendas, have sought to assert the primacy and novelty of their particular approach to the past: the political history of the nation state during the 1900s; diplomatic and economic history during the inter-war years; social and women's history during the 1960s and 1970s; and cultural and global history since then.[25] Time and again, the young turks have insisted that their hidebound forbears did history narrowly and badly; that their own new and original approach provided the one essential key that unlocked the whole of the complexities and processes of the past; that conferences, journals and societies were necessary to proclaim and assert this good news; and that all future departmental appointments must be made so as to help further this exciting and innovative agenda. Yet each such novel approach has invariably gone the way of its predecessors, being in its turn superseded, downgraded and marginalized, from being the all-powerful, unifying insight insisted upon by its protagonists and propagandists, to being one additional sub-specialism among many. Depending on your point of view, the cumulative effect of these successive 'new' versions of the past, piled one on top of the other, has been either a growing enrichment of the subject, as ever more sub-specialisms proliferated, or its fatal fragmentation.[26]

But what, meanwhile, of the broader world of popular history (or, as we would now say, public history) that had also seemed in such a parlous (if potentially promising) state at the beginning of the twentieth century? Across the inter-war years, there was some growth in preservationist activity, as the National Trust and the Royal Commission on Historical Monuments were joined by the Council for the Preservation of Rural England and the Georgian Group; and during the same period, writers such as G.M. Trevelyan, Lytton Strachey, John Buchan and Winston Churchill reached a large public audience. But once again, it was in the post-war era that popular history took off as never before. The wireless, film and (especially) television, brought history alive in new, vivid and exciting ways, from Kenneth Clark and Alastair Cooke in an earlier generation to Simon Schama and David Starkey in our own day. Conserving what now became widely known as the national heritage became something of a secular religion, urged on by (among others) the Victorian Society and English Heritage, and the new procedures for listing and preserving historic buildings. For a time, and thanks to the National Trust and Mark Girouard, the cult of the English country house became almost a national obsession.[27] Museums expanded, not only in London but in the provinces, and were given over to new subjects, from the Industrial Revolution to rock and pop; and the fashion for memorials, for anniversaries and commemoration, as well as for local history and family history, shows that the popular desire to remember things past is both powerful and insatiable.[28]

This necessarily abridged account of the rise and rise of public history in Britain closely parallels the rise and rise of history in British universities, and such a conjunction and coincidence makes it difficult to share the pessimism of those authorities quoted earlier, who insist that the subject is once again in a state of terminal decline. Today, there are 15,000 sixth-formers taking A Level history, 30,000 undergraduates reading history, 3,000 research students studying for higher degrees, and a similar number of university teachers. Today, history is described as the 'new gardening', the National Archives at Kew can barely cope with popular interest in family history and census data, and politicians remain obsessed with what they believe will be the 'verdict of history' – even though no simple, single, monolithic judgement is ever likely to be forthcoming.[29] Today, more history than ever before is being taught, researched, written and read, and (in belated corroboration of Bryce) it is concerned with a larger part of human experience, and embraces a wider spread of the globe, than ever before. But it bears repeating that this is a wholly unusual and unprecedented state of affairs, and that most of this explosion has happened very recently, in the sixty years since the end of the Second World War.[30]

II

Across the last one hundred years, then, the doing of history in Britain, both within universities and far beyond, has changed, evolved, developed and expanded to such an extent that those seemingly vain hopes expressed in Bryce's day, both for rigorous training in graduate work, and for a broad conception of the subject, are now accepted practices and widespread commonplaces. Much that has happened to the discipline during the second half of the twentieth century, especially the widening of its scope and the proliferation of its sub-fields, may best be explained in terms of the unprecedented amount of state funding that has been made available for the subject via universities, and the unprecedented numbers of people who have thus been able to become professional historians and none of this could have been foreseen in 1900 – or even in 1950. But while there is thus a fundamental transformation to report, there is also considerable continuity that should be recognized, for many of the controversies concerning the nature and purpose of history, over which scholars disagree now and have disagreed during the intervening hundred years, remain essentially the same, despite the changes that have taken place elsewhere in the scale and substance of the subject. 'Professors' quarrels', G.M. Trevelyan once observed, are 'always ridiculous and unedifying.' Maybe so: but that has not prevented them from happening, and although they have sometimes been concerned with very specific topics, they have often polarized around similar general issues.[31]

During the first decade of the twentieth century, British historians were particularly exercised as to whether their subject was a science or an art. Indeed, one of the reasons for establishing the British Academy in 1902 was to encourage 'the exercise of scientific acumen' in the humanities, so they might take their rightful place beside the 'sister sciences' represented by the Royal Society. And in 1903, in his famous inaugural lecture at Cambridge, J.B. Bury pronounced history to be 'not a branch of literature', but 'a science no less and no more'.[32] Those claims have been regularly re-stated by historians of Rankean persuasion and pretensions, they were reasserted by the founders of *Past & Present*, who insisted (at least to begin with) that theirs was a journal of 'scientific history', and they have been repeated more recently by the quantifiers and self-styled 'Cliometricians', who urged they were bringing unprecedented statistical rigour to the subject. But there has also been the alternative tradition, harking back to Macaulay, and represented across the twentieth century by (among others) G.M. Trevelyan, J.H. Plumb and Simon Schama, that has rejected what they see as archival fetishism and arcane self-absorption, and has stressed instead the literary and imaginative side of the historian's art. These are venerable disagreements, still unresolved; yet on closer inspection, they turn out to be nothing of the kind. For most historians readily concede that history is *both* a science *and* an art. There was, as even Trevelyan himself long ago admitted, no point in them 'forever abusing each other as Dry-as-Dusts on the one hand, and shallow featherheads on the other'. 'Let us guard', agreed Marc Bloch, 'against stripping our science of its share of poetry.'[33]

There are similar, over-stated disputes between those who favour analytical history, which stresses static structure, and those who prefer dynamic narrative, which tells a story – alternatives exemplified and polarized by those friends-turned-enemies Sir Lewis Namier and A.J.P. Taylor. Namier excelled at structural investigation, as in his studies of English politics during the 1750s and 1760s, and in his analysis of the European revolutions of 1848; but he was constitutionally incapable of creating an animated, mobile story of past events unfolding across time. Taylor, by contrast, was the most fluent writer of his generation, who produced scintillating chronicles of the nation state and international relations, but had little feel for the deeper forces of historical change.[34] Throughout the twentieth century, the battle between these two ways of doing history ebbed and flowed; but once again, these extreme positions were exaggeratedly opposed. This was partly because, as most historians recognize, analysis without narrative loses any sense of the sequencing (and unpredictability) of events through time, while narrative without analysis fails to convey the structural constraints within which events actually take place. And it is partly because, as Peter Burke has reminded us, there is in practice a long continuum extending from 'pure' narrative to 'pure' analysis, which means that the best history is situated somewhere between these extremes, seeking simultaneously to animate structure and contextualize narrative, as well exemplified in Garrett Mattingly's *Defeat of the Spanish Armada* (London, 1959), or Keith Thomas's *Religion and the Decline of Magic* (London, 1971), or Linda Colley's *Britons: Forging the Nation, 1707–1837* (London, 1992), or Christopher Clark's *Iron Kingdom: The Rise and Downfall of Prussia, 1600–1947* (London, 2006).[35]

This excessive polarization between the narrative and analytical modes has also fed into another long-standing debate, between those scholars who prefer to stress transformations and those who lay greater emphasis on continuity. 'If history is not concerned with change', Lawrence Stone once observed, 'it is nothing.' But much of what seemed like change was, according to Fernand Braudel, no more than the ephemeral trivia of political events, while at the deeper level of geography, climate, resources and demography, things moved very slowly, if at all: and '*l'histoire événe-mentielle*' was far less important than this '*l'histoire immobile*'.[36] To be sure, both approaches have their advocates. For some historians of seventeenth-century England, for instance, that was a time of fundamental, revolutionary upheaval; for others, it was a period when very little changed. And while some scholars see the eighteenth century as an epoch of progress and modernity, of self-made entrepreneurs and secular enlightenment, others insist that it was an old regime, dominated by the traditional triad of monarchy, aristocracy and established religion.[37] But this merely reminds us that historians are better employed trying to establish a balance between continuity and change, rather than insisting on the importance of one to the exclusion of the other. Striking that balance is not easy, and it no doubt differs from period to period: indeed, since 1986, an entire journal, named *Continuity and Change*, has been devoted to the subject.[38]

Yet striking a balance, like recognizing a continuum, is something which many perennially disputatious historians seem extremely reluctant to do. Consider, in this regard, the further distinction which is often drawn between those scholars allegedly described by LeRoi Ladurie as parachutists and those he called truffle hunters: the former surveying the broad historical landscape from a great and Olympian height, the latter grubbing around in dense thickets of local detail.[39] This distinction, too, endured for the whole of the twentieth century: at the beginning, between those who wrote general surveys and those who were antiquarian scholars; in the middle between admirers of the *Annales* school and adherents to traditional English empiricism; and at the end between such practitioners of micro history as Robert Darnton, Carlo Ginsburg and Natalie Davis, and such advocates of global history as William McNeill, John Roberts and Felipe Fernandez-Armesto.[40] But once again, these are excessively polarized positions. Micro history only works if there is a sense of the broader context which particular events illuminate, and are themselves illuminated by; global history loses its edge without concrete detail and local specifity. Now, as always, one of the most important tasks of the historian is to make connections, as Ranke long ago urged, between the particular and the general. Of course, there are many different ways of doing this: but again, the matter is best resolved by envisaging a continuum of expositional strategies, rather than by launching offensives from hostile and opposing camps.[41]

The same conclusion suggests itself if we examine another familiar Manichean formulation, that between high and low, elite and popular, be it in politics, society, culture or anything else. Those who concern themselves with the doings of the elite rightly insist that we cannot understand the past if we ignore those people who were in power, made the rules, possessed the wealth, and set the tone. Those who wish to rescue humbler figures from what Edward Thompson memorably described 'the enormous condescension of posterity' reply that it is more important to recover the lives of that far greater number of ordinary people who were the victims of history rather than those in charge who were the makers of it.[42] It is also sometimes (though not always) the case, that those on the right prefer to study people in authority, within the confines of the nation state, while those on the left are more interested in people lower down the social and political scale, and have a more internationalist outlook. But for all the admirable work which these two approaches have generated, they pay inadequate attention to the *inter-connectedness* of things: partly by failing to explore how elites are invariably circumscribed in the exercise of power; partly by giving insufficient attention to the framework of law and authority by which the lower classes were constrained; and all too often (and from both perspectives) by giving insufficient attention to the complexities of social structures and the significance of social interactions. For all its alliterative appeal, few societies in practice have ever been polarized – politically, economically, socially or culturally – between two hermetically-sealed and mutually-antagonistic collectivities labelled the 'patricians' and the 'plebs'.[43]

Yet despite these counsels of compromise and consensus, the same entrenched positions have often been taken up when historians have turned from their activities and their approaches to their audience. Those of a 'scientific' persuasion, often invoking Maitland as well as Ranke, insist that their work is of considerable technical complexity, requiring specialized language, concepts and calculations, which is only intended for fellow scholars. But for those brought up in the tradition of Macaulay and Trevelyan, the prime purpose of history is not to write for an exclusive coterie, but to reach as broad a public audience as possible. Here is the distinction, famously formulated by Hugh Trevor-Roper in his inaugural lecture as Regius Professor of Modern History at Oxford University, between history for the professionals and for the laity.[44] Again, this is a long-running dispute, between those who assert the primacy of scholarly learning, and those who fear that scientific history will be lost to the general public. But it is also another exaggerated disagreement. For in practice, there is a continuum of historical writing, extending all the way from arcane technical works to best-sellers, and our most distinguished historians have invariably spanned it. Trevor-Roper himself wrote articles in the *Economic History Review*, which were read by very few, as well as *The Last Days of Hitler* (London, 1947), which was read by very many; and while G.R. Elton wrote scores of detailed studies of sixteenth-century politics, and urged his colleagues to disclaim and disavow any public, educative function, or espouse any broader social purpose, he also published *England Under the Tudors* (London, 1955), and *Reformation Europe, 1517–1559* (London, 1963), general surveys which sold in their hundreds of thousands.

It would be easy, but also wearisome, to explore other excessively adversarial formulations of the practice and purpose of history. Is the past a foreign country, where they do things differently from us here and now, or a familiar country, where they do things the same?[45] Are historical developments inevitable, the outcome of long-term forces over which men and women have no control, or are they accidental, the result of caprice and contingency? Is history fiction by another name, in which the author makes it all up, or is it about fact, truth and certainty? And so on. Like the controversies outlined above in more detail, these scholarly disagreements raged back and forth across the twentieth century; and like them, again, the polarization is both appealing yet also misguided. In defiance of the first of these formulations, Jacques Barzun long ago observed that the task of the historian was to discover 'the familiar within the strange, without losing sense of either'. In answer to the second, Marx famously observed that men and women do indeed make their own history, but they do not do so under circumstances of their own choosing. And in answer to the third, Trevelyan rightly noted that the very essence of history was not 'the imagination roaming at large, but pursuing the fact and fastening upon it'.[46] All of which leads to the conclusion that throughout the twentieth century, too much discussion of history by historians has been dogmatically polarized, and insufficient attention has been given to exploring the gradations, continuums and common ground where most of the best history writing has in practice always been found. In deploring, as he has recently done, the 'baneful consequences' of this excessively adversarial approach to the past (and also to the present), Stefan Collini is surely right.[47]

III

Perhaps a brief recapitulation is by now in order. First, and from a narrative perspective, it is worth repeating that the second half of the twentieth century was unique in witnessing the unprecedented state sponsorship of (and public enthusiasm for) the study of history in this country. This vast proliferation of interest in the past, and of the study of the past, is something wholly extraordinary and without precedent in Britain as, indeed, it has also been elsewhere in the west (though in the United States, the leading universities which have driven forward the study of history have usually been private rather than public institutions). Those of us who have benefited from these developments, by having been able to sustain lifelong academic careers as a result, are naturally inclined to think they are right and good and should therefore be permanent. But at the same time, we ought also to recognize that there is absolutely no guarantee that this relatively recent state of affairs will endure indefinitely. Second, and in more analytical mode, it is important to remember that when historians have described how they do what they do, and when they have written about what history is about, they have often taken up extreme and entrenched adversarial positions, when in practice there is more agreement and common ground between many of them than this might suggest. Perhaps, then, we ought to think about what history is now, and about where history is going in the future, in this more positive and nuanced way.

In seeking to survey the present historical scene, and to offer some speculations as to possible future developments, some caution and circumspection are both in order. To begin with, we need to beware the present-minded parochialism which assumes that we live in the best of all possible worlds: for, as Blair Worden has recently reminded us, 'the certainties of one age, *in historical interpretations as in other walks of life*', often have a disconcerting habit of 'becoming follies to the next'.[48] Our present approaches to the past may seem self-evidently good and right and sensible and true, and better than anything that has gone before: but it is highly unlikely that historians writing fifty years from now, let alone one hundred, will share that view. If nothing else, that should engender some healthy and humble scepticism about the claims we make on behalf of ourselves and of what we are doing.[49] In the aftermath of post-modernity, we historians constantly assert that we are more self-aware and self-reflexive than ever before, and that self-scrutiny and self-examination are the prevailing modes. But before we congratulate ourselves on being so much more wise and mature and sophisticated than our scholarly forbears, we should also recognize the accompanying dangers of self-absorption, self-regard, self-satisfaction and self-importance. Moreover (and as Joyce Appleby has recently reminded us) 'it is the conceit of all contemporaries to think that theirs is a time of particularly momentous changes' – an option which she strongly urges us to decline. And no historian should set out to engage with the future without being reminded that it never unfolds in ways that can be predicted.[50]

Nevertheless, having sought to anticipate such objections and head off such criticisms, it is time to offer some predictions and prescriptions, which draw on arguments already advanced and suggestions already made. To begin with, historians need to emancipate themselves from the spurious thralldom of dichotomized modes of thinking, both about ourselves, and about the way we approach the past. If we are to think more creatively and constructively about what we are doing, we should be more concerned with gradations, continuums and nuances than with postulating mutually-exclusive alternatives. For example, instead of seeing our audience as being either professional or lay, we might consider what Stefan Collini calls the 'academic public sphere' which is neither exclusively academic, nor inclusively generalist, but something in-between.[51] And when we look at the past, perhaps we should consider more critically those beguiling binaries of religion, nation, class, gender, race and civilization, built around the notions of collective categories eternally in conflict. They are, to be sure, a significant (and often depressing) part of the human story. But they are only a part. Throughout history, Christian and Infidel, Briton and German, 'us' and 'them', men and women, black and white, 'the west' and 'Islam' have also got by, done business, rubbed along, co-existed, and in so doing have often embraced a sort of common humanity, and we urgently need to find a way of writing about the past from this important but neglected perspective.[52]

But if we are to do so, then a related issue that we are going to have to address is what we think our chief (though not sole) concern, namely humanity, actually was and is. In writing about this subject, many of us follow David Hume: 'Mankind are so much the same in all times and places, that history informs of nothing new or strange in this particular. Its chief use is only to discover the constant and universal principles of human nature.' But *are* the principles of human nature thus constant and universal?[53] Thanks to psycho history, we know a great deal more about the importance of the unconscious in human behaviour and motivation: but most history writing disregards it. Thanks to cultural history, we know that people in past times saw both their world, and themselves, differently from how we see our world and ourselves: but we understand very little about how human outlooks and human nature actually connect and change.[54] Nor have historians yet begun to engage with the work being done by geneticists, neuro-scientists, evolutionary biologists and evolutionary psychologists, which insists that human minds, human behaviour, human artefacts and human culture, in short everything we understand by human nature, and everything we write about as human history, are all biologically determined. The cross-disciplinary debate about what it means to be human, both in the physical and the social sense, has barely begun, not least because historians have been so unwilling to intrude themselves into it. It is time we did: for we can no longer take an unproblematic, Humean notion of humanity and human nature for granted.[55]

In addition to rethinking our notions of humanity, we are also going to have to address the vexed question of the changing territorial and political units within which men and women have operated and organized themselves. Much of the history that was written during the twentieth century, especially when concerned with high politics and international relations, unthinkingly took for granted the existence of the nation state. But now, in the early twenty-first century, that collectivity seems altogether more precarious and problematic, which means that we are going to have to rethink the sort of history that we write and teach – not by disregarding the nation state completely, but certainly by laying more stress on its contingent and constructed nature, as historians have increasingly been doing since the 1980s.[56] Yet we shall also need to de-parochialize it – partly (in the British case) by doing more to address international interconnections and by re-integrating metropolitan and imperial history, but also by engaging with the issue of what is termed globalization. To be sure, the phenomenon of globalization has been around for a long time, but only in the 1990s did it become a buzz word, and historians need urgently to connect with this issue: partly to provide the beef behind the buzz, and partly to emphasize that globalization has non-western as well as western origins, aspects and implications.[57]

One reason why the nation state looks significantly less secure than it did has been because of the transformative and subversive impact of the revolution in IT during the last two decades, and it has had, and is still having, a correspondingly transformative and subversive effect on the way in which history is being written and taught. Thanks to the net and the web, academic history is a much less exclusive and hierarchical enterprise than it once was: witness the debate, hosted on the IHR website, in response to Richard Evans's book *In Defence of History* (London, 1997) – despite its title, a book more in defence of historical method than a justification of the importance of history itself.[58] At the same time, massive data bases are now being assembled which are widely available, which in turn means that information about the past can be globally co-ordinated and globally accessed on a scale and in ways that were literally unthinkable a quarter of a century ago.[59] Of course, it is not only history, but the whole of the humanities, which are being transformed in this way; but the impact on the researching and writing of history may well turn out to be the most significant, and it has not yet run its course. Indeed, it may well be that it has scarcely begun, and that we are only at the beginning of the process whereby unprecedented quantities of information about the past are going to become electronically (and thus internationally) available. Within a decade, it also seems highly likely that the pattern of academic publishing will be altered, certainly as regards journals and monographs. If this is so, then the whole enterprise of historical research and writing may be further and fundamentally transformed in directions that at present it is impossible to foresee.[60]

Nor is this the only way in which IT is re-making history. During the last one hundred years, the pace of change, at least in the western world, has accelerated almost exponentially, and the IT revolution is merely its latest manifestation. And so, notwithstanding Joyce Appleby's wise and prudent warning against assuming that ours is a time of uniquely momentous changes, there *is* a case for saying that our world in 2008 has far, far less in common with most of human history than our predecessors did a century ago, in the days of James Bryce. The result, as one historian has recently observed, is that 'the gulf between a liberal, democratic, secular, collectivist, feminist present, and a non-liberal, non-democratic, non-secular, non-collectivist, non-feminist past grows more impassable by the year'. Or, as another scholar remarked in the 1950s, in words which have even greater resonance today, 'previous generations *knew* much less about the past than we did, but perhaps *felt* a much greater sense of identity and continuity with it'.[61] Today, indeed, many people feel so distanced from the (even relatively recent) past that they find it impossible to 'deal with'. Hence the blanket condemnations of previous eras and societies as classist, racist, sexist, imperialist, xenophobic, and homophobic; hence the demands for apologies for past events now deemed unacceptable, such as the Irish Potato Famine and the Treaty of Waitangi; hence the agitation for tangible rectifications of historical 'wrongs', be it compensation for the slave trade or the restitution of the Elgin Marbles; and hence the increasing involvement of historians in commissions, tribunals and court cases intended to establish 'the truth' about the past.[62]

These are difficult, complex and sensitive public issues (and often difficult, complex and sensitive political issues), into which historians are now finding themselves drawn, and it is a curious irony that they are increasingly being asked to deliver an authoritative version of 'the truth' to judges and politicians at the very same time that some post-modernists continue to insist that they cannot deliver any such thing as the 'truth' at all.[63] But then, whoever claimed that being an historian was easy or straightforward? In one guise, we are the handmaids of conventional wisdoms, explaining how we got from there to here; in another, we are the sceptics and the disbelievers, constantly in rebellion against the tyranny of present-day opinion; and in a third, which avoids yet another dichotomous formulation, we try to do both. We make our living by looking into the follies and horrors of the past, but it is also our duty to urge that people living in different centuries, inhabiting different cultures, and belonging to different civilizations, saw things and did things very differently from how we see things and do things today. And are we, in Marc Bloch's words, 'so sure of ourselves and of our age as to divide the company of our forefathers into the just and the damned', depending on how far they did, or did not, anticipate or share our own (and no less time-bound and place-specific) contemporary values?[64] More than ever, then, the justification for the study of history remains what it has always been: to teach the virtues of perspective and proportion, tolerance and humanity, breadth of vision and generosity of view – in short, to provide what is so often derided as a genuinely liberal education. For as John Carey has recently reminded us, 'one of history's most important tasks' is to bring 'home to us how keenly, honestly and painfully past generations pursued aims that now seem to us wrong or disgraceful'.[65]

IV

The following observation, by three distinguished American scholars, aptly summarizes much of what has been written and argued here so far:

> Essays on the state of the discipline [they note] often have a canonical form all their own: first a narrative of the rise of new kinds of history, then a long moment for exploring the problems posed by new kinds of history, followed by either a jeremiad on the evils of new practices, or a celebration of the potential of the overcoming of all obstacles.[66]

It cannot be denied that the first part of this chapter is very much as Professors Appleby, Hunt and Jacob describe it, and that section two also bears more than a passing resemblance to their 'long moment'. But while the third part has undoubtedly been concerned with both the problems and the possibilities of history now and in the future, it has sought to eschew the polarities of depression and euphoria, and has offered instead a more nuanced (though not necessarily a more accurate) set of predictions. And they are certainly offered in corroboration of the view that, 'in good times or bad, critical ones, transitional ones, or normal ones, history can help human beings think better, live more richly, and act more wisely'.[67] So, indeed, it can; so, indeed, it must: and it is up to us as historians to make sure that it can and that it does.

In more ways than one, and for the worse as well as for the better, the years from 1900 to 2000 were a century of history to an extent that had been true of no earlier era – in one guise a time of unprecedented terror and tragedy, horror and holocaust, when history-writing was regularly abused and repeatedly misused; but also a time of unexampled progress and accomplishment, improvement and opportunity, one sign of which was that in some countries history flourished and flowered, both in public and in academe, as it had never done before. From one perspective, the twentieth century was indeed an age of extremes and of anxiety, in which Africa was not alone in being the dark continent; from another it was an age of affluence, abundance and achievement, for more people, in more parts of the world, than ever before.[68] Whatever else may be said, both for it and against it, the second half of the twentieth century witnessed the greatest age of history writing the western world has so far seen: certainly in terms of the numbers of practitioners and the size of the public audience, and arguably in terms of the quality of writing as well. We must hope that the twenty-first century will continue to be at least as good. But as the record of the past makes plain, as does the experience of other countries in our own time, there is no guarantee that this will happen. Geographically and chronologically, this recent historical glut is 'a most restricted and unusual phenomenon, and there is as little reason to have any more confidence in its survival and spread in the future as there is in that of democracy itself'.[69] As historians should never need reminding: only time will tell. But in the meantime and for now, we should be guardedly grateful, both for what has been achieved, and for what is still being accomplished.

2

Monarchy:
Crowns and Contexts, Thrones and Dominations[1]

We are sometimes told, by those who believe that their prime scholarly task is to study 'history from below', that it is a mistake to concern ourselves with kings and queens, courts and coronations, art-patrons and palace-builders, flummery and mummery, because the whole glittering yet tawdry subject is at best elitist, and at worst boring. But throughout most of the human past, peoples, tribes, nations and empires have organized themselves, or have been forcibly organized, on the basis of royal rule, sovereign authority and hereditary succession.[2] Moreover, most monarchies have been generically male, and most monarchs have fulfilled a remarkable and powerful range of generically masculine roles, as god, priest, lawgiver, judge, warrior, philosopher, patron and benefactor, which have significantly influenced the societies over which they have presided.[3] If, then, we are to come to any settled understanding of the ancient, medieval and early modern history of Europe, to say nothing of the longer-term history of the majority of the globe beyond, we should recognize the importance of monarchy, and we need to study it – not as a wearying and meaningless succession of names and dates and roman numerals, but with all the varied insights and diverse approaches that have been developed by historians, and by those working in neighbouring disciplines, during the last half century.

For most of European history, and most of world history, monarchs have been at the centre (and also at the summit) of human affairs and events. Of course, the system did not always function smoothly or effectively: there were varied and sometimes disputed rules of succession; there were problematic relations between princes and prelates, between the crown and the church; there were dynastic rivalries, family squabbles, court intrigues;

there were bad kings, foolish kings, wicked kings, idle kings; there were long-lived dowagers, domineering wives, wicked uncles, faithless brothers and feckless cousins; there were usurpers, bastards, impostors and pretenders; and there were over-mighty subjects, disloyal dukes and baronial rebels.[4] Indeed, it is just such royal imbroglios and dynastic disputes that form the mainspring of so many of Shakespeare's plays, which taken together constitute (among many other things) the greatest sustained meditation across ancient, medieval and early modern monarchy ever carried out and carried off by one individual. But as Shakespeare so often makes plain, in *Hamlet* and *Macbeth*, in *Richard II* and *Richard III*, in *Henry V* and *Henry VI*, the battles and disagreements of the pre-modern period were about who should be king, about how the king should be chosen, and about what the king should do, rather than about whether there ought to be a king or not. Rarely was that an issue in his time, or before his time.[5]

To be sure, there was also in existence an alternative republican tradition, extending from the city-states of ancient Greece to those of Renaissance Italy, which offered a radically different and potentially subversive vision of how human affairs should be managed and organized; but although Charles I lost both his throne and his head in England in the 1640s, this was very much the minority view until the eighteenth century.[6] Since then, of course, it has become the conventional wisdom, with royal regimes, as distinct from specific sovereigns, being overthrown and discarded around the world: 1776 in much of north America, and the 1820s in much of south America; 1789, 1830 and 1848 in France, 1917 in Russia, 1918 in Germany and Austria-Hungary, and 1946 in Italy; and 1912 in China, 1949 in India, and 1950 in Indonesia. Some of these dynasties have disappeared because of internal political convulsions, often (but not invariably) following failure and defeat in war; others because of the gaining of independence from a royal colonial empire, leading to the establishment of an indigenous republican constitution. Either way, the mid eighteenth to the mid twentieth centuries witnessed a revolution wholly unprecedented in human history, as monarchical regimes ceased to be the norm, and became increasingly the exception in world affairs. By definition, the era of the common man has not been a good time to be a crowned head. And those thrones which did survive only managed by accommodating themselves (with varying degrees of reluctance, resignation, recognition, agility, enthusiasm and success) to the increasingly democratic and egalitarian trends of the times. It was no longer acceptable for kings (and, occasionally, queens) to *rule*; the best they could hope for was that they might be allowed to continue to *reign*.

But what do modern monarchs do when they reign, and how should we most appropriately write about what they do? In part, they continue their traditional functions, although usually in a scaled-back or altered way. But those of us who write on modern monarchies know less than we should about their ancient, medieval and early modern predecessors, and so fail to appreciate sufficiently what those traditional functions were, or just how much they have been diminished and adapted in more recent times.[7] Indeed, many of these customary activities have been appropriated and absorbed by other individuals and institutions, which means that modern monarchy is primarily about doing new things, finding new functions, and creating new rationales for its continued existence in societies no longer rural, religious and hierarchical (where kings were charismatic and authoritarian leaders), but instead urban, secular and democratic (where they are re-positioned as heads of state). If we are to understand the working of the modern British monarchy (which for convenience may be taken as beginning with the accession of Queen Victoria in 1837), then we need to strike the appropriate balance between attenuated and adjusted historical functions, and newly-created activities and justifications. How far have writers on the modern British monarchy grasped, recognized, comprehended and addressed these issues?

I

Until relatively recently, and to a much greater extent than for earlier periods, the majority of writing on the modern British monarchy has been in essentially biographical mode, and in many ways, the case for such treatment of sovereigns has always been, and remains, very strong.[8] Because they customarily occupy the throne alone, and because their period of occupancy constitutes a unique and discrete period of historical time, monarchs deserve to be treated as the significant historical individuals they undoubtedly were. That was certainly true for those far-off days when monarchs ruled, and it is arguably still true in more recent times, when monarchs reign. For, clearly, if we want to know what modern British monarchs do when they reign, then we need to follow them through their regal and regnal lives from beginning to end. And since the royal archives at Windsor house the papers of kings and queens reign by reign, this is something it is both possible and proper to do. Indeed, it was from these archives, and urged on by Lord Esher, that there issued forth in the early part of the twentieth century the fullest edition of the correspondence of any recent British sovereign yet to appear: the nine volumes of extracts from Queen Victoria's journals and letters. They are an indispensable source, and they have subsequently been augmented by additional publications.[9] But they have to be used with caution: much of the Queen's journal was destroyed, and those extracts from it deemed appropriate to put between hard covers are but a small, and far from wholly representative, sample of what has survived.

These volumes of letters appeared between 1908 and 1932, and it was also during those years that the standard form of official royal biography of recently-deceased monarchs had largely been settled, although interestingly enough the gas-lit Gloriana herself was not thus commemorated. But Victoria had effectively initiated the enterprise and defined the genre by commissioning Theodore Martin to produce a massive, five-volume biography of Prince Albert, which duly and dutifully appeared between 1875 and 1880, and which printed a great deal of primary material, some of it revealing more about the prince's political ambitions for himself and for the monarchy than might have been thought altogether wise or prudent.[10] Nevertheless, its overall tone and conclusions were excessively and predictably reverential, since it was not only written at the queen's behest, but also under her firm and determined editorial control, and she was convinced that Albert had been incapable of ever doing any wrong. By contrast, Sir Sidney Lee's biography of King Edward VII, published in a mere two volumes in 1925 and 1927, was noticeably less obsequious in tone, and more balanced in judgement; but most of the sovereign's papers had been destroyed on his own instructions, courtly and political pressure was brought to bear on the author, and the book was predictably discreet about the king's private life and personal habits. So, when describing Edward's voracious and gargantuan passion for multi-course meals, Lee coyly observed that the king 'never toyed with his food'. Inevitably, in the deflating era of Lytton Strachey's *Eminent Victorians*, this excessively tactful approach appeared both unconvincing and anachronistic.[11]

Thereafter, during the reign of King George V, official royal biography went more or less into an abeyance which lasted until after the Second World War. But after a trio of royal deaths between 1937 and 1952, there was then a sudden surge of commissioning, overseen by Sir Alan Lascelles, the sovereign's private secretary, which meant that during the 1950s, three royal biographies appeared in rapid succession: Harold Nicolson on King George V, James Pope-Hennessy on his wife Queen Mary, and John Wheeler-Bennett on their son King George VI.[12] In each case, the author was given privileged access to the royal archives, and a great deal of new information was published as a result: about (for example) the formation of the National Government in 1931 in the case of George V, and about Churchill's appointment to the premiership in 1940 in the case of George VI. These biographies were, and to some extent remain, works of serious scholarship and real historical significance. But for all their abiding worth, they also illustrated the limitations of the genre. Many politicians associated with these events were still alive, and so was Edward VIII as duke of Windsor; and George VI and George V were, respectively, the father and grandfather of the new young Queen Elizabeth II, which further limited what could candidly or critically be said about them.

Yet this sanitized discretion was precisely what those who commissioned these biographies intended and expected: indeed, all three authors were specifically instructed to write nothing that was embarrassing to the institution of monarchy, or critical of the particular individual who was being thus commemorated and memorialized.[13] As a highbrow liberal sceptic, Harold Nicolson did not always find this easy. During his years as Duke of York, the future King George V devoted most of his time to shooting and philately at York Cottage on the Sandringham estate, activities that were hardly to Nicolson's refined and fastidious taste. 'These years', he wrote with self-denying urbanity in his biography, 'succeeded each other with placid similitude. He lived the life of a privileged country gentleman, unostentatious, comparatively retired, almost obscure.' But such tact and emollience were much less in evidence off the record in Nicolson's diary: he thought York Cottage a 'horrible little house', no better than a Surbiton villa; where, 'for seventeen years', the future king 'did nothing at all but kill animals and stick in stamps'. As Sir John Wheeler-Bennett was later to observe, official royal biography as then undertaken was best described in sacred rather than scholarly terms, as an enterprise, like matrimony, 'not to be entered into inadvisedly or lightly; but reverently, discreetly, advisedly, soberly and in the fear of God'. As this suggests, he himself was wholly at ease with this genre, and his biography of George VI was courtly and obsequious, and written in orotund and ponderous prose. Even Nicolson, who had been consulted about Wheeler-Bennett's appointment, and was both a friend and mentor, found the result both toadying and dull.[14]

Thereafter, with a young monarch on the throne, and with no major deaths, official royal biography went into abeyance again, and it would be the 1980s before the passing of another generation meant that two further instalments appeared. By then, the climate of public opinion, towards the monarchy as towards everything else, had become noticeably less deferential and more intrusive, with the media both reflecting and encouraging these more sceptical patterns of behaviour and expectation. The House of Windsor was obliged to come to terms with these changes, and one sign of this was that the two most recent official royal biographies – of Lord Mountbatten and King Edward VIII, both brilliantly written by Philip Ziegler – broke much new ground, being far less sycophantic in tone, and more inquiring in scholarship.[15] They treated their subjects as individuals rather than as icons; they discussed their finances and their highly eventful private lives; they drew attention to their character flaws and career failures; and they admitted to tensions and disagreements within the royal family itself. Of course, it could scarcely have been otherwise: Edward VIII abandoned the throne for a twice-divorced American; and Mountbatten was by turns inordinately devious and colossally vain. Both, in their way, were black sheep in the royal family: Edward because he gave up his job and ran away; Mountbatten because he succeeded in sustaining a lengthy, significant and controversial public career. In part, then, because of changed circumstances, and in part because the subjects were the people they were, these two official biographies set new standards for candour and openness. It will be interesting to see, another generation on, whether William Shawcross will be able to maintain these standards with the latest of such commissions, in his official biography of Queen Elizabeth the Queen Mother.

The final serious mode of recent royal biography is that which may best be described as unofficial and non-commissioned, but sometimes with approved access to the royal archives. Pre-eminent in this genre is Elizabeth Longford's life of Queen Victoria, which was subsequently followed by Philip Magnus on King Edward VII, Georgina Battiscombe on Queen Alexandra, Frances Donaldson on King Edward VIII, Kenneth Rose on King George V and Sarah Bradford on King George VI.[16] Of these, Longford's was in many ways the commissioned biography the great queen never got, and drew extensively on the royal archives, while Donaldson's, which came

out before Ziegler, made great use of interviews with the dwindling band
of abdication survivors. Both Rose and Bradford represented a serious
advance on, respectively, Nicolson and Wheeler-Bennett: in part because
the passage of time enabled them to be more candid and less courtly; and
in part because more non-royal archival material had become available.
Rose demonstrated that George V deliberately refused to sanction the
rescue of his cousin the tsar, and Bradford showed how strongly King
George VI and Queen Elizabeth were for Neville Chamberlain and against
Winston Churchill in 1940. To these important volumes should be added
the (happily interim) biographies of the present Queen by Ben Pimlott
and Sarah Bradford: the best lives of a currently-reigning monarch ever
written, but inevitably constrained by the fact that Elizabeth II is still very
much with us, that the time is not yet ripe to attempt an overall appraisal
of her life, and that access to her archives will not be granted to an official
biographer until after her reign is over.[17]

Self-evidently, much of the history of the modern British monarchy would
be incomprehensible without these major biographical studies.[18] They evoke
a character, describe a life, encapsulate a reign and, with varying degrees of
authority and conviction, place it in the setting of its times. But as Sir Ian
Kershaw has recently observed, biography, however well done, runs 'the
natural risk of over-personalising complex historical developments, over-
emphasising the role of the individual in shaping and determining events,
[and] ignoring or playing down the social and political context in which
those actions took place'.[19] And if that is true of biographies in general, and
even of biographies of sovereigns when they rule, then how much more is
it true of biographies of monarchs who merely reign? To be sure, modern
British kings and regnant queens are often busy people, but they are not
busy in the same substantive or significant ways that their forbears were
busy: compared to Henry VIII or Elizabeth I, for instance, it is clear that
Edward VII and Elizabeth II were and are responding to events rather than
initiating them, and that they were and are presiding over a period of time
but not dominating it. So it is scarcely surprising that much of the best and
most innovative work that is now being undertaken on the modern British
monarchy is in a historical rather than a biographical mode.[20]

As such, this growth in scholarly interest constitutes something of a
minor historiographical revolution – and a relatively recent one at that.
Despite the expansion of the university-based historical profession during
the thirty years following the end of the Second World War, both in terms

of the increased numbers of practitioners and the new approaches to the past they pioneered and adopted, the modern British monarchy remained an essentially off-limits subject: courtly writers got on with their royal biographies, and historians of nineteenth-century politics paid some attention to such matters as the bedchamber crisis and Queen Victoria's vexed relations with Gladstone, but beyond that, they did not venture.[21] Although by the 1960s and 1970s, the modern British aristocracy was beginning to come into focus as a serious scholarly area of inquiry, the modern British monarchy still seemed too marginal to be worthy of academic concern and focused investigation.[22] It was only during the 1980s that some historians began to sense that there was important work to be done in this arena: perhaps because the Thatcher decade was a great stimulus to re-examine many aspects of patriotic Britain that had hitherto largely gone accepted and unquestioned; perhaps, too, because in the aftermath of the Queen's Silver Jubilee in 1977, attitudes towards the House of Windsor became less reverential and more critical.[23] The result has been an unprecedented quarter of a century's right royal research and writing, which means there is much to report, but also much left to do.

II

One of the new ways in which the modern British monarchy has been approached by historians is that they have begun to treat it, not so much as a glittering cavalcade of kings and queens, but as a successfully self-perpetuating elite institution. That description was valid in earlier times, and is still true today; but not necessarily in the same way. Take, for example, the issue of the attenuation of royal political power. In a long-term perspective, Walter Bagehot's famous definition of the prerogatives of what he termed constitutional monarchy – to warn, to encourage and to be consulted – was an attempt to codify creatively what was left of royal power after the crown had been compelled to give up most of its historical rulership and leadership functions during the eighteenth and early nineteenth centuries. But Victoria, and even more so Albert, were very reluctant to part with what remained of those historical rights, and on occasions they were significantly more interfering than Bagehot's oft-quoted formulation suggested. How was it, then, and when was it, that the monarch ceased to be an active participant in politics, and became a referee located somewhere above them?[24] But this is not the only form of residual and attenuated power which modern British monarchs still possess. They are no longer major benefactors in the manner of the three kings bearing their gifts to the stable at Bethlehem; but any charity with a royal name on its letterhead knows that such patronage is worth a substantial amount in terms of additional public subscriptions. Indeed, this shift in the exercise of royal power – from political intervention to philanthropic persuasion – has given rise to what has rightly been called the 'welfare monarchy'.[25]

As befits its historical antecedents, this welfare monarchy may also be studied as a warfare monarchy, although again not in the way, or to the extent, that it was in medieval or early modern times. No British monarch has led the troops into battle since the mid eighteenth century, but the sovereign remains head of the armed forces and some form of military service is still routinely expected of members of the royal family. Queen Victoria took pride in being a soldier's daughter; King Edward VII and King George V were much involved, respectively, in military reforms during the 1900s and military appointments during the First World War; the Duke of Cambridge, the Duke of Connaught and Lord Mountbatten were significant military-cum-political figures, who owed their careers in part to their royal connections; and many high-ranking officers subsequently hold senior positions in the royal court and bureaucracy.[26] This is not exactly King Henry V at the Battle of Agincourt, or even King George II at the Battle of Dettingen, but it is a recognizable and important theme, albeit once again attenuated, which needs to be examined historically as well as biographically. And the same may be said of the sovereign's relations with the Church of England: for while the recent royal past affords no church-and-state drama on the scale of Henry II and Thomas Becket, the monarch remains supreme governor, and relations between the crown and the church – at all levels, from theology and doctrine to episcopal appointments – need more investigation than they have so far received. We know that Queen Victoria entertained characteristically trenchant views on both military and religious subjects, but for the twentieth-century British monarchy these matters have so far gone largely unexplored.[27]

In terms of those traditional royal functions of political, philanthropic, military and ecclesiastical power, the history of the modern British monarchy is thus one of attenuation, adaptation and the creation of new roles. But across the centuries, monarchs have also been expected to be the richest, as well as the mightiest, people in their lands, and the recent history of

royal wealth is both complex and inadequately treated. We know that in
the mid nineteenth century, the monarchy was relatively poor (certainly
compared to the greatest landed magnates), but that by the mid twentieth
century, it had become relatively rich (ditto); and we also know a little
about the history of the modern civil list, and about the changes in royal
tax arrangements during the last one hundred years. But this scarcely
amounts to a comprehensive history of the crown's finances, either public
or private; and the recent and welcome openness by Buckingham Palace
in the provision of current royal accounts needs to be projected back into
the past.[28] Yet by definition, wealth is not just a matter of income, it is
also a matter of expenditure. As befitted their exalted status, many British
monarchs have been the greatest builders and patrons and collectors of
their time, and Queen Victoria and Prince Albert also discharged this
task on an appropriately regal scale.[29] But no sovereign since them has
done so, and it is surely worth asking why. Perhaps it is because of the
changing structure of twentieth-century patronage of the arts, away from
monarchs and notables and towards cities and the state. Or perhaps it
is because of the changing nature of twentieth-century art, architecture
and music (and costume), whose increasingly abstract, modernist, atonal
(and utilitarian) and thus non-representational forms are less useful for
buttressing the prestige of royalty than was the case with more traditional
modes in earlier times.[30]

The safeguarding and perpetuation of royal prestige has not just been
about the accumulation and disbursement of wealth and the cultivation
and projection of an artistically-enhanced image: it has also been under-
girded (and sometimes undermined) by the royal court and directed (and
sometimes misdirected) by the royal bureaucracy – two subjects of great
familiarity to historians of monarchy in the ancient, medieval and early
modern worlds, but which have been all but neglected for the recent period.
To be sure, the contemporary court is no longer the centre of political
power that it had been in earlier times.[31] But we do need to know how it
has functioned during the nineteenth and twentieth centuries. What was
the process whereby once-great offices of state, such as Earl Marshal and
Lord Chamberlain, became instead great offices at court? When, how
and why did the functions of the mistresses of the robes and of ladies in
waiting evolve from being quasi-political to being primarily sartorial and
secretarial? How has the royal civil service been recruited, and how have
its functions changed and evolved? How far is the political history of the

modern British crown, not so much the history of particular monarchs, but rather the history of successive private secretaries to successive sovereigns?[32] And who has been responsible for conceiving and orchestrating the monarchy's evolving ceremonial image, and – to the extent that they are able to determine it – for managing and overseeing its changing relations with the media? Who, in short, has been in charge of the right royal road-show as it has evolved and adapted from the early years of Queen Victoria to the later years of Queen Elizabeth?[33]

Power, wealth and prestige concern the public aspects of this successfully self-perpetuating elite institution; but what of the private lives and private relationships which are an essential precondition for that successful perpetuation? What, for example, was it like – and what is it like – to be born and bred and brought up as a member of the royal family? Or to be recruited into it? How does royalty view itself, and the world around – politically, socially and historically? How have the patterns and philosophies of royal education changed?[34] How is it, as befits their cultured and privileged background, that some sovereigns have been sensitive to the arts, while others have been wholly indifferent to them? The book has yet to be written that gives a convincing answer to these questions for the modern period. There is also the vexed subject of monarchy and matrimony. Despite the image of middle-class domesticity that was often projected, the children of Queen Victoria and Edward VII were mostly involved in arranged marriages with other European dynasties: love rarely entered into it, at least initially, and often subsequently; and some of these unions worked, while others did not.[35] Since the First World War, however, British royalty has virtually ceased to marry into foreign royalty, and has chosen its partners primarily from the indigenous aristocracy and middle class. Most of these alliances have been less deliberately (or less overtly) arranged, and some may even have been for love. But like those of an earlier style and era, some of them have worked, while others have not. Before the next royal generation embark on their matrimonial adventures, it might be helpful if these changes were better known and better understood.

At the most basic level, the history, functioning and perpetuation of monarchy is, as it always has been, about the social and sexual interaction between men and women. But it is not about men and women equally, and nor is it about men and women typically. Up to a point, it was (and is?) about the conventional gender roles of male superiority and female inferiority: as evidenced by the discussion at the time of the marriage of the Prince of Wales to Lady Diana Spencer, when it was deemed wholly appropriate that he had what was euphemistically called a 'past', whereas it was considered equally important that she did not. But only up to a point: for in Britain, the rules of succession are such that, on occasions, women have been able to cross the gender divide to play the male role of sovereign, and among the most moving and revealing of Queen Victoria's journals and letters are those in which she attempts to comprehend and come to terms with the fact that she was biologically a (female) mother but occupationally a (male) monarch.[36] Here is a rich field of study, where feminist scholars are following paths already blazed by historians of medieval and early modern monarchies. But there is more to do: for the modern British monarchy has often been described as a matriarchy, with a succession of dominant and/or charismatic women: Queen Victoria, Queen Mary, Queen Elizabeth the Queen Mother, the present Queen and Princess Diana. How are we to explain this?[37] Perhaps it should be in terms of the accidents of birth, succession, personality and good looks; but it might also be that constitutional monarchy is in fact emasculated monarchy, and thus a *feminized* version of an essentially male institution. For constitutional monarchy is what results when the sovereign is deprived of those historic male functions of god and governor and general, and this in turn has led – perhaps by default, perhaps by design? – to a greater stress on family, domesticity, maternity and glamour.

It should scarcely need saying that many of these historical issues are also subjects of great contemporary concern in the media; yet that current interest is at best historically under-informed, and at worst historically un-informed. This is partly because virtually all the public discussion of the British monarchy today takes place with scarcely any reference to a past before yesterday. But it is also because much of that relatively recent royal history does not yet exist in the way that it does for earlier royal periods and pasts. To be sure, there are hints and snatches and suggestions which can be found in the royal biographies already mentioned. But it is a besetting weakness of the genre for the modern period that it takes the institution of monarchy for granted, when it is precisely the structure, operation, functioning, development, evolution and legitimacy of that institution that we most need to know about. By its nature, and throughout its existence, monarchy is as much about institutions as it is about individuals; which is why the modern British monarchy, like its predecessors, needs to be treated historically as well as biographically, thematically as well as chronologically, analytically as well as anecdotally. And that is the treatment which it is now, belatedly but encouragingly, beginning to receive.[38]

III

That is not the only reason why such treatment is required, and has increasingly been undertaken since the 1980s: for while it is both necessary and appropriate to discuss the workings of the modern British monarchy as a self-perpetuating elite institution, it has not successfully perpetuated itself across the last two hundred years purely and exclusively of its own dynastic and dynamic volition. That, surely, is the lesson of the post-1776 and post-1789 past: for during the last two centuries, monarchies have functioned or ceased to function, have survived or have fallen, not so much on the basis of how particular monarchs did (or did not do) their jobs, nor because of how well (or how badly) the institution has collectively comported itself. They have succeeded, or failed, to the extent that they have seemed, or not seemed, broadly credible and convincing to the subjects of the nation over which they have reigned. This, in turn, has obliged successive sovereigns to take on new functions and do new things, even as old functions have been attenuated, adapted or appropriated elsewhere. As a result, the modern British monarchy has (on the whole) successfully embedded itself in a wider web of relationships and connections, which are themselves a rich amalgam of history and geography, sociology and ethnicity, dynasty and territory: the British nation, the European royal cousinhood, and the Empire and (more recently) the Commonwealth beyond the seas.

In the case of the British monarchy and its position in relation to the British nation, a series of questions demand attention, and some of them have recently been getting it.[39] How have the sovereign's relations with the aristocracy, the middle classes and the working classes developed and evolved since the accession of Queen Victoria? This inquiry raises complex issues, concerning both the changing circumstances and the developing aspirations of those three groups, and also the evolving and targeted appeal of the monarchy to them. Is (for example) the decline in the role of the crown as a significant patron of the arts, and the increased attendance by successive sovereigns at football cup finals and royal variety performances, in part to be explained by the nation's evolution from an aristocratic to a democratic polity? (It seems highly likely that it is.)[40]

And what part has the media played in all this, by turns manipulating the monarchy and also being manipulated by it? Clearly, the development of the national press, from the Liberal intellectual dailies of the mid-Victorian period to the Tory tabloids of our own time, is a major subject; and so is the impact of photography, the cinema, the wireless and television. In the case of the newspapers, the crown never seems to have wielded much influence with proprietors, editors or journalists; but over visual and broadcast images, it has generally been more successful in asserting some degree of control.[41]

Queen Victoria once famously declared that she would never become the queen of a 'democratical monarchy'; but by the end of her reign, she reluctantly was, and her successors have had no more choice in that matter than she did. Yet this remains a difficult subject to bring into sharp or clear historical focus. In the past, most monarchies were not of the democratic kind; in the present, most democracies are not monarchies. So what exactly is democratic monarchy? In part, it bears repeating, it is welfare monarchy; but it is also peripatetic monarchy. To be sure, medieval and early modern monarchs famously progressed around their realms, beating the bounds of their dominions, and often ruining their subjects on whom they descended for hospitality that might be demanded for weeks at a time. But the practice whereby, on any given weekday, many members of the royal family will be found undertaking public duties in towns and cities across the length and breadth of the country is a relatively recent development, and it seems likely that it is connected with the near-simultaneous extension of the franchise.[42] Likewise, the honours system, of which the monarch is both fount and sovereign, has developed during the last 150 years from being (largely) exclusive and aristocratic to being (in some ways) more meritocratic and democratic. Critics of the current practices might be surprised at that description; but there can be no doubt that the system was pushed firmly in this direction during the early part of the twentieth century, and it would be interesting to know more about the part played in these changes by successive British sovereigns.[43]

These are important and difficult questions, and one of the reasons they are difficult is that they cannot convincingly be answered with reference to a monolithic *British* nation. For across the last two hundred years, the British monarchy has enjoyed (if that is the right word) very different relations with the constituent parts of what is revealingly called the United *Kingdom*. Our modern and ostensibly unifying crown is, in many ways, the old, historic English monarchy – so powerfully identified with the Tower of London, Windsor Castle and Hampton Court – extended and writ large. But how is this so, and what remains uniquely English about it?[44] As for the Welsh: theirs was the first throne to be absorbed by the English nation and crown. But Victoria did not like the Welsh all that much (not least because they would persist in voting for Gladstone); there is no royal residence west of Offa's Dyke, and no Welsh order of chivalry; and the investiture of the Prince of Wales at Caernarfon is one of the more fanciful pieces of recently-invented royal tradition.[45] In the case of Scotland, it was Prince Albert who created the kilt-wearing, stag-hunting, Balmoral-living image of the royal family. But in many ways, this was pure fiction: he bought Balmoral because it reminded him of *Germany*, and it was not until Lady Elizabeth Bowes-Lyon married into the royal family this century that significant post-Stuart Scottish blood was brought in.[46] In Ireland, the story is different again: Queen Victoria disliked the Catholics and refused to countenance a royal residence across the sea; and the Irish nationalists whole-heartedly reciprocated this hostility; but for Ulster unionists, loyalty to the British crown was (and is) seen as essential to their identity and survival.[47]

Thus regarded, the relations between the crown and the nations, nationalisms and nationalities of England, Wales, Scotland, Ireland and Britain is a subject of great variety and complexity, and in our era of devolution and power sharing, it is still unfolding.[48] But throughout most of its existence, the British monarchy has always been a continental crown as well as a national dynasty, and not only (indeed, not primarily) because Britain has itself always been a European nation. From 1714 to 1837, British kings were also Electors of Hanover, and that close link across the North Sea was only severed on Victoria's succession because women could not rule in the Electorate.[49] Thereafter, and on into the reign of Edward VII, the British monarchy remained an integral part of the extended, cosmopolitan cousinhood of European royalty, which encompassed the ruling houses of Germany, Austria-Hungary, Russia, Spain, Portugal, Italy, Scandinavia and the Low Countries.[50] It was into the Protestant parts of this vast, single, extended family that both Victoria and Edward VII married off their children; both sovereigns were regular visitors to the continent, who spoke French and German fluently; and royal weddings, coronations and funerals in the great European capitals were family reunions on an international scale. In writing the history of the modern British monarchy, we need to give more attention to this continental dimension: not only because of its intrinsic (and under-rated) importance; but also so that we can appreciate better how it resembled, and how it diverged from, the other great European dynasties and thrones.[51]

Before 1914, these continental connections, comparisons and contrasts were essential to the identity and functioning of the British monarchy. But in Britain, as elsewhere, it became ever more difficult to reconcile them with the crown's increasingly important function as the symbol and cynosure of mass, democratic national identity; and this historical royal cosmopolitanism was no antidote to the intensifying great-power rivalries which erupted on the outbreak of the First World War.[52] With European royalty split down the middle, King George V was compelled to choose between his cousinhood and his country, and he unhesitatingly opted for his country, changing his family name from Saxe-Coburg-Gotha to Windsor. It was a wise move, for soon after, the monarchies of Russia, Austria-Hungary and Germany tumbled, leaving the British crown surviving in splendid isolation as the last authentic great-power European monarchy: a development which, in turn, explains why a younger royal generation looked primarily to aristocratic Britain rather than royal Europe for their husbands and wives. Since the First World War, only two members of the British royal family close to the throne have married continental royalty – the Duke of Kent (who wed Princess Marina of Greece) and the present Queen (who married Prince Philip, Marina's cousin). As a result, the family connections between the House of Windsor and the remaining royal houses of Scandinavia, the Low Countries and Spain have become ever more distant, which means that the British monarchy is now significantly less European than it was in the time of Queen Victoria or her predecessors. Yet even if the continental context has weakened, the continental comparisons remain important – and all too rarely drawn.[53]

One reason why George V was willing to distance himself from his European cousins was that he knew he would not be confining his throne to the relatively circumscribed compass of the British Isles. For the British crown, as it had evolved during the nineteenth century, was not only archipelagic and continental in its geographical reach and roots, it was also global and transoceanic. To be sure, it had been a maritime monarchy since the days when the first Elizabethans reached and settled Virginia; but it was only during the reign of Queen Victoria that a whole new clutch of imperial functions and world-encompassing justifications were heaped upon it, and successive sovereigns became empresses and emperors of India, rulers [sic] of British dominions beyond the seas, and the heart of an expanded imperial realm on which the sun never set. Yet we know relatively little about the process whereby the British monarchy became an imperial monarchy again in the long aftermath of the loss of America.[54] What were its differing relations with the dominions, with India, and with the colonies? How did British kingship connect with and relate to those many indigenous rulers in numerous parts of the British Empire, who were thus simultaneously fellow sovereigns but also imperial subjects?[55] And to what extent did the Empire (and subsequently the Commonwealth) provide a new justification for the post-divine, post-governing, post-fighting monarchy, not only in London, but also in the colonies, in terms of royal pro-consulates and extended overseas tours?[56]

These are significant historical questions, which biographies of British kings and queens can certainly help us with, but which also need to be considered on their own terms as scholarly problems which transcend particular reigns and individuals. By definition, lives of monarchs tend to concentrate on where they happen to be at any particular time, which means they are generally written from the viewpoint of Buckingham Palace or Windsor Castle or Sandringham or Balmoral (or Osborne). That is entirely understandable; but it is also very limiting, since the history of the modern British monarchy cannot properly or plausibly be written from such a constrained geographical perspective. For that history has also taken place – and to some extent is still taking place – all over this country, and also in the wider world beyond: not just in Mayfair and Tower Hamlets and Birmingham and Tunbridge Wells; but also in Belfast and Dublin and Glasgow and Cardiff; in Canada and Australia and New Zealand and South Africa; in Gibraltar and Malta and Cyprus and Egypt; and in India and Nigeria and Singapore and Jamaica. In each of those countries, the institution that we properly but parochially call the British monarchy has its own specific existence, locally-grounded history, and particular meaning; and these are histories, by turns place-bound yet cumulatively global, which are only now beginning to be written.[57]

As such, the scholarly treatment of the modern monarchy as an *imperial* institution is an even more recently-realized academic subject than the history of the monarchy as a *British* institution. Earlier generations of imperial historians, preoccupied with such issues as the economic motivation for expansion and the constitutional evolution from Empire to Commonwealth, were not much concerned with monarchy; more recent post-colonialist writers have their own very different agendas, but again the monarchy is not high on their list of interests; and even the magnificent multi-volume *Oxford History of the British Empire* left the subject very much alone. Once again, there was pioneering work on the role and rep-resentation of the imperial crown in India and in Africa published during the 1980s,[58] but it has only been since the 1990s that a substantial body of research has begun to build up, which rightly treats the modern British monarchy as an essential theme in the history of what is now called the 'British world'; and there is clearly a great deal more that needs doing, both from the particular perspectives of individual colonies and dominions, and also from the broader vantage point of the Empire and the Commonwealth as a whole.[59] Moreover, it was essentially that late-Victorian imperial monarchy, by turns new-old, public-private, English-British, military-maritime, transoceanic, local-global, low-tax and high-ceremony, that Queen Elizabeth II inherited from her father, King George VI, in 1952. Despite Indian independence, it was still very much a going concern: small wonder historians have not until recently begun to look into it.

IV

That inheritance and that accession took place well over fifty years ago, but although there are still many survivors from that era and that monarchy, including the Queen herself and Prince Philip, we do not and cannot inhabit that earlier royal, national or imperial world today. This, in turn, means that although her reign is not yet history, it is already an era of historic royal time. How, then, in the light of the arguments advanced here, and of events and developments during the intervening half century, might we begin to try to make historical sense of the reign of Queen Elizabeth II? Contemporary history is a notoriously easy subject to do badly, but a very difficult one to do well, since there is simultaneously too much documentation, yet also too little distance on it.[60] But it may be worth venturing two tentative observations. The first is that the most marked national transformation since the early 1950s has been Britain's slow, painful and not-yet-completed adjustment to the loss of imperial dominion and great-power status; and that the most marked royal transformation during the same period has been the slow, painful and not-yet-completed adjustment from being an imperial monarchy and great-power throne to something necessarily less and necessarily different. As we all know, downsizing is never easy, whether it be in a firm or a university or a nation – or a monarchy. Yet it is sometimes not only inescapable and unavoidable, but also salutary and stimulating as well. So it has been – and so it still is – during the reign of the present queen, where downsizing, and thus de-Victorianizing, has been in many ways the dominant theme.

Thus approached and apprehended the second Queen Elizabeth's reign cannot be properly understood purely and exclusively in terms of herself: now as always, there are deeper and more complex historical forces at work. But that is not the only dominant, if somewhat impersonal, theme. Here, then, is a second. On any reckoning, the survival of the British monarchy during the twentieth century must be deemed rather extraordinary, and almost exactly half of the period since the death of Queen Victoria is accounted for by the present Queen's reign. The monarchy may primarily have endured, as some insist, because the British people are deeply and abidingly and fundamentally loyal, so that republicanism has rarely been more than a fringe activity.[61] But it may also have lasted because Britain – unlike Germany and Austria-Hungary during the First World War, and Italy and Yugoslavia during the Second – was lucky enough to be on the winning side in both those conflicts.[62] Indeed, it is a nice irony that King George VI may have owed his throne to the military exertions of two nations – the USA and the USSR – that had both been created in revolutions during which monarchies were rejected and overthrown. In any event, and for whatever amalgam of reasons, the British monarchy is still here – largely (although not entirely) shorn of its traditional priestly, governing and warrior roles; reinvented during Victoria's time as an imperial, ceremonial, welfare and family monarchy; and now, during the present Queen's reign, perhaps in search of new functions and justifications once again.

As *The Times* rightly opined in a leading article that appeared ten years ago, 'the management of the monarchy has never been a comfortable task', and in undertaking it, a sense of history, along with practicality, is essential.[63] So, indeed, it is, though that is far from being a universally-held opinion. The left – certainly the far left – finds the very idea of monarchy baffling, indefensible, and thus of no significant interest. But monarchy has been around in this country for much more than a millennium, which means the subject demands to be taken seriously, whatever one's own opinions about it may be. On the other hand, the right – and certainly the far right

– believes monarchy to be self-evidently the best of all possible worlds, an unchanging symbol of national unity and continuity. But monarchy in Britain has changed and evolved and developed over time, and it can be shown, historically, to have done so: here again, the subject demands to be taken seriously, whatever one's own opinions about it may be. If we are to get the modern British monarchy in any sort of true, realistic and convincing historical perspective, then we must approach it with a mixture of sympathy (which the left does not like) and detachment (which the right does not like) – recognizing that it is, indeed, something of real historical significance, but always treating that history and that significance with appropriate scholarly scepticism.[64] Much work has been done since the 1980s, in this mode, and to this end; but there is a great deal still left to do. If we want to understand the modern British monarchy better, then we need to know yet more about it. *Pace* Walter Bagehot, it is not clear that magic and daylight are altogether incompatible.

3

Parliament:
Past History, Present History, Future History[1]

Like the British monarchy, the Westminster parliament has been around for a long time but, like the monarchy again, the writing of its history is a relatively recent (though a slightly more venerable) phenomenon. The great enterprise that is known as the *History of Parliament* is an iconic British undertaking which, in its scale, scope and significance, may fittingly be grouped with such cognate co-operative ventures as the *Dictionary of National Biography*, the *Survey of London*, the *Victoria County History*, and the *Buildings of England* series.[2] All of these great enterprises are multi-volume productions, inaugurated by dedicated and (sometimes, but not always) charismatic founders, which have subsequently evolved into major schemes of collective and collaborative inquiry, and all of them are (rightly and of necessity) still very much works in progress. Long may they continue to be so. From the outset, these massive projects have been informed by a strong sense of educational purpose as well as of academic aspiration, and across the decades since the late nineteenth century, when the earliest of them were first established, they have become increasingly integral to our national life and public conversations, encompassing (as they do together) London and the regions, the natural and also the man-made environment, people as well as places, power along with culture. As such, they combine perspective, popularity and prestige in a uniquely resonant way: they help us understand where we have come from, how and where we live now, and who we are today; they are the envy of many other countries around the globe who lack such splendid series; and no serious library, anywhere in the English-speaking world, can afford to be without their magnificent volumes.

From this perspective, the *History of Parliament* is one among several great engines of national historical endeavour and collective historical memory, and in reviewing its past achievements, contemplating its present circumstances, and considering its future prospects, this broader general context should never be lost sight of. It is (to switch metaphors) not the only great beast that is roaming in our historical jungle, and all these mammoth endeavours have certain characteristics in common. (How often, indeed, do the editors and directors of these mighty undertakings meet to discuss matters of common interest and mutual concern? Problems shared are not invariably problems solved; but it sometimes helps.) Moreover, in recent years, they have faced similar challenges and sensed common opportunities: concerns about levels of income, whether derived from government, from the Heritage Lottery Fund, or from private sources; the need to rethink (and in some cases re-establish) their relations with a much-expanded higher education sector and with universities, both old and new; the imperative to widen access to a broader public audience that is more fascinated by history than ever before; and the challenge of combining an instantly-recognizable (and much-loved) physical product, beautifully bound between hard covers, with the growing demands for online publication and immediate availability.

I

Yet for all their common characteristics, these scholarly leviathans are also (and rightly) strongly individualistic enterprises, in their mission, their organization, their financing, and their personnel. One way in which the *History of Parliament* is thus unique is that it has been, from the very outset, an essentially official enterprise: supported by peers and MPs alike during the 1930s, and funded by the taxpayer since it was re-established in 1951. It also bears the stamp of the two remarkable men who were its inspiration: Colonel Josiah Wedgwood, MP, and Professor Sir Lewis Namier, FBA. As their titles, their names and their post-nominal letters suggest, they could scarcely have been two more different begetters. Wedgwood was born in 1872 at the heart of England's entrepreneurial and intellectual aristocracy; he was a self-taught historian with a passion for genealogy and local history; he was a long-serving MP for Newcastle under Lyme, and he ended his days, ennobled by Winston Churchill in 1942, as Lord

Wedgwood of Barlaston.[3] Namier, by contrast, was born a Polish Jew in 1888 and was a disinherited landowner; he was subsequently exiled to England, where he studied history at Balliol College, Oxford, and where he fell in love with its traditional ruling classes and their great houses; but he was always a loner and an outsider, and he never obtained the sort of high-end professorship for which he yearned, despite the undoubted originality of his best scholarly work.[4]

The differences between the two men went deeper than that, for while Wedgwood was high-spirited, gregarious and convivial, Namier was bitter, joyless, and the prince of bores. (This, indeed, along with the prevailing anti-semitism in British academe, may explain his repeated professorial disappointments in Oxford, Cambridge and London.) Even more importantly, Wedgwood was a lifelong Whig, whereas Namier was a no-less-committed Tory, and it was out of this political contradiction and disagreement (or, alternatively, from these bipartisan impulses) that the *History of Parliament* eventually emerged in the form we know it today.[5] As befitted a friend and admirer of George Macaulay Trevelyan, Josiah Wedgwood believed passionately that the history of England was the history of liberty, and that the history of liberty was coterminous with the history of parliament: the pre-eminent national institution which had, across the centuries, won freedom for the people from the crown and nobility, and had nurtured it and safeguarded it against challenges from within and without.[6] Although too contrary, bloody-minded and individualistic to be a success in politics (he held office only briefly in the Labour government of 1924, having been an advanced Liberal earlier in his career), Wedgwood was much liked by MPs of all parties, and his desire to promote a history of parliament was inspired as much by his affection for the people as by his regard for the institution.

'To me, personally', he once wrote in a revealingly eloquent paragraph, which he re-worked, embellished and re-printed elsewhere,

Parliament is everything; the members are the staunchest friends man ever had; the life combines the mental gymnastics of college with the fresh wind of the outer world; only the recesses are intervals of stagnation.... The man who steps into the English Parliament takes his place in a pageant that has ever been filing by since the birth of English history.... And they one and all pass on the same inextinguishable torch – burning brightly or flickering – to the next man in the race, while freedom and experience ever grow. These men who have gone by, who have had the glimmer of the torch on them for a little time, are those

> whose memories I want to rescue, and in so doing reincarnate a small section
> of the Parliaments who made us.[7]

Hence Wedgwood's initiation of the history of parliament project during the 1930s, which was supported by a mixture of public and private money, and overseen by a committee including both politicians and academics. Hence his considered belief that such a history should cover the years from 1264 to 1918, and should contain biographies of all MPs and peers, detailed studies of constituencies, and also a general survey tracing the workings of parliament and through it, the rise, development and progress of liberty.[8] And hence the two volumes which he himself produced, covering the 2,500 known members of the House of Commons between the years 1439 and 1509, which were published in 1936 and 1938. They were appropriately bound in covers of Wedgwood blue, they celebrated parliament as a 'true mirror' of the nation, and they showed how, 'five hundred years before our day... the foundations of freedom were laid by Englishmen'.[9]

Such was Wedgwood's romantic, whiggish view of Britain's legislature and its past, which he hoped his great collective historical scheme would both promote and project. But from almost the very outset, he had fallen out with the academics and the professors, whose approval and assistance were essential if his enterprise was to move forward; and with no academic did he fall out more completely than with Lewis Namier. For Namier regarded the Colonel's unabashed whiggism as the embodiment of everything that he himself detested. He dismissed freedom and liberty as mere ideologies, which he scorned as 'cant', 'flapdoodle', or 'wobbling of the brain'. Men seeking or wielding power were not, he believed, motivated by any such lofty ideas or ideals, but by material self-interest, and by the psychological consequences of their upbringing and temperament.[10] Moreover, Namier's attack on whiggism was not just at the level of generality, but also of detail. In 1929, he had published a book entitled *The Structure of Politics at the Accession of George III*, which undermined the prevailing whiggish view that English politics had always been dominated by the two-party system; and in the following year, he produced *England in the Age of the American Revolution*, which refuted the Whig 'myth' that George III had been a tyrant, determined to undermine liberty in the American colonies as well as in Britain itself.[11] In both these works, Namier insisted, detailed scholarly research corrected the inaccurate, self-serving generalizations by which the Whigs had for so long distorted the nation's past. 'The pageant of history', he would later write, in riposte to Wedgwood, 'must not be arranged under capital letters.'[12]

Namier, then, did not regard the history of parliament as the heroic, patriotic story of liberty unfolding, he was not much concerned with the lives of the members of the Lords, and he had little interest in how the upper and lower houses exerted power, by passing (or refusing) legislation, or by making (or unmaking) governments. Instead, his overriding fascination lay with the particular personnel and personalities of the Commons. Who were these MPs? What were their social and religious backgrounds? How were they brought up? What were their occupations? Who were their relatives? Which constituencies did they represent? Why (and this issue especially intrigued him) did they decide to go into parliament?[13] What did they say, and how did they vote when they got there? These were the questions that Namier believed a history of parliament should address, not so much because of what they would reveal about *parliament*, but rather because of what they would reveal about *England*. For he was less concerned to study the evolution of a political institution over time than with studying the evolution of an elite group over time: the thousands of men who (unlike the hereditary peers) had voluntarily and deliberately set their sights on going to Westminster. 'The social history of England', he once famously and provocatively observed, 'could be written in terms of the membership of the House of Commons', and that was what Namier believed the history of parliament ought to do: to provide a long-term collective biography (or prosopographical analysis) of the membership and personnel of the lower house, from which he believed there would emerge 'a social and economic history of the nation as has never yet been attempted'.[14]

To be sure, Namier eventually came to share Josiah Wedgwood's regret at the inter-war decline of Britain's traditional grandee and gentry governing families; he echoed the Colonel's concern at the rise of authoritarian regimes across much of Europe at the expense of parliamentary democracy; and he would later pay tribute to his friend-cum-adversary as 'a passionate lover of his country, jealous of its honour and moral integrity, a knight-errant of Englishry'. But Namier also shared his fellow-professionals' disappointment at the many shortcomings of Wedgwood's two volumes, and he thought him an inadequate and naive scholar: 'sometimes inconsistent in argument, confused in thought, inaccurate in his "facts" – not a painstaking historian'.[15] Lord Wedgwood died in 1943, but three years earlier, a History of Parliament Trust had been established to carry his project forward, which eventually resolved to focus on MPs and their constituencies, and leave out the upper house and more general matters. The trustees were drawn from the Commons and the Lords, a separate academic editorial board was set up (so as to avoid any repetition of the earlier disagreements between the politicians and the professors), and in February 1951, the then Chancellor of the Exchequer, Hugh Gaitskell, guaranteed £17,000 annually for the project over the next twenty years. The aim, he insisted, in apparent contradiction of the remit that had recently been agreed, would be 'to give a detailed record of the personnel of Parliament, both Lords and Commons; an outline of the principal transactions in each of the recorded Sessions; and, built up from these details, a survey of the development and continuity of parliament through the centuries as an integral part of the British Constitution'.[16]

This broad-ranging mission statement, with its undeniable (if more muted) whiggishness, sounded rather like an updated version of Wedgwood's earlier conception of the form the history of parliament ought to take. It was scarcely consistent with what had been agreed during the Second World War, and given that public money was to be involved, it seems odd that the remit of the re-established enterprise was never fully settled or precisely specified. Nevertheless, the funding had been secured from the Treasury, and the editorial board now began its work, under the chairmanship of Sir Frank Stenton. But as Wedgwood had earlier discovered, it soon became clear once again that the task was far greater than had originally been envisaged, that the sum of money would be insufficient, and that twenty years would not be long enough to complete the project. This may have surprised the scholars, but it should not have shocked the civil servants. 'Estimates by historians', one official had warned the Secretary of the Cabinet back in 1949, 'whether as regards time or cost or staff have in our experience to be treated with the greatest reserve. They are nearly always exceeded.'[17] Accordingly, the whole scheme was reassessed in 1956–57, and the fifteen sections into which the *History* had originally been divided were reduced to six, in the hope they might be completed by the time the money ran out in 1971. But although extra funds were made available, progress continued to be slow: only two sections were published within the first twenty years of the revived *History*'s existence, and four of the section editors – Professors Bindoff, Neale, Namier himself, and Aspinall – died before their labours had been completed.

Among Stenton's most influential colleagues on the editorial board was the Tudor historian Sir John Neale, but it was Sir Lewis Namier, by now at the peak of his academic renown and public reputation, who became the dominant intellectual influence over the revived and reconstituted enterprise. Having been a fierce critic of what had seemed to him Wedgwood's amateur and anachronistic approach to the history of parliament, Namier devoted his final years to producing a much more rigorous, focused and scholarly version, which reflected his own interests and concerns, as well as the priorities of the trustees, rather than those of Hugh Gaitskell. For the best part of a decade, he laboured nine hours a day at the Institute of Historical Research in London, working on the biographies of eighteenth-century MPs and on the histories of their constituencies. (At this time, the men's lavatory at the IHR was provided with two hand towels, one exclusively for Namier's use, the other for everyone else, a privilege which no other historian, before or since, has ever enjoyed.[18]) Namier was helped by three assistants and several unpaid volunteers, but he found the work increasingly burdensome, and by the time he died in 1960, nothing had yet appeared in print. Four years later, three volumes were published, covering the House of Commons between 1754 and 1790, co-edited by Namier himself and by his long-time collaborator John Brooke.[19] Thus was the *History of Parliament* re-launched, with books that set the precedent and the pattern for virtually everything that has been accomplished since then.

II

As if to signal that this was indeed a new beginning, the three volumes of the *History of Parliament* that appeared in 1964 were bound, not in Wedgwood blue, but in a much darker hue of the same colour. They ran to 2,000 pages, they sold at 21 guineas the set, and the initial print run of 1,500 copies proved to be more than adequate.[20] They were well received by Namier's protégés, by those who shared his conservative politics, and by some senior officials in the Palace of Westminster.[21] The first volume contained a general introduction by John Brooke which distilled his master's mature thoughts on eighteenth-century politics, analysed the backgrounds of MPs and described the general elections that took place during the period; and it was followed by detailed surveys of the 314 parliamentary constituencies in England, Wales and Scotland. Volumes two and three were devoted to the biographies the 1,964 MPs who had sat in the British parliament between 1754 and 1790 – a number which, by remarkable arithmetical coincidence, was exactly the same as the year of the work's publication.[22] Many reviewers were fascinated by the biographies of the great (among them both Pitts, both Foxes, John Wilkes and Lord North) and also of the not so great (such as John Bentinck, Bamber Gascoigne, and Edward Eliot), and by the powerful light beamed on to the constituencies; and the prodigious labours that the work embodied were also rightly acclaimed (Namier's own contribution, by far the largest, amounted to half a million words). As such, the three volumes furnished 'the finest memorial to a great scholar', and they were also 'a unique tribute to a unique institution'. Indeed, according to the anonymous reviewer in the *Times Literary Supplement* (who was in fact John Carswell) they were 'magnificent'.[23]

But even those who wrote appreciatively of these three majestic volumes were often also critical of them, while other reviewers expressed outright disapproval and disappointment.[24] Namier's enemies (and he had made plenty) saw this posthumous publication as an irresistible opportunity to pay off old scores against him; there was much resentment at (and exaggeration of) the 'formidable squadrons' of protégés and the substantial sums of public funding he was alleged to have controlled via the *History of Parliament*; and his own scholarly views on eighteenth-century politics no longer commanded the unthinking acceptance they had enjoyed for much of the 1950s.[25] The knives were out for Namier, just as they had been for Wedgwood a generation earlier, and between them, the critics produced a litany of complaints. John Brooke's introduction seemed uneven and erratic in its coverage, caught in a historiographical time-warp where Namier's negative views of political parties still held unchallenged sway. For all its evidential richness and anecdotal fascination, the remorseless detail provided about MPs and constituencies meant the books seemed drained of every vestige of historical colour or imagination. This may have been consistent with the remit that had been devised for the *History* during the Second World War, but many reviewers found it unacceptably limiting and myopic. For it meant there was no discussion of the Commons as an institution: of what it did or how it worked, of how it made law and policy, or of how it made and unmade administrations. It meant there was no treatment whatsoever of the personnel or of the functioning of the House of Lords. And it meant there was no attempt to assess parliament's place in the evolving British constitution or in the broader political life of the nation.[26]

These were serious and substantial objections, which would be repeatedly rehearsed when subsequent volumes of the *History of Parliament* appeared. But it was Namier's former colleague and friend, A.J.P. Taylor, who provided the most damning (and oft-quoted) verdict in a review in *The Observer*, provocatively entitled 'Westminster white elephant'. Namier and Taylor had been colleagues at the University of Manchester during the 1930s, and they were both admirers of Winston Churchill. Moreover, Taylor's books on European history shared Namier's loathing of the Germans, and in 1956 he co-edited Namier's festschrift with Richard Pares. But by then, Taylor was turning against his mentor, and in the same year, he also wrote a devastating review in the *Manchester Guardian* of *The Chatham Administration, 1766–68*, which had been written by John Brooke.[27] Namier did not forgive this attack on his favourite protégé and close collaborator, and in the following year he declined to support Taylor for the Regius Professorship of Modern History at Oxford, when Harold Macmillan (who was not only the Prime Minister but also Namier's publisher) asked his advice. Thereafter, the two men never spoke, and Taylor allegedly refused Namier's offer of a death-bed reconciliation.[28] So it was scarcely surprising that he was unsympathetic to the Namier and Brooke volumes. They were not history, Taylor insisted in his review, but rather a vast quantity of undigested historical raw material. Most of the MPs thus biographied, he went on, were 'persons of no importance in their own day and certainly none in ours'. History, he concluded, was supposed to be a record of what was significant in the past; these volumes, by contrast, were merely 'a record of what was insignificant' in the past.[29]

These scholarly criticisms (and personal vendettas) soon spilled over into a broader public debate, over both the concept and the cost of the *History*, which was led off by an editorial in *The Listener*, and which continued during the general election held in October 1964. Two medievalists, H.G. Richardson and G.O. Sayles, damned the whole enterprise in a ferocious and not wholly-relevant letter as 'something more than a waste of effort' which would 'serve to obscure rather than to illuminate' the history of parliament.[30] John Brooke and Ian R. Christie (another Namier protégé) replied in the *History*'s support, and the debate was concluded with a second *Listener* editorial, guardedly endorsing the scheme, and rightly insisting that the sums of public money being spent on it (less than £250,000 over more than twenty years) were by no means large.[31] Two contemporary comments, which took a broader and longer view of the *History*'s purpose and prospects, and which turn out to have been remarkably prescient, are also worth mentioning. The first was by William Ferguson in a belated notice of the Namier and Brooke volumes in the *Scottish Historical Review*, which predicted that the *History*'s 'real worth will be cumulative rather than immediate'. The second, by *The Times* journalist Philip Howard, opined that the *History* 'may turn out to be one of the cultural and academic landmarks of our century' (he might have added 'and of the next century' as well).[32]

The forty-odd years that have intervened since the appearance of the Namier and Brooke volumes have in many ways borne out these more optimistic predictions concerning the future and the fate of the *History*. During the late 1960s, when Harold Wilson was Prime Minister, there was reiterated criticism in parliament and in the press of what was termed 'Britain's most expensive literary enterprise', and there were calls for the whole *History* to be closed down when the original twenty-year grant expired in 1971. But additional funding was eventually provided by the Chancellor of the Exchequer early in 1970. The grant-giving was subsequently transferred from the Treasury to parliament itself; it now stands at approximately £1.5 million per year; and the *History*'s finances, staff and publishing schedule are now organized with a realism, efficiency and focus that would have been inconceivable half a century ago.[33] As a result, the rate of output has markedly speeded up, with the production of seven more instalments, initially by Her Majesty's Stationery Office, subsequently by commercial publishers, and most recently by Cambridge University Press. This means that all the sections that had been agreed upon in the late 1950s have been completed, along with additional sections devoted to the years 1660 to 1690 (privately funded by an American and edited by Basil Henning of Yale University), and also covering the period from 1690 to 1715. Together, they comprise 28 volumes amounting to 20,000 pages, which contain 20 million words, and they include biographies of more than 17,000 MPs.[34]

These volumes have largely conformed to the pattern of the original volumes by Namier and Brooke, and some scholars have continued to lament the narrowness and rigidity of this approach: ignoring the Commons as a functioning legislature, disregarding the Lords in its entirety, and showing little interest in the broader history of parliament in the life of the nation. Moreover, the quality and content of the sections has varied, in terms of the general introductions, the surveys of constituencies and the biographies of MPs.[35] By common consent, the two volumes edited by Romney Sedgwick covering the years 1715 to 1754 are the weakest: they were rushed into print in 1970, in the hope that this might increase the likelihood (as it did) of the renewal and augmentation of the Treasury grant; the biographies of MPs and histories of constituencies are the least substantial of any in the *History*; and the general survey was distorted by an obsession with Jacobite MPs which the evidence did not warrant.[36] The introductions to the Hasler and Henning volumes, covering, respectively, the years 1558–1603 and 1660–90 have also been criticized for being rather insubstantial, while the Bindoff books, which deal with the period 1509–58, have no introduction at all, as the editor died before he was able to write it. Nor have these been the only problems: for many years, work on the period 1558 to 1603 was overseen by Sir John Neale, but he died before the section was completed, and his name was scarcely mentioned when the volumes finally appeared. By contrast, the most recent sections, edited by Thorne (1790–1820), Roskell et al. (1386–1421), and Cruickshanks et al. (1690–1715), have been widely praised, for being the most muscular and substantial yet produced, and for the high quality of their introductions, which range far beyond the narrower remits of their predecessors.

There has, then, been continued and justified criticism of the *History* – for its uneven scholarly standards, for its inconsistencies of approach and format, and for the rigid limitations imposed on it by the original Namier and Brooke straitjacket. But the personal animus against Namier has died away with the passage of time, and the continued regrets at the *History*'s shortcomings have been accompanied by a growing appreciation of the sheer scale, the meticulous scholarship and the cumulative significance of what *has* been achieved: namely the most detailed, authoritative and comprehensive account yet undertaken of the personnel of any legislature, at any time, in any part of the world. And it is an account whose worth and accessibility have been greatly increased since 1998, when the contents of all the volumes thus far published was made electronically available on a CD-ROM.[37] Moreover, the remaining sections, covering the Commons for the years 1421–1504, 1604–60, and 1820–32, are well on their way to completion, which means the entire history of the lower house from 1386 to 1832 will be finished, sometime after the end of this decade.[38] To be sure, it will have taken far longer to accomplish, and will have cost much more

money, than was originally envisaged when the History of Parliament Trust
was established over half a century ago; yet as reviewers have increasingly
come to appreciate, it *is* an extraordinary achievement, and all those in
politics and in academe who have helped sustain and support it across the
decades may feel justly proud of what has been done.[39]

III

With the completion of the history of the Commons (in terms of general
introductions, constituency surveys and collective biographies) now a
real and increasingly foreseeable prospect, this is an appropriate time to
pause, reflect, take stock, and consider what else is being done, could be
done and ought to be done, bearing in mind both the accomplishments
of the *History* so far, as well as its undeniable limitations. This seems, for
example, a propitious time to return to Namier's original vision, by turns
idiosyncratic yet commanding, that the collective biography of all MPs
would provide the raw material for writing a wholly original history of
Britain over the long term. From one perspective, that has always seemed an
absurd and perverse contention: how can the history of one section of the
legislative elite be regarded as constituting a history of the broader nation as
a whole?[40] Yet from another viewpoint, the proposition is as suggestive as it
is wrong-headed: already, since the appearance of the *History of Parliament*
CD-ROM, it has become possible to track the long-term patterns in (among
other things) MPs' social backgrounds and social mobility, their education,
their professional careers and their party affiliations, thereby gaining a
vivid and vital picture of the continuities and changes in the membership
of the Commons across more than half a millennium. *Pace* Namier, this
scarcely constitutes a comprehensive history of our nation; but it does
furnish many of the essential materials for constructing a long-durational
history of a significant segment of its elite; and in recent years there have
been encouraging indications that scholars are beginning to appreciate the
possibilities and grasp the opportunities that this unrivalled treasure house
of data and information provides.[41]

At the same time, the impending completion of the Commons volumes
from the thirteenth century to the early 1830s also opens up vistas of which
Namier and his contemporaries could never have dreamed, thanks to the

intervening revolution in information technology. One indication of this quantum change in the availability of knowledge is that the whole of the *Oxford Dictionary of National Biography* is already available online, and it can only be a matter of time (and, also, of money) before the *Victoria County History*, the *Buildings of England* series, the *Survey of London* all follow suit – along with the *History of Parliament* itself. Once this stage of electronic grace has been attained, both the audience for and the use of the completed Commons volumes of the *History of Parliament* will expand almost exponentially, in part because access will become so much easier and cheaper, but also because of the broader cross-searching which will then become practicable. It will, for instance, be possible to read a *History of Parliament* biography of an MP alongside (where it exists) an *Oxford DNB* biography. Even more usefully, it will be possible to move from a *History of Parliament* study of a constituency to a *Buildings of England* account of the county in which it was located, or to a *VCH* or a *Survey of London* history of a parish that formed part of it. Of course, such connections can already be made by pulling off the shelves the appropriate volumes in these different collective projects. But many people do no have easy access to all these works in hard copy, or lack the necessary physical strength to lift them, and so the opportunity to access them all electronically will significantly increase both their appeal and their utility – and from this development, as and when it happens, the *History of Parliament* will benefit substantially.[42]

We are, then, at a point in the *History*'s evolution when the riches contained within the completed Commons volumes are on the brink of becoming much more readily available, to a broader and more diverse audience, and also to greater scholarly effect, than ever before. This is an exciting prospect, but it also leaves a great deal still to be accomplished, as those glaring omissions in the *History*'s coverage, to which critics have so frequently (and so rightly) alluded, need to be made good. One such area is already being addressed, namely the House of Lords, which had been disregarded in the wartime remit devised by the History of Parliament Trust. In 1998, that decision was reversed by the trustees on the recommendation of the editorial board, and since 1999 (the very same year, by ironic coincidence, that most of the hereditary peers were expelled from the upper house) work has been progressing on the Lords between the years 1660 and 1832. This represents a major (and long-overdue) expansion of the *History*'s scope, and it has also necessitated a serious rethinking of its methodology. For unlike MPs, members of the second chamber did not represent constituencies, they became legislators by hereditary right rather than individual choice or election (or nomination), and their biographical details may already be gleaned from *Burke*, or *Debrett* or *The Complete Peerage*. Moreover, the upper house also accommodated bishops and law lords, and until the Parliament Act of 1911, it had the power to reject all bills sent to it by the Commons, except (by convention) those dealing with finance. Accordingly the history of the Lords will contain different sorts of biographies from those found in the Commons volumes, and there will be extensive introductions, not only analysing this material, but also explaining the functioning of the Lords as a legislature and a judicature, as well as its collective and institutional life.

These pioneering volumes on the upper house will begin to appear before 2010, and it is to be hoped that resources will become available to complete this parallel parliamentary history of the Lords, extending back to 1386, within the next ten years. If and (dare one add?) when this is accomplished, it will mean a significant widening of the scope of the *History*, beyond the trustees' narrow wartime remit and Namier's own restricted vision of the enterprise, to something more closely aligned with Josiah Wedgwood's more spacious original scheme. And at some future date, there might also be commissioned a general survey of the Commons across the centuries, to rectify the shortcomings of some of the section introductions that have been published, and also to deal with the lower house's institutional and collective history and its broader part in the life of the nation. This is not to advocate a return to the Colonel's ardent and naive whiggism, but it would go some way to meeting the repeated criticisms that there is more to the history of parliament than the biographies of MPs and the studies of their constituencies.[43] With any luck, the result will be a selective but appropriate synthesis of the seemingly irreconcilable priorities of Wedgwood and Namier: a detailed history of the Commons and the Lords, which also addresses more general themes. As such, the *History* would certainly merit the praise which has increasingly been lavished upon it in recent years: 'it is larger than life, and has at its heart a sense of purpose that takes the breath away'; and when concluded, it 'will constitute, in erudition, comprehensiveness and sheer size one of the major collective achievements of British historical scholarship'.[44]

IV

It is, then becoming increasingly possible not only to envisage, but also to anticipate, the completion of a comprehensive history of parliament, covering uninterruptedly all the years from 1386 to 1832. Yet such a work would still leave unaddressed two major periods, and it is to them that the editorial board has recently been turning its attention.[45] The first is the history of parliament during the years before 1386. This is a highly important project, dealing as it does with the medieval origins of the institution, and it is essential for the integrity of the enterprise that it should be undertaken in due course. In the interests of completeness and consistency, it would need to include both the Commons and the Lords at the same time, and the research for it would constitute a major (and very difficult) undertaking. This is partly because there were approximately ten thousand men who were returned to the lower house during this period, and there were also more than a thousand men in the upper house: these are very large numbers indeed, equal to more than three quarters of the Commons biographies that it has already taken more than forty years to produce. But it is also because the lack of archival sources may mean it will be difficult to establish even the basic biographical details of many of these MPs and peers. To complete the history of parliament for the thirteenth and fourteenth centuries as one single enterprise would thus be likely to take much longer than ten years. It therefore needs to be planned as a series of separate yet interconnected projects, and in due course the editorial board hopes that they may be both outlined and undertaken.

The second missing area of the history of parliament is, by agreeable symmetry, at the other end: namely the years from 1832 to as near to the present day as it is practicable and possible to get. It was Josiah Wedgwood's ultimate aim to bring his history down to 1918, and there are widespread demands that it should now be brought to the close of the twentieth century, when it would become a history of parliament in our own time. By agreeable coincidence, another ten thousand people were returned to the Commons during these years, so that as with the pre-1386 period, the numbers would once again be very large. But in other ways, the history of parliament for the modern period would be a very different undertaking from that for the medieval period. The challenge for researching the thirteenth and fourteenth centuries will be the lack of sufficient evidence, but the challenge for researching the nineteenth and twentieth centuries will be its daunting, intimidating and overwhelming abundance, both in terms of manuscript sources and available printed material. This is a very real problem, with which we are in some ways already familiar: for it has taken five volumes and more than three thousand pages to cover the Commons during the thirty years from 1790 to 1820, and the conclusion to be drawn from this experience is clear, namely that any attempt to bring the *History of Parliament* up to the present day conceived on the existing model would require massive resources and would take many decades to complete.

Bluntly put, this is simply not going to happen: we cannot cover the post 1832 decades in the same way that we have covered the pre 1832 years if there is to be any realistic prospect of bringing the *History of Parliament* up to date this side of eternity. Instead, the editorial board is in the process of discussing and developing a wholly new approach for the modern period, both in terms of research methodology and in terms of publishing strategy, while at the same time aiming to preserve the traditional values and virtues of the history, and making the treatment of the years after 1832 as consistent as possible with everything that has gone before. For now, we are focusing exclusively on the Commons, and we have set the Lords aside: in all conscience, the lower house is more than enough to be going on with. And as we consider how best to devise appropriate research projects, our thinking is informed by two very significant (and also very positive) considerations. The first is that the basic biographical material is already available, in published form, for all the MPs who have sat since 1832, which means that time will not have to be spent, as so much of it has been for earlier periods, trying to track down the obscure and the elusive. The second is that the revolution in information technology now makes it possible to process and present larger quantities of historical data than was previously the case, and also opens up the possibilities of new publication formats, in addition to the blue volumes, and thus wider public access.

In the light of these considerations, it is the present view of the editorial board that the years since 1832 cannot be divided into periods along traditional lines (such as 1832 to 1885, 1885 to 1918, 1918 to 1945, and so on), but should be treated in a more thematic way, with the aim of constructing a modern history of the House of Commons in discrete but interlocking and cumulative phases. The first stage might involve the creation of an online collection of essential sources, including *Hansard*, published obituaries of MPs, and election records. This material could be linked together so that users would be able to construct their own biographies of MPs and histories of constituencies. The second stage would be to enhance this electronically-available data by providing additional contextual information, concerning (for example) parliamentary debates, individual biographies, and constituency affairs. This in turn would make it possible at a third stage to build up a comprehensive picture of the operation, activities and personnel of the Commons which, in addition to being made available electronically, might be published as blue volumes. Along the way, there would be possibilities for collaboration with other institutions and individual scholars, and attention is also being given to inaugurating an oral history of parliament for the years since 1945. It bears repeating that our thinking on these matters is only at a preliminary stage, and was helped and refined by a consultative conference held in London in January 2006.

Even thus vaguely sketched, this is a hugely exciting project and prospect, and it is one of which Josiah Wedgwood would himself have wholeheartedly approved. For as he had finally come to conceive the *History of Parliament*, the years from 1885 to 1918 were crucial: indeed, the Colonel regarded the publication of books on those years as a bait to draw in living MPs to subscribe, at a time when funding was a major issue. To make these volumes as appealing as possible, Wedgwood originally hoped that his friend Winston Churchill would 'supervise' the history extending from the Third Reform Act to the First World War, and some of the correspondence between them on the subject, which took place in September 1934, has survived. Wedgwood was convinced that Churchill's name would 'be the making of the whole series', he insisted that his active involvement would be limited to exercising general oversight, and he was willing to make £2,000 available to him so that he could employ the necessary research assistants. The result, Wedgwood believed, would be a great monument to the great wartime parliament, and to those of its members who had died on active service during the conflict.[46] Churchill regarded it as 'a great compliment' to be asked to edit what he described as the Colonel's 'admirable symposium', and he sent a cheque of two guineas towards the enterprise; but he insisted that he was 'taxed to the limit of my capacity with my literary and political work', and he twice declined Wedgwood's invitation.[47]

In May 1935, the Colonel approached H.A.L. Fisher, the Warden of New College, Oxford; but he was also in the middle of a major writing project, namely his multi-volume *History of Europe*. Accordingly, he, too, refused, although he was willing to act in an advisory capacity. By early 1936, Wedgwood was getting seriously worried that no progress was being made on the modern period, and decided to take matters into his own hands. He dedicated the first of his own published volumes to the 22 MPs killed on active service between 1914 and 1918, and while working on the second of them, he also resolved to take up the recent history of the Commons himself. He chose a novel means of investigation, though one which was becoming increasingly popular during the 1930s, namely the questionnaire (Mass Observation, which relied heavily on this investigative technique, was founded in 1937[48]). During the autumn of 1936, Wedgwood sent out his survey to the 550 men who had survived from the 2,363 who sat in the Commons between 1885 and 1918, and he also despatched another 200 to the relatives of those who had not. All told, Wedgwood received 600 replies, and he worked on them until the middle of 1938. He closely analysed 130 of them, which he used as the basis for the biographical entries of MPs that would be an essential part of his history of the Commons during the late nineteenth and the early twentieth century. That history was never written. But the questionnaires and the biographies survive, and they make rewarding and enlightening reading.[49]

V

As he explained in the preamble to his survey, Wedgwood believed that it was 'desirable for living Members or ex-Members of Parliament to assist in the compilation of their own biographies'; and he was particularly keen that MPs should fill in the forms themselves: 'No biographer,' he insisted, rather portentously, 'only the man himself, can answer such questions.'[50] There followed a list of 24 queries, seeking out information on a wide range of personal and political matters: professional background, religious affiliation, preferred newspaper, and financial resources; early interest in politics, reasons for becoming an MP, prior experience of public work, and the cost of getting elected; the pleasures and downside of parliamentary life, and the speeches and statesmen they had most admired; chief political interests, major realms of parliamentary activity and endeavour, and so on. Some of his questions were characteristically trenchant: 'What was your

annual income, earned or unearned, when you first stood for parliament?';
'What did you dislike most [about parliamentary life], apart from being
re-elected?'; 'How did being an MP affect your earning capacity?'; 'Did
speeches affect your vote?'; 'If you are no longer in parliament, why did
you leave?' And for close friends, he pencilled in an additional inquiry,
perhaps reflecting his own lifetime's experience of disappointment: 'Why
have you failed?' (Lord Beaverbrook, in answering, declared that he had
not.)[51] Although he had consulted his fellow-MP Leonard Darwin, who was
a eugenicist and a statistician, Wedgwood's questions were not formulated
with any methodological rigour or sophistication. They were very open-
ended, and he had no intention of subjecting the answers to quantitative
analysis: he was more interested in stories than in statistics.

Wedgwood himself set an example, by completing his own questionnaire
on 28 July 1936. As he hoped would be the case with other MPs, his
answers are revealing. He became a Liberal in politics because of his parents
and his education at Clifton College. The two authors who helped form his
political views were Lord Macaulay and Henry George. He described his
religious convictions as 'agnostic and puritanical, mixed', and his favourite
newspapers were the *Daily Chronicle* and the *Manchester Guardian*. He
wanted to be an MP because he 'thought it the finest thing in the world
– and it is'. His annual (unearned) income when he stood for parliament
was £2,500, while his earned income was nil. It cost him £850 to contest
his seat in 1906, but only £300 in 1929. Before 1914, his prime political
concerns had been the taxation of land values, 'the interests of Indian
freedom and the protection of natives'. But they were superseded by
'winning the war, then saving the world from tyrants, and the weak from
being bullied'. Among living statesmen, Wedgwood's ideal was Sir Edward
Grey, among the dead, Cromwell (presumably Oliver) and Lincoln. His
greatest pleasure in parliamentary life was having delivered 'a good speech',
and his greatest dislike was 'not being called by the speaker'. He could
not decide which was his own best speech: on the declaration of war in
1914, or in the secret session debate on Passchendaele, or urging going
off the Gold Standard in 1931, or on India. In truth, he was spoiled for
choice, for as he explained, he had 'made more speeches than any of my
contemporaries, save Lloyd George and Winston Churchill'. And although
in conventional terms, his own political career had not been a success, he
had certainly learned along the way: 'I know now that vested interests

are too strong for abstract justice; and that one can only hope to modify injustice and protect liberty.'

Yet while Wedgwood was perfectly willing to answer his own questions, some recipients were distinctly unamused by what they regarded as such difficult, impertinent or time-consuming inquiries. 'I should be completely bowled out by your questionnaire', Lord Astor replied, 'and would have neither the knowledge nor the desire, nor the nerve to answer 95% of your queries.' Baldwin, then prime minister, thanked 'my dear Jos' for 'sending me the two forms', but there is no record that he filled them in. Churchill was still too busy to be involved with the scheme: 'Alas, I cannot undertake to answer this questionnaire. It is all I can do to get through my present work.'[52] Lord Monsell refused at greater length: 'I managed to retain my seat in parliament in spite of refusing to fill up every questionnaire that was put before me, and I do not propose to start now.' Sam Hoare also declined, in words that reveal something of his 'slippery' character: 'I have the greatest disinclination for circulating details and impressions about myself.' Lord Lee of Fareham was more cavalier than cagey: 'I really cannot bring myself to believe that the answers to most of the questions which you have drafted – at any rate in my own case – could be of the faintest interest to posterity.... Indeed, I am not sure looking back that the least said about my parliamentary career the better!'[53] Ramsay MacDonald gave several reasons for refusing an 'impossible' request, and ended by regretting 'how that sensible man Josiah Wedgwood has at last become infected by an interest in the vulgar trivialities of a personal character which are now being scattered abroad by a debased and debasing popular press'.[54]

Others did reply, but also sent revealing covering letters. 'I don't like making these "confessionals" even to such a broad-minded high-priest as yourself', wrote Sir Percy Harris, though he did so, all the same. 'You must have taken on a devil of a job in editing this parliamentary history', Lord Snowden wrote perceptively. 'But I will not go so far in my abomination for your questions as to refuse to answer them.' He was one of several correspondents who only did so out of personal affection for Wedgwood himself. 'If this request had not come from you', Lord Bingley wrote, 'I should have put it in the waste paper basket.'[55] 'Some of your questions are positively impertinent', Lord Kennett observed, 'and many for all that I can see very irrelevant. But I don't like to disappoint you!' Sir Norman Lamont came up with a particularly ingenious explanation for sending in his answers belatedly: 'I thought that as the *History* had only got down to

1509, it would be some time before you reached 1905, and that there could therefore be no great hurry.'[56] Others co-operated more promptly, but were sceptical of the whole enterprise. 'Are you so incredibly unsophisticated', Austin Hopkinson inquired, 'as to believe that MPs will tell you anything but lies about themselves?' 'You have got a big job on', George Barnes wrote, putting the same point another way. 'Our descendants may be led to believe that we parliamentarians were great fellows.'[57]

Detailed analysis of these questionnaires is presently being undertaken, but some general impressions may be worth reporting.[58] In reply to the question 'what were your religious convictions?' the overwhelming majority declared that they had been (and still were) believers. There was, unsurprisingly, a closer connection between nonconformity and the left, and between the Church of England and the right; but within these broad allegiances there were many shades of opinion, ranging from 'very low church', via 'a broad evangelicalism', and 'moderate High Anglican' to 'C of E Tractarian' on the one side; and from 'Nonconformist – Congregationalist', via 'Baptist' and 'Unitarian' to 'Presbyterian' on the other. (By contrast, Catholics, Jews and unbelievers were a distinct minority.) There was a similar broad division when it came to the 'favourite newspapers' the MPs had read when young or were reading now: those on the right generally opted for The Times or the Daily Telegraph or the Morning Post; those on the left preferred the Manchester Guardian, the Pall Mall Gazette or the Westminster Gazette. But there were also more idiosyncratic responses. Some MPs could not remember what they had read, or just answered 'none'; a few of them thought they had a duty to peruse a wide range of newspapers; others took the opportunity to denounce the Harmsworth regime at The Times. Henry Bowles had liked Punch 'as in those days it had a sense of humour'; Carlyon Bellairs, himself a journalist, preferred the papers to which he himself contributed; Henry Gooch took The Times, but only read the correspondence columns; while George Lansbury dismissed all newspapers as 'one-sided, unfair and partisan, with no idea of giving the public any other view except what they are established to propagate, and I say this of myself as an Editor'.[59]

One other division stands out: those on the left tended to go into politics with the intention of changing the world, while those on the right did so out of a sense of patriotic duty. Many would-be reformers regretted that they had not achieved much; some on the right thought their experience in parliament had taught them tolerance of views that differed from their own. But other aspects of parliamentary life seemed scarcely inflected by partisanship. Many MPs reported that speeches in the House had rarely swayed their votes, and they were often almost disconcertingly modest about their own oratorical performances. In answer to the question 'which speech do you think was your best?', Sir Archibald Weighill replied: 'equally disappointed with all'. An earlier bearer of the name William Whitelaw felt he had done little better: he recalled delivering only one notable speech, and that was his first, 'made against the views of his own party on the subject of the importation of Canadian cattle'. Most MPs seem to have enjoyed their time in the Commons, but the businessman Sir Eric Geddes (who was briefly an MP from 1917–22, when Lloyd George brought him into his coalition government) loathed it. He had 'never' thought of being an MP, he only went into parliament 'because I had to', and he 'got out as soon as I could', because he 'disliked the whole thing'. Among living statesmen, he most admired himself, but no one else who answered Wedgwood shared that preposterous opinion.[60] Other complaints about parliament were less self-serving: Sir Percy Alden regretted that being an MP meant wasting so much time; Christopher Addison deplored 'flummery of all kinds', of which there was plenty in the Palace of Westminster; while Sir Henry Bowles most disliked 'dinner in the members' dining room', and he left parliament on the bizarre grounds that 'my doctor said I must have all my teeth out'.

Wedgwood intended to use the answers to his questionnaire as the raw material for the biographical sketches he himself would write. They are diverting reading, for in addition to providing essential factual information, the Colonel added his own personal impressions. Indeed, according to Austin Hopkinson, the result was not so much a biographical register as a 'jest book'.[61] Here is Wedgwood on Lord Beaverbrook: 'since the war, his politics have been mostly wrong, but furiously energetic. He is the Churchill of the press.' Here he is on William Brace: he 'had the manners of gentleman, the candour of a child, and the complete honesty of the chapel'. Here he is on Lord Hugh Cecil: 'he has achieved nothing, save in the minds of men. His school is authoritarian yet he is the apostle of liberty.' And here he is on Sir Percy Harris: 'we even have his permission to say he is a Jew' (though the question 'have we?' is scrawled in the margin).[62] As this suggests, not everyone liked the sketches which the Colonel scrupulously sent back to their subjects for vetting. 'You may, of course, say that I am a poor speaker', John Clynes complained. 'I know of no one else who has said it.' Wedgwood was asked to delete this final sentence on Frederick

Guest: 'he always thought of himself first, but it was not a bad first'.[63] Lord Bingley did not mind being called stupid, but he took serious exception to being described as mean. And Frances Stevenson went out of her way to seek changes in Wedgwood's unflattering (but not inaccurate) description of Lloyd George as being lazy in his work habits. It is easy to see why Lord Bingley worried that the Colonel might find himself involved in libel actions if the work ever made it into public print.[64]

VI

But it never did so. Wedgwood initially hoped to publish the results of his survey in June 1937, scarcely nine months after the questionnaires had first been sent out. As so often in the early stages of the *History of Parliament*, this was a wildly over-optimistic timetable. Wedgwood continued working on the material until the middle of 1938, but thereafter he was distracted by more pressing commitments: the publication of the second volume of his parliamentary history covering the years 1439 to 1509 was met with much scholarly scepticism, and he became deeply involved in increasingly acrimonious correspondence with highly critical academics; and as a passionate anti-appeaser, he was much preoccupied with the events leading up to the Munich settlement in the autumn of 1938. Then came the Second World War, the whole *History of Parliament* project went into abeyance, and it was not revived until after Wedgwood's death.[65] But his questionnaires and biographical sketches survive, covering almost one quarter of all MPs who sat between 1885 and 1918. They contain important and valuable material about the men and their parliamentary experiences of a kind that cannot be found elsewhere, and which does not exist for earlier periods – or, indeed, for later times either. They are a unique, remarkable and challenging source, and as such they are an appropriate legacy to the *History of Parliament* from a unique, remarkable and challenging man.

As the *History* now begins to contemplate extending its coverage to the modern period after 1832, it is comfortingly reassuring to recognize that our first founder has in some ways already been there before us, and we must hope that a way will be discovered of putting his questionnaires, his biographies and his character sketches to good use as our work moves forward. It was Namier who insisted on the importance of primary sources, but it was Wedgwood who actually created such materials. And this is one more reason why, when contemplating the history of the *History of Parliament*, guarded homage to the Colonel is as appropriate as (no less) guarded homage to the Professor. They were both difficult and disputatious men, and it was entirely predictable that they should have fallen out over how the *History* should be researched and written. But with the lengthening perspective that time affords, we can surely agree that the result is indeed a daunting and imposing achievement, which owes much to both of them. And as we draw strength and inspiration from what these two men, and those who came after, have accomplished, we should also look to the future with buoyancy and hope: not only because, as Philip Howard recently put it, the magnificent blue volumes already produced will 'still be read centuries from now', but also because the most challenging and exciting phase in the history of the *History of Parliament* is only now beginning.[66]

4

Economy:
The Growth and Fluctuations of the
Industrial Revolution[1]

Throughout the twentieth century, Britain was engaged in a dialogue with what increasingly came to seem the much greater, more confident Victorian era; and while one of these many past-and-present national conversations was about the history of parliament, another of them, which began considerably earlier, concerned the causes, the nature, the consequences, the meaning and the moral status of those events, inventions, transformations and developments which took place during the late eighteenth- and early nineteenth-century economy, and which from the 1840s became known as 'the Industrial Revolution'. For as the British economy evolved and changed, declined and fell, survived and adapted, between 1900 and 2000, it did so against a historical background of earlier industrial prowess and global supremacy that was being constantly re-interpreted, re-evaluated and re-assessed, both by public commentators and, increasingly, by academics, who were economists, historians and economic historians.[2] As such, they had agendas and interests which were partly determined by the internal imperatives and academic dynamics of their own professions or sub-specialisms. But those agendas and interests were also externally influenced by the changing circumstances and contemporary conditions of Britain's twentieth-century economic performance and, on occasions, by the performance of the global economy as a whole. The result was that in every generation, one particular interpretation of the British Industrial Revolution was both more pervasive and more resonant than any other, not only within universities, but also in the broader public realm of punditry and policy making.

   This chapter seeks to describe and explain how and why this was so, by outlining four distinct phases into which these interpretations may be divided during the long one hundred years since Arnold Toynbee's *Lectures on the Industrial Revolution*, first published posthumously in the mid 1880s, effectively began modern discussion of the subject.[3] The first section examines the years to the 1920s, when contemporary pre-occupations with social surveys and working-class poverty influenced the prevailing interpretation of the Industrial Revolution, which emphasized (and criticized) its disagreeable human consequences. By contrast, the second generation of economic historians, writing from the mid 1920s to the mid 1950s, reflected current international concerns with war and economic fluctuations, by stressing the cyclical, up-and-down nature of the industrialization process. Their successors, who wrote from the mid 1950s to the early 1970s, were influenced by the rise of development economics and by the general post-war efflorescence of western capitalism, and re-wrote Britain's Industrial Revolution as the first instance of modern 'economic growth'. Finally, since 1974, the pursuit of economic growth became less fashionable, de-industrialization occurred, and Thatcherism came and went, with the result that Britain's Industrial Revolution has been given another new identity, as something less spectacular and more evolutionary, but also less parochial and more global, than had previously been supposed. The Industrial Revolution may be long since gone, but it keeps reappearing in new-old guises. Like so many aspects of the British past, it was not only something that happened then, but is also something that is still very much happening now.

                                           I

The years from the 1880s to the early 1920s were the first period in which a significant number of writers, pundits and historians investigated Britain's Industrial Revolution, and they did so against a complex background of anxieties about the economy and society of the time which significantly influenced the perspective they took on it. For politicians, businessmen and landowners, the prospects seemed distinctly gloomy: prices were falling, profits were correspondingly reduced, farmers were unable to pay their rents, and foreign competition was growing. The confident, optimistic faith in the possibility of unlimited economic progress, which had been reaffirmed only a generation earlier at the Great Exhibition of 1851, was suddenly and ominously diminished.[4] Royal Commissions investigated depressions in industry, trade and agriculture; the Boer War revealed a nation whose military were incompetent and whose manhood was unfit; and tariff reform was partly based on the recognition that there were, in the economy, unmistakable signs of decay. At the same time, the labouring classes were forcing their attention on their political masters: trade-unionist membership exploded between the 1880s and the early 1910s, and there were major outbreaks of industrial unrest in both of those decades; after the Third Reform Act of 1885, more members of the working class had the vote than ever before; the Liberals were increasingly challenged by Labour as the party of the ordinary man (though not yet woman); and there was a growing demand that government must be more actively interventionist in economic and social matters.[5]

More particularly, from the 1880s, there was a major revival of interest in what was termed the 'condition of England' question, concerning the health, housing and poverty of those at the lower end of the social scale. The reasons for what has been described as this 'remarkable flowering in the social concern of the English middle classes', and the extent to which it did (or did not) represent a new departure in social and sociological thought, remain sources of academic controversy.[6] But what is not in dispute is the massive outpouring of best-selling literature on the subject in the thirty years before the First World War, including the Royal Commission on the Housing of the Working Class, the surveys by Charles Booth and Seebohm Rowntree, the investigative journalism sparked off by Andrew Mearns's *The Bitter Cry of Outcast London: An Inquiry Into the Conditions of the Abject Poor* (London, 1883), the evocations of slum life in such novels as Arthur Morrison's *A Child of the Jagow* (London, 1894), and the writings of such members of the Liberal intelligentsia as C.F.G. Masterman. Together, these publications constituted a guilt-ridden, fearful recognition that working-class poverty and squalor was not the product of individual shortcomings, but was endemic in an economic system which created so much want in the midst of so much plenty. It was, as the radical Henry George put it in a memorable juxtaposition, 'this association of poverty with progress' which was 'the great enigma of our times'.[7]

Such contemporary revelations and polemics exerted a powerful influence, diverting the attention of many commentators, pundits and academics towards social concern with economic conditions.[8] For the majority of

British people, it now seemed, the Industrial Revolution had not delivered and had not worked, and it was the desire to discover what had gone wrong with it which prompted many of the pioneering studies of the late eighteenth- and early nineteenth-century economy. Indeed, it was Arnold Toynbee himself who formulated this close link between contemporary circumstances (and challenges) and the earlier Industrial Revolution. 'It would be well', he argued,

> if in studying the past we could always bear in mind the problems of the present.... You must have some principle of selection, and you could not have a better one than to pay special attention to the history of the social problems which are agitating the world now, for you may be sure that they are problems not of temporary but of lasting importance.[9]

As Lord Milner later explained, Toynbee 'was on fire with the idea of a great improvement' in the material condition of the working classes, and his upper-middle-class sense of guilt was both anguished and articulate:

> We – the middle classes, I mean, not merely the very rich – we have neglected you; instead of justice we have offered you charity; and instead of sympathy we have offered you hard and unreal advice; but I think we are changing.... We have wronged you; we have sinned against you grievously...; but if you will forgive us... we will serve you, we will devote our lives to your service.[10]

Toynbee's desire to locate the historical origins of unacceptable contemporary social conditions in the time (and the troubles) of the Industrial Revolution was shared by those two progressive husband-and-wife writing teams: J.L. and Barbara Hammond, and Sidney and Beatrice Webb. To be sure, the Hammonds did make an effort at objectivity which gave their work its real scholarly value; but at the same time they were also deeply committed radicals. *The Village Labourer, 1760–1832*, published in 1911, argued that the landowning classes, excited by the prospects of parliamentary enclosure, behaved with scarcely a thought for their social inferiors. The book was described by the Longmans reader as 'sound historically, though written from a radical point of view'; Gilbert Murray thought it showed 'how blind the whole upper and middle class can be to the condition of the poor'; and as an anti-landlord polemic, it provided historical validation for the 'land campaign' that Lloyd George would soon launch. Likewise, its sequel, *The Town Labourer, 1760–1832*, which appeared in 1917, was strongly anti-capital and anti-laissez-faire, thereby 'destroying', according to R.H. Tawney, 'the historical assumptions on which our modern slavery is based'.[11] In their portraits of rapacious landlords and heartless capitalists, the Hammonds' books lent strong support to the intensifying contemporary view that free enterprise must be controlled, that the state ought to be more interventionist, and that trade unions should be protected and strengthened.

The Webbs' writings on the Industrial Revolution contained a similar prescriptive thrust. As she explained in *My Apprenticeship*, Beatrice was profoundly influenced by her early work for Charles Booth, she was as racked with guilt as Arnold Toynbee about the sufferings of the lower classes, and she, too, drew explicit links between the unacceptable conditions of the present and the earlier horrors of the Industrial Revolution:

> A study of British blue books, illuminated by my own investigations into the chronic poverty of our great cities, opened my eyes to the workers' side of the picture. To the working class of Great Britain in the latter half of the eighteenth and first half of the nineteenth century – that is four-fifths of the entire population – the 'Industrial Revolution'... must have appeared... as a gigantic and cruel experiment which, insofar as it was affecting their homes, their health, their subsistence and their pleasure, was proving a calamitous failure.[12]

For Beatrice, as for Sidney, both past history and present circumstances made plain that what was needed was 'collective regulation of the conditions of employment... by legislative enactment or by collective bargaining': in short, an end to laissez-faire, by promoting stronger unions and greater state intervention. For the Webbs as for the Hammonds, their writings about the Industrial Revolution were essentially historical prefaces to contemporary problems. As Beatrice explained, their *History of Trade Unionism*, first published in 1901, was 'little more than a historical introduction to the task we had set before us: the scientific analysis of the structure and function of British trade unions', and their history of local government, the first volume of which appeared in 1906, was merely the prologue to 'an analysis of English local government as it existed in our own time for the use of would-be reformers'.[13]

Thus influenced and motivated, Toynbee, the Hammonds and the Webbs established the dominant interpretation of the British Industrial Revolution in their generation as 'the history of the social problems which are agitating the world now'. For them, it was a three-fold disaster, so it was scarcely surprising that its long-term impact should have been so negative: it was rapid; it was terrible; and it was rapid and terrible because selfish and inhumane governments refused to intervene to mitigate or even modify its evils and excesses. According to Toynbee, the old order 'was suddenly broken in pieces by the mighty blows of the steam engine and the power-loom'; innovations 'destroyed the old world and built a new one'; and the late eighteenth and early nineteenth centuries were a period of 'economic revolution and anarchy'.[14] Likewise, for the Webbs, the Industrial Revolution was characterized by 'wholesale adoption of power-driven machinery and the factory system', which suddenly 'took place around 1780'. And for the Hammonds these events at this time 'separated England from her past as completely as the political revolution separated France from her past'; the 'history of the early years of the Industrial Revolution' was 'a history of vast and rapid expansion'; it was 'a departure in which man passed definitely from one world to another'.[15]

But it was the horrific human consequences, with which they were still living in their own time, that most gripped them. 'We now approach', Toynbee wrote in his most famously apocalyptic passage,

> a darker period – a period as disastrous and as terrible as any through which a nation ever passed; disastrous and terrible because, side by side with a great increase in wealth was seen an enormous increase in pauperism; and production on a vast scale, the result of free competition, led to a rapid alienation of classes and to the degradation of a large body of producers.[16]

The Hammonds agreed. 'The history of England', they wrote,

> at the time discussed in these pages reads like a history of civil war…. Surely, never since the days when populations were sold into slavery did a fate more sweeping overtake a people than the fate that covered the hills and valleys of Lancashire and the West Riding with… factory towns.

As they described it, the Industrial Revolution created 'a profane and brutal system that spared neither soul nor body, and denied to men and women the right to human treatment', and gave rise to slavery on a scale comparable to ancient Egypt, the Roman Empire or the American plantations.[17] It was the same for Sidney and Beatrice Webb, who insisted that the years 1787–1837 witnessed 'a positive decline in the standard of life' of the workers, left 'the labourer a landless stranger in his own country', and created towns where 'paving, cleansing, lighting and watching were all lacking', and where 'the crowding together of tens of thousands of poverty-stricken persons was creating unspeakable nuisances'.[18]

Described and denounced from this hostile, enraged, engaged perspective, the Industrial Revolution produced 'results to the common people more terrible in prolonged agony than those of any war'; and it did so because the 'evils of unrestricted and unregulated capitalism' were callously ignored by the ruling, landowning and capitalist classes, who eagerly embraced the new ideology of laissez-faire, which denied to the labourer the fruits of his work, and condemned him to a life of poverty, misery and squalor. For Toynbee, 'complete and unhesitating trust in individual self-interest' was the same as 'the weak being trampled under foot'. 'This kind of competition', he concluded, 'has to be checked.'[19] In *The Town Labourer*, the Hammonds devoted two chapters to the minds of the ruling class, condemning them as the 'generation that left the workmen to their fate in the Industrial Revolution', when they were 'powerless and helpless, needing the protection of the law and parliament' – which, of course, they did not obtain. And the Webbs, too, argued that laissez-faire, 'fully established in Parliament as an authoritative industrial doctrine of political economy', was responsible for the squalid conditions in industrial towns and also for the brutal suppression of trade unions. 'With free competition', they concluded, 'and private property in land and capital, no individual can possibly obtain the full fruits of his own labour.'[20]

During the thirty years before the First World War, this interpretation of Britain's Industrial Revolution as rapid, terrible and laissez-faire, was not only articulated by other historians who were generally radical in their political views, but also by those who were not; and similar interpretations may be found in the once-popular but now largely-unread books by such contemporary writers and commentators as Sir William Ashley, the Rev. William Cunningham, Charles Beard, Henry de Bettgens Gibbins, J.E. Thorold Rogers and G. Townsend Warner.[21] Such was the conventional wisdom that this first generation of writers had established, and it was to their views that Sir John Clapham riposted weightily and explicitly in the first volume of his *Economic History of Modern Britain*, published in 1926. To begin with, he sketched out a very different chronology from that which had been generally accepted since Toynbee. Insisting that the Industrial Revolution was gradual in its timing and localized in its early impact, Clapham stressed 'the diversity of the national economic life', examined in great detail the predominant and non-mechanized industries, and noted how little change had taken place by 1851. His book was, in Herbert Heaton's memorable phrase, a 'study in slow motion', which repeatedly insisted that 'no single British industry had passed through a complete technological revolution before 1830'. 'The Lancashire cotton operative', Clapham noted, 'was not the representative workman of the Britain of King George IV'; 'the man of the crowded countryside was still the typical Englishman'; 'the steam engine itself... was still small and, outside a limited group of leading industries, comparatively little used'.[22]

Clapham also disputed the claim that the Industrial Revolution was terrible, and attacked 'the legend that everything was getting worse for the working man', by presenting statistics which showed, on the contrary, that in the decades after 1790, 'for every class of urban or industrial labourer about which information is available except – a grave exception – such dying trades as common hand loom cotton weaving, wages had risen markedly during the intervening sixty years'. Finally, he examined the record of the government and the legislature, not in the light of criticisms retrospectively (and anachronistically) levelled, but by the more realistic criterion of what the options were at the time:

> Judged as governments are perhaps entitled to be judged, not by what proved practicable in a later and more experienced day, not by what reformers and poets dreamed and were not called upon to accomplish, but by the achievement of other governments in their own day, that of Britain... makes a creditable showing.[23]

Clapham's reinterpretation of the Industrial Revolution drew on earlier statistical work, and also on other writings of a tentatively optimistic nature.[24] But he was the first major, university-based scholar to offer an alternative interpretation, and he was soon followed by Arthur Redford, who insisted that 'the whole trend of modern research has been to show that the economic changes of the eighteenth century were less sudden, less dramatic and less catastrophic than Toynbee and his disciples thought', and by Ephraim Lipson, who concluded that 'the "Industrial Revolution" constituted no breach in the existing order, but was part of a continuous movement which had already made marked advance'.[25]

Taken together, the work of Clapham, Redford and Lipson constituted a formidable assault on the Toynbee–Hammond–Webb interpretation of the Industrial Revolution. But in two ways, the novelty and the appeal of what they were saying was minimized. In the first place, they all wrote, and all acknowledged that they were writing, within the terms of reference and the interpretational framework, already specified by these earlier writers. The need to attack 'the premature generalizations of text books', which stated that the Industrial Revolution was rapid, terrible and laissez-faire, only served to show how powerful those generalizations had been in defining the problem and the period. Moreover, whatever the intrinsic academic force of this dissenting argument, it was to be many years before developments in the contemporary economy made its stress on slow and gradual change, and on long-term improvement sufficiently 'relevant' for it to be taken up more generally. In the meantime, in the next generation, the dramatically changed circumstances of the contemporary economy encouraged another interpretation of the Industrial Revolution, which had little more in common with the Clapham, Lipson and Redford view than it did with that of Toynbee, the Hammonds and the Webbs against which they were reacting.

II

The period from the mid 1920s to the early 1950s marks the second distinctive phase in the historiography of Britain's Industrial Revolution. Like the era before, it was characterized by pessimism about the economy and the future of capitalism, but this time it was cyclical rather than social, and global rather than merely national. For the international system which had worked relatively smoothly in the halcyon days of the Gold Standard had collapsed beyond recovery after the First World War. In 1923, the Webbs had published *The Decay of Capitalist Civilisation*, which argued that, since 1850, 'it has been receding from defeat to defeat'.[26] But, as the young M.M. Postan pointed out a decade later, the 'ossification of the system' was so widespread that such pessimism was no longer the monopoly of the anti-capitalist left:

> Among the many things which have affected the position of socialists in the postwar world has been the loss of their exclusive rights in 'the decline of capitalism'.... However much they differ about the origin and the causation, they all agree about the reality of the disease and its symptoms. The dwindling of international trade, the cessation of international migrations, the strangulation of international credit, recur in official speeches and in letters to the press.[27]

This anxiety was further fuelled by the Second World War, as Joseph Schumpeter explained in 1943. 'It is', he observed, 'a commonplace that capitalist society is, and for some time has been, in a state of decay.'[28]

The result was that contemporaries were most concerned, not with those elements of growth which economic historians have retrospectively come to discern in the inter-war economy, but with the destabilizing effects of war, the decline of the great staples, the unprecedentedly high level of unemployment, and the violent cyclical fluctuations. The immediate post-war boom collapsed in the slump of 1921–22 (when the Webbs wrote *The Decay of Capitalist Civilisation*), and was succeeded by a weak and uneven upswing, which reached its high point in 1929. There followed the unprecedented international meltdown of the great crash and the even greater depression, with its financial and industrial trough reached in 1932 (shortly after which Postan wrote his article), and then a gradual revival, which lasted until 1937, after which there was a sharp downswing, only arrested by the greater disaster of the Second World War. The period immediately after 1945 were almost as uncertain: the odd-numbered years were in general bad (especially with devaluation in 1949), and the even-numbered years were generally good (especially with the Korean War boom of 1950), while the early 1950s were clouded by the fear of a major slump in the United States, which stimulated John Kenneth Galbraith to write the history of the *last* great crash, in the hope that it might provide some useful insights for the future ups and downs of the international economy.[29]

Not surprisingly, the main work of professional economists during these years was concerned with trying to measure, explain and predict these cyclical fluctuations. Most of the statistics of such movements were compiled in the United States where, under the directorship of Wesley C. Mitchell and A.F. Burns, the National Bureau of Economic Research produced a series of books of ever-increasing quantitative precision and refinement. Attempts were made to establish how far there was an international economic cycle, to discern what features successive cycles had in common, and to measure the duration and amplitude of such movements.[30] Explaining them, however, proved to be more difficult. One approach was to look for exogenous causes, so-called 'random shocks', such as war (obviously attractive in the aftermath of 1914–18), climate change or political crisis. But in general, endogenous explanations, which sought to discern the dynamics of the cycle within the economy itself, proved to be more popular. Yet there remained ample scope for disagreement and debate. For Ralph G. Hawtrey, the business cycle was essentially a credit cycle which could best be explained in monetary terms. For John Maynard Keynes, by contrast, the causes of such ups and downs were to be found in the levels of consumer demand and business investment. But for Joseph Schumpeter, it was the long-term economic cycles which mattered most, and these were related to the clustering of innovations.[31]

To economists with a historical interest, there was an obvious appeal in seeing whether these contemporary business cycles could be traced back as far as the late eighteenth and early nineteenth centuries; and for the historian familiar with economic theory, there was an equally strong temptation to apply it directly to the period of the Industrial Revolution to see what might emerge if it was viewed as a cyclical rather than as a social phenomenon. Either way, these concerns and approaches served to stimulate new interpretations of the Industrial Revolution itself, which were neither indebted to, nor derived from, the earlier apocalyptic-pessimistic interpretation. More specifically, the obvious parallels between the wars of 1793–1815 and 1914–18, and also between the phases of readjustment and depression which followed in both cases, served to focus attention on the period from the 1790s to the 1820s. At a time when the Gold Standard had broken down in the twentieth century, there was an obvious temptation to look at the last period, almost exactly one hundred years before, when money, currency, banking and finance had been in a similarly confused and unstable state. As Theodor Emanuel Gregory explained, 'the economic and, in particular, the monetary problems which we are facing today have a startling resemblance to those which were the subject matter of contention for two generations a century ago'.[32]

The first sustained study of the Industrial Revolution as a cyclical phenomenon was undertaken in Britain by William Beveridge. During the 1900s, he had surveyed business cycles in the second half of the nineteenth century, and he had concluded that they were primarily a monetary phenomenon, largely determined by the ups and downs of the credit cycle, and that there were no comparable fluctuations in the years before 1858.[33] But during the late 1930s, Beveridge returned to this subject, and he changed his mind on both counts. Having recently constructed indexes of industrial production for the years 1785 to 1849, he now concluded that the 'fluctuations of economic activity' reproduced 'so many of the features of the modern trade cycle that we are bound to regard the trade cycle as having been in operation, in essentials, at least from 1785'. And in recognizing and analyzing 'the essential unity of the phenomenon' of cyclical fluctuations from the 1780s to the 1930s, he now concluded that it was the vicissitudes of the export industries which was a better explanation than the ebb and flow of credit.[34] In his wartime book, *Full Employment in a Free Society*, published in 1944, Beveridge brought these findings together: 'the cyclical movement from 1929 to 1938', he concluded, 'is a lineal descendant of the successive fluctuations which have brought insecurity to all advanced industrial countries with an unplanned market economy ever since industry took its modern form'.[35]

Like Toynbee, the Hammonds and the Webbs before him, Beveridge's interpretation of the Industrial Revolution was the almost incidental by-product of his contemporary political and welfare concerns. But a larger, transatlantic study of cyclical fluctuations in the Industrial Revolution undertaken in the 1930s was both more historical and also more theoretical.[36] In 1940, a young American named W.W. Rostow completed his Yale doctoral dissertation on the fluctuations of the British economy during the second half of the nineteenth century. It was, he explained, 'a conscious attempt... to employ modern economic theory' and it reached an appropriately Keynesian conclusion: 'as current trade cycle theory would lead one to expect, the amount and character of new investment was found to be the most important force in fluctuations in output and employment'.[37] By then, Rostow had joined a larger, collaborative project, which had been begun in 1936 under the direction of A.D. Gayer, and which was funded by the Columbia University Council for Research in the Social Sciences. Gayer, Rostow and their assistants assembled statistics on prices, trade, investment, industry, agriculture, finance and labour; they analysed and processed them in accordance with the most sophisticated techniques of the National Bureau of Economic Research; and they interpreted them on 'the assumption that theoretical concepts developed in modern business cycle theory are relevant to an analysis of the course of events in our period'.[38] The project was completed in 1941; but the Second World War delayed publication until 1953 when its findings were brought out by Oxford University Press as the two-volume *Growth and Fluctuations of the British Economy, 1790–1850*.

Yet in some ways, this was a misleading title, for as one reviewer correctly observed, the book was 'much more concerned with fluctuations than with growth': indeed, the authors themselves admitted that their aim had been to provide 'a general economic history of Great Britain from 1790 to 1850 written from the perspective of business fluctuations'. Their interest in the 'recurrent characteristics of ebb and flow' meant that they were undertaking a 'different line of inquiry' into the Industrial Revolution from the economic and social historians of the previous generation, whether Toynbee, the Hammonds and the Webbs, or their critics. 'This study', they rightly noted, 'asks a set of questions quite different from those addressed to the data, for example, by Professor Clapham.'[39] Moreover, it was, in its theoretical underpinnings and explanatory structure a quintessentially Keynesian book. The credit cycle was dismissed: 'monetary phenomena', the authors concluded, 'can be most usefully regarded... as a reflection of more deep-seated movement'; and the fundamental force underlying the cycles was not so much harvests or exports (except with the minor cycles) but fluctuations in investment. One particularly perceptive and influential reviewer of *Growth and Fluctuations* was Professor T.S. Ashton of Manchester University, and as he observed, in recognition of its Keynesian theoretical underpinnings, 'we can almost see the multiplier at work'.[40]

Ashton himself, in the Ford Lectures he delivered at Oxford University in 1953–54, directed his later endeavours along similar channels, as he studied the earlier fluctuations of the eighteenth-century British economy. Although he disclaimed any extensive use of trade cycle theory on the grounds that the data were inadequate, and although he found political crises, trade, harvests and the elements to be more important than investment, the book was as much a work of its time as the volumes of Gayer, Rostow et al. Its indebtedness to trade cycle theoreticians was, in fact, considerable, and the publisher marketed it as a work of applied economics, rather than of history, hoping that 'economists may find interest in the demonstration that what was later to be known as the trade cycle has an ancestry longer than some had supposed'.[41] At almost the same time as Ashton lectured and Gayer, Rostow et al. appeared, R.C.O. Matthews published his more detailed study of the ups and downs of the British economy during the 1830s which, by 'subjecting a single brief period to close study', sought to make clear 'the complexity of the fluctuations experienced'. Again, the author was concerned with the cyclical, rather than the developmental, aspects of the Industrial Revolution: 'an inquiry along the present lines', he insisted, 'does not by itself permit us to assess the place of the fluctuations studied in the longer run evolution of the national economy'; and, unsurprisingly, it concluded that 'the mainstay of the British cycle was domestic investment'.[42]

Like Toynbee, the Webbs and the Hammonds in their generation, these historians of the trade cycle were writing the history of the Industrial Revolution as 'the history of the social problems which are agitating the world now'.[43] There was the same search for the historical origins of contemporary problems: it was just that 'the problems of the present' had changed, the direction of inquiry into the past had changed along with them, and the people undertaking them were academics rather than public teachers, who were more interested in economic theory than in social history. And for the first time, but not for the last, many of them were Americans, who were increasingly fascinated by the British Industrial Revolution as somehow marking the beginning of the modern capitalist world of which their own country was now the foremost exemplar. But, like the earlier interpretation in its time, the cyclical view of the Industrial Revolution was paramount in its generation, yet never all-pervasive. Ephraim Lipson, for instance, in his new general survey, not only continued to assault the Toynbee et al. interpretation, but also offered a more ample perspective on the Industrial Revolution as a whole by suggesting that 'the population of England more than trebled in the nineteenth century, yet at the end of the century, the masses were in a material sense better off than at the beginning'.[44]

But the most seminal formulation of this broader, more optimistic and more cosmopolitan view had already come from T.S. Ashton who, in his brief, best-selling study, first published in 1948, had explored the long-term changes which industrialization brought with it, and also proclaimed its manifold benefits. As any comparison with nineteenth-century Ireland or with the contemporary underdeveloped world served to show, Ashton argued, only the Industrial Revolution held out the prospect of raising the standards of living for the majority of the people. 'There are', he concluded:

> today on the plains of India and China men and women, plague-ridden and hungry, living lives little better, to outward appearance, than those of the cattle that toil with them by day and share their places of sleep by night. Such Asiatic standards, and such un-mechanized horrors, are the lot of those who increase their numbers without passing through an Industrial Revolution.[45]

At the time of writing, when general pessimism about the British and global economy was further darkened by the vicissitudes of post-war fluctuations, such optimistic confidence in the long-term benefits of industrialization, not just for Britain and the west, but for the world beyond, was unusual and unfashionable. But within a decade, the improved circumstances of the western economies, and the change of interest from internal anxieties to external development, meant that these words became, for the next generation of economic historians, almost a sacred text.[46]

III

Between the mid 1950s and the early 1970s, the unexpected and remarkable efflorescence of western capitalism transformed Ashton's words into 'one of the most influential paragraphs in the writing of economic history in the present generation'.[47] Two decades of sustained economic growth, resulting from increased investment, rising productivity and technological progress, combined with limited inflation and full employment to create a rapidly rising standard of living for the majority of the people of the western world. Of course, rates of growth differed, both between the United States and Europe and within Europe itself: but all western nations benefited, and Britain was no exception.[48] The result was equally unprecedented optimism on the part of contemporary commentators. In the United States, John Kenneth Galbraith abandoned his interest in slumps, and announced that the 'affluent society' had arrived, which meant that the problems of poverty and production had been overcome, that economic growth was a certain solvent of inequality, and that inter-war anxieties about unemployment had been eliminated. Economists, he argued, must give up their professional (and historically-conditioned) predilection for misfortune and failure, and come to terms with prosperity and success.[49] In Britain, where the economy seemed to be growing faster than at any time since Victoria's heyday, Galbraith's picture seemed equally applicable. R.A. Butler, when Chancellor of the Exchequer, predicted that the standard of living would double in 25 years, and Harold Macmillan, when Prime Minister, claimed (or warned) that 'You've never had it so good.' Thus was western capitalism transformed, 'from the cataclysmic failure which it appeared to be in the 1930s into the great engine of prosperity of the post-war western world'.[50]

For economists, policy makers and those in government, these improvements in the west's post-war economic performance had a major impact on their thinking and aspirations: first, they were no longer as interested in the ups and downs of the business cycle as their immediate predecessors had been; second, they were much more concerned with the successful and sustained pursuit of economic growth at home than the social pessimists and radical activists had been in the decades before the First World War; and third, they became increasingly captivated by the possibilities of economic development in what was now becoming the rapidly decolonizing Third World. The sense of relief and euphoria that the inter-war and immediate post-war cyclical fluctuations had gone was palpable. As Andrew Schonfield observed, in words which stand proxy for many of his generation: 'there is no reason to suppose that the patterns of the past, which have been ingeniously unraveled by the historians of trade cycles, will reassert themselves in the future'.[51] So, as the cyclical model of western economic activity was dethroned, the growth model was put in its place. Going for growth became the consuming obsession of western governments, the shared aim of ostensibly opposed political parties, and a major preoccupation of applied economists who, extending Keynes's work on capital and investment in the business cycle, now assigned to them a crucial role in the growth process as well.[52] 'In all European countries', M.M. Postan remarked, 'economic growth became a universal creed, and a common expectation to which governments were expected to conform. To that extent, economic growth was the product of economic growth-man-ship.' Or, as Sir Roy Harrod put it in 1967, the pursuit of economic growth now had 'priority over all other objectives'.[53]

One consequence of the west's buoyancy about its own prosperity and about its public and private capacity to engineer and manage that prosperity was the burgeoning belief that it might be possible to accomplish similar economic miracles of development in the Third World, via technical assistance, trade and (especially) the injection of capital. As President John F. Kennedy proclaimed in his inaugural address, in the heady high noon of post-war western optimism: 'To those people in the huts and villages of half the globe struggling to break the bonds of mass misery, we pledge our best efforts to help them help themselves.' In practice, this meant a massive expansion in foreign aid programmes, to be deployed according to the prescriptions laid down by development economists, who were the first cousins of growth economists, and who were mainly to be found in the United States rather than in the United Kingdom.[54] The success of the Marshall Plan in reviving war-weary and war-ravaged Europe seemed to augur well for parallel American endeavours further a-field; the affinity between the problems of post-war unemployment in the west and post-independence underemployment in the Third World seemed clear; and it appeared but a short step from encouraging investment for growth at home to promoting investment for development abroad. The result was a commitment to global economic growth, which could be brought about by 'a massive injection of capital', though development economists would become (and remain) divided as to whether 'balanced' or 'uneven' growth was the more likely way forward.[55]

This change in the performance of post-war western economies, and in the perceptions of post-war western statesmen, profoundly influenced and profoundly changed the way in which economic historians on both sides of the Atlantic assessed and addressed Britain's Industrial Revolution during the 1950s and 1960s.[56] Among those who had earlier been interested in eighteenth- and nineteenth-century business cycles, W. W. Rostow now shifted his interests, and in the first edition of a book entitled *The Process of Economic Growth*, published in 1953, he noted how 'the issues of economic development from relatively primitive beginnings have increasingly occupied the minds of economists and policy makers in the west'.[57] And seven years later, in a new edition of the same work, he reported 'a most remarkable surge of thought centred on the process of economic growth'. 'A good part', he added, 'of the contemporary effort in economic history is directly shaped by the concern with public policy designed to accelerate growth in the underdeveloped regions of the world, which emerged in the decade after World War Two.'[58] As a result, Britain's Industrial Revolution was no longer seen as something terrible or cyclical because unregulated, but as the first example of sustained economic growth which was pioneered in England by private enterprise, and subsequently emulated and enjoyed across the western world, and which must now be promoted in the Third World by government (and, especially, American) agency. It ceased to seem something *bad* which should have been *tamed* in Britain by government intervention, and became instead something *good* which must be *replicated* around the globe by government aid.

Accordingly, and as Rostow further observed, 'the major common task and meeting place of economists and historians are to be found in the analysis of economic growth'; and, in his best-selling book, *The Stages of Economic Growth*, which appeared in 1960, he offered his own contribution, as an economic historian concerned about public affairs, and who would soon become a member of the Kennedy–Johnson administrations, 'to the formation of a wiser public policy'. It was, explicitly, 'a non-communist manifesto', which argued how and why the west could bring economic development to the Third World more efficiently and satisfactorily than Soviet Russia. It was addressed, not only to policy makers at home, but also to 'the men in Djakarta, Rangoon, New Delhi and Karachi; the men in Tehran, Baghdad, and Cairo; the men south of the desert too, in Accra, Lagos, and Salisbury'. And its message was simple: that the study of industrial revolutions in the past, beginning with the pioneering and prototypical British example, offered the best guide to the promotion of economic growth in the future. 'It is useful, as well as roughly accurate', Rostow noted, 'to regard the process of development now going forward in Asia, the Middle East, Africa, and Latin America as analogous to the stages of preconditions and take-off of other societies, in the late eighteenth, nineteenth, and early twentieth centuries.'[59]

Thus were past, present and future, economic theory, economic history and economic development, brought together in what seemed a powerful, universalizing and persuasive synthesis. For the policy maker, *The Stages of Economic Growth* was a prescriptive essay, which drew support from historical examples; for the economic historian, it was a reinterpretation of the industrialization process in general (and that of Britain in particular) which drew on contemporary development theory. By assigning to capital accumulation and investment a crucial role in the 'take-off into sustained economic growth', it gave historical validation to the 'massive injection of capital' theory. And by its stress on 'leading sectors', which abruptly and successfully pulled the economy forward, it offered historical support to the proponents among development economists of unbalanced growth. But by citing Britain as the pioneering and paradigmatic case of industrialization, with capital accumulation, leading sectors and energetic entrepreneurs, as the initiators of economic growth and, hence, the modern world, it produced a picture of the Industrial Revolution fundamentally different from that which had prevailed in the two earlier generations of interpretation.[60] Instead of being the historical tap-root of contemporary problems, it was the past guide to present endeavours, the historical precedent for future aspirations. 'What Professor Rostow has tried to do', observed Phyllis Deane, 'is to interpret British economic history in a way that has immediate policy implications for those concerned with the problems of today's pre-industrial economies.'[61]

During the expansive days of the 1960s and early 1970s, when higher education in Britain boomed and blossomed as never before, a new, numerous and confident generation of economic historians on this side of the Atlantic portrayed the Industrial Revolution in general terms – if not always in precise details – that were clearly indebted to Rostow and the recent work of the growth and development economists.[62] 'The focus of the economic history of the 1950s and 1960s', noted Michael Flinn, 'reflecting the switch of theoretical studies from short-term to long-run movements, has shifted sharply towards the study of economic development in its historical context.' Phyllis Deane described her own survey, entitled *The First Industrial Revolution*, published in 1965, as 'a product of the current interest in economic development', and as 'an attempt to apply the concepts and techniques of development economics to a vital section of the historical record'. Peter Mathias wrote his textbook, called *The First Industrial Nation*, which appeared in 1969, hoping it might appeal to 'the economist interested in development', and noted at the outset that, 'in many senses, all nations concerned with economic growth at the present time are treading the path Britain first set foot on in the eighteenth century'.[63] Eric Hobsbawm admitted that his Marxist account reflected 'the interests of the present... the problems of economic development and industrialization'. And from a very different ideological perspective, Max Hartwell summarized the consequential shift in opinion in words that echoed T.S. Ashton's by-now oft-quoted formulation: 'today, in a world in which two-thirds of mankind are still desperately poor, and are finding it difficult to improve their lot, the English Industrial Revolution is seen more as a spectacular and successful example of growth than as a catastrophe'.[64]

So, in economic history as in economic theory, the cyclical model of Britain's Industrial Revolution was dethroned and the growth and development model substituted in its place. 'There is no doubt', noted Hartwell, 'that the economists' preoccupation with growth has jolted the historian into a more careful and more explicitly theoretical analysis of the causes of English growth.' Regardless of ideological approach, the Industrial Revolution was now re-written and re-presented as 'a fundamental discontinuity in world economic development', in which there was 'a radical shift in the structure of the economy, in the composition of total output, and in the distribution of employment, which gives concrete meaning to the idea of an Industrial Revolution'.[65] As a result, the authors of this new generation of textbooks published in the 1960s wrote little of social consequences or of the trade cycle. Their bibliographies included the works of development economists. They made extended references to contemporary underdeveloped countries (especially Nigeria and India) when describing pre-industrial England. They adopted sectoral analysis, and wrote of a shift of productive resources away from agriculture and towards industry and service.[66] And they saw Britain as blazing the trail which the Continent, the United States and – given time and planning and resources – the rest of the world were ultimately to follow.

Thus was economic growth established as the predominant interpretation, and the specifics of the Industrial Revolution – as they related to such matters as banking and entrepreneurship – were researched and presented in accordance with the current and evolving theories of economic development.[67] Yet, even as this happened, there was also a recognition among those who employed it that the theory was not entirely appropriate, that the model did not fit completely, that Britain was first to industrialize and therefore at least as unique as it was paradigmatic and exemplary. In part, these qualifications arose from the rapid rejection of the more specific parts of W.W. Rostow's 'take-off', as detailed studies of capital accumulation and the role of cotton suggested evolutionary rather than revolutionary progress.[68] More generally, Phyllis Deane conceded that there was little to be gained from analysing pre-industrial England as if it was like a contemporary underdeveloped country: it had not been over-populated, it was not overwhelmingly agricultural, it was a society rich in resources, high in literacy, and with a well-developed market system.[69] Yet it was also the case that by 1851, as Mathias, Deane and David Landes all admitted, the overall picture of the country and economy was very different from that suggested by a look at the most advanced productive sectors: agriculture was still (if diminishingly) dominant, and the textile and metal industries employed a relatively small proportion of the labour force. Indeed, Hartwell went even further, not only suggesting that the facts of British industrialization did not accord to the theories of growth, but also that, if they showed anything, it was that 'any simple theory of, or policy for, growth is absurd'.[70]

Other scholars, working on topics such as banking, railways and the steam engine, offered detailed support for these qualifications, and there were also more general warnings against the 'growth' and 'development' approach to Britain's Industrial Revolution during the 1960s and early 1970s.[71] But such was the mood of the times that they were no more widely heeded than were the results of such detailed researches as also pointed to the same conclusion. For even if the authors of textbooks were careful to build in reservations, they still approached the Industrial Revolution from the standpoint of development economics, hoped that their findings might be of use to those planning growth in the Third World, and (albeit perhaps unintentionally) left many generations of undergraduates with the sense that it was sudden, successful and largely connected with investment and entrepreneurship. As long as 'the problems of the present' remained those of growth at home and development abroad, this unprecedentedly optimistic picture of the Industrial Revolution, so very different from that given in the two preceding generations, prevailed. Only when contemporary circumstances altered again would the reservations made in the growth generation, which themselves harked back to Clapham's earlier work, become enthroned in their own right, and in their entirety, as the new interpretation.

IV

During the mid 1970s, the economic climate again altered profoundly in the west. The two decades of unprecedented post-war prosperity and confidence, already dented by the impact of the Vietnam War from 1968 onwards, came to an abrupt end with the energy crisis of 1973–74, and this was followed by a new menace, stagflation, to which Keynesian economics appeared to offer no antidote. And, at just the time when the certainty of continued growth was being undermined, the very appropriateness of it was also being brought into question. According to the newly-influential environmentalist lobby, most famously exemplified by E.E. Schumacher, economic growth *should* not continue to happen: 'one of the most fateful errors of our age', he wrote, in explicit attack on Galbraith, 'is the belief that "the problem of production" has been solved'.[72] And from another perspective, the ecological, as articulated in the Club of Rome report, economic growth *could* not continue to happen because the world's resources would give out: 'for the first time, it has become vital to inquire into the cost of unrestricted material growth, and to consider the alternatives to its continuation'.[73] As W.W. Rostow summarized this new and very different climate of economic performance and of public opinion, 'suddenly, in the 1970's, the inevitability, even the legitimacy, of economic growth was questioned'.[74]

The result was a return of the sort of professional pessimism that had generally prevailed among economists and economic historians from the 1880s to the late 1940s. 'The most remarkable two decades of economic growth in modern history', Rostow explained, by which he meant the 1950s and 1960s, had been superseded by what now seemed to be 'the greatest challenge to industrial civilisation since it began to take shape two centuries ago'.[75] Once again his own interest shifted in consequence – this time from writing historically-grounded development manifestos to evolving 'specific lines of policy which might permit the world community to transit with reasonable success the next quarter century'. For him as for others, the change in circumstances had been remarkable:

> An important turning point occurred in the world economy and, indeed, in industrial civilisation during the first half of the 1970's. A pattern of economic and social progress which had persisted for almost a quarter century was broken. Politicians, economists and citizens found themselves in a somewhat new and uncomfortable world. Familiar modes of thought and action were challenged as they no longer seemed to grip the course of events. Expectations of the future became uncertain.[76]

John Kenneth Galbraith expressed similar sentiments in similar words, recording the shift from *The Affluent Society* (London, 1956) to *The Age of Uncertainty* (London, 1977). Whereas the years 1945–65 had been 'good and confident years, a good time to be an economist', the last decade had demonstrated once more 'the disarming complexity of the problems mankind now faces'.[77]

Nor was this the only shift in mood and perspective from the mid 1970s onwards: for at just the same time that economic growth in the west became both more uncertain and more unacceptable, economic development became less confident as a discipline and less credible as a policy as applied to the Third World.[78] In part, this resulted from the assaults mounted on the subject by the neo-Marxist left (who argued that development merely led to further underdevelopment, increased inequality and the growth of western neo-imperialism), and by the neo-classical right (who asserted with equal vigour that development merely led to misallocation of resources and to balance of payments deficits, but not to economic growth). But it was also because development economics did not seem to have worked: in many African countries, income distribution had become *more* unequal not less; the promotion of economic development led to some spectacular retrogression in human rights; and the whole process of modernization seemed stressful rather than beneficial. Moreover, there was the gradual and humbling discovery that there was no such thing as a typical under-developed country any more than there was a typical Industrial Revolution: a country's size, population, resources and politics differed so widely that there could be no single recipe for economic transformation. As a result, the confidence with which development economists had turned to their tasks in the 1950s and 1960s was much reduced.[79]

Within this generally pessimistic global climate, as regards both performance and perception, the British economy suffered more than most in western Europe. 'No subject', noted John Kenneth Galbraith in 1977, 'is so lovingly discussed in our own time as the economic problems of Britain.' 'The British deceleration of the late 1960s', agreed Rostow, had been 'more marked than for most of the other major industrial economies, and the subsequent impact of the price revolution of 1972–7 more acute.' Just as Britain had shared in the prosperity of the post-war years to a lesser extent than many western countries, so it had fared worse in the renewed age of uncertainty beginning in 1974, with higher rates of inflation and greater unemployment.[80] For the pessimists, who now lamented the crisis of a nineteenth-century industrial world whose very existence their predecessors had deplored, this meant regret at the broken and fragmented working class, the weakened and marginalized trades unions, and (until 1997) a revived and rampant Conservatism, and a divided and defeated Labour Party. For the escapists, it resulted (as had the depression of the 1930s) in a nostalgia boom, as evidenced by such best-sellers as *Life in the English Country House* and *The Country Diary of an Edwardian Lady*, and by the unprecedented expansion in such conservation organizations as the National Trust. And for the optimists, it saw the beginning of 'a future that works', based on leisure, culture and education, which was not a warning, but 'a model for others in the post industrial age'.[81]

Either way, by the 1980s, it was clear that Britain was in the midst, not just of a new and severe cyclical depression reminiscent of the inter-war years, but of a transformative and searing process of 'de-industrializing' that was occurring more rapidly than anywhere else in the western world. Its factories and mills were going out of business; its coal mines were closing down in the aftermath of the miners' strike of 1984; and the consequent decay of its once-great and once-proud Victorian cities was well evoked by David Lodge in his novel *Nice Work* (1988, set in Birmingham), and by Peter Cattaneo in his film *The Full Monty* (1997, set in Sheffield). For many commentators, the message was clear: Britain's industrial past was merely an ephemeral episode: a 'flirtation with factory culture', a time when a 'factory class of manual workers' was 'temporarily' in being, no more than a 'passing phase'. Accordingly, 'the explosion of energy around 1750, at the start of the first industrial revolution' could 'now be seen for what it really was: for Britain a flash in the pan'.[82] In this very changed climate of economic performance, public perception and academic opinion, Britain's Industrial Revolution was no longer regarded as the shining start of the great western success story leading to self-sustaining economic growth and individual prosperity and security. Instead, it was fundamentally re-written and down-sized, as the dissenting views of the 1960s, which were themselves indebted (whether knowingly or not) to Sir John Clapham's earlier work during the 1930s, became the new and very different orthodoxy.[83]

Accordingly, Britain's Industrial Revolution was no longer confidently (and proudly) presented as the paradigmatic case, as the first and most famous instance of modern economic growth: instead, it was depicted in a more negative light, as a limited, restricted, piecemeal phenomenon, in which various things did *not* happen, or where, if they did, they had far less impact than had previously been supposed. Thus reinterpreted, the typical businessman was not the fabled heroic entrepreneur, but a small-scale and un-heroic operator, and there were also real structural and geographical constraints which prevented even the greatest of British entrepreneurs from rivalling their American counterparts in their accumulation of wealth.[84] The importance of steam power was deemed to have been much less than had been previously supposed, while one of the paradoxical consequences of the advent of the railways was that they led to an *increase* in the number of horses employed throughout the nineteenth century.[85] And Martin J. Wiener's best-selling study, *English Culture and the Decline of the Industrial Spirit*, which appeared in 1981, stimulated by the 'economic Sargasso Sea' in which the British economy found itself, stressed the limits to industrial advance by 1851, and the ruling elite's lack of enthusiasm for economic growth. The nation's transition to an industrial society, he argued, 'was marked by admirably peaceful gradualism, but also, thereby, by a certain incompleteness'. 'In the world's first industrial nation', he went on, 'economic growth was frequently viewed with suspicion and disdain', 'industrialisation did not seem quite at home', and the survival of patrician values 'restrained rather than stimulated economic growth'. Again, it was what did not happen that was important: the limits to growth during the Industrial Revolution, rather than the achievement of it.[86]

These detailed findings contributed to broader shifts in interpretation. Instead of stressing how *much* had happened in Britain by 1851 (whatever the qualifications), it became commonplace for economic historians to note how *little* had actually altered (whatever the qualifications).[87] This change in emphasis – from what had been accomplished by mid-century to what had not, from the 'take-off into sustained growth' to the 'limits to growth', from a few large and successful businessmen to many small and faltering entrepreneurs – was accompanied by the dethroning of two of the central props to the earlier interpretation, one statistical, the other diffusional. Thanks to the painstaking calculations of Professors Feinstein and Crafts, it became clear that the increase in the rate of capital accumulation from 1780 to 1800 was about one third slower than W.W. Rostow's 'take-off' model hypothesized and required.[88] These new calculations mortally undermined the heroic picture painted during the 1950s and 1960s, and they also lead to the abandonment of the view that Britain, as the pioneering case of industrialization, was also the paradigmatic example. On the contrary, it was an 'idiosyncratic industrializer', and those countries alleged to have 'emulated' its experience, among them Germany, the United States and Japan, in fact took their own, more rapid paths to the modern economy. There was, then, no single, British-originated and British-dominated typology of industrialization which served as the model for the rest of the world: it happened differently everywhere. Even if 'the first industrial nation' hadn't industrialized first, the rest of the developed world would have managed to work it out, and to do it, for themselves.[89]

This gradualist, localist, separatist interpretation soon established itself as the new orthodoxy, as earlier textbooks were revised and new syntheses were produced.[90] The result was a de-industrialized history of the Industrial Revolution that was fit for (and inspired by) the de-industrialized nation that Britain was becoming during the late 1970s, 1980s and early 1990s: as one commentator observed, this meant 'the Industrial Revolution' was 'now a concept on the defensive'. For some economic historians, this was a new and much more healthy state of affairs, and they welcomed the belated advent of this gradualist and de-internationalized interpretation, which cut the whole thing down to size and sanity. 'One way or another', exulted Patrick O'Brien, 'the heroic, quintessentially British Industrial Revolution as a seminal episode in world history has been re-configured. The Industrial Revolution "aint what it used to be"', and '"triumphalist" books with such titles as *The First Industrial Revolution* and *The First Industrial Nation* will probably no longer be published by historians with posts in higher education'.[91] Some scholars even suggested that the 'Industrial Revolution' was a 'fictitious entity'; that the phrase should be abandoned when writing about the economic transformation of western Europe; and that it should be added 'to the list of spurious revolutions which are deleted from our accounts of social change by the act of quantifying'.[92]

But not all economic historians were exhilarated at the prospect of Britain's once-great Industrial Revolution being downsized and diminished in this way. For the 1980s and 1990s were not only decades of de-industrialization: they were also decades of post-modernism, a way of looking at the world which eschewed and positively disdained one single, all embracing 'master narrative', even when it was a master narrative of minimality. And so, as in previous generations, the new 'limits to growth' orthodoxy soon provoked its own critics and generated its own reaction. Some historians were worried that the essential statistical underpinning to the 'limits to growth' interpretation rested on ever more sophisticated manipulations of intrinsically speculative and unreliable figures, while others feared that this 'quantitative minimalism' was too narrow and too anachronistic a way of approaching the subject, and that 'too much of the currently modish treatments are limited in range and a-historical in approach'.[93] Others, like Sir Tony Wrigley, regretted that a subject 'whose intrinsic interest should make it the most exciting topic among the big issues of the history of the development of the modern world' had 'become a dull subject that slips into focus and out again, uncomfortably peripheral to the vision of many historians'. And the American economic historian Joel Mokyr was an unrepentant (indeed, messianic) believer in Britain's Industrial Revolution as a momentous event and defining process: 'its importance in economic history stands undiminished', which meant that Britain remained 'the Holy Land of industrialism', and that the period 1750 to 1830 still stood out as 'the years of miracles'.[94]

The most original and convincing of these new anti-gradualists was Wrigley, who insisted that between 1750 to 1830, there was indeed a 'radical break with the past', as Great Britain sustained a doubling in its population, without enduring the sort of Malthusian catastrophe which happened when numbers outrun resources (as they would do in Ireland in the 1840s). But it was only possible for Britain to 'cross a threshold into a new era' because its economy was growing at an unprecedented rate, thanks to the eclipse of the 'advanced organic economy', based on land and agriculture, and water- and wood- and wind-power, by the advent of the new, 'mineral-based energy economy' of coal and iron, which made available unprecedented amounts of mechanical energy. With productive resources increased in this novel, transformative and apparently exponential way, Britain became the first nation that was able to sustain both a much larger population, and a more prosperous economy, than ever before.[95] Other critics of the 'limits to growth' approach insisted that the recently-calculated aggregate figures concealed significant local variations and sectoral shifts which added up to very important changes in some parts of the country; that much economic development was not in the direction of factory production, but was based in the household and the workshop, and had been neglected by the quantifiers; and that there were major adjustments in the labour force, especially in the employment of women and children, and in the shift of the population from the countryside to the towns, which had also been disregarded. If the Industrial Revolution was approached in such a broad and humane manner, rather than in a narrow and statistical way, they insisted that it remained an amalgam of 'fundamental and in many respects unique changes'.[96]

There was one final quarter from which rehabilitation was offered and that, rather unexpectedly, came from the global historians. Theirs was a new subject, peopled by a new generation of scholars, but insofar as they were concerned about the British Industrial Revolution, there was a bridging figure in the American historian David Landes, who still adhered to the views he had earlier expressed in *The Unbound Prometheus* in the 1960s, and who now set out, in *The Wealth and Poverty of Nations*, to explain why some parts of the world (mostly western Europe and its transoceanic offshoots) became rich, while the rest remained poor. The explanation he offered was the (by then) highly traditional and (to some) unfashionable one that the Industrial Revolution was pioneered in Britain, spread to Europe, and then to those areas beyond, where a combination of resources, politics and culture offered a receptive environment.[97] Thereafter, Landes's argument (and also Wrigley's) was corroborated by historians writing from an extra-European perspective, such as Jack Goldstone, Kenneth Pomeranz and Roy Bin Wong, who insisted that until the late eighteenth century, much of Asia boasted organic economies which were as advanced as any in Europe. Only when Britain moved towards a 'mineral-based energy economy', and when other nations followed suit, was the balance of power between 'the west' and 'the east' tilted away from the latter towards the former. From this viewpoint, Britain's Industrial Revolution again appears as a great watershed in human history.[98]

V

There, towards the end of the first decade of the twenty-first century, the matter rests, uneasily and (as ever) unconcluded, with the quantifiers convinced they have cut Britain's Industrial Revolution down to size, and with the non-quantifiers unwilling to accept this. Respectively truffle hunters and parachutists, their very differing perspectives lead them to very different conclusions, although there is also some evidence that there is more common ground between them than either side is generally minded to admit.[99] But either way, there is little sense now that Britain's Industrial Revolution is the place to look for the source or the solution of today's economic and/or social problems, in Britain itself, in the west more generally, or in the still-developing world. At the same time (can this be just coincidence?), economic history has become a markedly less buoyant subject in universities in Britain than it had been from the 1950s to the 1970s – partly because the separate departments that had been set up in the booming 1960s had been closed or merged during the more austere 1980s; partly because it has become increasingly insular and introverted, especially in the hands of the quantifiers and the 'Cliometricians'; and partly because it has been overtaken as a young, vigorous, exciting, accessible subject by social history, cultural history and women's history.[100] For some economic historians, indeed, the business of sustaining the British Industrial Revolution has thus become inseparable from the business of sustaining their subject itself: for if the central episode in modern economic history disappeared, what are they left with to justify their continued sub-disciplinary existence?

Since the British Industrial Revolution has been discussed and debated for more than a century, by economists, economic historians, social historians, pundits and journalists, and not just in Britain, but also in the United States, that may well turn out to be too pessimistic a view of its future prospects as a major field of scholarly inquiry, public interest and international concern. At different times, and from different perspectives, the Industrial Revolution has been presented as 'social consequences', as 'cyclical fluctuations', as 'economic growth' and as 'the limits to growth'; and between them, the proponents of and dissenters from these views have depicted it as being slow or fast, good or bad, cyclical or linear, local or global, big or small, of great relevance to the contemporary world or of no relevance whatsoever: a veritable overload of polarized interpretations and binary formulations, each of which gives a vision and version of the truth, but none of which does full justice to its protean complexity.[101] Now that Britain's industrial age is over, with the coal mines closed, the steel mills silent, and their physical remains embraced in a national heritage that was originally conceived in opposition to everything that the Industrial Revolution was deemed to have done and to have meant, it may well be that the concept is passing beyond history into oblivion. Yet even in a de-industrialized nation, there are still those who insist that 'there was an Industrial Revolution, and it was British', and that it was 'the great event in world history'.[102] To be (no doubt) continued...

5

Heritage:
The Historic Environment in Historical
Perspective[1]

When Sir Kenneth Clark concluded his thirteen-part television series *Civilisation*, which was first broadcast on BBC 2 in 1969, he did so with a programme entitled 'Heroic Materialism', in which he explored and explained how engineering, technology and science had transformed the greater European world during the nineteenth and twentieth centuries – in many ways beyond recognition, and in some ways (as he saw it) beyond redemption. 'Heroic' described both the achievements of such visionary, titanic, creative individuals as Thomas Telford, James Watt and Isambard Kingdom Brunel, and also the massive scale of the change their endeavours had wrought on the landscape and environment; while 'Materialism' signalled that the creation of prodigious, unprecedented wealth, and its unhappy social consequences of poverty, misery, hypocrisy, cruelty and exploitation, were the dominant themes of the times.[2] But it was not just the nature and scope of these developments by which Kenneth Clark was impressed (and personally much perturbed): it was also their traumatically disruptive speed, as ever more rapid, alarming and irreversible change, at a seemingly incremental and exponential rate, and with far-reaching consequences for the world around us, became a permanent, built-in feature of modern life. 'Imagine', he urged his audience, in words it might have seemed tasteless to use a generation later in the aftermath of the events of 9/11, 'an immensely speeded up movie of Manhattan Island during the last hundred years.' 'It would', Clark insisted, 'look less like a work of man than like some tremendous natural upheaval. It's godless, it's brutal, it's violent.'[3]

Much the same could be said of the United Kingdom, which invented and pioneered 'Heroic Materialism' long before it reached its most extended and highly-developed manifestation in the United States, as William Blake's once 'green and pleasant land' was blighted by 'dark, satanic mills', by coal mines and by factories, and transformed by the mid nineteenth century into the first industrial nation and the workshop of the world. Across the length and breadth of England, and long before Manhattan exploded into skyscrapers and imploded into subways, there was 'brutal, godless, violent' change, which damaged and polluted, transformed and remade the national landscape.[4] One indication of such transformation is that between 1800 and 1900 the population of England and Wales more than tripled, from slightly fewer than 9 million to roughly 32 million people, and they were increasingly crowded into large towns and growing cities. At the beginning of the period, 25 per cent of English men and women were urban dwellers, while the majority still lived in the country. One hundred years later, 80 per cent of the population resided in London, or in such great cities as Leeds, Liverpool, Manchester and Birmingham, or in the industrialized villages of the Potteries, or in the mining communities of south Wales, or in the hills and dales of south Yorkshire. And during this period, change was as much evident in the English countryside as in the towns: as parliamentary enclosure was followed by the era of 'high farming', and then by the proliferation of barbed wire and by the advent of agricultural depression, and as the last great age of country-house building also came and went. At the same time, and thanks to the expansion of the railways, rural and urban England were joined up and interconnected as never before – by 1852 there were almost 6,000 miles of track, by 1875 the network had doubled and by 1912 it had almost trebled.[5]

The result of such unprecedented economic growth and population expansion was that when Queen Victoria died in 1901, England had become the most industrialized and urbanized nation in the world, and its towns and cities were linked by the most comprehensive system of railway transport that any country has ever possessed. Nor was there any letup during the twentieth century, as the national landscape, both rural and urban, was unmade and remade, again and again. England's population continued to grow, from 32 million to above 50 million; cities expanded and suburbanized during the 1920s and 1930s, and again and even more extensively after 1945; while a whole network of new towns was created, from Stevenage to Milton Keynes to Telford. By the year 2000, England's urban areas accounted for 90 per cent of the nation's population, economic output and employment. The heavy industries that had been associated with the country's nineteenth-century economic pre-eminence – iron and steel, cotton textiles, shipbuilding, coal mining – had largely disappeared since 1945, and they were largely superseded by a new service economy, built around finance and IT. Meanwhile, the railway system has been nationalized, rationalized and privatized, and since the 1960s, motorways and new roads have proliferated across the landscape. This amounted to another revolution in transport: in 1930 there were 1 million cars in England, by 1960 there were 6 million, in 1990 there were 20 million, and today there are more than 25 million. As a result, most English towns and cities have been redeveloped, with their centres re-planned around the motor car, and with their working-class housing cleared. And since the Second World War, there has been parallel and equivalent change in the countryside, as farming has become increasingly scientific, mechanized, intensive, large-scale, market-driven – and marginalized.[6]

From one perspective, these changes to the national environment, both rural and urban, have been all to the good: for they helped bring about, and they were themselves the consequences of, unprecedented improvements in the standards of living of millions of ordinary people. Today in England men and women are better fed, better educated, better housed, better travelled and better paid than at any time in our nation's history. They live longer, their working conditions are more congenial, and their social and geographical mobility are greater than ever before. But there has also been a significant downside, as more people, more cities, more industry, more railways, and more cars have exerted immense pressure on the natural and built environment across the last two hundred years, thereby undermining many of the material gains in the standard of living that have occurred during the same period. Nineteenth-century industrial cities were notorious for the squalor of their working-class housing, and for their polluted atmosphere. Late twentieth-century cities were no less notorious for their poorly planned central areas, their crime-ridden housing estates, their suburban sprawl, and their gridlocked traffic.[7] And the turn-of-the-millennium countryside has its own problems: retreating from rapidly advancing motorways, bypasses and shopping malls; denuded of many of its birds, animals, flowers and hedgerows; and facing the seemingly inexorable decline in village life and local amenities.[8]

'Heroic Materialism', as Kenneth Clark recognized, has thus been a mixed blessing for our civilization – for no environment, be it urban or rural, can survive the traumatic disruptions of the last two centuries unaltered or unscathed. Today as in the past, the challenges and dilemmas that face the public, the planners, the pundits and the politicians in looking after our small part of the planet are clear: how to reconcile use with delight, profit with pleasure, development with conservation, the needs of the town with the interests of the country, the wishes of individuals with a broader notion of the common good.[9] But while these challenges to our landscapes and cityscapes are easily specified, they have never been easily addressed or answered. For the unfinished history of conservation in England has an unnervingly equivocal non-ending to it. To be sure, many voluntary societies and pressure groups have sought to safeguard the natural and built environment, and to urge the same course of action on successive governments which, since the Second World War, have been increasingly involved in such activities. But the outcome of these endeavours has been at best half-hearted. If we are to make further (and much-needed) progress in protecting and nurturing our national (and global?) environment during the twenty-first century, both natural and man-made, we would do well to ponder the successes and failures of these earlier efforts, and also the reasons for them.

I

By 1800, and thanks to a profound shift in sensibilities that had taken place across the preceding three centuries, it no longer seemed self-evidently right for English men and women to dominate, exploit and subdue their environment, as experience and reflection increasingly suggested that they should be more concerned to preserve and appreciate the joys and delights of the natural world around them. It was already recognized that towns were becoming polluted, overcrowded and insalubrious, whereas the countryside seemed by contrast to be clean, quiet and spiritually regenerating; that the fields and forests were in danger of excessive exploitation and cultivation, and should be looked after and taken care of as natural wilderness; and that instead of conquering the environment citizens should protect its species and its spaces.[10] These attitudes towards the natural environment would intensify during the next two centuries, they still inform our

contemporary debates about conservation, and most people today would
at least pay lip service to them. In the middle of the nineteenth century
John Ruskin famously spelt out the parallel case for the appreciative and
sympathetic conservation of the built environment in *The Seven Lamps
of Architecture*. 'It is', he asserted, 'no question of expediency or feeling
whether we shall preserve the buildings of past times or not. *We have no
right whatever to touch them*. They are not ours. They belong partly to
those who built them, and partly to all generations of mankind who are
to follow us.'[11] Here were Edmund Burke's views of society and politics,
as being a compact between generations dead, generations living, and
generations yet unborn, transferred and applied to the realms of design,
construction and architecture.

Nevertheless, it was a big step from sensibility to safeguarding, from
aspiration to action, for the protection of the natural and built environment
requires that limits be set to the freedom of individuals or business
organizations, especially in regard to the ownership of their property
and the size of their profits, in the pursuit of a greater, collective, public
good. Before 1914 the very idea that the national landscape might be
safeguarded by legislative action would have seemed bewildering and
incomprehensible to most people in power. Private property was private
property and government interfered with it as little as possible. As Peter
Mandler has rightly noted, parliament did not set out to legislate for
historic preservation and environmental conservation; and 'the British had
fewer powers in this area than any other Western European state, both at
local and central levels'.[12] In 1905, the art historian Gerard Baldwin Brown
published *The Care of Ancient Monuments*, in which he examined the
legislative provision and institutional support (both private and public) for
such activities across Europe. His conclusions were sombre. After looking
at France and Germany, and also Greece and Denmark, he concluded that
'our official machinery, judged by continental standards, is defective'. He
may have exaggerated in making these comparisons and in drawing these
conclusions, as writers and campaigners in other countries often did at
this time, but he did not do so by much.[13]

To be sure, the British parliament did sometimes legislate to regulate
property rights, notwithstanding the conventional laissez-faire wisdom of
the time; but it rarely did so for what we would now term conservationist
or environmental reasons. Throughout the nineteenth century, it regularly
passed measures to control the planning, building, sewage arrangements

and water supplies of houses, and in the 1870s, 1880s and 1890s, it passed acts in favour of slum-clearance schemes. Yet most of this legislation was permissive rather than mandatory: even when it was applied it could usually be evaded, and the motivation was sanitary rather than environmental.[14] Parliament also intervened in the countryside, as when it passed the Ground Game Act of 1831, which preserved grouse and partridge and pheasant; but it did so only to ensure that landlords could enjoy the exclusive right of shooting them, and the population of game-threatening vermin and birds of prey was much reduced in consequence. There was also legislation concerning the welfare of animals, passed between 1822 and 1835, and further extended thereafter, which outlawed bull-running, cock-fighting and bear-baiting. But the motive was more to prevent cruelty than to promote conservation and it was blatantly class biased: for while the aristocracy and gentry continued to enjoy their own blood sports of hunting and shooting, the plebeian versions of such recreations were increasingly denied to their social inferiors.[15]

Only towards the end of the nineteenth century was parliamentary legislation passed that was more explicitly concerned with conservation of both the natural and the built environment. Some of it was to do with wildlife. In 1869 the Seabirds Protection Act imposed a closed season from 1 May to 1 August for 43 species of bird, and during the next thirty years these provisions were more broadly extended. In 1914 the Grey Seals Protection Act safeguarded mammals for the first time, making it illegal to kill them in their breeding season.[16] There was also one landmark piece of law-making to protect buildings, passed in 1882, when Sir John Lubbock obtained an Act for the Preservation of Ancient Monuments, which was designed to prevent landowners from destroying such venerable artifacts located on their property, on the grounds that the state had an obligation to protect them for the common good. As a result an inspector was appointed, some monuments were brought under public guardianship, the act was twice renewed and extended in the next thirty years and, in 1908, the Royal Commission on Historical Monuments was created to list and describe buildings and monuments of historical importance throughout Britain for the period before 1700.[17] Concern about the relations between the city and the country was expressed in the Town Planning Act of 1909, which enabled local authorities to prepare schemes for land that was about to be developed, and as such it followed the views of Raymond Unwin, who constantly urged 'the drastic and planned improvement of both natural and urban environment'.[18]

But this did not amount to all that much, and as Baldwin Brown noted, it seemed an unimpressive record compared to what had been accomplished during the same period by the more progressively preservationist nations of continental Europe.[19] The legislation concerning birds and seals was difficult to implement and could be easily evaded. It had taken Sir John Lubbock more than a decade to get his ancient monuments measure through parliament (for which reason it became known as the 'monumentally ancient bill'); its definitions were loose and it gave inspectors little real power; and many landowners resented it as an unwarranted invasion of their rights of property. As for the Town Planning Act, scarcely a handful of schemes had been formally approved before the outbreak of the First World War.[20] Overall, then, little was achieved in terms of preservation and even less was accomplished in terms of safeguarding or increasing public access. There were many radicals who looked to parliament to remedy a long and deeply felt grievance, namely that ordinary men and women were unable to enjoy many of the most beautiful parts of the country because landowners guarded their property rights so zealously, and insisted that trippers and ramblers were trespassers who could – and should – be prosecuted. Yet they did so in vain. Between 1884 and 1905, James Bryce presented his Access to Mountains Bill eight times in the Commons – but he always did so unsuccessfully.[21]

With the British parliament largely indifferent during the years before the First World War, most of what would now be termed the work of environmental conservation was undertaken by voluntary organizations. In 1865 the Society for the Preservation of the Commons of London was founded, and within a decade it had saved open spaces at Wimbledon, Wandsworth and Putney, and also Hampstead Heath. Twelve years later, William Morris founded the Society for the Protection of Ancient Buildings, primarily to safeguard England's churches from the heavy-handed 'restoration' of Sir George Gilbert Scott. The Society for the Protection of Birds began as a ladies' pressure group to oppose the wearing of plumage (although ostrich and game birds were excluded), and it received a royal charter in 1904. The National Trust was founded in 1895, by Octavia Hill, Sir Robert Hunter and Canon Charles Hardwicke Rawnsley, to hold land and to preserve places of historic interest or natural beauty, and in 1907 such land was declared inalienable by act of parliament. In 1897 the *Survey of London* was established, with support from the London County Council (LCC), partly to provide an inventory of the capital's buildings, but also in the hope that this would make it easier to preserve them at a time when large areas of the city were being demolished and redeveloped.[22]

Yet for all their high-mindedness, crusading ardour and good intentions, these voluntary societies and pressure groups made no more impact on popular opinion or on the natural and built environment than did the limited parliamentary legislation of the time. Their memberships were small, their influence was tiny, and their public profile was minimal. The Society for the Protection of Ancient Buildings was supported mainly by artists and architects, but apart from influencing ideas and techniques of church restoration, it achieved little. By 1910 it had only 443 members and when the government appointed the Royal Commission on Historical Monuments it deliberately excluded the Society's chief spokesman as 'faddist' and 'extremist'. By this time the National Trust had attracted less than eight hundred supporters, and there were real doubts as to whether it would survive the deaths of its founding triumvirate (Hill in 1912, Hunter in 1913, and Rawnsley in 1920). It was regarded by landlords as a threat to private property, and by government as wet and skittish.[23] Even in the era of the Liberal welfare-state reforms, conservation of the historic environment was seen as a threat to laissez-faire, and it was also deemed to be too backward-looking for a nation that still regarded itself as being both powerful and progressive. As a result, the pattern established in the years before 1914 – of limited, largely ineffectual legislation, of small and crankish pressure groups, and of little sympathy or contact between them and the government or the general public – remained the prevailing and predominant pattern in England throughout the inter-war years.[24]

II

At first glance, such lack of progress during the 1920s and 1930s seems surprising, for the dominant figure in national politics during this period was the Conservative leader Stanley Baldwin, who was three times prime minister, and a man who constantly sang the praises of the countryside and the hedgerows. 'To me,' he once observed in his most-frequently quoted speech, 'England is the country and the country is England.' He took a genuine delight in being a Worcestershire squire, his favourite novelist was Mary Webb, and among his friends were Sir Edward Grey, the former foreign secretary and a renowned naturalist and birdwatcher, Lord Halifax, a great northern landowner, fox-hunter and believer in 'spiritual values', and John Buchan and G.M. Trevelyan, two famous writers whose deep attachment to the countryside was well known.[25] But although it was undoubtedly sincere, Baldwin's interest in rural matters was more political than conservational. For him, the countryside spelt decency and respectability, the qualities he was determined to bring back into public life after the corrupt excesses of the Lloyd George coalition; and it also spelt neighbourliness and consensus, attitudes he was eager to promote among the broader public in the difficult years of the slump and high unemployment. In short, Baldwin was more interested in using the countryside to the advantage of his politics than he was eager to use his politics to the advantage of the countryside.[26]

Once again, then, the result was a legislative record in support of conservation that was distinctly meagre. In the immediate aftermath of the First World War, the Lloyd George coalition government set up the Forestry Commission, which soon began to plant upland areas with conifers and pines. The primary motivation, however, was to grow timber on a sufficient scale to relieve England of the danger of being starved of a strategic resource in the event of another war, and almost from the beginning there were bitter rows between the advocates of commercial forestry and those who wanted to preserve amenity and promote outdoor recreation.[27] In 1932 a Town and Country Planning Act was passed by the National Government, but it was scarcely more important than its 1909 predecessor: it encouraged local authorities to designate planning schemes for specific areas, but once again its clauses were permissive rather than mandatory, and by the outbreak of the Second World War virtually nothing had been accomplished under its provisions.[28] The Restriction of Ribbon Development Act of 1935 was an ineffectual effort to control the construction of new housing along arterial roads, while the Access to Mountains Act of 1939 was another legislative non-event. To be sure, it was a measure in the liberal tradition of James Bryce, but it failed to grant any general right of access, left decision-making in the hands of the Ministry of Agriculture, and was soon rendered irrelevant by the outbreak of the Second World War.[29]

This lack of interest may seem all the more remarkable because, as the need for a Ribbon Development Act suggests, the towns and the countryside of England were undergoing dramatic changes and (as it seemed to some) unprecedented spoliation during the 1920s and 1930s. In London, many of the capital's eighteenth-century architectural glories were demolished to make way for new developments of shops and offices, including Lansdowne House, Devonshire House, Nash's stuccoed facades on Regent Street, Soane's magnificent Bank of England building, Old Waterloo Bridge and the Adelphi. In the countryside, building blight seemed to be everywhere, as 4 million new houses were put up during the inter-war years, and as towns and cities expanded on the ground at an unprecedented rate, gobbling up 60,000 acres of rural land a year.[30] The result was a new world of council house estates and white-collar suburbia, and of seaside bungalows and holiday homes, as the working and lower middle classes leapfrogged their way out into the country. And they were accompanied by advertising signs, petrol stations, telephone boxes, pylons and cinemas. There was also the arrival of the automobile in unprecedented numbers: between 1924 and 1936 the price of a car fell by 50 per cent and production increased by 500 per cent. Coach parties and day-trippers brought yet more noise and litter to previously tranquil scenes and localities, while the aristocracy and gentry, the traditional guardians of the countryside, were in social and political retreat and many were selling their estates in what was described as a 'revolution in landowning'.[31]

Naturally, there were protesting voices against these trends, and they came mostly (and predictably) from the upper echelons of society. One of them was Clough Williams-Ellis, who produced two books, *England and the Octopus* (London, 1928), which he wrote himself, and *Britain and the Beast* (London, 1937), containing essays by such luminaries as J.M. Keynes, E.M. Forster and Patrick Abercrombie, inveighing against what they deplored as the ruination of the countryside. Another was G.M. Trevelyan, who became a staunch supporter of the National Trust and spoke out powerfully against the wounding of the landscape in two crusading lectures revealingly entitled *Must England's Beauty Perish?* (London, 1926) and *The Calls and Claims of Natural Beauty* (London, 1931). With Trevelyan's help, and under the leadership of John Bailey, R.C. Norman and Oliver Brett, the scale of the Trust's activity significantly expanded, as both its membership and its holdings increased, from 713 to 6,800 people and from 13,200 to 68,544 acres.[32] In 1926 the National Trust was joined by the Council for the Preservation of Rural England, which was set up to co-ordinate conservation activities, and to bring pressure to bear on the government. And in 1937 the Georgian Group was inaugurated, to campaign against the demolition of so much of London's architectural heritage, with active support from Douglas Goldring, Robert Byron, Osbert Sitwell, John Betjeman, the young, pre-television Kenneth Clark and James Lees-Milne.[33]

These were very establishment and well-connected names, and one of the reasons they achieved relatively little was that they were too paternal, too exclusive, too elitist for the mass democracy that England had recently become in the aftermath of the Fourth Reform Act of 1918. They were more interested in preservation than in access – in safeguarding great buildings and in keeping the suburbs and the trippers out of their beloved hills and fields. 'The people's claim', C.E.M. Joad argued in *Britain and the Beast*, 'upon the English countryside is paramount.' But, he went on, 'the people are not as yet ready to take up their claim without destroying that to which the claim is laid'. And so the landscape must be kept inviolate 'until such time as they *are* ready'.[34] But this was not how those in government saw things, now that they were answerable to a mass electorate. Why should the working classes be denied access to those rural places and pleasures that the upper classes had always enjoyed? 'The countryside', the preservationists were sternly reminded in an official memorandum of 1937, 'is not the preserve of the wealthy and leisured classes.' On the contrary, it was a source of pride that since the war, 'there has been unparalleled building development, a development which every government has done its utmost to stimulate, and whose effect has been to create new and better social conditions for a very large number of persons'. From this populist, laissez-faire perspective, 'homes fit for heroes' were much more important than elite 'spiritual values'.[35]

In such a climate of official and popular opinion the crusading conservationists again achieved little. The Council for the Preservation of Rural England put forward ideas concerning green belts to throttle suburbs, strict planning controls to preserve agriculture and scenery, and the appointment of landowners as 'trustees' for the public good. They came to nothing. It did succeed in 1929 in persuading the government to set up a committee to look into the idea of establishing national parks, but its report was lost in the financial and political crisis of 1931, and Baldwin was not prepared to touch it thereafter. The National Trust tried to encourage landowners to join a trusteeship scheme, but they rebuffed it as being pretentious and socialistic. On the whole, both the public and the politicians were indifferent (and sometimes hostile) to these preservationist efforts, and so it was scarcely surprising that there was little legislation, and that what there was continued the nineteenth-century practice of being enabling but not mandatory. In 1927, a senior mandarin at the Office of Works noted that England had fewer provisions to preserve historic buildings 'than any other country in Europe, with the exception of the Balkan states and Turkey'. And after the Town and Country Planning Act of 1932, which contributed nothing to urban containment or rural development, controls of the built and natural environment remained among the weakest in Europe.[36]

III

During the Second World War and its immediate aftermath there was dramatic change, not so much because the preservationist lobby triumphed, but because the climate of public and political opinion in England shifted towards greater planning of the rural and urban environment, and also towards wider access to it. This was partly because war wrought havoc with towns and cities: in Coventry and Southampton, 30 per cent of the housing stock was wiped out, and a similar proportion of LCC council houses was destroyed or harmed. Most country mansions and palaces were requisitioned, many suffered lasting damage, and it seemed unlikely that their owners would be willing or able to return at the end of the war.[37] But it was also because Labour dominated the home front in Churchill's coalition government and won the election in 1945, and so set in train a series of inquiries, which served as the blueprint for its management of the environment in its years of power, not so much as individual property, but rather as collective heritage. Among them were the Barlow Commission (1940) on the distribution of the industrial population, the Scott Committee (1942) on planning in rural areas, the Uthwatt Report (1942) on land values, the Dower Committee (1945) on national parks, the Hobhouse Committee (1947) on national parks and access, and the Gowers Committee (1948–50) on houses of outstanding historic importance or architectural interest.[38]

From these reports and inquiries came a flood of legislation that set the framework for conservation in England for a generation. The Town and Country Planning Act of 1944 authorized the listing of individual buildings of historic significance, going far beyond the narrow category of scheduled monuments. In 1946 Hugh Dalton set up a £50 million National Land Fund, 'to buy some of the best of our still unspoiled open country and stretches of coast, to be preserved forever, not for the enjoyment of a few private landowners, but as a playground and a national possession for all our people'.[39] A further Town and Country Planning Act of 1947 introduced the concept of comprehensive development plans across the whole urban and rural landscape. In 1949 the National Parks and Access to the Countryside Act was passed: it gave provision for the designation of National Parks and Areas of Outstanding National Beauty, and a Nature Conservancy was set up to establish a network of National Nature Reserves and Sites of Special Scientific Interest. And in 1953, in the aftermath of Gowers, the Historic Buildings and Ancient Monuments Act established the Historic Buildings Council, which distributed repair and maintenance grants to the owners of great but threatened mansions in return for guaranteed public access.[40]

These wide-ranging and interlocking measures were intended to usher in a whole brave new world of active conservation on behalf of everyone, in marked contrast to the limited legislation and paternal preservationism of the early twentieth century and the inter-war years. Looking after the environment, both rural and urban, natural and man-made, was now the responsibility of government, and during the next two decades, regardless of whether Labour or the Conservatives were in power, the range of that responsibility further increased. In 1951 the Rivers (Prevention of Pollution) Act was passed, and in 1956 the Clean Air Act received royal assent, which within a decade transformed the environment of industrial towns and cities. In the following year, Duncan Sandys established the Civic Trust, which co-ordinated the activities of local amenity societies working to preserve the built-up landscape, and which became an urban equivalent of the Council for the Preservation of Rural England. Subsequently, Sandys piloted through the Civic Amenities Act, which made it possible to establish conservation areas in cities, towns and villages across the length and breadth of the country. Yet another Town and Country Planning Act, in 1968, tightened up the listed-building procedure, the Countryside Act of the same year gave the Countryside Commissioners a general responsibility for safeguarding the landscape, and the Conservation of Wild Creatures and Wild Plants Act of 1975 established a statutory framework for the protection of all types of wildlife.[41]

But these well-meaning attempts to safeguard and plan the national environment seem to have met at best with limited success. In the cities there was destruction and redevelopment on a massive and wholly unprecedented scale. Between 1955 and 1975, 1.3 million people were re-housed, moving from slum dwellings into high-rise flats, which were hugely subsidized, but were soon disliked as unfriendly and unwelcoming council houses in the sky. Neighbourhoods were demolished, communities destroyed, and historic street patterns obliterated: in 1970 the Greater London Council acknowledged that 67,000 houses that it had bulldozed could and should have been renovated.[42] At the same time, ancient city centres were wiped out, and replaced with soulless office blocks, multi-storey car parks, and impenetrable ring roads. For this was the era of property developers like Jack Cotton and Charles Clore, and of large-scale building contractors such as Bovis, Wimpey and Taylor Woodrow. Many famous and historic buildings were razed to the ground, among them the Birmingham Public Library, its Midland Institute, and the Doric Arch at Euston Station. Despite public pressure, much of it organized by the recently founded Victorian Society, the Prime Minister, Harold Macmillan, had personally authorized the destruction of the Euston Arch in 1961, on the grounds that conservation was only a minority interest, and that such obsession with the past would sap the nation's vitality.[43] Small wonder that in 1975 Colin Amery and Dan Cruickshank published a book on what was described as the 'devastating' vandalizing of cities entitled *The Rape of Britain*.[44]

At the same time, the destruction of English country houses also reached unprecedented levels. The 1950s and early 1960s were peak years for demolitions: at least 10 per cent of the national stock disappeared completely, including such illustrious piles as Eaton Hall (the Dukes of Westminster) and Panshanger (the Earls Cowper). Some great houses were much reduced in size, like Bowood (the Marquesses of Lansdowne) and Woburn (the Dukes of Bedford), others were taken over by the National Trust under its country houses scheme, and many more were sold off for institutional use as schools, colleges, hospitals and nursing homes. Some finance was initially made available from the National Land Fund to pass a dozen or so properties to the National Trust, but by the early 1960s the Fund was essentially moribund. In such a climate of devastation, John Harris and Marcus Binney mounted an exhibition at the Victoria and Albert Museum in 1974 on 'The Destruction of the Country House' and soon after, a new pressure-group was formed called SAVE Britain's Heritage.[45] It was far more publicity-conscious than the inter-war organizations had been, but all the campaigning and lobbying in the world could not prevent the sale of Mentmore Towers in 1977, in the aftermath of the death of the sixth Earl of Rosebery, and the dispersal of its fabulous collections – as a result of which the by-now defunct National Land Fund was revived as the National Heritage Memorial Fund.[46]

Nor did the English countryside fare any better, for as in the towns, the protective legislation was simply not strong enough. Because of the overriding need to produce food and timber domestically, in the aftermath of the war, agriculture and forestry were both exempted from the development control of the new Town and Country Planning Act. Although ten national parks had been established in England and Wales by 1960, there were none in Scotland, they were never nationally owned, they were inadequately administered and overseen, and it proved impossible to prevent economic development and intensive farming. Copper mining was allowed in Snowdonia, an oil terminal was established on the Pembrokeshire coast, and the early-warning station was built at Fylingdales on the North Yorkshire Moors.[47] Despite 3,000 Sites of Special Scientific Interest having been designated by 1975, this proved to be little more than a label stuck on the ground, and which the farmer could disregard at will. In the same way, the Countryside Commissioners had been given inadequate powers to exert any serious form of control, and the Conservation of Wild Creatures and Wild Plants Act listed too few species, many of which had already disappeared altogether.[48] In the cities, it seemed, the planners had been given too much power; in the countryside, by contrast, they did not seem to have enough.

In many ways the real threat to the rural environment in these post-war years came not so much from continuing urban encroachment (although there was, indeed, plenty of that) but from newly-mechanized farming, which soon began to wreak havoc on the flora and fauna of the countryside. In the aftermath of war it was thought essential that Britain should continue to be self-sufficient in food, and the Agriculture Act of 1947 brought about guaranteed markets and assured prices for farmers, which lasted for a generation. This was accompanied by the revolution in agricultural technology, in which horses were replaced by tractors, and by the unprecedented use of fertilizers and pesticides. In 1940 there were 1,100 tractor-mounted sprayers in England and Wales; by 1981 there were 74,000. In 1944 there were 63 products approved for use by farmers as pesticides; by 1976 there were 819. Increased mechanization made for bigger fields, which meant the destruction of meadowlands, grasslands, downlands and hedgerows.[49] Between 1947 and 1985 hedgerow length fell by 25 per cent and this, combined with the growing use of chemicals, had a devastating effect on flowers, trees, animals and birds. By 1964 peregrines were at 44 per cent of their pre-war numbers, and many other species suffered similar fates.[50] In 1977 the Nature Conservancy Council produced a report emphasizing the damaging effects that new-style agriculture was having on the biodiversity of the environment, and in 1980 Marion Shoard published an angry, wounded book lamenting what she termed *The Theft of the Countryside*. 'The English landscape', she gloomily insisted, 'is under sentence of death.'[51]

Underlying all this was a growing dissatisfaction on what might, during this period, be termed the two evolving sides of the great conservation divide. For those who cared about the natural and the built environment, it seemed that the initially-welcomed increase in government involvement had gone terribly wrong. In *The Making of the English Landscape*, W.G. Hoskins regretted that the countryside he had known and loved was vanishing, and was being replaced by the planners, the politicians and the vandals with a new, horrible, 'barbaric England' of 'the arterial by-pass, treeless and stinking of diesel oil, murderous with lorries'.[52] For their part, those in government, regardless of political affiliation, were no less annoyed that the growing cult of conservation was being used as a brake on what they saw as much-needed progress and improvement. In a speech he delivered in 1962, Lord Hailsham (himself no philistine), urged that 'all the really artistically healthy societies of the world have been marked with a supreme artistic self-confidence'. 'Mattocks and sticks of dynamite' were their watchword, 'to clear away the rubble of the past, often of exquisite beauty, and to make way for the beauties of the future.' In a later Tory government, Peter Walker deplored the public's sentimental tendency 'to retain all that exists and to oppose all that is new', while for Labour, Anthony Crosland took the populist line that the conservationists were elitist, 'hostile to growth and indifferent to the needs of ordinary people'.[53]

IV

During the last 25 years it has become much more difficult for opponents of conservation to make such accusations of class bias and elitism, as the urge to protect both the natural and built historic environment has simultaneously become unprecedentedly popular in its appeal, and

unprecedentedly global in its reach. Hence Greenpeace and Friends of
the Earth, hence the growing concern about global warming, hence the
Prince of Wales's advocacy of organic farming, and hence the growing and
increasingly widespread use of the word 'heritage' to describe the nation's
historic environment, both rural and urban. Such activities encompass
a broad spectrum of political opinion, and an equally broad swathe of
society. During the 1980s, there was an unparalleled rise in the number
of people joining such English conservationist organizations. In 1945, the
Royal Society for the Protection of Birds had a membership of only 5,900;
by 1980 the figure was 320,000 and by 1997 it had more than trebled to 1
million. The figures for the National Trust show a similar trend: 200,000
members in 1970; 1 million in 1980; 2 million in 1990; 2.7 million in
2001; and 3.5 million by 2007.[54] No political party in Britain today can
remotely compete with such large-scale popular support and involvement.
Even Margaret Thatcher recognized the direction in which the conservational wind was now blowing. 'We are all no more than life tenants of our
heritage', she observed in a speech to the Royal Fine Arts Commission in
1989, expressing views that would have done credit to Ruskin, but in the
vocabulary of her own time, 'and we have a moral duty to pass it on in as
good a condition as that in which we received it.'[55]

Beyond any doubt, the conservation climate did become much more
benevolent during the 1980s, as those in favour, and those previously
against, seemed eager to reach some measure of mutual understanding
and political accommodation. For its part, the government became more
sympathetic. The National Heritage Act, passed in 1983, replaced the Historic
Buildings Council with a new organization, appropriately named English
Heritage, which was 'an independent body devoted to the conservation and
presentation of England's inheritance of ancient monuments and historic
buildings'. As Secretary of State for the Environment, Michael Heseltine
was a powerful advocate of the comprehensive listing of historic buildings,
and in the mid 1980s the National Heritage Memorial Fund gave £25
million to 'save' the three great houses of Kedleston, Nostell and Weston,
and to prevent any repetition of the Mentmore debacle.[56] And after the
planning excesses that had blighted so many inner cities, ancient and
modern, during the 1960s and 1970s, there was now a growing recognition
that the conservation of a more human and appealing urban environment
was the precondition for renewal, not the enemy of it.[57] Accordingly, when
Marcus Binney published *Our Vanishing Heritage* in 1984, he noted that

conservationists were now more willing and able to 'stand up and speak out for endangered buildings', and his book was not so much a lament for what had been lost as an account of country houses, public buildings, churches, terraces, town houses and factories that had been successfully saved and often put to new and imaginative uses.[58]

Underlying these changes was a deeper shift in the public and political mood against the ethos of planning and control that had been the guiding (though not always effective) force in conservation for a generation since the Labour government had taken office in 1945. One indication of this was the intervention of the Prince of Wales in public debates. Between them, he claimed, the planners and architects had done more damage to England's towns and cities than the Luftwaffe, and in *A Vision of Britain* (London, 1989) he set out an alternative view of urban and rural landscapes in which a sense of the past, of place, and of human scale was given higher priority than utopian, ahistorical and anti-human blueprints. Viewed in the longer perspective afforded by this chapter, such royal intervention is best understood as the reassertion of the patrician aesthetic of Clough Williams-Ellis and his inter-war friends.[59] But now the planners were equally assailed from the other side of the political spectrum by the free-market populism of Margaret Thatcher. For she regarded them with the same loathing with which she regarded bishops, academics and civil servants: they were wet, elitist, self-perpetuating, irresponsible, out of touch, and arrogantly indifferent to the needs and views of ordinary men and women. It was 'the planners', she told the Conservative Party Conference in 1987, who had 'cut the heart out of our cities'. Accordingly, the construction of inner-urban motorways was brought to an end, no more municipal flats were built, many existing blocks were demolished, and council houses were sold off.[60]

The result of these changes in outlook and action was that between 1979 and 1997 there was an increasingly relaxed attitude towards planning. In some ways this improved the prospects for conservation, but in other ways the effect was decidedly adverse. By the late 1980s the Secretary of State for the Environment, Nicholas Ridley, was bullying local authorities into granting planning permission for new developments on green-field sites at the edge of many towns (while objecting to similar practices in his own neighbourhood). This in turn led to a new and largely unregulated suburbanization of the countryside, concentrated around shopping malls and housing estates. In 1986 Britain contained 432 superstores; in 1996 there were 1,034. Since 1986 the retail giant Sainsbury's has added more than two hundred new supermarkets: 10 per cent in town centres; 23 per cent in suburbs; 67 per cent on outside sites.[61] At the same time, the major house-building contractors covered the adjacent fields with homes in standardized and repetitious style that are insensitive to the local built environment and traditional materials, and thus are unappealingly reminiscent of Lego. 'No continental European country', the historian Richard Rodger claims, 'has cloned private housing on such a scale in the last quarter of a century.'[62]

In all these ways, planning deregulation has been more the enemy than the handmaid of conservation: both in the town and in the country, the increasingly unfettered free market, driven by populist impulses and laissez-faire ideology, has blighted the environment in recent times to an even greater extent than during the inter-war years. As stores have moved out from city centres to city peripheries, the variety and vibrancy of downtown life have been much diminished, as smaller shops close down and many buildings become derelict, thereby compounding the mistakes made by the planners in earlier decades. More out-of-town shopping means more out-of-town car journeys: since 1980, road traffic has increased by two-thirds and is still growing. As a result, Britain's newly sprawling towns and cities are more gridlocked and more polluted than ever before. Indeed, according to Lord Rogers' Urban Task Force, which reported in 1999, the quality of urban life in Britain has fallen far behind that enjoyed by much of Europe.[63] And towns and cities are not only sprawling outwards, but upwards, too, as high-rise office blocks and apartments threaten historic views and overwhelm local neighbourhoods. Meanwhile, the advance of the urban frontier into the country seems both inexorable and irresistible. At present, England is losing 27,000 acres (nearly 11,000 hectares) annually to urban development and if this trend continues until 2050, the total built-up area will be twice as great as it is today.[64]

Nor are these the only problems that beset the conservation of the countryside. Today, agriculture contributes only 1 per cent to the nation's gross domestic product, and it employs a mere 1 per cent of the labour force. Yet these employees are responsible for the stewardship of 80 per cent of England's land surface. In lowland regions, and notwithstanding restrictions on the use of chemicals, over-subsidized farming continues to ruin the landscape. Hedgerows still disappear at an alarming rate, the number of starlings halved between 1972 and 1997, and many other species have similarly declined.[65] Meanwhile, and as the outbreak of foot-and-mouth disease in 2001 searingly demonstrated, much upland farming, in the West Country, the Lake District and the Pennines, is scarcely viable economically: if this section of the English landscape is to be maintained and conserved new ways will probably have to be found to finance it.[66] Small wonder there are many who cry that 'the countryside' is in 'crisis'. It certainly is from a conservation point of view. 'The landscape', Oliver Rackham wrote in 1986, in words that have become even more pertinent in the twenty-odd years since, 'is a record of our roots and the growth of civilisation.' 'Almost every rural change since 1945', he goes on, 'has extended what is already commonplace at the expense of what is wonderful or rare or has meaning.'[67] This is not exactly an encouraging appraisal of our contemporary environment, and it demands attention.

Yet at the same time, it is also fair to observe that more of the English landscape and countryside is enjoyed (and valued) by more people than ever before; while recognition of the significance, attractiveness and potential of the historic built environment has never been as great as it is today.[68] Here, indeed, is a major paradox. For much of the period with which this chapter has been concerned, the seemingly inexorable extension of the built and industrial environment, in the form of factories and houses, coal mines and steel mills, was seen as the greatest threat to the countryside, and thus to a national heritage that was defined (and defended) in essentially rural terms. But with the demise of the old British industrial economy from the 1970s onwards, its once-hated (and feared) buildings and artefacts are now themselves deemed worthy of conservation, and in recent decades they have been welcomed and enfolded into a much broader notion of a national heritage, which is as much urban as it is rural, as much built as it is natural.[69] The terraced house in Liverpool where John Lennon was born now belongs to the National Trust, and English Heritage actively concerns itself with the preservation of collieries in Staffordshire, while tall buildings now present as great a threat to London's historic skyline as the expansion of the 'great wen' once presented to the surrounding countryside. As now regarded and re-defined, the post-industrial national heritage embraces those very 'dark satanic mills' which once seemed so threatening. 'Heroic Materialism', in Britain at least, has had its day, and it no longer threatens our heritage, but has become part of it.

V

It should by now be clear that the history of conservation in twentieth-century England has, at best, an equivocal outcome, for it is in many ways a story of lost causes, disappointed hopes, and failed endeavours, as a result of which both the urban and rural landscape, the man-made and the natural environment, have suffered irreversible damage. On the other hand, we should not lose sight of the fact that in conservation, as in everything, the best is often the enemy of the good. For notwithstanding the traumatic changes to which our landscapes and cityscapes have been subjected during the last two hundred years, the fact remains that many parts of England, both town and country, are still extraordinarily beautiful, and even today, after a century of unprecedented urban encroachment, nearly 90 per cent of the nation's surface area is still classified as being rural.[70] We should also remember that constraint and control, which are the essential keys to conservation, are exceptionally difficult political (and philosophical) issues. As Simon Schama has rightly observed, there are 'profound problems' that beset any democracy seeking both 'to repair environmental abuse and to preserve liberty'.[71] Today, the most effective way to improve our environment at a stroke would be to reduce pressure on it by banning second children, second cars, and second homes. In a few years this would transform our cities and our countryside for the better. But such draconian measures are not possible in a contemporary democracy such as ours; and nor should they be.

By definition, democracy is a cumbersome instrument for dealing with vexed, protracted, complicated issues, and that is certainly so in the case of conservation. 'The planners' are blamed: sometimes for having too much power, sometimes for having insufficient. 'The market' enables individuals to satisfy their own desires (and who are any of us to gainsay *that*?), yet it takes no account of the broader, general, public good. Inevitably, the result is a bewildering array of half-thought-out and half-completed initiatives by a no less bewildering array of voluntary societies, government departments and (increasingly) EU directives and global imperatives. As Oliver Rackham notes, 'historic landscapes and historic buildings are similar in many ways, and both should have the same kind of legal protection'. But, he adds, 'the case for conservation is weakened by lack of co-ordination between those concerned with scenery, wildlife, antiquities and freedom'.[72] This is true not only in terms of voluntary societies, but also in terms of government, as exemplified by the seemingly endless re-configuring (and re-naming) of those many departments (transport, agriculture, defence, environment, rural affairs, heritage, communities and Deputy Prime Minister) that have a legitimate concern with conservation. The results are those shuffles and scuffles, the compromises and bargains of politics, which 'so enrage the most zealous friends of the earth', for whom the death of nature is imminent, and for whom the stark alternatives are those (most likely) of extinction but (just maybe) of redemption.[73]

Put less apocalyptically, this means that in the future as in the past, there will always be a conflict between the use of the historic environment to sustain our material way of life and the enjoyment of the historic environment to nourish our other (but no less important?) needs.[74] What are the prospects for the countryside, when subsidized and mechanized farming has wrought such damage to our lowland landscape, when upland agriculture is in economic crisis, and when the advance of the urban fringe continues un-halted? How will our country and our cities cope with the projected 4.4 million new homes which will, apparently, be needed by 2021, and which will be the equivalent of 25 additional towns the size of Milton Keynes? And how can new life be brought back into the centre of our cities, and the planning mistakes and excesses of the 1960s and 1970s be remedied, at a time when road traffic is set to increase by another third in the next twenty years?[75] During the past decade and a half, a succession of governments has produced a succession of white papers on Environmental Strategy, Urban Life, and Rural Conditions. But so far their impact has been negligible. The preservation of our historic environment requires serious political engagement, committed public involvement, and the achievement of consent and consensus. But as the history of the twentieth century's efforts at conservation shows, these are not easily obtained.[76]

Yet can we afford to conclude by being thus resigned, indifferent, detached, non-apocalyptic – and parochial? As the world's rainforests disappear for ever, as tigers are threatened with extinction across Asia, as Venice seems set to sink beneath the Mediterranean waves, and as global warming intensifies with consequences that seem increasingly clear, the answer may well be that we cannot. For the conservation of our own national environment is but a small part of the larger and increasingly urgent enterprise of conserving our whole global environment. Yet if it is difficult to reach an agreed and viable policy within *one* nation, how will an agreed and viable policy ever be evolved between *all* nations, when

President George W. Bush is viscerally hostile to taking serious measures to combat global warming in the United States, and when the demand for cars in China and India grows explosively and pollutingly, year on year? Faced with such pressing and seemingly intractable problems, all the historian can do is to point out the successes and failures of the past, and offer some tentative explanations as to why some things happened (for good or ill) and why others did not (ditto). Like all historical accounts of contemporary issues, this chapter is 'less a recipe for action than an invitation to reflection, and as such it is meant as a contribution to self-knowledge rather than a strategy for ecological rescue'.[77] But for all that, a better understanding of 'how we arrived at our current local predicaments might, just possibly, help to clear our heads about which directions to take in the future'.[78] For if the history of conservation efforts in twentieth-century England proves anything, it is that clear heads are at least as important (but rarely as much in evidence) as good intentions.

6

Tradition:
Inventing and Re-Inventing the 'Last Night
of the Proms'[1]

Like many ostensibly ancient British rituals and observances, the Promenade Concerts were founded – by the manager Robert Newman and by the young, aspiring orchestral conductor Henry J. Wood – towards the close of the nineteenth century, two years after the Queen's Hall had opened as a new concert venue and event space in London in 1893. As such, they may be regarded as a classic instance of what is sometimes called 'invented tradition', where venerable antiquity is less in evidence than is often popularly supposed; and where change and adaptation are at least as important as continuity and survival, even though the former are often deftly disguised or mistakenly perceived as the latter.[2] This in turn means that there are many ways of writing the history of what have long been colloquially known as the 'Proms' (a word which has a very different connotation in Britain from its popular meaning in the United States), and there are many aspects of this remarkable series of concerts that deserve and require to have their histories written. From what economists call the 'supply side', any comprehensive account of the Proms must encompass composers and compositions, orchestras and conductors, concerts and buildings, funders and sponsors, programmes and organizers. From what might be termed the 'demand side', the story of the Proms should be concerned with the audiences: with their numbers, motivation, social background, education, occupations, nationality, gender balance and ethnic mix; with their geographical location, whether in the concert hall in London, or elsewhere in Britain, or even across the seas and around the world; and with the varied and advancing technologies by which the Promenaders, or more distant listeners, or viewers, or spectators are reached: by live performance, via the wireless, through television, on the big screen, and so on.[3]

Thus regarded, the history of the Proms is an important, knotted, intricate, multi-faceted and many-stranded subject; and to make it even more complex and protean, these varied themes which constitute the supply and demand sides inter-connect and inter-act in different ways and at different times, and each of them also has its own separate pace, tempo and chronology. In terms (for instance) of its performing space, the crucial dates in the history of the Proms were 1893 (when the Queen's Hall was opened) and 1941 (when it was destroyed and the concerts were relocated at the Albert Hall); but in terms of sponsorship and organization, the key dates were 1927 (when the BBC first became involved) and 1942–44 (when the Corporation's commitment was reaffirmed and effectively became permanent). Moreover, the evolving 'supply' and production of the Proms, along with the developing 'demand' and audience for them, must be set in a broader historical and geographical context: namely the state and self-image of the nation in which the concerts have taken place uninterruptedly across a century and more. For clearly the imperial Britain in which Henry Wood's Proms began in the summer of 1895 (when Queen Victoria's Diamond Jubilee was only two years away) was a very different place from the post-imperial Britain in which the BBC Proms were performed in the summer of 2007 (when Queen Elizabeth II's Diamond Jubilee was only five years away), and this in turn helps explain why the Proms, like other regularly-repeated rituals, have not only meant (and mean) different things to different people, but have also meant (and mean) different things at different times.[4]

These considerations apply to the Promenade Concerts taken as a whole, performance on performance, year on year, and decade on decade; but they are of especial relevance to the annual 'Last Night' jamboree which brings the season to a climax and to a close, and which for many years has concluded with a virtually immutable (and thus 'traditional') programme, which has acquired a near-sacrosanct popular significance. The first half of the concert consists of several items of serious music, each usually fairly short, and sometimes including the first performance of a newly-commissioned piece. But during the second half, which is televised live on BBC 1 and is also watched and listened to by a global audience of millions, the mood of the evening lightens considerably, as some less demanding works are performed immediately after the interval. There then follows what have long been regarded as the 'traditional' closing items: Elgar's 'Pomp and Circumstance' March No.1, better known as 'Land of Hope and Glory'; Henry Wood's 'Fantasia on British Sea Songs', including the sailor's hornpipe; 'Rule Britannia!' composed by Thomas Arne, with orchestration by Sir Malcolm Sargent; and finally 'Jerusalem', set to music by Sir Charles Hubert Hastings Parry, and later re-orchestrated by Elgar. All of these numbers involve active participation by the audience which, as the second half advances, becomes ever more boisterous, noisy and irreverent, with loud and lusty singing, as well as a deafening stamping of feet. And before 'Jerusalem' is sung, the conductor of the BBC Symphony Orchestra makes a farewell speech of thanks and good wishes, sometimes struggling to make himself heard amidst the din of shouts and cheers, whistles and trumpets, football rattles and bursting balloons.

For some people this remarkable occasion is the very embodiment and quintessence of the Proms as a great, patriotic, unchanging British 'tradition', by turns moving and memorable, flamboyant and festive, splendid and spectacular; for others it is a deplorable display of boorish behaviour, mindless nostalgia and jingoistic xenophobia, which bears no relation whatsoever to the liberal values, cosmopolitan reach and international-ist ethos of the Proms series as a whole.[5] Yet despite their very different verdicts, these entrenched and contradictory assessments of the 'Last Night of the Proms' both share and assume a permanence of programming and a constancy of purpose which are wholly belied by the historical evidence. For the 'Last Night' as it is played, sung, conducted, transmitted, commentated on, listened to, watched, acclaimed and loathed in our day is as different from the final concerts which were initially staged in Henry Wood's time as is the British nation over which the present Queen reigns compared with that over which her great-great grandmother presided. Across the years which separate – yet also connect – the Proms then and the Proms now, there are three phases into which the history of the 'Last Night' may be usefully divided: from 1895 to 1946, the inaugural half-century dominated by Sir Henry Wood, when the last night was merely the final concert of the series; from 1947 to 1967, when Wood's successor, Sir Malcolm Sargent, effectively invented the 'tradition' of the 'Last Night of the Proms'; and from 1968 until the present day, when a succession of BBC Controllers of Music have tried – with varying degrees of determination and success – to rein in, tone down, modify, adapt, reform, revive and reinvigorate what they have increasingly come to regard as an outmoded tradition and as an embarrassing anachronism.[6]

I

When Robert Newman and the young Henry Wood inaugurated their eight-week season of Promenade Concerts at the recently-built Queen's Hall in London on 10 August 1895, they were not doing anything very novel, and nor were they setting out to create a great, long-lasting British 'tradition': for while there were abundant metropolitan precedents for their new enterprise, they were not wholly encouraging.[7] Such 'promenades' had been a permanent yet ephemeral part of London cultural life for the best part of sixty years, and as originally conceived, the Newman–Wood venture was just the latest in that long line. Public concerts had been a feature of eighteenth-century metropolitan life in places like Vauxhall, Marylebone and Ranelagh Gardens, but promenade concerts had originated in Paris, and they were imported to Britain during the late 1830s. They were held in such London theatres as the Drury Lane, Her Majesty's, the Lyceum and Covent Garden, they were usually presided over by foreign conductors (often French: among them Philippe Musard and Louis Antoine Jullien), and they were attended by a youthful, lively, diverse and convivial audience, who stood up and walked around while the music was being played (hence the name 'promenade'), and who paid less to listen to the music than they would have done had they sat down at a formal concert. The programmes were appropriately light, enjoyable and undemanding, consisting of songs, waltzes, marches and other short pieces, the playing was often of a low standard, and most of these early promenades fizzled out after a few years.[8]

Newman's aim, when he engaged Wood to conduct another such series of concerts, was primarily commercial: to fill the recently-completed Queen's Hall, for whose finances he was responsible, and thus to generate some additional income during what would otherwise be the empty summer season. The tickets might be cheap, especially for those who stood and promenaded in the body of the hall rather than sitting in the galleries above, but at least they brought in revenue. Wood, by contrast, saw the promenade enterprise differently and more imaginatively: as a way to raise performing standards by creating what would be known as the Queen's Hall Orchestra, which he would rehearse more rigorously than was customary in London at the time; and as a means of 'democratising music', by slowly elevating the taste, broadening the interests, and improving the knowledge of his essentially metropolitan audience. To this end, Wood resolved to conduct every concert personally, to select and arrange all the programmes himself, and to make them gradually more sophisticated, innovative and demanding. As a conductor, impresario and public educator, he would eventually establish a remarkable rapport, both with his players, and with his audience, to whom he would become known as 'Old Timber', an affectionate play on his name that also celebrated his famed staying power and reliability.[9] But despite what was later claimed, neither Newman nor Wood could initially have foreseen (or intended?) that their promenade concerts would establish themselves as a permanent annual fixture in the cultural life of the capital (initially) and of the nation (subsequently); and it is only in retrospect that they can be seen to have invented something that would later be celebrated as an enduring and 'living' British 'tradition'.[10]

Indeed, the prospects were not exactly encouraging during the 1890s, for as the failure of earlier promenading ventures in London made plain, classical music was far less central to the lives of most people – in Britain and throughout the western world – then than it has subsequently become. The wireless, television, gramophone, record player, tape recorder, cassette, compact disc or iPod did not then exist, which meant that most people's knowledge of music was confined to such live events as they might attend, ranging from oratorios in the local town hall to patriotic songs in the nearby music hall, or to the hymns they sang in church or had learned at school, or to such works as they might play themselves. Live performance was the only way in which music could be encountered, but that by its nature was ephemeral. Moreover, nineteenth-century Britain had been famously dismissed as the 'land without music': there had been no great composers since Purcell and Handel; provincial festivals and London concerts and opera were of a generally low standard; there were scarcely any established orchestras in London or the regions; the leading role of the conductor had only recently been established, by Sir Michael Costa (who was Italian) and Sir Charles Halle (who was German); Sir Arthur Sullivan's best years were past, and he had failed to receive serious international recognition as a major European composer; the teaching of Parry and Stanford at the recently-founded Royal Academy of Music had yet to bear fruit; and Elgar

had not yet composed the 'Enigma Variations', while Vaughan Williams
had composed scarcely anything at all. The 'English Musical Renaissance'
might already be in its early stages, and the Newman–Wood promenade
concerts would eventually help sustain and reinforce it; but at the time of
their foundation, it was not clear that money could be made out of music,
or an audience for it sustained, on a regular let alone permanent basis.[11]

Not surprisingly, then, during the first half-century of their existence,
the Proms seemed neither a secure nor a permanent institution, as their
finances were often so precarious, and their sponsors so unreliable, that
it seemed as though the current season might well be the last. Robert
Newman went bankrupt in 1902, and the series was only saved by the
intervention of Sir Edgar Speyer, who put together a syndicate to finance
the Queen's Hall Orchestra and the Promenade Concerts themselves.
But Speyer in turn was forced out of Britain in 1915 by the prevailing
anti-German sentiment of the First World War, and the Proms had to be
rescued for a second time, by William Boosey, the managing director of
Chappell & Company. Nine years later, financial pressure forced Chappell
to terminate its support, at which point the BBC 'saved' and took over the
running of the Proms. But in 1940 and 1941, the Corporation abruptly
withdrew its sponsorship, and it was only the largesse of Keith Douglas
which kept them going, until the BBC renewed its commitment in 1942.[12]
In retrospect, these are transition points in the long-running history of the
Proms from one sponsoring financial regime to another; but at the time,
they were wrenching moments of anxiety and disruption, when the series
might have folded entirely: the 1940 Proms, for example, were billed as
Wood's 'forty sixth and farewell season'.[13] In this uncertain climate, which
endured for half a century, the final performance was not a triumphant
celebration of the ending of one season and a confident looking forward
to the next; rather, it was something that would happen if the money
ran out, necessitating a definitive last night, when the series would close
down, and when the whole enterprise would go out of business for good
and for ever.

This was the immediate financial and managerial context within which
Henry Wood created both his Promenade programmes in general, and the
closing concert of the Proms in particular. He himself was a remarkable
combination of chauvinist and cosmopolitan. Like Elgar, he was a
tradesman's son, and like Elgar again, Wood unthinkingly accepted the
established social order into which he had been born, and the legitimacy and

importance of the monarchy and the royal family at its apex. Significantly, when his mother taught the young Henry to memorise the lines of the treble staff (E, G, B, D, F) it was not as 'Every good boy deserves a favour', but as 'Every good Briton deals fairly'; and his 'uncomplicated patriotism' was subsequently reinforced by such turn of the century events as the Queen-Empress's jubilees and funeral, the Boer War (especially Mafeking Night), and the Coronation of King Edward VII.[14] Yet at the same time that Britain was experiencing (and Wood was enjoying) its imperial high-noon, Wood himself was also passionately devoted to European music, from the Baroque period onwards, and all his life he would be a tireless champion of works by new composers. As the Proms developed (albeit falteringly) season on season, Wood's aim was to familiarize his audience not only with the great standards of the European repertory, such as the symphonies of Beethoven and Brahms, but also to educate them in new musical trends, and major new works by Stravinsky and Schoenberg and Richard Strauss were premiered at the Proms before the First World War.[15] But in the beginning, his programmes were much less demanding, often consisting of many short items, so as not to bore the audience. This was especially true of the early final concerts, and it has remained true of the 'Last Night' to this day.

There was, then, nothing special about Henry Wood's original end of season concerts, which tended to offer a light programme with many short and popular items, rather than the concertos or symphonies or new works that were being increasingly played during the preceding weeks: as such, they embodied the commercial and recreational side of Newman's and Wood's Proms rather than the uplifting and educational one, and they were also the means of bringing the series to an end on a festive and convivial note. The programme for the first final concert, on Saturday 5 October 1895, was published in *The Times*, and it listed nine items, including works by Gounod (music from his ballet 'Polyecute'), Verdi (selections from 'Aida'), and Hubert Parry (the 'Idyll' from his 'Suite Moderne'); and it concluded (stirringly but not patriotically) with the 'Grande Marche' from Schloesser's 'Les Enfants de la Garde'. Two years later, the last performance occurred on Saturday 16 October, and it had already become a longer (but still essentially popular) affair: it was divided into first and second halves, and there were 21 items on the programme, among them Wagner's 'The Ride of the Valkyries', Sullivan's 'The Lost Chord' and 'Take a Pair of Sparkling Eyes' from 'The Gondoliers', and Beethoven's Overture 'Leonora'

No.3; and the evening ended (again rousingly but not nationalistically) with Rossini's Overture to 'William Tell'. The latter was an especial favourite during these early final concerts, as were Grieg's 'Peer Gynt' Suite, along with Wagner's Overture to 'Tannhauser' and his Prelude to Act III of 'Lohengrin'.[16] The result was an eclectic mixture, but it was much more European than British, and the programmes were conspicuously devoid of those military, nautical, jingoistic or imperial overtones which were so much in evidence in Britain during those years.

But while such sentiments were absent from the early closing concerts, they were certainly on display during other performances of these pioneering Proms. Indeed, both Newman and Wood regarded 'rousing, military-style music' as a proper component of their Promenade programmes. Jullien's 'British Army Quadrilles' was revived during the opening season; Beethoven's 'Wellington's Victory' was played in the following year (though Wood dismissed it as 'an appalling work'); in 1896 Mackenzie's 'Britannia' Overture was performed as part of a tribute to Queen Victoria's reign that took place on 23 September; and it was repeated in the first week of the 1900 Prom season in a Thanksgiving Concert to celebrate the victory of imperial troops in South Africa.[17] Both 'Wellington's Victory' and Mackenzie's Overture included the melody from Thomas Arne's 'Rule Britannia!', which had been composed in 1740 for the masque 'Alfred', and was first played in London five years later. The song was an exhortation to naval greatness, rather than a celebration of it ('rule' not 'rules' the waves); but it subsequently took on a life of its own, as a paean of praise to Britain's nineteenth-century maritime might, and as such, it was the only one of the four patriotic compositions which would eventually become 'traditionally' associated with the 'Last Night' that was then in existence.[18] In 1895, Elgar's 'Pomp and Circumstance' March No.1 was six years off, Wood's own 'Fantasia on British Sea Songs' was ten years away, and Parry's setting of William Blake's poem 'Jerusalem' would not appear until 1916. Moreover, none of these pieces was composed with the 'Last Night of the Proms' specifically in mind, and it would not be until the sixtieth season, which took place in 1954, that all four items would be featured together on the printed programme.

Elgar's 'Pomp and Circumstance' March No.1 was first performed at the Promenade Concerts on 22 October 1901, having been premiered in Liverpool four days earlier. On this as on other subjects, Henry Wood's later published recollections were not wholly accurate: he claimed the work was unique in the history of the Promenades in that it received two encores; but the press reported only one. Be that as it may, the March had as yet no words attached to it (they were not written by A.C. Benson until the following year), and Wood was surely right when he recalled that 'little did I think then that the lovely broad melody of the trio would one day develop into our second national anthem – "Land of Hope and Glory"'.[19] Almost precisely four years later, on 21 October 1905, Wood put together an appropriately nautical programme as his contribution to the widespread celebrations of the centenary of the Battle of Trafalgar, including Mackenzie's 'Britannia' once again, along with the 'Flying Dutchman' and '1812' Overtures. For 'a real popular climax' to the same concert, he also composed his 'Fantasia on British Sea Songs', beginning with the Bugle Calls, and ending with 'Rule Britannia!' – not as a separate item for a vocal soloist and chorus, but allotted to the orchestra only, with the organ joining in at the end, and with audience participation confined to singing the final refrain.[20] In the case of 'Jerusalem', Sir Charles Parry set Blake's words to music in 1916, one of the worst years of the First World War, and it was initially sung at a Fight For Right campaign meeting in the Royal Albert Hall. Eight years later, Elgar produced his superbly-orchestrated version for the Leeds Festival, which George V allegedly preferred to 'God Save the King', and 'Jerusalem' later became the unofficial anthem of the Women's Institute.

Only very gradually did two of these three 'traditional' works become associated with the closing programme of the Promenade Concerts during this first, uncertain period of their existence. As 'Land of Hope and Glory', 'Pomp and Circumstance' No.1 was played at the concluding performance in 1905, along with items by Grieg, Wagner, Rossini and other short, popular works by European composers that formed the majority of the programme, and it was played again in 1909. The year before, the 'Sea Songs' had been first performed at a final concert, and in 1909 they were played at both the first night (14 August) and also at the closing evening (3 October). By this time they had become a regular fixture at the Proms: indeed, on the one subsequent occasion that Wood left his 'Fantasia' out, he was forced by popular pressure to reinstate it. In 1916, 1917 and 1918, the 'Sea Songs' were joined by 'Land of Hope and Glory': the first recorded occasions on which both works were performed together at the final concert.[21] During the 1920s and 1930s, the 'Sea Songs' became an almost permanent fixture of the last night, but not 'Land of Hope and

Glory', although it may have been played during the evening as an encore. According to the programmes, 'Pomp and Circumstance' No.2 was played along with the 'Sea Songs' in 1927, and only in 1928, 1929, 1936 and again in 1939 were both the 'Sea Songs' and 'Land of Hope and Glory' performed on the last night; but then, as previously, they were not played seriatim, but were separated by other short and more sober pieces. 'Rule Britannia!' was never performed as a separate item during these years, but only as the finale to the 'Sea Songs', and Parry's 'Jerusalem' with Elgar's orchestration was not heard at the Proms before the Second World War.[22]

To the limited extent, then, that the inter-war last night of the Proms was a celebration of patriotism and continuity, that was largely as a consequence of Sir Henry Wood's personal presence on the podium (he had been knighted in 1911), and of the regular performance of his 'Sea Songs'. But the remainder of the programme continued to be the same cosmopolitan miscellany of popular European items that had characterized the final concerts from the outset: on Saturday 3 October 1931, for instance, the first half included three Wagner pieces, and short works by Verdi, Bach, Liszt and Grainger; and the second half was given over to Chopin's 'Nocturne and Etude' and Rossini's 'William Tell' Overture, as well as to the 'Sea Songs'.[23] But amidst this continuity, there was one very significant change: for the impact of the BBC's sponsorship, beginning in 1927, was not merely financial. Classical music was an essential part of Sir John Reith's conception of the Corporation's purpose to inform, to educate and to entertain, and this had also been Sir Henry Wood's vision of the Proms from the very beginning.[24] Accordingly, and in exchange for the Corporation's subsidized support, the Promenade Concerts were broadcast across the country, to what was very rapidly becoming a mass listening audience. In 1927 there were less than 2.5 million licence holders (20 per cent of households); by 1939 there were more than 9 million (70 per cent). Not all concerts were broadcast, but the closing programme invariably was. The result was that what had previously been an exclusively London-based performance for a (predominantly) London-based audience of a few thousand was now transformed, in a way that the founders Wood and Newman could never have conceived or predicted, into a national event with a listening audience across the length and breadth of the country. Put in the terminology of our own time, the 3,000 'real' Promenaders in the Queen's Hall were now joined, and vastly outnumbered, by the millions of 'virtual' Promenaders huddled round their wireless sets across Britain.[25]

Even before the BBC took them over, the Proms had been recognized as a 'national institution' – an accolade bestowed in 1924, on the occasion of a special visit by King George V and Queen Mary towards the end of the season, when they enjoyed an undemanding programme culminating, at the king's request, in the 'Sea Songs' (His Majesty found 'Rule Britannia!' a 'jolly fine tune', infinitely to be preferred to 'The Red Flag'). The Corporation's sponsorship and transmissions significantly consolidated that position. But at the same time, in musical terms, the Proms remained an essentially cosmopolitan enterprise. To be sure, and like Sir John Reith of the BBC, Wood was a devoted and lifelong monarchist, who relished his knighthood, and delighted in ceremonial occasions, and he saw the sovereign as the embodiment of patriotic pride and national tradition. He had conducted a command performance for Queen Victoria at Windsor Castle in 1898, he had participated in a Festival of Empire held at the Crystal Palace to honour the coronation of King George and Queen Mary, and in 1936 he would share the podium at the Albert Hall with Malcolm Sargent at a concert in memory of the late monarch.[26] But as in the years before 1914, so throughout the 1920s and 1930s, Wood was no jingo or chauvinist when it came to compiling his Promenade programmes. Although he gave more time to premiering the works of English composers during the inter-war years than he had done previously, he continued to give many first performances of continental music, by such avant-garde composers as Bartok, Hindemith, Ibert, Janacek, Kodaly, Prokofiev and Shostakovich.[27] Even at the final Prom, the patriotism which expressed itself in his 'Sea Songs' was kept firmly in check until the very end of the evening.

Nevertheless, it seems to have been during the 1930s that the Promenaders themselves became more noisy and assertive as each season reached its close.[28] By the end of the decade, what Sir Henry Wood himself revealingly called 'the ritual of the "Last Prom of the Season"', had now become 'established' as a 'gala night' (though it was not yet known as the 'Last Night'). During the first part of the programme, the audience listened intently, but as the second half reached its climax with the 'Sea Songs', Wood admitted that the scenes 'must strike anyone witnessing them for the first time as unique'. 'The young Promenaders', he noted,

> stamp their feet in time to the hornpipe – that is until I whip up the orchestra into a fierce accelerando which leaves behind all those whose stamping technique is not of the first quality. I like to win by two bars, if possible; but sometimes have to be content with a bar and a half. It is good fun, and I enjoy it as much

as they. When it comes to the singing of 'Rule Britannia!' we reach a climax that only Britons can reach, and I realize I can be nowhere in the world but in my native England.

'I think of the days of the Great War', he went on, 'when "Rule Britannia!" was sung with a depth of feeling that brought tears to the eyes. Britain's navy', he concluded, 'meant something to us all in those days, for on it did our safety depend – and still does depend.' And his final reflections on the subject left no doubt as to his true-blue feelings:

> When I look down on that sea of faces before me and conduct my great, amateur, untrained choir, I know that I am British, I know that I am in my native London, and I know that in *them* the spirit of Horatio Nelson still lives and will never die.[29]

Although the Proms had now been in existence for more than forty years, the rituals of the closing concert were more those of the 'semi-riotous' audience than those of a definite, fixed programme of patriotic songs.[30] The Promenaders applauded the heads of each orchestral section as they took their seats on the platform, but they reserved their greatest ovation for the leader of the orchestra and for Wood himself. (Since 1930, the Queen's Hall Orchestra had been replaced by the newly-established BBC Symphony Orchestra, whose Chief Conductor was not Wood, but Adrian Boult.[31]) In 1938, Wood celebrated his fiftieth anniversary on the podium, and he conducted a special jubilee Prom in his own honour on 5 October, of which the second half was broadcast, concluding with 'Pomp and Circumstance' No.1.[32] But before the Second World War, there were no last night remarks from the conductor: Wood disliked public speaking, preferring to communicate through his baton, and at the end of the final concert each year he just put on his coat and left. But when hostilities broke out against Germany once again, Wood felt compelled to make a brief statement at the end of the concert on 1 September 1939, ironically to announce that 'the Promenade Concerts will close down until further notice', which meant there would be no 'Last Prom'.[33] It was the same in 1940, when the heavy bombardment of London during the blitz meant the Proms (now sponsored by Keith Douglas, and featuring the London Symphony Orchestra rather than that of the BBC) were abruptly ended on 7 September, only half way through their intended eight-week run. Once again, the final Promenade Concert of the season actually took place several weeks before the closing night that had been planned but in the event was never played.[34]

The following year, in the aftermath of the destruction of the Queen's Hall, the Proms were moved to the much larger and less intimate Royal Albert Hall (which held an audience twice the size of that which the Queen's Hall had been able to accommodate) for a six-week season, and there, on 16 August 1941, the series having been brought forward to tempt patrons with longer hours of daylight, Wood delivered the first formal last night speech, in which he thanked his many collaborators and supporters, although he pointedly did not mention the series sponsor, Keith Douglas, with whom his relations had recently turned sour.[35] In 1942, the BBC resumed its support (and broadcasting) of the concerts, which was a great relief to Wood, as Douglas had been greatly chagrined by Sir Henry's deliberate refusal to thank him publicly. Having set a precedent for a last night speech at the end of the previous season, Wood could hardly refuse this time to thank his collaborators and his audience – including those listening on the wireless. To laughter, cheers and applause (but no horns or whistles), he spoke with pride of 'our glorious season', he praised the Promenaders ('how you listen!'), and he looked forward to meeting next year in what he hoped would be 'days of peace'. For a quarter of an hour, the cheers of the audience, accompanied by the singing of 'For he's a jolly good fellow', were transmitted by the BBC; and after the broadcast ended, they continued for another fifteen minutes.[36] Here was the template for all subsequent 'Last Night' speeches, which Wood's successors would deliver from the rostrum in the Royal Albert Hall; but the Proms were already in their 48th season before the precedent set in the previous year became a 'tradition'.

In 1943, Wood delivered a third formal 'last night' speech in the Albert Hall, which was now definitely established as the Proms' new home; but since his health was visibly failing, and he needed to conserve his energy for conducting the concert, it was pre-recorded, and Wood absented himself from the podium while his words were being relayed. Once again, he rendered thanks, he praised the audience for its youth and for being the most 'wonderful' in the world, he spoke of music as a beneficent force for 'harmony and good will', and he looked forward to the 1944 Proms, which would witness both their 50th season, and his own 75th birthday. Once again, the audience sang 'For he's a jolly good fellow', and Wood's car was mobbed as he drove away from the Albert Hall.[37] His birthday was duly celebrated in March 1944, and he was subsequently appointed a Companion of Honour, the first British conductor to be so recognized, though there were many who regretted Wood had not been given the Order of Merit.[38] Soon after, he made over the title 'Henry Wood Promenade Concerts' to the BBC, to be used by them in perpetuity, and the golden jubilee season duly began on 10 June. But it did not run as Wood and his audience had hoped. At the end of the month, the remaining concerts were cancelled because of the new menace represented by the V-1 'flying bomb', and those that should have been broadcast from the Albert Hall were transmitted instead from Bedford, where the BBC Symphony Orchestra was based for the duration of the war. Yet again, there was no closing concert; and even if there had been, Sir Henry would not have been present to deliver a speech, for he died on 19 August 1944, nine days after the anniversary of the first Promenade Concert he had conducted in 1895.[39]

Wood's final years had already witnessed some significant changes, as the BBC Symphony Orchestra had been joined by the London Philharmonic and the London Symphony Orchestras, and as he himself had begun to share the heavy conducting load with Adrian Boult and Basil Cameron.[40] After Sir Henry's death, Boult and Cameron (along with Constant Lambert) conducted the Proms for the 1945 season, including the final concert, but this was an occasion which neither Boult nor Cameron enjoyed, as they were 'pelted with flowers' by the audience. Nor were they alone in regretting what was becoming the increasingly boisterous behaviour of the Promenaders, which some commentators, recalling the Nuremberg rallies of Nazi Germany, lamented as un-British displays of 'mass hysteria'. A young music critic named William Glock wrote a harsh notice of the proceedings in *The Observer*, and the bureaucrats at the BBC also wanted to calm things down, while at the same time, they sought to 'de-personalize' the cult of the conductor now that Wood was no longer there.[41] In fact, nothing of the kind happened, for in 1947, the Corporation appointed an additional conductor for what were now styled their 'Henry Wood Promenade Concerts', who would eventually make the 'Last Night' entirely his own, and who would refashion it into an even more rumbustious, nostalgic, patriotic occasion than it had become by the final years of Henry Wood. His name was Sir Malcolm Sargent, he had recently been knighted after sustained lobbying of the Labour government by his friend and sometime lover Edwina Mountbatten, and by agreeable coincidence, he had been born in 1895, the very year in which the Promenade Concerts had begun. As Sargent would later joke, in one of his inimitable 'Last Night' speeches, Sir Henry Wood, hearing of his birth, had created the Proms so as 'to give me something to do when I grew up'.[42]

II

At first glance, it may seem odd that the so-called 'traditional' 'Last Night' of what now became known as the 'Henry Wood Promenade Concerts', with its four stirring musical items, its balloons and whistles, flags and streamers, and mannered speeches from the podium, should have been created and established by Sargent as a 'British tradition' during the period between 1947 and 1967. For in many people's minds, the leitmotif of those years was not so much 'hope and glory' but rather 'decline and fall'. In the post-war, bi-polar world that had now come into being, dominated by the United States and Soviet Russia, Britain was ceasing to be the great imperial or naval power it had once been. The independence of India in 1947 had been a momentous portent, and the Suez fiasco nine years later made Britain's diminished status in the world plain for all to see. During the next decade, most of what remained of the British Empire was rapidly dismantled, and Churchill's state funeral in January 1965 was not only the last rites of the great man himself, but also a requiem for Britain as a great power.[43] 'Wider still and wider' was a more apt description of the country's growing balance of payments deficit than of its much-diminished imperial dominion, and Britannia no longer ruled the waves, except in the vividly escapist pages of C.S. Forester's Hornblower novels. Indeed, by the early 1960s, this process of de-Victorianization was not only international but also domestic, as youth culture, pop music, student protest, flower power, drug taking, the sexual revolution and what some called (and others condemned as) the 'permissive society' took hold. This was scarcely the world of Sir Henry Wood or Lord Reith – or of Sir Malcolm Sargent.[44]

Yet while these diminishing and transformative trends seem virtually self-evident in retrospect, matters were never quite that clear cut at the time: certainly not before the end of the 1950s. There were many Britons who had been proud to sing 'Land of Hope and Glory', 'Rule Britannia!' and 'Jerusalem' during the darkest days of the Second World War, and they felt neither guilt nor embarrassment about continuing to do so in the hard-won and austere years of peace that followed, or in the 'affluent society' that succeeded them. Internationally, the issue of Indian independence and membership of the Commonwealth seemed to have been successfully handled; Churchill himself returned to 10 Downing Street in 1951 and would still be there on his eightieth birthday; and two years later, a British expedition conquered Mount Everest, and Queen Elizabeth II was crowned in a ceremony which seemed to affirm both the nation's past greatness and hope and pride in its future.[45] One reason that her Coronation made such an extraordinary impact was that it was the first great state occasion to be televised by the BBC. It was a technological triumph, which reaffirmed the Corporation's importance in the life of the nation, and as an essential part of what would soon be called the 'establishment', and which shared and helped articulate the prevailingly consensual, conservative and patriotic mood of the times.[46] From now on, the televising of great ceremonies of state would become one of the ways in which the BBC held the nation together, and the individual who would become most closely associated with these activities and these attitudes was Richard Dimbleby, who would be the dominant public embodiment of the Corporation until his death in 1965, just two years before Sargent's, and in his case, too, of cancer.

During the same period, and again via the BBC, Sir Malcolm Sargent would become to the nation's musical life something of what Richard Dimbleby became to its ceremonial life. In some ways, the two men were very different: they were half a generation apart in age, and Sargent had grown up in lower-middle-class Stamford, whereas Dimbleby was the scion of a comfortably-off home-counties family. But their similarities were more significant. Neither of them received a university education, they distrusted intellectuals and often felt uncomfortable in their presence, both were deeply and unreflectively patriotic, and they accepted the nation's established order unquestioningly, especially (like Elgar and Wood and Reith) the British monarchy that glittered at its summit, and the ritual and display that went along with it. They had both become widely-known public figures during the Second World War: Sargent with the popular classical concerts he had conducted across the length and breadth of the country, Dimbleby with his increasingly esteemed broadcasts, which vividly depicted the horrors of armed conflict and Nazi occupation.[47] They both consolidated their national reputations in peacetime through the wireless: Sargent appeared regularly on *Any Questions* (later *The Brains Trust*), and Dimbleby was a stalwart of *Down Your Way* and *Twenty Questions*. Both of them were eager for additional fame and recognition, and they soon grasped the

exciting potential of television; and unlike others who had originally made
their mark on the wireless, they adapted to the new medium with relish,
confidence and ease, and would prove themselves consummate performers
on the small screen during the 1950s and early 1960s.[48]

Like Richard Dimbleby, Sir Malcolm Sargent adored spectacle and
ceremonial – especially if royalty was present and he himself was at the centre
of the show. In July 1948, resplendent in morning dress and his doctoral
gown from Durham University, Sargent conducted a choir of 3,000 voices
and the massed bands of the Grenadier Guards, at the formal opening of the
Olympic Games at Wembley Stadium in the presence of King George VI. A
year later, and once again thanks to the lobbying of Edwina Mountbatten,
Sargent was appointed Honorary Advisor in Music to the Royal Marines,
a post created especially for him, and which he held until his death, when
it disappeared. He conducted massed bands at Portsmouth (where he later
dined on board HMS *Victory*), and in the Coronation summer at Valetta
(Malta was the headquarters of the British Mediterranean Fleet, of which
Lord Mountbatten was then C-in-C), in programmes of short nautical and
patriotic items, including 'Rule Britannia!' and 'Land of Hope and Glory',
which were guaranteed 'crowd-pleasers'.[49] In June 1956, Sargent led the
BBC Symphony Orchestra on a tour to Scandinavia, where the climax was
a concert he conducted at the Konserthuset in Stockholm on 12 June, in
the presence of the Queens of Sweden and England, with Prince Philip,
Princess Margaret and members of the Swedish royal family. Sargent was
in his element, the concert was a triumph, he received a great ovation, and
the following day he was made a Commander of the Order of the North
Star by the King of Sweden.[50] Such open-air and concert-hall spectaculars
were for Sargent the musical equivalents of the great state occasions on
which Dimbleby commentated from the coronation of Queen Elizabeth
II to the state funeral of Sir Winston Churchill.[51]

But Sargent's greatest and most sustained efforts went into the Promenade
Concerts, where he eventually established himself as the dominant figure
after Sir Henry Wood, to whose memory and example he always remained
devoted. With Wood's encouragement, Sargent had conducted his own
compositions at the Proms in the early 1920s, and he had gone on to
establish a great reputation, both in London and the provinces, especially
as the conductor of choral works and choral societies.[52] Orchestral players
never liked him much, and nor did BBC bureaucrats or arts administrators, while his fellow conductors resented his social success and his public

fame, complaining that he lacked profundity in his interpretations, and (unlike Sir Henry Wood) that he was increasingly conservative and insular in his horizons and repertoire.[53] But choirs loved him, and so did concert audiences, with whom he established a remarkable rapport, and who invariably greeted his appearance on the platform with applause and cheers. By the end of the Second World War, Sargent had travelled a long way from his lowly provincial origins: although his private life was lonely and tainted by tragedy, in public he was charming, witty, articulate and immaculately groomed, he was the confidante of politicians, duchesses and royalty, he loved smart parties, late-night dancing and seducing upper-class women, his attire was faultlessly tailored and impeccably debonair, and he was an unrivalled showman on the podium, with a riveting stage presence that combined dynamism and poise, friendliness and authority. His nickname, 'Flash Harry', was a very different soubriquet from Henry Wood's 'Old Timber': a double-edged acknowledgment, not only to his popular celebrity, but also to what his critics regarded as his professional limitations.[54]

From the time of his initial appointment to co-conduct the Proms, it took Sargent seven years to establish his dominance over the concerts as a whole, culminating in his creation of what soon became accepted as the 'traditional' 'Last Night'.[55] At the closing concert of the 1947 series, the recently-appointed Sargent, who had made an immediate impact on his first Prom season, shared the podium with Sir Adrian Boult, Basil Cameron and Stanford Robinson (who had replaced Constant Lambert). During the first half, Sargent conducted the Mendelssohn Piano Concerto No.1, and Mars and Jupiter from Holst's 'The Planets', but the whole of the second half was conducted by Cameron, concluding with Wood's 'Fantasia on British Sea Songs'. This was the first final Prom to be (partly) televised, and it provoked the biggest public response for any television programme at the time; and when those with TV sets saw most of the first half in their homes, it was Sargent who was 'the man of the hour': in a way that was true of no other British conductor of his generation, he possessed 'star quality'.[56] The following year, when Boult gratefully withdrew, there was an all-British programme: Basil Cameron directed the first half, which included works by Vaughan Williams, Ireland and Delius; then Stanford Robinson conducted Boughton and Walton; and Sargent concluded the programme with Elgar's 'Cockaigne' Overture and 'Serenade for Strings', followed by both 'Land of Hope and Glory' and the 'Sea Songs'. For this 1948 last night, some Promenaders queued for more than twenty hours outside the

Albert Hall so as to be able to stand as close to the orchestra as possible: and they did so as much for Sir Malcolm as for the music. When, at the end, he simply thanked everyone and announced a forthcoming series of winter concerts, he unleashed what one journalist described as 'an almost hysterical outburst from the packed crowd'.[57]

Writing soon after in the *Radio Times*, Sargent described the Promenaders' antics as being no more than a 'mild rag'; but others were less impressed by their increasingly boisterous behaviour. One of them was Lady Jessie Wood, who thought that standards were being lowered, and that the 'audience was there more for a good time than for self-improvement'. *The Times* agreed: 'hooliganism was rather too evident', its reporter noted; 'high-spirited gratitude must not be confused with sheer bad manners'.[58] The BBC held an inquest, which recognized and regretted that behaviour was getting out of hand. Basil Cameron thought it might help to omit the repeat of the hornpipe, while Stanford Robinson thought the 'Sea Songs' might be dispensed with altogether. Instead, it was Sir Malcolm Sargent who was dispensed with: he made his final appearance in the Albert Hall a fortnight before the 1949 season ended, and in an attempt to return to a more restrained atmosphere, Sir Adrian Boult was entrusted with conducting the last night. But he was the 'wrong man': he lacked Sargent's visible energy, debonair panache and showmanly rapport, he found the experience uncomfortable and disagreeable, and he conspicuously failed to restore order. In the following year, Boult was compulsorily retired as the Chief Conductor of the BBC Symphony Orchestra, and after some doubts and delays, and further lobbying from Edwina Mountbatten, Sargent eventually succeeded him.[59] He now stamped his personality indelibly on the Proms, conducting the first nights, more than half of the concerts during each season, and the whole of what soon became the 'Last Night'; and while others deplored the exuberance of an audience which Sargent came to describe as 'my beloved Promenaders' (why *his*?, Eric Blom asked), he himself welcomed and encouraged it.[60]

Beginning in 1950, when he returned to the podium at the final concert, Sir Malcolm Sargent established and perfected the sequence of musical numbers which have ever since been regarded as constituting the 'traditional' 'Last Night of the Proms'. Yet the key episode in the evolution of this programme took place, not in the Royal Albert Hall, but in another London venue, the Royal Festival Hall, where Sargent and Boult conducted the dedication concert for the new building on 3 May 1951, in the presence of King George VI, Princess Elizabeth, the Prime Minister, the Archbishop of Canterbury, and almost the entire British establishment. The highlight of the evening was when Sargent conducted 'Land of Hope and Glory', followed by 'Jerusalem', and by his own arrangement of 'Rule Britannia!', which had been so rapturously received at Portsmouth and Valetta, and which was for soloist, chorus, state trumpeters and full orchestra. Sharing the melodic tastes of his father, the King was overwhelmed, later informing Sargent that he had never been so moved by any music, the audience stood and cheered, and it was several minutes before a visibly-discomfited Sir Adrian Boult could get on the stage to conduct the next part of the programme.[61] In 1953, which was coronation year, these three items were transferred wholesale from the Royal Festival Hall programme to the 'Last Night' of the Proms, the second half of which was televised for the first time since 1947, and which Sargent alone conducted. But in what may have been a last, desperate attempt to prevent the recurrence of what were still being lamented at the BBC as 'a dangerous exhibition of high spirits by the promenaders', the Corporation's Head of Music, Maurice Johnstone, left out the 'Sea Songs' from the programme, deeming them 'an unworthy end to a fine series'. There was a public outcry, and Sargent duly played an abbreviated version (minus the finale of 'Rule Britannia!') as an encore.[62]

The following year, 1954, was the diamond jubilee season, and the 'Last Night' of the Proms settled into what has become its 'traditional', near-immutable form. Sir Malcolm Sargent directed the whole of the second half, and the BBC Symphony Orchestra and massed choirs performed 'Land of Hope and Glory', the 'Sea Songs' (in abbreviated form), 'Rule Britannia!' (to Sargent's arrangement), and 'Jerusalem'. All these items were on the programme together for the first time; and the conductor made a witty and appreciative speech. It was Sargent's evening and event and, unlike his more strait-laced conductor-colleagues, he revelled in it. 'If people can get as enthusiastic about music as about football', he opined, 'that is all to the good.'[63] And it was not only the audience in the Albert Hall and listening to the wireless which was delighted: for as in all subsequent years, the second half of the 'Last Night' was televised live by the BBC, and it brought out all of Sargent's showmanly bravura, thereby establishing him as the only British orchestral conductor who was also a media celebrity. And as Sargent himself appreciated, it was television which was the essential ingredient in creating, magnifying and projecting what now became an instant national tradition. On the wireless, the cheers, the laughter, the horns, the whistles and the popping balloons often seemed little more than a tiresome distraction from the music; but on television, they became an integral part of the occasion and the performance. Indeed, it was only after the 'Last Night' became an annually televised event that the Promenaders began to wear ever more outlandish clothes, and to bring their union jacks and streamers and bunting and umbrellas and funny hats. The result, as Sargent intended, was a television spectacle which made for unmissable viewing for millions of people, not just in Britain, but around the world: according to the composer Robert Simpson, the Proms now boasted 'an audience one seventh the size of Islam'.[64]

By the mid 1950s, when the Henry Wood Promenade Concerts had been in being for sixty years, the 'Last Night', as created and choreographed by Sir Malcom Sargent, and as transmitted by BBC television, had become an instant yet timeless British 'tradition': fashioned, to be sure, out of elements that were in some cases old (though with the exception of 'Rule Britannia!' and the Albert Hall itself the remainder were not that old), but also needing the televised images to make its greatest impact. Thanks to Sargent, 'Pomp and Circumstance' No.1, the 'Sea Songs', 'Rule Britannia!', and 'Jerusalem' now became both a mixture and a fixture; the exuberant audience and their adored conductor were united in mutual admiration; and the 'Last Night' was established as an iconic national occasion, transcending party loyalties (it may have helped that 'Land of Hope and Glory' was associated with the Conservatives, whereas 'Jerusalem' was identified with Labour). As such, and in a decade where the impact of commercial television was only beginning to be felt by the very end, the 'Last Night' soon became an integral part of a new British calendar of public events, which the BBC fashioned and which brought the whole nation together in a succession of observances blending recreation, ritual, royalty and religion in an appropriately uplifting Reithian amalgam, including the Boat Race, the Cup Final, the Trooping of the Colour, Wimbledon, Remembrance Day, the Festival of Nine Lessons and Carols from King's College, Cambridge, and the Queen's Christmas broadcast (first televised in 1957). Into this broadcast patriotic schedule, which was further embellished by Richard Dimbleby's commentaries on royal events and great state occasions, the new-old 'tradition' of the 'Last Night of the Proms' fitted perfectly.[65]

Although this post-war national calendar was very much the BBC's creation, there were those at the Corporation who were not happy with Sargent's part in it, just as there were others who were not happy with Dimbleby's (even more substantial) contribution to it. To many in Broadcasting House, Sir Malcolm was an impossible prima donna, who was more interested in his own reputation than in developing and nurturing the BBC Symphony Orchestra, and he was often away conducting abroad. Moreover, he lacked Henry Wood's interest in contemporary music, and his own tastes and interests stopped with Sibelius (who died in 1957) and Vaughan Williams (who passed on in the following year). From this perspective, the 'Last Night of the Proms' was merely the most self-indulgent and flamboyant expression of Sargent's vanity, conservatism and insularity.[66] There was some truth in these accusations, especially his dislike of 'modern composers' as a 'very uninspired lot', but there was more to the falling-out than that. For the BBC was simultaneously a Corporation, run and staffed by bureaucrats, yet it also needed charismatic figures to bring broadcasting alive and connect it with the public; but this was something the administrators only grudgingly and resentfully admitted. (Sargent's difficulties with the BBC, over terms and conditions, were very like those which Richard Dimbleby was experiencing with the Corporation at the same time.[67]) In 1957, the bureaucrats triumphed, and Sargent was abruptly relieved of his Chief Conductorship of the BBC Symphony Orchestra. But although he was much shaken to be thus peremptorily dismissed, he could not be relieved of his dominant position at the Proms, where he was conducting well over half the concerts each season, and of which he now became (like Sir Henry Wood before him) Conductor-in-Chief.[68]

Nevertheless, by the early 1960s, the national mood *was* beginning to change, and the BBC was changing along with it. The new cult of youth, epitomized by John F. Kennedy in the United States, and by Harold Wilson in Britain, made anyone born in the nineteenth century (as both Harold Macmillan and Malcolm Sargent had been) seem hopelessly 'square' and 'past it', however dapper and debonair their appearance. The 'Profumo Scandal' lent further credence to those who believed that the whole national 'establishment' was out of date and out of touch, and both hypocritical and corrupt. The rise of pop music, epitomized by Elvis Presley and Cliff Richard, by the Beatles and the Rolling Stones, brought into being a mass and increasingly globalized popular culture, which scorned classical music as irremediably old-fashioned and old hat. And the growing success of what had once been derided as 'commercial television' meant the BBC could no longer count on an automatically loyal audience, or continue to present itself as the unchallenged and undisputed voice of the nation. Accordingly, when Hugh Greene became the new Director-General in 1959, he was determined to update and re-position the Corporation, by lessening its ties with and deference towards the establishment, and by bringing it into the new era of what would soon become known as the 'swinging sixties'. Hence his employment and promotion of bright young university graduates, often with left-leaning political views; hence his support for such satirical programmes as *Beyond the Fringe* and *That Was the Week That Was*; and hence his appointment, very soon after he himself had arrived at Broadcasting House, of William Glock as Controller of BBC Music.[69]

In accordance and agreement with Greene's policy of change and innovation, Glock was determined to shake up the Proms from what he regarded as their insular and complacent conservatism, epitomized by Sargent himself and by the 'Last Night', which Glock had disliked as far back as 1945, when he had been reviewing for *The Observer*. 'Nothing', he later wrote, 'needs renewing more than a tradition.' Gradually but determinedly, Glock brought in more orchestras and foreign conductors (he particularly admired Pierre Boulez), he extended the repertoire backwards to the Renaissance and forwards into the second half of the twentieth century, and he sought to make the Proms more 'relevant' to the contemporary world.[70] This meant serious confrontation with Sargent, as Glock reduced the number of concerts that he was allowed to conduct, and he also urged Sargent to limit himself to the first half of some programmes, leaving the second and more experimental part to younger conductors more in sympathy with the modern musical scene. Although he spoke warmly of Glock, Sargent was unhappy with these developments, by which he was effectively being sidelined, and which merely reinforced his growing anxiety that by the early 1960s he was becoming out of date, and that his values were no longer the BBC's values. (Richard Dimbleby came to feel the same thing at the same time, as he was similarly marginalized at *Panorama*.)[71] He made plain his dislike of intellectuals, of modern music, of Frank Sinatra, and of groups like the Beatles, and he denounced 'mods' and 'rockers' as 'mads' and 'rotters' in one 'Last Night' speech. As a result, Sargent was increasingly seen as an Edwardian anachronism, with an old-fashioned and unadventurous repertoire, who could not adapt to the changing times.[72]

Yet on into the mid 1960s, Sargent's rapport with his 'beloved Promenaders' remained unbroken, bringing him the sort of affection and admiration that was withheld by many of his professional colleagues;

and as long as he lived, his 'Last Night' jamboree continued essentially unaltered.[73] His capacity to encourage and tease and goad the audience into a near-frenzy of enthusiasm, exuberance and excitement, while never losing control of the proceedings, was indeed extraordinary; and his speech at the end of the 1961 season was a vintage performance, which he began with the words 'ladies and gentlemen, and babies with horns and toy trumpets'.[74] The Promenaders loved it, as Sargent played off his audience with a skill, assurance and quick-wittedness that other conductors could only envy – or, alternatively, deplore. 'I like these interruptions', he observed at one point. 'It gives me time to think of the next sentence.' When one balloon went off with a particularly loud pop, he instantly assured his listeners on the wireless that all was well and that he had not been assassinated. He presented the statistics of the number of orchestras which played, conductors who appeared and new works commissioned with great style and skill, he insisted that music was 'for the glory of God and the recreation of man', he flattered the Promenaders as 'the most appreciative audience in the world', and he looked forward to seeing them again at the next first night which would take place on 21 July 1962. Here was Wood's valedictory formula, invented during the Second World War, and now enlivened and embellished by Sargent; and however much the BBC bureaucrats loathed the proceedings which it climaxed and concluded, the Promenaders could never get enough, chanting 'We want Flash!' and singing chorus after chorus of 'For he's a jolly good fellow'.

But by now his eyesight and hearing were becoming impaired, and he was visibly ageing. In September 1965, there was a special Prom to celebrate Sargent's seventieth birthday; at the end of the season, the Promenaders loyally voted him their favourite conductor; and the first night of the 1966 series was celebrated as his 500th Promenade Concert (in fact, it was only his 473rd, but who would have checked?).[75] No one in the audience would have guessed that this, his nineteenth consecutive season, would be his last on the podium. On the eve of the 1967 Proms, he was struck down by illness, he reluctantly withdrew from the first night, and he conducted no concerts thereafter; but he resolved to appear at the 'Last Night'. Dressed in one of his immaculate suits, Sargent made a brief speech, by turns charming and witty, in his accustomed style, praising the BBC Symphony Orchestra and its 'new and very gifted conductor Colin Davis'. Nearing the end of his remarks, he insisted he had 'one more thing' to say: 'next year the Promenade concerts begin on 20 July, and I have been invited to be here that night'. To roof-raising cheers, he added: 'I have accepted the invitation; God willing, we will all meet again then.' It was a brave and bravura performance, and Sargent remained the consummate showman and crowd-pleaser to the very end. But it was his last appearance at the Proms and in public, for within two weeks he was dead. At his memorial service in Westminster Abbey, the whole of the nave was set aside for the Promenaders; and on the first anniversary of his death, a group of them made a pilgrimage to Stamford to place a wreath on his grave.[76] Such observances marked the end of an era in the history of the Proms, and especially in the history of the 'Last Night', which would prove Sargent's most enduring, difficult and controversial legacy.

III

Immediately after his death, what remained of Sargent's professional reputation abruptly went into a steep decline from which it has never subsequently recovered, despite the support of Neville Cardus and the publication of two sympathetic biographies, one soon after his death, and another much more recently.[77] For while his audiences and his choirs had adored him to the end (and, indeed, beyond), it was the musicians, the critics and the arts administrators who would most determine how posterity would ultimately come to view him. The initial omens were not good. When, in the first season after his death, some Promenaders inquired whether a bronze bust of Sargent might be placed alongside that of Sir Henry Wood in the Royal Albert Hall for the duration of the series, William Glock refused point blank.[78] Nor did Sargent's reputation revive after a decent interval. During the 1970s and 1980s, Cecil Beaton in his diaries, and Susanna Walton (Sir William's widow) in her memoirs, damned and excoriated him both as a person and as a conductor. According to Michael Kennedy, summing up the generally-received view, Sargent was a 'bargain basement' music-maker, by which he meant 'a star musical propagandist, not a great conductor'.[79] He was superficial, unadventurous and stuck in an Edwardian mind-set, and his creation and enjoyment of the 'Last Night' of the Proms exemplified these faults and failings all too readily. '"I'm not up to much, really"', William Glock recalled Sargent telling him at the end of one late-evening dinner in his flat following a Promenade concert. 'For all his showmanship, his high-handed manner with orchestral players, and glorying in the control of vast assemblies of choristers,' Glock concluded, with perhaps a touch of *schadenfreude*, Sargent knew in his heart of hearts 'that he did not approach the noblest level of music-making.'[80]

Be that as it may, in retrospect, the Sargent years at the Proms should most appropriately be seen as a bridge (or a buffer?) between two very different creative and managerial regimes: an earlier period, characterized by one conductor (and programmer) and many sponsors, and a later era, where the mode was one sponsor (and programmer) and many conductors.[81] To be sure, many of the tensions during Sargent's time were personal (as they were with Richard Dimbleby and the Corporation): between BBC bureaucrats who resented what they regarded as Sargent's conservatism, vanity, charisma and selfishness, and a conductor who thought the Corporation insufficiently appreciative of his unique talents, his remarkable popularity, and his unrivalled capacity to attract young people to classical music. But taking the long view, this was also the period when the relationship between the BBC and the Proms was being fundamentally re-formed and re-structured, as the balance of power tilted away from conductors and towards the Corporation: and Sargent was increasingly uncomfortable with changes and arrangements which he did not like but in the end could not resist. Yet he also scored one major victory in his battles with the bureaucrats: for in the 'Last Night of the Proms', Sir Malcolm Sargent had bequeathed to the BBC a Janus-faced legacy: in one guise, a popular, iconic national 'tradition' with which the bureaucrats and administrators would tamper at their peril; in another an embarrassing anachronism which was urgently in need of a make-over. Either way, the result has been that across the forty years since Sargent's death, the issue of what the BBC should 'do' with or to the 'Last Night' of the Proms has been simultaneously impossible to avoid, yet also very difficult to address.

To many, the arguments in favour of change have been and still are overwhelming, in part because the British nation has changed, and in part because the Proms have changed along with it, which means in turn that the 'Last Night' should change as well. In the forty-odd years since Sargent's death, the Empire on which the sun never set and the waves which Britannia once ruled have both passed into history, and Britain has evolved into the secular, liberal, post-imperial, multi-cultural, multi-ethnic nation that it is today. In such changed circumstances, the flag-waving jamboree of Sargent's ossified 'Last Night' now seems to many to be at best an uncomfortable and inappropriate display of deluded, mindless and escapist nostalgia, and at worst a pandering to the xenophobia and racism of football hooligans and the far right.[82] Meanwhile, and as planned and developed by successive BBC Controllers of Music, the Proms themselves have responded to these global and domestic developments by becoming more cosmopolitan and internationalist (with many orchestras and conductors from overseas), more innovative and experimental (with new works commissioned, late night concerts, and an unprecedented range of early and contemporary music), and with more varied locations (among them the Round House, Covent Garden and Westminster Cathedral in addition to the Albert Hall). This in turn means that in recent decades, the 'Last Night' has become increasingly detached, both from the contemporary circumstances of the British nation and people, and also from the Promenade Concerts as a whole; and when it is beamed and broadcast around the world, it conveys a deeply misleading impression and image of both.[83]

In deference to Sargent's memory, and to his continuing hold on the Promenaders, the first 'Last Night' after his death, in September 1968, was left largely intact. Some commentators doubted whether the young, diffident Colin Davis had the glamour or confidence or panache to carry off the evening as his own, rather than as Sargent's understudy; and their anxieties were borne out when he appeared on the platform, not in full evening dress, but in the sort of white dinner jacket then worn by wine waiters on cruise ships, and when he seemed diffident and hesitant in making the customary speech at the end. Moreover, Davis was on record as saying that the 'jingoism, the patriotic flag-waving and exhibitionism' were now out of date, that the 'Last Night' smacked too much of 'Earl Haigery', and that it needed serious reshaping and reconsideration.[84] In the following year, Glock and Davis made their first effort at reform, by deleting 'Land of Hope and Glory' from the 'Last Night' programme; but so great was the press and public outcry that in the end it had to be reinstated. In 1970, the controller and conductor attempted an alternative modification: Malcolm Arnold was commissioned to write a modern equivalent of Wood's 'Sea Songs', which included audience participation and the traditional hornpipe, this time in 5/8 rhythm, demanding an exceptional facility in the stamping from the audience; but perhaps for this reason, it did not catch on. Twelve months later, there was another new commission in the form of Malcolm Williamson's 'instant opera' entitled 'The Stone Wall'; but it, too, was not a success. And in 1972 there was yet a third attempt to produce a modern substitute for the 'Sea Songs' in the form of a work entitled 'Celebration', by Gordon Crosse; but this, also, failed to resonate with the audience in the Albert Hall or with the public beyond.[85]

By this time, Colin Davis had had enough of the 'Last Night': although a more profound interpreter of music than Sargent, he lacked the panache of 'Flash', and he had never enjoyed the occasion, either in terms of music-making or speech-making: 'I haven't really anything very interesting to say', he wanly informed the Promenaders in September 1972. 'Can I go on?', he asked plaintively after one noisy interruption; 'Enough for now', he concluded his speech, rather lamely. With Davis's departure, this first (and so far only) sustained attempt to move the 'Last Night' of the Proms into the post-Sargent era effectively came to an end. In 1973, which was also William Glock's last season as Controller, the podium was occupied by Norman Del Mar, who opted for a more 'traditional' programme, and thereafter, until 1990, the 'Last Night' was presided over by a different 'guest conductor' each year, among them Sir Charles Groves, James Loughran, Vernon Handley, Raymond Leppard, Mark Elder and Sir John Pritchard. This was partly a matter of necessity: after Davis, no chief conductor of the BBC Symphony Orchestra was eager to take on the job, least of all the Frenchman Pierre Boulez, who would scarcely have been at ease with the 'Sea Songs' that had been written to celebrate the centenary of Nelson's victory at Trafalgar.[86] But it was also a matter of design: as more orchestras and conductors performed at the Proms, the BBC management had no wish that any individual should dominate the 'Last Night' as Sargent had done, and as Wood had done for more than twice as long before him. In this sense, the 'de-personalization' policy, first sketched out in the late 1940s, had finally been implemented. Insofar as the Proms were dominated by anyone, it was no longer by any single conductor, but by successive BBC Controllers of Music.[87]

Although Andrew Davis would direct the 'Last Nights' from 1990 to 1992, and again from 1994 to 2000 as Chief Conductor of the BBC Symphony Orchestra, his long tenure of the podium was exceptional in the post-Sargent era; and no single figure has stamped his personality on the occasion as both Sargent and Henry Wood did in their time. *Their* command of the 'Last Night' derived from their dominant position across the Promenade Concerts as a whole, concert after concert, week after week, year after year, and series after series, which meant they built up a close relationship and continuing rapport with the audience. But with more and more conductors, making fewer and fewer appearances, those relationships and that rapport have significantly weakened. Most 'Last Night' speeches since Sargent's day follow his formula, which in turn had derived from Wood's three original speeches: thanks to the BBC and the BBC Symphony Orchestra for bearing the brunt of the work; a list of statistics enumerating the orchestras, conductors and soloists who have performed in the series; some jokes and witticisms of varying quality and originality; flattery of the Promenaders for being such a wonderful, loyal and discerning audience; some words in praise of music in general; and the announcement of date of the first night of the next series. But while Sargent carried off his 'Last Night' speeches with effortless confidence, verve, and brio, most of those who have followed him would probably agree with William Glock that 'conducting this final concert of the Proms is one of the most nerve-racking assignments imaginable' (although in 2000, Andrew Davis actually *sang* his 'Last Night' speech as a Gilbert and Sullivan patter song). As David Cox has written, 'it's rather like teachers having to cope with an unruly class. There are some [conductors] who by a combination of personality, air of authority and sense of purpose, can keep order. Others can't.'[88]

For successive BBC Controllers of Music, this meant that, after the abortive Glock–Davis attempts at modernization, the 'traditional' 'Last Night' had become a headache that had to be endured because it could not be cured.[89] Robert Ponsonby, who succeeded William Glock, and held that position from 1972 to 1985, disliked the occasion so much that he habitually left the Albert Hall before the second half even began. But in Thatcher's Britain, with its new-found self-confidence after the Falklands War, and with the Prime Minister presenting herself as a latter-day Britannia and as the champion of 'Victorian values', Sargent's 'traditional' 'Last Night' remained largely unaltered, except for the addition of 'Auld Lang Syne' from the late 1970s, which was sung impromptu at the very end. Indeed, the programme had become so sacrosanct that in September 1990, Mark Elder was abruptly replaced as the conductor, because he had questioned the playing of such patriotic music when the Gulf War was about to be waged, at a time when 'the public would be better disposed than ever to bellow their way through "Land of Hope and Glory"'[90] By then, Ponsonby had been succeeded by John Drummond, who was Controller from 1985 to 1995 (he was also given the additional title of Director of Promenade Concerts), and he saw the Proms through both its centenary season of 1994 and its hundredth anniversary the following year. Drummond shared

Ponsonby's 'distaste' for the 'Last Night': he regretted that it perpetuated the 'jingoistic isolationism' of the Sargent years, and he later recalled that he moved 'from tolerant enjoyment to almost physical revulsion as the behaviour of the audience inexorably took over from the music. It was no longer Britannia who ruled, but exhibitionism.' As for 'Land of Hope and Glory': by the early 1990s, 'few things sounded more hollow as "Make thee mightier yet" in the last years of John Major's government'.[91]

Drummond had been particularly appalled by one 'Last Night' when so many balloons were popped and klaxons sounded as to render the conductor Andrew Davis inaudible, forcing him to abandon his speech. Accordingly, for his final 'Last Night', in 1995, he decided to assert himself, as no Controller had done since William Glock in the near-aftermath of Sargent's death, and he resolved to put an end to this 'silliness'. He urged the Promenaders, via the Proms prospectus, to leave their 'balloons, klaxons and pop-guns at home', and to listen 'without extraneous noises', since 'the music and the speech must be heard'.[92] Drummond also commissioned a new work from Harrison Birtwistle, which was originally intended for the more conventional and less high-spirited first half of the 'Last Night'. But as composition proceeded, the piece grew significantly in scale, and the finished score necessitated elaborate seating changes on the platform for the orchestra, which could only be accomplished during the interval. As a result, and for the first time ever, a major new, avant-garde work was premiered in the *second* half of the 'Last Night' programme. It was entitled 'Panic', it was a concerto for saxophone and orchestra, it lasted a very long eighteen minutes, and it was the composer at his most energetic, violent, abrasive, strident and dissonant. It was 'tough' on the players and audience alike, and immediately afterwards, the BBC was inundated with complaints that the piece was 'a disgrace and an insult to the British public', that 'a wonderful nationalistic occasion had been turned into a terrible nothing', and that the banned balloons would have sounded a great deal better than the blasted Birtwistle. But Drummond was unrepentant: 'if the mummified corpse of the Last Night ever experiences any sort of re-animation', he wrote in his autobiography, 'Birtwistle's Panic may have played its part.' (It has not done so yet.)[93]

As these very different responses suggest, the 'Last Night' of the Proms had become a deeply controversial issue in the post-Sargent years that extended from Glock, via Ponsonby to Drummond. Those who defended the 'traditional' form did so on a variety of grounds: that it was a good night out and a fun event; that it was an end of season party when hair should be let down; that it was a 'timeless' and harmless occasion; that it was a celebration of patriotic pride; that it was the essence of 'Britishness' or (alternatively) 'Englishness'. But the critics had their answers: they saw the evening as (increasingly) rowdy and disruptive; as dominated by the antics of a very different public from that which regularly attended the Proms; as being out of date and out of touch in a post-imperial world; and as projecting a wholly distorted image of the British people and of the Promenade Concerts. Be that as it may, any suggestion of large-scale reform of the 'Last Night' invariably provoked the wrath of more conservative broadsheets, as well as of the tabloids. For them, Sargent's last four items – 'Land of Hope and Glory', the 'Sea Songs', 'Rule Britannia!' and 'Jerusalem' – were sacrosanct, and any attempt to interfere with them was, as they saw it, but further proof that since the time of Sir Hugh Greene, the BBC had abandoned its establishment ethos and patriotic remit, and had been infiltrated and taken over by Oxbridge-educated, left-leaning subversives, who had only contempt for the robust and wholesome loyalty of ordinary people. These perspectives were (and are) not easily reconciled: indeed, just about the only thing they have in common is an almost complete ignorance of precisely when, how, why and by whom the 'traditional' and 'timeless' 'Last Night of the Proms' was actually created.[94]

Among those who attend the 'Last Night' (1,400 standing in the Albert Hall arena, the remaining 4,600 seated), opinions were equally varied. In the early 1980s, many Promenaders, who bought season tickets and showed up regularly to the concerts during the series, resented the fact that other season ticket holders just appeared for the first and (especially) the final programmes. Indeed, some of them deliberately stayed away from the 'Last Night', because it had 'so degenerated in recent years', while others delighted in bringing their sleeping bags and queueing for hours before to get a place at the very front of the hall, closest to the conductor and orchestra. In 1983, a scheme was introduced to restrict 'Last Night' attendance to those who had already attended several other Proms. Another anxiety, which John Drummond felt particularly, was that tickets might be obtained for a whole block, which meant the 'Last Night' might be 'taken over by an extremist group such as the British National Party', and this has resulted in ever more complex arrangements concerning sales and standing and seating in the Albert Hall.[95] Yet despite these concerns, there are many who find the occasion moving, inspiring, even uplifting: 'there is no sound quite like it anywhere else in the world…. A chorus of over seven thousand voices…. It makes the hairs tingle at the back of your neck, and a prickle creep along your spine.' Or, as another Promenader put it, in more chauvinistic but less awe-struck terms: 'It's all about having fun, waving the flag, being proud of being British, without feeling a complete prat.'[96]

In the light of such widely-held opinions, the lesson drawn from what many saw as the debacle of the 'Panic' episode was: 'mess with the "Last Night" and you risk scuppering a big part of audiences' sense of what the Last Night of the Proms means'. In any case, Drummond's (frustrated) desire both to rein in the 'Last Night' audience and to reform the 'Last Night' programme was not shared by his successor, Nicholas Kenyon, who assumed responsibility in 1996. 'I am a "Let joy be unconfined" man myself', he told the press, and throughout his period in charge he took the 'Last Night' in a different direction, aiming neither to calm down nor shock existing audiences, but to attract and draw in new ones – priorities well reflected in the changed title of his job: Controller, BBC Proms, Live Events and TV Classical Music.[97] Indeed, by the time Kenyon assumed office, a blueprint was already available, for during the early 1990s, there had been discussions about the possibility of staging a simultaneous open-air, crowd-pulling concert in Hyde Park on the final evening. Drummond had been against: partly because he feared it would reduce the demand for tickets in the Albert Hall and detract from the main proceedings; partly because he regarded such an open air concert as 'the essence of mindless populism imposed on an event which is already dangerously rabble-rousing'; and partly because such a stunt seemed to him redolent of all that was most philistine about John Birt's regime as BBC Director-General. (The only Prom that Birt regularly attended during his years at Broadcasting House was the 'Last Night' when, as Drummond disdainfully put it, he filled his box in the Albert Hall 'with Conservative politicians and right-wing journalists'.)[98]

But Kenyon embraced such proposals enthusiastically: he saw them as an opportunity, in the tradition of Wood and Sargent, to involve as many people in music as possible, and to draw in new audiences; he regarded it as a way of competing with Classic FM, which had begun broadcasting on commercial radio in 1992; and he also sensed a new opportunity to rebut the long-standing criticism that the final Prom was too crudely nationalistic. Accordingly, in 1996, the 'traditional' 'Last Night' at the Royal Albert Hall was accompanied by a parallel live concert in Hyde Park. The first half of this 'Prom in the Park' was a separate programme, in which classical artists performed alongside names drawn from the worlds of popular and light entertainment. But thanks to new big-screen technology, there was a live link-up to the Albert Hall for the second half, so that thousands in Hyde Park could join in 'Land of Hope and Glory', the 'Sea Songs', 'Rule Britannia!' and 'Jerusalem'. In subsequent years, these 'Proms in the Park' were extended to Belfast, Swansea and Glasgow, thereby connecting the 'Last Night' with the British public beyond London in a wholly new way, and also acknowledging the importance of, and the differences between, the four constituent nations of the United Kingdom. And this technological dis-aggregation of a previously monolithic British national identity has in turn led to modifications of the 'Last Night' programme in the Albert Hall itself – but modifications within, rather than opposed to, the Sargent 'tradition'. For the successful extension of the 'Proms in the Park' across the British Isles has been accompanied by the insertion of English, Welsh, Scottish and Irish melodies into the 'Sea Songs', thereby making the 'Last Night' a yet more popular and yet more authentically 'British' event – although David Mellor took exception to 'the addition of glutinous settings of Celtic ditties, from an entirely different aesthetic to Wood's virile evocation of our nation's glorious naval past'.[99]

Yet on two occasions in recent years, the concluding programme of the 'Last Night' has been more substantially altered, in response to sudden and unexpected events.[100] In 1997, after the death of Diana, Princess of Wales, it was modified to include Jupiter from 'The Planets', which contained her favourite hymn tune, 'I vow to thee my country'; and John Adams's (unfortunately titled) 'Short Ride in a Fast Machine' was replaced by Aaron Copeland's 'Fanfare for the Common Man'. But in 2001, in the aftermath of 9/11 and the destruction of the twin towers of the World Trade Center in New York, something more fundamental was deemed necessary than the simple substitution of works within the conventional framework of the 'traditional' 'Last Night'. Triumphalism would have seemed tasteless; and quite by chance, the conductor that night was the first-ever non-Briton to be in charge, and he also happened to be an American: Leonard Slatkin. Accordingly, the programme in the second half was substantially re-designed. Out went 'Land of Hope and Glory', the 'Sea Songs', 'Rule Britannia!' and (once again) 'Short Ride in a Fast Machine', to be replaced by Samuel Barber's 'Adagio for Strings', and by the finale to Beethoven's Ninth Symphony, after which 'Jerusalem' was sung. The revised programme was both a popular and critical success, creating an intense yet dignified evening with music that 'rose to the occasion'. For some critics of the 'traditional' 'Last Night', this necessary 'ditching' of the patriotic finale seemed the long-awaited opportunity to change the established formula in a decisive and permanent way.[101] But in 2002, 'Land of Hope and Glory', the 'Sea Songs' and 'Jerusalem' were all back on the programme, rather to Slatkin's regret, and there they remained for the rest of Kenyon's tenure. Who can predict how, or in what direction, the 'Last Night' will evolve under his successor?[102]

IV

That is for the future which the BBC Proms (as they are now called, instead of the 'Henry Wood Promenade Concerts') seem certain to enjoy, and this means that any conclusions that can be reached concerning the extraordinary occasion that is the 'Last Night' can be no more than interim and provisional. In their pioneering study, *The English Musical Renaissance*, Merion Hughes and Robert Stradling lament that 'music history, in our view, is still written with too much "music" and too little "history"'.[103] In recent years, music and history have been drawing much closer together, to their great mutual benefit, and it is to be hoped that these earlier strictures do not apply to this account: in part because some would insist that 'Land of Hope and Glory', the 'Sea Songs', 'Rule Britannia!', and 'Jerusalem', the 'traditional' elements of the 'Last Night of the Proms', scarcely amount to 'music' at all (one BBC official in 1950 claimed they made for 'execrable broadcasting'); in part because the account of how the closing promenade concert of Henry Wood's day evolved across a century and more into the 'Last Night of the Proms' of our time is necessarily and inescapably an historical matter.[104] For what has been re-constructed and described here is the gradual evolution and development of an annual performance event, initially taking place under the baton of its long-lived founder, which in the hands of his successor was suddenly and deliberately crystallized into a particular set form, which almost immediately acquired all the accoutrements of a national 'tradition' and which, despite its relatively recent invention, then became extremely difficult to change: partly because it rapidly became a popular and resonant and much-enjoyed occasion, and partly because it was widely believed that it had been in existence, *in that particular form*, for a very long time.

Indeed, it may well be that much of the popularity and resonance of the 'Last Night of the Proms' derives from this vague, powerful and (in historical terms) largely erroneous sense that it has existed in what seems to be its present immutable form for many decades. To be sure, there can be few Britons who would share the ignorantly-awe-struck response of an American visitor on attending the 'Last Night' in 2005: 'The Proms, they go back to 1400, right?'[105] But there is much about the popular perception of this annual jamboree that rests on the sort of historical amnesia that is, indeed, an essential characteristic and a defining attribute of many nations' so-called 'traditions'. In this regard, it bears repeating that when Henry Wood began his Promenade Concerts in 1895, three of the four musical items which are regarded as essential to the programme of the 'traditional' 'Last Night' had not yet even been composed. In the same way, the BBC Symphony Orchestra, which is invariably associated with the 'Last Night', did not then exist, and would not come into being for more than a third of a century. Although the Queen's Hall was the home of the Proms for the best part of fifty years, it was already being claimed, within ten years of its destruction, that the Proms had never been staged anywhere except the Royal Albert Hall.[106] And it is an intriguing irony that the 'Last Night', which celebrates (for many) British patriotism and identity, and which reminds us of Nelson's triumph at Trafalgar, brings to an end a series and a style of musical concert whose origins are *French* rather than British.[107]

Yet whether it is derided as 'ossified' or applauded as 'traditional', perhaps the most remarkable aspect of the 'Last Night of the Proms', beyond the extraordinary narrative of its creation and survival, change and continuity, has been the inexorable, exponential growth in its audience, to which the words 'wider still and wider' may, indeed, appropriately be applied. The initial audience for Henry Wood's first final concert at the Queen's Hall in 1895 was but a few thousand. By the Second World War, thanks to the wireless and the BBC, the Proms were being acclaimed as the 'Possession of the Whole Nation', and from the 1950s onwards, 'Last Night' concerts would be replicated in many towns and cities across Britain.[108] By the closing decades of the twentieth century, the 'Last Night' was reaching a global audience of millions, and no other musical event, not even the annual New Year's Day Concert from Vienna, attracts so many viewers. As such, it is a fitting finale to a series rightly described as 'the world's greatest music festival'. In Japan, people get up in their millions at four o'clock in the morning to marvel at what they believe to be the authentic antiquity of the tradition and the moving sincerity of the sentiment.[109] In May 2002, Sir Andrew Davis took the BBC Symphony Orchestra to Kuala Lumpur, where they played a brief Prom season, including a 'Last Night'. Although adjusted for local tastes and sensibilities, the second half of the programme included 'Land of Hope and Glory' and the 'Fantasia on British Sea Songs'. In Berlin, thousands of Germans stage 'British parties', as they view the 'Last Night', and eat bangers and mash to the strains of 'Rule Britannia!'[110] And such is the Antipodean appeal of the event that even the greatest living Australian, Dame Edna Everage, has taken note: one of her most memorable television programmes was entitled 'The Last Night of the Poms'. What would Sir Henry Wood, or Sir John Reith, or Sir Malcolm Sargent, or Sir William Glock, or Sir John Drummond, have made of *that*?

7
Nation:
British Politics, British History and British-ness[1]

During the national campaign to elect British members to the European Parliament in Strasbourg, which was fought out in May 1994, the then Conservative Prime Minister, John Major, offered this version of the history of the country whose government he led:

> This British nation has a monarchy founded by the Kings of Wessex over eleven hundred years ago, a Parliament and universities formed over seven hundred years ago, a language with its roots in the mists of time, and the richest vocabulary in the world. This is no recent historical invention: it is the cherished creation of generations, and as we work to build a new and better Europe, we must never forget the traditions and inheritance of our past.[2]

Albeit in less strident form, these rather idiosyncratic comments echoed those made by his predecessor, Margaret Thatcher, in Paris at the bicentennial of the French Revolution, when she spoke with more force than accuracy about Magna Carta, about the 'quiet revolution' of 1688, and about the 'English tradition of liberty' which 'grew over the centuries'.[3] Taken together, their remarks suggest that when it comes to producing a contemporary account of our nation's past, the most unreconstructed and uncompromising form of Whig history has been that preached from 10 Downing Street by Tory Prime Ministers. In more ways than one, it is a suggestive and significant irony.

For their account was not only Whig history implausibly masquerading as Conservative propaganda: notwithstanding their ritual invocation of the word 'Britain', it was also emphatically 'Little England' history. Both Margaret Thatcher and John Major were asserting the essential Englishness of the United Kingdom, its separateness from the rest of Europe, the long and unbroken continuity of its traditions and precedents, and its unique characteristics and institutions. But the reason that they had felt obliged to reaffirm these beliefs was that recent developments abroad and at home seemed to have thrown virtually every one of them into question. Moreover, those developments did not merely change the contemporary political landscape; they also inspired many scholars to look again and anew at our nation's past. During the last four decades, an emerging school of self-consciously 'British' historians has been evolving a very different interpretation of Britain's past from that espoused by Major and Thatcher. Indeed, it is an interpretation *so* different that it is doubtful whether either of them would readily understand what 'British history', as it is now defined, practised and understood by professional historians, actually is.

Inasmuch as Thatcher and Major were both reacting to the same external stimuli, provided by growing demands in Wales and Scotland for some form of devolution or even for the 'break-up of Britain', there was a real and important connection between these two Conservative premiers on the one side, and the 'new' British historians on the other. But they were reacting to the same stimuli in significantly different ways: the two top Tories responded by reviving and restating the traditional view of the national past; the 'new' British historians responded by redefining and rethinking it. And so, while Thatcher and Major will reappear occasionally in the course of this chapter, to be succeeded and superseded, in its later stages, by Tony Blair and Gordon Brown, the chief concern of what follows is to explain, explore and evaluate the results of this scholarly labour of redefining and rethinking our national identity and our national past. The first section discusses the 'traditional' Whig interpretation of English history, against which the new British historians have been reacting. The second part examines changes in the international, domestic and academic environments, which in the final decades of the twentieth century rendered English history less compelling, and helped to bring this new form of British history into being and into prominence. The third section considers the strengths and weaknesses which characterized this new approach to the national past, as it was championed and undertaken during the 1980s and 1990s. Finally, this chapter explores how both the political and the scholarly agenda of Britishness have changed in the ten years since New

Labour won the general election on (among other things) a programme
of devolution in May 1997.

I

One problem in discussing the traditional Whig interpretation of English
history is in knowing just when and where to begin. After all, the Venerable
Bede completed his *History of the English Church and Nation* in AD
731, and there is a more or less continuous tradition of national history
writing thereafter. For present purposes, it may be most useful to confine
discussion to books which appeared between the middle of the nineteenth
century and the outbreak of the Second World War, the years which are
generally regarded as having marked the zenith of the modern nation-state.
This was the period which saw the reconstruction of the United States
in the aftermath of the Civil War, the creation of new nations in Europe
in 1870 and again in 1919, the partition of Africa by the Great Powers
during the last decades of the nineteenth century, and the Confederation
of Canada, the Federation of Australia and the Union of South Africa. It
also witnessed mass electorates, mass political parties, mass education,
mass transport, mass mobilization – and mass war. And one result of these
developments, which further helped to define and consolidate the identities
of these new countries, was the rise of nationalist history in Germany, in
France, in the United States – and also in Britain itself – the aim of which
was to provide a coherent and uplifting narrative engendering appropriate
patriotic pride.[4]
   All these national narratives were built around some sense of national
exceptionalism, and Britain was no exception in these claims to being
exceptional: for as elsewhere in the west, there was striking evidence of the
unprecedented consolidation and consciousness of the territorially-based
nation-state.[5] The years from 1800 to 1922 saw the creation, survival and
modification of the United Kingdom of Great Britain and Ireland. They
witnessed the inexorable expansion of that greater Britain beyond the
seas, as the Empire reached its territorial zenith in the years immediately
after the First World War. W.E. Forster's Education Act of 1870 created
a mass literate public; the Reform Acts of 1885 and 1919 created a mass
voting public. Both internationally, in terms of dominion, and domestically,
in terms of citizens, the boundaries of the nation were (as A.C. Benson

observed in 'Land of Hope and Glory') being set wider than ever before. And in Britain as elsewhere, one of the ways in which this new-old nation was defined, its unity asserted, and its mission proclaimed was by giving unprecedented attention to its past. At elementary schools, grammar schools and public schools, the history of the nation became an essential subject; at Cambridge, a History Tripos was inaugurated, and at Oxford a History School, which meant that Clio soon superseded the Classics as the most appropriate training for statesmen; and in London, Oxbridge and the new provincial universities, scholarly, rigorous, academic history was established for the first time.[6]

From the standpoint of the British reading public, the national past came presented and packaged in three different versions. Initially, pride of place went to those multi-volume single-authored works, written by gentlemen amateurs, which were so fashionable during the reign of Queen Victoria. The most famous and most successful was Lord Macaulay's *History of England*, published in four volumes between 1855 and 1861. But he was far from being alone: during the same period, H.T. Buckle began (but, like Macaulay, did not live to finish) his large-scale *History of Civilisation in England*. Then, between 1873 and 1878, Bishop William Stubbs produced his *Constitutional History of England* in three volumes; and in 1902 S.R Gardiner completed his *Student's History of England* at the same length, a work spanning the whole of British history, from Caesar's invasion to the death of Queen Victoria. But Gardiner also published in much greater detail on the seventeenth century, and other writers likewise concentrated on shorter periods: among them J.A. Froude (*History of England from the Fall of Wolsey to the Defeat of the Spanish Armada*, twelve volumes, 1856–70); E.A. Freeman (*History of the Norman Conquest*, six volumes, 1867–79); and W.E.H. Lecky (*History of England in the Eighteenth Century*, eight volumes, 1878–90).

Towards the end of Victoria's reign, these lengthy, leisurely surveys were going out of fashion, and they were replaced by new single-volume histories, which were better suited to the mass public audience that had recently come into being. They were less expensive, they told the whole of the story from beginning to end, they were ideal text books for schools and universities, and they genuinely seem to have reached that long since defunct category, the general reader. The most important was J.R. Green's *Short History of the English People*, first published in 1874, so soon after the passing of W.E. Forster's Education Act that it surely cannot be coincidence. For two generations, Green's book held the field: it was endlessly reprinted and updated, and a multi-volume illustrated edition was later brought out by his wife Alice.[7] For millions of Britains across two generations and more, this may have been the only book they ever read about their national past. Not until 1926 was it superseded, when G.M. Trevelyan published his *History of England*, which served its day and more than one generation as effectively as Green had done, selling 200,000 copies during the next twenty years. Such was its appeal and its renown (and its eirenic whiggishness) that it may even have inspired the publication of that most memorable and affectionate parody of the one-volume text-book history, Sellar and Yeatman's *1066 and All That*, which appeared four years later, in 1930.[8]

By this time, the third version of the nation's history was also well established: the multi-volume, multi-authored series, written by a team of academic professionals, most of whom confined themselves to their realm of scholarly expertise. Here was emphatic indication not only of the increased quantity and complexity of historical knowledge, but also of the expanding market for detailed histories which had come into being. These collaborative ventures first appeared during the early years of the twentieth century, just as the single-author multi-volume histories were beginning to fade from the scene. Methuen produced *A History of England* in seven volumes, edited by Sir Charles Oman, with contributions from H.W.C. Davis (who wrote *England Under the Normans and Angevins*) and G.M. Trevelyan (who produced *England Under the Stuarts*). Longman replied with a twelve-volume *Political History of England*, co-edited by William Hunt and Reginald Lane Poole, with books by T.F. Tout, Sir Charles Oman, H.A.L. Fisher, A.F. Pollard and Sir Richard Lodge. Finally, the early 1930s witnessed the launch of the most comprehensive and authoritative multi-authored work, *The Oxford History of England*, under the general editorship of Sir George Clark, which was eventually completed, in fifteen volumes, thirty years later, with the appearance of A.J.P. Taylor's *English History, 1914–1945*.

These three different versions of the national past varied greatly in their scale, their content, their quality, and their argumentation.[9] But they also had much in common. To begin with, it cannot be too much stressed that they were all conceived, written and marketed, like the Venerable Bede in an earlier millennium, as histories of *England*. The word Britain did not appear in the title of any of the series that have been mentioned. These years may have witnessed the zenith of the *British* nation-state, of the

United Kingdom, and of the British Empire, but the nation whose history they recounted and whose identity they helped to proclaim was *England*. (For much of the eighteenth and early nineteenth centuries, by contrast, histories of Britain and of its constituent parts were readily available. When, how and why they came to an end are subjects still awaiting their historian.[10]) Moreover, these books were almost without exception *in praise* of England. They celebrated parliamentary government, the Common Law, the Church of England, ordered progress towards democracy, and the avoidance of revolution. They took this evidence of what they believed to be English exceptionalism for granted: it existed, it was good, and it was the historian's task to describe it, to explain it and to applaud it. And they generally supposed that this history was a success story: as the authors of *1066 and All That* argued, when England ceased to be top nation, at the conclusion of the First World War, history came to a full stop – a termination proclaimed much earlier, and defined very differently, from Francis Fukuyama's subsequent declaration of the end of history.[11]

These characteristics formed the commonplaces of the Whig interpretation of English history which is now so much derided in professional academic circles, even if it retained its allure for Margaret Thatcher and John Major, and as it allegedly did so and does so for their successors as Conservative leader. In retrospect, it is also easy to dismiss these books and these series as having been wholly devoid of any awareness of the separate identities and the separate histories of England, Ireland, Scotland and Wales, let alone those of Great Britain, of the United Kingdom, of the British Isles and of the British Empire. Almost without exception, the authors indiscriminately interchanged the words England and Britain, as if they were no more than different names for the same country, to be used contrapuntally in the interests of stylistic variation. And to the extent that they did deal with the British Isles, these authors wrote from a very anglocentric perspective: insofar as they possessed any geographical range and territorial teleology, they were concerned to describe the gradual expansion of England, slowly but inexorably overwhelming, absorbing and dominating its Celtic neighbours. The history of Britain was but the history of England as and when it took place elsewhere: initially in the British Isles, subsequently in the British Empire.

Nowadays, these attitudes, assumptions and arguments seem unacceptable and outmoded. But before we dismiss this earlier historiography completely out of hand, it should be said in its defence that some of these books and some of these authors were not so unthinkingly anglocentric as it is now fashionable to deride them for having been (this was even true, in an earlier millennium, of the Venerable Bede himself).[12] Nor should this come as any surprise, given that from the 1880s to 1914, there was almost constant discussion in political circles about adjusting the constitutional relationship between the United Kingdom and Ireland and also, albeit to a lesser degree, that between the United Kingdom and Scotland and Wales.[13] Among the single-author multi-volume writers, Macaulay was exceptionally sensitive to the histories of the three kingdoms (he was, after all, of Scottish descent), and Lecky devoted considerable attention to relations between Great Britain and Ireland during the eighteenth century. The same can be said of some of the single-author single-volume surveys, and of the multi-author multi-volume series. They treated Roman Britain as Roman *Britain*. The books or chapters on the twelfth and thirteenth centuries dealt in detail with the changing relations between England, Ireland, Scotland and Wales. And the same was true when it came to the 'long' seventeenth century, from the advent of James VI and I, via the Civil War, to the Act of Union with Scotland.[14] Only thereafter did interest in greater Britain somewhat diminish – the very time, it bears repeating, when greater Britain itself was undeniably at its greatest, at least in terms of territorial extent.

Despite these significant qualifications, the fact remains that during the heyday of the *British* state, nation and Empire, it was the *English* version of Whig history which was very much the prevailing mode, and it proved remarkably tenacious, long outliving the era in which it had blossomed, and the circumstances which had given it such resonance. The last single-author multi-volume chronicle appeared during the late 1950s: Sir Winston Churchill's aptly named *History of the English-Speaking Peoples*, a time-warp work, owing much to such best-selling authors of his youth as Lecky and Green. Sir Keith Feiling and Sir George Clark produced single-volume histories of England, in 1949 and 1971 respectively, which were very much in the Trevelyan mould, though less beguilingly written. The last volume of the *Oxford History of England* contained A.J.P. Taylor's celebrated (or notorious) denial that such a thing as Britain had ever existed: England, he insisted, could and did mean 'indiscriminately England and Wales; Great Britain; the United Kingdom; and even the British Empire'.[15] And in the post-war, welfare-state era, there was a veritable glut of multi-authored, multi-volume series: from Penguin, Nelson, Longman, Paladin and Edward

Arnold. All of them were conventionally styled *Histories of England*, and they continued to appear as late as the 1970s and 1980s. But by then, this traditional English history no longer seemed as confident or as convincing or as resonant or as unchallenged as it had been in earlier decades.

II

What were the changes in context and circumstance during the quarter century from the 1970s to the mid 1990s, which led to the rethinking of national history, and not only in Britain, but also elsewhere? The most significant international development was the unexpected and unprecedented break-up of some of those nation-states whose existence had been increasingly taken as part of the indissoluble order of things. Many of the independent countries which emerged in Asia and Africa in the aftermath of the unravelling of the European colonial empires failed to sustain their (often artificial) territorial unity or their democratic viability, as examples as varied and depressing as Zaire and Iraq testified.[16] The demise of Communism since 1989 brought an end to the Union of Soviet Socialist Republics, and saw the establishment or re-establishment of many states in Eastern Europe and Central Asia. But as new nations were brought into being, older countries fell apart: in Czechoslovakia, the break-up was relatively amicable, in Yugoslavia, it was horrendous. By the mid 1990s, the world seemed to be full of what would soon be called 'failed states', and around the globe, ethno-linguistic nationalism came stridently and aggressively alive; but much of the most fervent national feeling – or 'identity' as it was revealingly called – was no longer consistent with the units of nationhood as they had been created and consolidated between 1870 and 1919. As a result, the unstable politics of identity seemed set to supersede the more structured politics of the nation, and a glut of publications, by historians and political scientists, on nations and nationalism, provided abundant evidence that these two subjects were no longer aligned as closely as they had previously been.[17]

This meltdown of some countries into smaller and less stable units was not the only way in which political developments undermined earlier national identities during these years. The enlargement of the European Union (from the Common Market to the EEC to the EU), and the seemingly inexorable shift of power away from national capitals, national governments and national legislatures to the Strasbourg Parliament and the Brussels bureaucrats, meant that state sovereignty was significantly curtailed and substantially undermined. The advent of a single currency and a central European bank eroded both the symbols (coins and bank notes) and the substance (separate monetary policies) of national autonomy, and Britain's disengagement from these developments was merely the exception that proved the rule. But this was not simply a political erosion, confined to the once-sovereign states of Europe, and nor is it over yet. For the increasing globalization of the world economy meant that decisions affecting particular nations or regions of Europe were as likely to be taken in New York or Tokyo or Hong Kong as they were in Berlin or Birmingham or Barcelona, while the (as yet incomplete) revolution in communications technology only served to break down national identities still further. As the multinational, multi-media empire of Rupert Murdoch so vividly demonstrated, the new information superhighway recognized no national boundaries or barriers.

Not surprisingly, then, the nation-state was widely regarded as being one of the most significant casualties of the emerging post-modern world. Fernand Braudel devoted the last years of his life to trying to find *The Identity of France*. It eluded him – albeit in two volumes. The reunification of Germany, instead of stemming the tide of national dissolution, seemed to renew, rather than lessen, German anxieties about their identity.[18] More generally, Benedict Anderson argued that nations should properly be understood as 'imagined communities': as invented associations, encompassing a multitude of shifting boundaries and subjective identities. This did not make them any less 'real', but it did suggest that there was nothing absolute, unchanging or immutable about the late nineteenth- and early twentieth-century nation-state. On the contrary, it was merely one provisional, temporary and contingent way of organizing, governing and identifying large numbers of people, which invariably rested on manufactured myths and invented traditions, and which was never as homogeneous or as unified as those national historians who had helped create its national narratives had been inclined to insist.[19] By deconstructing these myths and traditions, historians of the 1970s and 1980s were no longer reinforcing national identity as many of their nineteenth and early twentieth-century predecessors had done: instead, they were themselves contributing to, and intensifying, the very identity crisis through which many countries now seemed to be passing.[20]

In a manner which further undermined the claims to national exception-alism made by Margaret Thatcher and John Major, Britain fully shared in these developments and erosions: for both internationally and domestically, its identity, independence and sense of nationhood seemed increasingly problematic and uncertain during the closing decades of the twentieth century. On the global stage, Britain no longer enjoyed the comforting reassurance of being a great power: after 1945, the nation's standing in the world declined with astonishing rapidity, and for all Thatcher's bluster and bravura, this was a decline which she conspicuously failed to reverse.[21] It no longer had the secure satisfaction of being the metropolis of a greater Britain flung far beyond the seas: the Empire was gone, the Commonwealth had become multi-racial, and apart from the Queen, there seemed to be few people who believed in it, or even knew what (or where) it was. In different but equally vivid ways, the Suez crisis, the Falklands War and the two Iraq wars showed how subordinated to the United States British foreign policy had become, notwithstanding the country's allegedly 'independent' nuclear deterrent. And relations with 'Europe' were fundamentally changed: in 1973, Britain joined the EEC, bringing to an end, as some feared 'a thousand years of history', while the subsequent construction of the Channel Tunnel meant the ties to the rest of the Continent became even closer. For a nation that had, throughout so much of its history, defined itself over and against 'Europe' as something different, something exceptional, and something superior, this was at best unsettling, at worst traumatic.[22]

These globally-conditioned anxieties about Britain's late twentieth-century identity were reinforced by three very significant domestic developments. First, the obverse of post-war decolonization was a massive influx of immigrants into this country, especially from South Asia and the Caribbean, and to these overseas arrivals were subsequently added people from eastern Europe, seeking work and opportunity in the west in the aftermath of the fall of Communism and the extension of the EU. This meant that to an unprecedented degree, Britain was becoming a multi-racial, multi-ethnic, multi-cultural society, where (for instance) there were more Muslims than Methodists. Second, the 'troubles' in Northern Ireland, which began in the late 1960s and lasted for the best part of forty years, combined with the resurgence of Welsh and Scottish nationalism from the 1970s onwards, led many commentators to predict (and some to hope for) the 'break-up of Britain' as a nation-state into its separate, historic, constituent parts of England, Scotland, Wales and (presumably) a re-united Ireland – a possibility first seriously (or ominously) mooted with the ill-fated devolution legislation of James Callaghan's Labour government in 1976–78.[23] Third, many once-great British institutions which had seemed for so long the very embodiment of national identity, national values and national success lost much of their sense of purpose and the confidence of the public – among them the monarchy, parliament, the Church of England, the police and the BBC.[24]

At the same time, and partly influenced by these broader trends, there were also significant changes and developments in British historical scholarship, away from the earlier concern with, and celebration of, the English nation-state. In England itself, university-based history greatly expanded during the immediate post-war years, and again during the 1960s and 1970s. But although traditional English political and constitutional history was still taught, with the aid of the new multi-authored series that were then being produced, it was no longer as unchallenged as it had been.[25] For the new, burgeoning, fashionable sub-disciplines which came to prominence and maturity during those years were little concerned with asking questions about the past that needed to be answered within the conventional units of national territoriality or national identity. Economic historians preferred to deal with smaller areas (especially Lancashire) or larger (usually Europe). Local historians and urban historians concentrated on particular regions and individual cities (often Birmingham or Manchester). Social historians were more interested in classes than in nations (especially industrial workers). And historians of ideas, of culture, of capitalism, of technology, of population, of race, of sex, of gender and of religion were rarely concerned with specific national boundaries at all.

Elsewhere in the British Isles, the hegemony of the traditional English history narrative was faced with a different, but no less powerful challenge: the energetic emergence of Irish, Welsh and Scottish history as separate self-conscious academic subjects.[26] The post-war expansion of universities, combined with the Irish 'troubles' and the upsurge of Scottish and Welsh nationalism, undoubtedly gave a great impetus to non-English (and sometimes anglophobic) historical studies in these three nations. One indication of this development was the advent of a cohort of outstanding scholars, including T.W. Moody, J.C. Beckett and F.S.L. Lyons in Ireland, Rosalind Mitchison, Gordon Donaldson and Geoffrey Barrow in Scotland, and Glanmor Williams and Gwyn A. Williams in Wales, who spent their careers studying the histories of their nation: and their nation was emphatically not England. Another was the proliferation of separate scholarly journals devoted to similar ends, which effectively toppled the claims of the *English Historical Review* to pan-British inclusiveness: the *Scottish Historical Review* was revived and rejuvenated after 1945; *Irish Historical Studies* became the major forum for rethinking Irish history; and they were joined by the *Welsh History Review* in 1961. Yet a third development was the appearance of new single-volume histories of the three nations, consolidating the detailed research now being done, and establishing new, non-anglocentric interpretations.[27]

Together, these international, domestic and scholarly changes during the last quarter of the twentieth century substantially undermined the easy presumptions and unspoken presuppositions which had characterized so much English history-writing during the heyday of the nation-state, and especially during the heyday of Britain as the top nation-state of them all. 'What virtue can there be', Geoffrey Elton inquired in 1984, in his inaugural lecture as Regius Professor of Modern History in the University of Cambridge, 'in studying the muddled history of a small off-shore island whose supposed achievements have turned out illusory?' Elton thought he had an answer to this by-then pressing question, but others were not so sure.[28] Globally, it no longer seemed convincing to depict the history of England as the successful and still unfinished epic of the rise of a great power and the winning and consolidation of a great transoceanic empire. Continentally, it no longer seemed convincing to depict the history of England as one of providential exceptionalism, intermittent involvement, and ordered and detached progress. Domestically, it no longer seemed convincing to depict the history of England as the process whereby it inexorably came to dominate and assimilate the rest of the British Isles. And academically, it no longer seemed convincing to write the history of England without some awareness of the separate but interlocking histories of Ireland, Scotland and Wales, and without giving thought to the different identities (and histories) implied by the words England, Great Britain, the United Kingdom, the British Isles, and the British Empire.

Accordingly, and even as Thatcher herself was reasserting it, the 1970s and 1980s witnessed the gradual abandonment of the old-style whiggish history of England, and the first tentative moves towards a new and more sophisticated form of genuinely British history. Michael Hechter's study of England and the Celtic fringe seems retrospectively too anglocentric, but at the time it appeared, it was the British dimension of the work which rightly impressed. As if turning its back on the presumptions underlying the multi-volume national history culminating in A.J.P. Taylor's coruscating 'little Englandism', Oxford University Press published a one-volume history which had Britain in the text as well as the title, and Cambridge duly responded with an encyclopaedia which embraced both Britain and Ireland.[29] Most importantly, J.G.A. Pocock produced two seminal articles, which urged the creation and recognition of British history as what he called 'a new subject'. It should, he urged, be concerned for the early period with the British archipelago ('these islands') as a whole. It should be concerned for the seventeenth and eighteenth centuries with the greater British transatlantic world, which was irretrievably shattered by what was thus the civil war of American Independence that began in 1776. And it should be concerned for the nineteenth and twentieth centuries with what then became a new imperial Britain, encompassing North America, large parts of Africa, much of South Asia and beyond, India, and all the Antipodes.[30]

This was a powerful programmatic polemic, motivated by Pocock's concern, as a New Zealander, that Britain's entry into the Common Market might lead to the termination of interest in its complex global past; and he accordingly urged historians of England to raise their game, broaden their horizons, de-parochialize their subject and engage with a wider world in which, significantly, Europe itself did not seem to fit or figure. Not surprisingly, there were those who scorned such a challenging call (A.J.P. Taylor, predictably, among them), and it was some time before Pocock's manifesto significantly influenced the course of historical thinking, research and writing.[31] As late as 1986, the highly-sympathetic Professor Rees Davies lamented that

> British history has been much in the air of late; but it still seems strangely reluctant to come down to earth.... British history has not in truth arrived. The programmatic rhetoric, as is usual in these matters, has been more impressive than the practical achievement.[32]

So, indeed, at the time it was. But within ten years, there was scarcely a scholar left in 'these islands' who would still unthinkingly interchange the words England and Britain, who would be ignorant of the work done in Irish, Scottish and Welsh history, or who would fail to recognize that 'British history' was something substantively different from 'English history' writ larger. Indeed, during the 1980s and 1990s, articles, monographs and general surveys regularly appeared, proclaiming their commitment to, or their exemplification of, the 'new British history'. The next section considers them in more detail.

III

In so doing, it may be helpful to recall an observation of the late but sympathetically-disposed Conrad Russell, made in the early 1990s, namely that 'British history', as it was then developing, could not and should not be undertaken for every century of our nation's past with the same methodological approach, or with the same degree of plausibility, conviction, success or scholarly benefit.[33] Two of the pioneering historians who did engage with the new subject, and who produced books which were outstanding examples of it, were Rees Davies for the twelfth and thirteenth centuries, and Russell himself for the seventeenth century.[34] The appeal and plausibility of investigating these periods in this way should not have come as any great surprise: for if we look back on the many English histories of the past, be they the single-author multi-volume works, the single-author single-volume surveys, or the multi-author multi-volume series, it was for precisely these same centuries that most attention was lavished on the affairs, not just of England, but also of Wales, Scotland and Ireland. And how could it have been otherwise, given that the histories of the four (or the three) kingdoms interacted more intensely and intensively at these times than beforehand or afterwards? From this perspective, the 'new British history' that was initially undertaken, covering the period of what might be termed the first Pocockian paradigm, was not always quite as new or as original as some might be inclined to think; but beyond any doubt, the work of Davies and Russell was of exceptional quality and sophistication, and was justly influential.

When it came to the new history undertaken on the broader, transatlantic British world that had been established, flourished and fell apart during the seventeenth and eighteenth centuries, the new, British, paradigm yielded significant and novel insights. The great English historians of the past had not viewed these things from a Pocockian perspective: they wrote about the settlement of the 13 colonies on the eastern seaboard, and about the American War of Independence, but they did not see these places and events as constituting a discrete phase (or interconnected field) of

British history as a whole. But during the 1980s and early 1990s, this period and this community became much studied: a great array of self-styled 'Atlanticist' scholars began exploring the demographic, economic, social, political and ideological links which bound together, and eventually drove apart, this greater British realm located on both the eastern and the western perimeters of the Atlantic Ocean.[35] And for a later period, Peter Marshall and C.A. Bayly led the investigation of the beginnings of a new British Empire that was being founded in India. There were also pioneering studies of Britishness itself, a developing sense of national identity that was explained in terms of Protestantism, dislike of the French, and the growth of Empire.[36] Only Ireland seemed to have received rather less attention than perhaps it should have done, and its ambiguous position makes it easy to understand why this was so. Was it part of the British Isles, or part of the British Empire? Was Ireland an integral component of Britain, or something tangential, even hostile? Then as now, these have never been easy questions to answer unequivocally, and it was a problem that the early practitioners of the 'new' British history did not satisfactorily resolve.[37]

By the nineteenth and twentieth centuries, the period of Pocock's third and most expanded British community, which was global rather than 'merely' archipelagic or transatlantic, the picture of work done in response to his manifesto changed again; but this time not for the better. It is worth repeating that the histories written in the heyday of the United Kingdom and the British Empire were generally indifferent to that Kingdom and that Empire, in the sense that they simply took them for granted. Since the Second World War, the ending of this most extended and most recent phase of British history-making might have been expected to have led to an upsurge in British history-writing about it. But this was rarely the case. With the exception of the work of Keith Robbins, there was very little authentic, self-conscious 'British history' of the British Isles – and as he was the first to admit, his work did not extend much to Ireland or the Empire. Peter Cain and A.G. Hopkins audaciously reconnected metropolitan Britain and its Empire; but they never addressed, let alone resolved, the central contradiction of their magnum opus, namely that they saw the *British* Empire as the result of exporting the *English* gentlemanly ideal overseas. Beyond that, there was next to nothing.[38] How odd that the 'new British history' as a subject should have been at its weakest for the very period when British history itself in many ways reached its zenith.[39]

Thus practised and written during the 1980s and 1990s, the early offerings of the 'new' British history, as Conrad Russell rightly observed, meant very different things to different historians working in very different centuries. But this was not just in terms of when and where British history could be deemed to have taken place, nor in terms of just how much of it there could – or should – be. For this new, fashionable, generic heading also concealed – or encompassed – a variety of very different problems and issues, approaches and methodologies. Rees Davies showed how the kings and aristocracy of England sought to extend their dominion, by military conquest, over Wales, Scotland and Ireland during the twelfth and thirteenth centuries. Conrad Russell sought to explain what used to be called the English Civil War, not in terms of ideology or class or religion or localism, but as an essentially British War of the Three Kingdoms. Linda Colley looked at the many ways in which a new sense of British national identity was created and forged at all social levels during the long eighteenth century, and the long years of war with France, beginning with the Act of Union in 1707 and ending with the Great Reform Act of 1832. And Keith Robbins investigated the integration of nineteenth-century Britain from a different perspective, via the arts, religion, business, education and recreation, in addition to politics.[40] These are excessively oversimplified summaries of works of great subtlety, insight and complexity; but it is surely correct to note that these historians were looking at very different forms of what might be termed Britishness, and so were writing very different forms of the 'new' British history.

There was, in short, no one single, dominant methodology for doing this 'new British history', and nor should there have been. Put another way, this meant that the approach, which was so brilliantly pioneered at this time by Hugh Kearney, of seeing the history of Britain as the interaction of the 'four nations' that constituted it, did not come to dominate the subject, even though for a time it seemed as though it would.[41] Clearly, there were some aspects and some centuries of the British past which this way of looking at it illuminated with unique force and power. But, as Kearney himself admitted, this was not the whole of the story of the two islands. The four nations of England, Wales, Scotland and Ireland evolved in different ways and at different speeds, and their borders and boundaries were often contested and shifting. At certain stages in their histories, they possessed different state structures, different monarchies, different religions, and different national identities. There were also important internal divisions in each country, between the north and the south of England, between the Lowlands and Highlands of Scotland, between Protestant and Catholic Ireland. Moreover, England's eventual incorporation of Wales was different from its subsequent union with Scotland, which was different again from Britain's later merger of Ireland. The danger with the 'four nations' methodology was that it sometimes paid insufficient attention to the important dis-similarities between the countries, and also to the significant variations within each one of them.[42]

Indeed, in the opening pages of his book, Kearney came close to subverting the very conceptual framework which, thereafter, he utilized with such brio and élan: for, as he pointed out, there were other ways of dividing up the British Isles, and thus of envisioning its history, than that embodied in the 'four nations' approach. Suppose, for instance, a history of the British Isles was organized, not around the varying political relations between England, Ireland, Scotland and Wales, but around the economic and social differences between lowland and upland regions across the archipelago.[43] This might lead to an alternative form of 'British history', which had, indeed, been briefly suggested by Pocock, but which had not been taken up. For as Kearney rightly noted, the 'new British history' did not have to be primarily political and constitutional and military and diplomatic. It could, he seemed to be implying, be social history, or economic history, or cultural history, or demographic history, or environmental history, or maritime history – though in what sense then it would be still be 'British' remained unclear. It could – and this was Kearney's own shorthand term – be a sort of Braudellian history, concerned with the *longue durée* as much as with *l'histoire événementielle*: and as such it would provide a much more broadly-conceived history of the British Isles than that provided by political historians, whether they used the 'four nations' approach or not.[44]

That was an important early challenge to the 'new' British history, paradoxically mounted by one of its foremost early practitioners: namely that conceiving and doing it as political history had run far ahead of other, but no less essential, ways of looking at the British past. In this sense, there was a need for more 'British history', not less, though whether a history of these islands with the politics and the constitution taken out would be recognizably British at all was, perhaps, a moot point. Like many forms of 'new' history in their early, crusading, proselytizing phases, there was a danger that more was being promised by the 'new' British history than it could realistically be expected to accomplish or deliver.[45] Nor was this the only problem. One additional danger was that it might merely replace the political teleology of ordered constitutional development, and the sociological teleology of an ever-rising middle class, with an indentificational teleology which merely and mindlessly claimed that, in any particular century, the British were actively engaged in the process of becoming more British than they had ever been before. Another was that an excessive concentration on 'Britishness' might lead some historians to ignore those many alternative identities, sometimes complementary, sometimes contradictory, which were more locally – but no less powerfully – articulated. Even in the post-modern era of de-centred discourse, it was important to remember that the creation of a British identity did not necessarily entail or require the abandonment of alternative but also complementary English or Scottish or Welsh or Irish identities, or of more regional loyalties to county, city or village.

It was, then, neither surprising nor wrong that separate histories of England, Ireland, Scotland and Wales continued to flourish alongside newly-conceptualized and newly-commissioned histories of Britain during these years.[46] As Rosalind Mitchison noted, 'for those who live within the British Isles, it is reasonable to assume that British history means the history of the separate nationalities which at one time or another have joined up to make a single state, that is, Scottish, Welsh and Irish, as well as the politically dominant English'.[47] Far from being mutually exclusive, these separate histories (like the identities they traced) were compatible with and even complimentary to, the 'new', more expansively-conceived British history. Accordingly, the 1980s and 1990s witnessed the appearance of Edward Arnold's *New History of Scotland* in eight volumes; of Oxford University Press's *New History of Ireland*, to be in a projected ten volumes; and of the Oxford University Press/University of Wales Press *History of Wales*, of which four volumes have so far appeared.[48] Nor was the history of England going into terminal decline. Practising what he had preached in his inaugural lecture as Regius Professor, while simultaneously insisting that the Whig interpretation of history was dead, Sir Geoffrey Elton's single-volume survey, *The English*, celebrated English virtue, institutions and exceptionalism with an enthusiastic ardour that G.M. Trevelyan (or Margaret Thatcher) barely equalled.[49] And despite OUP's audacious venture into the single-volume *History of Britain*, the first volumes of the *New Oxford History of England* seemed scarcely more British-minded and British-ranging than was the old series it has been designed to replace.[50]

There was, then, still a great deal of anglocentric history being produced in some English quarters, and there was also a great deal of anglophobic history being undertaken in some of the more distant reaches of the British Isles; these, too, had their own curious complementarity, for they were united in their shared lack of interest in (and sometimes their hostility to) matters British.[51] Yet despite the alternative and broader approach which its exponents advocated and exemplified, the 'new British history', whether it was the history of Britain, or of Britishness, or of the United Kingdom, or of the British Empire, could not be a denial of those separate histories and separate identities of England, Ireland, Scotland and Wales. All too often in the past, histories of England, Ireland, Scotland and Wales ignored (or resented) the British dimensions. It would have been an unhappy irony if the newly-emergent histories of Britain had ignored (or resented) the continuing English, Welsh, Scottish and Irish dimension.[52] Beyond any doubt, there were some aspects of our past where the 'new British history' was successful and illuminating, and there were others where it urgently needed to be undertaken. But it was also necessary to insist that more should not be claimed for British history 'as a new subject' than it was right, sensible and appropriate to be doing.[53]

IV

Such was the promising yet tentative state that British history as a 'new' subject had reached by the mid 1990s, a time when the dogmatic certainties of Thatcherism were giving way to the distinctly uncharismatic and unsure Major years – characterized by a preponderantly English Tory Party in agonized and divided meltdown over (among other things) Britain's relations with 'Europe', and by a Labour Party sensing that there might at last be a political future for the taking and the winning, which was dominated by a group of Scottish 'modernizers' in the form of Messrs Smith, Blair and Brown. At the same time, the 'new' expanded, archipelagic and imperial conception of British history, by which was meant something very different from, and much broader than, the old, narrow, little England, whiggish history, had definitely established itself on the scholarly agenda. As such, it seemed to be an innovative, exciting and challenging way of conceiving what had increasingly become a rather staid and outdated version of the national past; and it also provided some prospect that the history of 'these islands' might retain a global (especially north Atlantic) appeal at a time when the old, universalized episodes of English history, that had been so popular and resonant during the 1960s – the political revolution of the mid seventeenth century, the political stability at the beginning of the eighteenth century, and the Industrial Revolution at the end of it – no longer seemed to be of such public significance or to carry such scholarly conviction as they once had.[54]

The exact relation between the rise of the new British history, and the simultaneous advent of the new British politics, is not yet clear, but it cannot have been just coincidence that they happened at the same time: for while English history was being re-formulated as British history during the 1970s and 1980s, English politics was simultaneously becoming preoccupied with the British question. As a neophyte Tory leader, Margaret Thatcher had been deeply hostile to James Callaghan's scheme for Scottish and Welsh devolution, and it was his parliamentary defeat on that issue which paved the way for her subsequent electoral victory in 1979. As Prime Minister and as the leader of the Conservative and Unionist Party (the name had been expanded in the late nineteenth century to accommodate those renegade Liberals such as Joseph Chamberlain and the Marquess of Hartington, who opposed Gladstone's Home Rule scheme for Ireland as subverting the Union), Thatcher was a convinced defender of the constitutional status quo, despite (or because of?) the fact that the Conservative Party's popular support north of the border was visibly dwindling. 'Scottish values are Tory values – and vice versa', she informed the General Assembly of the Church of Scotland in May 1988, but neither they nor most of their compatriots agreed with her, and even she was compelled to admit that her Caledonian overtures were 'rebuffed'.[55] John Major was no less committed to the maintenance of the Union: convinced that it was in the best interests of the English and the Scots, and that the dismantling of the 1707 settlement would be disastrous for both countries and both peoples. 'If I could summon up', he observed during the general election of 1992, 'all the authority of this office, I would put it into a single warning: the United Kingdom is in danger.'[56]

Since the Conservative Party was by the 1990s winning scarcely any seats in Scotland, this was a strangely paradoxical position for the Tories to hold: insisting on a constitutional arrangement for the United Kingdom from which they did not benefit in electoral terms, and when it would have been more sensibly self-interested for them to advocate the complete devolution of Wales and Scotland, by making them independent nations, thereby leaving a no less independent England in which they would have a much greater prospect of enjoying a permanent, in-built majority.[57] The position of the Labour Party was scarcely less paradoxical by the mid 1990s, although in an exactly opposite way. Historically, the Conservatives had used (and needed) England to dominate the rest of Britain, but Labour, like the Liberals before it, had used (and needed) the rest of Britain to dominate England. Yet it was Labour, anxious not to be upstaged by the increasingly popular and strident nationalist parties in Wales and Scotland, that most wholeheartedly embraced devolution during the early and mid 1990s, even though it had no clear legislative programme, and even though the resulting loss of any Scottish and Welsh parliamentary seats at Westminster would do harm to its chances of winning any more general elections.[58] Just as the Tories should have ceased to defend the Union, and advocated complete independence for Wales and Scotland, so Labour should not have embraced devolution, but should have insisted on defending the Union.

Tony Blair and New Labour duly won the general election in May 1997, when the Conservatives obtained *no seats whatsoever* in Wales or Scotland. Not surprisingly, then, devolution was high on Blair's political agenda, and he was also trying to reach some sort of permanent settlement in Northern Ireland, but he insisted that these were the means whereby the United Kingdom would be strengthened, not weakened. Referendums were duly held in Wales and Scotland and, despite the slim majority in the former, devolution went ahead, and a Scottish Parliament and Welsh Assembly were established on the basis of proportional representation.[59] These were among the most significant legislative accomplishments at the beginning of Blair's decade in office, just as the Northern Ireland settlement, and the re-establishment of the hitherto-suspended Stormont Parliament, was a major achievement in the final months of his premiership. (In-between, and quite by coincidence, public attention was further focused on these matters with the 200th anniversary of the Act of Union with Ireland (2001), the 400th anniversary of the union of the English and Scottish crowns (2003), and the 300th anniversary of the Act of Union between the English and Scottish nations (2007).[60]) The result was a new but inconsistent constitutional settlement, with differing forms of devolved government for Wales, Scotland and Northern Ireland, with no devolved government whatsoever for England, and with Scottish, Welsh and Ulster MPs able to vote on certain English matters at Westminster, whereas English MPs could not vote on similar issues for Scotland, Wales and Ulster, because they were now reserved to the legislatures in Cardiff, Edinburgh and Stormont.

As at present constituted, the United Kingdom is thus neither a newly-nor a coherently-constructed federal state, yet nor is it any longer an historically-continuous unitary state: the constitutional arrangements embodying and expressing such contemporary 'Britishness' as may now exist are thus decidedly messy.[61] As Tony Blair was to discover (and as the Tories had always insisted), devolution has not satisfied the more vehement nationalists in Scotland, and the prospects of unco-operative colleagues in Cardiff, or of a hostile nationalist government in Edinburgh, 'doing something different from the rest of Britain', were outcomes he does not seem to have contemplated or considered in advance.[62] Small wonder that his successor, Gordon Brown, has espoused the mantra of a 'Britishness' built around what he believes to be shared values, grounded in a shared past, which is a way of defending the Anglo-Scottish Union without actually saying so explicitly. Meanwhile, the Tories seem unable to make up their minds what position to adopt. For all their vehement defence of the Union, both Thatcher and Major seemed to many Welsh and Scots to be incorrigibly English and anglocentric. Moreover, the party that had once championed the British Empire is now more inclined to dismiss the whole imperial adventure and its Commonwealth aftermath as a distorting aberration from English history.[63] And it bears repeating that its own electoral prospects would be better served by advocating and implementing full independence for Wales and Scotland, thereby leaving it in a much stronger position as the party of English nationalism in an independent England.[64] Yet is this a policy which a party that has also been historically-pledged to uphold the Union can espouse? William Hague, Michael Howard and Iain Duncan-Smith all hedged their bets: small wonder that David Cameron has yet to make up his mind.

Just as 'British' politics has moved markedly on in the decade since Blair's election victory in 1997, so the 'new' British history has also moved on, one indication of which was that within a year of Blair's occupancy of 10 Downing Street, Oxford University's prestigious Ford Lectures, previously defined as being in English history, were now re-named as encompassing British history.[65] But whereas the politics of British-ness have become more significant (and also more unpredictable) in the aftermath of devolution, the history of Britishness, although being produced in much greater quantity than before, seems to have been going through a largely reactive (and recognizable) phase of consolidation, controversy and criticism, after the earlier years of manifesto-production and pioneering publications. It is more than a quarter of a century since J.G.A. Pocock wrote his first programmatic articles, and more than fifteen years since the seminal works of Kearney, Davies, Russell, Colley and Robbins demonstrated by example that British history was a serious and important subject that could and should be done – and could and should be done in a variety of ways. Rees Davies continued to deepen and extend his own work on the medieval period, but the most significant new development has been the production of general surveys which have been self-consciously British: especially, and unsurprisingly, for the medieval period, for the seventeenth century, and for the 'long' eighteenth century. More ambitiously, in a book aptly entitled *The Isles*, Norman Davies set out to construct an entire history of the British archipelago from pre-historic times to the present day.[66] Together, such volumes are an emphatic expression of the fact that the 'new' British history has now become part of the scholarly main stream.

But even as the subject has achieved unprecedented recognition, it has also become increasingly mired in controversies, some of which threaten to undermine its very existence. Well over a dozen edited volumes have appeared in recent years, devoted to the 'new' British history for the early modern period alone, sending out a range of contradictory messages.[67] There are those historians who insist that it is a serious, viable field of study, and that it should continue to focus on war and state building and political relations. There are those who urge that identity formation and multiple identities are exceptionally slippery concepts, both definitionally and historically, and that more attention should be given to weighing the relative significance of such different variables as religion, race and institutional influences. There are well-disposed critics who regret that the new British history is still preoccupied with high politics and statecraft, and pays inadequate attention to social, demographic, economic and cultural history. There are others, much more hostile, who insist that even in its most recent guise, this not so 'new' British history remains tainted by the usual unthinking and imperialist anglo-centricism, and that as such should be disowned and denounced by all right-thinking historians (and inhabitants) of Wales, Scotland or Ireland.[68] And there are those who insist that English history is still the most significant subject, not least because for most of the time, the majority of the English did not think in 'British' terms. Not surprisingly, then, many books are still being written which are determinedly English (or Welsh or Scottish or Irish) in their focus, sometimes in deliberate defiance of the 'new' British history, sometimes in determined refusal to engage with it at all, and sometimes because their authors plausibly insist this remains a serious and significant subject.[69]

There is a further issue that has recently come into play, and which harks back to Pocock's original formulation of the 'new' British history, and to his motives for advocating it in the way he did. It bears repeating that he was prompted to sketch out this newer, larger way of conceiving the British past out of anxiety at the likely consequences, both for history and for his native New Zealand, of Britain's turning away from its own imperial narrative by its entry into the Common Market. Britain might be going 'into' Europe in the future, Pocock seemed to be saying, but that was no reason for writing Britishness out of its past. Europe, then, scarcely figured in Pocock's vision of the new British history and many scholars since then, focusing either on the history of Britishness, or on the history of the British Empire, have tended to leave 'Europe' out of the picture.[70] Yet in truth, there was no historical zero-sum game that was being played between Britain and Empire on the one hand, or between Britain and Europe on the other. The relations between England and Europe, Wales and Europe, Scotland and Europe, Ireland and Europe, and Britain and Europe were many and varied, there may have been occasions when they were more important than relations between Britain and its Empire, and they are only now beginning to get the attention they merit.[71] Just as the 'new' British history involved a rethinking of the history of England, so a 'new' European history may involve a rethinking of the history of Britain. Indeed, one of the most salutary consequences of the entry of Britain into the EEC and the construction of the Channel Tunnel is that these are but the most recent and vivid reminders that throughout its history, England/ Britain has been a European nation at least as much as it has been an imperial nation.

V

There, for now, the new British history and the new British politics may be said to be – though they can scarcely be said to be resting. No historian should ever be rash enough to predict what is going to happen next, either in terms of the new directions historical research will take, or in terms of how future political events will unfold. After a generation of 'new' British history, there are those who think the subject jaded and passé, while there are also those who think there is still a great deal of life left in it; and in their different ways, they may both be right.[72] By the same token, while the predicted or hoped-for or despaired-of break-up of Britain may yet occur, it also seems possible that it may not – or, at least, that it may not do so just yet. Nor should we lose sight of the broader perspective that lies beyond the horizon of British history however expansively this new-old subject is defined. In the first decade of the twenty-first century, nations that have survived far outnumber nations that have recently dissolved, and the forces holding the United Kingdom together may turn out to be stronger than those pulling it apart. So while the 'new British history' has been significantly stimulated by what has sometimes seemed to have been the impending dissolution of Britain, there is now a sufficient body of published work to ensure that the continued validity and vitality of the subject no longer depends upon such an apocalyptic political and constitutional outcome. All that can be said with certainty at present is that Britain still exists, that British history is still being made, both in these islands and beyond, and that it will continue to be made for the foreseeable future. This is not the only reason why scholars should continue to study and to rethink 'British history'; but it is certainly a serious and compelling one.

8

Dominion:
Britain's Imperial Past in Canada's
Imperial Past[1]

As the previous chapter has suggested, there is much to be said for regarding the period from 1870 to 1914 as witnessing 'the zenith of the nation state', seeing as it did the reconstruction of the United States in the aftermath of the Civil War, the unification of Italy and Germany, and the consolidation of the great industrial democracies of France and Britain.[2] But as was also made plain, from the standpoint of the early twenty-first century, this no longer seems quite so complete or convincing a picture, even for Europe, let alone for the wider world beyond. At the beginning of the twentieth century, there were relatively few sovereign states then in being, compared with the massive increase in numbers that would take place from 1945 onwards, and again after 1988, and many of those which did then exist were so complex in their histories, so sprawling in their jurisdictions, and so elaborate in their governing arrangements that the phrase 'nation state' describes them very inadequately and very incompletely. Britain, Russia, Germany, Spain, Italy, Austria-Hungary, China (and the United States) were all multi-national entities, each with a bewildering number of lands, regions and territories, inhabited by many different ethnic groups with fierce and sometimes competing national aspirations, and all of them held together under a no less bewildering variety of laws and constitutions. All of these essentially composite countries had been put together across the centuries, often as the result of dynastic arrangements and royal ambitions, and as such, they were not so much nation states as multiple monarchies, latter-day survivals (and developments) from the early modern European world.[3]

But it is not just that these European, Asiatic and north American countries were different from many of the nation states of our own time in terms of their complex internal structures, their contorted domestic histories, their multiple identities, and their polyglot ethnic make up, all of which denied, rather than embodied, simplistic notions of homogeneous nationhood. It is also that they were all imperial powers, with far-flung empires stretching across continental land masses (in the case of Russia, China, Austria-Hungary and the United States), and beyond the seas (in the case of the rest). The existence and expansion of these empires – whether land-based or sea-borne – further complicated the nature and structure of the countries which governed and controlled them. For these imperial holdings came in a multiplicity of different guises, with many and varied relationships to the metropolis itself. In the case of Britain, there were protectorates, naval bases, colonies of conquest, League of Nations mandates, the Indian Empire, and the great dominions of settlement.[4] To a lesser or greater degree, they were all extensions of the British state and nation (and monarchy) overseas; and what was true for Britain was mimicked by all the other colonial powers of late nineteenth-century Europe, Asia and north America, even if they were republics. In short, they were not only unlike the modern nation-state model in that they were multi-national composite constructions: they were also unlike it because of their lengthy imperial reach and their extensive and often world-wide colonial appurtenances.

If these great global powers of the nineteenth and early twentieth century were in some ways more, but in other ways less, than modern nation-states, what does this imply about the constituent parts of their empires, and especially about those great British settlements beyond the seas: Canada, which was Confederated in 1867; the Australian Federation, which was inaugurated in 1901; the Union of South Africa, which came into being in 1911? (New Zealand should also be included here, although it was neither a confederation, nor a federation, nor a union.) In the history of the British Empire, these transplanted, transoceanic communities were unique: the thirteen American colonies joined together only after they had thrown off British rule; the federal scheme embodied in the Government of India Act of 1935 was never implemented; and the post-war years saw a succession of abortive or incomplete federations: in Central Africa, East Africa, the West Indies and Malaysia.[5] But these three great British dominions of settlement, ranging from a loose federation, via a much stronger confederation, to a tightly-knit union, were atypical survivals and successes; and since their creation coincides with the alleged 'zenith of the European nation state', it is tempting to see Canada, Australia, and South Africa as outstanding examples of European nation-building and state-making overseas.

I

It is a strong and understandable temptation; but it is also a temptation which should be questioned and resisted – certainly in the case of Canada, and arguably in the other two cases as well. For if we are to get Canada's history in the most appropriate and helpful perspective, we need to appreciate that in certain important ways, it never was a nation at all, and nor is it yet. To begin with, there is the problem of its boundaries, most of which are unnatural, irrational, or difficult to discern.[6] The Maritime provinces are really an outcrop of the Appalachians, and belong both economically and geographically to New England and thus the United States. The St Lawrence lowlands merge imperceptibly into the old industrial heartland of America: Pennsylvania, Michigan, Ohio and Illinois. Out on the Prairies, along the 49th parallel, it is often impossible to know whether you are in Canada or the United States. Further west, heading through the Rockies, either to Seattle or Vancouver, the same is true. Much of what should be Canada's natural Pacific coastline is part of Alaska, and the northern frontier vanishes into the snows and ice of the Arctic. If clear, demarcated boundaries define a nation, then Canada is not much of a nation: it has been wilfully and unnaturally created, in defiance of geography and history, rather than in collaboration with them.[7]

Likewise, if racial and ethnic homogeneity defines a nation, then Canada does not score well under this heading. The Inuit and the Indians were there long before their European conquerors, and they are still there. The French were there before their British conquerors, and they, too, are very much still there. The fond nineteenth-century hopes that they might be assimilated have proved vain. Lord Durham's 'two nations warring in the bosom of a single state' are still in many ways in conflict, albeit politically rather than militarily. Thus described, Canada has always been an ethnic melting pot – which has intermittently come to the boil, but which has invariably refused to melt or meld.[8] For these different communities have their different histories, which defy homogenization into one coherent and all-encompassing national account. Take, as an illustration, the McCord Museum of Canadian history in Montreal. It is a fascinating place, full of good exhibits, imaginatively displayed, and much new work has been done there in recent years. But it is a museum which subverts the very idea it ostensibly exists to articulate and project. For what it shows is that there is no such thing as a single grand narrative of Canadian history.[9] There is the history of the British in Canada, to which the separate histories of the French and the Indians and the Inuit have been recently added. But they do not coalesce into anything recognizable as the history of *the* Canadian nation.

We must also remember that when the British assisted in the making of Canadian confederation, they were not creating, and no one who mattered there thought they were creating, an independent nation. 1867 was not 1776 carried out belatedly and by peaceful means, north of the 49th parallel. The title of the measure was the *British* North America Act, and that was indeed the community which was brought into being: of the British in North America. Thus established, Canada was a dominion under the British crown, the British privy council and the British parliament, it was a dominion with a British constitution, and it was a dominion over whose foreign policy the imperial metropolis retained full control. *Pace* Nicholas Mansergh, it was not 'an experiment in nationhood'.[10] To be sure, there was a strong, unified, central state, of which more later. But supreme political authority remained in London, and that imperial subordination was a long time in going. Indeed, it is not easy to be clear when – if yet – Canada became a fully autonomous nation. The separate signing of the Treaty of Versailles, the Balfour Declaration, the Statute of Westminster, the appointment of native-born Governors General, the new maple-leaf flag and national anthem, the patriation of the Canadian constitution: all of these are possible candidates.[11] But this is a long, unfinished journey to sovereign nationhood. For most of its history, Canada was not a fully-independent nation-state in the sense we in the early twenty-first century understand that phrase.

Moreover, this long process of gradual yet incomplete emancipation from British influence was accompanied by an increased degree of subordination to the United States. Many parts of Canada are more closely tied to America than to other parts of Canada itself. Ninety per cent of Canada's population lives within two hundred miles of the US border. In military terms, Canada has always depended on American goodwill and leadership, especially since the Second World War; and as America overtook Britain as the biggest and most vigorous economy in the world, it was bound to extend its influence across its northern border into Canada. By 1940, the United States was the preponderant investor, and its economic power is now overwhelming; and since the Second World War, American cultural 'imperialism' has been added to its military and commercial dominance.[12] The expansion of higher education during the 1960s led to a vast influx of US trained graduate students, and American cinema and television and coffee are all alike irresistible. The fact that many Americans think Canada is boring, and that Canadians hate being mistaken for Americans, is a sign of both the closeness and of the difficulties of this superior–subordinate post-colonial relationship. For many Canadians today, the most depressing aspect of their history is that they seem to have gone from British dominance in the nineteenth century, to American dominance in the twenty-first, without ever having gone through autonomous, self-sufficient nationhood on the way.[13]

Not surprisingly, then, Canada has few of the sentimental or cultural appurtenances that are customarily associated with the achievement and assurance of autonomous nationhood. It has no defining moment of independence and freedom, like 1776 for the United States, or 1947 for India: the Durham Report and Confederation are by comparison singularly un-epic things.[14] There is no central, cathartic past event on the importance (though not the meaning) of which everyone can at least agree: as with 1789 in France or 1917 in Russia. There are no national heroes, like Washington or Jefferson or Lincoln, and the fact that Wolfe and Montcalm were sworn enemies presents something of a problem. There are no towering, home-grown cultural figures, like Shakespeare or Molière or Goethe. There is no national character such as Uncle Sam or John Bull or Marianne – figures not only recognized inside the United States, Britain and France, but also outside as well.[15] In short, Canada conspicuously lacks national monuments, national myths, national heroes and national traditions. It has never come alive or taken off or achieved credibility as one of Benedict Anderson's 'imagined communities'. Its sense of national identity is neither strong nor shared. Thus regarded, Canada is much more a state than it is a nation.[16]

II

To say this is not to draw up a long and demanding list of the essential attributes of modern day nationhood, and to take condescending and unsympathetic pleasure in pointing out that Canada does not meet up to all of these exacting requirements. It bears repeating that many nineteenth-century countries – whether European or extra-European – have been described as nation states when in fact they were no such thing. So it is scarcely surprising that the achievement of nationhood has been so difficult for those British communities transplanted across the seas. For Canada was not – is not – unique in having been, and in still being, a less than 'inevitable nation'.[17] In Australia, there were native peoples; the federal structure was very weak; there is no agreement on when, if yet, the country became independent; and its own identity between Asia and America is still uncertain. In South Africa, there were British, Boers and native Africans; and although it achieved a certain sort of independence by leaving the Commonwealth in 1961, there clearly remains, after forty years of apartheid, and its subsequent overturning, much nation building still to do. In this sense, it has been harder for these three old dominions to achieve nationhood and independence than it was for the thirteen American colonies before them, or for India and the African colonies in the twentieth century.[18]

If this characterization of Canada is correct, then it is bound to be difficult to tell the history of this incomplete and unimagined nation in a way which does justice to its incomplete and unimagined nationality. This was clearly the case with the great narrative histories ostensibly constructed in the 'from colony to nation' paradigm. Some, like Arthur Lower, wrote of the influence of the environment in forming the national community and the national soul. Some, like Donald Creighton, saw Confederation as the great event in the story of nationhood, rounded off by the tariff and transport policies of John A. Macdonald.[19] Others regarded the achievement of nationhood as the accomplishment of William Lyon Mackenzie King, as he successfully campaigned to remove vestiges of colonial subordination during the inter-war years. But while there was disagreement between these historians as to exactly when Canada became a nation, and who deserved the credit for it, there was also the shared presumption that Canada did indeed evolve from a subservient colony to an independent nation-state. As such, this view was too partial, it confused statehood with nationhood, and it tried to force Canada's complex and unusual history into a national straitjacket which it did not fit.[20]

From this perspective, the more recent trends in Canadian historiography have not helped all that much. Since the 1960s, the high-politics, nation-building interpretation has been disregarded, as Canadian historians have shifted their interests, like their colleagues elsewhere in the western world, to economic history, labour history, regional history, social history, urban history, cultural history, the history of women and of minorities.[21] As a result, there have been many gains. We know much more about the lives of native peoples and French Canadians. We know much more about the Maritimes, the Prairies, and about the Canada beyond the Rockies. In J.M. Bumsted's two-volume history of *The Peoples of Canada* (Toronto, 1992), we have a brilliant synthesis of this new work. He is 'much less concerned with the traditional concentration on nation building, presented in chronological narrative', but prefers to structure his account around 'multiplicities', giving especial attention to 'maginalized invisibles': women, blacks, native people, Quebecois.[22] Thanks to such writings, we have a stronger sense of the diversity and pluralism of Canadian life. But since most of this 'new history', like its counterparts everywhere else, has been little interested in politics or power or the state, that still leaves unaddressed the problem of Canada's incomplete nationhood.

Yet it is this very incompleteness in Canada's nationhood which lies at the centre of its history, and which should therefore lie much closer to the centre of its historiography. How, then should it be dealt with? Any attempt to do so will have to address two complementary but seemingly contradictory issues. The first concerns the structure of the Canadian state which, from the very outset of Confederation, was exceptionally strong. It was strong in that it was primarily a unitary government, with all residuary authority reserved to Ottawa, not the provinces.[23] This was very different from what had previously been established in the United States, and from what was subsequently to be done in Australia. It was strong in that it played a very active role in the economic and social life of the country – initially in transport and development, subsequently in welfare and social services. And it was strong in that the constitution has possessed extraordinary powers of survival. New provinces have been admitted, the balance between the centre and the regions has been changed, the problem of Quebec has been contained for thirty years, and fears that the Confederation would break up have become a way of life. Notwithstanding these deeply divisive internal divisions, and despite the lack of a collective sense of Canadian national identity, the Canadian state has endured – and may endure long into this new millennium.

Yet it bears repeating that this powerful, unitary, infrastructural Canadian state was not (and is not) accompanied by a corresponding sense of a shared Canadian nationhood. The Canadian nation has never been – and is not today – an autochthonous 'imagined community'. But this does not mean that, for much of its history, the majority of Canadians were without such an imagined life, or were lacking for such an imagined nationhood. It did not receive its due in histories written in the 'colony-to-nation' mode, because it would have contested and subverted that very narrative and trajectory; and it has not received its due in the new history which has superseded it, because its practitioners have primarily been interested in other matters. But if we are to understand Canada, we must pay greater attention to this powerful, resonant, appealing imagined community which was so important for so much of its history: and that community was, of course, the British Empire.[24] From a north American perspective, 'imperial Canada' is the most appropriate shorthand term to describe the deep sense of belonging to this greater British transoceanic world. But what exactly was 'imperial Canada'? Who were the 'imperial Canadians'? When and how did it happen? And when and why did it end?

III

From 1867 to 1917, material circumstances played a large part in moulding and maintaining this imperial Canadian identity. Although the connections between Confederation, nation building and foreign investment now seem more complex and contingent than it was once fashionable to suppose, no one has denied that the infrastructural investment during this period was of the greatest importance, and that it was Confederation which helped to make possible and make credible such investment. The financing of the transatlantic shipping lines from Liverpool and Glasgow to Montreal, and of the Grand Trunk, the Canadian Pacific and the Canadian National Railways, was all undertaken through London, with merchant banks like Barings playing a major part. Between 1900 and 1914, Canada absorbed £500 million of overseas capital, of which more than 70 per cent came from Britain. And this investment not only made Canada's economic development possible, for by being so closely tied to the London money markets, the threat of American economic dominance was diminished and (for a time) postponed. This in turn meant that while Canada gradually moved towards a degree of political independence within the Empire, it was also becoming more subordinate to Britain economically.[25]

It was this massive British investment which underpinned imperial Canada; but it was not a matter merely of figures and finance, for the men in Canada who created the infrastructure and industries out of British investments were among the most important imperial Canadians. Consider the case of Donald Alexander Smith, who arrived in Canada, a penniless Scott, in 1838. For 26 years, he worked in the Hudson's Bay Company. He then moved to Montreal, and became a major figure in the Canadian Pacific Railway and in national politics. In 1895, when already long past seventy, he became the official representative of Canada in London, where he died in harness in 1913. He piled up colossal wealth, was ennobled as Lord Strathcona and Mount Royal, and lived in great state on both sides of the Atlantic. He was Chancellor of McGill University, Montreal; he equipped at his own cost a troop of horse during the Boer War; he presided in London at an annual banquet on 1 July to commemorate Canadian Confederation; and he spent $40,000 to celebrate his election to the Lord Rectorship of Aberdeen University. Thus described, this was an authentic imperial Canadian life, with a touch of self-help romance: from Scotland to Canada, fame and fortune, and then a triumphant return to the land of his birth.[26]

Or consider, in a later generation, the life of William Maxwell Aitken, born in Ontario in 1879, the son of a Presbyterian minister who had himself emigrated to Canada from West Lothian. Aitken's first and greatest hero was Joseph Chamberlain, who championed the British Empire and Tariff Reform, and having spent much of his youth in the maritime province of New Brunswick, he looked to London more than he looked to New York or Toronto. He made a fortune in banking and business before he was forty, and having conquered Montreal, it was only natural that he should set his sights on the conquest of Britain. Within a decade of his arrival, Aitken was a Member of Parliament, a baronet, a peer, the owner of the Express newspapers, and the friend and confidant of that other son of the Canadian manse, Andrew Bonar Law. For fifty years, Beaverbrook lived in England, eventually achieving a certain kind of immortality as Churchill's Minister of Aircraft Production in 1940. Yet he never really liked or understood the British, by many of whom he was understandably distrusted as an unscrupulous adventurer and corrupt mischief maker, and he remained at heart an imperial Canadian all his life. Hence his 'Empire crusade' of the 1930s; hence his hatred of Lord Mountbatten, who had sent thousands of

Canadian troops to their deaths at Dieppe and who later 'gave away' the
Indian Empire; and hence his opposition to Britain's proposed entry into
the Common Market. Like most imperial Canadians, Beaverbrook loved
the British Empire more than the British did themselves.[27]

Any imperial system worthy of the name tends to draw the most ambitious
figures from the colonies to the metropolis, where they are incorporated
into the new imperial establishment; and, as these examples suggest, the
British Empire was no exception.[28] But this also worked the other way,
as the metropolitan aristocracy was exported to the colonial periphery.
From Lord Dufferin to the Duke of Devonshire, the Governor-Generalship
of Canada was the most glittering pro-consular position available in the
whole of the British Empire, with the exception of the Indian Viceroyalty.
Canada was the senior dominion and anyone representing the monarch
there was expected to be a peer, and although not all Governors General
were statesmanly figures of the first rank, they were on average of a higher
level of distinction than those sent out to Australia, New Zealand and
South Africa.[29] Moreover, the increasingly grand court over which they
presided was expected to embody those links which bound the dominion to
Britain, and to mimic the ordered, stable hierarchical world of the British
court. Much more than today, the Governor General was at the apex of
anglophile, imperial Canadian society, and invitations to his residence
at Rideau Hall in Ottawa were sought after to an extent we can now
scarcely imagine. Even more sought after were British titles and honours,
for which the Governor General was often importuned. Ambitious imperial
Canadians expected to receive the recognition provided by the bestowal of
imperial honours, and down to the inter-war years, many of them did.[30]

At an even higher social level than the British aristocracy was the
British monarchy which, from Confederation onwards, was central to the
existence of an imperial Canadian identity, marking the dominion off from
its rebellious, royalty-rejecting, equality-worshipping, civil-war fighting
neighbour to the south.[31] For reasons connected with its lesser geographical
distance, and its unchallenged status as the senior dominion in the Empire,
relations between imperial Canada and the British monarchy were closer
than they were between Australia, New Zealand or South Africa and the
imperial crown. It was the only dominion before the First World War to
which members of the royal family were sent as pro-consuls: one Governor
General, Lord Lorne, was Queen Victoria's son in law, another, the Duke
of Connaught, was her favourite son.[32] A further indication of the close

link was that Canada was the first dominion to receive a royal visit from Britain, by the Prince of Wales (the future King Edward VII), in 1860, and the subsequent tour by the Duke and Duchess of York (the future King George V and Queen Mary) in 1901 was also a major event.[33] Nor was the appeal of the imperial monarchy in Canada confined to Britons transplanted overseas to Toronto or Ottawa or Halifax or Winnipeg or Vancouver. The French in Quebec, who were descendants of pre-1789 immigrants, respected the crown as a symbol of the pre-revolutionary, ancient regime society with which they still identified, and they were flattered that successive Governors General paid so much attention to 'their' city of Quebec; while the native peoples saw in the sovereign a bulwark against encroachment, since their chiefs claimed direct relations with the imperial monarch, whom they looked upon as their protector.[34]

This world, of international finance capital, of ennobled plutocracy, of pro-consular aristocracy, and of imperial monarchy, may seem a long way from the lives and imaginings of ordinary men and women in Canada between 1867 and 1917. But the British connection pervaded Canadian life at all levels. In conformity with the British North America Act, most Canadians thought of themselves as Britons, who just happened to be living in British North America. There were too many Scots for them to be English: rather, it was their shared sense of Britishness which held them together and linked them to the land of their birth or of their forbears. As Jan Morris has noted: in 1897, 'there was no exact dividing line between a Canadian Briton and a British Briton.... They carried the same passports, and usually honoured the same ideals.'[35] Nor was this all they kept in common. For as the Rev. Canon Norman Tucker observed, the association between Canada and the Empire enabled Canadians 'to share in the traditions of the motherland; to say that Shakespeare is our poet, and that the great men of England are our brethren, and that the great deeds of England, the battles of Trafalgar and Waterloo, were our battles'. The fact that there were no Canadian heroes hardly mattered: British heroes were in plentiful supply and easily available. If there was a Stratford in England, then why should Canada not have one, too?[36]

These pieces of evidence not only help us understand why post-Confederation Canada had no indigenous myths, heroes or culture: they also remind us that most Canadians *did not need them*, because they maintained a sense of identity, but it was of belonging somewhere else, of living their imaginative lives in another place. And, with a few continentalist exceptions such as Goldwin Smith, that place was Britain. For the majority of Canadians at this time, nationalist sentiment and ethnic identity were not Canadian but British. Small wonder, then, that there was a Canadian state, but not a Canadian nation. How could there have been when, for most Canadians, separation from Britain was literally unthinkable?[37] Moreover, this imagined community did not imply Canadian subordination to Britain, and therein lay both its appeal and its utility. 'I am an imperialist', thundered Stephen Leacock in 1907, 'because I will not be a colonial.' The logic may seem odd today, even non-existent. But for contemporary Canadians, imperialism was not the denial of their political independence: it was something better, something bigger, enabling them to participate in the largest global community the world had ever seen. This was a captivating prospect: as long as Britain remained the greatest power and pre-eminent empire in the world, most Canadians wanted to belong to it, and to be in on the act, for both sentiment and reason urged that they should.[38]

All this emerges clearly in the events of 1914–17. Canada took up arms because it was part of the British Empire, and because Britain declared war on the Empire's behalf. This was, it bears spelling out, to fight battles half a world away from Ottawa, against the Kaiser's Germany and Franz Josef's Austria-Hungary. Yet no part of the Empire, proportionately, made so great a contribution as did Canada, in terms of the number of men who joined up, and in terms of the number of men who were killed. Of all the war years, the grimmest and greatest for Canada was 1917, the fiftieth anniversary of Confederation, which coincided with the Battle of Vimy Ridge and the passing of the Military Service Act. It also saw the advent to power of Sir Robert Borden's Unionist Government, and his active participation in the policy making of the Imperial War Cabinet. Here was the apogee of imperial Canada and the British connection: 'a national consensus based on the ideal of national service and a homogeneous British-Canadian nationalism'. Lloyd George should not have been surprised to learn that Borden had a remarkable knowledge of British cathedrals.[39]

IV

This may have been the high point of imperial Canada, but as both a sentimental and a substantive construct, it still had almost another half-century to run. To be sure, American investment came to supersede British investment there during the inter-war years; but since most Canadians much preferred the British connection to the American, this went some way to reinforcing imperial Canada even as in other ways it was undermined.[40] This was also the era of William Lyon Mackenzie King, who was regarded in many quarters as anti-British and pro-American, and who was responsible for asserting dominion sovereignty. Yet recent work on King suggests that this is an excessively simplistic picture: for King was also recognizably, proudly and unrepentantly an imperial Canadian. He sought 'to draw England and Canada closer together'. His heroes were British Liberals: Gladstone, Grey and Asquith. In his home, pride of place went to the two seats which he had brought back from Westminster Abbey after the coronation of 1937. 'I was prepared', he once observed, 'to lay down my life at their feet [he meant King George VI and Queen Elizabeth] in helping to further great causes which they had at heart.' And for all his supposed anti-Britishness, he did bring the country into the Second World War on Britain's side with the minimum of domestic discord or dissent.[41]

As the case of Mackenzie King implies, the British and imperial monarchy remained central to this continued sense of British and imperial Canadian identity. For much of the First World War, the Duke of Connaught served as Governor General. Soon after, the Prince of Wales, later King Edward VIII, paid the first of his sensational imperial tours to the senior dominion. So captivated was he by it that he even bought property there, and he made several subsequent trips. By the same token, prim Scots Presbyterian sentiment was outraged at his affair with Mrs Simpson: this was not how the King, who was also a 'Canadian farmer', should behave. Two years later, the state visit of King George VI and Queen Elizabeth was the most sensational event in the history of the dominion.[42] Today, when royal tours have become commonplace, it is hard to realize what an extraordinary episode this was. But as the first expedition ever by a reigning British monarch to one of the four great dominions, it brought imperial Canada alive as never before. And in 1940, on the death of John Buchan, Lord Tweedsmuir, another royal proconsul was appointed: the Earl of Athlone, who was the brother of Queen Mary and had previously been Governor General of South Africa. Even Mackenzie King was ecstatic. Appropriately enough, the connection between the British monarchy and the senior dominion remained closer than it was with any other part of the British Empire.[43]

Notwithstanding the Chanak incident and the passing of the Statute of Westminster, most Canadians in the 1920s and 1930s still thought of themselves as British, and still thought of Britain as their home – which for more than half of them it was or once had been. Culture and education were still largely British. When the young Alistair Buchan accompanied his father to Canada in 1935 on John Buchan's appointment as Governor General, he was amazed to discover just how British the country still was. 'If', he later recalled, 'you asked anyone in Toronto or Vancouver about his nationality, he was as likely to say "British" as "Canadian".'[44] The national anthem was still 'God Save the King', and the national flag still had the Union Jack on it. When Lord Tweedsmuir had the temerity to suggest that Canada should develop a greater sense of national identity, and that a Canadian's first loyalty was to Canada (not Britain), he was roundly condemned in certain sections of the Ontario press. For most people, imperial Canada remained their imagined community, and Britain and its Empire their spiritual and sentimental home. The British connection was still essential to most Canadians' sense of themselves, and they wanted to keep their country 'dominated by British ideals, with British institutions, and predominantly British in population'.[45]

Nor did the Second World War bring imperial Canada to an end as completely and as immediately as is sometimes supposed. Consider the career of Vincent Massey: born in 1887, Golden Jubilee year, he was the scion of one of Ontario's richest industrial dynasties, who married the daughter of Sir George Parkin, the secretary and first administrator of the Rhodes Scholarships. Like many imperial Canadians, Massey was educated at Balliol College, Oxford, the Valhalla of the British Empire. While there, he acquired an attachment to upper-class British life and to British traditions which never left him, and he came to regard Britain as his real home. And so it proved to be. From 1935 to 1946, Massey was Canadian High Commissioner in London, and for much of this time he was also Chairman of the Trustees of the National Gallery. From 1952 to 1959, he was Governor General of Canada – the first who was Canadian born, but his vice-regal style yielded nothing to his British patrician forebears. In 1961, he delivered the Romanes Lecture in Oxford, on the subject of Canadians and their Commonwealth, a deft synthesis of 'colony to nation' history, close ties to Britain, the importance of the Commonwealth, and all joined together by a benevolent and revered monarchy. Not for nothing did Claude Bissell call the second volume of his biography of Massey *The Imperial Canadian*.[46]

Even a generation later, this tradition and these attitudes still survived, most notably in the life and work of Robertson Davies. He was born in 1913, of Scots and Welsh (but not English) ancestry. Like Massey, Davies was educated at Balliol College, Oxford, and thanks to his patronage, Davies eventually became the first Master of the newly-established Massey College at the University of Toronto. Much of his writing, especially in the Salterton trilogy and *World of Wonders*, was concerned to explore the ways in which inter-war Canadians were exiles in matters of the spirit, and still lived their imaginative lives across the Atlantic.[47] And his last works may be read as both a celebration of, and a requiem for, the still-close British connections of his youth, as in these closing words of *The Cunning Man*:

> To have watched my city [Toronto] change from a colonial outpost of a great Empire to a great city in what looks decidedly like a new empire; to have watched the British connection wither as the Brits grew weary under Imperial greatness, and the American connection grow under the iron hand beneath the buckskin glove – that was to have taken part in a great movement of history. And to have watched the paling of a Checkovian colonial social order, as new values and new heroes supplanted old manners and outworn ideals of heroism.

There, perhaps for the last time, is the authentic voice of imperial Canada.[48]

V

Today, there are many Canadians who dismiss Vincent Massey and Robertson Davies as old-fashioned, irrelevant, anachronistic, Tory elitists – which is but another way of noting that since their time, much in Canada (and in Britain) has changed.[49] The last vestiges of imperial Canada have gone: the British flag, the British national anthem, the appeal to the British privy council in London, the British-located constitution and legislative supremacy. As Britain has declined as a great imperial power, the old connections – and the opportunities which those connections gave – count for much less than they did.[50] The remaining attraction of the monarchy today is not so much that it is a way of continuing to be British or imperial, but rather that it is a symbol of Canada's continued determination not to succumb to being or becoming American.[51] In Canada itself, regionalism is rife and rampant in the Maritimes and the west. The Quebec Party and its demands for independence are a seemingly intractable problem.[52]

The massive, non-British immigration since the Second World War means Canada is now a multi-ethnic and multi-cultural nation, and the decline in the traditional British connection was as much evidenced by the arrival of garlic and curry in Canadian restaurants as by the flying of the maple-leaf flag. And this new world has not only banished imperial Canada from the mainstream of public life and personal sentiment: it has also brought into being the new history in which, like the old history, but for different reasons, imperial Canada does not figure as much as it should.

So, while there is a need to be more sensitive than the old 'colony to nation' historians were to the limitations of Canadian nationhood, there is also a need to give more attention than the new historians tend to do to the imagined community of 'imperial Canada' and to the far from imagined people, things, institutions and connections which underlay it – not just down to 1917, but for a considerable time beyond. 'What makes you feel Canadian?', Robert MacNeil heard one of his fellow countrymen asking another recently. 'It's the Britishness', came the answer. 'It's that wonderful little Britishness at the heart of everything.'[53] Today, this is very much a minority view. Imperial Canada has faded away, leaving behind French Canada, which is arguably a nation but not a state, and the rest of Canada, which is arguably a state but not a nation. Imperial Canada, by contrast, was never a state: it was a state of mind, and a state of being, and a state of identity. And it is because these states of mind, of being and of identity were once so powerful and pervasive, but have only relatively recently receded so completely into the distance, that historians of Canada should be more concerned with recovering and retrieving them; indeed, there have recently been most encouraging indications that that is precisely what they are now beginning to do.[54]

This is an important and welcome development in the evolving history of Canada; but it is also an important and welcome development in the evolving history of Britain: for just as Britain was a major theme in imperial Canada's past, so imperial Canada was a major theme in Britain's past. To be sure, it was not a theme which played out on the same scale in both countries: Britain was the one great imperial presence in Canada, whereas Canada was one of many imperial presences in Britain.[55] But despite this undeniable asymmetry, Canada was an important presence, nonetheless, and with the exception of India, it was the most important imperial presence in London, as exemplified by the prime position of Canada House on the west side of Trafalgar Square. Opened by King George V and Queen Mary in 1925, it was next door to the National Gallery, opposite the Army and Navy Club, and near to the offices of Sun Life, Canadian Pacific and the Canadian National Railway, in the very heart of imperial London. Yet the significant part played by successive Canadian High Commissioners in the political, economic, social and cultural life of London and the nation beyond, as well as in mediating the evolving imperial relations between the mother country and the senior dominion, has only recently begun to receive the recognition it deserves.[56] And the support given by Canada to Britain when it stood 'alone' during the Second World War in the long, anxious months before Pearl Harbor, in terms of men, materials and money, is also a theme of major historical significance.[57]

Not surprisingly, then, British political figures generally regarded Canada as being more important and more friendly than the United States for most of the half century from the 1880s to the Second World War, and some of them believed that Canada was of comparable importance in imperial terms to India itself – perhaps, indeed, more so. Joseph Chamberlain, who was certainly of this view, insisted that it was Canada that was the 'flagship' of the Empire; Andrew Bonar Law was Canadian by birth, and was brought up in a remote manse in rural New Brunswick; Stanley Baldwin was a regular visitor, from the time he went as a young man seeking orders for his family iron company until he lectured there as an elder statesman after he had retired as prime minister; Ramsay MacDonald valued his Canadian contacts, and his son Malcolm would be British High Commissioner in Ottawa during the Second World War; Neville Chamberlain shared his father's views, toured Canada extensively in 1922, and was a major figure at the imperial economic negotiations held at Ottawa ten years later; and Winston Churchill visited 'the great dominion' more frequently than any other part of the British Empire, regarding it as 'the master-link in Anglo-American unity'. Canada, he assured his audience in the radio broadcast with which he concluded his final visit as Prime Minister in June 1954, occupied 'the place of honour' in 'British hearts'.[58]

VI

It may indeed be true, as recent revisionist scholars have suggested, that even at the heady high noon of Queen Victoria's Diamond Jubilee and the Relief of Mafeking, the British Empire had a lower profile in Britain itself than it did overseas, both as a global construct and in terms of specific colonies or dominions or territories.[59] And such views lend support to those historians of Canada who wish to down-play the importance of the British imperial connection in their own country, too. Yet for good or ill, indeed, for good *and* ill, the influence of Britain on Canada's development was deep and significant; and the importance of imperial Canadians in London, from Confederation to the Second World War and beyond is only now being fully appreciated; while the part played by Canada in the imagination of Britons, both prime ministerial and others, still awaits its historian. When all this work has been done, we shall not only know more about the British element in the history of imperial Canada, but we shall also know more about the Canadian element in the history of imperial Britain.[60] And as if that will not be gain enough, we might also then be able to understand how and why it was that the Toronto newspaper proprietor, Conrad Black, determined to follow his press-lord compatriots and predecessors, Lords Beaverbrook and Thompson of Fleet, and obtained a seat in Britain's upper house. Apparently Baron Black of Crossharbour is a great believer in what is termed the 'Anglosphere': but that is a far cry from the earlier, and largely vanished, world of imperial Canada and of imperial Britain.

9

Empire:
Some Anglo-American Ironies and Challenges[1]

Paradoxical though it may appear at first sight, empire is a pervasive phenomenon and a very big thing when it happens, yet as an area of historical study, or of contemporary political concern, it is usually approached parochially and understood narrowly. It is a pervasive phenomenon because from the ancient Egyptians, the Assyrians and the Romans, via the Arabs, the Holy Romans, the Ottomans and the Incas, to the Spanish, the Portuguese, the Dutch and the British, and now in our own time to the Russian, the Chinese and the American empires, there has been (and still is) a great deal of it about. By definition, empires tend to be large, and there are usually several of them in being at any given moment. Indeed, according to *The Times Atlas of World History*, there have been at least seventy of them, they have existed in virtually every century and continent of human history, and they have often encompassed the majority of the world's population.[2] Yet at the same time, the study of empire is almost invariably (perhaps unavoidably?) restricted and confined, normally written from the standpoint of one example, but rarely making comparisons between empires at any given time, or exploring common themes which characterize them across cultures and civilizations.[3]

The approach adopted in this chapter will, alas, exemplify exactly such a limited and circumscribed perspective, since what follows will be confined to considering the relatively recent history of the British Empire, while making some connections with and comparisons to the American empire during the same period; and it will also be concerned with the different attitudes taken to the history of the British Empire by scholars working in the United Kingdom and (increasingly) by those based in universities across the Atlantic in the United States. But while it is undoubtedly confined in the viewpoints it offers, this chapter is scarcely addressing a small subject. It begins by offering some general observations about the evolving ways in which the history of the British Empire has been approached, especially by American scholars who in recent years have come to constitute such a significant force in the field. Next, it considers how Americans understand, or do not understand, their own imperial history and continuing imperial presence in the contemporary world. Then it explores some additional American conventional wisdoms, which also carry implications for the ways in which empire is studied in the United States – and also not studied. And finally, it offers some suggestions as to how, in the light of these reflections, the history of the British Empire might be made even more complex – but also more convincing – than it already is.

I

In Britain itself, it was only during the half century after the ending of the Second World War that the history of the British Empire became an obituary for a national and international enterprise that was gradually (or in some cases, abruptly) coming to an end. Before then, and as exemplified in the multi-volume *Cambridge History of the British Empire*, which had been begun in the late 1920s, it had been assumed that some form of dominion over palm and pine would endure as far into the future as it was possible to foresee.[4] Even into the 1950s, there was some attempt to disguise this 'decline and fall' of Empire by celebrating its transmogrification into a voluntary, post-imperial association called 'the Commonwealth', which was presented, rather imaginatively, as the point to which both the history and the evolution of the British Empire had always been tending from the very beginning. But even though this gave a certain whiggish tinge and upbeat conclusion to some of the writing that was then being carried on, the main impetus to the *expansion* of British imperial history was the simultaneous *contraction* of the British Empire itself, beginning with the independence of India in 1947, and ending with the handover of Hong Kong to China just fifty years later.[5] The result was an approach to Britain's immediate imperial past which stressed the economic, social, military and religious imperatives towards overseas expansion, and which explored the Empire's constitutional evolution towards 'responsible government' in some cases, and towards 'independence' in others.

Many of the historians who wrote about the British Empire had themselves spent time living in it, defending it and, occasionally, administering it, during the Second World War and its immediate aftermath. As writers and university teachers, they tended to inhabit separate intellectual worlds from historians of mainland Britain, and their notion of what was then called the 'imperial metropolis' was very undifferentiated and uninflected: economically, socially, politically, religiously, ethnically and geographically. Empire, as they wrote about it, was understood and explained as an emanation of impulses from the British metropolis, perhaps directed by 'the official mind', or undertaken by 'gentlemanly capitalists'.[6] But these historians were much more interested in the overseas impact and dynamic of those imperial emanations than in their metropolitan structures or formations and also, as time passed, in the limitations and constraints on those impulses and projections in distant places. Significantly, this lack of interest by historians of Empire in Britain was paralleled by a lack of interest by historians of Britain in Empire. Indeed, during the boom years of the 1960s, when history flourished in universities as never before, only two scholars working on modern Britain sought to link these subjects together: Asa Briggs, in his marvellously suggestive chapter on Melbourne, Australia, as a 'Victorian community overseas', in his *Victorian Cities*; and Eric Hobsbawm, who addressed the interconnections of the subject head on in two books revealingly entitled *Industry and Empire* and *The Age of Empires*.[7]

But many of the foremost historians of that remarkable post-war generation were wholly uninterested in the British Empire, or, indeed, in Britain itself as distinct from England. This could be said of scholars with such varied interests and outlooks as Geoffrey Elton, Christopher Hill, Lawrence Stone, E.P. Thompson, J.H. Plumb and A.J.P. Taylor. To be sure, there was an unprecedented concern for dealing with 'English' history in such a way as to appeal to a broad (and especially American and Third World) audience, but this was not done by writing about Britain as the global nation it had been during the long heyday of its empire. Instead, these historians claimed that *particular* instalments of the English national past were of *universal* historical relevance and significant contemporary resonance: among them the political revolution of the mid seventeenth century, the political stability of the early eighteenth century, and the Industrial Revolution of the late eighteenth and early nineteenth centuries.

Taken together, so the argument ran, these episodes and events signalled the beginning of the modern world, they helped to explain the present, and they offered guidance for the future. Thus packaged and projected, English history needed to be studied, not only in Leeds and Liverpool, but in New York and Washington, and in Cairo and Calcutta, and not only for what it implied about many other pasts in addition to its own, but also for what it implied about how the contemporary world might develop and evolve in the years ahead.[8]

By the 1990s, these powerful and resonant interpretational paradigms, which flourished in universities on both sides of the Atlantic, had been largely broken down, their particular significance in England's national past had been undermined by a generation of ferociously 'revisionist' scholarship, and their global relevance had also been largely discredited as the liberal, optimistic sixties *zeitgeist* was superseded by the conservative reaction of the 1980s. Moreover, in the aftermath of the debates on devolution, the demand for representative institutions for Scotland and Wales, and what were euphemistically termed the 'troubles' in Northern Ireland, 'English' history had been superseded by something that was more broadly and more self-consciously 'British' history.[9] This adjustment represented both a conceptual advance and territorial broadening; but it was not enough by itself to guarantee the continued appeal of the subject outside Britain. To retain some wider interest, and to continue to compete successfully for funding and positions in university history departments in the late twentieth and early twenty-first centuries, its north American practitioners, who included substantial numbers of Britons eager to teach and project and enlarge their country's history overseas, felt a pressing need to find a new way to universalize it. Accordingly, they re-invented British history: not as the specific national repository of world-historical happenings with contemporary policy relevance, but rather as the history of one nation's encounter with the cultures and continents of the wider world through its centuries-long and globally-extended imperial activities.[10]

This change in approach and expansion of horizons was vividly signalled by two historians. The first was J.G.A. Pocock, whose call for a new and more imaginative version of British history, during the late 1970s and the early 1980s, and which would encompass the whole of the British Isles, has already been discussed. But as befitted someone of his New Zealand origins and antipodean anxieties, Pocock was also concerned with that greater Britain overseas, and he additionally urged that its maritime empire, expanding and contracting across six centuries, needed to be brought to the centre of what was otherwise a rather parochial national narrative. Thus understood, British history was not only archipelagic (the British Isles), but transoceanic (the British Empire) as well.[11] The second historian in question was Peter Stansky, who chaired a committee for the North American Conference on British Studies, which produced a report in 1999 on the future of British history in US universities. Its conclusion, echoing and extending Pocock, was that the best way to ensure the continued survival and resonance of that field was for British *insular* history to re-brand, re-invent and re-position itself as British *imperial* history.[12] It cannot be coincidence that in the aftermath of Pocock and Stansky, most new posts in modern 'British' history that have recently been advertised in American university history departments have insisted on an imperial component – sometimes seemingly to the exclusion of anything else. The result is that in many universities in north America, the history of the British Empire is now being taught more, and taught more enthusiastically, than the history of the British nation; and practitioners of this new, expanded, world-encompassing form of British history are confident that this change is also a significant improvement.[13]

This shift in interest on the part of British historians – away from univer-salizing episodes in the national past, and towards the globalized history of the nation as the cynosure of a world empire – had already been signalled more substantively by a symposium that took place under the auspices of Lawrence Stone, which was held at Princeton University in the autumn of 1990. Sensing, as he so often did, the beginnings of a new scholarly trend, Stone had begun to broaden his own horizons beyond the confines of England to encompass British history overseas, and he duly edited the book of the conference, significantly entitled *An Imperial State at War*.[14] To be sure, some of the contributors, such as C.A. Bayly, had been lifelong historians of particular parts of the Empire; but the book also marked the beginning of a new phase of interest by historians of modern mainland Britain in the bigger and broader history of the British Empire beyond. The most emphatic sign of this has been the glut of books that have recently emerged from scholars who have been transferring and extending their interests from what used to be called the imperial metropolis to the imperial periphery: among them Jeremy Black, Linda Colley, Niall Ferguson, Catherine Hall and Kathleen Wilson. Their historical approaches and their individual politics varied; but all of them were moving from a national and a European perspective on the past to an imperial and global one.[15]

In turn, these works connected – and sometimes collided – with two other modes of writing on the British Empire, the one by now seemingly 'traditional', the other more recent and 'innovative'. The first mode has been that of British 'imperial' historians who have continued to work on their subject, largely detached from the evolving history of England/Britain, and whose many and varied labours have recently been codified, consolidated and collected in the multi-volume *Oxford History of the British Empire*. The result is an extraordinary entrepreneurial and editorial achievement, which has been widely and rightly recognized as such. (Significantly, the enterprise had been initiated and overseen from America rather than Britain, a sign and a portent of the growing engagement of United States scholars with the history of the British Empire.) But the books were also criticized from a variety of perspectives: for their continued concentration on military or constitutional or economic or political history; for their lack of interest in the history of imperial, mainland Britain; for their unwillingness to give sufficient attention to such matters as language, ethnicity and gender; and for evidencing a certain hostility to more recent academic developments which portended a further rethinking of how to undertake the history of empire.[16]

These latter criticisms came from a new but growing group of scholars who form the second constituency with whose work the recent books of Professors Black, Colley, Ferguson, Hall and Wilson converge and connect, though to varying degrees and in different ways. Some in this second constituency are 'post-colonialist' writers, while others are cultural historians or critics; many drew their inspiration from the writings of Edward Said or Michel Foucault or E.P. Thompson; and they often work in university departments devoted to language and comparative literature, to the history of art, to cultural studies or to the history of gender, rather than in what might be called 'conventional' history departments.[17] They are especially concerned to explore issues of gender and race and identity; to recover the voices and lives of those peoples and groups who rarely appeared in the official records of empire (hence the burgeoning field of 'subaltern studies'); and to investigate the structures of knowledge and representations of empire which played so central a part in the creation of what they regard as the crucial experiences of imperial dominance and imperial subservience.[18]

The consequence of these developments is that more scholars are now working on the history of the British Empire than ever before, and they are undoubtedly approaching it from a wider variety of perspectives. It is too soon to know whether this will result in the successful prolongation in north America of the study of British history by other means, not least because many of those who approach the British imperial past, whether from a traditional or a post-colonial perspective often, though not invariably, show limited interest in the British colonial metropolis – or, indeed, in Britain's relations with Europe.[19] But it is additionally important to notice that a majority of those historians of Britain who have extended their interest to encompass the British Empire, and of those who form the burgeoning ranks of post-colonialist scholars and cultural historians of empire, are to be found working in the United States of America. This is both a marked and also a relatively recent development. What are the implications of this for the present and future study of the history of the British Empire – and, at least by implication, for the study of empires more broadly?

II

It is always something of a challenge for British historians of the British Empire to write about how its history is being approached – and should and should not be approached – in the United States. This is partly because one of the major narratives of the global twentieth century has been the supercession of the United Kingdom by the United States as the greatest power in the world – a supercession simultaneously predicted, lamented and encouraged by Rudyard Kipling at the end of the nineteenth century. In 'Recessional', he warned that the British Empire would not last for ever, and in 'The White Man's Burden', he urged Uncle Sam to assume the imperial task which a faltering John Bull would not be able to sustain indefinitely.[20] Two global conflicts, and the downfall and dismantling of all the great European empires in their aftermath, have wrought just the very changes that Kipling had predicted, and the United States has been both a participant and a beneficiary in these developments. At the end of the First World War, President Woodrow Wilson was determined to assist in the break-up of the great land-based empires of Europe (Russia, Austria-Hungary and Germany), and during the course of the Second World War,

President Franklin D. Roosevelt was equally determined to do all he could to speed up the ending of the British (and also the French) Empire.[21]

This in turn means that there are those in Britain, and they are to be found on the left and the right of both the political and the scholarly spectrum, who both regret and resent the fact that America climbed to twentieth-century global greatness on the ruins of the British Empire – a ruination which many in Britain insist the United States deliberately sought to accelerate and bring about.[22] Indeed, the fact that the history of the British Empire may now be more studied and taught and researched in the United States than it is in the United Kingdom is taken as one more sign of the extent to which America has superseded Britain, not only as the global, but also as the academic hegemon. As a result, the United States sustains many more universities than the United Kingdom, and the richest of them are substantially better resourced on the American side of the Atlantic than on the British, which in turn means that virtually *any* historical subject flourishes more in the United States than in the United Kingdom.[23] But in addition, the history of the British Empire now seems so vexed, controversial and guilt-ridden in the former imperial metropolis that it is rarely taught in high schools, and is widely regarded as something that is best avoided. This helps explain (but does not excuse) why the British government unconscionably refuses to help fund the British Empire and Commonwealth Museum, despite the fact that it is widely supported by many non-white Britons and Commonwealth citizens.[24]

The result of these developments is that the study of the British imperial past is becoming increasingly Americanized, and while in many ways this is both an exciting and beneficial development, its implications and consequences need to be thought about carefully and deliberately. One reason why they need to be thus pondered is that empire in America, and especially the *British* Empire in America, is an even more problematic subject than it is in Britain. Throughout most of its own history, and in many quarters today, America proudly sees itself as the prototypical and quintessential anti-colonial nation. The United States was, after all, the first country which regarded itself as having been 'conceived in liberty' and thus in opposition to the reactionary colonial powers of 'old Europe', especially Britain. Since independence, hostility to empire has remained a constant theme in American political life and popular discourse, whether in the form of determined isolationism and the avoidance of any form of foreign entanglement, or in the form of occasional engagement with the world beyond which is habitually presented as the export of freedom rather than as the imposition of dominion. As Colin Powell recently put it, 'The United States does not seek a territorial empire. We have never been imperialists. We seek a world in which liberty, prosperity and peace can become the heritage of all peoples, and not just the exclusive privilege of a few.'[25] From this perspective, other, lesser nations may 'do' empire, but the United States, true to its founding beliefs, which were essentially revolutionary and essentially libertarian, never does.

Yet this widely-shared and self-congratulatory assumption is in many ways utter delusion: for the United States has been an empire throughout its history and, rather unusually, it has been (and still is) an imperium in two senses, being both an overland and an overseas dominion.[26] During the first hundred years or so of America's existence, the original thirteen colonies, initially huddled on the eastern Atlantic seaboard, expanded into a transcontinental, territorial empire, extending from one shining sea to another – and they did so by buying up or gobbling up large masses of land from Louisiana to Texas to Alaska, and by exterminating most of the native inhabitants, and much of the wildlife in the process, in ways that would later be replicated by other emigrant Britons in Canada, Australia, New Zealand and South Africa.[27] By the 1880s, when Sir John Seeley wrote his book on *The Expansion of England*, he warned the British that the future lay with the great land-based empires, and not with the maritime empires, for which he (rightly) predicted a much less assured life-span, and the three great land-based empires with which he was concerned were Germany, Russia – and the United States. (He did not mention China.) Seeley was, of course, quite right in his analysis and prediction. The United States is many things: but one of the things it is emphatically, but is rarely admitted by its rulers and citizens to be, is a massive, land-based, imperial agglomeration, with an appropriately (and increasingly) multi-ethnic population.[28]

As well as being a territorial behemoth, the United States is also an overseas empire: in the formal sense, its transoceanic dominion was initially based on naval might, but has subsequently been sustained by the unrivalled strength of its air force; and in the informal sense, American resources and American culture seem to have swept the globe. There are many indications of this urge to overseas dominance: the authorship by the American Admiral A.T. Mahan of a book entitled *The Influence of Sea Power Upon History, 1660–1783* (Boston, 1890); the desire (not always fulfilled) to acquire or control territory, from the Philippines and Puerto Rico, or to 'liberate' peoples from Vietnam and Iraq; the massive projection of weaponry and force and fire power overseas, involving military bases in many nations, and fleets of hyper-sized aircraft carriers; the global extension of American enterprise, from McDonald's to Starbucks, Coca-Cola to Microsoft, to the distant corners of the earth; the international dominance of American culture via film and television and computer games and IT; and a whole series of informal means of exerting influence (not always successfully), among them the United Nations, NATO, the International Monetary Fund and the World Bank.[29] By these means, Kipling's injunction has indeed come to pass, which means that the United States is both a great land-based imperial power, and also a great transoceanic imperial power, which has not only superseded the British Empire, but also seems to be in the process of taking over that empire's history as well.

To anyone familiar with the conventional wisdoms that flourished and thrived in the nineteenth-century heyday of British greatness, the similarities between that empire then and the American empire now, while not total, are nevertheless both striking and suggestive.[30] Then, as now, there was an underpinning of unrivalled global economic superiority allied to the latest and most sophisticated weaponry available. Then, as now, there was the belief in the importance, and sometimes the necessity, of unilateral behaviour: Lord Palmerston sending a gunboat, George W. Bush sending a stealth bomber. Then, as now, there was a belief in the unique merits of laissez-faire economics and constitutional democracy, which should be exported overseas so that other places and peoples might be similarly enlightened, not by the imposition of empire but by the gift of freedom. Above all, both nineteenth-century Britain and twenty-first-century America believed that they were unique and *exceptional* nations, providentially blessed by a discerning God who spoke their language, and inspired by the zealous faith of Protestant Christianity, which meant they were not, and are not, as other (and lesser) nations were, or are.

Consider, by way of illustration, these observations of Ronald Robinson and John Gallagher, in their celebrated and pioneering study of nineteenth-century expansion, *Africa and the Victorians*, in which they tried to summarize the values and beliefs that impelled the British towards empire at that time:

> The Victorians regarded themselves as the leaders of civilization, as pioneers of industry and progress.... They were sure that their ability to improve the human condition everywhere was as tremendous as their capacity to produce wealth....

Their secret seemed to lie in releasing private enterprise from the dead hand of the state. Social energy appeared to flow from the happy play of free minds, free markets and Christian morality.... The... mid-Victorian outlook on the world... was suffused with a vivid sense of superiority and self-righteousness, if with every good intention.... All over the world, the Canningites and Palmerstonians exerted their strength to bring about conditions favouring commercial advance and liberal awakening.[31]

If modern Americans are substituted for mid-Victorian Britons, and the names of Presidents John F. Kennedy and George W. Bush replace those of George Canning and Lord Palmerston, the parallels are arresting, indeed unnerving.

These are suggestive and stimulating comparisons, and it may be easier for Britons to draw them than for Americans to do so, because their nation has already been through the whole process of making, running and losing their own empire, which means they can usually recognize another empire when they see one. (In some cases, too, Britons enjoy a certain amount of *schadenfreude* when, as in Iraq, America turns out to be no more successful an imperial power than Britain did.)[32] Beyond any doubt, many of the exceptional claims which America makes about and for itself seem almost comfortingly familiar to historically-minded Britons, especially the implausible insistence that America is not an imperial nation. Although American presidents behave as imperialists, they never admit to *being* imperialists, and while American history is taught in high schools and universities across the land, it is scarcely ever taught as American *imperial* history. In both public and academic life, the shared presumption is that empire happens elsewhere, but not in the United States itself, and certainly not where America has outposts and bases overseas.[33] Empire is what other nations 'do' or 'have done', or what happens to other people on the receiving end of it. And the conclusion is clear and inescapable (and circular and wrong): empire, which others do, is 'bad'; but because America doesn't do empire, it is somehow 'good'; and because it is 'good', it cannot admit to being imperial.

III

But empire is not the only subject about which large swathes of American public and academic life are (depending on your point of view) in denial or which they simply take for granted. There are other matters which are insufficiently discussed in the political, the public and parts of the academic realm, and these absences become particularly significant when American scholars approach the history of the British Empire. Take, for example, the history of wealth. During the late nineteenth and early twentieth centuries, the American economy suddenly became the strongest and most thriving in the world – initially on the basis of coal, iron, steel and railroads, subsequently on the basis of chemicals, electronics, oil and the motor car – and one hundred years later, and notwithstanding the present and future challenges presented from India and China, the United States remains the most successful wealth-generating nation the globe has ever seen.[34] One does not have to be an economic determinist to recognize that this may also help explain America's overwhelming military, political, imperial and cultural impact on the rest of the world in recent times. Yet despite its undeniable importance and massive enabling significance, the history of the American economy, and by extension the study of the economic pasts of other nations (and other empires), receive scant attention in the history departments of universities in the United States.

This inattention to the subject of wealth in certain parts of American academic life which ought to know better, and also in certain parts of American public life (ditto), means in turn that the closely-connected subject of inequality also receives less consideration than it should. Despite the ringing hopes of the Declaration of Independence, the United States is economically a very (and increasingly) unequal nation: its rich are on average substantially richer than their equivalents in western Europe, and its poor are noticeably poorer and receive significantly less attention and support from the state. Yet on both the left and the right, inequality is less discussed than it ought to be: on the left because phrases such as 'the poor' or 'working class' are no longer deemed to be politically correct, which makes it virtually impossible to discuss the disadvantaged social groups these phrases (however imperfectly) once described; and on the right because the master narrative of American self-help and business success leaves no room in it for any losers, and because policy-makers eager to reduce the federal deficit are casting predatory eyes on both Medicare and Social Security, those welfare provisions of which many millions of people at the bottom of the economic scale are the prime beneficiaries.

The result is that Americans who incline to champion the adoption of a radical or progressive agenda (again, in government, in academe and beyond) tend to do so more in the realm of *race* than in the realm of *class*. Since the collapse of Lyndon Johnson's 'Great Society' programme, and with the advent of affirmative action under Richard Nixon, the impulse (where it has existed) to bring about a less inegalitarian American society has been much more concerned with eliminating the inequities which are deemed to be a consequence of colour rather than those which are derived from economic circumstance. The ambition to achieve what is called 'diversity' is a widely held and wholly admirable goal: in government, in business, in the professions and in academe. But these days, in the United States, diversity is much more often construed and conceived of in terms of broadening the *ethnic* mix than it is in terms of broadening the *economic* (and thus the social) mix. To cite but one example: Ivy League universities boast increasingly diverse student bodies in terms of their racial composition, but for all their many financial aid packages, they are much less successful in attracting students from poor backgrounds and deprived neighbourhoods.[35]

Americans do not think or talk much about inequality any more, and this in turn means that they do not think or talk about class, another subject about which they are in increasingly serious denial, especially serious *historical* denial.[36] To be sure, the United States does not possess a crowned head of state, or a structure of noble titles, or an hereditary aristocracy: features of 'old Europe' which were abolished in the name of equality when the founding fathers brought their great republic into being. And most Americans, when asked to state their social position, apparently reply that they are 'middle class', on the grounds that there is thus no upper class, and that it would be admission of failure to admit to belonging to the working class. But such perspectives and perceptions are clearly misleading. At the upper levels, hereditary and dynastic politics (as exemplified by the Rockefellers, the Kennedys, the Bushes, the Gores and the Clintons) are far more important in the United States today than in most western European countries, and it is also a much greater advantage (or necessity) in getting to the top in American politics to be rich than it is in, say, Britain or Germany. Moreover, there *is* a large working class in the United States: to be sure, it is no longer overwhelmingly unionized and working in traditional heavy industry, but it is still very much present in a large range of low-paid and low-esteemed manual and service occupations. Yet scarcely anyone, on either the left or the right of the political divide, now seems to want to talk or write about them.[37]

There are two further subjects whose central importance in American life and elsewhere is not appropriately reflected in some parts of its historical academy. The first of these is religion. To any western European observer, the significance of religion as a public issue and personal preoccupation is both extraordinary and pervasive, from its influence in the still-continuing debates on abortion and stem-cell research to the regular and ritual invocation 'God bless America' made by presidents and other political figures. This has serious, and contradictory, implications for American universities: they feel obliged to go to great lengths to articulate their institutional respect for the varied religious faiths professed by individual students and faculty; but they are also (and rightly) dedicated to the rational pursuit of truth, and as such they embody a deep professional scepticism towards religious faith and belief and superstition. One consequence of this unresolved contradiction is that the history of religion – be it the history of religion in the United States or anywhere else in the world – receives far less attention than its significance merits, and it is too often marginalized in theology departments and divinity schools. In fact, the history of religion ought to be taught and studied as an integral element of the American past and as an essential way of understanding the American present.[38]

The second presence-cum-absence is a declining interest in politics, and this has resulted in a declining interest in the history of the political past on the part of many academic historians in the United States. No one (except perhaps Gertrude Himmelfarb) would wish to turn the clock back to the pre-1945 world when, in America as in Europe, a training in history was deemed to be above all else a training in statesmanship and public life, and when history was often construed and taught and written in narrowly political (and elitist) terms.[39] But while each subsequent post-war wave of the 'new' history – economic, social, quantitative, feminist, cultural – has undoubtedly increased our understanding of the past and our appreciation of its multi-faceted complexities, these successively innovative approaches have also dethroned, diminished and ultimately marginalized the study and appreciation of political history. These days, the lives of American presidents are more likely to be written by professional biographers than by academic historians; history departments struggle (or else give up the fight) to offer basic narrative outlines of the American revolution, the civil war, the New Deal and the war in Vietnam; and courses on 'the American presidency' are more likely to be found in schools of government or political science than in history departments.[40]

What have these present-yet-absent subjects in American life and American academe got to do with the writing of the history of the British Empire as it is being carried on by increasing numbers of scholars in the United States today? The answer may seem to be not much, but is in fact a great deal. Negatively, these absences may help us understand why so many aspects of the British imperial past are not studied in the United States as extensively as they ought to be – among them the economic history of empire, the social history of empire, the religious history of empire and the political (and ideological) history of empire. And they may also help us understand why, more positively, so much of the history of the British Empire, as currently undertaken in the United States, is concerned with culture, which might negatively be described as what is left after these other subjects have, for varying reasons, been ignored or abandoned. Of course the cultural history of the British Empire needs doing, and is being done – and often in important, imaginative and exciting ways. But despite some of the more unselfconsciously imperialist assertions of its most impassioned champions, who insist it is the key to understanding every other form of history, culture is but one approach to the (British) imperial past – as to any other past, whether imperial or otherwise.[41] Empires by definition are big tent phenomena; and to get them in appropriate perspective, they need correspondingly big-tent histories and correspondingly big-tent historians.

IV

Today, it bears repeating, the history of the British Empire is being more vigorously undertaken in the United States than it is in the United Kingdom, and for now there seems every reason to suppose that it will continue to be more vigorously undertaken on the other side of the Atlantic rather than on this one. But as American scholars approach the British imperial past in increasing and unprecedented numbers, there is a case for urging them to be more self-aware about their own presuppositions, and about those of their own country – especially as regards its sense of providential exceptionalism, the historic hostility of the United States to the British Empire, and its no less historic (but also contemporary) denial about the existence (and, indeed, recent expansion) of its own empire.[42] At the same time, American historians of the British Empire (or, indeed, American historians of any other empire) might be more concerned than they generally are about the lack of interest evinced by cultural historians in such crucial subjects as wealth, inequality, class, religion, politics and ideology. Indeed, they might want to question the increasingly-widespread assumption that if the history of empire is written about as cultural history, there is no need to write about it in any of these other ways. The remaining section of this chapter explores these questions and develops these points in more detail.

To begin with, it is important to question the presumption, which certainly pervades much writing by American scholars on the British Empire, that the whole expansionist enterprise, from beginning to end, was intrinsically evil and irredeemably *bad*: for that is merely the latest iteration of a conventional, anti-imperial wisdom that is as old as the United States itself, and which therefore needs to be subjected to serious and sceptical historical analysis. Moreover, those Americans who espouse such hostile views of *Britain*'s empire might pause to consider how they reconcile them with the existence of *America*'s empire, both past and present. For as the record makes plain, Americans have no historical or moral grounds to justify their habitual condemnation of other nations as being imperialist. It ought also to be possible to recognize that while there was much about the British Empire (as there is about the American empire today) that strikes us as evil and abhorrent, it was far from being wholly devoid of virtue or decency.[43] The over-dichotomization of public and historical discourse is one of the banes of our time, and the history of empire has suffered disproportionately from it, as those who seek to argue that empire was not completely bad all too often find themselves pilloried for somehow 'defending' it.[44] Yet what the history of empire most urgently needs is not to be approached in the stark and adversarial alternatives of 'good or bad' or (literally) 'black or white', or 'colonizer or colonized', but with a greater recognition of nuance, complexity, ambiguity, paradox and contingency.

This point may be illustrated another way. Post-colonial scholars, and practitioners of cultural histories of empire often assume that there was a monolithic entity and enterprise called 'the imperial project', which originated in, and emanated from, the imperial metropolis, and which was not only purposeful, unified and coherent but also overwhelmingly powerful (as well as being unrelievedly evil). This image of the British Empire as unified and invincible had earlier been anticipated in those Mercator maps where so much of the world was coloured red in what appeared to be a striking display of imperial cohesiveness and of maritime power and military force.[45] Yet in many ways, this earlier representation was precisely that: it was only an image, and as such it was largely a cartographic illusion. For even at the level of its London-based government, the British Empire at its greatest extent was a bewildering amalgam of competing jurisdictions and authorities; while other interested parties in empire – the military, the church, business, banking – had their own agendas too; and so did the multifarious realms, colonies, dominions, protectorates, mandates, bases and condominiums, whose varied patterns of subservience to the 'mother country' were constantly being modified by such considerations as distance, personalities, nationalist politics and (in some cases at least) the evolution of representative institutions.

Moreover, while it was the case that for some of their history the British had got the Gatling gun, while other nations and peoples had not, the projection of imperial power over land was sometimes more challenging than expected, and the realization of the so-called 'imperial project' across the oceans was often exceptionally difficult.[46] Even at the height of the so-called 'Pax Britannica', there were certain parts of the world where the British were simply unable to prevail, as in Afghanistan, and other places where their rule was never more than tenuous, as in Egypt; and even when they did secure their imperial dominion, they had very limited resources, especially in terms of military and civilian manpower, to enforce it. Like other empires, both before and since, the British needed allies in their expansionary and proconsular endeavours, since they depended significantly on consent and collaboration. And what was true for the British as imperialists has been no less true of their transatlantic imperial successors. Since 1950, America's resources of wealth and manpower, and its ever-increasing military superiority, have far surpassed anything that Britain could boast in its imperial heyday. Yet even at the apogee of the 'Pax Americana', the ability of the United States to coerce Third World countries, from Vietnam to Iraq, has been far from convincing or complete.[47] In writing about empires, in the (American) present or the (British) past, these intrinsic constraints and ineradicable weaknesses should never be lost sight of.

In terms of the functioning and operation of the British Empire, the will to dominate was neither monolithic nor omnipotent, and it was invariably modified and constrained by the need to compromise and incorporate: co-option and conversation were often more successful than coercion or confrontation, and the only alternative to them. There may have been British strategies of imperial rulership, and a few men like Joseph Chamberlain, Lord Curzon, Lord Milner and Leopold Amery may for a time have believed in the British 'imperial project'. But these strategies and these beliefs were often so undermined by distance, weakness and circumstance that it is seriously distorting to express them in such assertive pro-consular (or post-colonial) terms. The nature of the societies over which the British aspired to rule, or found themselves obliged to rule, are thus of exceptional importance in understanding how the British Empire worked, and in demonstrating the real limits to its only notionally-hegemonic power.[48] Yet the structure of indigenous societies, the functioning of their economies, and the material circumstances of native people's lives tend to receive less attention from imperial historians than they ought to; and the interconnections between the social structures (and social perceptions) of the imperial metropolis and its far-flung dominions has received scarcely any attention at all. The study of gender and empire, and of race and empire are both thriving subjects; but these days the subject of class and empire is rarely considered.[49]

Nor is sufficient historical attention given these days to issues relating to what might be termed the material life and workings and circumstances of the British Empire. To be sure, this was a subject that was very fashionable in the immediate post-war phase of imperial historiography, as the economic imperatives to imperial expansion that were provided by trade and investment were extensively studied.[50] And these were followed by more sophisticated – but largely inconclusive – attempts to calculate and to weigh up the costs and benefits of the British Empire – at least to the British themselves. But since the large-scale synthesis of Peter Cain and A.G. Hopkins, which argued that throughout its history, the British Empire was largely the creation of 'gentlemenly capitalists', very little work has been done on this topic.[51] Indeed, cultural historians of empire, and post-colonial scholars, concerned above all with texts and knowledge and representations and identities, show little interest in the demographics or the material conditions or the economic functioning of the British Empire. Yet one does not have to be an economic determinist to recognize that these are subjects of major significance in the history of the British Empire or, indeed, of any other such dominion. Life and death, getting and spending, trading and investing, mobility and migration: these were the material forces shaping and constraining imperial constructs and imperial lives, and they were at least as important as culture, if not more so.

Religion and empire is likewise a subject in which post-colonial scholars and cultural historians might show more interest than they generally seem inclined to do. For as the events of 9/11 vividly demonstrated, there are many aspects of human behaviour, both present and past, metropolitan and imperial, which cannot be explained in terms of the secular trinity of class, gender and race, and nor can religion be subsumed or dissolved or elided into a reified category called 'culture'. To be sure, work has been done on British missionaries overseas, and on certain religious encounters that took place within the empire, as between Protestants and Catholics in Canada and Hindus and Muslims in South Asia.[52] But there is much that remains unstudied. How, for example, did the Anglican Church operate in Australia and India and South Africa? What was it like to be bishop of Sydney or Calcutta or Cape Town? And how did an empire built around metropolitan notions of providential Protestantism come to terms with the fact that the vast majority of its subjects were people of other faiths, whose views of the world, and of life and death were, as a result, often fundamentally different?[53]

Finally, there is the issue of what might loosely be called the politics of empire. This certainly encompasses 'strategies of rulership', but also much more besides. It ought to include a fuller consideration of imperial ideologies (from authoritarian to democratic, royal to republican) than cultural historians of empire seem minded to provide.[54] It ought to include a broader consideration of the constituent elements of empire, so that, say, Australia is looked at alongside India, or Canada alongside South Africa. It ought to recognize the importance of the circulation of peoples around the empire, from the colonies to London, but also from colony to colony: not just the pro-consular elites, but also social elites, professionals and (increasingly) intellectuals.[55] It ought to give attention to how different empires related to each other and interacted with each other: among them the British and the United States in North America, the British and the French in Africa, the British and the Russian (and the British and the Chinese) in Asia, and so on.[56] And it ought to give as much attention to the making and the ending of empire as to how it operated while it actually existed. In part because of its indebtedness to anthropology, cultural history is not always very convincing at dealing with change; but throughout its existence, the British Empire was perpetually changing, and we need to write histories which pay appropriate attention to that constant state of flux.

V

Doubtless there are as many ways of thinking about empire historically (and in our own time) as there are empires that have existed (and still exist). Although the focus of this chapter has been on the (past) British Empire and on the (present) American empire, this is not to suggest that the United States is the only imperial power in existence (and in denial) today. Like America, China is both a land-based empire (as instanced by its recent construction of a roof-of-the-world railway to strengthen its hold on neighbouring Tibet), and it also harbours expansionist impulses overseas (as evidenced by its purchase of railways and other utilities in Angola and Nigeria, and by the large holdings it has acquired of the US government debt). Such modes of imperial operation were commonplace among the imperial powers of the nineteenth century. Indeed, China has been an empire for much of its long history; but like the United States today, it has invariably denied this. And although the Soviet Empire has disappeared in the aftermath of the fall of the Berlin wall, the older Russian Empire still endures, even as Vladimir Putin denies its existence.[57]

Like scholars who are based and working in the United States, today's Chinese and Russian historians are living in empires of their own – whether they know it or not, or whether they will admit it or not. But so far as it is possible to know, they are not writing about the British Empire in the way that American historians are doing in increasing (and increasingly influential) numbers. It is, then, a serious and urgent task to reflect on what it means that so much of the history of the British imperial past is now being written by scholars based in the United States – a nation which is both a land-based and a transoceanic empire, but whose inhabitants have experienced, and still experience, profound difficulties in coming to terms with that empire's very existence. And it also bears repeating that there are further constraints on the agenda of American public discussion, which carry over on to (and in part derive from) the agenda of academic inquiry, which also limit the historical approaches to empire that are presently being taken across the Atlantic. One consequence of the Iraq war is that it may change the way American citizens think about their (imperial) place in the world, and this may in turn change the way American historians write about the British Empire, and also about their own. Once again, only time will tell.

Meanwhile, we should never forget that empires have been, across the centuries and around the globe, among the most persistent and pervasive modes of human association, and if they are indeed 'the default mode of political organization throughout most of history', then there seems every likelihood that they are going to remain so for the foreseeable future – and beyond. We may live in post-colonial times in the contemporary academy, but we certainly do not live in post-imperial times in the contemporary world.[58] Is this constant continuance of empire on our planet merely conclusive evidence that all men and women are either unavoidably sinful or irremediably suffering? Or does it suggest that, whether we like them or not, empires are one essential means of managing (and also mis-managing) the multifarious aspirations and even the multicultural identities of humankind? These are not easy questions to answer, but as we approach the many variants and versions of the imperial past, provided by other empires in addition to the British, and as we ponder the vexed and troubling problems of the imperial present (and of what seems likely to be a continuing imperial future), we might do well to keep them firmly – if unsettlingly – in mind.

10

Recessional:
Two Historians, the Sixties and Beyond[1]

If history, as Jacob Burckhardt once remarked, 'is on every occasion the record of what one age finds worthy of note in another', then the 1960s was a doubly noteworthy decade. On both sides of the Atlantic, it was a vigorous and innovative time for the researching and writing of English history (and it was, then, very much *English*, not British history that was being produced).[2] In the Tudor period, the Eltonian revolution was in full and fertile flower. The Civil War was receiving unprecedented attention, in part stimulated by broader notions of a general European crisis of the mid seventeenth century. The Hanoverian era was reviving after the long interlude of Namierite torpor and atomization, with renewed interest being shown in popular politics, political ideas, and economic and social change. The nineteenth century was coming alive for the first time as a field of scholarly interest, replacing Strachey's squibs and sarcasm with something altogether more solid and substantial. Even the early twentieth century was beginning to receive serious scrutiny, as public and private records were becoming available for the first time in large quantities. This was, in short, the decade when historians such as Christopher Hill, E.P. Thompson, Asa Briggs, Eric Hobsbawm, Ronald Robinson and Jack Gallagher, and A.J.P. Taylor produced major works of lasting importance, exceptional quality and widespread appeal.[3]

Even in such a vigorous and creative decade (which Arthur Marwick rightly suggests actually lasted from 1958 to 1974), two particularly resonant and significant books were Lawrence Stone's *The Causes of the English Revolution, 1529–1642* (London, 1972) and J.H. Plumb's *The Growth of Political Stability in England, 1675–1725* (London, 1967).[4] They were written by outstanding scholars at the peak of their powers and renown, they sold well on both sides of the Atlantic, and they crystallized and defined important problems in ways that were influential and provocative, not only among historians, but also among academics working in other disciplines, and not just within higher education, but also far beyond its ivory towers and ivy-clad walls. They were clever books, addressing historical issues that for a time appeared to be of global significance in the past, and which also seemed to be of substantial contemporary 'relevance' (a very sixties word and concept). And although dealing with what looked like completely different subjects, at opposite ends of the human and historical spectrum – in the one case the breakdown of political order in the mid seventeenth century, and in the other the re-establishment of political order in the early eighteenth century – they were in fact very similar (and, again, very sixties) in their conceptual frameworks, their methodological approaches and their explanatory structures.

In the decades that have passed since these two books first appeared, the sixties have vanished into the distance, while historians have moved on, as they always do, always must, and always will, to new subjects, new problems and new approaches. Inevitably, this means that *Revolution* and *Stability* are much less central to the current historiographies of the seventeenth and the eighteenth centuries than once they were: they are works to be savoured or dismissed, but they are no longer setting the contemporary scholarly agenda.[5] Yet they are more than mere academic curiosities, mouldering away un-thumbed on library shelves and in second-hand bookshops. They are still, and rightly, read, and in the best and truest senses, they are period pieces, which need to be set against the broader background of their times – which means both the political culture of Anglo-America, and the academic world of sixties history. But they also need to be understood as the creations of particular scholars, with their own intentions and interests, who were subject to specific influences and inspirations. They are, in short, texts with contexts, and it is those contexts that this chapter seeks to explore, in the hope that they will shed new light on these books and their authors, and also on the varied, evolving and disputatious ways in which historians wrote about seventeenth- and eighteenth-century England, primarily in the 1960s, but also more generally in the sixty years after the Second World War.

I

In many ways, the 1960s was an unprecedentedly prosperous, buoyant, confident and optimistic decade – a time of hope on both sides of the Atlantic, the like of which had not been seen since the *belle epoque* of the Edwardian era, or perhaps not been seen ever. Economically, they witnessed the climax of the long boom which had begun tentatively in 1945, extended and intensified through the 1950s, and reached its peak around 1968. This was the era which bore out Harold Macmillan's claim (or warning) of 1959 that the British people had 'never had it so good', and which gave rise to John F. Kennedy's confident assertion two years later that it was now possible for the west to abolish all forms of human poverty. This, in turn, meant unprecedented prosperity for the middle and working classes, freed from the anxieties of 1930s depression and 1940s world war, who now enjoyed a time of consumer abundance and material well-being that their forebears had never known: cars and fridges, foreign holidays and televisions, mortgages and hire purchase agreements, James Bond novels and films. It was, in short, the era memorably described by J.K. Galbraith as witnessing the arrival of the 'affluent society' in the United States, and by British sociologists as portending the permanent 'embourgeoisement' of what had previously been the traditional, manual working class.[6]

This economic growth and social advancement were defined and exploited by the progressive politicians of the sixties, who did much by their phrases and their legislation to consolidate and confirm the optimistic mood of the time. On both sides of the Atlantic, after the years of Eisenhower torpor and Macmillan scandal, the stress was on novelty and action, and on moving things forward again, in a hundred or a thousand days, by utilizing the combined resources of national wealth and confident state power, as exemplified by John Kennedy's 'new frontier', by Harold Wilson's 'white heat of technological revolution', and by Lyndon Johnson's 'great society' programme. In the United States, these reformist impulses meant sweeping domestic legislation concerning welfare provision for the disadvantaged and civil rights for blacks, and of massive overseas aid to the Third World. And in rapidly decolonizing Britain, the progressive agenda was more concerned with domestic social issues: the reform of race relations, the modification of the divorce laws, and the legalization of homosexual activities between consenting adults in private, and of abortion. Truly, as the late Roy Jenkins observed, in words that apply equally to the United Kingdom and the United States, the 1960s was 'the liberal hour'.[7]

One indication of this was that American and British universities enjoyed unrivalled public esteem: John F. Kennedy took pride in appointing to his administration such Harvard luminaries as McGeorge Bundy, Arthur Schlesinger Jr, and J.K. Galbraith; and Harold Wilson's government was full of first-class Oxford minds – not just himself and Roy Jenkins, but also Anthony Crosland, Richard Crossman, Douglas Jay and Denis Healey.[8] And with buoyant economies and burgeoning tax revenues, which meant unprecedented public funding and private means, higher education in the era of the Robbins Report was in confident and creative mode. Old campuses expanded to accommodate more students studying a greater variety of subjects; new universities were founded in England in deliberate reaction to the elitism and traditionalism of Oxbridge; and Harold Wilson's Open University was even more innovative. As Lawrence Stone would later write, the 1960s was 'one of the eras of greatest expansion, and of greatest optimism about higher education, that have ever existed', and in these leviathans of light and learning, the social sciences seemed set to carry all before them.[9] Economics provided the key to sustaining growth at home, and to the ending of poverty in the Third World; sociology held out the hope of understanding the world as it was; and political science offered visions of the world as it might be. All these disciplines were intellectually fertile and publicly engaged: seeking both to understand the world and to change it, for the better, outlooks and aspirations well exemplified in Barrington Moore's book, *Social Origins of Dictatorship and Democracy*, published in 1966. It was sub-titled *Lord and Peasant in the Making of the Modern World*; it surveyed the process of capitalist modernization in England, France, the United States, China, Japan and India; and it ended with a section on 'Theoretical Implications and Projections'.[10]

In such a buoyant and heady atmosphere, where the social sciences seemed poised to overtake the humanities in offering the best guide to comprehending (and controlling?) life on earth, the study and teaching of the past were transformed both in substance and in scale. For the history which thrived on the old and new campuses of the 1960s was not primarily concerned, as it had previously been, with England's political and constitutional evolution, which now seemed to many an outmoded and obscurantist subject. Instead, and stimulated by these challenges to compete and to adapt, it took sustenance from the social sciences, and also sought to engage with them.[11] Economic history charted the transition, via industrialization, to the modern world – transitions beginning in late eighteenth-century England, and diffusing across Europe and the Atlantic, which also provided guidance as to how the developing world might now best catch up. And social history built on this revived materialist foundation, partly by exploring the new class formations to which these economic changes gave rise (first in England, then spread more widely); partly by recovering the protests and dissidence of those who were the victims of economic development (ditto); and partly by offering a better way of understanding and explaining political behaviour, by setting it in a broader social context which set the limits to individual freedom of choice, and also informed the decisions that were taken. Here was social history, not as a narrow and sectarian sub-discipline, nor as anecdotal and bucolic nostalgia, but rather as the total history of human society.[12]

There were many exemplars and practitioners of what seemed to be this broader, more exciting, more relevant brand of sixties history. The *Annales* school, based in Paris, had been extending historical inquiry in these directions since the days of Marc Bloch, and Fernand Braudel's work on the Mediterranean at the time of Philip II opened up a whole new way of seeing the past, in which long-term trends in the economy and society were given precedence and priority over day-to-day political decision making. The journal *Past & Present*, founded in 1952, soon became England's closest equivalent to the *Annales*, stressing economic and social change more than high politics: as such, it was in rebellion against the more traditional *English Historical Review*, and the *Historical Journal*, and it enjoyed unprecedented renown in the 1960s.[13] In *The Stages of Economic Growth*, W.W. Rostow offered the British industrializing experience between 1780 and 1800 as the paradigmatic case of economic transformation, through which all modernizing nations had subsequently to pass. In *The Making of the English Working Class*, E.P. Thompson explained the rise of proletarian political consciousness in the light of the economic and social changes wrought by the Industrial Revolution. In *The Origins of Modern English Society, 1780–1880*, Harold Perkin told essentially the same story with reference to the middle class. And in *Victorian Cities*, Asa Briggs explained how nineteenth-century urban England (especially Manchester and Birmingham) might best be understood in terms of their different economies, different social structures and thus different politics.[14]

These books were very much the products of their times in their approach to the past (and the present) and in their methodology. Like many other works of history published in the same decade, on both sides of the Atlantic, they took it for granted that economic history must be connected to social history, which in turn must be connected to political history. This was how change might best be understood in all its multifarious and interlinked complexities. For as their titles implied, these books were concerned with deeply-rooted, long-term causes, with origins, with growth, with making, with stages, and with becoming: in sum, with economic transformation, which brought about social development, which in turn set the parameters and determined the possibilities of political outcomes. This was how, in the past, something had become something else, how we had got from there to here, and during the 1960s it was the historian's business to explain how these advances had taken place: both for their own intrinsic interest, and also because such accounts might provide guidance for those wishing to contemplate and bring about similar transformations in society, now and in the future. 'If history is not concerned with change', Lawrence Stone observed, 'it is nothing.' And such change was generally assumed to be improving and beneficial: towards modernity, prosperity, democracy. 'The one certain judgement of value that can be made about history', agreed J.H. Plumb, 'is the idea of progress.'[15]

Having discerned the outlines of progress in the past, these sixties historians were eager and active contributors to the encouraging and forwarding of progress in their own time. Among those just mentioned, W.W. Rostow served in the White House under Presidents Kennedy and Johnson from 1960 to 1968; E.P. Thompson established the Centre for Social History at Warwick University, and then became an active campaigner against nuclear weapons; Harold Perkin was a founding father of the University of Lancaster, where he was the first Professor of Social History in Britain; and Asa Briggs was Vice-Chancellor of the University of Sussex, the most innovative and interdisciplinary of the new British universities.[16] Here was a hopeful, optimistic world of higher learning and active engagement where, for a time, everything seemed possible – even for historians. It was widely believed that the combination of power, money, technology and ideas would enable the governments of the west to transform their own societies, and those of the rapidly decolonizing Third World. But to improve the human condition, both at home and abroad, it first had to be better understood, and in that enterprise of comprehension and comparison, history – broadly and imaginatively conceived – had a key part to play, not only (and as always) in making the past yield up its secrets, but also in drawing lessons from past circumstances, situations and events, which the economists, sociologists and political scientists might then apply to their studies of the contemporary world and plans for the future.

For many historians of the 1960s, that seemed an exciting possibility: the dual function of history, exulted E.H. Carr, was 'to enable man to understand the society of the past, and to increase his mastery over society in the present'.[17] But not everyone was captivated, least of all Geoffrey Elton who, in 1967, became Professor of English Political and Constitutional History at the University of Cambridge. It was an ad hominem chair and he chose his title deliberately and provocatively. For as befitted a lifelong admirer of F.W. Maitland, he believed passionately in the traditional history of government and administration; he stressed the primacy of painstaking, empirical research into the sources in the archives; he was vehemently hostile to inter-disciplinary approaches to the past; he was deeply unsympathetic to economics, sociology and political science; and he despised what he regarded as the overweening self-confidence of planners and visionaries and reformers, who sought to change the world before they had even begun to understand it. In his inaugural lecture, and at greater length elsewhere, Elton berated his colleagues for running after such false, ephemeral and fashionable gods; the historian was not, he insisted, 'a teacher to society, to his time'; it was not for them to be 'finding an answer to the future'; they should be concentrating on the past, and on the political past at that. As Elton saw it, he was fighting a battle for the soul and mind of history and of the historical profession. It did not seem as if he was winning it, and so he did not share the widespread euphoria of the 1960s.[18]

As if to bear out his gloomy forebodings, there were many who ended the decade less optimistic than they had begun it: for there was a darker side to the sixties, which intensified as those years drew on. This was partly because the Kennedy and Wilson cohort, which had come to power with such youthful confidence and new-generational ardour, was soon turned on by its own children, who became unprecedentedly assertive and disruptive, as affluence (rather unexpectedly and disappointingly) bred discontent rather than satisfaction.[19] For the sixties was also the decade of the Beatles and the Rolling Stones, of jeans and long hair, of drugs and flower power, of contraceptives and pre-marital sex, of live-ins and love-ins: in short, of a fundamental revolution in youth culture and adolescent lifestyles, which left their parents enraged, dismayed, bewildered and uncomprehending. The sterling qualities which had seen the United Kingdom and the United States through to success in the Second World War – duty, courage, patriotism, restraint, selflessness and self-sacrifice – were rejected by an unprecedentedly privileged, well-educated and disaffected generation, and across America and Europe, university campuses erupted in student riots, protests and demonstrations from 1967 onwards, as the 'civilised society' of the 'liberal hour' became the 'permissive society' of liberal excess.[20]

Underlying these alienated responses was a deeper sense of dissatisfaction and disillusion, as the early political hopes of the decade were (as in 1906 and 1945) soon disappointed. In Britain, the initial optimism of Harold Wilson's first one hundred days and his massive election victory of 1966 were soon dissipated; there were persistent economic crises leading to the devaluation of the pound; his government failed to carry through fundamental, modernizing reforms; and he went down to defeat at the hands of Edward Heath and the Conservatives in the general election of 1970. In France, the student demonstrations in 1968 seemed for a time to be a portent of genuine revolution, but after precipitating the resignation of President de Gaulle, little fundamentally changed. And in the United States, the assassinations of Martin Luther King and Robert F. Kennedy in 1968, the escalating demonstrations against America's involvement in the Vietnam War, and Lyndon Johnson's enforced withdrawal from the presidential race, seemed to bring the country to the very brink of anarchy. The election of Richard Nixon to the White House signalled a serious shift in opinion to the right, and by the mid 1970s the earlier sense of liberal optimism was largely extinguished, not only in America, but throughout western Europe.[21]

II

This was the general, transatlantic climate in which Lawrence Stone and J.H. Plumb were moving, living and working during the 1960s, and both felt themselves to be in tune with the progressive (rather than the depressive) mood of the times, which were in marked contrast to the years of slump and struggle in which they had grown up.[22] Stone had been born in 1920, he was educated at Charterhouse and Christ Church, Oxford, and his undergraduate studies were interrupted by war service in the Navy. On his return to Oxford in 1945, he began research into the economic, social and political history of Tudor and Stuart England, a fashionable subject at the time, encompassing as it seemed to do the transition from feudalism to capitalism, the decline of the aristocracy and the rise of the bourgeoisie, and thus what were termed the 'social origins' of the Civil War. This work brought Stone into contact with R.H. Tawney, the Christian-socialist scholar whose 'century' extended from 1540 to 1640, and whom Stone always thereafter admired (though as a lifelong agnostic he did not share his mentor's religious convictions). Stone was elected a Fellow of Wadham College in 1950, and during the next decade undertook a full tutorial teaching load, most of it in medieval and early modern English history. He was also publishing extensively, including a biography of an unscrupulously appealing Elizabethan financier, Sir Horatio Palavicino, and a series of articles, owing much to Tawney, which set out to analyse the financial weakness of the late-Elizabethan and early-Stuart aristocracy.[23]

These were all conventional steps in the making of a conventionally donnish Oxford career. But by the late 1950s, Stone had become restless: he found the history he was obliged to teach, with its narrow and insular stress on English high politics, to be increasingly parochial and stultifying, and he had also clashed bitterly with Hugh Trevor-Roper in what became known as the 'storm over the gentry', when his work on the aristocracy was ferociously attacked by his former Christ Church tutor.[24] There was more to this than mere historical disagreement, for as befitted an admirer of Tawney's, Stone was a man of the (non-Marxist) left, whereas Trevor-Roper was a Tory and the biographer of Archbishop Laud, who was well connected in Conservative Party circles. In 1957, Harold Macmillan, then Prime Minister, appointed Trevor-Roper Regius Professor of Modern History at Oxford, and three years later he returned the compliment by securing the Chancellorship of Oxford University for Macmillan. With his own prospects there effectively blocked, Stone moved to Princeton University in 1963, where he was captivated by what seemed to him the more open, flexible, confident, inter-disciplinary environment, and where he felt an optimism and sense of possibilities he had not known since the Labour victory of 1945. But he continued to write English history, and he retained his English links: he regularly returned to Oxford; he still published with Oxford University Press; and he was a frequent and influential contributor to *Past & Present*, whose editorial board he had joined in 1958.[25]

Plumb's background was less establishment than Stone's, being provincial, dissenting and working class. He was born in Leicester in 1911, and only reached Cambridge as a graduate student after taking an external London degree at his local university college. He began research on the social structure of the House of Commons in the reign of King William III, and he was supervised by George Macaulay Trevelyan, the then Regius Professor, for whose whiggish histories and sympathetic biographies, which reached a large and appreciative audience, he conceived a lifelong admiration. But there were no jobs in Cambridge in the late 1930s, and it was only after war years spent at Bletchley that Plumb was elected a Fellow of Christ's College and subsequently appointed a University Lecturer in history, specializing in the late seventeenth and eighteenth centuries.[26] He, too, seemed on the way to a conventional academic career, publishing conventional scholarly articles about local politics, the cabinet and parliament; and in the late 1940s and early 1950s, he came under the influence of Sir Lewis Namier, who sought to appoint him to the *History of Parliament* project, based at the Institute of Historical Research in London, where he was the dominant and directing force.[27]

But as befitted a protégé of Trevelyan, Plumb was not wholly enamoured of such dry-as-dust scholarship, and nor did he find the Christian and conservative tone of the History Faculty at Cambridge altogether to his taste. Not surprisingly, he soon fell out with Geoffrey Elton, the other rising historical star in the university. As a Jewish immigrant to England in the late 1930s, Elton was even more of an outsider than Plumb, and all his life he disliked what he saw as Trevelyan's patrician grandeur, amateur history and liberal attitudes. Plumb's eventual assumption of his mentor's Whig mantle deepened his rift with Elton; and throughout the 1950s and 1960s, they were bitter professional rivals in Cambridge for promotion and preferment.[28] Moreover, Plumb preferred writing general surveys and evocative biographies in vigorous, lively prose, which reached a wide public readership, whereas Elton specialized in technical, austere, self-consciously scholarly history, exclusively concerned with politics and the constitution. Plumb saw himself as radical, progressive, secular, modernizing, the lifelong enemy of 'bigotry, national vanity and class domination'; he adored America in the Kennedy years, was a frequent visitor to university campuses across the country, and wrote regularly for *Horizon* and the *Saturday Review*.[29]

By the mid 1960s, Stone and Plumb were at the peak of their creative powers and scholarly renown, and they were 'commanding and controversial figures in the world of Anglo-American historiography'.[30] Stone was happily (and influentially) ensconced at Princeton, where he was Dodge Professor of History, chairman of his department from 1967–70, and from 1968 the founding Director of the Shelby Cullom Davis Center for Historical Studies, a position which he retained until his retirement in 1990. He was also a frequent contributor to the *New York Review of Books*, the in-house journal of the liberal, east coast, anglophile intelligentsia, as their regular commentator on early modern Britain, and he took great delight in bringing academic history to a general audience.[31] In Cambridge, Plumb was promoted to Reader (1962) then Professor (1966) of Modern British History, he was chairman of his Faculty Board (1966–68), and he was elected a Fellow of the British Academy (1968). He, too, was writing prolifically in the newspapers and weekly journals, and became historical adviser for Penguin Books. Both men were also involved in the progressive politics of the time, albeit in different ways: Stone took part in the demonstrations at Princeton against the Vietnam War, and was a fascinated witness to '*les événements*' in Paris in May 1968; and Plumb was a strongly-committed supporter of Harold Wilson's government, where his friend C.P. Snow was briefly a junior minister.[32]

Moreover, both of them had big and successful projects behind them. Stone's mammoth *The Crisis of the Aristocracy, 1558–1641* had been completed just before he left Oxford for Princeton, and it was published in 1965, to widespread (but not universal) acclaim, and in most people's eyes (though never all) it more than atoned for his earlier mistakes in the 'storm over the gentry' controversy.[33] In more ways than one, it was a radical and audacious book. At the outset, Stone made plain both his abiding curiosity about England's aristocratic elite, and his personal detestation of 'an antipathetic group of superfluous parasites', who enjoyed what he regarded as an unacceptable monopoly of wealth, status and power. He paid a warm tribute to R.H. Tawney; he urged historians to study sociology and statistics; and he reiterated (in modified form) his mentor's view that *social* change lay at the heart what was ostensibly of the English *political* revolution. Based on massive research in private archives, supported by a vast array of figures and calculations, and ranging across economic, social, political, cultural and architectural history, *The Crisis of the Aristocracy* was (and remains) the most elaborate and comprehensive study of the English parliamentary peerage ever attempted for any period; and, by tracing and explaining the aristocracy's collective decline from the age of Elizabeth I to that of Charles I, Stone believed he was offering both 'a prolegomoneon to, and an explanation of, the Civil War'.[34]

Shortly before Stone's magnum opus appeared, Plumb published the first and second volumes of his full-dress biography of Sir Robert Walpole, effectively England's first minister from 1721 to 1742. They were more traditional works than Stone's self-consciously innovative study, and they owed much to the example of Trevelyan and his great uncle, Lord Macaulay. The lavish treatment, intended to be in three volumes, was on the same ample scale as Trevelyan's Garibaldi trilogy, and each book began with panoramic surveys, respectively of Walpole's England and Walpole's Europe, modelled on the famous opening chapters of Macaulay's *History of England*.[35] The biography was widely praised, for its vigorous evocation of life at the time, and for its convincing portrayal of Walpole himself. This was partly because Plumb closely identified with his subject: in his conquest of provincial obscurity, his delight in patronage and power, his enjoyment of food and wine, and his pleasure in collecting works of art. (Elton, by contrast, preferred Thomas Cromwell, another provincial outsider who also made it to the top, but a much nastier and more ruthless character.) Together, the Walpole volumes established Plumb as the leading authority on English history from the Restoration to the Hanoverian Succession and beyond, and it was on the strength of them that he was invited, in 1965, to deliver the Ford Lectures at Oxford, which were subsequently published as *The Growth of Political Stability*.[36]

In moving on from these big projects to *Revolution* and *Stability*, which would be synoptic surveys in a much briefer compass, Stone and Plumb were changing their mode of exposition more than the subject. For they had long brooded on the periods about which they were writing, they drew on their recent experiences as professors and teachers, and they also sought to remedy shortcomings in their earlier work. Stone's *Revolution* was dedicated 'to my students at Princeton, under whose relentless but friendly criticism these ideas have taken shape', it was informed by his observations of undergraduate protest in Paris and in Princeton, and it was put together from earlier articles in which he had explored the history and sociology of revolution.[37] In venturing again into an historiographical 'battle-ground, which has been heavily fought over, and is beset with mines, booby-traps and ambushes manned by ferocious scholars prepared to fight every inch of the way', Stone admitted he was offering a 'highly personal interpretation', which he did not expect to 'meet with general acceptance'. But he was anxious to 'make amends for a deficiency in my previous writing', namely that in stressing the importance of social change in the 'storm over the gentry' and in the *Crisis of the Aristocracy*, he had 'unduly neglected the religious, political, administrative and constitutional elements' of the revolution, to which he now gave attention.[38]

By the mid 1960s, Plumb had been thinking about late seventeenth- and early eighteenth-century England since his days as Trevelyan's research student, and he had been deeply influenced by his mentor's trilogy *England Under Queen Anne* (3 vols, London, 1930–34), with its stress on war and government and the importance of party conflict. But he also recognized the need to specify the bigger and broader historical problem which lay behind his biographical treatment of Walpole's rise to power, and later political dominance.[39] It was these issues which he sought to confront in *The Growth of Political Stability*, thereby providing a sort of retrospective prologue to his Walpole books, setting the great man's life in a broader and more analytical historical context than he had done in the panoramic surveys which opened the two volumes that had so far appeared. *Stability* also drew extensively on Plumb's pre-war Ph.D. thesis (which he had never published), it made good use of his earlier, scholarly writings on the localities, parliament and the cabinet (which owed something to Namier's influence), and it incorporated the recent work of research students, close associates and college friends (which provided many of the building blocks for the broader interpretation he would advance).[40]

But while, in this sense, both *Revolution* and *Stability* were deeply personal books, they were also very much the products of their time. Like most sixties historians, neither Stone nor Plumb was much concerned with Britain (as distinct from England) or its Empire. But they were eager to break down the barriers dividing economic from social from political history, and they were unusually well and widely read. Plumb had edited a book on the Renaissance and was the general editor of a multi-volume *History of Human Society* which ranged across the whole of recorded time. Stone had admired the *Annales* school of history since studying at the Sorbonne in 1938; his first book had been on English medieval sculpture; and on his arrival in America he took up quantification, sociology and political science, those rising disciplines which fertilized the 'new history' in the 1960s.[41] And so, in the manner of the time, both men made large claims for their subjects, insisting that they were addressing problems of general significance and contemporary relevance. Stone thought the English revolution was 'an event of fundamental importance in the evolution of Western civilization'; and Plumb believed the establishment of stability was 'part of social and political change to which western Europe has been extremely prone this last five hundred years', as in 1930s Mexico, 1950s Russia, and de Gaulle's France.[42]

Such broad claims, which resembled those being made by Anglo-American historians working on the British Industrial Revolution, were very much *à la mode* in the 1960s, when the history of England was being transatlanticized and intruded into contemporary discussions as never before – both in terms of the people who were working on it, and in terms of the influences that were feeding into it.[43] Indeed, the Anglo-American academic world which Stone and Plumb had joined was very much a creation of that decade, not least because air travel made regular and rapid to-ing and fro-ing across 'the pond' possible for the first time, especially for those based in Oxford or Cambridge, or on the east coast of the United States. Both Stone and Plumb greatly enjoyed being among the earliest scholarly jet-setters, and their evident delight in these new opportunities enhanced their confidence as historians, and gave them a broader perspective on the English past and its relation to other disciplines and to contemporary events. In all these ways, Stone's *Revolution* and Plumb's *Stability* were related to their authors' lives, and to the circumstances of the time, and both men had reached a stage of seniority when they thought they had considered and significant things to say about the periods they had made their own, and about the times in which they lived. What, exactly, were they?

III

Stone's *Causes of the English Revolution* began in characteristically combative mode by asserting the superiority of 'analytical' over 'narrative' history, and with a dismissal of the sort of political history he had been obliged to teach in Oxford as 'one of the most sterile and meaningless ways of cutting into the tangled thickets of historical change'. *His* aim, by contrast, was to situate the political upheavals of the 1640s in a much broader economic and social context, and also to draw on the insights of social scientists as 'a corrective to the antiquarian fact-grubbing to which historians are so prone'. From their work, he emphasized two points: that rapid economic growth often led to social instability, and that 'a lack of harmony between the social system on the one hand and the political system on the other' brought about what he called 'a condition of multiple dysfunction' which habitually made revolution possible.[44] He then turned to survey the long-running debate on the social origins of the English revolution, in which he himself had been a not-wholly-happy participant, and concluded that 'every historian, whatever his political persuasion, lays great stress on social forces as operative factors in history'; that 'the future of history lies in a cautious selective cross-fertilisation with the methods and theories of the social sciences'; and that 'since it looks as if the twentieth century above all others is going to be the age of revolutions', this was 'a matter of some interest to politicians and planners as well as to historians'.[45]

These were Stone's presumptions and presuppositions, and having made his claim to broader public notice and attention, he set out to explain how the English revolution had happened. He did so on three different levels, beginning with what he called the 'preconditions', those long-term causes and structural forces which made revolution possible, but not inevitable. In the century after 1529, he argued, England duly moved into a state of 'disequilibrium' (or multiple dysfunction): the economy boomed and prospered in terms of population, overseas trade and capitalist enterprise; the aristocracy declined while the gentry prospered, consolidating its position in the localities and in parliament; there was a growth of puritanism among an increasingly affluent professional and merchant class, who wanted a larger say in the affairs of the nation; an opposition, drawn from the gentry and the middle classes, successfully established itself in the House of Commons; there was a mounting feeling of dissatisfaction at the integrity and moral worth of those in high office; and the crown failed to establish or retain control of the army or the government of the localities. The result, by 1629, was an ever more unsettled and insecure society, characterized by both upward and downward social mobility, which was confronting an inadequate and inflexible government, and it was this 'growing inability of the state to adjust to new social forces' which made revolution a distinct possibility.[46]

Having 'dealt in forces and trends, social, economic, political and religious, and in long-term government policies', in those 'broad sweeps of history [which] move in inexorable patterns', Stone turned his attention to 'the interconnection of forces and events', by considering the 'precipitating' developments of 1629–39, which meant that revolution was no longer merely possible but became probable.[47] As he saw it, the key to these years was 'the ruthless and uncompromising nature of the royal policies', characterized as 'Thorough', which 'drove more and more of the silent majority into the arms of the opposition' during the 1630s: a religious reaction, in favour of the established church (and, perhaps, of Catholicism?), pressed furiously forward by Archbishop Laud; a political reaction, signalled by Charles I's decision to try to rule without parliament; a social reaction, as the monarch and archbishop threw their weight behind the traditional aristocracy in an effort to overawe the rising gentry and ambitious middle classes; and an economic reaction, as royal control was reasserted over numerous crafts and trades. Here was a menacing royal policy of paternalist absolutism, which conceded nothing to the parliamentary opposition, and which took its most assertive and authoritarian form in Ireland under Strafford. The result was that an already unsettled society became increasingly polarized: thus did 'the precipitants of the 1630s turn the prospects of political breakdown from a possibility to a probability'.[48]

Finally, between 1640 and 1642, there took place 'a series of unfortunate accidents and misguided personal decisions' which 'triggered' the English revolution itself, turning probability into certainty.[49] Desperate for money, Charles was obliged to recall parliament in 1640, but by this time he was bereft of allies, and faced a united opposition. Parliament duly removed from the crown its powers of taxation without consent and of arrest without trial; it abolished the main organs of central government; it reversed Laud's religious policies; and it punished those who had implemented the king's wishes. The result was a virtual collapse of government and a power vacuum at the centre of affairs, characterized by an unprecedentedly active press, and 'virtual religious anarchy'. And it was in this frenzied environment that the Irish rebellion erupted in November 1641, that the king vainly tried to arrest the five leading members of the parliamentary opposition in January 1642, and that the City of London turned against their monarch early in the following year. By mid 1642, the whole country was riven between a royal party and the parliamentary opposition. As a result of what Stone described as 'multiple helix chains of causation more complicated than those of DNA itself', the Civil War had begun, the king would be executed, the monarchy would be terminated, the House of Lords would be swept away, and the bishops would be abolished. Thus was initiated 'the first of the "Great Revolutions" in the history of the West'.[50]

As befitted the biographer of Walpole, Plumb's *Growth of Political Stability* was, at least superficially, a more traditional sort of book. It did not parade its model of historical causation, and it contained more substantial historical detail and archival research than Stone displayed in *Revolution*. There was no extended methodological preliminary, and only a brief historiographical discussion, where Plumb set out what he was trying to do. In ascending order of generality, he wanted to clear up the growing 'confusion' that had recently arisen about late seventeenth- and early eighteenth-century English political history; he hoped to do so by restoring 'concepts' in a post-Namier world, in this case that of 'political stability'; and he urged that, in Augustan England as elsewhere, stability was not so much the 'given' product of inertia, tradition and evolution, but 'becomes actual through the actions and decisions of men'. Plumb's aims, then, were to offer a coherent and convincing interpretation of the contorted and complex politics of late Stuart and early Hanoverian England; to explain how the 'conspiracy, plot, revolution and civil war' of the seventeenth century was replaced by the 'adamantine strength and profound inertia of the eighteenth'; and so to provide a case study of the means by which political stability – which he defined as the 'acceptance by society of its political institutions, and of those classes of men or officials who control them' – was deliberately brought about and made to happen.[51]

Part of the answer, Plumb began, was to be found in 'deep social causes', and in 'certain long term factors' which were 'driving English society to a closer-knit political and constitutional structure' as, in the fifty years from 1675 to 1725, the country moved towards economic and social stability 'without which political stability would always be an illusion'.[52] There was population growth, a commercial revolution, a consolidation of landownership, an expansion in inland and overseas trade, and an ever-enlarging government bureaucracy, as a result of which, 'local economic isolation' was gradually 'obliterated', and social mobility increased. This, in turn, meant there were more prosperous people than ever before, with a greater interest in order, security and stability: country mansions were built and rebuilt; Queen Anne houses proliferated in market towns and seaports; there was a richer and more varied life. 'These factors', Plumb concluded, 'were constantly building and strengthening pyramids of power'; there was 'a drift towards the formation of urban and rural oligarchies', consisting of progressive landowners, great merchants and self-made men; and this was 'bound to secure, sooner or later, a more stable society.' But such an outcome could not be guaranteed, for 'the political events of the last half of the seventeenth century were largely at cross purposes with this general drift': if economic and social stability were to be transformed into political stability, then political structures, institutions and conditions had to be changed.[53]

Between 1675 and 1714, Plumb argued, there were some tentative steps in this direction, but for much of the time, it was an uphill struggle. For England was a nation where local government, including the City of London, was fiercely hostile to centralization, and it was also riven by 'raging' party political differences between Whigs and Tories, over the succession (Hanoverian or Stuart), over foreign policy (to fight Louis XIV or not), over religion (Dissent versus the Established Church), and over deeper issues of power and purpose.[54] Accordingly, passions ran high across the nation, encompassing both rulers and ruled, and they were intensified by the unprecedentedly large size of the popular electorate (which it was impossible for patrons to manage), by the recalcitrant conduct of parliament (a 'medieval institution' which could not be disciplined or controlled), and by the disunited nature of the cabinet (which meant there was no single, unified policy). In dealing with these obstacles to political stability, some progress was made: the 'growth of oligarchy' lessened local hostility to the centre, and reduced partisan dissent among many men of power; this gradually contributed to the rise of a more unified executive; and this in turn made it possible to begin taming the electorate. Here were the still-uncertain beginnings of the process whereby the long-term economic and social forces making for stability were made actual and concrete in particular political situations and arrangements.[55]

But even then, Plumb insisted, the 'long-term forces making for political stability' still lacked 'the full support' of the 'institutions of government', and it was only with the decisive events of the years 1714–22 that political stability was successfully established. To begin with, the succession was settled, as the Hanoverians arrived and the Jacobite rebellion failed. In 1716, the Septennial Act was passed, which reduced the frequency of elections and thus the power of the electorate to interfere. In 1720, Sir Robert Walpole re-joined the Whig government, and soon came to dominate it. He created an effective and unified executive, and through ruthless exploitation of patronage, he was able to tame parliament and bring the localities to heel.[56] After the 1722 election, the Whigs, who enjoyed the support of commercially-minded aristocrats and new men of business, were firmly in power; the Tories and minor gentry had been cast into utter darkness; there was a united ruling class of 'natural oligarchs' sharing 'social and political cohesion'; and the way was open to the single party government and political torpor which characterized the 1750s. And so political stability had been achieved, as the strife of the seventeenth century gave way to a new system, built around patronage, privilege and inheritance, and the merging of 'political and social authority', in which 'the rage of party gave way to the pursuit of place', and which would last, with modifications, extensions and patchings-up, 'almost to our own day'.[57]

IV

In defining their subjects as they had, and in treating them as they did, Stone and Plumb sought to show, and succeeded in showing, that historians could tackle big issues with boldness and bravery – meeting the economists, the sociologists and the political scientists of the 1960s on their own ground. They demonstrated that, in appropriately gifted, imaginative and ambitious hands, the history of what might seem to be no more than particular episodes in the parochial English past could be transatlanticized, globalized and universalized, and be made to yield suggestive insights into the studies of revolution and of stability in France and Russia, the United States and Mexico, and even the world of their own time.[58] Of course, there were differences of style and emphasis between the two authors. Stone was eager to parade his inter-disciplinary credentials, to make plain his methodological presuppositions, and to write in language that derived from the social scientists. Plumb disdained all such activities, eschewing sociological jargon, and wrote with his customary verve, zest, brio, colour and élan.[59] For Stone, population growth, increasing prosperity and greater social mobility lead to instability, and thus to the possibility of revolution; for Plumb, they meant more people with an interest in order and thus a greater chance of stability. And according to Stone, the English aristocracy was in deep crisis by 1640, whereas for Plumb, it was back in charge fifty years later.

But in this latter case at least, there was no substantive contradiction: for Stone and Plumb were self-consciously working at the opposite ends of what seemed in the sixties (and into the seventies) to be a single, interconnected and extremely important historical problem: how had order become disorder in the middle of the seventeenth century, and how had that disorder become order again early in the eighteenth century? For his part, Stone reluctantly admitted that in the short run, the English Revolution 'ostensibly failed', as the monarchy, peerage and church were restored within a generation (indeed, he would later write an essay on precisely this theme).[60] And Plumb recognized that stability was the mirror image of revolution: 'stability', he observed in words which bear repeating and completing, 'becomes actual through the actions and decisions of men, *as does revolution*'. 'Societies', he noted, 'can move as quickly into stability as into revolution.' 'We are more than dimly aware of the causation of revolutions', he went on; 'some of the greatest historical minds of many generations have subjected them to fruitful analysis.' But, he concluded, 'there is as great a need, if not greater, to study how societies come to accept a pattern of political authority and the institutions that are required for its translation into government'.[61]

In formulating the problem in this way, Plumb was making a connection which also provided the solution. For in explaining political stability, he resorted to the same causal mechanism that Stone was using to explain political revolution. To be sure, he did not label them 'preconditions', 'precipitants' and 'triggers'; but he did structure his argument (though not his book) around what were essentially the same sequence of long-term forces, medium-term developments, and short-term events. And this three-tiered, 'stage by stage' model of historical causation was not only shared by Stone and Plumb: it was the conventional wisdom in the 1960s for explaining historical change. It drew on the social sciences; it linked together different types of history; and it was concerned with origins, with processes and with outcomes (indeed, in the United States, Plumb's book was called *The Origins of Political Stability*, not *The Growth*). As such, it was also clearly indebted to Fernand Braudel's famous tripartite time scheme of *longue durée*, *conjoncture*, and *histoire événementielle*. Nor should this come as any surprise, for as a sixties icon to scholars on the left, Braudel was much admired by Stone and Plumb; and they both applauded his ambition in tackling big subjects in a broad and imaginative way, which recognized the real limits which context and circumstance set on personal choice and individual freedom of action.[62]

Like many historians writing in the sixties, Stone and Plumb assumed that economic change spelt and determined social change, and that such moves towards modernity were pregnant with political possibilities. But it also followed that these political possibilities were more likely to be recognized and exploited by those who were whiggish and progressive, by those who were working with the grain of events, rather than by those who were Tory, reactionary and backward looking, and thus were vainly defying the trends of the time. Behind Stone stood Samuel Rawson Gardiner and Wallace Notestein, with their accounts of the rise to prominence (and permanence) of the early Stuart parliaments, just as behind Plumb stood Trevelyan, with his belief in the abiding importance of the two party system: here was Whig political history into which Stone and Plumb elided their model of economic and social change.[63] And from this analysis of past events they also derived a clear and shared contemporary message: as then, so now, the task of the responsible, perceptive statesman (be he Kennedy in America or Wilson in England) was 'not to perpetuate civil strife by attempting the impossible task of making history run backwards'. It was 'to accept the results of developments which he is powerless to reverse, to stabilize by legislation the social situation created by them, and to adjust the political system to the conditions which it imposes'.[64] Failure to do so meant revolution; success in doing so meant stability.

According to R.H. Tawney, this view of men and events had first been systematically elaborated by James Harrington in *Oceana*, a contemporary analysis of the causes of the civil war, and Stone shared his mentor's opinion that this was a fundamental historical insight.[65] As Stone understood him, Harrington believed that 'a constitution is a direct reflection of the distribution of social and economic power; and consequently the two must alter in step together if major upheavals are to be avoided'. But since the economy and society evolved of their own accord, it was the polity and the constitution which had to be changed when they no longer reflected economic and social realities. 'The view', Stone insisted, 'that there must be a direct relationship between social structure and political institutions, and that the former tends to dictate the latter' was 'widely accepted today', even by 'historians and politicians of a strongly anti-Marxist cast of mind.' It was certainly accepted by J.H. Plumb, who agreed that 'law and custom must give way to the needs of a changing world'; and it also provided the basis for the traditional explanation of the passing of the Great Reform Act in 1832, when the British constitution had to be remodelled and updated to take account of the disruptive economic and social changes of the preceding fifty years.[66]

Within this Harringtonian interpretation, which was preoccupied with the primacy of economic and social change, Stone's book stressed the 'critical importance of the response of those in authority in determining whether or not the revolutionary mood will lead to physical violence and destruction, or to peaceful accommodation and constructive adjustment'.[67] This was scarcely a surprising conclusion for a lifelong historian of the English aristocratic elite to reach, but it had also been reinforced by his observations of riot and protest in Paris and Princeton, and of the ways in which they had been handled (or not) by those ostensibly in charge. The worst response of those in authority to the disturbances and political demands arising from long-term economic and social change was 'intransigence', the failure 'to anticipate the need for reform', which blocked the possibility of peaceful, constitutional adjustment, united the opposition, polarized opinion, and opened the path to violence. By contrast, 'timely – as opposed to untimely – political concessions may win over moderate opinion and isolate the extremists'. And so in Stone's book, the 'triggers' to revolution were the 'misguided personal decisions' taken by Charles I and his advisers between 1640 and 1642, which led to 'physical violence and destruction'. Had they acted more flexibly and more imaginatively, the result might, instead, have been 'peaceful accommodation and constructive adjustment' – as the Whigs managed between 1714 and 1722, and again between 1830 and 1832.[68]

Stone also insisted that the long-lasting effects of the English revolution were significant and widely beneficial. He did not deny that the Restoration brought back the crown, the peers and the established church: 'England at the end of the revolution in 1660 was barely distinguishable from England at the beginning in 1640'. But he was equally certain that the radical *ideas* generated by the revolution *did* matter: indeed, they were so important and so portentous that they distinguished it from the mere rebellions taking place elsewhere in Europe at the same time.[69] For they were ideas about 'liberty not liberties, equality not privilege, fraternity not deference', which would 'live on, and… revive again in other societies in other ages' – ideas 'about religious toleration, about limitations on the power of the central executive to interfere with the personal liberty of the propertied classes, and about a polity based on the consent of a broad spectrum of society'. The 'establishment of these ideas as the common property of the nation was something quite new', which 'prepared the way for the extension of these privileges down the social scale at a later date, and something which could serve as a model in other times and places'. Thus did the English 'export political revolution all over Europe' and beyond, just as their successors would export industrial revolution to other far-off destinations. Here was *English* history as *world* history, and as history with a happy ending, and as such *Revolution* was a very euphoric, optimistic, sixties book.[70]

So, though in a more specifically directed way, was Plumb's. In its celebration of progress, and its evident sympathy for Walpole and the Whigs, *Stability* reflected the anti-Tory euphoria of those briefly optimistic years of 1964–66, when Harold Wilson seemed to have vanquished the corrupt, inept and anachronistic party of Profumo, Macmillan and Douglas-Home. According to Plumb, late-Stuart Tories were religiously bigoted, constitutionally obscurantist, economically backward, culturally xenophobic, and politically maladroit, and there was a joyous relish with which he described their demise thereafter:

> The Tory party was destroyed... by its incompetent leadership, by the cupidity of many of its supporters, by its own internal contradictions.... By 1727, Tories were outcasts, living on the frontiers of the political establishment.... By 1733,... Toryism... had become quite irrelevant.[71]

But it was not only the Tory Party that Plumb was attacking: it was also the Tories' favourite philosopher. For by insisting that stability had been deliberately made and consciously created, through the particular 'actions and decisions of men', rather than being of 'slow, coral like growth, the result of time, circumstance, prudence, experience, wisdom, slowly building up over the centuries', Plumb was explicitly questioning the political doctrines of Edmund Burke, whom he would dismiss elsewhere as being a purveyor of 'utter rubbish and completely unhistorical'. Indeed, according to Plumb, Burke offered no understanding of human society, being the supporter of prejudice, inequality and the status quo, and the enemy of reason and progress.[72]

Moreover, *Stability* did not confine its attacks to the Tory Party and to Tory philosophy. For it was also an assault on 'conservative historians', who constituted (surely Plumb was wrong about this?) 'the bulk of the historical profession', and of whom the outstanding example was Sir Lewis Namier, with his 'veneration for monarchy, aristocracy and tradition', his 'reverence for inherited status', and his 'belief in the authority of possessions'.[73] Plumb did not criticize Namier directly in his book; but he did severely chastise

Namier's disciple, the American scholar Robert Walcott, whose *English Politics in the Early Eighteenth Century*, had sought to 'atomize' the 1700s in the same way that Namier had earlier 'atomized' the 1750s. After a painstaking examination of the personnel of the Commons, Walcott had concluded that there were no political parties, no deeply divisive issues: only faction, connection and family relationship – in short, a very different, and far less agitated world than that which Trevelyan had depicted in *England Under Queen Anne*. But Plumb would have none of this: there *were* two parties at war with each other, there *were* great issues, and they *did* preoccupy the whole country, not just narrowly in the Commons, but across the length and breadth of the nation. Walcott's greatest sin (and it was an appropriately Burkeian and Tory one) was that he 'mistook genealogy for political history'.[74]

Plumb's final task in *Stability* was to get England from the early 1720s, where he left Walpole triumphant, to the mid 1960s, where it seemed as if Harold Wilson was triumphant. But there was a difficulty. For if the Whigs, on the side of progress and modernity, had triumphed under Walpole, why was it that British society had become so enervated and hide-bound (as Plumb believed it had) during the subsequent period? His answer was ingenious. For having thwarted the forces of reaction and obscurantism, the Whigs in turn became reactionaries, settling for the very world of patronage and place, inherited status and gentlemanly values, that Edmund Burke was to describe and celebrate later in the same century. And so, perhaps surprisingly, it was the increasingly conservative Whig oligarchy which created that long-lasting and highly inert political culture which failed 'to adjust its institutions and its social system to the needs of an industrial society'. And that belated adjustment, for Plumb as for many supporters of Harold Wilson, was precisely what they hoped and expected the Labour governments of 1964–70 would achieve.[75] Thus understood, *Stability* was not only an account of England from 1675 to 1725: it was also offering historical validation for Wilson's attempts to get Britain moving again by the application of the 'white-heat' of technology.

V

On publication, these two works were widely read and discussed, and they soon made their way on to reading lists in schools and universities on both sides of the Atlantic, where they remained for the best part of a generation. As befitted books whose authors were attempting to do many things, both historical and contemporary, and who sought to make history exciting and relevant, they were adjudged successes at many levels. Stone's *Revolution* was hailed as a dazzling display of interdisciplinary learning, as a brilliant summary of half a century of detailed scholarly investigation, as an audacious synthesis of economic, social, political, intellectual and cultural history, and as a cogent explanation of a very complex problem in the past which also seemed to be the most preoccupying problem of the present.[76] Plumb's *Stability* was equally acclaimed: for introducing a wholly new concept into historical inquiry; for specifying and for solving a particular problem which, once he had defined it, seemed both obvious and crucial, but which no one had previously been able to pin down; for bringing clarity and recognition to a period of English history which in recent decades had been both confused and neglected; for combining an awareness of long-term change with an appreciation of the importance of individual personalities; and for making the politicians, the planners and the policy makers more aware of what a complex, problematic and unusual thing 'stability' actually was.[77]

But there were also critics, and they mostly came from the right. In Stone's case, they were led by Geoffrey Elton, who had been deeply disturbed by the progressive mood and student unrest of the 1960s; who championed the very sort of narrow political and constitutional history that Stone so detested; who hated the *Annales* for downgrading his own brand of scholarship into mere *histoire événementielle*; who had no time for the 'social origins' interpretation of the Civil War or of anything else; who disliked Notestein and Gardiner as much as he disliked Trevelyan and Plumb; and who despised Tawney and loathed Stone.[78] And Elton was supported in his strictures by Blair Worden, a protégé of Hugh Trevor-Roper's, whose festschrift he would one day co-edit, and who shared Elton's dislike of Stone and sociology and social history.[79] For them, *Revolution* was a disaster and a disgrace. They did not derive any enlightenment from Stone's jargon or his discussion of the theories of revolution; they were unimpressed by his claims about the superiority of analytical over narrative history; they thought he gave too much attention to long-term causes, and insufficient to immediate political events; and they ridiculed his claim to be dealing with 'problems of general relevance'. In short, they were unimpressed by his three-stage model of historical causation which, stripped of its fashionable sixties pretentiousness, was essentially the same explanatory mechanism that had been used by Notestein and Gardiner; and they saw no good reason why these outmoded Whigs should be rehabilitated. This might be a 'highly personal interpretation', but it was scarcely an original one.[80]

Stone had anticipated that his book would not command universal assent, and he had been proven immediately and emphatically right, as Elton and Worden sketched out the general case against his interpretation which would be developed in detail by the next generation of self-styled 'revisionist' scholars. In the short run, Plumb did not fare so badly, not least because he had prudently given fewer hostages to fortune than Stone. But there were those (especially in Oxford) who wondered (in the manner of Elton and Worden) whether the 'modish New Look' that Plumb advanced went significantly beyond the 'traditional interpretation' of Trevelyan's era. Was stability suddenly brought about as a self-conscious and deliberate political act? They were not convinced. What about the impact of the change of dynasty, from the Stuarts to the Hanoverians in 1714, to which Plumb gave but scant attention? Surely this mattered. Did patronage really have the marked effect of subduing the opposition under Walpole? This was not convincingly demonstrated. Was the passing of the Septennial Act as important as Plumb claimed? It seemed unlikely. Was it right to inflate a peaceful change of dynasty and subsequent change of government into a world-historical scenario about the creation of political stability? Probably not. And in any case, what exactly did the concept of 'political stability' mean, and how valid was it? In both cases, they seemed to be implying, the answer might be 'not much'.[81]

These quick-fire criticisms of Stone and Plumb also hinted at deeper issues and unresolved problems. One concerned methodology. Did great events have to have correspondingly great and deep and multiple causes? Could long-term economic and social developments be elided into short-term high political events to help 'explain' them? How exactly, if at all, did such economic and social changes *lead* to political changes? Another anxiety concerned the scale of what was being described and explained. For was it so self-evident that these were great events? How truly revolutionary was the mid seventeenth century? How seriously unstable was Restoration England? How much more stable was Walpole's Robinocracy? Yet a third difficulty was that of diffusion and emulation. How far were all revolutions comparable? Did stability 'break out' everywhere it happened according to the same pattern? Did the rest of the world later follow down these two paths that England had pioneered?[82] A final issue was that of teleology: of working back from a known end point in the story. Stone and Plumb were interested in winners, in progress, in modernity: but what about the losers? Surely this stress on change, on processes, on things becoming something else, rather than on being what and remaining as they were, neglected the evidence (and experience) of continuity? 'To analyse a period', observed one reviewer of *Stability*, in words equally applicable to *Revolution*, 'in terms of what it was to lead to, deprives it of some of its characteristics.'[83]

By the mid and late 1970s, these vague doubts were beginning to crystallize, especially in the case of Stone's book. For in bringing together the Harringtonian interpretation of the civil war as 'social origins' with the Whig analysis of it as constitutional conflict, he presented an irresistible target to a new generation of scholars who were 'viscerally angry and frustrated' at what they regarded as its 'utter falsity' of this secular, anachronistic and over-generalized approach.[84] By contrast, these self-styled revisionists were, according to Geoffrey Elton, 'empiricist and non-ideological'. They looked at local and parliamentary sources which Stone and his generation had neglected; and they did not share the modish, whiggish, progressive, sixties mentality. (Of course, this did not mean that they had no ideology: but for Elton the only people who had 'ideology' were those with whom he disagreed.)[85] Taking their cue from Clarendon (who in opposition to Harrington had focused on short-term, political contingencies), such scholars as Conrad Russell, John Morrill, Mark Kishlansky, Kevin Sharpe and Anthony Fletcher rejected the siren-songs of the social sciences, turned against long-term explanations, and searched for answers in politics and religion. And in so doing, they did much to render out of date these words of Herbert Butterfield, with which he had indicted all Whig historians nearly half a century before: 'Much greater ingenuity and a much higher imaginative endeavour have been brought into play upon the Whigs, progressives and even revolutionaries of the past, than have been exercised upon the elucidation of Tories and conservatives and reactionaries.'[86]

From this very different perspective, the revisionists subjected the Stone interpretation to what they believed were devastating criticisms. There were, they insisted, no long-term 'preconditions' for 'revolution': developments in the economy and society and government were not one way but multi-directional, and the idea that the parliamentary opposition constituted a 'high road to civil war' was simply incorrect. Nor were there any 'precipitants' between 1629 and 1639: parliament was not 'rising' so much as weak and impotent, and there was limited opposition to royal policy. And so the breakdown, when it came, was as unexpected as it was unpremeditated: a high political crisis, as relations between the monarch and MPs suddenly collapsed, and as government imploded at the centre. As for the ensuing Civil War, it was not so much the first modern revolution, but the last old-fashioned war of religion. Or it was about disconnected local upheavals in the provinces. Or it was a baronial revolt. Or it was a *British* conflict, a war of the four kingdoms, precipitated by events in Ireland and Scotland rather than England. Or the whole thing was simply an accident.[87] In sum, Stuart England was not the setting for great events, with great causes and consequences: it was, according to Conrad Russell, *Unrevolutionary England*. At the very same time that the English Industrial Revolution, conceived as a big and much-emulated event, was being undermined and overturned, the same fate was befalling to the English political revolution, which had been conceived (or inflated?) in precisely the same way.[88]

Stone's book was the summation of a whole generation's approach to the seventeenth century which the young revisionists were determined to destroy. Plumb, by contrast, had sketched out an agenda for a hitherto much-less crowded field, which was eagerly and appreciatively taken up. In the next decade or so, many of his occasionally-speculative arguments were supported and fleshed out: the scale of the commercial revolution, the significance of military expenditure and government employment, the power of ideas and ideology, the nature of party politics in the reign of Queen Anne, the depth of divisions in the localities and constituencies, and the importance of the electorate.[89] Not for nothing was *Stability* described as 'one of the most fertile and truly original historical works written in the past thirty years', and it spawned an unprecedented number of edited volumes, taking up and elaborating the themes Plumb had outlined.[90] And it provided the inspiration for Derek Hirst's study of the seventeenth-century electoral system, the interpretive scheme for J.R. Jones's survey of the late Stuart era, the underlying structure for W.A. Speck's account of early Hanoverian England, the basic framework for Roy Porter's eighteenth-century social history, the essential background for John Brewer's analysis of the high and low politics in the 1760s, and it coincidentally corroborated Bernard Bailyn's account of the origins of modern American politics.[91]

But as the tide of revisionism swelled in seventeenth-century history writing, it eventually spilled over into the eighteenth: for if Stuart England was no longer seen as revolutionary, but as fundamentally stable, then the problem that Plumb had so imaginatively specified and solved ceased to be a problem at all. One of the long-term forces potentially making for stability, by which Plumb had set great store, was the consolidation of the land market in favour of the elite. But subsequent research cast grave doubt on this view of things.[92] Nor did his depiction of England from 1675 to 1714 as being on the brink of collapse and disintegration seem right. To be sure, there were serious disagreements about religion, the succession and foreign policy: but the system successfully contained these divisions; there was *already* 'a general acceptance by society of its political institutions, and of those classes of men or officials who control them'; many of the boroughs and constituencies were even then being brought under patron control; and the Tories were often as progressive and modernizing as the Whigs. And his depiction of England after 1714 was no less misleading: the Tory Party survived as a more coherent and credible force than Plumb had allowed; the Jacobite threat was real, not only in 1715, but again thirty years later; and popular politics continued virtually unabated.[93]

In short, pre-1715 England was less unstable, and post-1715 England was less stable, than Plumb had argued: his great 'before-and-after' drama in which 'adamantine' stability was hard won out of chaos was little more than a rhetorical (and ideological) creation. Such, at least, was the opinion of J.C.D. Clark who, spurred on by Geoffrey Elton, sought to construct a coherently revisionist interpretation of the seventeenth and eighteenth centuries, built around continuity rather than change, religion rather than modernity, and politics and the constitution rather than the economy and society. 'In the changed climate of the 1980s', Clark noted, it was now appropriate to stress 'the virtues of loyalty, diligence, discipline, subordination and obedience.'[94] From this essentially Thatcherite perspective, both seventeenth- and eighteenth-century English society were dominated by the traditional props of any ancien régime: the monarchy, the aristocracy and the church. Revolution, progress and secularization had no place in this scheme of things where divine right, providential subordination and religious belief remained the natural state of affairs. This, in turn, enabled Clark to reject the Harringtonian model which implied that economic and social change must lead to political and constitutional change. This was wrong for the 1640s, wrong for the 1720s, and wrong for the 1830s. For politics operated largely autonomously from the economy and society: it had its own internal dynamic, and was best explained in terms of accident and contingency – or, if something more substantial was needed, then by religion.[95]

By the mid 1980s, this was close to becoming the new orthodoxy – not only because this was the way the logic and dynamic of scholarly inquiry were going, but also because the broader political and cultural climate had changed dramatically (and influentially) since the 1960s. The seventies had been an era of failed administrations in the United Kingdom and the United States, both on the right (Heath and Nixon) and on the left (Wilson–Callaghan and Carter), signalling the breakdown of the post-war liberal consensus. The eighties, by contrast, saw new, confident, energized, messianic right-wing governments installed on both sides of the Atlantic, dominated by Reagan and Thatcher, which were strongly ideological. Both the prime minister and the president hated liberals and hated 'the sixties', which they regarded as a 'third rate decade', 'insufferable, smug, sanctimonious, naive, guilt-ridden, wet [and] pink', with big spending governments, permissive legislation, self-indulgent secularism, and pampered and protesting universities, full of 'tenured radicals', who would later deny Thatcher her honorary degree at Oxford. *They*, by contrast, believed in religion, order and duty; they hated consensus and compromise, and spurned accommodation and retreat; they provided firm, decisive and (where necessary) confrontationalist leadership; and in defiance of the Harringtonian view of the world, they were even willing to 'attempt the impossible task of making history run backwards'.[96]

In this very different political climate, the academic landscape, and the trajectory of historical inquiry were both bound to change. This was partly a matter of passing generations. In politics, as Noel Annan noted, Thatcher led the hissing and booing which saw 'his age' – the liberal, secular and accommodationist generation that had dominated Britain and America since the Second World War – leave the stage. And in the academy, it became fashionable to depict historians of that generation – not just Stone and Plumb, but also Christopher Hill and Rodney Hilton, Edward Thompson and Eric Hobsbawm – as 'yesterday's men': the 'class of '68', as J.C.D. Clark dismissively (and mistakenly) called them.[97] And it was partly that economics, sociology and political science, having conspicuously failed to provide the means whereby the world might be transformed for the better, were no longer the confident, creative disciplines they had been two decades before. But it was also a matter of ideology: for while not all the revisionists were Thatcherite, and few were as enamoured of her as Clark (who likened her to Gloriana), there was a definite tinge of Thatcherism in revisionism. Thatcher thought high politics mattered; so did the revisionists, who once again made *histoire événementielle* the main event. Thatcher thought religion mattered; so did the revisionists, whether they believed in God or not. Thatcher thought there was no such thing as society; the revisionists thought there was no such thing as sociology. Thatcher hated the wets; the revisionists hated the Whigs. The result was a very different political and intellectual climate from the 1960s, and Stone and Plumb now found themselves out of touch with their times, rather than being in harmony with them.[98]

VI

Of the two authors, Stone's response to his critics was, predictably, the more defiant, as he made plain in an unrepentant postscript to a new edition of *Revolution*, published in 1985. He had no time for 'the writings of the new British school of young antiquarian empiricists', who wrote 'detailed political narratives which implicitly deny that there is any deep-seated meaning to history except the accidental whim of fortune and personality'; he thought the revisionists were merely the 'very erudite and intelligent chroniclers of the petty event, of *l'histoire événementielle*'; and he urged that their 'neo-namierite' attitude to political history stemmed 'from a sense of disillusionment with the capacity of the contemporary parliamentary system to grapple with the inexorable economic and power decline of Britain'.[99] Their case, he insisted, was weak and unconvincing – too obsessed with detail, incapable of grasping the larger landscape, and unwilling to recognize that historical causation was a complex, multi-faceted phenomenon, in which the detailed events of high politics had to be contextualized more broadly and in a longer time span. And he remained convinced that the English revolution *was* a big and portentous event: 'the first of the so-called great revolutions of the world... one of the great central episodes of the western world', which must necessarily have great causes, by which he meant it must have both important causes, and also multiple causes.[100]

But even Stone had to take some account of the changing climate of political opinion and scholarly interests. On second thoughts, he admitted that *Revolution* was too riddled with jargon; he felt he should have begun the precipitants in 1625 rather than 1629, when relations between the king and parliament began to deteriorate; he conceded that, while recognizing the importance of religion, he was not, as a non-believer, happy 'working on something which I have not had any personal experience of'; and he came to doubt the value of the 'three-tiered model of causal factors in history' that he had employed. Indeed, by the 1980s, Stone had begun to wonder whether the social sciences could still provide helpful insights for the historian: he was worried by the inaccessible excesses of quantification and psycho-history, he feared the *Annales* school was atrophying into methodological rigidity, and he lamented that arid social science history was reaching an ever smaller audience. He was, then, not altogether surprised that a younger generation of scholars were rejecting the structural analysis that had been so fashionable among the 'new historians' of the 1960s, and were returning to more conventional narrative modes.[101] Only Robert Brenner, his most loyal American disciple, and a dwindling number of sociologists, continued to believe that the 'social origins' interpretation of the English revolution was the most fruitful way to approach the problem.[102]

Not surprisingly, Stone's later work moved in different directions, and to much bigger projects which were more research-based than synthetic, and which left politics very much to one side – to a study of the family, sex and marriage in the early modern period (which denoted a shift in his interdisciplinary interests from sociology to anthropology, and from political science to psychology); to the quantitative history of country houses and upward social mobility (which inadvertently corroborated the revisionists' views that not much changed in England between the fifteenth and the nineteenth centuries); to a history of divorce (which gave more attention to case studies than to an over-arching explanatory framework); and finally to a consideration of Britain as an imperial state at war in the long eighteenth century (in which he belatedly turned his attention to state power, the military and overseas expansion).[103] By then, Stone had fully embraced the new narrative mode he had earlier and presciently discerned, once describing himself, towards the end of his career, as being no more than an old man, sitting by the fireside, telling stories; and for all his earlier openness to new approaches and methodologies, he vehemently disapproved of what he saw as the irresponsible (and ahistorical) excesses of post-modernism. But he remained to the end a liberal trans-atlanticist, the self-styled 'last of the Whigs', and on his death in 1999 he was uniquely honoured with memorial services both at an Ivy League university and in an Oxford college.[104]

For Stone, *Revolution* was thus a brief and bravura pause between much bigger and more varied projects, and he continued writing and working almost until his death. But for Plumb, *Stability* was both his first and his last sustained work of history (amplified in two subsequent articles dealing with the electorate and popular politics), and his next book was entitled, with inadvertent prescience, *The Death of the Past* (London, 1969), in which he reaffirmed his view that 'the purpose of historical investigation is to produce answers, in the form of concepts and generalizations, to the fundamental problems of historical change in the social activities of men'.[105] But thereafter, he lost his momentum. The third volume of the Walpole biography was started but not finished. He toyed with a project on eighteenth-century leisure (modernity and progress once again), but although there were several essays, no book ever appeared. And a study of the British seaborne Empire, for his own *History of Human Society* series, was not even begun. Instead, Plumb turned his attention to television, writing the scripts for a series on British monarchs as builders and collectors, which was presented by Huw Wheldon, and which portended Plumb's transformation from radical sceptic to pillar of the establishment, as admiring of 'monarchy, aristocracy and tradition' as Lewis Namier had ever been. And he began (but again, did not complete) an edition of his collected essays, linked together by auto-biographical recollections, in which he paid off old academic scores, and claimed he had always been a Thatcherite – even before Thatcher.[106]

Part cause, part consequence of this loss of momentum was that Plumb resigned his Cambridge chair in 1974, so that he could spend more time in the United States and also devote himself to writing *Royal Heritage*. Having discharged that task, he was elected Master of Christ's College in 1978, where he entertained in appropriately regal (and Walpolean) style, and where his earliest guests included the now-retired Harold Wilson and Marcia Falkender, to whom he was still (if diminishingly) close. For Plumb had been disappointed not to receive a peerage in Wilson's famous resignation honours of May 1976, when his name had been crossed off the controversial 'lavender list' at a late stage, and as Labour descended into fratricidal unelectability, he moved rapidly to the right, throwing in his lot with the now seemingly-omnipotent Thatcher.[107] He was belatedly knighted after the expiration of his mastership in 1982, but the hoped-for peerage never materialized, in part because the true Thatcherite believers were never wholly convinced by his conversion to their creed and cause. His sixties attitudes were always held against him and, despite his disclaimers, they were amply (and unwisely) paraded again in his two volumes of collected essays. They were not well received on the right, which may partly explain the project's abrupt demise, and Plumb published nothing else before his death, shortly after his ninetieth birthday, in 2001.[108]

Meanwhile, the revisionist impulses had reached their zenith in the mid 1980s, when they seemed poised to carry all before them in their 'frontal challenge to the whiggish canon', and when there was little the old Whigs could do except protest ineffectually. Geoffrey Elton was appointed Regius Professor of Modern History at Cambridge in 1983, and in his (second) inaugural lecture he pronounced the Whig interpretation of history dead for good (in both senses). Lawrence Stone lamented that so much blood, 'a great deal of it mine', had been shed by those who were determined to re-write the history of the seventeenth century; and Sir John Plumb was visibly disconcerted by the ferocity of the attacks launched on him by J.C.D. Clark from those two bastions of 'thinking Thatcherism': Peterhouse, Cambridge, and All Souls College, Oxford.[109] Not since the 'storm over the gentry' or the 'standard of living' controversy had modern British historians seemed so riven. In fact, revisionism had taken different forms in the two centuries. Those working on the Stuarts had less of a contemporary political agenda, they were more concerned with archives than with printed sources, they produced a substantial body of work, and they were not altogether happy about what was being done to the Hanoverian era. And so seventeenth-century revisionists became mainstream in a way that eighteenth-century revisionists never did. But these distinctions were not so apparent at the time as they have since become.[110]

In any case, and like many self-styled scholarly revolutionaries, the revisionists soon began to lose their sense of purpose and identity, in part because the political climate changed with the retirement of Reagan in 1988 and the fall of Thatcher two years later, and in part because the more detailed the research they themselves undertook, the less convincing (or consistent) their arguments became. Many historians of the seventeenth century became so preoccupied with the 'exultation in sources, the more arcane the better', and with relishing detail and decrying generalization, that they were left with a disconcerting number of mono-causal explanations for the outbreak of the Civil War which it has so far proved impossible to fit together, and which are of little interest to non-specialists in seventeenth-century English history, let alone to that broader readership for whom Stone sought to write.[111] Indeed, some self-styled 'post-revisionists' are now daring to suggest that early Stuart England did witness severe conflict; that 'long-term social, ideological and political developments' leading up to the outbreak of the Civil War should be reconsidered; and that Stone may have been right in urging the need to think carefully and comprehensively about the problems of historical causation.[112]

In the same way, among historians of the eighteenth century, the Jacobite obsession soon ran its course, work on the Whigs and the Tories lost momentum, and studies of popular politics reached a consensus that there may have been more activity during the early Hanoverian decades than Plumb had been inclined to allow, but not sufficient to make it as unstable as mid or late seventeenth-century England had been.[113] More generally, interpretations were soon put forward by John Brewer, Linda Colley, Julian Hoppit, Paul Langford and Roy Porter (many, but not all, of them recent protégés of Sir John Plumb) which reasserted the importance of trade, commerce, urban growth, modernity, rationality and middle-class culture: all the themes which Clark had so roundly rejected in Plumb's own account.[114] And so the attempt to depict Hanoverian society as an unchanging 'ancien régime' as a result of what G.R. Elton had prematurely called 'the Jonathan Clark revolution', has scarcely carried the day. Indeed, after a period of calm and mature reflection, Clark's arguments have been dismissed in the most authoritative recent account of eighteenth-century England as frequently 'tilting at windmills'.[115]

VII

What conclusions might we draw from this account of the genesis, appearance and reception of Stone's *Revolution* and Plumb's *Stability*, these two landmark works of 1960s history? For reasons that should by now be clear, no modern historian is likely to be impartial in this matter; but here is an attempt at an even-handed summation. To their critics, both in the 1960s and increasingly thereafter, these were glib, superficial, modish, misleading books, which exemplified many of the fashionable scholarly faults of the highly unsatisfactory time in which they were produced. They were too preoccupied with economic and social change, and they underestimated the importance of continuity, religion, contingency and politics. They were too whiggish, too materialist, too teleological, too secular, too present-minded, too concerned with causes, processes and outcomes. Both were attempting, as Conrad Russell put it in another Stone-breaking context, to 'explain events which did not happen in terms of a social change for which the evidence remains uncertain'.[116] And as a result, it seemed to their detractors that they over-inflated the subjects they dealt with, they over-extended their contemporary relevance, they over-determined the results, and they over-explained the causes. Not surprisingly, then, 'the causes of the English revolution' and 'the growth of political stability' now reside on the scrap heap of sixties history, along with such other clichéd casualties as 'the take off into self-sustained growth', and 'the making of the English working class'.[117]

But a more positive and appreciative conclusion would be that these were clever, thoughtful, exciting and original works, full of fertile hypotheses and suggestive generalizations which ought, in J.H. Hexter's words, 'to be licensed to put on their covers in bold type *Pay attention! Listen to me! Follow along! Have fun!*' 'Books as lively, as intelligent, as clever, as bubbling with ideas as these', Hexter went on, 'deserve to be read for themselves and for the intellectual excitement they generate.'[118] That was true of *Revolution* and *Stability* when they first appeared; and it remains true today. For notwithstanding the criticisms subsequently levelled at them, Stone and Plumb *were* on to important things. They saw the big picture: not completely, not fully nuanced, not entirely convincingly. But the big picture, nevertheless. 'How much', Glenn Burgess asked in 1990, 'have we lost in reaction to [Plumb] and Stone? For all their many faults, both integrated into one picture economic, social, political, religious and intellectual history. Who does that any more?' It is a good question. 'What exactly', he inquired elsewhere, 'is wrong with Whig history?'[119] The answer, as for Tory history is, no doubt, a great deal. But neither Stone nor Plumb could be reproached for narrow-mindedness, intellectual timidity, or public indifference. 'The test of an historian', Lawrence Stone once wrote of R.H. Tawney, in words equally applicable to himself and to J.H. Plumb, 'is not so much the final validity of his theories, as the originality of his approach, his talent for devising new and more fruitful ways of looking at the past.' Judged by that criterion, both *Revolution* and *Stability* still stand up well.[120]

Of course, and thanks in part to the revisionists themselves, we *do* now know more about the mid seventeenth and early eighteenth centuries than we did in the 1960s, and there was a time when the revisionist approach was itself 'a new and more fruitful way' of looking at the past. But that, too, has now largely had its day, as revisionism in its turn has also become (as some perceptive observers foresaw that it would) part of the settled historiographical landscape of an earlier era.[121] From the longer perspective afforded by the new century, it is clear that many of the revisionists were as much the creatures of the 1980s as Stone and Plumb were of the 1960s, and their much-vaunted, Eltonian claims to non-ideological truth, to a higher order of scholarly rectitude, and (on occasions) to superior moral worth, were little more than the standard war cries of young turks, which have long since ceased to be credible or convincing.[122] Once more, history has moved on. Today, the most exciting work on seventeenth- and eighteenth-century Britain is again turning outwards, this time towards the wider Atlantic and imperial world. But who can know how long this new impulse will last, or what will, eventually, replace it?[123]

To be sure, fashions in history change and evolve, come and go, but some things seem more enduring.[124] For this particular episode also bears out the general proposition that some historians (usually on the left) prefer complex explanations of large-scale problems associated with great leaps forward, while others (usually on the right) prefer detailed scholarship and believe it convincingly demonstrates that little in the past ever changes very much. This distinction – between Harringtonians and Clarendonians, Whigs and Tories, parachutists and truffle-hunters, lumpers and splitters; between those who believe it important to write for a general audience, and those who prefer to write for fellow scholars; between those who seek to link particular historical episodes with broader attempts at human understanding, and those who disdain such activities; and between those 'who try to make sense of history and those who see nothing in it but the play of the contingent and the unforeseen' – this distinction has existed for as long as history has been made and been written, and since it is based on faith and belief rather than fact and certainty, on politics and ideology rather than on truth and proof, there seems no reason to suppose it will ever end – even though there are some very good reasons why it should.[125]

All that can be ventured on the basis of this survey is that historians have an obligation to recognize that this is the way history works, to try to be as clear and candid as possible (as Lawrence Stone himself always was) as to just where we ourselves fit in to this scheme of things, and also to recognize that there are broader, complementary explanations as to how and why history writing seems to move forward in this essentially adversarial and generational fashion. During the second half of the twentieth century, as in earlier periods, the Whig interpretation of history was in the ascendant at some times, and the Tory interpretation of history at others, both within the academy and outside. And if we are to understand how and why this has been so, then we need to look, not just at the internal logic of evolving scholarly inquiry, at the historians who were writing, the methodologies they were employing, the questions they were posing, and the subjects they were treating: we also need to recognize the broader public culture and political climate by which they are influenced (sometimes consciously, sometimes not), which give different approaches different resonances at different times.

But as the revisionists repeatedly insisted, and as Stone and Plumb both accepted in their own way and day, we should always seek to modify broad-brush generalizations with appreciation of individual contingency, and that is as true when writing about historians as when writing history. To be sure, many disagreements between scholars can be explained in terms of Whig and Tory predispositions, but (at the risk of imitating Walcott) there are also what might be termed genealogies of amity and animosity, individual alliances and antipathies, both within and across academic generations: Trevelyan to Plumb, Tawney to Stone, Trevor-Roper to Worden, Elton to Clark, are all instances of the torch being passed on; Trevor-Roper versus Stone, Stone versus Elton, Elton versus Plumb, Plumb versus Clark, are all examples of the fuse being lit.[126] But that is not the only way in which partisan generalizations need to be carefully qualified and individually inflected. For among historians, as among politicians, there are those who defy these easy and appealing partisan categories. Conrad Russell was the leading revisionist of his generation. But as the son of a great Whig philosopher, who took the Liberal Democratic whip in the House of Lords, he could hardly be regarded as the embodiment of revisionism as Thatcherism. As for the latter-day Gloriana herself: she may have hated Whigs and liberals; but her own view of her nation's history was even more complacent and self-regarding than that of Macaulay or Gardiner.[127]

The urge to see patterns in the past, and the impulse to deny that any such patterns exist, are both as old as history writing itself. But here is one final generalization which is surely beyond contention or dispute. A generation from now (or perhaps, who knows, even before that?) those of us writing in the 2000s will no doubt seem to have been as much the time-bound and outmoded creatures of our decade as Plumb and Stone seem now to have been of the 1960s, and the revisionists of the 1980s. There is, then, much by way of interest to be learned from exposing and exploring the temporal limitations (and inspirations) of our professional predecessors. But there is nothing to be gained by way of comfort. To accuse them of being 'deeply engaged in the political and intellectual movements of [the] day', to dismiss them with a supercilious air for having been 'present-minded', will not prevent others in the future from pointing the same accusing finger at us. In the light of this, and as Hugh Trevor-Roper rightly observed, 'some humility is in order'. 'For if we all date,' he goes on, 'who can claim exemption from a universal law?'[128] In more ways than one, history remains, as it always has been and always will be, wiser than any of us who do the best we can to try to write it.

Epilogue:
Making History, Then?[1]

On 1 May 1997, Tony Blair kissed hands as Prime Minister of the United Kingdom of Great Britain and Northern Ireland, and exactly twelve months later, to the very day, on 1 May 1998, I took office as Director of the Institute of Historical Research here in the University of London. It must seem by turns both presumptuous and bathetic to link together these two very different events and these two very different positions, for this was a potential historical coincidence that stubbornly refused to happen, and one that few people would have noticed even if it had occurred. Yet if we give or take twelve months or so at either end of it, the fact remains that my ten-year association with the IHR has been virtually coterminous with Blair's New Labour decade at 10 Downing Street. Nor is that the only such near-but-not-quite-happenstance in terms of comings and goings, or of beginnings and endings, for during the same period, J.K. Rowling commenced and completed her world-conquering cycle of best-selling novels, starting with *Harry Potter and the Philosopher's Stone*, published in June 1997, and concluding with *Harry Potter and the Deathly Hallows*, which appeared in July 2007. There seems no reason to suppose that either Blair or Rowling will reciprocate by relating their respective years of power and of productivity to my decade at the Institute. Nevertheless, these close but near-miss coincidences do remind us that all academics live and work in particular periods of historic time, that those times invariably exert a greater influence on us than we ourselves exert on them, and that what we do is thus inextricably linked with when we do it.

In any event, Tony Blair is gone from British politics, the Harry Potter saga has been triumphantly concluded, and my time here at the IHR is also drawing rapidly to a close: hence this valedictory occasion. But before I get to the substance of my remarks, I must observe that such farewell lectures by professors of history in this country are even less common occurrences than inaugurals – and those are not exactly frequent happenings, either. Indeed, in recent decades, there seem to have been only two valedictions of any substantial significance, and both of them, as it happens, were given by Regius Professors vacating their chairs in Oxford. Yet for powerful (albeit opposite) reasons, neither of them provides models or precedents which I am willing or able to emulate. The first was delivered by Hugh Trevor-Roper, who took his leave by lecturing on the subject of 'History and Imagination'; but this was a phrase which would later come back to haunt him, when he mistakenly authenticated the forged Hitler diaries, and his resonant but risky title is a hostage to fortune I would prefer not to give.[2] The second was delivered by his successor, Sir Michael Howard, who bade his farewell by discoursing on 'Structure and Process in History'; but, like Trevor-Roper before him, he declined to furnish a narrative of his time and tenure as Regius Professor, although he has subsequently done so, and with characteristic urbanity, wisdom and generosity, in his splendid autobiography, *Captain Professor*.[3]

Unlike these two great and illustrious Oxonian illuminati, and for reasons which I anticipated in my own inaugural lecture here as Director, I *do* feel a strong obligation to provide some report of my work during my decade here at the IHR; for I thought then, and I still think now, that British universities and British academics should do more and work harder when it comes to the task of explaining – and thus of justifying – to our paymasters and to the public what it is that we actually do and why it is that we actually do it. Accordingly, I offer this lecture as a pioneering contribution to this strangely-neglected and under-developed field of academic endeavour and (as it might seem) professorial (and institutional) self-justification; and in so doing, I shall be taking up some of the closing words of my inaugural, delivered in the far-off past of an earlier millennium, where I urged that there was not only life to be lived, but that there was also work to be done, that there was history to be written and that there might even, perhaps, in some small way, be history to be made.[4] Across the intervening decade at the IHR, I have sought to keep these injunctions and imperatives constantly in mind; and having set myself, and having been set by others, certain tasks and targets when I began here, I should like to describe how I have tried to undertake them, and what I have done to achieve them. And I shall furnish this account of the different ways in which I have sought to make history in the three sections into which any lectures I deliver seem invariably to be divided: first, my reforming, fund-raising and entrepreneurial work for the Institute itself; then my scholarly and literary activities as an administrator, author, writer and broadcaster; and finally my participation in the wider national realm of academic endeavour, cultural engagement and public service.

I

When I became the eighth Director of the Institute of Historical Research in what still seemed, in the spring of 1998, the heady aftermath of New Labour's new dawn, I found an organization which in some ways appropriately mirrored the nation of whose affairs Tony Blair had recently taken charge, for it was a place where problems aplenty co-existed on an approximately equal scale with real potential and great possibilities.[5] The good news was that the IHR had been an admired and respected fixture on the scholarly historical landscape – local, national and international – for the best part of three quarters of a century; that it boasted a marvellous working library, an unrivalled array of conferences and seminars, and two important research units (the *Victoria County History* and the Centre for Metropolitan History); that many of its staff were long-serving, distinguished and devoted; and that there was a great deal of goodwill towards the place and also, I sensed, towards me. The bad news was that the IHR was housed in accommodation which it would be polite to describe as dishevelled and depressing; that the staff, though not all of them were dishevelled, were themselves in many cases understandably depressed, and with good reason; that the HEFCE funding allocated through the School of Advanced Study was inadequate for the tasks the Institute was expected to discharge; and that the structure of management and oversight left a great deal to be desired. Moreover, although two members of staff had recently produced a lively and informative history of the place, there was (as we would now say) no mission statement or institutional narrative: of why the IHR had been established by Professor A.F. Pollard in 1921, of what exactly it had been doing since then, of what was going on there now, of where it wanted to be in ten years' time, or of how it intended to get there.[6]

It was made plain to me when I was appointed that I was expected to propel the IHR vigorously into the twenty-first century which would very soon be arriving; and that to do so, I must provide strong leadership and a firm sense of direction, which also meant that it would be necessary for me to raise some substantial sums of money. In retrospect, I am not only appreciative, but also amazed, at the combination of confidence, audacity, foolhardiness and sheer desperation which had been displayed by the appointments committee in recommending me. For at that time, my experience of senior academic administration was limited to one term as acting chairman of the History Department at Columbia University, and I had not raised a penny in my life for anything, let alone for history. On the other hand, I enjoyed a reasonably high professional profile, I had published books which had created something of a stir, I was relatively well-known in the London and New York media, I had a broad range of friendships and connections on both sides of the Atlantic, I had spent enough time in the United States to believe that fund-raising was not only desirable but also possible, and the challenge of the post and of the place had in some intangible but definite way captured my imagination.[7] It was a job I very much wanted, and I was eager to make a success of it, not least because, at 47, I was the youngest Director since V.H. Galbraith, and like him, but unlike all my other predecessors, I was determined to go on to do other things, and not to ease my way towards retirement in the IHR.

Among the most urgent tasks I faced was that of doing something to improve and brighten up the building, and in this I was lucky, because soon after I began as Director, the Vice-Chancellor paid an official visit to the Institute, and clearly found the ambience as gloomy and miserable as I did. He rapidly agreed to provide a major sum which enabled us to refurbish large parts of the basement, all of the ground floor, and much of the third floor; and this imaginative gift was subsequently followed by generous donations from the British and the American Friends of the IHR, which enabled us to refurbish the Common Room and the Periodicals Room; and also by a substantial grant from the Wolfson Foundation which enabled us to redecorate the British Local History Room, and to carve out of it two new spaces, exclusively dedicated to meetings, which we named the Wolfson and the Pollard Rooms. These improvements were not only important in making many areas of the IHR more cheery and more welcoming: they also showed that with luck and leadership we could get beyond complaining that things were not good, and actively change our working environment for the better. At the same time, I also sought to create a much clearer management structure built around the IHR's activities: the library, publications, events and premises, the *Victoria County History*, the Centre for Metropolitan History, and the Centre for Contemporary British History, which I succeeded in incorporating formally and fully into the IHR, where it had previously lodged, but as an independent entity. Having reformed the internal administration, and having been able to make some excellent promotions and new appointments, I set about pulling the place together, by breaking down the regrettable division that existed between 'academics' and 'administrators', and by trying to engage all the staff in the challenging but exhilarating task of institutional regeneration, revival and renewal.

To achieve this end, I also needed to reduce in size the well-meaning but unwieldy Advisory Council which, after two years' hard and persistent labour, I eventually succeeded in doing (things did not always move rapidly, I soon learned, in the Senate House). As slimmed down and reconstituted, the Advisory Council was peopled by representatives of our three most significant constituencies: the colleges of the University of London, the historical profession across the United Kingdom, and the broader scholarly-cum-public world, as personified by the Director of the National Portrait Gallery, the Chairman of English Heritage, and a former President of the British Academy, all of whom generously accepted my invitation to serve. I also orchestrated and co-ordinated all the meetings of the IHR committees which oversaw its six separate sections, to ensure that they reported to the Advisory Council, which was thus able, for the first time, to get a comprehensive picture at the end of each term of what had been going on during the preceding months. And by providing ample documentation, and by constructing the agenda so as to allow extensive room for discussion of several major items each meeting, the level and the energy of participation were both significantly raised. Above all, I was exceptionally lucky in the two chairs of the reformed Advisory Council, Professors Jinty Nelson and Peter Marshall, both of them lifelong devotees of the IHR, and both of them people of outstanding scholarly distinction and personal integrity. They provided support, advice and guidance in generous and unstinted abundance; and their backing for what I was trying to do convinced many other historians in the University of London, who might otherwise have been inclined to wonder what this brash outsider was up to, that change needed to happen and that change indeed had to happen.

By such measures and such means, I succeeded in re-furbishing, re-structuring and re-forming the IHR – not completely, but to a significant extent. But I didn't just want the place to look better and to function better, important though these considerations were: I also wanted it to do more things than it had been doing, and to reach out to a wider public audience as it did so. Situated in the heart of Bloomsbury, the Institute had always been a place where outstanding scholarly work had the potential to engage a broader constituency, and it was that potential which I sought to realize, in the first instance by expanding our conference programme. The starting point was the annual Anglo-American Conferences of Historians which had taken place here every July for well over half a century. I sought to re-energize a rather tired format, by embracing such big subjects as 'Monarchy', 'Race and Ethnicity', 'War and Peace', 'The Sea', and 'The Body', and also by organizing a special gathering to mark the fiftieth anniversary of the periodical *Past & Present*. I persuaded a succession of high profile speakers to give plenary lectures, from John Elliott, Eric Hobsbawm and Michael Howard to Roy Jenkins, John Tusa and Tom Phillips. I obtained sponsorship from publishers and friends, which enabled us to hold receptions at the Cabinet War Rooms, the Theatre Museum, the National Portrait Gallery and the Wallace Collection, and on these occasions I made a speech outlining what we had achieved at the IHR during the previous twelve months. There was always, and increasingly, plenty to say. And I did all I could to involve the Americans as well as the Anglos, especially the representatives of our largest and loyalist overseas constituency, the North American Conference on British Studies.

These Anglo-American gatherings soon began to generate a new buzz and energy, and thus encouraged, I resolved to add a January conference to these reinvigorated summer events. I began by co-organizing a meeting with the Royal Historical Society exploring how Winston Churchill's reputation would be regarded during the twenty-first century, and I also persuaded Mary Soames, Bill Deedes, Peter Carrington and Tony Benn to offer their own reminiscences of the great man.[8] But the seating for their panel got rather muddled, which gave me the (surely unique?) opportunity, when introducing these distinguished guests, to begin by saying 'on the far right is Mr Tony Benn'. I followed this with a conference on 'What Is History Now?', to mark the fortieth anniversary of the publication of E.H. Carr's classic work, and later convened a meeting to consider the past and future prospects of the country house, not just in England, but in Scotland and Ireland as well. But the most successful of these January conferences was that which I organized in 2003 on the subject of 'History and the Media', when I persuaded (among others) Jeremy Isaacs, Simon Schama, Tristram Hunt, Ian Kershaw and Melvyn Bragg to appear.[9] The ensuing dialogue between academics and media people was engaged and exhilarating, and occasionally surprising; and in this last category was Kate Adie, who gave a vivid and vigorous account of her time covering the war in Bosnia. In the middle of a battle-scarred landscape, she came across a combatant, who looked like a bandit, and might have been an assassin, sporting a Che Guevara moustache, the look of blood lust in his eyes, two magazines of bullets slung across his chest, and two pistols at the ready. Greatly daring, but fearing the worst Adie inquired as to his profession. 'Madam,' he replied, as if the answer was self-evident, 'I am a librarian.'

These conferences helped raise the IHR's profile, not only in the academic profession, but also in the broader public realm: as Melvyn Bragg kindly put it, 'you called us all in, and because it was you we all came'. Yet as I had realized at the outset, the Institute's activities could only be substantially expanded and enhanced if our income was significantly increased, which meant that I needed to undertake some serious fund-raising; and I set out the case in my inaugural lecture, where I came up with a target of £20 million.[10] At that time, there was no one working in the Senate House who knew much about raising money, and like many academics and administrators, they inclined to regard it with a mixture of benevolence, indifference, scepticism and outright disapproval. Accordingly, I sought advice from two good friends, who knew more about this subject than anyone else in London: Claus Moser and Jacob Rothschild. Both made it plain that fund-raising was hard and exhausting work; that it had to be done seriously and persistently, or not at all; that in order to get money, it was necessary to spend money first; that without a development office, there would be no chance of achieving anything; and that it would be necessary to set up a separate IHR Trust to hold any sums we might eventually receive. With a hard-pressed budget, I had no choice but to raise the money needed for a development office and, rather to my surprise, I soon succeeded in doing so. This in turn enabled me to appoint a director of development, and to establish the IHR Trust, and we were in business. Since then, we have raised a sum which is fast approaching £15 million: not quite, and not yet, the £20 million I initially wanted, and scarcely petty cash in comparison with the sums that American universities routinely generate. Nevertheless, by British standards, it is a significant figure: indeed, the largest sum that any university has succeeded in raising for history.

Among the many gifts and benefactions we have so gratefully received in recent years, I must mention (again) the donations from the Vice-Chancellor, from the British and American Friends of the IHR, and from the Wolfson Foundation which enabled us to refurbish substantial parts of our building; the Professorships in Metropolitan History and in Contemporary British History that were funded by the Leverhulme Trust; the massive grant from the Heritage Lottery Fund for the *Victoria County History*; and the constant support from the Andrew W. Mellon Foundation of New York for, among other things, the digitization of many of our primary printed sources.[11] These are some of the grants and gifts which fundamentally changed our lives at the IHR, by transforming the work we were able to do, just as I had hoped and believed that they would. In the first place, they enabled us to raise our intellectual credibility, with the appointment of professors who provided academic leadership for each of the three research centres which had previously been lacking.[12] In the second place, they made it possible for us to engage more fully with the challenges and opportunities of IT, and with the new political agenda of access and outreach. In the third place, this meant we were able to fulfil, more effectively than hitherto, our mission to promote the best scholarly work in history, and to make it available to a broad public audience. And finally, such successes as we enjoyed transformed the culture of the IHR itself: instead of complaining at what we couldn't do because the HEFCE grant was not big enough, we now took charge of our own agenda and affairs, decided what we wanted to do, and then set about raising the money which would enable us to do it.

One indication of our success in raising these substantial, external sums of money is that over the last ten years, our turnover at the IHR has doubled, from roughly £1.5 million to more than £3 million; and during the same period, on that rising trend, the proportion of our annual income which is provided by the HEFCE grant has gone down from 56 per cent to less than 30 per cent. Put the other way, this means that we now obtain two thirds of our annual income from outside sources, and this greatly enhances not only what we do, but also our capacity to determine and our freedom to decide what it is we want to do. Of all the things that have happened at and to the IHR during the last ten years, this change in the size and the structure of our income has been the most innovative, the most enabling, the most liberating and the most significant in its consequences. And it is not at all coincidence that this diversification of our income stream parallels and replicates (albeit on a much smaller scale) the sort of changes that have been happening to the revenue patterns of our museums and galleries, where a similar trend is clear across the same period: away from total dependence on government, and towards diversification and self-help. At the same time, this widening of our sources of funding also bears out an argument that is increasingly being made in the higher echelons of higher education, namely that the strongest and most secure universities are those with the most varied and diverse sources of income, not least because it means they are no longer wholly dependent on hand-outs (and thus subject to regulation) from the state.[13]

All this is true, and I like to think that in a small but significant way, the IHR has helped to pioneer a more energetic and pro-active approach to development, for history in particular, and for university fund-raising more generally. But such self-satisfaction has its limits. To begin with, and specifically in relation to the Institute itself, we are in danger of becoming victims of our own success: for the IHR now functions on the presumption that we can raise more than half of our income every year in this way, which means that doing so is no longer an option, but has become an unrelenting necessity, if we are to sustain the higher levels of activity and of quality to which we (and others) have become accustomed. And although we have raised substantial sums, they have all been earmarked for specific projects and posts: we have not so far been able to create an endowment which would itself generate some of our much-needed additional annual revenue. In short, we have yet to turn our success into sustainability, and that remains the great challenge for our fund-raising in the future. More generally, I am far from clear whether what we have accomplished at the IHR can be replicated elsewhere, though I naturally hope it can be and will be. We are located in London, and we do history in a certain sort of academic-cum-public way, and this may make us more attractive to potential donors than conventional history departments, especially those located in universities in the regions. Moreover, I was able to give the sort of time and attention to development that hard-pressed heads of department and their senior staff rarely have the opportunity to do; I was also lucky enough to enjoy the support and guidance of a brilliant director of development, who taught me much about doing my own job, while also doing hers; and the powers that be in the central university kindly left me alone to get on with things.

While I was raising money for the Institute, I often called to mind some words that were used to describe Oliver Lyttelton, first Viscount Chandos. He was a major figure in British business and then in politics (he was a great friend of Churchill's), and during his final decades he was one of the most powerful cultural panjandrums in London, when he was a formidable chairman of the National Theatre. It was said of Lyttelton, who was very good at raising money, that in doing so, he was 'pitiless in pressing the claims of friendship'.[14] I fear, but I also hope, that similar accusations have been levelled at me during the last ten years, because without friends, there can be no funds, and we have had friends and funds in gratifying and generous abundance. One such friend, who knows about raising money, and also about giving it away, is David Rockefeller, and in his autobiography, he insists that successful fund-raising requires a combination of 'leadership, persistence and creativity'.[15] He is absolutely right, and to his list I would add some extra temperamental traits and anatomical attributes: determined patience, tireless stamina, incorrigible optimism, a thick skin, a very strong liver, and a clear and commanding vision of where you want your organization to get to, along with a capacity to communicate that vision eloquently and convincingly. Another such friend, who is similarly knowledgeable on these matters, is Lord Wolfson, and on more than one occasion, when I was seeking his support and advice, he said to me, 'You're a good salesman.' I doubt if that was how A.F. Pollard ever envisaged the job of being Director of the IHR; but that, in significant part, is what it now entails – and what, indeed, it now requires.

II

No one who is privileged to serve as Director of the Institute of Historical Research should ever forget that this is one of the four senior posts in the English historical profession, along with the Regius Professorships of Modern History at the Universities of Oxford and Cambridge, and the Presidency of the Royal Historical Society (I exclude Scotland, which boasts another equally illustrious position, with a much more splendid title and venerable pedigree, namely that of Her Majesty's Historiographer).[16] But unlike the two Oxbridge professorships, the Directorship of the IHR carries with it specific and extensive administrative responsibilities; and unlike the Presidency of the Royal Historical Society, it is a full time academic job here in the University of London. So while I was busily engaged, as Director, in actively reforming and re-energizing the Institute, and in raising money for it, I had to run the place even as I sought to change it, and I also thought it important to take on my share of those academic tasks and obligations which tend to go with a certain level of professorial seniority. At the IHR itself, there were committees to chair, meetings to attend, grants to disburse, fellowships to award, staff to manage, jobs to fill, budgets to be apportioned, and accounts to be balanced, as well as a growing amount of paperwork that had to be processed. And there were also those more generic activities which are the bread and butter of our profession: supervising and writing references for graduate students, presiding over seminars and examining doctoral dissertations, refereeing manuscripts for publishers and articles for journals, advising on appointments and promotions in British universities, and evaluating cases for tenure across the Atlantic.

Accordingly, while part of my job at the Institute required me to be a reformer, fund-raiser and entrepreneur, I also became a bureaucrat and an administrator, and I assumed extensive editorial responsibilities, both within the Institute and beyond. As Director, I was editor of two in-house journals, *Historical Research*, and *Reviews in History*, and I devoted considerable effort to raising the quality and extending the range of the articles which were accepted; I set up a publications committee at the IHR, to oversee and advise one of our most rapidly growing and financially robust sections; and I helped Blackwells inaugurate a new online journal entitled *History Compass*, which aimed to make the subject accessible for the first time to a genuinely global audience. In addition, and as by-products of some of the conferences we were putting on at the Institute, I found myself editing what amounted to a series of books for Palgrave Macmillan, on subjects ranging from *What Is History Now?*, via *History and the Media*, to *Empire, the Sea and Global History*; and I helped establish a new *Journal of Maritime History*, along with a seminar at the IHR devoted to the same subject.[17] Beyond the confines of the Senate House, I also continued my editorial work for three series at the Penguin Press: a history of Britain, an economic history of Britain, and a history of Europe, and their volumes began to appear at regular intervals during my time at the Institute.[18]

But editing other people's articles and essays and books is no substitute for doing those things yourself, and although there were now many claims on my time and attention, I was determined, as Director, to remain an active and productive scholar. But there was one form of history-writing which I soon gave up almost completely, and that was the regular production of book reviews: both as extended essays in such publications as the *London Review of Books*, the *New Yorker*, the *New York Review of Books* and the *Times Literary Supplement*, and as shorter notices for weekly journals and weekend newspapers on both sides of the Atlantic.[19] Although I had greatly enjoyed the discipline of producing to length, the buzz of meeting non-negotiable deadlines, and the opportunities to reach a broad general audience, I felt it was time for younger historians to have their chance 'on the page' just as I had been lucky enough to have had mine. I also thought it inappropriate to continue writing in a mode which would involve public criticism of professional colleagues, while I was holding a position where I wanted to be welcoming and hospitable to all serious and engaged practitioners of history. So when I got to the Institute, one of the first things I did was to gather together a second (and final) collection of my full-length reviews, which I published as *History in Our Time*.[20] Soon after, I was invited to present the annual Longmans-*History Today* book awards, and I spoke on the challenges and hazards of reviewing – and of being reviewed. Oscar Wilde once observed: 'I never read a book I must review; it prejudices you so.' I, by contrast, insisted that the most important obligation of any reviewer was indeed to *read the book* – an injunction which clearly came as a surprise to some members of my audience.[21]

I also gave up reviewing because there were other forms of writing I wanted to try, and which I was increasingly being asked to undertake. Some of them were mournful tasks, as I was asked to produce obituaries and more extended memoirs of friends, colleagues and benefactors, many of whom had been enthusiastic supporters of the IHR, among them Noel Annan, Roy Jenkins, Harold Perkin, J.H. Plumb, Lawrence Stone and Giles Worsley.[22] More festively, and as the national cult of the anniversary intensified, I became involved in a variety of commemorative enterprises, which necessitated the writing or editing of books, or the production of articles and essays, or the delivering of lectures, looking back on such landmark events as the 500th anniversary of the foundation of Christ's College, Cambridge; the 400th anniversary of Guy Fawkes and the Gunpowder Plot; the 200th anniversary of the Battle of Trafalgar and the death of Nelson; the 150th anniversaries of the establishment of the National Portrait Gallery and of the birth of Sir Edward Elgar; and the centenary of the setting up of the British Academy.[23] And at the invitation of Mark Damazer of the BBC, I became a regular contributor to the slot on Radio 4 that had previously been occupied by Alistair Cooke's *Letter from America*, but which was now re-named *A Point of View*, and which gave me another opportunity to offer historical perspectives on contemporary events, and to a different (and larger) sort of audience. One of the many outstanding producers with whom I have been fortunate enough to work on these broadcasts is a former student of mine. When he was an undergraduate, he wrote essays for me; now I am a professor, I write essays for him ....

While I have been at the IHR, people have often asked me if I missed teaching undergraduates. The answer was partly 'yes', because it was something I had greatly enjoyed doing, both in Cambridge and at Columbia; but it was also 'no' in that my days were now fully taken up with other tasks. Yet although I stopped giving lecture courses, I was determined to keep lecturing as often as I could. There was ample opportunity to so in London, both within the academy and beyond and, given the Institute's national remit and international role, I was eager to get out of the capital as frequently as possible. In London, I spoke in such varied locations as the National Gallery, the British Museum, the Public Record Office, the London Library, the Paul Mellon Centre for British Art, and the Newcomen Society; beyond the confines of the M25, I lectured at (among others) the Universities of Cambridge, Cardiff, Central Lancashire, Essex, Glasgow, Leicester, Nottingham, Sheffield and York; and I travelled and spoke extensively in the United States.[24] Nor did I neglect the IHR itself: during my time as Director, I gave papers to eight of its seminars, ranging from the history of parliament, via the history of empire, to the history of music. In some of these lectures and papers, I explored aspects of the political, cultural and social history of modern Britain, as I sought to explain how our nation successfully defended its Victorian inheritance during the first half of the twentieth century, but thereafter gradually (and in some cases reluctantly) let it go. This strikes me as a major theme in our recent history, to which I want to return; but for now I gathered together the essays most closely related to it in a book I called *In Churchill's Shadow*, which was published in 2002.[25]

In my preface to that volume, I noted that historians write essays for many reasons, one of which may sometimes be to avoid the greater and more challenging task of writing books. But I have never subscribed to that view, for I wholly agree with G.M. Trevelyan that one of the most significant things historians can do and ought to do is to write what he called important books of enduring quality.[26] When I returned to Britain, I already had one major project in the pipeline, which had originated as a series of public lectures that I had delivered in my closing months at Columbia University, and which I published in 1998 as *Class in Britain*. In that book, I attempted to evaluate, and also to move forward, the debates about the social structure and social history of our country, as they had evolved – or not evolved – in the aftermath of what was called the 'linguistic turn', and I also sought to relate this essentially (and increasingly arcane) academic discussion to the broader public issues of the rise of Thatcherism and the fall of Communism. As I tried to show, class could (and should) be seen as a way of analysing economic inequality; but it could (and should) also be seen as a way of understanding social perceptions of that inequality. It was class in this second sense that was my primary concern, as I argued that it might helpfully be understood as being what culture did to social structure; and I traced the three different ways of looking at British society which had been most prevalent across the last three hundred years: the binary ('us' and 'them'), the tripartite (upper–middle–lower), and the hierarchical (which, I suggested, was the most enduring and pervasive, and which, perhaps for this very reason, had received less attention than it should have done).[27]

As I reached the end of *Class in Britain*, I realized that I could not leave the subject at that point, for there were clearly important and complex relationships, which I wanted to explore more fully, between perceptions (and workings) of social structures in the British imperial metropolis, and perceptions (and workings) of social structures in the British Empire overseas. And so I wrote *Ornamentalism*, published in 2001, as an act of sceptical homage to Edward Said's *Orientalism*, in which I argued that class needed to be intruded or (in some cases) re-intruded into the histories of the Empire that were now being written, where excessive concentration on the categories of race and gender seemed to leave insufficient room for alternative approaches. I also urged that the Empire needed to be understood as a place where the cultivation of affinities was as worthy of historical study as the assertion of difference, and where ceremony and spectacle were an integral part of the means whereby the British co-opted those local elites and indigenous collaborators on whom their imperial rule ultimately depended.[28] In some ways, this book looped back to my earlier work on ceremonial and the British monarchy: for 'ornamentalism' was the 'invention of tradition' made visible, palpable and imperial. But I also wanted to open up some new issues in the history of Empire that only came into focus by looking at the whole of it, rather than at specific areas or individual colonies: among them the themes of imperial aristocrats, imperial monarchs, royal tours, and imperial honours. These were, it seemed to me, important but neglected aspects of the greater British world that was the British Empire, and other historians are now taking up in detail the subjects that I was only able to sketch out in general terms.[29]

The researching and writing of *Class in Britain* and *Ornamentalism* kept me busy at the IHR while I was Director, but at the same time, I was overseeing a much larger research project, which I was eager to bring to completion, namely the official life of the American banker, businessman, politician, art collector and philanthropist, Andrew W. Mellon. I had agreed to take on this task in 1994, while I was still at Columbia University, at the behest of Andrew's son, Paul Mellon; and thanks to the generosity of the Andrew W. Mellon Foundation, I was able to recruit and oversee a team of research assistants who, under my supervision, combed the 78 archival collections in the United States and Europe where Mellon's papers, correspondence and business records were to be found.[30] I did not find the shy, sad, silent Andrew Mellon an easy man to warm to, his deeply conservative politics were not exactly mine, and because there were so many themes to his long and controversial life, I knew his biography would not be an easy one to construct. But I had no doubt that he was a major figure in the history of America during the period from the Civil War to the Great Depression; his business, his art collecting and his philanthropy meant his life formed a sort of upside down coda to my *Decline and Fall of the British Aristocracy*; and I thought it would be a fascinating challenge to render historically credible someone whom I didn't altogether like, but whom I did come (at least in some ways) to admire. Once I had relinquished the Directorship, and with the chance to hold Visiting Fellowships at the Australian National University in Canberra, and the National Humanities Center in North Carolina, I was able to get on with writing the biography, which I completed early in 2006. *Mellon* ran to eight hundred pages, it was the last big life of an American capitalist of that generation to be written, and in the *Wall Street Journal*, Vartan Gregorian, the President of the Carnegie Corporation, included it on his list of the best plutocratic-cum-philanthropic biographies, along with Jean Strouse on J.P. Morgan, Ron Chernow on John D. Rockefeller, and David Nasaw on Andrew Carnegie.[31]

I calculate that during my ten years at the Institute of Historical Research, I published seven books, edited another six, wrote more than twenty essays and articles, and gave scores of lectures, papers and broadcasts; and in so doing, I had several objectives in view. Since I was in charge of an organization devoted to the undertaking and dissemination of historical research, I was eager to set an example by remaining an engaged and creative and accessible scholar; and since the words and phrases and paragraphs still kept flowing most mornings, I really had no alternative but to keep on writing them down. And from the privileged podium and bully pulpit that the IHR provided, I was determined to reach as wide an audience as I could, from those people in universities who attended lectures and seminars, via the general reading public who still bought history books and attended literary festivals, to the millions of listeners who regularly tuned in to Radio 4 on Friday evenings or Sunday mornings. In these endeavours, I must have achieved a modicum of success, because in the August 2004 issue of *Prospect* magazine, I was one of the historians included on their list of Britain's foremost one hundred public intellectuals.[32] But my moment of rejoicing was brief. Soon after, a friend (at least, he had been a friend up until then) telephoned to say he had been more than a little surprised to see my name included in such illustrious, distinguished and high-powered company as Eric Hobsbawm and Amartya Sen. He had, he went on, absolutely no problem in my case with the 'public' part of that designation; but the additional accolade of 'intellectual' had caused him very serious anxiety, concern and distress ....

III

In late 2002, I gave notice of my intention to resign the Directorship of the Institute of Historical Research, to take up the Queen Elizabeth the Queen Mother Professorship of British History, which had been generously and imaginatively created especially for me. In the meantime, it was necessary to produce a new job description before the post of Director could be advertised and my successor appointed, and I was kindly invited by those in charge to offer my comments on a draft, drawing on my own recent experience. I looked over the text, and suggested that insufficient attention had been given to what I termed the pro-consular and ambassadorial aspects of the post; but I was firmly (and rightly) told that this was far too pompous and pretentious a term to describe what I had been doing since May 1998, or what would be expected of my successor; and I was accordingly invited to come up with another, less grandiose and more low-key, form of words. Thus provoked (and having only recently published *Ornamentalism*), I suggested 'vice-regal', whereupon this well-meant exercise in informal consultation understandably came to an abrupt halt. Yet in truth, the Directorship of the IHR has always involved a significant representational and senatorial element, beginning with the School of Advanced Study, where I had soon found myself sitting on the Advisory Councils of the Warburg Institute, the Institute of English Studies, the Institute of American Studies, the Institute of Latin American Studies, and where I was also appointed to the University's Honorary Degree Committee. These were no sinecures, and I recall with pride and pleasure the small part I played in helping create a new, merged Institute for the Study of the Americas as a whole, and also that during, or shortly after, my time on the committee, honorary degrees were bestowed by the University on Roy Jenkins, Frances Partridge, Amartya Sen, Jacob Rothschild, Keith Thomas and John Elliott.

These were agreeable domestic forays into what might be termed the local government of the University of London; but here as in so much else, the Senate House was also an ideal base from which to venture into the broader world beyond. When appointed Director, I was already a vice-chair of the Editorial Board of the journal *Past & Present*, I was soon elected a vice-president of the Royal Historical Society (where I chaired the committee that gave out grants to graduate students), I was later appointed to the Editorial Board of the *History of Parliament*, and I also became a judge of the Wolfson History prize. In a further effort to avoid becoming too tied to London, I joined the Management Committee of the Centre for Research in the Arts, Social Sciences and Humanities at Cambridge, and as a loyal son of the West Midlands, I accepted the Presidency of the Worcestershire Historical Society (which in earlier days had been held by local, broad-acred grandees, but times and circumstances had clearly changed). I also found myself drawn into the world of archival management and administration: I was put on the Advisory Council of the Public Record Office (subsequently The National Archives), I was elected a Trustee of the Rothschild Archive, and in 2002 I became a member of the Archives Task Force.[33] My final area of academic pro-consulship concerned the furthering of Anglo-American relations: I was the first Director of the IHR to sit on the Council of the North American Conference on British Studies; I persuaded the Andrew W. Mellon Foundation of New York to sponsor a programme of fellowships for North American graduate students, working in the humanities, who wanted to visit Britain; and as a Trustee of the Kennedy Memorial Trust, I have helped to send some of our best and brightest graduates (including some especially talented historians) in the other direction, to study at Harvard University and at the Massachusetts Institute of Technology.

To these new and challenging ways to be doing and making history should be added my involvement with the British Academy, to whose Fellowship I was elected in 1999, and where I subsequently served on the standing committee of my section, on the committee which appointed the Raleigh Lecturer in History, and on a working party devoted to studying the issue of academic copyright.[34] I also found myself in demand to offer historical advice, on a variety of subjects and to a variety of audiences: on radio and television, as a talking head commentating on multifarious contemporary events; to the British Museum, when it sought external evaluation of its research activities and culture; to the Cabinet War Rooms, as they extended and enlarged their Churchill display; to Sir Hayden Phillips and to the Committee on Public Administration as they sought to improve and re-model the honours system; to the Imperial War Museum, when they put on an exhibition to mark the centenary of the birth of Ian Fleming; and to the Prime Minister, when he asked me to take part in the review he commissioned late in 2007, to look into the thirty-year rule that governed the transfer and opening of official records that were held in The National Archives.[35] Such activities reinforced my view that historians can make – and should make – a significant contribution to the formulation of wiser and better informed policies, as they were being formulated, rather than after the event, and regardless of which party might be in power; and to this end, I helped set up the History and Policy Unit at the IHR, which was launched in December 2007, to an encouragingly warm reception by both politicians and the media.[36]

Such were my 'pro-consular' activities, in the University of London, and in the broader academic world beyond, but I also believed that the Director of the IHR should play a wider part in the cultural and public life of the nation, and I found opportunities aplenty to do so. Having written a brief history to mark its centenary, I was already familiar with the work of the National Trust, and in 2001 I was recruited to its Eastern Regional Committee, which provided another good excuse for getting out of my office, and gave me first hand experience of the challenges and opportunities of conservation in ways that sitting on London boards never could.[37] While on the committee, I helped push forward a programme of research and restoration at Blickling, scheduled to be completed by 2012, to coincide with the 75th anniversary of the Country House Scheme, which had been conceived being by its proprietor, the eleventh Marquis of Lothian, and under which Blickling itself had been the first great mansion to go to the Trust on his death in 1940. In tandem with this regional conservation work, I also became a Commissioner of English Heritage, where I supported the efforts of its outstanding chairman, Neil Cossons, and its brilliant chief executive, Simon Thurley, to render that great but flawed organization fit for purpose. One of their most significant innovations was to schedule Commission meetings out of London, so we could see the efforts being made (and, sometimes, not being made) to protect and regenerate the historic environment, in places as varied as Carlisle, Manchester and Bath; and at such resonant sites as Hadrian's Wall, Dover Castle and Osborne House. These outings were enormous fun, but being a Commissioner was a serious job, as we struggled at our meetings with an unending succession of complex, important and controversial issues, ranging from the effect of tall buildings on the London skyline, to the implications of global warming for the conservation of historic structures that had been put up in a very different climatic environment.[38]

As a result of my connection with English Heritage, I was appointed chairman of its Blue Plaques panel, which evaluates the proposals that are submitted by the general public to commemorate famous people at a residential address in London where they spent a significant portion of their lives. The committee is a pleasure to chair, but it needed some initial attention: I brought in some new members, the backlog of case-work was reduced, and we disengaged ourselves from a national scheme into which we had entered with insufficient consideration or resources. We try to unveil between five and ten plaques a year, on buildings located anywhere in London, with the exception of the City itself. Many such plaques are to be found, very close by, in Bedford Square, but that is pure coincidence, and none have been unveiled there in my time as chairman. Blue plaques are one form of circumferential homage to important figures in our national past, and so are commemorative coins, of which the Royal Mint has been producing increasing numbers in recent years. The subjects are selected, and the designs decided, by an Advisory Committee which, in an earlier time had been chaired by the Duke of Edinburgh, and had included such high-end luminaries as Kenneth Clark. When I was sounded out as to whether I might be appointed to it, I was given the unnerving reassurance that since those patrician days, the Committee had gone so down-market sociologically that even I had a fighting chance of getting on, which I duly did in 2004. Such is the lead time required, that commemorative coins are agreed well in advance, so it has only been with those issued since 2006 that I have had any input. That year, coins were minted celebrating the bicentennial of the birth of Isambard Kingdom Brunel, the 150th anniversary of the inauguration of the Victoria Cross, and the Queen's eightieth birthday. This year, special coins commemorate the 450th anniversary of the accession of Queen Elizabeth I, the centenary of the first Olympic Games held here in London, and the sixtieth birthday of the Prince of Wales.[39] During the same period, the Mint Committee has also overseen a comprehensive redesign of the reverse sides of the whole of the national coinage, and they have recently been issued.

The Blue Plaques Panel and the Royal Mint Advisory Committee offered new opportunities and new ways of trying to help make history, and so did my trusteeships of two museums, the first of which was the National Portrait Gallery, of which I became a trustee in 2000, and of which I was elected chairman five years later. From the outset, when Lord Macaulay was one of its founding fathers, the Gallery has been concerned to display images of those who have made a major contribution to British history and British life, and this helps explain why historians have always played a prominent part in its affairs, among them G.M. Trevelyan, J.H. Plumb, Owen Chadwick and Colin Matthew.[40] It has been a pleasure to work with two brilliant Directors, Charles Saumarez Smith and Sandy Nairne, and in 2006, the Gallery celebrated its 150th anniversary, which makes it the oldest of its kind in the English-speaking world. As my contribution to those celebrations, I wrote a brief history, in which I tried to get beyond what often tend to be the claustrophobic confines of such in-house, institutional accounts.[41] By then, I had also joined the board of the British Empire and Commonwealth Museum, which was located in Bristol, and was entirely dependent on private funding and revenue from admission fees. Its collections and exhibitions were of a very high standard, it dealt sensitively and even-handedly with complex and controversial historical issues, and it won numerous awards. But although the imperial phase of the British past was widely admitted to be of the utmost importance, both nationally and globally, it has proved impossible to generate sufficient income to make ends meet in Bristol, and it is to be hoped that the museum's projected relocation to London will enable it to do so.

When I wrote *The Decline and Fall of the British Aristocracy*, one of the issues I wanted to get on to the agenda of historical inquiry, and which has, indeed, been taken up by other scholars since, was the part played by lords and landowners as the self-appointed definers and guardians of national culture, by virtue (among other things) of their trusteeships of the great galleries and museums of London. One such figure was the 27th Earl of Crawford and Balcarres who, during the inter-war years, acquired interlocking directorships across a great swathe of London's cultural establishments.[42] Times have changed since then, and in a world where Nolan rules now apply, trusteeships and other such public appointments turn over more rapidly than they used to do, and they are offered to people of more varied and diverse social background than was the case even thirty years ago. Quite by chance, I arrived in London at just the time when these changes were being implemented, and this may well explain why I have been appointed to such a range of boards and committees. But I also firmly believe that these are the sort of jobs which Directors of the IHR ought to be called upon to undertake, for they offer yet another way of doing and making history in the public realm. Despite constant temptations to the contrary, no academic should join committees just for the sake of doing so, or to provide yet another alibi for not researching or writing books. But such work as I have just been describing does enable historians to make some sort of contribution to the broader cultural life of our nation, and I hope that more of them will be asked and will agree to do so in years to come.

Looking back, I realize that I have been exceptionally lucky in that such work was becoming more widely available than ever before to people like me; and I was also fortunate in having been given these opportunities at just the time when public spending on the arts, both from the Department of Culture, Media and Sport and via the Heritage Lottery Fund, has been greater than ever before. One indication of such unprecedented state support was that during the early years of my Directorship, it seemed as though scarcely a month passed by without an invitation to attend yet another grand opening: the new British Library, the Ondaatje Wing at the National Portrait Gallery, Neptune Court at the National Maritime Museum, Tate Modern on the South Bank, and the Great Court at the British Museum. These splendid new buildings house splendid collections, and their unprecedented popularity in recent years is but one facet of the history boom which has taken place, not only in our museums and galleries and at our historic sites, but also on television and across the media more broadly. This is much to be applauded, but I am not sure that we understand what this trend signifies, or how long it will last, so perhaps a few caveats are in order. The teaching of history in schools still gives cause for widespread anxiety, in terms of the restricted hours made available for it, and the limited subjects and periods covered; and the media-driven celebration of history as 'the new gardening' is also cause for some concern. To be sure, many people read history books, and visit historic sites, for recreation; and so they should. But history is not just part of the leisure or the entertainment industry: it is also a serious academic pursuit, and it has a serious public purpose; and after a decade spent in the Senate House, I am more convinced than ever of the essential inter-connectedness of those endeavours, and of the pivotal part the IHR plays in helping to join them up.

IV

Such, then, have been my activities during my decade at the Institute of Historical Research; and although I have not achieved everything I initially set out to do, I can report that many of my original objectives have been accomplished, and that we have certainly been making a great deal of history, and in many different, varied and exciting ways. Thus have the imperatives of my inaugural become the retrospectives of this valedictory. I began it by noting the not-quite-exact coincidence between the span of my years here at the IHR, the duration of Tony Blair's premiership, and the publication of J.K. Rowling's Harry Potter novel cycle, and as I move towards my closing remarks, it seems appropriate to cite the precedents of their own recent farewells. When Blair said his goodbye, at the finish of his last question time in the House of Commons, it was with the brief and incontrovertible observation, 'That is that. The end'; while J.K. Rowling concluded her last book no less economically, remarking that for an older and wiser Harry Potter, 'all was well'.[43] Thus, then, in their time, their adieus; what, now, in my time, of mine? Midway through my years here at the IHR, when I was often in Washington working on my Andrew Mellon biography, I would end a day in the archives by heading down the marble steps of the National Gallery of Art, at which point I would turn right and walk along the Mall, out beyond the obelisk commemorating America's first president, and past the calm, placid waters of the reflecting pool, until I reached the memorial to Abraham Lincoln that closes off its western end. On its interior walls are carved some of that president's most eloquent and immortal phrases, and some of them, from his second inaugural, are much in my mind as I take my farewell tonight.

Here is one: 'with malice toward none [and] with charity for all'.[44] If you conducted a poll of historians practising their art and their craft in British universities today, I'm not entirely sure that they would come up with those words as a description of their collective mentality, or of their shared professional outlook; but as a summary of my present mood and feelings, they are not far wide of the mark. It has been my great good fortune to have spent ten years here which have been busy, crowded, creative, productive, enjoyable, rewarding and fulfilling, and it would be unpardonably churlish, unconscionably mean-spirited, grotesquely small-minded, and just plain wrong, if I did not take this occasion to express my heartfelt thanks and abiding gratitude to those colleagues and friends and institutions to whom those thanks and that gratitude are due: to the University of London for having given me the opportunity and the challenge of being Director of the Institute of Historical Research; to the Linbury Trust and the Andrew W. Mellon Foundation of New York for enabling me to stay here when I ceased to be Director; to the staff, members, friends and benefactors of the IHR, and to the trustees of the IHR Trust, without whom nothing significant would have been achieved during these last ten years; and to the many people I have been lucky enough to encounter, in publishing, in the media, in the arts, in higher education, in business, in philanthropy, in politics, in government and in the civil service, from whom I have learned so much about so much, and whose kindness, support and generosity have been unfailing.

And so to my second and final quotation from Lincoln: 'with high hope for the future,… let us strive on to finish the work [that] we are in'.[45] I have always been optimistic about the future; I was always optimistic about the future of the Institute these past ten years; and I have never been more optimistic for its future than I am now, with the exhilarating prospect of a new and vigorous and brilliant Director, who will surely lead it to levels of academic achievement, public engagement and financial well-being never attained before. As for the work that we are in: those endeavours, whether in history or in politics, are never finished in single lifetimes. Politics goes on, and history goes on, and those of us playing our small, brief part do what we can, where we can, when it is our time, our turn, our task and our try. Thus it has been for me, here at the Institute of Historical Research, as my ten years come to a close: I have had my time, I have served my turn, and I have tried to discharge my tasks; I leave this place with real regret but with lasting, devoted and enduring affection; and I draw comfort and resolve from the thought that endings, however final they might seem, are often new beginnings, for individuals and institutions alike. That, at least, is how it seems to me, here, now, tonight, as I look backwards with gratitude, and forwards with hope, and as I say: I did what I could; but I haven't finished yet; and nor, I feel certain, have any of you.

Appendix:
On Reviewing – and Being Reviewed

As anyone knows who has tried their hand sufficiently at both activities, it is a great deal easier to review books on history than it is to write them. Even the most turgid and mediocre volume about the past is likely to show traces of expertise, curiosity, stamina, empathy and creativity – qualities that are sometimes conspicuously lacking in historical reviews, and in historical reviewers. But since reviews are quick, short and cheap, whereas books are by comparison slow, long and expensive, they are often thought to exert an immediate influence out of all proportion to their length and merit. Such, at least, are the opinions of all literary editors, some publishers, and most authors – and of many reviewers themselves. Of course, they would say that, wouldn't they? But whether they are right or wrong, it cannot be denied that for the best part of two hundred years, since the launching of the *Edinburgh Review* in 1802, history reviews and history reviewing have been an integral part of the public and academic culture of Britain. Whether we know it or not, like it or not, or are intimidated by it or not, those of us who turn our hands to this task are standing and scribbling in a direct line of succession which reaches back to the young Macaulay, who first made his public reputation as a coruscating writer in the 1820s.

To be sure, Macaulay was a genius. As a poet, reviewer, essayist, historian, parliamentary orator, conversationalist, letter-writer and author of state papers, he was never less than a scintillating stylist and consummate rhetorician. He was also prodigiously learned, across a far wider spectrum of human knowledge than is possible for any professional historian or full time writer to be today. The result was that he fashioned and projected an inimitable authorial voice – by turns jaunty, authoritative, vigorous, ebullient, highly-coloured and warm-hearted – which can still catch and captivate the ear, and compel the reader to keep turning the pages. No one since Macaulay has ever written historical reviews quite like he did, and no historian could, or should, try to do so now. But when I was learning about history in the 1960s and 1970s, scholars such as J.H. Plumb, Lawrence Stone, A.J.P. Taylor and Hugh Trevor-Roper were at the peak of their powers and their productivity, and they were regularly reviewing in newspapers and periodicals on both sides of the Atlantic. They, too, were accomplished and confident stylists, with distinctive and opinionated voices, who reached a broad public audience, and as such they were Macaulay's direct and legitimate descendants.

I am not sure that the same can be said today, of the later generation of historians to which I myself belong, let alone of those younger scholars coming up fast behind us. Although there are now more professional historians in this country than ever before, there are some ways in which they impinge less on the public and cultural life of the nation than their forbears did a quarter of century ago, and one indication of this is the decline in serious historical reviewing, in the Saturday and Sunday papers. There are many explanations for this. One is that, as historical knowledge becomes more specialized, it becomes increasingly difficult to write confidently across a range of subjects sufficiently broad to establish a public identity as a regular and distinctive reviewer. Another is that the Research Assessment Exercise takes no note of such brief, ephemeral and un-footnoted activities, which means there is a strong disincentive for hard-pressed historians to undertake them. And as even the broadsheet newspapers 'dumb down' and tabloidize their pages, there is less space and scope for serious historical reviewing than once there was. Yet there remain many opportunities: in the ever-proliferating number of scholarly journals; in the 'literary' periodicals on both sides of the Atlantic; and (albeit diminishingly) in the 'quality' press.

This inevitably means that historical reviews come in a wide variety of shapes and sizes, lengths and weights. Short notices, between five and eight hundred words, are usually little more than a (very inadequate) précis of the book. Reviews of one thousand to fifteen hundred words allow more scope for discussion and debate. And in a review-essay of two thousand words or more, there is opportunity to venture beyond the confines of the book, into a more general treatment of the subject it deals with, in the way that Macaulay pioneered and perfected. In short, different word limits do imply very different reviews, and from the outset, it is important to be clear which sort is being written. But this is not the only way in which historical reviews vary: for they are also aimed at readers who are themselves very diverse. Those produced for scholarly journals can take for granted an expert, professional audience; those appearing in the 'literary' periodicals can assume most of their readers are academics or intellectuals, but not necessarily experts; those written for the 'quality' press are intended for the 'intelligent general reader', which in our day usually (but not exclusively) means university graduates in any subject. Writing reviews for each of these different audiences requires rather different expositional strategies.

But notwithstanding these variations of length and readership, there are two further aspects of historical reviewing which should remain constant, and be constantly borne in mind. Neither should need spelling out, but there are occasions when it is helpful and necessary to state the obvious, and this is surely one of them. The first is that the prime purpose of any review should be to evaluate the book, the author and the subject. Even if the reviewer is more famous than the author, with a long-established reputation and a distinctive style, the historical work that is being discussed is the thing that matters. The review is parasitic on the book, and so is the reviewer, and this should always be remembered. The second is that, regardless of the precise number of words required, or the particular nature of the audience, there are several essential tasks that any serious reviewer must always conscientiously seek to discharge. Again, these should scarcely need spelling out, but perhaps it is appropriate to do so here. They are as follows: read the book; place the book; describe the book; judge the book. It is worth examining these four aspects of reviewing in more detail.

It may seem absurd to insist that any book to be reviewed must first be read by the reviewer. Surely, this is self-evident? No serious work of history can be completed in less than two years, and some take more than a decade: out of common decency, any author who has laboured thus hard and long is entitled to a full reading and a fair hearing. This, in turn, means that no conscientious reviewer should venture into print without having read the book in question at least once and preferably twice. Yet many reviews are often less thorough than they ought to be. Sometimes this arises from the unavoidable pressure of tight deadlines, as in the case of the first volume of the Thatcher memoirs. The book was embargoed before publication, but most newspapers carried their notices within 48 hours, which means that none of them could have been based on a thorough reading. But all too often, such lapses occur for the simple reason that the reviewer has not bothered to read the book carefully, but has merely dipped into it or idly skimmed it. Most experienced authors can easily identify such cursory and unprofessional reviews of their books, because the telltale signs are obvious: excessive concentration on the introduction, conclusion and a few particular chapters, and confusion or ignorance about the general argument.

Only when the book has been read, pondered and understood, should the review of it be begun, and this must be done in such a way as to catch the reader's attention. It can be with a memorable and arresting anecdote, picked up along the way; but when the word-count is limited, there is often insufficient space. It is usually better to open with an outline of the broader historical and contemporary issues with which the book engages, and with some remarks about who the author is, and how the subject is being approached. When publishing in the professional historical journals, some of this scene-setting can be dispensed with; but the closer towards the 'general reader' the review is directed, the more important and essential it becomes. For one of the prime purposes of such non-academic reviewing is to bring to the notice of the non-academic public those outstanding works of scholarly history about which they might not otherwise know, and the only way to do this is to begin by explaining why the subject, the book and the author matter. A classic instance of this is G.M. Trevelyan's review of Lewis Namier's *England in the Age of the American Revolution*, which he published in *The Nation* in 1930. Trevelyan wanted to draw attention to the novelty of Namier's approach, and the importance of his findings, in the hope that this might encourage a British university to give him a much-needed academic job. Soon after, Manchester did just that.

Having read and placed the book, the next thing to do is to give some clear sense of what it is about. Here, again, there are snares and pitfalls aplenty. Many reviewers simply fail to discharge this responsibility: having neglected to read the work, they sound off on the subject which they believe it to be about, venting their feelings and parading their prejudices, but with virtually no reference to the book itself. The result is not so much a review as an intellectual or (more usually) emotional spasm. But even for the conscientious reviewer, this sort of summary is no simple a task. For it is virtually impossible to describe any work of many thousand words in a mere few hundred: with the best will in the world, the argument will be simplified and abridged to the point (or beyond the point) of caricature. And if the volume is an edited collection, such as a festschrift, it is difficult to avoid a laundry-list enumeration – author by author, subject by subject, in a remorselessly comprehensive catalogue which may please the contributors, since none will feel slighted by having been left out, but which usually sends the reader away in search of more exciting fare elsewhere on the page. Dullness in reviews is unforgivable, but describing books in ways that are not dull can tax the expositional resources of the most experienced and accomplished reviewer.

All that remains is to give some verdict – an activity which provides the greatest scope for fun and irresponsibility and for causing offence. The desire to trash a book can sometimes be very strong, because one dislikes the volume or the author or both. On the whole, this desire should be resisted – partly because few books are completely contemptible, and if they are, why bother to review them?; and partly because it is better to be generous than to be negative, since in reviewing as in life, one should do unto others as one would wish to be done by oneself. Of course, there should be some criticism and disagreement: the work of history that is so perfect as to be without fault or flaw has yet to be written, and reviews that are unrelievedly hyperbolic rarely carry conviction. Above all, it is essential to *engage* with the book – to argue with it, agree with it, dissent from it – and thereby to convey the flavour of the work, and of what the author is trying to do: in short, to take it seriously. And in doing this, it is no less essential to engage with the volume *as written*: to see how far the author has accomplished what he (or she) set out to do, rather than chastise him (or her) for not having written a different sort of book.

These, it bears repeating, are the elementary rules for good reviewing, which any responsible, conscientious, professional and self-respecting reviewer should seek to observe and to follow. It might be protested that these rules are absurdly naive: they might be what reviewing *ought* to be about, but they are not what reviewing *is* actually about. In practice, it might be argued, reviewing is really about showing off, or about furthering one's own career at the price of someone else's, or about demonstrating that the author of the review is so much cleverer than the author of the book, or about the continued pursuit of deeply-felt and long-running scholarly vendettas, or about the waging of party-political battles by other means, as in the (Whig) *Edinburgh* and the (Tory) *Quarterly* early in the nineteenth century. The lengthy conflict between Geoffrey Elton (a Tory empiricist) and Lawrence Stone (a Whig generalist) certainly came within both of these last two categories, and as such it provided gladiatorial entertainment of a high order. But while these personal, polemical and political temptations can be difficult (and sometimes impossible) to resist, they should ideally be kept within bounds, and be firmly subordinated to the serious business of placing, describing and judging the book.

The fact that they are so often unresisted and uncontrolled may explain why many authors fear and hate being reviewed. Of course, there are some authors who fear and hate *not* being reviewed: no one enjoys having laboured long and hard, to produce a work which they believe to be of major importance, only to discover that this view is not widely shared by literary editors. But being reviewed can be an even worse ordeal than not being reviewed. Even when a book is well received, being subjected to the caprice of the critics remains for many authors a nerve-racking experience, as they open the Sunday papers, half hoping, but also half dreading, what they will read about themselves. And few books receive (or deserve) unalloyed praise, while many are routinely trashed, not just in one review, but again and again. It may be as true for authors as for actors or politicians that there is no such thing as bad publicity: that it is better to be loathed than ignored. But few authors enjoy reading hostile things about themselves in the public print, and they rarely forgive or forget what they regard as wicked reviews. And reviews can be very hostile indeed: scornful, dismissive, vituperative, mendacious, dishonest, misleading. Even for the most thick-skinned writer (and most productive writers are obliged to develop thick skins), this is no fun. And if, like Virginia Woolf, you don't have a thick skin, it can be a nightmare.

Here is one more recent example. In the summer of 1998, Victoria Glendinning, who is by any reasonable yardstick an accomplished and successful writer (and, incidentally, reviewer), took a whole column of *The Spectator* to describe how badly she felt she had been treated by Terry Eagleton's highly critical review of her biography of Swift in *The Sunday Times*. She was clearly very upset, and it was difficult not to feel some sympathy with her. But it was also difficult not to feel that in parading her pain, she had made a big mistake. For while there are many rules about how to review, there is only one rule about how to respond to being reviewed. And that is, quite simply, never reply. Well, as W.S. Gilbert would have said, hardly ever. There is nothing wrong in thanking someone for a generous or thoughtful review, provided the letter is not too sycophantic in tone. Alternatively, if a review is libellous and defamatory, then there are traditional recourses available to which it might seem tempting to resort: namely a horsewhip or the courts. But even under those circumstances, litigation is usually best avoided, while physical retribution is a very high-risk strategy. And if the review is merely critical or hostile or antagonistic but not actionable, it is much more prudent and seemly to suffer it in silence.

But many authors are incapable of maintaining such a dignified and taciturn front, and are easily provoked into responding and replying. The obvious way to do this is to write in to the journal in which the offending review appeared. One reason this is an unwise strategy is that on many occasions, the editors simply refuse to publish the letters, which merely serves to intensify authorial outrage still further, because the obvious conclusion is that the editor is on the side of the reviewer not the author. And such rebuttal is even more galling because the leading literary periodicals actually thrive on their correspondence columns, and academic journals are also increasingly allowing authors the right of reply. These exchanges – often displaying petulance, wounded pride, bad temper and bloody mindedness in equal quantities on both sides – can be great fun to read. But no self-respecting author should ever resort to such misguided epistolary combat. However unfair or inaccurate or distorting the offending review may have been, all letters of protest invariably sound peevish and whinging. And since the rules of engagement in the correspondence columns usually allow the reviewer the last word, it is almost inconceivable that any author will get the better of the exchange.

An alternative mode of redress is for the author to write a private letter of protest or remonstrance to the reviewer. This avoids the unseemly spectacle of parading one's hurt or outrage publicly, but it is, again, an unwise and unedifying stratagem. To the recipient, it always seems a cheap form of rejoinder: the reviewer upsets the author, so the author responds in kind by trying to upset the reviewer. I once found myself on the receiving end of such ill-judged retaliation after reviewing Geoffrey Elton's study of Maitland. I do not think that his most ardent admirers would regard it as his best book, and in my review I disregarded several of the precepts I have outlined above in pointing this out. 'Elton's Maitland', I rightly but intemperately concluded, 'bears a remarkable resemblance to Elton's Elton.' 'And', I added, scaling new heights of tactlessness, 'we have already had rather a lot of that.' A scorching letter arrived by return, denouncing and ridiculing the review, and inquiring how much Lawrence Stone had paid me to write it. I replied proposing it would be a good idea for us to have a drink together, to which Geoffrey retorted that it would be insufferably effronterous for him to presume to take refreshment with someone who had recently told the world we had had enough of Elton.

On this absurdly pompous and petulant note, the correspondence ended. I later learned that Elton was notorious for writing such bullying and hectoring letters: although exceptionally brave and bold when berating other historians for not doing the subject his way, he became astonishingly touchy and tender when anyone dared to try to mete out the same treatment to him. This was not – and is not – a sensible or grown-up way to respond to being critically reviewed. Even worse is the lengthily-delayed private letter, which is ostensibly about something else, but which is really a long-pondered, and long-postponed protest. Thus: 'I'm sorry, I cannot attend your meeting next week and, by the way, while I am writing, I ought to add that I hope when next you review a book of mine, you will be less gratuitously hostile than you were last time.' Such letters, whose laboured afterthoughts are in fact their real purpose, deceive no one except the sender. And, far from upsetting them, they invariably give the recipients exquisite and unalloyed pleasure: for there are few things that make a reviewer happier than knowing a critical notice has hit home, and that it has rankled and festered with the author for many months thereafter. No self-respecting writer should ever give a reviewer such satisfaction.

With very rare exceptions, therefore, authorial silence is always the best policy in the face of hostile and disobliging reviews. Whatever the provocation, and however unfairly treated the author may feel, it accomplishes nothing useful to parade one's outrage, hurt, annoyance and insecurity: far better to take mute consolation in Sibelius's rightly reassuring remark that 'no statue was ever put up to a critic'. For, as this observation reminds us, it is much more important (albeit sometimes much more painful) to be an author than a reviewer. Good reviews should cheer up an author for half an hour; bad reviews should depress an author for a morning: but in the end, it is the book the author has written that matters. Moreover, as most publishers reluctantly recognize, books sell, or do not sell, on the basis of word of mouth rather than on the basis of good or bad reviews in the press or the periodicals. Put the other way, this means that when a book is launched into the public domain, the author is powerless to influence how the public will react to it, and there is no point in trying to do so. It will, inevitably, take on a life of its own, and people will respond to it as they will, and these things have to be recognized and accepted.

When done well, responsible reviewing can be a worthwhile and rewarding activity: a way of ensuring important books get known and discussed and read by a wider public audience than they might otherwise reach; a means of summarizing scholarly trends and historiographical debates, and of suggesting new developments and approaches; and, under really inspired editorship, an opportunity for promising young writers to learn to put sentences together in a more vivid and vigorous way than is usually encouraged in doctoral dissertations. But at its worst, reviewing is often a carping, mean-spirited, axe-grinding exercise in academic envy and scholarly resentment, as narrow-minded, uncreative historians set out to disparage the achievements of those of much greater gifts and accomplishments than themselves. When writing my biography of G.M. Trevelyan, I compiled an extensive anthology of the reviews his many books had received. Most of them were negative, carping and sometimes downright hostile, written by second-rate figures who had seized their chance to belittle an historian of incomparably greater abilities than they, before returning to the mediocre obscurity from which they should never have emerged. Trevelyan ignored these scholarly snipers: and he was right to do so.

It bears repeating that even at its best, reviewing is by its nature an ephemeral activity, and this in turn helps explain why no major historian (not even Macaulay) has ever made a lifelong reputation primarily, let alone exclusively, from doing it. It looked for a time as though Jack Hexter might be the exception who would prove the rule, since he fashioned almost an entire literary career from reviewing other people who, unlike him, were themselves writing real history. But although he wrote with an engaging combination of wit and style, humour and savagery, these pieces remain ultimately confined, earth-bound and dependent on the greater and more imaginative works of scholarship that they discuss, dissect, and sometimes dismiss. And that is just as it should be: for the real business of our profession is not to write reviews of each other's work (which is relatively easy), but to produce what Trevelyan called important books of enduring quality (which is much more difficult). In the end, creativity is much more significant than criticism, which means that in the long run, books rightly matter much more than reviews. These are things which no historian – and no reviewer – should ever forget.

Acknowledgements

The author is grateful to the following journals, publishers, learned societies and editors for permission to reproduce the essays and articles which, in revised form, comprise the following chapters:

1. J. Morrill (ed.), *The Promotion of Knowledge: Lectures to Mark the Centenary of the British Academy, 1902–2002* (Oxford University Press, 2004)
2. *Historical Research*, lxxvii (2004)
3. *Parliamentary History*, xxvi (2007)
4. *Past & Present*, no. 103 (1984)
5. J. Jenkins (ed.), *Re-Making the Landscape: The Changing Face of Britain* (Profile Books, 2002)
6. *Historical Research*, lxxx (2008)
7. *Welsh History Review*, xvii (1995)
8. C.M. Coates (ed.), *Imperial Canada, 1867–1917* (Centre for Canadian Studies, University of Edinburgh, 1997)
9. *Common Knowledge*, xi (2005)
10. *Historical Research*, lxxv (2002)

Appendix: *History Today*, March 1999

Notes

PROLOGUE, pp. 1–18

1. In preparing this lecture, I have benefited greatly from conversations with many scholars here in Britain since my return eleven months ago. But inaugural lectures are, by their nature, very personal utterances, and so it is more than usually important to observe that I am alone responsible for what follows. At the same time, I must take this opportunity to set down my thanks to my colleagues at the Institute of Historical Research for their assistance, support and encouragement, especially Debra Birch, Joyce Horn, Clyve Jones, Cathy Pearson and Jane Winters. [This lecture was delivered in Beveridge Hall of the Senate House of the University of London on 21 April 1999, and it was subsequently published. Apart from some slight stylistic modifications and embellishments, I have left the text unaltered; additions to the original footnotes, such as this one, have been placed in square brackets.]
2. M. Gilbert, *Winston S. Churchill*, vol. vi, *Finest Hour. 1939–1941* (London, 1983), pp. 900–3.
3. D. Cannadine (ed.), *The Speeches of Winston Churchill* (Harmondsworth, 1990), p. 194; idem, *The Pleasures of the Past* (London, 1989), p. 305. It was to answer the same question ('What is the use of history?'), posed at almost the same time by one of his younger sons, that Marc Bloch wrote *The Historian's Craft* (New York, 1953), p. 4.
4. A recent and honourable exception is Quentin Skinner, in *Liberty Before Liberalism* (Cambridge, 1998), pp. 107–8: 'We ought, I think, to be prepared to ask ourselves quite aggressively what is supposed to be the practical use, here and now, of our historical studies.... We must expect to be asked, and must not fail to ask ourselves, what is supposed to be the point of it all.'
5. A.G. Hopkins, *The Future of the Imperial Past* (Cambridge, 1997), p. 2; R.J.W. Evans, *The Language of History and the History of Language* (Oxford, 1998), pp. 33–4. For one outstanding example of the genre, which manages to encompass all three objectives within the confines of a single lecture, see P.K. O'Brien, *Power Without Profit: The State and the Economy. 1688–1815* (London, 1991).
6. This obligation to 'speak to the world at large' was the reason F.W. Maitland refused the Regius Professorship of Modern History at Cambridge in 1902: see G.R. Elton, *F.W. Maitland* (London, 1985), p. 14.
7. Pollard's creation and its subsequent history is fully dealt with in D.J. Birch and J.M. Horn (eds), *The History Laboratory: The Institute of Historical Research 1921–96* (London, 1996), to which I am much indebted. The phrase 'a world centre for research' was used by G.M. Trevelyan in his article on the IHR in *The Times*, 16 December 1937. The chief benefactor to the IHR in Pollard's time was Sir John Cecil Power, for whom see J.G. Edwards, 'Sir John Cecil Power,

Bart, 1870–1950', *Bulletin of the Institute of Historical Research*, xxiii (1950), pp. 139–46; *Dictionary of National Biography, 1941–1950* (Oxford, 1959), pp. 694–95; [*Oxford DNB*, vol. xlv, p. 137].

8. Militant conservative empiricists have never warmed to Pollard (a lifelong Victorian Liberal), preferring to stress what they regard as the shortcomings of his scholarly method, rather than recognizing his massive (and unique) contribution to history and the study of history: see, for example, G.R. Elton, *Return to Essentials: Some Reflections on the Present State of Historical Study* (Cambridge, 1991), pp. 57, 115; idem, *Henry VIII: An Essay in Revision* (London, 1962), pp. 3–11; idem, 'Introduction' to A.F. Pollard, *Wolsey* (London, 1965 edn), pp. xi–xxxvii; J.P. Kenyon, *The History Men: The Historical Profession in England since the Renaissance* (2nd edn, London, 1993), pp. 204–6, 211–15, is slightly more balanced. See also L. Stone, 'The Revival of Narrative: Reflections on New Old History', *Past & Present*, no. 85 (1979), p. 20; Q .Skinner, 'Sir Geoffrey Elton and the Practice of History', *Transactions of the Royal Historical Society*, 6th Ser., vii (1997), pp. 313–16.

9. L.F. Salzman, 'The Victoria County Histories', *Bulletin of the Institute of Historical Research*, xii (1935–36), pp. 65–8; R.B. Pugh, 'The Structure and Aims of the Victoria History of the Counties of England', *Bulletin of the Institute of Historical Research*, xl (1967), p. 5.

10. Regrettably, there is no full-length study of Pollard, but the outlines of his life may be found in *The Times*, 5 August 1948, and in the following obituary notices: J.E. Neale, *English Historical Review*, lxiv (1949), pp. 198–205; C.H. Williams, *Bulletin of the Institute of Historical Research*, xxii (1949), pp. 1–10; V.H. Galbraith, *Proceedings of the British Academy*, xxxv (1949), pp. 257–74; *Dictionary of National Biography, 1941–1950* (Oxford, 1959), pp. 679–81. [See also D. Cannadine, *In Churchill's Shadow: Confronting the Past in Modern Britain* (London, 2002), pp. 134–58; *Oxford DNB*, vol. xliv, pp. 746–8; also below, Chapter 3, pp. 60–3.]

11. Galbraith, obituary notice of Pollard, in *Proceedings of the British Academy*, p. 262.

12. History of Parliament, Col. Josiah Wedgwood MSS: Box A46, A.F. Pollard to J.C. Wedgwood, 25 October 1936. Pollard ceased to be Director of the IHR in 1931, but continued as Honorary Director until 1939. He was followed by Cyril Flower who was Acting Director until 1944, when Galbraith replaced him as the second Director.

13. For some earlier thoughts, set down just before I left the United Kingdom for the United States, see D. Cannadine, 'British History: Past, Present – and Future?', *Past & Present*, no. 116 (1987), pp. 169–91.

14. J. Horn, *Teachers of History in the Universities of the United Kingdom* (London, 1980); J.M. Horn and J. Winters, *Teachers of History in the Universities of the United Kingdom* (London, 1999); Royal Historical Society, *Annual Bibliography of British and Irish History* (Oxford, 1990), p. ix; ibid. (Oxford, 1998), p. xiii.

15. *1992 Research Assessment Exercise: The Outcome* (Bristol, 1992), pp. 69–71; *1996 Research Assessment Exercise: The Outcome* (Swindon, 1996), pp. 103–5.

16. Elton, *Return to Essentials*, p. 41: 'We historians are, in a way, fighting for our very lives'; P. Novick, *That Noble Dream: The 'Objectivity Question' and the*

American Historical Profession (Cambridge, 1988), p. 628: 'As a community of scholars, united by common aims, common standards and common purposes, the discipline of history had ceased to exist'; F. Fukuyama, *The End of History and the Last Man* (London, 1992). [For a fuller discussion of these matters, see below, Chapter 1, pp. 20–1.]

17. R.J. Evans, *In Defence of History* (London, 1997); A. Ryan, 'Introduction', in A. Ryan et al., *After the End of History* (London, 1992), pp. 1–5.

18. R. Jenkins, *Gladstone* (London, 1995); I. Gilmour, *Riot, Risings and Revolution: Governance and Violence in Eighteenth-Century England* (London, 1992); A. Clark, *Barbarossa: The Russo-German Conflict, 1941–45* (London, 1965); J.G. Brown, 'The Labour Party and Political Change in Scotland, 1918–29: The Politics of Five Elections' (unpublished Ph.D. dissertation, University of Edinburgh, 1982); idem, *Maxton* (Edinburgh, 1986).

19. J. Keegan, *The First World War* (London, 1998); O. Figes, *The People's Tragedy: The Russian Revolution, 1891–1924* (London, 1997); R.J. Overy, *Russia's War* (London, 1998); N. Ferguson, *The Pity of War* (London, 1998). [S. Schama, *A History of Britain*: vol. i, *At the Edge of the World? 3000 BC–AD 1603* (London, 2000); vol. ii, *The British Wars, 1603–1776* (London, 2001); vol. iii, *The Fate of Empire, 1776–2000* (London, 2002).]

20. R. Pares, *The Historian's Business and Other Essays* (Oxford, 1961), p. 10; K.V. Thomas, 'History and Anthropology', *Past & Present*, no. 24 (1963), p. 18; M. Howard, *The Lessons of History* (Oxford, 1991), pp. 8–9; D. Cannadine, *G.M. Trevelyan: A Life in History* (London, 1992), pp. 183–4; J.L. Gaddis, *On Contemporary History* (Oxford, 1995), pp. 19–25; A.C. Grayling, *Moral Values* (London, 1997), pp. 52–4. The most famous (and influential) exposition of a 'liberal education' is in J.H. Newman, *The Idea of a University* (ed. F.M. Turner, New Haven, 1996), Discourses v and vi, pp. 76–108.

21. W.O. Chadwick, *Freedom and the Historian* (Cambridge, 1969), p. 39: 'History... does more than any other discipline to free the mind from the tyranny of present opinion'; B. Bailyn, *On the Teaching and Writing of History* (Hanover, New Hampshire, 1994), p. 12: 'History... is... a way of getting out of the boundaries of one's own life and culture and of seeing more of what human experience has been.' See also G.F. Kennan, 'The Experience of Writing History', *Virginia Quarterly Review*, xxxvi (1960), pp. 211–14: 'Every age thinks itself to be the most important age that ever occurred', a fallacy which only history can dispel.

22. The case for historians as a hegemonic power elite has been put by K. Jenkins, *Re-Thinking History* (London, 1991), pp. 19–21; idem, *On 'What is History?' From Carr and Elton to Rorty and White* (London, 1995), p. 22. For a powerful and persuasive riposte, see Evans, *In Defence of History*, pp. 204–23. In the early 1950s, writing about academic life in Cambridge during the 1930s, C.P. Snow (*The Masters* (London, 1952), p. 387) claimed dons lived 'the least anxious, the most comfortable, the freest lives' of any professional group he had encountered. Such a claim would be inconceivable today; but it was probably right then: see A. Flexner, *Universities: American, English, German* (New York, 1930), p. 288; [D. Cannadine, 'The Era of Todd, Plumb and Snow', in D. Reynolds (ed.), *Christ's: A Cambridge College Over Five Centuries* (London, 2004), pp. 214–15].

23. A.H. Halsey, *Decline of Donnish Dominion* (Oxford, 1992), esp. pp. viii, 2, 124–5, 134–7, 175–6, 268–70; J.R. Vincent, *An Intelligent Person's Guide to History* (London, 1995), p. 53.

24. Halsey, *Decline of Donnish Dominion*, p. 137, notes that since 1975, academic salaries have been stationary in real terms, while those in other professions have risen by one third.

25. M. Strathearn, 'From improvement to enhancement: an anthropological comment on the audit culture', *Cambridge Review*, November 1997, p. 123.

26. H. Swain, 'RAE can "corrupt" research', *The Times Higher Education Supplement*, 26 March 1999, p. 8.

27. Strathearn, 'From improvement to enhancement', pp. 123–4. [For a fuller discussion of J.H. Plumb's *The Growth of Political Stability in England*, see below, Chapter 10, pp. 235–73.]

28. H.R. Trevor-Roper, *History: Professional and Lay* (Oxford, 1958). The dangers of over-specialization were already being drawn attention to by C.N.L. Brooke, *The Dullness of the Past* (Liverpool, 1957), pp. 7–8, and by H. Butterfield, *The Present State of Historical Scholarship* (Cambridge, 1965), pp. 3–4.

29. Here, randomly culled from recent newspapers, are some opinions to this effect: R. Stummer, 'The eternal now', *The Guardian Weekend*, 21 November 1998: 'New Britain has history on the run – or, to be more precise, the old, liberal consensus that history is a worthwhile thing to know about, to value, something that enriches culture and strengthens democracy'; M. Marrin, 'We forget to remember', *The Sunday Telegraph*, 8 November 1998: 'It is not just that those who know no history are condemned to repeat it. It is also that independence and freedom depend on having sure sense of identity, which in turn depends on historical remembrance; and shared memory brings a shared sense of identity and values'; *The Times*, leading article, 23 November 1998: 'To be ignorant of what happened before one was born is to remain a child for the whole of one's life'; T. Benn, 'Let's have an elected head of state', *The Independent on Sunday*, 24 January 1999: 'New Labour regularly denounces everything that went before as old-fashioned, irrelevant and downright dangerous. A knowledge of, or even an interest in, the past is viewed with suspicion, and those who are thought to be studying it run the risk of being marginalised.'

30. For the general decline in academic authority, see Z. Bauman, 'Universities: Old, New and Different', in A. Smith and F. Webster (eds), *The Postmodern University? Contested Visions of Higher Education in Society* (Buckingham, 1997), pp. 21–4.

31. The argument that the prime 'social function' of the historian is to dispel such present-minded and parochial amnesia has been eloquently made by J.H. Elliott, *National and Comparative History* (Oxford, 1991), pp. 1–5. The case for politicians needing to know more history than they generally do these days has been cogently and convincingly advanced by R. Jenkins, 'Should Politicians Know History?', in idem, *Portraits and Miniatures* (London, 1993), pp. 206–13. For two recent examples of ahistorical discussion of contemporary issues, the reform of the House of Lords, and the removal of the Queen's head from British banknotes in the event of Britain joining the single currency, see *The Times*, 16 February 1996, and 23–26 September 1998.

32. R.W. Winks, *The Imperial Revolution: Yesterday and Tomorrow* (Oxford, 1994), p. 11.
33. D. Bythell, *The Handloom Weavers: A Study in the English Cotton Industry During the Industrial Revolution* (Cambridge, 1969). Happily, academic housing is not yet as bad as described in J.G. Timmins, *Handloom Weavers' Cottages in Central Lancashire*, Centre for North-West Regional Studies, occasional paper, no. 3 (Lancaster, 1977).
34. Howard, *The Lessons of History*, pp. 19–20.
35. The German Chancellor Helmut Kohl did not send his two sons to the Universities of Heidelberg or Munich. But nor did he send them to Cambridge or Oxford: they went to Harvard and MIT. See J. Joffe, *The Future of the Great Powers* (Phoenix, 1998), p. 40. I am grateful to David Goodhart for this reference.
36. 'Institutions Ranked by Fiscal Year 1998 Market Value of Endowment Assets', *National Association of College and University Business Officers* (February 1999), pp. 32–7. At present, there are 18 US universities with larger endowments than Oxford: R. Stevens, *Barbarians at the Gates: A View from Oxford's City Wall* (Washington DC, 1998), pp. 26–7. From this transatlantic perspective, the fundamental problem facing Oxford and Cambridge Universities today is not that their privileges are indefensibly excessive, but that they are woefully insufficient. [By 2007, Harvard's endowment was alleged to have grown to $35 billion: A. Delbanco, 'Academic Business: Has the modern university become just another corporation?', *New York Times Magazine*, 30 September 2007, p. 26.]
37. This helps explain why an American academic, James Axtell, recently published a book entitled *The Pleasures of Academe* (Lincoln, Nebraska, 1998). It is inconceivable that any British academic would publish a book with such a title, unless employing the ironic mode, as in D. Lodge, *Nice Work* (London, 1988).
38. Outstanding historians at American Ivy League universities are made University Professors, so they can get on unencumbered with their writing and teaching; outstanding historians at Oxford and Cambridge are made Regius Professors or heads of colleges, which means they spend more time on more committees.
39. For a cogent protest against them, see A. Broers, 'Diversity and quality which thrive under light touch', *The Times Higher Education Supplement*, 29 January 1999, p. 14. It is not coincidence that these are precisely the same problems at present facing the BBC.
40. British Library of Political and Economic Science, Passfield MSS: 2/4/D, G.M. Trevelyan to Sidney Webb, 22 May 1908.
41. Halsey, *Decline of Donnish Dominion*, p. 146: 'Their prestige, salaries, autonomy, and resources have been much humbled. Whether their quality as teachers and researchers has risen or fallen is an open question. Whether their creativity, in the past both celebrated and never fully understood, can be maintained into the future is a vital but unresolved issue.' Indeed it is.
42. Strathearn, 'From improvement to enhancement', p. 124.
43. This case has been well put by Stevens, *Barbarians at the Gates*. See also J. Cole, 'Balancing Acts: Dilemmas of Choice Facing Research Universities', *Daedalus*, cxxii, no. 4 (Fall, 1993), p. 33: 'The best of the research universities will continue to be a source of national pride – an American institution that remains superior

to its counterparts around the world.' There seems no reason to dissent from this view. Indeed, it has been strongly (and cogently) endorsed from this side of the Atlantic in C. Russell, *Academic Freedom* (London, 1993), p. 109: 'Even in Oxford and Cambridge, formal teaching may be taking up as much as twenty two hours a week which, after meetings, letters, reading books and so forth is likely to add up to a sixty hour week *even before any research can be attempted*. Few academics will long have the dedication to make the attempt, and already people are leaving Oxford and Cambridge for the USA in order to recover the opportunity to do research.' (My italics.)

44. For which see the letter of John Keegan in *The Times*, 12 December 1998.

45. It was something of a commonplace for professors in the 1960s to deplore increased government interference in universities. See especially, C. Wilson, *History in Special and in General* (Cambridge, 1964), p. 23: 'From reformers, politicians and government committees, comes a steady stream of exhortations, threats and sermons on our duties.' What, one wonders, would he make of things today?

46. I take this quotation from Lord Annan's forthcoming book, *The Dons*, which he kindly allowed me to read in typescript. [N. Annan, *The Dons: Mentors, Eccentrics and Geniuses* (London, 1999), pp. 3–4.]

47. B.H. Liddell Hart, *Reputations Ten Years After* (Boston, 1928), p. 163.

48. [It was subsequently re-named the Centre for Contemporary British History.]

49. The creation of the SAS has been admirably and instructively described by its present Dean in T. Daintith, 'A Change of Life? The Institute Joins the School of Advanced Study', in B. Rider (ed.), *Law at the Centre: The Institute of Advanced Legal Studies at Fifty* (London, 1999), pp. 31–46.

50. SAS Paper 11/98/9, School and Institute Accounts for 1997–98.

51. This figure is, I freely admit, plucked largely (but not wholly) out of the air. Under the inspired leadership of Sir Claus Moser, the British Museum has recently raised almost £100 million. But it is easier to raise money for British museums than for British universities, and in any case, Moser is universally acknowledged to be the best fund-raiser of his generation. To put this hypothesized endowment for the School of Advanced Study in perspective, it is worth mentioning that the present (30 June 1998) endowment of the Institute for Advanced Study at Princeton is slightly less than $400 million: Institute for Advanced Study, *Report for the Academic Year 1997–98* (Princeton, 1998), p. 103.

52. *The Public Papers of the Presidents of the United States: John F. Kennedy. January 1 to November 22 1963* (Washington DC, 1964), p. 537; T.C. Sorenson, *The Kennedy Legacy* (New York, 1967), p. 388.

53. A.F. Pollard, *Factors in Modern History* (3rd edn, London, 1932), pp. 252–3.

54. Pollard, *Factors in Modern History*, p. 250.

55. V.H. Galbraith, *Historical Study and the State* (Oxford, 1948), p. 19.

56. G.M. Trevelyan, *Clio, a Muse, and Other Essays* (London, 1930 edn), p. 196. There are many allusions in this paragraph which might be more fully teased out. The idea of 'imagination pursuing the fact and fastening upon it' recalls Keats: 'I am certain of nothing but of the holiness of the heart's affections and the truth of imagination' (Keats to Benjamin Bailey, 22 November 1817, in M.B. Forman (ed.), *The Letters of John Keats* (2nd edn, Oxford, 1935), pp. 66–70). I

am most grateful to A.S. Byatt for this suggestion and this reference. The phrase to 'scorn delights and live laborious days' is from Milton's *Lycidas:*

> Fame is the spur that the clear spirit doth raise
> (That last infirmity of noble mind)
> To scorn delights, and live laborious days.

And the injunction 'to know what really happened' clearly derives from Ranke: '*wie es eigentlich gewesen*': F. Stern (ed.), *The Varieties of History* (New York, 1972 edn), p. 57. For recent re-statements of the importance for history writing of controlled imagination, see H.R. Trevor-Roper, *History and Imagination* (Oxford, 1980); Bailyn, *On The Teaching and Writing of History*, pp. 72–3; Evans, *In Defence of History*, pp. 250–1.

CHAPTER 1, PERSPECTIVES, pp. 19–38

1. This chapter began as one of the lectures to celebrate the hundredth anniversary of the founding of the British Academy, which I delivered at the University of Sheffield on 14 March 2002. I am grateful to Professor Sir Ian Kershaw and his colleagues in the history department, and also to the Vice-Chancellor, Professor Robert Boucher, for their invitation, and for their helpful comments and criticisms of the original version.
2. Anon, 'A Brief Account of the Foundation of the Academy', *Proceedings of the British Academy*, i (1903–04), p. ix; S. Collini, *Public Moralists: Political Thought and Intellectual Life in Britain, 1850–1930* (Oxford, 1991), pp. 21–7.
3. W.R. Brock, 'James Bryce and the Future', *Proceedings of the British Academy*, cxv (2002), *Biographical Memoirs of Fellows*, i, pp. 3–30. For a recent reappraisal of Bryce, see J. Seaman, *A Citizen of the World: The Life of James Bryce* (London, 2006); S. Martin, *The Order of Merit: One Hundred Years of Matchless Honour* (London, 1907), pp. 312–13.
4. Viscount Bryce, 'Presidential Address', *Proceedings of the British Academy*, vi (1913–14), pp. 121–2.
5. J. Bryce, 'World History', *Proceedings of the British Academy*, ix (1919–20), pp. 189–92.
6. L. Stone, *The Present and the Past Revisited* (London, 1987), pp. 4–8; J.H. Robinson (ed.), *The New History* (New York, 1912); T.K. Rabb and R.I. Rotberg (eds), *The New History: The 1980s and Beyond* (Princeton, 1982).
7. L. Jordanova, *History in Practice* (London, 2000), p. 203.
8. R.J. Evans, *In Defense of History* (New York, 1999), pp. 1–8; J.W. Scott, 'History in Crisis? The Others' Side of the Story', *American Historical Review*, xciv (1989), pp. 680–92.
9. G. Himmelfarb, *The New History and the Old: Critical Essays and Reappraisals* (Cambridge, Mass., 1987); idem, *On Looking into the Abyss* (New York, 1994); S. Pedersen, 'What is Political History Now?', in D. Cannadine (ed.), *What Is History Now?* (Basingstoke, 2002), pp. 36–55; P. Novick, *That Noble Dream: The 'Objectivity Question' and the American Historical Profession* (Cambridge, 1988), p. 628.

10. F. Fukuyama, *The End of History and the Last Man* (London, 1992); A. Ryan et al., *After the End of History* (London, 1992); C.M. Andrew, 'Foreword' in A.G. Hopkins (ed.), *Globalization in World History* (London, 2002), p. vii.

11. F. Stern, 'A Note to the Second Edition', in idem (ed.), *The Varieties of History* (New York, 1972 edn), pp. 9–10.

12. For four recent attempts to address these issues, see P. Purke (ed.), *History and Historians in the Twentieth Century* (Oxford, 2002); J. Gardiner (ed.), *What Is History Today?* (London, 1988); B. Southgate, *History: What and Why? Ancient, Modern and Post-Modern Perspectives* (2nd edn, London, 2001); Cannadine, *What Is History Now?*

13. J.P. Kenyon, *The History Men: The Historical Profession in England since the Renaissance* (London, 1983), pp. 145, 164; P. Mandler, *History and National Life* (London, 2002), pp. 11–45; see also below, Chapter 7, pp. 173–4.

14. Lord Reay, 'Address by the President', *Proceedings of the British Academy*, ii (1905–06), p. 5; Collini, *Public Moralists*, pp. 216–20; see also below, Chapter 7, pp. 175–6.

15. P. Readman, 'The Place of the Past in English Culture, c. 1890–914', *Past & Present*, no. 186 (2005), pp. 147–99.

16. C.H. Firth, 'The Study of Modern History in Great Britain', *Proceedings of the British Aacademy*, vi (1913–14), p. 139.

17. Mandler, *History and National Life*, pp. 56–60; D. Cannadine, *The Pleasures of the Past* (London, 1989), pp. 92–3, 275–8; idem, *In Churchill's Shadow: Confronting the Past in Modern Britain* (London, 2002), pp. 225–9.

18. Firth, 'Study of Modern History', p. 142; T.F. Tout, 'The Present State of Medieval Studies in Great Britain', *Proceedings of the British Academy*, vi (1913–14), p. 156; Kenyon, *History Men*, p. 165.

19. Collini, *Public Moralists*, pp. 216–21; Kenyon, *History Men*, pp. 174–6.

20. P. Mandler, 'Against "Englishness": English Culture and the Limits to Rural Nostalgia', *Transactions of the Royal Historical Society*, 6th ser., vii (1997), pp. 155–75; P. Readman, 'Landscape Preservation, "Advertising Disfigurement", and English National Identity, c1890–1914', *Rural History*, xii (2001), pp. 61–83.

21. Kenyon, *History Men*, pp. 175, 180; J.H. Arnold, *History: A Very Short Introduction* (Oxford, 2000), p. 56. For the foundation of the IHR, see above, Prologue, p. 2.

22. J.H. Plumb, *The Death of the Past* (London, 1969), p. 108, made this point over thirty years ago: it is even more true today. For the figures in this and the preceding paragraph, I am much indebted to Dr Jane Winters of the Institute of Historical Research, who has derived them from two of the IHR's long-running annual publications: *Historical Research for Higher Degrees in the UK*, and *Teachers of History in the Universities of the UK*.

23. N. Annan, *Our Age: Portrait of a Generation* (London, 1990), pp. 3–18.

24. E.H. Carr, *What is History?* (London, 1961); G.R. Elton, *The Practice of History* (Sydney, 1967). Both works have been well discussed by R.J. Evans, in his introduction to the (London, 2001) edition of Carr, and in his afterword to the (Oxford, 2002) edition of Elton.

25. For economic history, see below, Chapter 4, pp. 83–111.

26. Evans, *In Defense of History*, pp. 173–5.

27. Cannadine, *Pleasures of the Past*, pp. 99–109, 256–71; idem, *In Churchill's Shadow*, pp. 233–7; Mandler, *History and National Life*, pp. 3–9, 97–100; see also below, Chapter 5, pp. 119–31.

28. Jordanova, *History in Practice*, pp. 141–71; D. Lowenthal, *The Past is a Foreign Country* (Cambridge, 1985); R. Samuel, *Theatres of Memory* (London, 1994); D. Cannadine, *National Portrait Gallery: A Brief History* (London, 2007), pp. 60–76.

29. Arnold, *History*, p. 118; Mandler, *History and National Life*, pp. 1–10. For Tony Blair's insistence that 'history' will 'forgive' him for invading Iraq, see *The Guardian*, 18 July 2003; *Financial Times*, 19 July 2003; L.J. Colley, 'What Blair Can Learn From History', *The Guardian*, G2, 29 July 2003, p. 8.

30. Nor should the current difficulties, concerning the under-funding and over-regulation of British universities, which were discussed above in the Prologue, pp. 5–8, be forgotten.

31. D. Cannadine, *G.M. Trevelyan: A Life in History* (London, 1992), p. 219.

32. Lord Reay, 'Address by the President', *Proceedings of the British Academy*, i (1903–04), pp. 1, 12; Kenyon, *History Men*, pp. 174–6; Collini, *Public Moralists*, pp. 216–21.

33. Arnold, *History*, p. 114; Cannadine, *Trevelyan*, pp. 214–17; M. Bloch, *The Historian's Craft* (Manchester, 1992 edn), p. 7.

34. L.B. Namier, *The Structure of Politics at the Accession of George III* (London, 1929); idem, *1848: The Revolution of the Intellectuals* (London, 1946); A.J.P. Taylor, *The Course of German History* (London, 1945); idem, *English History, 1914–1945* (Oxford, 1965).

35. P. Burke, 'History of Events and the Revival of Narrative', in idem (ed.), *New Perspectives on Historical Writing* (Oxford, 1991), pp. 233–48.

36. L. Stone, *The Crisis of the Aristocracy, 1558–1641* (Oxford, 1965), pp. 3–4; F. Braudel, *On History* (Chicago, 1980), pp. 3–4, 27–30.

37. C. Hill, *The Century of Revolution, 1603–1714* (London, 1961); C. Russell, *Unrevolutionary England, 1603–42* (London, 1990); R. Porter, *English Society in the Eighteenth Century* (Harmondsworth, 1982); J.C.D. Clark, *English Society, 1688–1832: Ideology, Social Structure and Political Practice during the Ancien Regime* (Cambridge, 1985).

38. 'Editorial Introduction', *Continuity and Change*, i (1986), pp. 5–6.

39. Stone, *Present and the Past*, p. 8.

40. R. Darnton, *The Great Cat Massacre and Other Episodes in French Cultural History* (London, 1983); C. Ginsburg, *The Cheese and the Worms* (Baltimore, 1980); N.Z. Davis, *The Return of Martin Guerre* (Cambridge, Mass., 1983); W. McNeill, *A World History* (Oxford, 1979); J.M. Roberts, *The Hutchinson History of the World* (London, 1976); F. Fernandez-Armesto, *Millennium* (London, 1995).

41. Stern, *Varieties of History*, pp. 59–61; G. Levi, 'On Microhistory', in Burke, *New Perspectives*, pp. 93–113.

42. E.P. Thompson, *The Making of the English Working Class* (London, 1963), p. 12.

43. P. Burke, 'Overture: The New History', in idem, *New Perspectives*, p. 19; E.P. Thompson, 'Patrician Society, Plebian Culture', *Journal of Social History*, vii

(1974), pp. 382–405; idem, 'Eighteenth-Century English Society: Class Struggle Without Class?', *Social History*, iii (1978), pp. 133–65.

44. H.R. Trevor-Roper, *History Professional and Lay* (Oxford, 1957); see also above, Prologue, p. 7.

45. Arnold, *History*, p. 6; Lowenthal, *Past is a Foreign Country*, pp. xvi, 191.

46. Stern, 'Introduction', in idem, *Varieties of History*, p. 27; Evans, *In Defense of History*, p. 162; Arnold, *History*, p. 85; Cannadine, *Trevelyan*, p. 196.

47. S. Collini, *English Pasts: Essays in History and Culture* (Oxford, 1999), pp. 2, 320.

48. B. Worden, *Roundhead Reputations: The English Civil War and the Passions of Posterity* (London, 2001), p. 344.

49. See also below, Chapter 10, pp. 272–3.

50. J. Appleby, 'The Power of History', *American Historical Review*, ciii (1998), p. 1; J.R. Vincent, *An Intelligent Person's Guide to History* (London, 2001 edn), p. 47; Worden, *Roundhead Reputations*, p. 339; E.J. Hobsbawm, *The Age of Empire, 1875–1914* (London, 1987), p. 340.

51. Collini, *English Pasts*, pp. 318–22.

52. For two recent examples of the 'collectivities in conflict' view of the past, see S.P. Huntington, *The Clash of Civilizations and the Re-Making of the World Order* (London, 1997); A. Wheatcroft, *Infidels: The Conflict between Christendom and Islam, 638–2002* (London, 2003). For the alternative approach, stressing individual co-operation rather than collective conflict, see M.R. Menocal, *The Ornament of the World: How Muslims, Jews and Christians Created a Culture of Tolerance in Medieval Spain* (London, 2002); W. Dalrymple, *White Mughals: Love and Betrayal in Eighteenth-Century India* (London, 2002), esp. pp. xl–xliii, 494–501. See also W.H. McNeill, 'Mythistory, or Truth, Myth, History and Historians', *American Historical Review*, xci (1986), p. 7.

53. Arnold, *History*, p. 51; N. Orme, *Medieval Children* (London, 2001), p. 10.

54. M. Rubin, 'What is Cultural History Now', in Cannadine, *What Is History Now?*, pp. 80–94.

55. The literature on this subject is vast, but I benefited much from the seminar series 'History and Human Nature', held at the Institute of Historical Research during the academic year 2000–01, and I have also been helped by K. Malik, *Man, Beast and Zombie: What Science Can and Cannot Tell Us About Human Nature* (London, 2000).

56. Mandler, *History and National Life*, pp. 7–8; see also below, Chapter 7, pp. 178–81.

57. A.G. Hopkins, 'Introduction: Globalization – An Agenda for Historians', in idem, *Globalization*, p. 5; C.S. Maier, 'Consigning the Twentieth Century to History: Alternative Narratives for the Modern Era', *American Historical Review*, cv (2000), pp. 807–31.

58. At http://www.history.ac.uk/projects/discourse/index.html.

59. L.J. Colley, *The Ordeal of Elizabeth Marsh: A Woman in World History* (London, 2007), p. xxviii.

60. On 7 July 2003, the Institute of Historical Research sponsored a conference on 'Examining the Impact of Digitisation Upon Scholarship in the Humanities', and the papers may be found at http://www.history.ac.uk/confernces/digitisation2003/index.html. See also below, Chapter 3, pp. 70–1.

61. Vincent, *Intelligent Person's Guide*, p. 53; M.I. Finley, *The Use and Abuse of History* (London, 2000 edn), p. 33.

62. H. Russo, *The Vichy Syndrome: History and Memory in France since 1944* (Cambridge, Mass., 1991); S. Falmer et al., *France at War: Vichy and the Historians* (Oxford, 2000); B. Niven, *Facing the Nazi Past: Unified Germany and the Legacy of the Third Reich* (London, 2002); R.J. Evans, *Telling Lies About Hitler: The Holocaust, History and the David Irving Trial* (London, 2002).

63. R.L. Brooks (ed.), *When Sorry Isn't Enough: The Controversy Over Apologies and Reparations for Human Injustice* (New York, 1999); A. Boraine, *A Country Unmasked* (Cape Town, 2000), esp. pp; 379–442; T. Hunt, 'In the Scales of History', *The Guardian*, 6 April 2002.

64. Bloch, *Historian's Craft*, p. 115.

65. J. Carey, 'The Last Flowering of the British Aristocracy', *The Sunday Times, Culture*, 17 March 2002, p. 38. See also above, Prologue, p. 5.

66. J. Appleby, L. Hunt and M. Jacob, *Telling the Truth About History* (New York, 1995), p. 228.

67. Appleby, 'The Power of History', p. 1.

68. E.J. Hobsbawm, *Age of Anxiety: The Short Twentieth Century* (London, 1994); M. Mazower, *Dark Continent: Europe's Twentieth Century* (London, 1998).

69. L. Stone, *The Family, Sex and Marriage in England, 1500–1800* (abridged edn, Harmondsworth, 1979), p. 428.

CHAPTER 2, MONARCHY, pp. 39–58

1. This chapter began life as my inaugural lecture as Queen Elizabeth the Queen Mother Professor of British History, which I delivered in the Beveridge Hall of the University of London Senate House on 12 January 2004. I am grateful to Charlotte Alston for essential research assistance, and to my former undergraduate students at the University of Cambridge and Columbia University, New York, with whom I discussed many of the thoughts and ideas that appear in these pages during the 1980s and 1990s. An abridged version of this lecture appeared in the *Times Literary Supplement*, 23 January 2004, pp. 11–13, which gave rise to a lively subsequent correspondence (*TLS*, 6 February 2004, p. 15; 27 February 2004, p. 17). I also record subsequent and special thanks to Walter Arnstein and Derek Beales.

2. S. Schama, 'Television and the Trouble with History', in D. Cannadine (ed.), *History and the Media* (Basingstoke, 2004), pp. 26–7.

3. M. Bloch, *The Royal Touch: Sacred Monarchy and Scrofula in England and France* (London, 1973); E.H. Kantorowicz, *The King's Two Bodies: A Study in Medieval Political Thought* (Princeton, 1957); H. Nicolson, *Monarchy* (London, 1962); D. Cannadine and S. Price (eds), *Rituals of Royalty: Power and Ceremonial in Traditional Societies* (Cambridge, 1987); G. Dagron, *Emperor and Priest: The Imperial Office in Byzantium* (Cambridge, 2003).

4. A.W. Lewis, *Royal Succession in Capetian France: Studies on Familial Order and the State* (London, 1981).

5. J.C. Bromley, *The Shakespearean Kings* (Boulder, 1972); C. Jordan, *Shakespeare's Monarchies: Ruler and Subject in the Romances* (London, 1997); P. Saccio, *Shakespeare's English Kings: History, Chronicle and Drama* (1st edn, Oxford, 1977; 2000); G. Wilson Knight, *The Sovereign Flower: on Shakespeare as the Poet of Royalism* (London, 2002).

6. M. van Gelderen and Q. Skinner (ed.), *Republicanism: A Shared European Heritage* (2 vols, Cambridge, 2003).

7. I tried to attempt something of this sort in D. Cannadine, 'The Last Hanoverian Sovereign? The Victorian monarchy in historical perspective, 1688–1988', in A.L. Beier, D. Cannadine and J.M. Rosenheim (eds), *The First Modern Society: Essays in English History in Honour of Lawrence Stone* (Cambridge, 1989), pp. 127–66. There are very few studies of the English/British monarchy which take a long view, among them J.H. Plumb and H. Weldon, *Royal Heritage: The Story of Britain's Royal Builders and Collectors* (London, 1977); J.A. Cannon and R.A. Griffiths, *The Oxford Illustrated History of the British Monarchy* (Oxford, 1988); D. Starkey, *The Monarchy of England* (1 vol. so far, London, 2004–), vol. i, *The Beginnings*. See also H. Hackett, 'Dreams or Designs, Cults or Constructions? The study of images of monarchs', *Historical Journal*, xliv (2001), pp. 811–24.

8. I have been much helped in preparing this section by R. Baldock, 'Publishing Monarchs and Publishing Monographs', paper presented to the Anglo-American Conference of Historians, Institute of Historical Research, 1 July 1998.

9. A.C. Benson and Viscount Esher (eds), *Letters of Queen Victoria, 1837–61* (3 vols, London, 1908); G.E. Buckle (ed.), *Letters of Queen Victoria, 1862–85* (3 vols, London, 1926–28); idem, *Letters of Queen Victoria, 1886–1901* (3 vols, London, 1930–32). For an outstanding study of the publication of the first series of the Queen's letters and journals, see: Y.M. Ward, 'Editing Queen Victoria: How Men of Letters Constructed the Young Queen' (unpublished Ph.D. dissertation, La Trobe University, 2005). For details of subsequent additional publications of the Queen's correspondence, see W.L. Arnstein, *Queen Victoria* (London, 2003), pp. 234–5.

10. Sir T. Martin, *The Life of H.R.H. The Prince Consort* (5 vols, London, 1875–80).

11. Sir S. Lee, *King Edward VII: A Biography* (2 vols, London, 1925–27); C.W. White, 'The Biographer and Edward VII: Sir Sidney Lee and the embarrassments of royal biography', *Victorian Studies*, xxvii (1984), pp. 301–19, esp. p. 318.

12. H. Nicolson, *King George V: His Life and Reign* (London, 1952); J. Pope-Hennessy, *Queen Mary, 1867–1953* (London, 1959); J.W. Wheeler-Bennett, *King George VI: His Life and Reign* (London, 1958). See also J. Gore, *King George V: A Personal Memoir* (London, 1941) which, as its title makes plain, dealt (very tactfully) with the king's private life.

13. N. Nicolson (ed.), *Harold Nicolson: Diaries and Letters, 1945–62* (London, 1968), pp. 142–5, 184; J. Lees-Milne, *Harold Nicolson: A Biography*, ii: *1930–68* (London, 1981), pp. 223, 238.

14. Nicolson, *Diaries and Letters*, pp. 174–6; Lees-Milne, *Harold Nicolson*, p. 268; J.W. Wheeler-Bennett, *Friends, Enemies and Sovereigns* (London, 1976), pp. 132–69, esp. p. 168. See also P. Quennell (ed.), *A Lonely Business: A Self-Portrait of James Pope-Hennessy* (London, 1981), pp. 207–70.

15. P. Ziegler, *Mountbatten: The Official Biography* (London, 1985); idem, *King Edward VIII: The Official Biography* (London, 1990). See also J. Morgan, *Edwina Mountbatten: A Life of her Own* (London, 1991); D. Cannadine, *The Pleasures of the Past* (London, 1989), pp. 58–67; idem, *History in our Time* (London, 1998), pp. 48–58.

16. E. Longford, *Victoria R.I.* (London, 1964); P. Magnus, *King Edward the Seventh* (London, 1964); G. Battiscombe, *Queen Alexandra* (London, 1969); F. Donaldson, *Edward VIII* (London, 1974); K. Rose, *King George V* (London, 1983); S. Bradford, *King George VI* (London, 1989). See also Cannadine, *Pleasures of the Past*, pp. 32–43; idem, *History in our Time*, pp. 59–67. Oddly enough, there is no satisfactory modern life of Albert (idem, *Pleasures of the Past*, pp. 12–21).

17. S. Bradford, *Elizabeth: A Biography of Her Majesty the Queen* (London, 1996); B. Pimlott, *The Queen: A Biography of Elizabeth II* (London, 1996). For a French perspective, see M. Roche, *Elizabeth II: La dernière reine* (Paris, 2007). See also J. Dimbleby, *The Prince of Wales: A Biography* (London, 1994); Cannadine, *History in our Time*, pp. 68–85.

18. I have confined myself here to royal biographies of monarchs and their consorts, but there are also lives of royal children, among which the following may be especially recommended: N. Frankland, *Prince Henry, Duke of Gloucester* (London, 1980); H. Pakula, *An Uncommon Woman: The Empress Frederick – Daughter of Queen Victoria, Wife of the Crown Prince of Prussia, Mother of Kaiser Wilhelm* (New York, 1995); J. Wake, *Princess Louise: Queen Victoria's Unconventional Daughter* (London, 1988).

19. I. Kershaw, *Hitler*, i: *1889–1936 – Hubris* (London, 1998), p. xxi; idem, 'Facts don't reflect myths of power', *Times Higher Education Supplement*, 16 January 2004, p. 23; G.R. Elton, *The Practice of History* (Sydney, 1967), pp. 169–70.

20. The pros and cons of biography are discussed in P.K. O'Brien and others, 'Is Political Biography a Good Thing?', *Contemporary British History*, x (1996), pp. 60–86; B. Pimlott, 'Once upon a lifetime', *Times Higher Education Supplement*, 6 November 1998, p. 24. For the growing interest of historians in the modern monarchy, see H. Richards, 'A right royal restoration', *THES*, 6 January 1995, p. 17.

21. For the post-war expansion of the historical profession in Britain, see above, Chapter 1, pp. 23–5.

22. F.M.L. Thompson, *English Landed Society in the Nineteenth Century* (London, 1963).

23. E.J. Hobsbawm and T. Ranger (eds), *The Invention of Tradition* (Cambridge, 1983); R. Samuel (ed.), *Patriotism: The Making and Unmaking of British National Identity* (3 vols, London, 1989); R. Porter (ed.), *Myths of the English* (Oxford, 1992).

24. W.L. Arnstein, 'Queen Victoria's Speeches from the Throne: A New Look', in A. O'Day (ed.), *Government and Institutions in the Post-1832 United Kingdom* (Lewiston, NY, 1995), pp. 127–53; V. Bogdanor, *The Monarchy and the Constitution* (Oxford, 1995); D. Cannadine, *In Churchill's Shadow: Confronting the Past in Modern Britain* (London, 2002), ch. 3; idem, *History in our Time*, pp. 19–24; P. Hennessy, 'Searching for the "Great Ghost": The

palace, the premiership, the Cabinet and the constitution in the post-war period', *Journal Contemporary History*, xxx (1995), pp. 211–31.

25. F. Prochaska, *Royal Bounty: The Making of a Welfare Monarchy* (London, 1995); Cannadine, *History in our Time*, pp. 25–32.

26. C. Carlton, *Royal Warriors: A Military History of the British Monarchy* (London, 2003); W.L. Arnstein, 'The Warrior Queen: Reflections on Victoria and Her World', *Albion*, xxx (1998), pp. 1–28; K.W. Farrell, 'The Monarchy and the Military: The case and career of the Duke of Cambridge in an age of reform' (unpublished Columbia University Ph.D. thesis, 1999); N. Frankland, *Witness of a Century: The Life and Times of Prince Arthur Duke of Connaught, 1850–1942* (London, 1993).

27. D.W.R. Bahlman, 'The Queen, Mr. Gladstone and Church Patronage', *Victorian Studies*, iii (1960), pp. 349–80; W.L. Arnstein, 'Queen Victoria and Religion', in G. Malmgreen (ed.), *Religion in the Lives of English Women, 1760–1930* (London, 1986), pp. 88–128; P. Hinchliff, 'Frederick Temple, Randall Davidson and the Coronation of Edward VII', *Journal of Ecclesiastical History*, xlviii (1997), pp. 71–99; G.I.T. Machin, 'Marriage and the Churches in the 1930s: Royal abdication and divorce reform, 1936–7', *Jour. Eccles. Hist.*, xlii (1991), pp. 68–81.

28. P. Hall, *Royal Fortune: Tax, Money and the Monarchy* (London, 1992); W.M. Kuhn, 'Queen Victoria's Civil List: What did she do with it?', *Historical Journal*, xxxvi (1993), pp. 642–65; Cannadine, *History in our Time*, pp. 11–18.

29. H. Hobhouse, *Prince Albert: His Life and Work* (London, 1983); S. Bayley, *The Albert Memorial: The Monument in its Social and Architectural Context* (London, 1981); C. Brooks (ed.), *The Albert Memorial* (London, 2000).

30. For a pioneering study, see P. Mansel, *Dressed to Rule: Royal and Court Costume from Louis XIV to Elizabeth II* (London, 2005).

31. For eighteenth-century studies of the royal court, to which there are no (much-needed) successors, see R.O. Bucholz, *The Augustan Court: Queen Anne and the Decline of Court Culture* (Stanford, 1993); J.M. Beattie, *The English Court in the Reign of George I* (Cambridge, 1967); H. Smith, 'The Court in England, 1714–1760: A Declining Political Institution?', *History*, xc (2005), pp. 23–41; idem, *Georgian Monarchy: Politics and Culture, 1714–1760* (Cambridge, 2006).

32. K. Rose, *Kings, Queens and Courtiers* (London, 1985); K. Reynolds, *Aristocratic Women and Political Society in Victorian Britain* (Oxford, 1998); J. Cannon, *The Modern British Monarchy: A Study in Adaptation* (Reading, 1987), pp. 15–19; W.M. Kuhn, *Henry and Mary Ponsonby: Life at the Court of Queen Victoria* (London, 2002).

33. J. Lant, *Insubstantial Pageant: Ceremony and Confusion at Queen Victoria's Court* (London, 1979); D. Cannadine, 'The Context, Performance and Meaning of Ritual: The British Monarchy and the "Invention of Tradition", *c.*1820–1977', in Hobsbawm and Ranger, *The Invention of Tradition*, pp. 101–64; W.L. Arnstein, 'Queen Victoria Opens Parliament: The Dis-invention of Tradition', *Historical Research*, lxiii (1990), pp. 178–94; W.M. Kuhn, *Democratic Royalism: The Transformation of the British Monarchy, 1861–1914* (Basingstoke, 1996); J. Wolffe, *Great Deaths: Grieving, Religion and Nationhood in Victorian and Edwardian Britain* (Oxford, 2000), esp. chs 7–9; K. Tetens, 'A Grand

International Durbar: Henry Irving and the Coronation of Edward VIII', *Journal of Victorian Culture*, viii (2003), pp. 257–91.

34. P. Gordon and D. Lawton, *Royal Education: Past, Present and Future* (London, 1999).

35. S. Schama, 'The Domestication of Majesty: Royal Family Portraiture, 1500–1850', *Journal of Interdisciplinary History*, xvii (1986), pp. 155–83.

36. D. Thompson, *Queen Victoria: Gender and Power* (London, 1990); L. Vallone, *Becoming Victoria* (London, 2001); Cannadine, *History in our Time*, pp. 39–47; V. McKendry, 'The *Illustrated London News* and the Invention of Tradition', *Victorian Periodicals Review*, xxvii (1994), pp. 1–24; N. Armstrong, 'Monarchy in the Age of Mechanical Reproduction', *Nineteenth-Century Contexts*, xxii (2001), pp. 495–536.

37. C. Campbell Orr (ed.), *Queenship in Britain, 1660–1837: Royal Patronage, Court Culture and Dynastic Politics* (Manchester, 2002); A. Munich, *Queen Victoria's Secrets* (New York, 1996); M. Homans and A. Munich (eds), *Remaking Queen Victoria* (Cambridge, 1997); M. Homans, *Royal Representations: Queen Victoria and British Culture, 1837–76* (London, 1998); B. Campbell, *Diana, Princess of Wales: How Sexual Politics Shook the Monarchy* (London, 1998); J. Burchill, *Diana* (London, 1998); T. Brown, *The Diana Chronicles* (London, 2007); Y.M. Ward, 'Queen Victoria and Dona Maria II da Gloria of Portugal: Marriage, motherhood and sovereignty in the lives of the young queens regnant (1828–53)', *Lilith: A Feminist History Journal*, xi (2002), pp. 117–30.

38. The first royal biography written by a professional historian is Arnstein, *Queen Victoria*. It builds on his work cited elsewhere in the notes to this chapter, and as such is an outstanding and pioneering example of how historically-informed royal biography can – and should – be written for the modern period.

39. A.J. Olechnowicz (ed.), *The Monarchy and the British Nation, 1780 to the Present* (Cambridge, 2007) sheds much light on this matter. For a suggestive continental comparison, see L. Cole and D. Unowsky (eds), *The Limits of Loyalty: Imperial Symbolism, Popular Allegiances, and State Patriotism in the Late Habsburg Monarchy* (Oxford, 2007).

40. The increased commercialization, commodification and commemoration of the monarchy is also of great importance in this context: see E. Darby and N. Smith, *The Cult of the Prince Consort* (London, 1983); J. May, *Victoria Remembered: A Royal History, 1817–61, Entirely Illustrated with Commemoratives* (London, 1983); T. Richards, *The Commodity Culture of Victorian England: Advertising and Spectacle, 1851–1914* (Stanford, 1990), esp. ch. 2; E. Allen, 'Culinary Exhibition: Victorian Wedding Cakes and Royal Spectacle', *Victorian Studies*, xlv (2003), pp. 457–84.

41. J.M. Golby and A.W. Perdue, *The Monarchy and the British People, 1760 to the Present* (London, 1988); R. Williams, *The Contentious Crown: Public Discussion of the British Monarchy in the Reign of Queen Victoria* (Aldershot, 1997); J. Plunkett, *Queen Victoria: First Media Monarch* (Oxford, 2003); F. Dimond and R. Taylor, *Crown and Camera: The Royal Family and Photography, 1842–1910* (London, 1987); R. Strong, *Cecil Beaton: The Royal Portraits* (London, 1988); R. Brunt, 'The Family Firm Restored: Newsreel Coverage of the British Monarchy, 1936–45', in C. Gledhill and G. Swanson (eds), *Nationalising Femininity: Culture, Sexuality and British Cinema in the Second World War*

(Manchester, 1996), pp. 140–51; R. Brown, '"It is a very wonderful process...":
Film and British royalty, 1896–1902', *The Court Historian*, viii (2003), pp. 1–22;
L. McKernan, '"The finest cinema performers that we possess": British royalty
and the newsreels, 1910–37', *The Court Historian*, viii (2003), pp. 59–71.

42.   The modern monarchy in the English provinces is a much neglected subject, but
      see E. Hammerton and D. Cannadine, 'Conflict and Consensus on a Ceremonial
      Occasion: The Diamond Jubilee in Cambridge in 1897', *Historical Journal*,
      xxiv (1981), pp. 111–46; and C. Gill and A. Briggs, *History of Birmingham* (2
      vols, London, 1952), ii, app. E, pp. 336–8. The research project on 'Monarchy,
      Nation and Region: The Case of the North-East since 1837', directed by Dr.
      A.J. Olechnowicz of the University of Durham, is a pioneering in-depth local
      study, whose findings are eagerly awaited.

43.   P.J. Galloway, *The Order of the British Empire* (London, 1996); idem, *The Order
      of St. Michael and St. George* (London, 2000); D. Cannadine, *Ornamentalism:
      How the British Saw their Empire* (London, 2001), ch. 7.

44.   J. Wolffe, *God and Greater Britain: Religion and National Life in Britain and
      Ireland, 1843–1945* (London, 1994), esp. ch. 6; N. Smith, *The Royal Image and
      the English People* (Aldershot, 2001); A. Rowbottom, 'Subject Positions and
      "Real Royalists": Monarchy and Vernacular Civil Religion in Great Britain', in
      N. Rapport (ed.), *British Subjects: An Anthropology of Britain* (Oxford, 2002),
      pp. 31–47; J. Baxendale, 'Royalty, Romance and Recreation: The Construction
      of the Past and the Origins of Royal Tourism in Nineteenth-Century Britain',
      Cultural and Social History, iv (2007), pp. 317–39.

45.   J.E. Davies, 'Victoria and Victorian Wales', in G.H. Jenkins and J.B. Smith (eds),
      *Politics and Society in Wales, 1840–1922: Essays in Honour of Ieuan Gwynedd
      Jones* (Cardiff, 1988), pp. 7–28; J.S. Ellis, 'The Prince and the Dragon: Welsh
      national identity and the 1911 investiture of the Prince of Wales', *Welsh History
      Review*, xviii (1996), pp. 272–94; idem, 'Reconciling the Celt: British national
      identity, empire and the 1911 investiture of the Prince of Wales', *Journal of
      British Studies*, xxxvii (1998), pp. 391–418; R. Lacey, 'Made for the Media:
      The 20th century investitures of the Princes of Wales', *The Court Historian*, viii
      (2003), pp. 31–40.

46.   H.R. Trevor-Roper, 'The Invention of Tradition: The Highland Tradition of
      Scotland', in Hobsbawm and Ranger, *The Invention of Tradition*, pp. 15–41;
      C.A. Whatley, '"Royal Day, People's Day": The Monarch's Birthday in Scotland,
      *c.*1660–1860', in R. Mason and N. Macdougall (eds), *People and Power in
      Scotland: Essays in Honour of T.C. Smout* (Edinburgh, 1992), pp. 170–88;
      idem, '"The Privilege which the Rabble have to be Riotous": Carnivalesque
      and the Monarch's Birthday in Scotland, *c.*1700–1860', in I. Blanchard (ed.),
      Labour and Leisure in Historical Perspective (Stuttgart, 1994), pp. 89–100; A.
      Tyrrell, 'The Queen's Little Trip: The Royal Visit to Scotland in 1842', *Scottish
      Historical Review*, lxxxii (2003), pp. 47–73.

47.   W.L. Arnstein, 'Queen Victoria's Other Island', in W.R. Louis (ed.), *More
      Adventures with Britannia: Personalities, Politics and Culture in Britain* (1998),
      pp. 45–66; S. Paseta, 'Nationalist Responses to Two Royal Visits to Ireland, 1900
      and 1903', *Irish Historical Studies*, xxxi (1999), pp. 488–504; J.H. Murphey,
      *Abject Loyalty: Nationalism and Monarchy in Ireland During the Reign of
      Queen Victoria* (Cork, 2001); Y. Wheelan, 'Performing Power, Demonstrating

Resistance: Interpreting Queen Victoria's Visit to Dublin in 1900', in L.J. Proudfoot and M.M. Roche (eds), *(Dis)placing Empire: Renegotiating British Colonial Geographies* (Aldershot, 2005), pp. 99–116; J. Loughlin, 'Allegiance and Illusion: Queen Victoria's Irish Visit of 1849', *History*, lxxxvii (2002), pp. 491–513; idem, *The British Monarchy and Ireland: From 1800 to the Present* (Cambridge, 2008).

48. See below, Chapter 7, pp. 190–2.

49. N. Harding, *Hanover and the British Empire, 1700–1837* (Woodbridge, 2007).

50. J. Paulmann, '"Dearest Nicky...": Monarchical relations between Prussia, the German emperor and Russia during the 19th century', in R. Bartlett and K. Schönwälder (eds), *The German Lands and Eastern Europe: Essays on the History of their Social, Cultural and Political Relations* (London, 1999), pp. 166–72; J. Paulmann, 'Searching for a "Royal International": The mechanics of monarchical relations in 19th-century Europe', in M.H. Geyer and J. Paulmann (eds), *The Mechanics of Internationalism: Culture, Society and Politics from the 1840s to the First World War* (Oxford, 2001), pp. 145–76.

51. D. Mack Smith, *Italy and its Monarchy* (London, 1989); A.W. Palmer, *Twilight of the Habsburgs: The Life and Times of Emperor Francis Joseph* (New York, 1995); R. Wortman, *Scenarios of Power: Myth and Ceremony in Russian Monarchy* (2 vols, Princeton, 1995–2000); D. Lieven, *Nicholas II: Emperor of all the Russias* (London, 1993); M.C. Hall, 'Alfonso XIII and the Failure of Liberal Monarchy in Spain, 1902–23' (unpublished Columbia University Ph.D. dissertation, 2003); J.C.G. Rohl and N. Sombart (eds), *Kaiser Wilhelm II: New Interpretations* (Cambridge, 1982); I.V. Hull, *The Entourage of Kaiser Wilhelm II, 1888–1918* (Cambridge, 1982); L. Cecil, *Wilhelm II: Prince and Emperor, 1859–1900* (London, 1989); idem, *Wilhelm II: Emperor and Exile, 1900–41* (London, 1996); J.C.G. Rohl, *The Kaiser and his Court: Wilhelm II and the Government of Germany* (Cambridge, 1994); idem, *Young Wilhelm: The Kaiser's Early Life, 1859–88* (Cambridge, 1998); idem, *Wilhelm II: The Kaiser's Personal Monarchy, 1888–1900* (Cambridge, 2004). It is also worth comparing developments in the British monarchy with those beyond Europe: T. Fujitani, *Splendid Monarchy: Power and Pageantry in Modern Japan* (Berkeley, 1996); M. Peleggi, *Lords of Things: The Fashioning of the Siamese Monarchy's Modern Image* (Honolulu, 2002).

52. D. Cannadine, 'Kaiser Wilhelm II and the British Monarchy', in T.C.W. Blanning and D. Cannadine (eds), *History and Biography: Essays in Honour of Derek Beales* (Cambridge, 1996), pp. 188–202; R.R. McLean, 'Kaiser Wilhelm II and the British Royal Family: Anglo-German dynastic relations in political context, 1890–1914', *History*, lxxxvi (2001), pp. 478–502; idem, *Royalty and Diplomacy in Europe, 1890–1914* (Cambridge, 2001); A. Green, *Fatherlands: Building and Nationhood in 19th-Century Germany* (Cambridge, 2001), ch. 2.

53. J.A. Cannon, 'The survival of the British Monarchy', *Transactions of the Royal Historical Society*, 5th ser., xxxvi (1986), pp. 143–64.

54. D. Bell, 'The Idea of a Patriot Queen: The Monarchy, the Constitution and the Iconographic Order of Greater Britain, 1860–1900', *Journal of Imperial and Commonwealth History*, xxxiv (2006), pp. 3–21; K. Jeffery, 'Crown, Communication and the Colonial Post: Stamps, the Monarchy and the British

Empire', ibid., pp. 45–70; P. Murphy, 'Breaking the Bad News: Plans for the Announcement to the Empire of the Death of Elizabeth II and the Proclamation of Her Successor', ibid., pp. 139–54; idem, 'The African Queen? Republicanism and Defensive Decolonization in British Tropical Africa, 1958–64', *Twentieth Century British History*, xiv (2003), pp. 243–63. For the British monarchy as an imperial monarchy in the 13 colonies before the American revolution of 1776, see B. McConville, *The King's Three Faces: The Rise and Fall of Royal America, 1688–1776* (Chapel Hill, North Carolina, 2006).

55. Cannadine, *Ornamentalism*, ch. 8; C. Newbury, *Patrons, Clients and Empire: Chieftancy and Over-Rule in Asia, Africa and the Pacific* (Oxford, 2003); J. Lonsdale, 'Ornamental Constitutionalism in Africa: Kenyatta and the Two Queens', *Journal of Imperial and Commonwealth History*, xxxiv (2006), pp. 87–104; J. Willis, 'A Portrait for the Mukama: Monarchy and Empire in Colonial Bunyoro, Uganda', ibid., pp. 105–22; S.C. Smith, 'Moving a Little with the Tide: Malay Monarchy and the Development of Modern Malay Nationalism', ibid., pp. 123–38.

56. The literature on the subject of royal overseas tours is now growing rapidly. For Canada: I. Radforth, *Royal Spectacle: The 1860 Visit of the Prince of Wales to Canada and the United States* (Toronto, 2004); P. Buckner, 'Casting Daylight upon Magic: Deconstructing the Royal Tour of 1901 to Canada', in C. Bridge and K. Fedorowich (eds), *The British World: Diaspora, Culture and Identity* (London, 2003), pp. 158–89; S.J. Potter, 'The BBC, the CBC, and the 1939 Royal Tour of Canada', *Cultural and Social History*, iii (2006), pp. 424–44; P. Buckner, 'The Last Great Royal Tour: Queen Elizabeth's 1959 Tour to Canada', in idem (ed.), *Canada and the End of Empire* (Vancouver, 2005), pp. 66–93. For Australia: K. Fewster, 'Politics, Pageantry and Purpose: The 1920 Tour of Australia by the Prince of Wales', *Labour History*, xxxviii (1980), pp. 59–66; D. Adair, '"On Parade": Spectacles, Crowds, and Collective Loyalties in Australia, 1901–38' (unpublished Flinders University Ph.D. dissertation, 1994); J. Connors, 'The 1954 Royal Tour of Australia', *Australian Historical Studies*, xxv (1993), pp. 371–82. For New Zealand: L. Cleveland, 'Royalty as Symbolic Drama: The 1970 New Zealand Tour', *Journal of Commonwealth Political Studies*, xi (1973), pp. 28–45; J. Bassett, '"A Thousand Miles of Loyalty": The Royal Tour of 1901', *New Zealand Journal of History*, xxi (1987), pp. 125–38. For South Africa: P. Buckner, 'The Royal Tour of 1901 and the Construction of an Imperial Identity in South Africa', *South African Historical Journal*, xli (1999), pp. 127–46, 326–48. For India: J. Woods, 'Edward, Prince of Wales's Tour of India, October 1921 – March 1922', *The Court Historian*, v (2000), pp. 217–21; C. Kaul, 'Monarchical Display and the Politics of Empire: Princes of Wales and India, 1870–1920s', *Twentieth Century British History*, xvii (2006), pp. 464–88. For elsewhere: A. Clarkson, 'Pomp, Circumstance and Wild Arabs: The 1912 Royal Visit to Sudan', *Journal of Imperial and Commonwealth History*, xxxiv (2006), pp. 71–86; K. Dodds, D. Lambert and B. Robison, 'Loyalty and Royalty: Gibraltar, the 1953–54 Royal Tour and the Geopolitics of the Iberian Peninsula', *Twentieth-Century British History*, xviii (2007), pp. 365–90.

57. P. Spearitt, 'Royal Progress: The Queen and her Australian Subjects', in S.L. Goldberg and F.B. Smith (eds), *Australian Cultural History* (Canberra, 1988), pp. 138–57; A. Taylor and L. Trainor, 'Monarchism and Anti-Monarchism:

Anglo-Australian comparisons, *c.*1870–1901', *Social History*, xxiv (1999), pp. 158–73; K. Munro, 'Canada as Reflected in her Participation in the Coronation of her Monarchs in the 20th Century', *Journal of Historical Sociology*, xiv (2001), pp. 21–46; W.A. Henry, 'Imagining the Great White Mother and the Great King: Aboriginal Tradition and Royal Representation at the "Great Pow-wow" of 1901', *Journal of the Canadian Historical Association*, new ser., ix (2000), pp. 87–108; idem, 'Royal Representation, Ceremony, and Cultural Identity in the Building of the Canadian Nation, 1860–1912' (unpublished Ph.D. dissertation, University of British Columbia, 2001); A. Clarke, 'With One Accord Rejoice on this Glad Day: Celebrating the Monarchy in Nineteenth-Century Otago', *New Zealand Journal of History*, xxxvi (2002), pp. 137–60; S. Constantine, 'Monarchy and Constructing Identity in "British" Gibraltar, c1800 to the Present', *Journal of Imperial and Commonwealth History*, xxxiv (2006), pp. 23–44. For a non-imperial transoceanic perspective on the British monarchy, see W.L. Arnstein, 'Queen Victoria and the United States', in F.M. Leventhal and R. Quinault (eds), *Anglo-American Attitudes: From Revolution to Partnership* (Aldershot, 2000), pp. 91–106.

58. B. Cohn, 'Representing Authority in Victorian India', in Hobsbawm and Ranger, *Invention of Tradition*, pp. 165–210; T.O. Ranger, 'Making Northern Rhodesia Imperial: Variations on a Royal Theme', *African Affairs*, lxxix (1980), pp. 349–73; idem, 'The Invention of Tradition in Colonial Africa', in Hobsbawm and Ranger, *Invention of Tradition*, pp. 211–62.

59. Bridge and Fedorowich, *The British World*; P. Buckner and R. Douglas Francis (eds), *Rediscovering the British World* (Calgary, 2005); idem (eds), *Canada and the British World: Culture, Migration and Identity* (Vancouver, 2006); S.J. Potter, *News and the British World: The Emergence of an Imperial Press System, 1876–1922* (Oxford, 2003). See also below, Chapter 8, pp. 205–8.

60. For other biographies of currently-reigning monarchs, see P. Preston, *Juan Carlos: A People's King* (London, 2004); P.M. Handley, *The King Never Smiles: A Biography of Thailand's Bhumibol Adulyadej* (London, 2006). For an outstanding biography of a recently-deceased sovereign, see A. Shalim, *Lion of Jordan: The Life of King Hussein in War and Peace* (London, 2007)

61. N.J. Grossman, 'Republicanism in 19th-century England', *International Review of Social History*, vii (1962), pp. 47–60; F. D'Arcy, 'Charles Bradlaugh and the English Republican Movement, 1868–78', *Historical Journal*, xxv (1982), pp. 367–83; A. Taylor, *'Down With the Crown': British Anti-Monarchism and Debates about Royalty since 1790* (London, 1999); F. Prochaska, *The Republic of Britain, 1760–2000* (London, 2000); D. Nash and A. Taylor (eds), *Republicanism in Victorian Society* (Stroud, 2000); A. Taylor, '"Pig-sticking Princes": Royal hunting, moral outrage, and the republican opposition to animal abuse in 19th- and early 20th-century Britain', *History*, lxxxix (2004), pp. 30–48; D.M. Craig, 'The Crowned Republic? Monarchy and Anti-Monarchy in Britain, 1760–1901', *Historical Journal*, xlvi (2003), pp. 167–85.

62. This generalization cannot, however, be pushed too far, since the Japanese monarchy survived devastating military defeat in the Second World War, even as other European thrones did not: see H.P. Bix, *Hirohito and the Making of*

Modern Japan (New York, 2000); K.J. Ruoff, *The People's Emperor: Democracy and the Japanese Monarchy, 1945–95* (Cambridge, Mass., 2001).

63. *The Times*, 10 March 1998.
64. W.G. Runciman, *A Treatise on Social Theory*, i: *The Methodology of Social Theory* (Cambridge, 1983), p. 312.

CHAPTER 3, PARLIAMENT, pp. 59–82

1. This chapter began as the annual History of Parliament Lecture, delivered in Portcullis House in London on 21 November 2006. I am grateful to the Trustees of the History of Parliament Trust, and especially to their chairman, Sir Patrick Cormack, for their kind invitation. In preparing this more substantial version, as with the lecture itself, I have been helped by Priscilla Baines, Helen McCarthy, Paul Seaward and Jane Winters. Although I am myself a member of the editorial board of the *History of Parliament*, the views and opinions expressed in this article are entirely my own. Two abbreviations have been used in the notes: HOP: History of Parliament; JCW: Colonel Josiah Clement Wedgwood.
2. D. Cannadine, *The Pleasures of the Past* (London, 1989), pp. 92–5; H.C.G. Matthew, *Leslie Stephen and the New Dictionary of National Biography* (Cambridge, 1997); K.V. Thomas, *Changing Conceptions of National Biography: The Oxford DNB in Historical Perspective* (Cambridge, 2005); F.H.W. Shepard, 'Sources and Methods Used for the *Survey of London*', in H.J. Dyos (ed.), *The Study of Urban History* (London, 1966), pp. 131–45; H. Hobhouse, 'Ninety Years of the Survey of London', *Transactions of the Ancient Monuments Society*, xxxi (1987), pp. 25–47; idem, *London Survey'd: The Work of the Survey of London, 1894–1994* (Swindon, 1994); R.B. Pugh, 'The Structure and Aims of the Victoria History of the Counties of England', *Bulletin of the Institute of Historical Research*, xl (1967), pp. 65–73; A. Fletcher, '"Englandpast.net": A Framework for the Social History of England', *Historical Research*, lxxv (2002), pp. 296–315; B. Cherry, *The Buildings of England: A Short History and a Bibliography* (Cambridge, 1983); S. Bradley and B. Cherry (eds), *The Buildings of England: A Celebration* (London, 2001); D. Matless, 'Topographical Culture: Nikolaus Pevsner and the Buildings of England', *History Workshop Journal*, no. 54 (2002), pp. 73–99.
3. The standard biographies of Wedgwood are: J.C. Wedgwood, *Memoirs of a Fighting Life* (London, 1940); C.V. Wedgwood, *The Last of the Radicals: Josiah Wedgwood MP* (London, 1951); D. Cannadine, *In Churchill's Shadow: Confronting the Past in Modern Britain* (London, 2002), pp. 134–58; *Oxford Dictionary of National Biography*, vol. lvii, pp. 925–27. See also N. Annan, 'The Intellectual Aristocracy', in J.H. Plumb (ed.), *Studies in Social History: A Tribute to G.M. Trevelyan* (London, 1955), pp 246, 260–5.
4. For Namier's life and work, see: J. Namier, *Lewis Namier: A Biography* (London, 1971); L.J. Colley, *Namier* (London, 1989); *Oxford Dictionary of National Biography*, vol. xl, pp. 134–7.
5. Colley, *Namier*, pp. 16–17; N. Annan, *Our Age: Portrait of a Generation* (London, 1990), p. 270; E.H. Carr, *What Is History?* (London, 1961), pp. 45–48.

6. Cannadine, *In Churchill's Shadow*, pp. 136–43.

7. J.C. Wedgwood, *Staffordshire Parliamentary History from the Earliest Times to the Present Day*, vol. i, *1213 to 1603*, in *Collections for a History of Staffordshire* (1917), pp. xxi–xxii.

8. Wedgwood, *Memoirs of a Fighting Life*, pp. 213–23; Wedgwood, *Last of the Radicals*, pp. 163–81; Cannadine, *In Churchill's Shadow*, pp. 143–50.

9. J.C. Wedgwood, *History of Parliament: Biographies of the Members of the Commons House, 1439–1509* (London, 1936), pp. xlv, lii–liii; idem, *History of Parliament: Register of the Ministers and of the Members of Both Houses, 1439–1509* (London, 1938), pp. cxxxiv–cxxxviii, cxlv.

10. L.B. Namier, *Conflicts: Studies in Contemporary History* (London, 1942), p. 72; idem, *Personalities and Powers* (London, 1955), pp. 1–4, 7; Namier, *Namier*, pp. 199–200; Colley, *Namier*, pp. 21, 26, 75, 77; Q. Skinner, 'Introduction', in idem (ed.), *The Return of Grand Theory in the Human Sciences* (London, 1985), p. 3.

11. L.B. Namier, *The Structure of Politics at the Accession of George III* (London, 1929); idem, *England in the Age of the American Revolution* (London, 1930); Colley, *Namier*, pp. 46–71.

12. L.B. Namier, *Crossroads of Power: Essays on Eighteenth-Century England* (London, 1962), p. 5.

13. Namier had first systematically addressed this question in the opening chapter of *Structure of Politics*.

14. Namier, *Namier*, p. 290; Namier, *England in the Age of the American Revolution*, p. 3; Colley, *Namier*, pp. 82–9. For prosopography, see L. Stone, *The Past and the Present* (London, 1981), pp. 45–73.

15. Cannadine, *In Churchill's Shadow*, pp. 142, 150–4; Colley, *Namier*, pp. 35, 76–8; L.B. Namier, *Avenues of History* (London, 1952), p. 171; Namier, *Namier*, pp. 284–5.

16. M. Lawrence, 'The History of Parliament Trust', *Parliamentary Affairs*, xviii (1964), pp. 460–1; *Hansard* (Commons), 20 February 1951, cols 1067–70.

17. Quoted in J. Hoppit, 'An Embarrassment of Riches', *Parliamentary History*, xviii (1999), p. 149.

18. For a brief and revealing glimpse of Namier at the IHR at this time, see: M. Howard, *Captain Professor* (London, 2006), p. 136.

19. Cannadine, *In Churchill's Shadow*, pp. 156–57; Lawrence 'History of Parliament Trust', pp. 458–61; A. Sandall, 'The History of Parliament', *The Table*, liv (1986), pp. 82–85; Sir L. Namier and J. Brooke (eds), *The History of Parliament: The House of Commons, 1754–1790* (3 vols, London, 1964).

20. Colley, *Namier*, p. 78

21. P.D.G. Thomas, 'La vie politique en Grand-Bretagne vers la fin du XVIIIe siècle', *Review Historique*, April–June 1967, pp. 415–32.

22. J.B. Owen, 'Small Men', *New Statesman*, 9 May 1964, pp. 736–7. See also the anonymous review in *The Economist*, 23 May 1964, p. 48.

23. A.P. Ryan, 'Honourable Member Over the Years', *The Times*, 1 May 1964; W. Rees-Mogg, 'Unreformed and Unrepentant', *The Sunday Times*, 3 May 1964; [J. Carswell], 'Calling the House to Order', *Times Literary Supplement* (*TLS*), 9 July 1964, pp. 581–2; C.J. Boulton, review of Namier and Brooke in *The Table*,

xxxii (1964), p. 175; Sir E. Fellowes, 'Introduction', *Parliamentary Affairs*, xvii (1964), pp. 450–3.

24. See, for example, J.H. Plumb, 'Members of the House', *The Spectator*, 22 May 1964, p. 699; P. Laslett, 'Namier's Parliament', *The Guardian*, 8 May 1964; [Carswell], 'Calling the House to Order', pp. 581–2; H. Butterfield, 'The History of Parliament', *The Listener*, 8 October 1964, pp. 535–7; idem, *English Historical Review*, lxxx (1965), pp. 801–5; J. Sainty, 'The History of Parliament: The House of Commons, 1754–1790', *Parliamentary Affairs*, xvii (1964), pp. 453–7.

25. See, for example: R. Pares, *George III and the Politicians* (Oxford, 1953); H. Butterfield, *George III and the Historians* (London, 1957); W.R. Fryer, 'King George III: His Political Character and Conduct, 1760–84: A New Whig Interpretation', *Renaissance and Modern Studies*, vi (1962), pp. 68–101; E.A. Reitan (ed.), *George III: Tyrant or Constitutional Monarch?* (London, 1964). See also J. Brooke, 'Namier and Namierism', *History and Theory*, iii (1963–64), pp. 331–47.

26. John Brooke suggested that parliament in the eighteenth century was not particularly concerned with legislation: in fact it passed some 10,000 acts: see J. Hoppitt, 'Patterns of Parliamentary Legislation, 1660–1800', *Historical Journal*, xxxix (1996), p. 201.

27. R. Pares and A.J.P. Taylor (eds), *Essays Presented to Sir Lewis Namier* (London, 1956). Taylor's hostile review of Brooke appeared in the *Manchester Guardian*, 16 November 1956.

28. Colley, *Namier*, pp. 99–100; A.J.P. Taylor, *A Personal History* (London, 1983), pp. 214–17; A. Sisman, *A.J.P. Taylor: A Biography* (London, 1994), pp. 247–52; K. Burk, *Troublemaker: The Life and History of A.J.P. Taylor* (London, 2000), pp. 207–12, 445; R. Davenport-Hines (ed.), *Letters from Oxford: Hugh Trevor-Roper to Bernard Berenson* (London, 2006), pp. 229–33.

29. A.J.P. Taylor, 'Westminster white elephant', *The Observer*, 3 May 1964.

30. 'Let them speak up!', *The Listener*, 16 July 1964, p. 78; H.G. Richardson and G.O. Sayles, 'History of Parliament', *The Listener*, 30 July 1964, p. 164.

31. 'A waste of effort?', *The Listener*, 8 October 1964, p. 538; J. Brooke and I.R. Christie, 'The History of Parliament', *The Listener*, 15 October 1964, p. 591.

32. W. Ferguson, review of Namier and Brooke, *Scottish Historical Review*, xlvi (1967), p. 164; P. Howard in *The Times*, 18 August 1967.

33. *Hansard* (Commons), 14 December 1965, col. 1059; *Daily Mirror*, 15 December 1965; *Evening News*, 10 August 1967; *Daily Express*, 28 March 1970.

34. In order of publication, the subsequent volumes in the *History of Parliament* are as follows: R. Sedgwick (ed.), *The House of Commons, 1715–1754* (2 vols, London, 1970); P.W. Hasler (ed.), *The House of Commons, 1558–1603* (3 vols, London, 1981); S.T. Bindoff (ed.), *The House of Commons, 1509–1558* (3 vols, London, 1982); B.D. Henning (ed.), *The House of Commons, 1660–1690* (3 vols, London, 1983); R.G. Thorne (ed.), *The House of Commons, 1790–1820* (5 vols, London, 1986); J.S. Roskell, L. Clark and C. Rawcliffe (eds), *The House of Commons, 1386–1421* (4 vols, London, 1993); E. Cruickshanks, S. Handley and D.W. Hayton (eds), *The House of Commons, 1690–1715* (5 vols, Cambridge, 2002).

35. For example, D.E.D. Beales, 'History and Biography: An Inaugural Lecture', in T.C.W. Blanning and D. Cannadine (eds), *History and Biography: Essays in Honour of Derek Beales* (Cambridge, 1996), p. 282.

36. J.M. Beattie, review of Sedgwick, *American Historical Review*, lxxvii (1972), p. 512; L.J. Colley, *In Defiance of Oligarchy: The Tory Party, 1714–60* (Cambridge, 1982), ch. 2; Hoppit, 'Embarrassment of Riches', pp. 197–8. But cf. I.R. Christie, 'The Tory Party, Jacobitism and the "Forty-Five": A Note', *Historical Journal*, xxx (1987), pp. 921–31.

37. Hoppit, 'Embarrassment of Riches', pp. 189–205; M.J. Daunton, 'Virtual Representation: The *History of Parliament* on CD-ROM', *Past & Present*, no. 167 (2000), pp. 238–61. See also the following reviews: M. Wheeler-Booth, *TLS*, 5 February 1999, p. 5; S. Taylor, *The Higher*, 2 October 1998, p. 33.

38. At the same time, substantial progress is also being made in Edinburgh and Belfast on the histories of the pre Act of Union Parliaments in Scotland and Ireland: for which see K.M. Brown and R.J. Tanner (eds), *Parliament and Politics in Scotland, 1235–1560* (Edinburgh, 2004); E.M. Johnson-Liik, *History of the Irish Parliament, 1692–1800: Commons, Constituencies and Statutes* (6 vols, Belfast, 2002).

39. See, for example: G.R. Elton, 'Members' Memorial', *London Review of Books*, 20 May 1982, p. 14; idem, 'The Grandmother of Parliaments', *The Spectator*, 22 May 1982, p. 19; G. Holmes, 'The Growing Presence of Parliament', *TLS*, 6 January 1984, pp. 3–4; J.J. Scarisbrick, 'Tudor MPs Biographied', *Parliamentary History*, iii (1984), p. 183; J.S. Morrill, 'Between Conventions: The Members of Restoration Parliaments', *Parliamentary History*, v (1986), p. 132; N. Gash, 'Between Court and Country', *TLS*, 24 October 1986, p. 81; M. Prestwich, 'Middle Age MPs', *TLS*, 4 June 1993, p. 30; R.B. Dobson, 'Members Only', *London Review of Books*, 24 February 1994, p. 25; S. Walker, 'Parliamentary History in Perspective', *Nottingham Medieval Studies*, xxxviii (1994), p. 172; G.L. Harriss, 'The Medieval Parliament', *Parliamentary History*, xiii (1994), pp. 206–26.

40. Colley, *Namier*, pp. 83–4; Daunton, 'Virtual Representation', pp. 243–4.

41. Colley, *Namier*, pp. 84–8. For some recent examples of such uses of the *History of Parliament*, see: J. Brewer, *The Sinews of Power: War, Money and the English State, 1688–1783* (London, 1989), pp. 44–5; I.R. Christie, *British 'Non-Elite' MPs, 1715–1820* (Oxford, 1995); E.A. Wasson, *Born to Rule: British Political Elites* (Stroud, 2000), esp. pp. 6–7. For some general comments on the broader ways in which the *History of Parliament* may be used, see: P. Seaward, 'Whigs, Tories, East Indiamen and Rogues: The History of Parliament, 1690–1715', *Historian*, lxxv (2002), esp. p. 9; C. Jackson, 'The Rage of Parliaments: The House of Commons, 1690–1715', *Historical Journal*, xlviii (2005), pp. 567–87.

42. Much of this material is already available through British History Online (BHO), a digital library of the key sources for the medieval and early modern history of the British Isles developed by the Institute of Historical Research with funding from the Andrew W. Mellon Foundation: http://www.british-history.ac.uk. At the time of writing, BHO has published 116 volumes of the *Victoria County History*, eight volumes of the *Survey of London*, 23 volumes of the *Journal of the House of Lords*, and 13 volumes of the *Journal of the House of Commons*. A full list of parliamentary material on the site can be seen at http://www.

british-history.ac.uk/subject.asp?subject=6. By the end of 2008, the 45 'area' or parish volumes of the *Survey of London* and a further 40 volumes of the *Victoria County History* will be digitized and published. All of the material in the BHO library is fully cross-searchable, and can be browsed by period, subject and place.

43. For a greater sense of the connection between constituencies and MPs for Namier's period, see N. Rogers, *Whigs and Cities: Popular Politics in the Age of Walpole and Pitt* (Oxford, 1989); P. Langford, *Public Life and the Propertied Englishman, 1687–1798* (Oxford, 1991). On the practice and procedure of the House of Commons during that time, see P.D.G. Thomas, *The House of Commons in the Eighteenth Century* (Oxford, 1971). For a much later re-articulation of Wedgwood's whiggish view of the history of parliament, see J.H. Hexter, 'The Birth of Modern Freedom', *TLS*, 21 January 1983, pp. 51–4.

44. Hoppit, 'Embarrassment of Riches', p. 205; N. Gash, 'Between Court and Country', *TLS*, 24 October 1986, p. 81.

45. This and subsequent paragraphs draw on discussion papers prepared for and by the editorial board of the *History*.

46. JCW to W.S. Churchill, 30 September 1934, printed in R.S. Churchill and M. Gilbert (eds), *Winston S. Churchill: Companion Volumes* (5 vols, London, 1966–82), vol. 5, pt. ii, pp. 878–89, 916–17.

47. W.S. Churchill to JCW, 14 September 1934, in ibid., pp. 871–2.

48. P. Summerfield, 'Mass-Observation: Social Research or Social Movement?', *Journal of Contemporary History*, xx (1985), pp. 439–44; N. Hubble, *Mass Observation and Everyday Life: Culture, History, Theory* (London, 2005), pp. 1–10. Mass Observation's first investigation was of popular responses to the Coronation of King George VI: C. Madge and H. Jennings (eds), *May the Twelfth: Mass-Observation Day-Surveys, 1937* (London, 1937).

49. Where no reference is given, all quotations in the next section come from the questionnaires and biographies in the HOP MS.

50. The whole of this section draws heavily on an unpublished discussion paper prepared for the editorial board of the *History* by Priscilla Baines.

51. Wedgwood, *Last of the Radicals*, p. 170.

52. HOP MS: Lord Astor to JCW, 10 July 1936; S. Baldwin to JCW, 16 July 1936; W.S. Churchill to JCW, 15 August 1936.

53. HOP MS: Lord Monsell to JCW, 30 November 1936; Sir S. Hoare to JCW, 24 August 1936; Lord Lee of Fareham to JCW, 14 December 1936.

54. HOP MS: J.R. MacDonald to JCW, 29 July 1936.

55. HOP MS: Sir P. Harris to JCW, 10 December 1936; Lord Snowden to JCW, 5 August 1936; Lord Bingley to JCW, 28 July 1936.

56. HOP MS: Lord Kennett to JCW, 14 August 1936; Sir N. Lamont to JCW, 27 November 1936.

57. HOP MS: A. Hopkinson to JCW, 8 August 1936; G.N. Barnes to JCW, 6 August 1936.

58. All the quotations in this paragraph are taken from the answers to questions 4 and 5 of JCW's questionnaire.

59. With Raymond Postgate, Lansbury had edited *Lansbury's Labour Weekly* between 1925 and 1927.

60. HOP MS: Sir E. Geddes to JCW, 16 July 1936.

61. HOP MS: undated comment scrawled by A. Hopkinson on letter to him from JCW, 27 April 1937.

62. For Harris's reply, see HOP MS: Sir P. Harris to JCW, 5 March 1937.

63. HOP MS: J.R. Clynes to JCW, 15 February 1937; J.G.H. Altham to JCW, 12 March 1937.

64. HOP MS: Lord Bingley to JCW, 5, 10 May 1937; F.L. Stevenson to JCW, 21 April 1937; JCW to F.L. Stevenson, 26 April 1937.

65. Cannadine, *In Churchill's Shadow*, pp. 150–6.

66. Hoppit, 'Embarrassment of Riches', p. 205; P. Howard, 'What parliament and public alike could do with is a lot more prosopography', *The Times*, 20 September 2002.

CHAPTER 4, ECONOMY, pp. 83–111

1. My interest in this subject was first aroused when I was a graduate student in Oxford in the early 1970s, where I was supervised by Professor Peter Mathias and took courses with Dr Max Hartwell, and it was further stimulated by a lecture given by Professor Albert Hirschman at the Institute of Advanced Study at Princeton in 1980. This chapter owes much to all three of them, and thanks are also due to the late Sir John Plumb, Professor Barry Supple, and Professor Patrick O'Brien.

2. N.B. Harte (ed.), *The Study of Economic History: Collected Inaugural Lectures, 1893–1970* (London, 1971).

3. A. Toynbee, *Lectures on the Industrial Revolution in England* (London, 1884); A. Bezanson, 'The Early Use of the Term Industrial Revolution', *Quarterly Journal of Economics*, xxxvi (1922), pp. 343–9; K. Tribe, *Genealogies of Capitalism* (London, 1981), pp. 101–20; D.C. Coleman, *Myth, History and the Industrial Revolution* (London, 1992), pp. 3–22; M. Teich and R. Porter, 'Introduction', in M. Teich and R. Porter (eds), *The Industrial Revolution in National Context: Europe and the United States* (Cambridge, 1996), pp. 3–10.

4. W.D. Fraser, *The Evolution of the British Welfare State* (London, 1973), p. 124; D. Winch, *Economics and Policy: A Historical Study* (London, 1972), pp. 33–4.

5. B.B. Gilbert, *The Evolution of National Insurance in Great Britain: The Origins of the Welfare State* (London, 1966), p. 83.

6. Winch, *Economics and Policy*, p. 34; G. Stedman Jones, *Outcast London: A Study in the Relations between Classes in Victorian Society* (Harmondsworth, 1976), esp. chs 11, 16, 17. But cf. E.P. Hennock, 'Poverty and Social Theory in England: The Experience of the Eighteen-Eighties', *Social History*, i (1976), pp. 67–91.

7. S. Hynes, *The Edwardian Turn of Mind* (Princeton, 1968), pp. 54–69; H.J. Dyos, 'The Slums of Victorian London', in D. Cannadine and D. Reeder (eds), *Exploring the Urban Past: Essays in Urban History* (Cambridge, 1982), pp. 133–9; H. George, *Poverty and Progress* (London, 1883), pp. 6–7; Gilbert, *Evolution of National Insurance*, p. 77, and ch. 1 generally.

8. G.N. Clark, *The Idea of the Industrial Revolution* (Glasgow, 1953), p. 27.

9. Toynbee, *Lectures on the Industrial Revolution*, pp. 31–2.

10. Lord Milner, 'Reminiscence', in ibid. (1908 edn), pp. xi, xxi; B. Webb, *My Apprenticeship* (London, 1926), pp. 182–3.

11. P.F. Clarke, *Liberals and Social Democrats* (Cambridge, 1978), pp. 154–63, 187–91, 243–52; S.A. Weaver, *The Hammonds: A Marriage in History* (Stanford, 1997), pp. 76–108.

12. Webb, *My Apprenticeship*, pp. 343–4.

13. Ibid., p. 348; Beatrice Webb, *Our Partnership* (London, 1948), pp. 147–52. See also V.L. Allen, 'A Methodological Critique of the Webbs as Trade Union Historians', *Bulletin of the Society for the Study of Labour History*, iv (1962), pp. 4–5.

14. Toynbee, *Lectures on the Industrial Revolution*, pp. 31–2.

15. S. and B. Webb, *The History of Trade Unionism* (London, 1911 edn), pp. 34–5; J.L. and B. Hammond, *The Town Labourer, 1760–1832: The New Civilization* (London, 1917), pp. 3, 98; J.L. and B. Hammond, *The Rise of Modern Industry* (London, 1925), p. 240.

16. Toynbee, *Lectures on the Industrial Revolution*, p. 84.

17. J.L. and B. Hammond, *The Skilled Labourer, 1760–1832* (London, 1919), pp. 1, 4; idem, *The Town Labourer*, pp. 31, 39, 59, 171; idem, *Rise of Modern Industry*, pp. 196, 232, 247.

18. S. Webb, *Labour in the Longest Reign* (Fabian tract no. 75, London, 1897), p. 2; S. Webb, 'Historic', in *Fabian Essays*, 6th edn (London, 1962), p. 69; S. and B. Webb, *The Decay of Capitalist Civilisation* (London, 1923), p. 8; S. and B. Webb, *English Local Government from the Revolution to the Municipal Corporations Act* (8 vols, London, 1906–29), i, *The Parish and the Country*, p. 63; Webb, *My Apprenticeship*, pp. 178, 207.

19. Toynbee, *Lectures on the Industrial Revolution*, pp. 83–7.

20. Hammonds, *Town Labourer*, chs 10–11, esp. p. 217; Webb, *History of Trade Unionism*, pp. 49–50, 91–2.

21. Winch, *Economics and Policy*, pp. 54, 63–6; A.M. McBriar, *Fabian Socialism and English Politics, 1884–1918* (Cambridge, 1962), pp. 51–7; J. Maloney, 'Marshall, Cunningham and the Emerging Economics Profession', *Economic History Review*, 2nd ser., xxix (1976), pp. 440–9; idem, 'The Professionalisation of Economics in Britain, 1870–1914' (unpublished University of Nottingham Ph.D. dissertation, 1981), chs 3, 6; B. Semmel, *Imperialism and Social Reform: English Social-Imperialist Thought, 1895–1914* (London, 1960), pp. 26–7, 67–73, 82, 131–3, and chs 10–11. For particular authors, see: W.J. Ashley, *The Economic Organisation of England: An Outline History* (London, 1914), pp. 159–61, 190; W. Cunningham, *The Growth of English Industry and Commerce in Modern Times*, 6th edn (Cambridge, 1907), pp. 613, 668, 737–45; C. Beard, *The Industrial Revolution* (London, 1901) , pp. 3, 23, 59; H. de B. Gibbins, *Industry in England: Historical Outlines* (London, 1896), pp. 34, 421, 423; J.E. Thorold Rogers, *Six Centuries of Work and Wages* (London, 1884), pp. 485, 492, 523–8; G. Townsend Warner, *Landmarks in English Industrial History* (London, 1889), pp. 313–14, 355.

22. J.H. Clapham, *An Economic History of Modern Britain* (3 vols, Cambridge, 1926–38), i, *The Early Railway Age, 1820–1850*, pp. viii, 41, 66, 142, 155.

23. Ibid., pp. vii, 315–16, 561.

24. G.H. Wood, 'The Course of Average Wages between 1790 and 1860', *Economic Journal*, ix (1899), pp. 588–92; A.L. Bowley, *Wages in the United Kingdom in the Nineteenth Century* (Cambridge, 1900); G.W. Daniels, *The Early English Cotton Industry* (Manchester, 1920), pp. 145–8; G. Unwin et al., *Samuel Oldknow and the Arkwrights* (Manchester, 1924), pp. 241–2.

25. A. Redford, *The Economic History of England, 1760–1860* (London, 1931), pp. v, 4, 12–13, 24, 57–65, 78–93, 111–17; E. Lipson, *The Age of Mercantilism* (2 vols [2nd edn of vols ii and iii of his *The Economic History of England*], London, 1934), i, pp. vi, 8, and ii, pp. 53, 249. See also idem, 'England in the Age of Mercantilism', *Journal of Economic and Business History*, iv (1932), pp. 691–3, 699, 705.

26. Webb, *Decay of Capitalist Civilisation*, p. 4.

27. M.M. Postan, 'Recent Trends in the Accumulation of Capital', *Economic History Review*, 1st ser., vi (1935), p. 1.

28. Quoted in D.S. Landes, *The Unbound Prometheus: Technological Change and Industrial Development in Western Europe from 1750 to the Present* (Cambridge, 1969), p. 536.

29. J.K. Galbraith, *The Great Crash, 1929* (2nd edn, Boston, 1961), pp. ix, 4, 193–5. The book was first published in 1955. For contemporary British expressions of concern, see Sir O. Franks, *Central Planning and Control in War and Peace* (London, 1947), p. 21; C.A.R. Crosland, *Britain's Economic Problems* (London, 1953), p. 183; E.A.G. Robinson, 'Industrial Fluctuations in the United Kingdom, 1946–52', in E. Lundberg (ed.), *The Business Cycle in the Post-War World* (London, 1955), pp. 37–8.

30. See, for example, W.C. Mitchell, *Business Cycles* (London, 1913); idem, *Business Cycles: The Problem and the Setting* (London, 1927); idem, *Business Cycles and their Causes* (London, 1950); W.L. Thorp, *Business Annals* (London, 1926); A.F. Burns and W.C. Mitchell, *Measuring Business Cycles* (London, 1946). For evidence of the continuing liveliness of trade cycle literature in the decade after the Second World War, see the works discussed in two review articles: H.M. Somers, 'What Generally Happens during Business Cycles – and Why', *Journal of Economic History*, xii (1952), pp. 270–318; H.H. Segal, 'Business Cycles: Methodology, Research and Public Policy', *Journal of Economic History*, xiv (1954), pp. 164–98. The best guide to this topic is the introduction in D.H. Aldcroft and P. Fearon (eds), *British Economic Fluctuations, 1790–1939* (London, 1972), esp. pp. 1–8, 14–25, 43–56.

31. R.G. Hawtrey, *Currency and Credit* (London, 1919); idem, *Capitalism and Employment* (London, 1937); J.M. Keynes, *A Treatise on Money* (London, 1930); idem, *A General Theory of Employment, Interest and Money* (London, 1936); J.A. Schumpeter, *Business Cycles* (2 vols, London, 1939).

32. T.E. Gregory, *An Introduction to Tooke and Newmarch's 'A History of Prices and of the State of the Circulation from 1792 to 1856'* (London, 1928), p. 8.

33. J. Harris, *William Beveridge: A Biography* (Oxford, 1977), pp. 116–19; W. Beveridge, *Unemployment: A Problem of Industry* (2nd edn, London, 1930), pp. 341–2.

34. W. Beveridge, 'Unemployment and the Trade Cycle', *Economic Journal*, xlix (1939), pp. 54, 57, 61–2; idem, 'The Trade Cycle in Britain before 1850', *Oxford*

Economic Papers, iii (1940), pp. 79, 102; idem, 'The Trade Cycle in Britain before 1850: A Postscript', *Oxford Economic Papers*, iv (1940), p. 75.

35. W. Beveridge, *Full Employment* in *a Free Society* (London, 1944), p. 27.

36. For earlier historical work and discussion, see N.J. Silberling, 'British Prices and Business Cycles, 1779–1850', *Review of Economic Statistics*, v (1923), supplement, pp. 219–62; W.O. Henderson, 'Trade Cycles in the Nineteenth Century', *History*, xviii (1933), pp. 147–53.

37. W.W. Rostow, 'British Trade Fluctuations, 1868–1896: A Chronicle and a Commentary' (unpublished Yale University Ph.D. dissertation, 1940), summary, pp. 454–60, 488–93, chs 3–7. See also idem, *British Economy of the Nineteenth Century* (Oxford, 1948), p. 54.

38. A.D. Gayer, W.W. Rostow and A.J. Schwartz, *Growth and Fluctuations of the British Economy, 1790–1850: An Historical, Statistical and Theoretical Study of Britain's Economic Development* (2 vols, Oxford, 1953), i, p. xxx.

39. R.C.O. Matthews, 'The Trade Cycle in Britain, 1790–1850', *Oxford Economic Papers*, vi (1954), p. 98; Gayer, Rostow and Schwartz, *Growth and Fluctuations of the British Economy*, i, p. xxxiii–xxxiv, 2.

40. Ibid., ii, pp. 532–3; T.S. Ashton, 'Economic Fluctuations, 1790–1850', *Economic History Review*, 2nd ser, vii (1955), pp. 380–1.

41. T.S. Ashton, *Economic Fluctuations in England, 1700–1800* (Oxford, 1959), publisher's blurb and pp. 29, 34, 105, 178.

42. R.C.O. Matthews, *A Study in Trade Cycle History: Economic Fluctuations in Great Britain, 1833–1842* (Cambridge, 1954), pp. xiii–xiv, 219.

43. Toynbee, *Lectures on the Industrial Revolution*, pp. 31–2.

44. E. Lipson, *The Growth of English Society: A Short Economic History* (2 vols, London, 1950), ii, p. 221.

45. T.S. Ashton, *The Industrial Revolution, 1760–1830* (London, 1948), p. 161.

46. Weaver, *The Hammonds*, p. 267.

47. P. Mathias, *The First Industrial Nation: An Economic History of Britain, 1700–1914* (London, 1969), p. 6.

48. M.M. Postan, *An Economic History of Western Europe, 1945–1964* (London, 1967), p. 11; Landes, *Unbound Prometheus*, p. 498.

49. J.K. Galbraith, *The Affluent Society* (London, 1962 edn), pp. 10–16, 30, chs 3, 7, 8, 23. For the background to this, see J.K. Galbraith, *A Life in Our Times* (Boston, 1981), pp. 335–7, 339–40.

50. M. Pinto-Duschinsky, 'Bread and Circuses? The Conservatives in Office, 1951–1964', and P. Oppenheimer, 'Muddling Through: The Economy, 1951–1964', both in V. Bogdanor and R. Skidelsky (eds), *The Age of Affluence, 1951–1964* (London, 1970), pp. 55–8, 118–20; A. Schonfield, *Modern Capitalism: The Changing Balance of Public and Private Power* (London, 1965), p. 3.

51. Schonfield, *Modern Capitalism*, p. 62; Postan, *Economic History of Western Europe*, pp. 18–19; R.A. Gordon, 'The Stability of the US Economy', and R.C.O. Matthews, 'Post-War Business Cycles in the UK', both in M. Bronfenbrenner (ed.), *Is the Business Cycle Obsolete?* (New York, 1969), pp. 4–5, 28, 99, 131–2; F.W. Paish, 'Business Cycles in Britain', *Lloyds Bank Review*, xcviii (1970), p. 1; M. Gilbert, 'The Post-War Business Cycle in Western Europe', *American Economic Review, Papers and Proceedings*, lii (1962), pp. 100–1.

52. Gordon, 'Stability of the US Economy', p. 26; Bogdanor and Skidelsky, *Age of Affluence*, introduction, pp. 10–11.

53. Postan, *Economic History of Western Europe*, p. 25; Sir R. Harrod, *Towards a New Economic Policy* (London, 1967), p. 70.

54. For the background to this, see A.O. Hirschman, 'The Rise and Fall of Development Economics', in his *Essays in Trespassing: Economics to Politics and Beyond* (Cambridge, 1981), pp. 7–13. For the early classics of development economics, see N.S. Buchanan and H.S. Ellis, *Approaches to Economic Development* (New York, 1955); H. Leibenstein, *Economic Backwardness and Economic Growth* (New York, 1957); G.M. Meier and R.E. Baldwin, *Economic Development: Theory, History, Policy* (New York, 1957); B. Higgins, *Economic Development: Prospects, Principles and Policies* (London, 1959); S. Kuznets, *Economic Growth and Structure* (London, 1965).

55. R.E. Cameron, 'Some Lessons of History for Developing Nations', *American Economic Review, Papers and Proceedings*, lviii (1967), p. 313. For the two views, see, respectively, R. Nurkse, *Problems of Capital Formation In Underdeveloped Countries* (Oxford, 1953); A.O. Hirschman, *The Strategy of Economic Development* (New Haven, 1958).

56. P.K. O'Brien, 'The Reconstruction, Rehabilitation and Reconfiguration of the British Industrial Revolution as a Conjuncture in Global History', *Itinerario*, xxiv (2000), pp. 17–31.

57. W.W. Rostow, *The Process of Economic Growth* (Oxford, 1953), p. 227.

58. Idem, *The Process of Economic Growth*, 2nd edn (Oxford, 1960), pp. v–vi, 335. For his other 'programmatic' books, see W.W. Rostow, *An American Policy in Asia* (London, 1955), pp. viii, 12–15, ch. 7; idem, *The United States in the World Arena: An Essay in Recent History* (New York, 1960), pp. 432, 444–6, 464; idem, *View from the Seventh Floor* (London, 1964), pp. 1–2, 14, 26, 29.

59. Rostow, *Process of Economic Growth* (2nd edn), p. 343; idem, *The Stages of Economic Growth: A Non-Communist Manifesto* (Cambridge, 1960), pp. 137, 139, 166. Between 1960 and 1972, *The Stages* sold 260,000 copies in the original English version alone: see J.D. Heyl, 'Kuhn, Rostow and Palmer: The Problem of Purposeful Change in the 'Sixties', *The Historian*, liv (1982), p. 300 n. 4.

60. Rostow, *Stages of Economic Growth*, pp. 10–11, 34–6. The central idea of the book was acknowledged to be indebted to W.A. Lewis, *The Theory of Economic Growth* (London, 1955), esp. pp. 208, 225–6, 235.

61. P. Deane, *The First Industrial Revolution* (Cambridge, 1965), p. 116.

62. Harte, 'Trends in Publications', pp. 23–8.

63. Flinn, *Origins of the Industrial Revolution*, p. 2; Deane, *First Industrial Revolution*, p. vii; Mathias, *First Industrial Nation*, p. 5. See also the review by W.H.B. Court in *Economic History Review*, 2nd ser., xxii (1969), p. 563.

64. E.J. Hobsbawm, *Industry and Empire: From 1750 to the Present Day* (Harmondsworth, 1969), p. 10; R.M. Hartwell, *The Industrial Revolution and Economic Growth* (London, 1971), p. 58.

65. Ibid., pp. 161–4; R.M. Hartwell, 'The Causes of the Industrial Revolution: An Essay in Methodology', in idem (ed.), *The Causes of the Industrial Revolution in England* (London, 1967), pp. 54, 79.

66. The key work here, to which all the late 1960s textbooks were indebted, was P. Deane and W.A. Cole, *British Economic Growth, 1688–1959* (2nd edn, Cambridge, 1967), esp. pp. xix, 3. The statistics they provided, on the basis of eight-sector disaggregation, made it possible to outline the main quantitative features of long-term economic change in Britain, especially the rate of growth and the shifts in structure. It is also noteworthy that the authors thanked Simon Kuznets 'who initiated the inquiry as one of a series of similar studies in different countries'. The book was published under the auspices of the University of Cambridge Department of Applied Economics.

67. C.H. Wilson, 'The Entrepreneur in the Industrial Revolution in Britain', *Explorations in Entrepreneurial History*, vii (1955), pp. 132–8; R.E. Cameron, *Banking in the Early Stages of Industrialization: A Study in Comparative Economic History* (New York, 1967), pp. ix, 3.

68. P. Deane and H.J. Habakkuk, 'The Take-Off in Britain', in W.W. Rostow (ed.), *The Economics of Take-Off into Sustained Growth* (London, 1963), esp. pp. 80–2. These findings were incorporated in all the 1960s textbooks. See Landes, *Unbound Prometheus*, pp. 77–9; Hobsbawm, *Industry and Empire*, p. 75; Hartwell, *Industrial Revolution and Economic Growth*, p. 28; Deane, *First Industrial Revolution*, pp. 107–8, 153–4; Mathias, *First Industrial Nation*, pp. 3, 13.

69. Deane, *First Industrial Revolution*, pp. 7, 15, 17. See also Landes, *Unbound Prometheus*, p. 13; Hartwell, *Industrial Revolution and Economic Growth*, p. 179; Mathias, *First Industrial Nation*, pp. 27, 30, 145.

70. Landes, *Unbound Prometheus*, pp. 105, 118, 120–2; Deane, *First Industrial Revolution*, pp. 150, 255, 263, 270–4; Mathias, *First Industrial Nation*, esp. pp. 259, 263, 271–2; Hartwell, *Industrial Revolution and Economic Growth*, pp. 8, 11, 20.

71. For specific criticisms, see: B.L. Anderson, 'Provincial Aspects of the Financial Revolution in the Eighteenth Century', *Business History*, xi (1969), pp. 11–22; idem, 'Money and the Structure of Credit in the Eighteenth Century', *Business History*, xii (1970), pp. 85–101; G.R. Hawke, *Railways and Economic Growth in England and Wales, 1840–1870* (Oxford, 1970), esp. p. 405; S.D. Chapman, 'The Cost of Power in the Industrial Revolution in Britain: The Case of the Textile Industry', *Midland History*, i (1971), esp. pp. 1, 6, 16, 19. For more general criticisms, see: E.A. Wrigley, 'The Process of Modernization and the Industrial Revolution in England', *Journal of Interdisciplinary History*, iii (1972–73), p. 259; D. Whitehead, 'The Industrial Revolution as an Example of Growth', in R.M. Hartwell (ed.), *The Industrial Revolution* (Oxford, 1970), pp. 24–7; H.J. Habakkuk, *American and British Technology in the Nineteenth Century: The Search for Labour Saving Inventions* (Cambridge, 1962), pp. 112–14, 142–7, 151, 174–89; B.E. Supple, 'Economic History and Economic Growth', *Journal of Economic History*, xx (1960), pp. 554–5.

72. E.E. Schumacher, *Small is Beautiful: A Study of Economics as if People Mattered* (London, 1974), pp. 10–11, 46–7.

73. W.H. Meadows et al., *The Limits to Growth* (New York, 1972), p. 191. For similar anti-growth views, see D. Bell, *The Cultural Contradictions of Capitalism* (New York, 1976), p. 237; R. Theobald and S. Mills (eds), *The Failure of Success: Ecological Values vs Economic Myths* (Indianapolis, 1973), p. xii. For a (much

less fashionable) restatement of the growth case, see W. Beckerman, *In Defence of Economic Growth* (London, 1974), esp. chs 1 , 9.

74. W.W. Rostow, *Getting from Here to There* (New York, 1978), pp. 1–2.

75. W.W. Rostow, *The World Economy: History and Prospect* (Austin, 1978), pp. 247, 294.

76. Rostow, *Getting from Here to There*, pp. 1, 19, 20.

77. J.K. Galbraith, *The Age of Uncertainty* (Boston, 1977), pp 7, 225. For the background, see Galbraith, *Life in Our Times*, pp. 528–34.

78. Hirschman, 'Rise and Fall of Development Economics', pp. 1, 16–24.

79. Cf. Galbraith, *Age of Uncertainty*, p. 280: 'There is no economic question so important as why so many people are so poor.'

80. Ibid., p. 295; Rostow, *World Economy*, p. 383; J.E. Alt, *The Politics of Economic Decline: Economic Management and Political Behaviour in Britain since 1964* (Cambridge, 1979), ch. 2, esp. p. 33.

81. E.J. Hobsbawm, *The Forward March of Labour Halted?* (London, 1981), pp. 3–4, 14–18; M. Girouard, *Life in the English Country House: A Social and Economic History* (London, 1978); E. Holden, *The Country Diary of an Edwardian Lady* (London, 1977); B.D. Nossiter, *Britain: A Future that Works* (Boston, 1978), pp. 104, 227, 231, 234.

82. R. Bacon and W. Eltis, *Britain's Economic Problems: Too Few Producers* (2nd edn, London, 1978), p. x; J. Bellini, *Rule Britannia: A Progress Report for Domesday, 1986* (London, 1981), pp. 5–6, 63, 69; Bairoch, 'International Industrialization Levels', pp. 304–5.

83. B.E. Supple, 'Economic History in the 1980s: Old Problems and New Directions', *Journal of Interdisciplinary History*, xii (1981), p. 203; C.P. Kindleberger, *Manias, Panics and Crashes: A History of Financial Crises* (New York, 1978), p. 3.

84. P.L. Payne, *British Entrepreneurship in the Nineteenth Century* (London, 1974), pp. 24–5, 30–34; S. Marriner, 'English Bankruptcy Records and Statistics Before 1850', *Economic History Review*, 2nd ser., xxxiii (1980), pp. 351, 366; J. Hoppit, *Risk and Failure in English Business, 1700–1800* (Cambridge, 1987); W.D. Rubinstein, *Men of Property: The Very Wealthy in Britain since the Industrial Revolution* (London, 1981).

85. G.N. von Tunzelmann, *Steam Power and British Industrialization to 1860* (Oxford, 1978); A.E. Musson, 'Industrial Motive Power in the United Kingdom, 1800–70', *Economic History Review*, 2nd ser., xxix (1976), pp. 416, 436; J.W. Kanefsky, 'Motive Power in British Industry and the Accuracy of the *1870 Factory Returns*', *Economic History Review*, 2nd ser., xxxii (1979), pp. 360, 374; R. Samuel, 'The Workshop of the World: Steam Power and Hand Technology in Mid-Victorian Britain', *History Workshop*, no. 3 (1977), pp. 7–8, 47–8; F.M.L. Thompson, 'Nineteenth-Century Horse Sense', *Economic History Review*, 2nd Ser., xxix (1976), pp. 64–6, 77–80.

86. M.J. Wiener, *English Culture and the Decline of the Industrial Spirit, 1850–1980* (Cambridge, 1981), pp. ix, 3, 7, 8, 10.

87. M. Fores, 'The Myth of a British Industrial Revolution', *History*, lxvi (1981), pp. 181–98.

88. C.H. Feinstein, 'Capital Formation in Great Britain', in P. Mathias and M.M. Postan (eds), *The Cambridge Economic History of Europe*, vol. vii, *The Industrial*

Economies: Capital, Labour and Enterprise (Cambridge, 1978), pt. i, pp. 28–96;
C.K. Harley, 'British Industrialization before 1841: Evidence of Slower Growth
During the Industrial Revolution', *Journal of Economic History*, xlii (1982),
pp. 267–89; N.F.R. Crafts, 'English Economic Growth in the Eighteenth Century:
A Re-Examination of Dean and Cole's Estimates', *Economic History Review*,
2nd ser., xxix (1976), pp. 226–35; idem, 'British Economic Growth, 1700–1831:
A Review of the Evidence', *Economic History Review*, 2nd ser., xxxvi (1983),
pp. 177–99; idem, *British Economic Growth During the Industrial Revolution*
(Oxford, 1985); idem, 'British Economic Growth, 1700–1850: Some Difficulties
of Interpretation', *Explorations in Economic History*, xxiv (1987), pp. 245–68;
N.F.R. Crafts and C.K. Harley, 'Output Growth and the Industrial Revolution:
A Re-Statement of the Crafts–Harley View', *Economic History Review*, 2nd
ser., xlv (1992), pp.703–30; C. More, *Understanding the Industrial Revolution*
(London, 2000), pp. 174–82.

89. N.F.R. Crafts, 'Industrial Revolution in England and France: Some Thoughts
on the Question "Why was England First?"', *Economic History Review*, 2nd
ser., xxx (1970), pp. 429–41; idem, 'Economic Growth in France and Britain,
1830–1910', *Journal of Economic History*, xliv (1984), pp. 46–69; P.K. O'Brien
and G. Keyder, *Economic Growth in Britain and France, 1780–1914* (London,
1978), pp. 21, 90, 146–50, 194; P.K. O'Brien, 'Do We Have a Typology for
the Study of European Industrializaton in the Nineteenth Century', *Journal of
European Economic History*, xv (1986), pp. 291–333; idem, 'Path Dependency,
or Why Britain Became an Industrialized and Urbanized Economy Long Before
France', *Economic History Review*, 2nd ser., xlix (1996), pp. 215–39; idem,
'The Britishness of the First Industrial Revolution and the British Contribution
to the Industrialisation of "Follower Countries" on the Mainland', *Diplomacy
and Statecraft*, viii (1997), pp. 48–67; J.A. Davis, 'Industralization in Britain
and Europe before 1850', in J.A. Davis and P. Mathias (eds), *The First Industrial
Revolutions* (Oxford, 1989), p. 67; S. Pollard, 'The Industrial Revolution – An
Overview', in Teich and Porter, *Industrial Revolution in National Context*,
pp. 371–87; G.D. Snooks, 'New Perspectives on the Industrial Revolution', in
G.D. Snooks (ed.), *Was the Industrial Revolution Necessary?* (London, 1994),
p. 15.

90. P. Mathias, *The Transformation of England* (London, 1979), pp. 10–14, 36, 43,
89–90, 140–2, 146; A.E. Musson, *The Growth of British Industry* (London,
1978), pp. 8, 62–5, 107–14, 139–42, 149. N.L. Tranter, 'The Labour Supply,
1780–1860', in R. Floud and D.N. McCloskey (eds), *The Economic History
of Britain since 1700* (2 vols, Cambridge, 1981), i, p. 226; D. McCloskey, 'The
Industrial Revolution, 1780–1860: A Survey', in ibid., i, pp. 104, 109, 124.

91. J. de Vries, 'The Industrial Revolution and the Industrious Revolution', *Journal
of Economic History*, liv (1994), p. 253; G. Clark and Y. van der Werf, 'Work
in Progress? The Industrious Revolution', *Journal of Economic History*, lviii
(1998), pp. 830–43; O'Brien, 'Reconstruction, Rehabilitation and Reconfiguration of the British Industrial Revolution', pp. 120, 131.

92. R. Cameron, 'A New View of European Industrialization', *Economic History
Review*, 2nd ser., xxxviii (1985), pp. 1–23; idem, 'Industrial Revolution: Fact
or Fiction', *Contention*, iv (1994), pp. 163–88; J.C.D. Clark, *English Society,
1688–1832: Ideology, Social Structure and Political Practice During the Ancien*

Regime (Cambridge, 1985), p. 4; idem, *Revolution and Rebellion: State and Society in England in the Seventeenth and Eighteenth Centuries* (Cambridge, 1986), p. 38.

93. J. Hoppit, 'Counting the Industrial Revolution', *Economic History Review*, 2nd ser., xliii (1990), pp. 173–93; R.V. Jackson, 'Rates of Growth During the Industrial Revolution', *Economic History Review*, 2nd ser., xlv (1992), pp. 1–23; R. Church, 'The Industrial Revolution', *Historical Journal*, xxxix (1996), pp. 535–43; Coleman, *Myth, History and the Industrial Revolution*, pp. 39–42.

94. E.A. Wrigley, *Continuity, Chance and Change: The Character of the Industrial Revolution in England* (Cambridge, 1988), p. 2; J. Mokyr, 'Editor's Introduction: The New Economic History and the Industrial Revolution', in idem (ed.), *The British Industrial Revolution: An Economic Perspective* (2nd edn, Boulder, 1999), p. 127; idem, *The Lever of Riches* (New York, 1990), p. 81. See also the following critiques of the 'Wiener thesis' that Britain was never fully enthused about industrialization: B. Collins and K. Robbins (eds), *British Culture and Economic Decline* (London, 1990); W.D. Rubinstein, *Capitalism, Culture and Decline in Britain, 1750–1990* (London, 1993); P. Mandler, 'Against "Englishness": English Culture and the Limits to Rural Nostalgia, 1850–1940', *Transactions of the Royal Historical Society*, 6th ser., vii (1997), pp. 155–75.

95. E.A. Wrigley and R.S. Schofield, *The Population History of England, 1541–1871: A Reconstruction* (London, 1981), pp. 410–12, 440–1; Wrigley, *Continuity, Change and Chance*, pp. 12, 34–97.

96. M. Berg and P. Hudson, 'Rehabilitating the Industrial Revolution', *Economic History Review*, 2nd ser., xlv (1992), pp. 24–50; P. Hudson, *The Industrial Revolution* (London, 1992), p. 5; M. Berg, *The Age of Manufactures, 1700–1820: Industry, Innovation and Work in Britain* (2nd edn, London, 1994), pp. 1–33. See also C. Sabel and J. Zeitlin, 'Historical Alternatives to Mass Production: Politics, Markets and Technology in Nineteenth-Century Industrialization', *Past & Present*, no. 108 (1985), pp. 133–76; D. Valenze, *The First Industrial Woman* (Oxford, 1995); S. King and G. Timmins, *Making Sense of the Industrial Revolution* (Manchester, 2001); Mokyr, 'Editor's Introduction', pp. 1–127; M.J. Daunton, *Progress and Poverty: An Economic and Social History of Britain, 1700–1850* (Oxford, 1995), esp. pp. 1–19, 127.

97. D.S. Landes, *The Wealth and Poverty of Nations: Why Some Are So Rich and Some So Poor* (London, 1999), pp. 187–257. See also idem, 'What Room for Accident in History? Explaining Big Changes by Small Events', *Economic History Review*, 2nd ser., xlvii (1994), pp. 637–56; idem, 'The Fable of the Dead Horse; or, The Industrial Revolution Revisited', in Mokyr, *British Industrial Revolution*, pp. 128–59. Landes's book has been subjected to widespread criticism: D.D. Buck, 'Was it Pluck or Luck that Made the West Grow Rich?', *Journal of World History*, x (1999), pp. 413–30; J. Goldstone, 'Efflorescences and Economic Growth in World History: Re-thinking the "Rise of the West" and the Industrial Revolution', *Journal of World History*, xiii (2002), pp. 323–90; C. Tilly, 'A Grand Tour of Exotic Landes', *American Historical Review*, civ (1999), pp. 1253–7; P. Vries, 'Culture, Clocks and Comparative Costs: David Landes on the Wealth of the West and the Poverty of the Rest', *Itinerario*, xxii (1998), pp. 67–89.

98. J. Goldstone, 'The Problem of the Early Modern World', *Journal of the Economic and Social History of the Orient*, xli (1998), pp. 249–84; K. Pomeranz, *The Great Divergence: China, Europe and the Making of the Modern World Economy* (Princeton, 2000); R. Bin Wong, *China Transformed: Historical Change and the Limits of European Experience* (Ithaca, 1997); J.L. van Zanden, 'The Great Convergence from a West-European Perspective', *Itinerario*, xxiv (2000), pp. 63–82.

99. The view that there was a fundamental transformation in the British economy between the mid eighteenth and mid nineteenth centuries, but that it was not so much rapid economic growth as rapid structural change, culminating in a uniquely small agricultural sector, seems generally shared: see N.F.R. Crafts, 'British Industrialization in an International Context', *Journal of Interdisciplinary History*, xix (1989), pp. 415–28; P. Temin, 'Two Views of the Industrial Revolution', *Journal of Economic History*, lvii (1997), pp.63–82; C.K. Hartley and N.F.R. Crafts, 'Simulating Two Views of the British Industrial Revolution', *Journal of Economic History*, lx (2000), p. 839; Daunton, *Progress and Poverty*, pp. 25–57; Church, 'Industrial Revolution', p. 542; J. Mokyr, 'Accounting for the Industrial Revolution'; S.L. Engerman and P.K. O'Brien, 'The Industrial Revolution in Global Perspective', both in R. Floud and P. Johnson (eds), *The Cambridge Economic History of Modern Britain* (3 vols, Cambridge, 2004), vol. i, *Industrialization, 1700–1860*, pp. 1–3, 450–3. For 'parachutists' and 'truffle-hunters', see above, Chapter 1, p. 30.

100. D. Cannadine, 'The Embarrassment of Riches: Historians and Wealth in Modern Britain', *The Rothschild Archive: Review of the Year 2001–02* (London, 2002), p. 18; P. Coclanis and D. Carlton, 'The Crisis of Economic History', *Challenge*, xliv (2001), p. 95; P. Hudson (ed.), *Living Economic and Social History: Historians Explain Their Interest in, and the Nature of Their Subject* (Glasgow, 2001); R. Floud and P. Johnson, 'Preface', in Floud and Johnson, *Industrialization, 1700–1860*, pp. xvii–xviii.

101. See above, Chapter 1, p. 32.

102. de Vries, 'Industrial Revolution and Industrious Revolution', p. 249; R.M. Hartwell, 'Was there an Industrial Revolution?', *Social Science History*, xiv (1990), p. 575; S.L. Engerman, 'The Industrial Revolution Re-visited', in Snooks, *Was the Industrial Revolution Necessary?*, pp. 112–23. For the most recent account, G. Clark, *A Farewell to Alms: A Brief Economic History of the World* (Princeton, 2007), pp. 8–12, 230–71.

CHAPTER 5, HERITAGE, pp. 112–34

1. I wrote this chapter at the invitation of Dame Jennifer Jenkins, and I am grateful to her, and also to Andrew Franklin and Merlin Waterson, for their helpful and constructive comments on an earlier draft. In the light of the arguments made, strictures levied, and hostages to fortune given in Chapter 7 below, I should stress that this chapter is concerned with England rather than Great Britain as a whole, that Scotland and Wales are only rarely mentioned, and that Ireland does not feature in it at all. For valuable discussions of these broader issues of landscape and competing nationalities, see D. Lowenthal, 'British National

Identity and the English Landscape', *Rural History*, ii (1991), pp. 205–30; S. Daniels, *Fields of Vision: Landscape Imagery and National Identity in England and the United States* (Cambridge, 1993).

2. For the engineer as hero, see C. Macleod, 'James Watt, Heroic Invention and the Idea of the Industrial Revolution', in M. Berg and K. Bruland (eds), *Technological Revolutions in Europe: Historical Perspectives* (Cheltenham, 1998), pp. 96–118; idem, *Heroes of Invention: Technology, Liberalism and British Identity, 1750–1914* (Cambridge, 2007).

3. K. Clark, *Civilisation: A Personal View* (London, 1969), p. 321.

4. It should be clear that this apocalyptic picture of Britain's Industrial Revolution derives from the first phase of interpretation discussed above, Chapter 4, pp. 84–91. But taking the whole of the nineteenth and twentieth centuries, the scale of the transformation to the environment has, indeed, been remarkable.

5. P. Hall, 'England circa 1900', in H.C. Darby (ed.), *A New Historical Geography of England after 1600* (Cambridge, 1976), pp. 374, 378; M. Reed, *The Landscape of Britain from the Beginnings to 1914* (London, 1990) pp. 302–3.

6. Hall, 'England circa 1900', p. 374; P. Waller, 'Introduction: The English Urban Landscape: Yesterday, Today and Tomorrow', in idem (ed.), *The English Urban Landscape* (Oxford, 2000), pp. 12, 15, 17.

7. H. Meller, 'Urban Renewal and Citizenship: The Quality of Life in British Cities, 1890–1990', *Urban History*, xxii (1995), pp. 63–84.

8. M. Sissons (ed.), *A Countryside for All: The Future of Rural Britain* (London, 2001); E. Holdaway and G. Smart (eds), *Landscapes at Risk? The Future for Areas of Outstanding Natural Beauty* (London, 2001).

9. For the historical antecedents to these vexed contemporary issues, I have drawn heavily and appreciatively on K.V. Thomas, *Man and the Natural World: Changing Attitudes in England, 1500–1800* (London, 1984); S. Schama, *Landscape and Memory* (New York, 1995); T.C. Smout, *Nature Contested: Environmental History in Scotland and Northern England since 1600* (Edinburgh, 2000).

10. See especially Thomas, *Man and the Natural World*, pp. 242–303.

11. J. Ruskin, *The Seven Lamps of Architecture* (New York, 1989 edn), p. 197; M. Hunter, 'Introduction', in idem (ed.), *Preserving the Past: The Rise of Heritage in Modern Britain* (Stroud, 1996), p. 7.

12. P. Mandler, 'Against "Englishness": English Culture and the Limits to Rural Nostalgia, 1850–1940', *Transactions of the Royal Historical Society*, 6th ser., vii (1997), p. 161.

13. M. Hunter, 'The Preconditions of Preservation: A Historical Perspective', in D. Lowenthal and M. Binney (eds), *Our Past Before Us: Why Do We Save It?* (London, 1981), pp. 23–4.

14. H. Carter and C.R. Lewis, *An Urban Geography of England and Wales in the Nineteenth Century* (London, 1990), pp. 193–211; R. Rodger, *Housing in Urban Britain, 1780–1914: Class, Capitalism and Construction* (Basingstoke, 1989), pp. 26–7, 48–51; idem, 'Slums and Suburbs: The Persistence of Residential Apartheid', in Waller, *English Urban Landscape*, p. 240.

15. B. Harrison, *Peaceable Kingdom: Stability and Change in Modern Britain* (Oxford, 1982), pp. 85–6; R.W. Malcolmson, *Popular Recreations in English Society, 1700–1850* (Cambridge, 1973), pp. 118–38.

16. Smout, *Nature Contested*, p. 34.

17. D. Pearce, *Conservation Today* (London, 1989), p. 16; Reed, *Landscape of Britain*, p. 340; Hunter, 'Preconditions of Preservation', p. 29.

18. Reed, *Landscape of Britain*, pp. 339–40; W. Ashworth, *The Growth of Modern British Town Planning: A Study in Economic and Social History of the Nineteenth and Twentieth Centuries* (London, 1954), pp. 167–90; A. Beach and N. Tiratsoo, 'The Planners and the Public', in M. Daunton (ed.), *The Cambridge Urban History of Britain*, vol. iii, *1840–1950* (Cambridge, 2000), pp. 529, 534.

19. For a broader comparative perspective, which suggests that such claims to national backwardness were commonplace across the continent, as heritage propagandists in each country insisted that theirs was the most backward nation of all, see A. Swenson, 'Conceptualising Heritage in Nineteenth- and Early Twentieth-Century France, Germany and England' (unpublished Ph.D. dissertation, University of Cambridge, 2006).

20. Ashworth, *Growth of Modern British Town Planning*, pp. 191–9.

21. A. Offer, *Property and Politics, 1870–1914: Landownership, Law, Ideology and Urban Development in England* (Cambridge, 1981), pp. 338, 340, 370; Smout, *Nature Contested*, p. 26.

22. D. Cannadine, *The Pleasures of the Past* (London, 1989), pp. 92–4; idem, *In Churchill's Shadow: Confronting the Past in Modern Britain* (London, 2002), pp. 225–8.

23. Cannadine, *In Churchill's Shadow*, pp. 228–9.

24. Mandler, 'Against Englishness', pp. 169–70; Harrison, *Peaceable Kingdom*, p. 84.

25. M.J. Wiener, *English Culture and the Decline of the Industrial Spirit, 1850–1980* (London, 1992 edn), pp. 98–111; D. Cannadine, *G.M. Trevelyan: A Life in History* (London, 1992), pp. 158–67; idem, *In Churchill's Shadow*, pp. 160–71, 229–30.

26. For differing appreciations of Baldwin's politics, see P. Williamson, *Stanley Baldwin: Conservative Leadership and National Values* (Cambridge, 1999); R.I. McKibbin, *The Ideologies of Class: Social Relations in Britain, 1880–1950* (Oxford, 1990), p. 270–300.

27. Smout, *Nature Contested*, p. 61.

28. Ashworth, *Genesis of Modern British Town Planning*, pp. 223–4.

29. J. Lowerson, 'Battles for the Countryside', in F. Gloversmith (ed.), *Class, Culture and Social Change: A New View of the 1930s* (Brighton, 1980), pp. 275–7.

30. D. Evans, *A History of Nature Conservation in Britain* (2nd edn, London, 1997), p. 56.

31. D. Cannadine, *The Decline and Fall of the British Aristocracy* (London, 1990), pp. 110–11; Lowerson, 'Battles for the Countryside', pp. 258–9, 263.

32. Cannadine, *Trevelyan*, pp. 151–8; idem, *In Churchill's Shadow*, pp. 230–2; Smout, *Nature Contested*, p. 158.

33. R.J. Moore-Colyer, 'From Great Wen to Toad Hall: Aspects of the Urban–Rural Divide in Inter-War Britain', *Rural History*, x (1999), pp. 112–21.

34. C.E.M. Joad, 'The People's Claims', in C. Williams-Ellis (ed.), *Britain and the Beast* (London, 1937), p. 64; Lowenthal, 'British National Identity and the English Landscape', p. 219; D.N. Jeans, 'Planning and the Myth of the English Countryside in the Interwar Period', *Rural History*, i (1990), pp. 259–60.

35. Mandler, 'Against Englishness', p. 174.

36. Ibid., pp. 172–4; Lowerson, 'Battles for the Countryside', p. 267.
37. Rodger, 'Slums and Suburbs', p. 257; Cannadine, *Decline and Fall*, pp. 627–9.
38. G.M. Young (ed.), *Country and Town: A Summary of the Scott and Uthwatt Reports* (Harmondsworth, 1943).
39. P. Mandler, *The Fall and Rise of the Stately Home* (London, 1997), p. 335.
40. Evans, *Nature Conservation in Britain*, p. 79; Mandler, *Fall and Rise of the Stately Home*, p. 347.
41. Evans, *Nature Conservation in Britain*, pp. 96–7, 143–50; Pearce, *Conservation Today*, p. 20.
42. Waller, 'English Urban Landscape', p. 21; Roger, 'Slums and Suburbs', pp. 261–2.
43. Cannadine, *Decline and Fall*, pp. 643–4; Pearce, *Conservation Today*, p. 236.
44. J. Betjeman, 'Foreword', in C. Amery and D. Cruickshank, *The Rape of Britain* (London, 1975), p. 7.
45. Mandler, *Fall and Rise of the Stately Home*, pp. 401–6; Pearce, *Conservation Today*, pp. 2–3; R. Strong et al. (eds), *The Destruction of the Country House, 1875–1975* (London, 1974).
46. Pearce, *Conservation Today*, p. 6.
47. Evans, *Nature Conservation in Britain*, pp. 79–99.
48. Smout, *Nature Contested*, pp. 163, 166.
49. Evans, *Nature Conservation in Britain*, p. 154.
50. Smout, *Nature Contested*, pp. 79–84, 166–7.
51. M. Shoard, *The Theft of the Countryside* (London, 1980), p. 9.
52. W.G. Hoskins, *The Making of the English Landscape* (London, 1985 edn), pp. 298–9; D. Matless, 'One Man's England: W.G. Hoskins and the English Culture of Landscape', *Rural History*, iv (1992), pp. 187–207; idem, *Landscape and Englishness* (London, 1998), pp. 274–7.
53. H. Newby, *Green and Pleasant Land? Social Change in Rural England* (Harmondsworth, 1980), pp. 255–6.
54. Cannadine, *In Churchill's Shadow*, pp. 237–41.
55. Pearce, *Conservation Today*, p. vii.
56. Ibid., pp. 27, 32.
57. M. Binney, 'Oppression to Obsession', in Lowenthal and Binney, *Our Past Before Us*, pp. 210–11.
58. M. Binney, *Our Vanishing Heritage* (London, 1984), pp. 8–10.
59. J. Dimbleby, *The Prince of Wales: A Biography* (London, 1994), pp. 451–4.
60. M. Thatcher, *Speeches to the Conservative Party Conference, 1975–1988* (London, 1989), p. 128; Beach and Tiratsoo, 'The Planners and the Public', p. 525; Pearce, *Conservation Today*, p. 5.
61. Waller, 'English Urban Landscape', pp. 23–4.
62. Rodger, 'Slums and Suburbs', pp. 264–8.
63. Waller, 'English Urban Landscape', pp. 27, 31.
64. Ibid., p. 21.
65. Smout, *Nature Contested*, p. 86.
66. P. Lowe, 'After Foot-and-Mouth: Farming and the New Rural Economy', in J. Jenkins (ed.), *Remaking the Landscape: The Changing Face of Britain* (London, 2002), pp. 165–82.
67. O. Rackham, *The History of the Countryside* (London, 2000 edn), pp. 25–7.

68. Appropriately, the most comprehensive treatment of the English historic environment may now be found in a series edited by Sir Neil Cossons, who was Chairman of English Heritage from 2000 to 2007: A. Winchester, *England's Landscape: The North West* (London, 2006); F. Aalen, *England's Landscape: The North East* (London, 2006); D. Hooke, *England's Landscape: The West Midlands* (London, 2006); D. Stocker, *England's Landscape: The East Midlands* (London, 2006); B. Cunliffe, *England's Landscape: The West* (London, 2006); R. Kain, *England's Landscape: The South West* (London, 2006); T. Williamson, *England's Landscape: East Anglia* (London, 2006); B. Short, *England's Landscape: The South East* (London, 2006).

69. See above, Chapter 4, p. 111.

70. Waller, 'English Urban Landscape', p. 21.

71. Schama, *Landscape and Memory*, p. 18.

72. Rackham, *History of the Countryside*, p. 28.

73. Schama, *Landscape and Memory*, p. 18.

74. Smout, *Nature Contested*, pp. 2–3, 32, 171–2.

75. Waller, 'English Urban Landscape', pp. 17, 21–3, 27.

76. Evans, *Nature Conservation in Britain*, pp. 210–11, 231.

77. Schama, *Landscape and Memory*, p. 18.

78. Evans, *Nature Conservation in Britain*, p. 252; Smout, *Nature Contested*, pp. 4–5.

CHAPTER 6, TRADITION, pp. 135–70

1. This chapter originated as a keynote lecture delivered to a conference entitled 'The Proms and British Musical Life', held at the British Library in April 2007, and jointly sponsored by the British Library, BBC Proms, and King's College, London. I am grateful to the participants for their comments, questions and suggestions, and especially to Stephen Banfield, Asa Briggs, Nicholas Kenyon, Patrick McCarthy and David Wright. I should also like to pay tribute to the work, inspiration and memory of Cyril Erlich. An abridged version of this chapter was published in the *London Review of Books*, 6 September 2007, pp. 21–4.

2. See E.J. Hobsbawm, 'Introduction: Inventing Traditions', in E.J. Hobsbawm and T. Ranger (eds), *The Invention of Tradition* (Cambridge, 1983), pp. 1–14.

3. Many of these issues have been brilliantly addressed in N. Kenyon, J. Doctor and D. Wright (eds), *The Proms: A New History* (London, 2007). Also of relevance are: A. Orga, *The Proms* (Newton Abbot, 1974); D. Cox, *The Henry Wood Proms* (London, 1980); B. Hall, *The Proms and the Men Who Made Them* (London, 1981); N. Kenyon, *The BBC Symphony Orchestra* (London, 1981).

4. D. Cannadine, 'The Context, Performance and Meaning of Ritual: The British Monarchy and the "Invention of Tradition", c.1820–1977', in Hobsbawm and Ranger, *Invention of Tradition*, p. 162; P. Kildea, 'The Proms: An Industrious Revolution', in Kenyon et al., *The Proms*, p. 22.

5. Compare, for example: M. Portillo, 'The promenaders don their headdresses and fly their flags', *New Statesman*, 20 September 2004; A. Holden, 'Time to ban the banners', *The Observer*, 11 September 2005.

6. For a pioneering study, to which this chapter is much indebted, see L. Tzidon, 'The Ritual of the Last Nights of the Proms and the Role of Invented Tradition' (unpublished MA dissertation in the Visual and Performing Arts, King's College, London, 2001).

7. The fullest treatment of this first, founding phase, is now L. Langley, 'Building an Orchestra, Creating an Audience: Robert Newman and the Queen's Hall Promenade Concerts, 1895–1926', in Kenyon et al., *The Proms*, pp. 32–74.

8. For the pre-Wood proms, see Cox, *Henry Wood Proms*, pp. 9–21; Orga, *The Proms*, pp. 9–40; T. Russell, *The Proms* (London, 1949), pp. 12–18.

9. R. Aldous, *Tunes of Glory: The Life of Malcolm Sargent* (London, 2002), pp. 19, 131–8; C. Reid, *Malcolm Sargent: A Biography* (London, 1968), pp. 400–1; Russell, *The Proms*, p. 26; Orga, *The Proms*, pp. 46–7.

10. Cf. Russell, *The Proms*, p. 10, which insisted that Wood 'was creating a tradition, and he knew it'. There is no evidence that Wood thought he was doing anything of the kind.

11. F. Howes, *The English Musical Renaissance* (London, 1966); M. Hughes and R. Stradling, *The English Musical Renaissance, 1840–1940: Constructing a National Music* (2nd edn, Manchester, 2001).

12. Cox, *Henry Wood Proms*, pp. 82–6, 109–26; A. Briggs, *The History of Broadcasting in the United Kingdom*, vol. ii, *The Golden Age of Wireless* (Oxford, 1965), pp. 63, 172–3.

13. Russell, *The Proms*, p. 58.

14. A. Jacobs, *Henry J. Wood: Maker of the Proms* (London, 1994), p. 4.

15. Ibid., pp. 41, 457, 459.

16. Tzidon, 'Ritual of the Last Nights', pp. 17–19.

17. H. Wood, *My Life of Music* (London, 1938), p. 92; Jacobs, *Henry J. Wood*, pp. 47–8; Cox, *Henry Wood Proms*, p. 47.

18. D. Armitage, *The Ideological Origins of the British Empire* (Cambridge, 2000), pp. 173, 185.

19. Wood, *My Life of Music*, p. 155; Jacobs, *Henry J. Wood*, pp. 73–4.

20. Jacobs, *Henry J. Wood*, pp. 104–5; Cox, *Henry Wood Proms*, pp. 51–2; Russell, *The Proms*, pp. 42–3. For the broader context of these national and imperial celebrations, see: J. MacKenzie, 'Nelson Goes Global: The Nelson Myth in Britain and Beyond', in D. Cannadine (ed.), *Admiral Lord Nelson: Context and Legacy* (Basingstoke, 2005), pp. 157–60; M. Czisnk, 'Commemorating Trafalgar: Public Celebration and National Identity', in D. Cannadine (ed.), *Trafalgar in History: A Battle and its Afterlife* (Basingstoke, 2006), pp. 146–7.

21. Hall, *The Proms*, p. 63.

22. Tzidon, 'Ritual of the Last Nights', pp. 3–7.

23. Ibid., p. 21.

24. For this phase in the history of the Proms, see J. Doctor, 'A New Dimension: The BBC Takes on the Proms, 1920–44', in Kenyon et al., *The Proms*, pp. 74–129.

25. Briggs, *Golden Age of Wireless*, p. 6.

26. Cox, *Henry Wood Proms*, pp. 72–4; Jacobs, *Henry J. Wood*, pp. 62, 127, 200–1, 280, 339.

27. Russell, *The Proms*, p. 21; Orga, *The Proms*, pp. 95–6; Jacobs, *Henry J. Wood*, pp. 166, 172, 204, 207, 236, 413, 442–61.

28. Kenyon, *BBC Symphony Orchestra*, p. 46; Hall, *The Proms*, pp. 80–1, 99; Doctor, 'A New Dimension', pp. 96, 114.

29. Wood, *My Life in Music*, p. 192.

30. Jacobs, *Henry J. Wood*, p. 281.

31. Kenyon, *BBC Symphony Orchestra*, pp. 15–57; Briggs, *Golden Age of Wireless*, pp. 174–5.

32. Jacobs, *Henry J. Wood*, pp. 328–9.

33. Ibid., pp. 341–2, 406–7; Kenyon, *BBC Symphony Orchestra*, p. 154.

34. Kenyon, *BBC Symphony Orchestra*, pp. 165–7; Cox, *Henry Wood Proms*, pp. 109–10.

35. Doctor, 'A New Dimension', pp. 125–6; Jacobs, *Henry J. Wood*, pp. 361–2.

36. Jacobs, *Henry J. Wood*, pp. 370–1.

37. Ibid., p. 380.

38. S. Martin, *The Order of Merit: One Hundred Years of Matchless Honour* (London, 2007), pp. 495–6; Jacobs, *Henry J. Wood*, p. 391.

39. Kenyon, *BBC Symphony Orchestra*, pp. 188–90; Cox, *Henry Wood Proms*, pp. 127–33, 137–8; A. Briggs, *The History of Broadcasting in the United Kingdom*, vol. iii, *The War of Words* (Oxford, 1970), pp. 709–10.

40. Kenyon, *BBC Symphony Orchestra*, pp. 180, 183; Cox, *Henry Wood Proms*, pp. 139–47.

41. A. Garnham, 'The BBC in Possession, 1945–59', in Kenyon et al., *The Proms*, pp. 130–48; Cox, *Henry Wood Proms*, p. 152.

42. Aldous, *Tunes of Glory*, pp. 129–31; Reid, *Sargent*, p. 446.

43. D. Cannadine, *In Churchill's Shadow: Grandeur and Decline in Modern Britain* (London, 2002), pp. 36–7.

44. B. Levin, *The Pendulum Years: Britain and the Sixties* (London, 1970); A. Marwick, *The Sixties: Cultural Revolution in Britain, France, Italy and the United States, c1958–c1974* (Oxford, 1998).

45. Cannadine, 'Context, Performance and Meaning of Ritual', pp. 153–4.

46. H. Thomas (ed.), *The Establishment: A Symposium* (London, 1959).

47. Aldous, *Tunes of Glory*, pp. 97–112; Reid, *Sargent*, pp. 270–81; J. Dimbleby, *Richard Dimbleby: A Biography* (London, 1975), pp. 88–203.

48. Aldous, *Tunes of Glory*, pp. 117–20; Reid, *Sargent*, pp. 309–31; Dimbleby, *Dimbleby*, pp. 205–23.

49. Aldous, *Tunes of Glory*, pp. 139–40, 170–6; Reid, *Sargent*, pp. 346–7, 375–81.

50. Kenyon, *BBC Symphony Orchestra*, pp. 268–9; Aldous, *Tunes of Glory*, p. 187; Reid, *Sargent*, pp. 387–8, 392.

51. Dimbleby, *Dimbleby*, pp. 234–64, 384–8.

52. Hall, *The Proms*, pp. 65–6; Aldous, *Tunes of Glory*, pp. 23–4; Reid, *Sargent*, pp. 99–102.

53. Reid, *Sargent*, pp. 220–8, 362–74.

54. Sir Thomas Beecham once described Herbert von Karajan as 'a sort of musical Sir Malcolm Sargent'.

55. Garnham, 'BBC in Possession', pp. 148–64.

56. A. Briggs, *The History of Broadcasting in the United Kingdom*, vol. iv, *Sound and Vision* (Oxford, 1979), p. 219; Aldous, *Tunes of Glory*, pp. 140–1; Cox, *Henry Wood Proms*, pp. 155–6; Hall, *The Proms*, p. 127.

57. Hall, *The Proms*, pp. 127–9.
58. M. Sargent, 'The Conductor Speaks', *Radio Times*, 14–20 September 1952; Tzidon, 'Ritual of the Last Nights', p. 8. See also Russell, *The Proms*, pp. 11, 71.
59. Kenyon, *BBC Symphony Orchestra*, pp. 215–29; Aldous, *Tunes of Glory*, pp. 154–65.
60. Hall, *The Proms*, p. 131.
61. Aldous, *Tunes of Glory*, pp. 167–8.
62. Briggs, *Sound and Vision*, p. 737; Cox, *Henry Wood Proms*, pp. 163–4.
63. Reid, *Sargent*, pp. 441–7; Cox, *Henry Wood Proms*, pp. 172–3; Hall, *The Proms*, pp. 133–6.
64. P. Mullen, *The History of the Proms: Celebrating 100 Seasons* (High Wycombe, 1994), pp. 66–7; Aldous, *Tunes of Glory*, pp. 142–4.
65. A. Briggs, The *History of Broadcasting in the United Kingdom*, vol. v, *Competition* (Oxford, 1995), p. 144; P. Scannel, 'Public Service Broadcasting and Modern Public Life', in P. Scannel, P. Schlesinger and C. Sparks (eds), *Culture and Power: A Media, Culture and Society Reader* (London, 1992), pp. 322–3; N. Kenyon, 'Planning the Proms: Yesterday, Today and Tomorrow', in Kenyon et al., *The Proms*, p. 273.
66. Kenyon, *BBC Symphony Orchestra*, pp. 238–43, 244–7, 252–5, 261–2, 266–8; Cox, *Henry Wood Proms*, pp. 159–60; Aldous, *Tunes of Glory*, pp. 160–6.
67. Dimbleby, *Dimbleby*, pp. 319–40.
68. Briggs, *Competition*, p. 230, note 13; Kenyon, *BBC Symphony Orchestra*, pp. 270–3; Aldous, *Tunes of Glory*, pp. 179–89.
69. Briggs, *Competition*, pp. 309–76. For a full account, see D. Wright, 'Reinventing the Proms: The Glock and Ponsonby Eras, 1959–85', in Kenyon et al., *The Proms*, pp. 168–95.
70. N. Edmunds, 'William Glock and the British Broadcasting Corporation's Music Policy, 1959–73', *Contemporary British History*, xx (2006), esp. pp. 241–4; Briggs, *Competition*, pp. 398–9; Kenyon, *BBC Symphony Orchestra*, pp. 289–94, 297–8, 304–8, 318–19; Cox, *Henry Wood Proms*, p. 152; W. Glock, *Notes in Advance* (Oxford, 1991), p. 118; idem (ed.), *Pierre Boulez: A Symposium* (London, 1986).
71. Glock, *Notes in Advance*, pp. 114–27; Aldous, *Tunes of Glory*, pp. 203–13; Reid, *Sargent*, pp. 405–10; Dimbleby, *Dimbleby*, pp. 391–402.
72. Aldous, *Tunes of Glory*, pp. 222–32.
73. Reid, *Sargent*, p. 468.
74. Ibid., p. 339.
75. Aldous, *Tunes of Glory*, pp. 229–33; Hall, *The Proms*, p. 158.
76. Aldous, *Tunes of Glory*, pp. xiv, 240–2; Reid, *Sargent*, pp. 459–62.
77. Reid, *Sargent*; Aldous, *Tunes of Glory*.
78. Hall, *The Proms*, p. 165; Aldous, *Tunes of Glory*, p. xiv.
79. Aldous, *Tunes of Glory*, pp. xiv–xvi.
80. Glock, *Notes in Advance*, p. 123.
81. Hall, *The Proms*, p. 16.
82. E.g. V. Lewis-Smith, 'Lager louts' big night', *Evening Standard*, 13 September 2004.

83. This point was being made as early as 1958: Garnham, 'BBC in Possession', p. 163.
84. Hall, *The Proms*, p. 168; Aldous, *Tunes of Glory*, p. xiv.
85. Kenyon, *BBC Symphony Orchestra*, pp. 347–8; Cox, *Henry Wood Proms*, pp. 192–4.
86. Wright, 'Reinventing the Proms', p. 195.
87. Orga, *The Proms*, pp. 158–9; R. Swinton, *The Proms and Natural Justice* (London, 1981).
88. Cox, *Henry Wood Proms*, pp. 194, 250.
89. P. Kildea, 'The Proms: An Industrious Revolution', in Kenyon et al., *The Proms*, p. 29.
90. J. Drummond, *Tainted by Experience: A Life in the Arts* (London, 2000), pp. 393–4; Hall, *The Proms*, pp. 190, 209; Tzidon, 'Ritual of the Last Nights', p. 11; Wright, 'Reinventing the Proms', pp. 195–8.
91. Drummond, *Tainted by Experience*, pp. xiv–xvii, 146.
92. Tzidon, 'Ritual of the Last Nights', p. 12; Drummond, *Tainted by Experience*, p. 389.
93. Drummond, *Tainted by Experience*, pp. xiii–xvi; T. Service, 'Branding the Postmodern Proms, 1986–2007: Reflecting on Three Last Nights', in Kenyon et al., *The Proms*, pp. 237–41; H. Wallace, 'Defining Moment: Birtwistle's "Panic", Last Night of the Proms, September 16 1995', *Financial Times Magazine*, August 11/12 2007, p. 46.
94. *The Guardian*, editorial, 9 September 2006.
95. Cox, *Henry Wood Proms*, pp. 229–32; Drummond, *Tainted by Experience*, pp. 386–7.
96. Hall, *The Proms*, p. 15; I. Hewett, 'Joining the Queue: The Proms Audiences', in Kenyon at al., *The Proms*, p. 227.
97. Service, 'Branding the Postmodern Proms', p. 241; Hewett, 'Joining the Queue', p. 227.
98. Service, 'Branding the Postmodern Proms', pp. 242–3; Drummond, *Tainted by Experience*, p. 424.
99. Service, 'Branding the Postmodern Proms', pp. 244–9; David Mellor in the *Mail on Sunday*, 17 September 2006.
100. Service, 'Branding the Postmodern Proms', pp. 249–52.
101. R. Morrison, 'No encore please for Last Night of jingoism', *The Times*, 15 September 2001; E. Seckerson, 'Music that rose to the occasion', *The Independent*, 18 September 2001; S. Pollard, 'Moved to Tears', *New Statesman*, 24 September 2001; R. Weight, *Patriots: National Identity in Britain, 1940–2000* (London, 2002), p. 725.
102. N. Kenyon, 'Planning the Proms, Yesterday, Today and Tomorrow', in Kenyon et al., *The Proms*, pp, 256–77.
103. Hughes and Stradling, *English Musical Renaissance*, p. 291.
104. Garnham, 'The BBC in Possession', p. 161.
105. Hewett, 'Joining the Queue', p. 231.
106. Briggs, *Sound and Vision*, p. 735.
107. Cox, *Henry Wood Proms*, pp. 9–11.
108. Garnham, 'The BBC in Possession', p. 131.
109. Tzidon, 'Ritual of the Last Nights', p. 12.

110. A. Sherwin, 'Land of Hope and Glory moves to Germany', *The Times*, 3 September 2004.

CHAPTER 7, NATION, pp. 171–95

1. This chapter began life as the opening plenary lecture delivered to the Anglo-American Conference of Historians held at the Institute of Historical Research in 1994. In revising it for publication, I have benefited greatly from the comments and advice of David Armitage, Linda Colley, Willy Malley and Kenneth O. Morgan. For some earlier thoughts on related issues, but which use the term 'British history' in rather a different way, see D. Cannadine, 'British History: Past, Present – and Future?', *Past & Present*, no. 116 (1987), pp. 169–91.

2. *The Times*, 24 May 1994. It is worth quoting the riposte by Lord Jenkins of Hillhead, who rightly took exception to 'some rather curious history': 'I'm not sure many parts of the United Kingdom regard their monarchy as being descended from Wessex, nor that it is very natural to cite our two seven-hundred-year-old universities, together with our languages, as being worthy signs of our ancient separateness and ancient insularity.... For a substantial number of centuries, the universities operated almost exclusively, not in the indigenous language, but in one which attempted a European universality' (*The Independent*, 26 May 1994). For Britain as an 'invented nation', see P. Scott, *Knowledge and Nation* (Edinburgh, 1990), p. 168.

3. M. Thatcher, *The Downing Street Years* (London, 1993), p. 753.

4. P.M. Kennedy, 'The Decline of Nationalistic History in the West, 1900–1970', in W. Laqueur and G.L. Mosse (eds), *Historians in Politics* (London, 1974), pp. 329–52.

5. C.S. Maier, 'Consigning the Twentieth Century to History: Alternative Narratives for the Modern Era', *American Historical Review*, cv (2000), pp. 807–31.

6. V. Chancellor, *History For Their Masters: Opinion in the English History Text Book, 1800–1914* (Bath, 1970); G. Kitson Clark, 'A Hundred Years of History Teaching at Cambridge, 1873–1973', *Historical Journal*, xvi (1973), pp. 535–53; D.S. Goldstein, 'The Organisational Development of the British Historical Profession, 1884–1921', *Bulletin of the Institute of Historical Research*, lv (1982), pp. 180–93; R. Soffer, 'Nation, Duty, Character and Confidence: History at Oxford, 1850–1914', *Historical Journal*, xxx (1987), p. 22; see also above, Chapter 1, pp. 77–104.

7. A.S. Green, 'Preface to the Illustrated Edition', and 'Introduction' to J.R. Green, *A Short History of the English People: Illustrated Edition* (2nd edn, London, 1902–03), i, pp. v–xxiii.

8. D. Cannadine, *G.M. Trevelyan: A Life in History* (London, 1992), pp. 109–14.

9. J.W. Burrow, *A Liberal Descent: Victorian Historians and the English Past* (Cambridge, 1981).

10. For some suggestive ideas, see P. Morgan, *A New History of Wales: The Eighteenth-Century Renaissance* (Llandybie, Glamorgan, 1981); and M. Ash, *The Strange Death of Scottish History* (Edinburgh, 1980).

11. W.C. Sellar and R.J. Yeatman, *1066 and All That* (London, 1930), p. 123. Cf. F. Fukuyama, *The End of History and the Last Man* (London, 1992).

12. A. Hastings, *The Construction of Nationhood, Ethnicity, Religion and Nationalism* (Cambridge, 1997), p. 37.

13. D. Cannadine, *In Churchill's Shadow: Confronting the Past in Modern Britain* (London, 2002), pp. 17–18; C. Harvie, 'The Politics of Devolution', in P. Addison and H. Jones (eds), *A Companion to Contemporary Britain, 1939–2000* (Oxford, 2005), pp. 427–31.

14. For the Longman series, see T.F. Tout, *From the Accession of Henry III to the Death of Edward III (1216–1377)* (London, 1920 edn), chs 8–11; and R. Lodge, *From the Restoration to the Death of William III (1660–1702)* (London, 1923 edn), chs 2, 3, 9, 13, 14. For the *Oxford History of England*, see R.G. Collingwood and J.N.L. Myers, *Roman Britain and the English Settlements* (Oxford, 1936), books 1–4; A.L. Poole, *From Domesday Book to Magna Carta, 1087–1216* (Oxford, 1951), ch. 9; F.M. Powicke, *The Thirteenth Century, 1216–1307* (Oxford, 1953), chs 9, 12; and G.N. Clark, *The Later Stuarts, 1660–1714* (Oxford, 1934), chs 12, 13.

15. A.J.P. Taylor, *English History, 1914–1945* (Oxford, 1965), pp. v–vi; K. Feiling, *A History of England* (London, 1949); G.N. Clark, *English History: A Survey* (Oxford, 1971).

16. C. Geertz, *Available Light: Anthropological Reflections on Philosophical Topics* (Princeton, 2000), pp. 231–45.

17. J. Breuilly, *Nationalism and the State* (2nd edn, Manchester, 1982); E. Gellner, *Nations and Nationalism* (Oxford, 1983); E.J. Hobsbawm, *Nations and Nationalism since 1870: Programme, Myth, Reality* (2nd edn, Cambridge, 1992); L. Greenfield, *Nationalism: Five Roads to Modernity* (Cambridge, Mass., 1992); Hastings, *Construction of Nationhood*.

18. F. Braudel, *The Identity of France* (2 vols, London, 1988–90); P. Burke, 'French Historians and their Cultural Identities', in E. Tonkin et al. (eds), *History and Ethnicity* (London, 1989), pp. 157–67; R. Gildea, *The Past in French History* (New Haven, 1994); R.J. Evans, 'The New Nationalism and the Old History: Perspectives on the West German *Historikerstreit*', *Journal of Modern History*, lix (1987), pp. 761–97; C.S. Maier, *The Unmasterable Past: History, Holocaust and German National Identity* (Cambridge, Mass., 1988); G. Eley, 'Nazism, Politics and the Image of the Past: Thoughts on the West German *Historikerstreit*', *Past & Present*, no. 121 (1988), pp. 171–208; H. James, *A German Identity, 1770–1990* (revised edn, London, 1990).

19. B. Anderson, *Imagined Communities: Reflections on the Origin and Spread of Nationalism* (London, 1983); P. Sahlins, *Boundaries: The Making of France and Spain in the Pyrenees* (Berkeley, 1989); D. Sayer, 'The Language of Nationality and the Nationality of Language: Prague, 1780–1920', *Past & Present*, no. 153 (1996), p. 182; idem, *The Coasts of Bohemia: A Czech History* (Princeton, 1998), pp. 29, 328 note 2.

20. For examples of such work, concerned with England, Wales, Scotland and Britain, see E.J. Hobsbawm and T. Ranger (eds), *The Invention of Tradition* (Cambridge, 1983); T. Curtis (ed.), *Wales: The Imagined Nation: Essays on Culture and National Identity* (Bridgend, 1986); D. Cannadine, *The Pleasures of the Past* (London, 1989); R. Samuel (ed.), *Patriotism: The Making and Unmaking*

of British National Identity (London, 1989); M.G.H. Pittock, *The Invention of Scotland: The Stuart Myth and the Scottish Identity, 1638 to the Present* (London, 1991); R. Porter (ed.), *Myths of the English* (Cambridge, 1992); and K. Robbins, *History, Religion and Identity in Modern Britain* (London, 1993).

21. Cannadine, *In Churchill's Shadow*, pp. 37–41.

22. L.J. Colley, 'Britishness and Otherness: An Argument'; J.G.A. Pocock, 'History and Sovereignty: The Historiographical Response to Europeanization in Two Cultures'; G. Eley, 'Culture, Britain and Europe': all in *Journal of British Studies*, xxxi (1992), pp. 309–29, 358–89, 390–414.

23. For contemporary polemics, see T. Nairn, *The Break-Up of Britain: Crisis and Neo-Nationalism* (London, 1977); T. Dalyell, *Devolution: The End of Britain?* (London, 1977). For more considered views, see V. Bogdanor, *Devolution* (Oxford, 1979); H.M. Drucker, *The Politics of Nationalism and Devolution* (London, 1980); J. Osmond, *The Divided Kingdom* (London, 1988); N. Evans (ed.), *National Identity in the British Isles* (Harlech, 1989); B. Crick (ed.), *National Identities: The Constitution of the United Kingdom* (Oxford, 1991). For historical treatment, see K.O. Morgan, *The People's Peace: British History, 1945–1989* (Oxford, 1990), pp. 367–75, 408–11; Harvie, 'The Politics of Devolution', pp. 434–35.

24. Morgan, *People's Peace*, p. 515; P.F. Clarke, *Hope and Glory: Britain 1900–2000* (London, 2004 edn), pp. 339–46.

25. For a vigorous protest against these developments, see G.R. Elton's (first) inaugural lecture, in 1968, as Professor of English Constitutional History at Cambridge, 'The future of the past': reprinted in G.R. Elton, *Return to Essentials: Some Reflections on the Present State of Historical Study* (Cambridge, 1991), pp. 75–98.

26. B. Lenman, 'The Teaching of Scottish History in the Scottish Universities', *Scottish Historical Review*, (1973), pp. 165–90; G. Williams, 'Local and National History in Wales', *Welsh History Review*, v (1970–71), pp. 45–56, T.W. Moody, 'The First Forty Years', *Irish Historical Studies*, xx (1977), pp. 377–83; R.F. Foster, 'History and the Irish Question', *Transactions of the Royal Historical Society*, 5th ser., xxxiii (1983), pp. 169–92; P. Jenkins, *A History of Modern Wales, 1536–1990* (London, 1992), pp. 407–29.

27. E.g., G. Williams, *A History of Modern Wales* (London, 1950); J.C. Beckett, *The Making of Modern Ireland* (London, 1966); R. Mitchison, *A History of Scotland* (London, 1970).

28. Reprinted in Elton, *Return to Essentials*, p. 112.

29. M. Hechter, *Internal Colonialism: The Celtic Fringe in British National Development* (Berkeley, 1975); K.O. Morgan (ed.), *The Oxford Illustrated History of Britain* (Oxford, 1984); C. Haigh (ed.), *The Cambridge Historical Encyclopaedia of Great Britain and Ireland* (Cambridge, 1985).

30. J.G.A. Pocock, 'British History: A Plea for a New Subject', *Journal of Modern History*, xlvii (1975), pp. 601–21; idem, 'The Limits and Divisions of British History: In Search of the Unknown Subject', *American Historical Review*, lxxxvii (1982), pp. 311–36. These, and his subsequent articles on the subject, have been collected in idem, *The Discovery of Islands: Essays in British History* (Cambridge, 2005).

31. Pocock, *Discovery of Islands*, pp. ix–x, 3–22; A.J.P. Taylor, 'Comments', *Journal of Modern History*, xlvii (1975), pp. 622–3; A.H. Williamson, 'Scotland and the British Revolutions', *Scottish Historical Review*, lxxiii (1994), p. 126.

32. R.R. Davies, 'In Praise of British History', in R.R. Davies (ed.), *The British Isles 1100–1500: Comparisons, Contrasts and Connections* (Edinburgh, 1988), p. 9.

33. C. Russell, 'John Bull's Other Nations', *Times Literary Supplement*, 12 March 1993, pp. 3–4.

34. R.R. Davies, *Domination and Conquest: The Experience of Ireland, Scotland and Wales 1100–1300* (Cambridge, 1990); C. Russell, 'The British Problem and the English Civil War', *History*, lxxii (1987), pp. 395–415; idem, 'The British Background to the Irish Rebellion of 1641', *Historical Research*, lxi (1988), pp. 166–82; idem, *The Fall of the British Monarchies, 1637–1642* (Oxford, 1991); idem, *The Causes of the English Civil War* (Oxford, 1991). For other work from this time in a similar vein, see: R. Frame, *The Political Development of the British Isles 1100–1400* (Oxford, 1990); J. Wormald, 'The Creation of Britain: Multiple Kingdoms or Core and Colonies?', *Transactions of the Royal Historical Society*, 6th ser., ii (1992), pp. 175–94; J. Morrill (ed.), *The Scottish National Covenant in its British Context* (Edinburgh, 1990); and B.P. Levack, *The Formation of the British State: England, Scotland and the Union, 1603–1707* (Oxford, 1987).

35. J.G.A. Pocock (ed.), *Three British Revolutions: 1641, 1688, 1776* (Princeton, 1980); idem (ed.), *The Varieties of British Political Thought, 1500–1800* (Cambridge, 1993); K.R. Andrews, N.P. Canny and P.E.H. Hair (eds), *The Westwards Enterprise: English Activities in Ireland, the Atlantic and America, 1480–1650* (Liverpool, 1978); N. Canny, *Kingdom and Colony: Ireland in the Atlantic World, 1560–1800* (Baltimore, 1988); N. Canny and A. Pagden (eds), *Colonial Identity in the Atlantic World, 1500–1800* (Princeton, 1987); J.P. Greene, *Peripheries and Center: Constitutional Development in the Extended Polities of the British Empire and United States, 1607–1788* (Athens, Georgia, 1986); idem, *Pursuits of Happiness: The Social Development of Early Modern British Colonies and the Formation of American Culture* (New York, 1988); B. Bailyn, *The Peopling of British North America* (New York, 1986); idem, *Voyagers to the West* (New York, 1986); D.H. Fischer, *Albion's Seed: Four British Folkways in America* (New York, 1989); B. Bailyn and P.D. Morgan (eds), *Strangers Within the Realm: Cultural Margins of the First British Empire* (Chapel Hill, North Carolina, 1991); D. Armitage, 'The Cromwellian Protectorate and the Language of Empire', *Historical Journal*, xxxv (1992), pp. 531–55; J.C.D. Clark, *The Language of Liberty, 1660–1832: Political Discourse and Social Dynamics in the Anglo-American World* (Cambridge, 1994).

36. C.A. Bayly, *Indian Society and the Making of the British Empire* (Cambridge, 1988); idem, *Imperial Meridian: The British Empire and the World, 1780–1830* (London, 1989); P.J. Marshall, *Problems of Empire: Britain and India, 1757–1813* (London, 1968); idem, *Bengal, the British Bridgehead* (Cambridge, 1987); L.J. Colley, *Britons: Forging the Nation, 1707–1837* (London, 1992).

37. L. Kennedy, *Colonialism, Religion and Nationalism in Ireland* (Belfast, 1996); M. Pittock, *Inventing and Resisting Britain: Cultural Identities in Britain and Ireland, 1685–1789* (Basingstoke, 1997). For more recent work on this

subject, see S. Howe, *Ireland and Empire: Colonial Legacies in Irish History and Culture* (Oxford, 2000); K. Kenny (ed.), *Ireland and the British Empire* (Oxford, 2004); T. McDonagh (ed.), *Was Ireland a Colony? Economics, Politics and Culture in Nineteenth-Century Ireland* (Dublin, 2005); D. Lloyd, 'Regarding Ireland in a Post-Colonial Frame', *Cultural Studies*, xv (2001), pp. 12–32; J. Cleary, 'Amongst Empires: A Short History of Ireland and Empire Studies in International Context', *Eire-Ireland*, xlii (2007), pp. 11–57.

38. K. Robbins, *Nineteenth-Century Britain: Integration and Diversity* (Oxford, 1988); P.J. Cain and A.G. Hopkins, *British Imperialism*, vol. i: *Innovation and Expansion, 1688–1914*; vol. ii: *Crisis and Deconstruction, 1914–1990* (London, 1993). For another attempt to write British history in the modern era, see D. Cannadine, *The Decline and Fall of the British Aristocracy* (New Haven, 1990).

39. For the impact of Pocock's paradigm on the modern history of the British Empire, see below, Chapter 9, pp. 217–18.

40. Colley, *Britons*; Robbins, *Nineteenth-Century Britain*.

41. H. Kearney, *The British Isles: A History of Four Nations* (Cambridge, 1989).

42. Colley, 'Britishness and Otherness', pp. 313–16. For some valuable works of comparative history, dealing with some, but not all, of the 'four nations', see L.M. Cullen and T.C. Smout (eds), *Comparative Aspects of Scottish and Irish Economic and Social History, 1600–1900* (Edinburgh, 1977); T.M. Devine and D. Dickson (eds), *Ireland and Scotland, 1600–1850: Parallels and Contrasts in Economic and Social Development* (Edinburgh, 1983); R.A. Mason (ed.), *Scotland and England, 1286–1815* (Edinburgh, 1987); and K. Wrightson, 'Kindred Adjoining Kingdoms: An English Perspective on the Social and Economic History of Early Modern Scotland', in R.A. Houston and I.D. Whyte (eds), *Scottish Society, 1500–1800* (Cambridge, 1989), pp. 245–60.

43. Kearney, *British Isles*, pp. 1–9. For some suggestive hints, see H.M. Jewell, *The North–South Divide: The Origins of Northern Consciousness in England* (Manchester, 1994).

44. Pocock, 'Limits and Divisions of British History', pp. 317–18.

45. See above, Chapter 1, pp. 25–6.

46. J. Davies, *A History of Wales* (London, 1993); M. Lynch, *Scotland: A New History* (London, 1991); R.F. Foster, *Modern Ireland, 1600–1972* (London, 1988).

47. R. Mitchison, *Why Scottish History Matters* (Edinburgh, 1993), p. i.

48. Though, slightly earlier, the decade 1965–75 saw the publication of the four-volume *Edinburgh History of Scotland*.

49. G.R. Elton, *The English* (Oxford, 1992), esp. pp. 213–14, 233–5; idem, *Return to Essentials*, especially pp. 110–15. Interestingly, one of Elton's last editorial projects was to preside over the inauguration of a multi-volume *History of the Modern British Isles*. For other studies of England dating from this time, see R. Colls and P. Dodds (eds), *Englishness: Politics and Culture, 1880–1920* (Beckenham, Kent, 1986); and G. Newman, *The Rise of English Nationalism: A Cultural History, 1740–1830* (London, 1987).

50. J. Roberts, 'General Editor's Preface', in P. Langford, *A Polite and Commercial People: England, 1727–1783* (Oxford, 1989), pp. vii–viii.

51. K.M. Brown, 'British History: A Sceptical Comment', in R.G. Ash (ed.), *Three Nations: A Common History? England, Scotland, Ireland and British History, c1600–1920* (Bochum, 1993), pp. 117–27.

52. For discussions of these separate histories and historiographies, see Mitchison, *Why Scottish History Matters*; G. Donaldson, *Scottish History: Approaches and Reflections* (Edinburgh, 1994); B. Bradshaw, 'Nationalism and Historical Scholarship in Modern Ireland', *Irish Historical Studies*, xxvi (1989), pp. 329–51; S.G. Ellis, 'Historiographical Debate: Representations of the Past in Ireland: Whose Past and Whose Present?', *Irish Historical Studies*, xxvii (1991), pp. 289–308; N. Evans, 'Debate: British History: Past, Present – and Future?', *Past & Present*, no. 119 (1988), pp. 194–203; and R. Merfyn Jones, 'Beyond Identity: The Reconstruction of the Welsh', *Journal of British Studies*, xxxi (1992), pp. 330–57.

53. For two interim discussions, see: A.H. Williamson, 'From the Invention of Great Britain to the Creation of British History: A New Historiography', *Journal of British Studies*, xxix (1990), pp. 267–76; D. Hirst, 'The English Republic and the Meaning of Britain', *Journal of Modern History*, lxvi (1994), pp. 451–86.

54. See above, Chapter 4, pp. 103–11, and below, Chapter 10, pp. 258–69.

55. H. Young, *The Iron Lady: A Biography of Margaret Thatcher* (New York, 1990), p. 528; Thatcher, *Downing Street Years*, pp. 618–24; Harvie, 'Politics of Devolution', pp. 435–6.

56. J. Major, *The Autobiography* (London, 2000 edn), p. 424.

57. Ibid., pp. 415–16, 421.

58. T. Blair, *New Britain: My Vision of a Young Country* (London, 1996), pp. 259–76; L. Andrews, 'New Labour, New England?', in M. Perryman (ed.), *The Blair Agenda* (London, 1996), pp. 125–46; N. Ascherson, 'National Identity', in G. Radice (ed.), *What Needs to Change: New Visions for Britain* (London, 1996), pp. 82–95.

59. Blair, *New Britain*, p. 261; Clarke, *Hope and Glory*, pp. 432–3.

60. T.C. Smout (ed.), *Anglo-Scottish Relations from 1603 to 1900* (Oxford, 2005); W.L. Miller (ed.), *Anglo-Scottish Relations from 1900 to Devolution and Beyond* (Oxford, 2005); see also the *Transactions of the Royal Historical Society*, 6th ser., x (2000), devoted to the Anglo-Irish Union.

61. J. Mohan (ed.), *A United Kingdom? Economic, Social and Political Geographies* (London, 1999), pp. 160–4, 176–9; R. Hazell (ed.), *The State and the Nations: The First Year of Devolution in the United Kingdom* (Devon, 2000).

62. Major, *Autobiography*, pp. 429–30, 739–41; Harvie, 'Politics of Devolution', pp. 438–41; P. Ashdown, *The Ashdown Diaries*, vol. ii, *1997–1999* (London, 2001), pp. 93, 439–49, esp. p. 446.

63. This was an especially pronounced theme in many of the speeches of Enoch Powell: see Nairn, *Break-Up of Britain*, pp. 256–91.

64. Elton, *The English*, pp. 233–5; R. Blake, *The Conservative Party from Peel to Churchill* (London, 1970), p. 273; idem (ed.), *The English World: History, Character and People* (New York, 1982).

65. R.R. Davies, *The First English Empire: Power and Identities in the British Isles, 1093–1343* (Oxford, 2000), p. v.

66. R.R. Davies, *The Matter of Britain and the Matter of England* (Oxford, 1998); idem, *First English Empire*; D. Carpenter, *The Struggle for Mastery: Britain,*

1066–1284 (London, 2004); M. Nicholls, *A History of the Modern British Isles, 1529–1603: The Two Kingdoms* (Oxford, 1999); D.L. Smith, *A History of the Modern British Isles, 1603–1707: The Double Crown* (Oxford, 1998); J. Smyth, *The Making of the United Kingdom, 1660–1800: State, Religion and Identity in Britain and Ireland* (London, 2001); A. Murdoch, *British History, 1660–1832: National Identity and Local Culture* (Basingstoke, 1998); N. Davies, *These Isles* (London, 1999). See also H. Kearney, *The British Isles: A History of Four Nations* (2nd edn, Cambridge, 2006); F. Welsh, *The Four Nations* (London, 2002).

67. B. Bradshaw and J. Morrill (eds), *The British Problem, c1534–1707* (London, 1996); L. Brockliss and D. Eastwood (eds), *A Union of Multiple Identities: The British Isles, c1750–c1850* (Manchester, 1997); R.J. Young (ed.), *Celtic Dimensions of the British Civil Wars* (Edinburgh, 1997); B. Bradshaw and P. Roberts (eds), *British Consciousness and Identity: The Making of Britain, 1533–1707* (Cambridge, 1998); T. Claydon and I. McBride (eds), *Protestantism and National Identity: Britain and Ireland, c.1650–1850* (Cambridge, 1998); J.P. Kenyon and J. Ohlmeyer (eds), *The Civil Wars: A Military History of England, Scotland and Ireland* (Oxford, 1998); G. Burgess (ed.), *The New British History: Founding a Modern State, 1603–1715* (London, 1999); S.J. Connolly (ed.), *Kingdoms United? Great Britain and Ireland since 1500* (Dublin, 1999); C. Kidd, *British Identities Before Nationalism: Ethnicity and Nationhood in the Atlantic World, 1600–1800* (Cambridge, 1999); A. Macinnes and J.H. Ohlmeyer (eds), *The Stuart Kingdoms in the Seventeenth Century: Awkward Neighbours* (Dublin, 2002); J. Hoppit (ed.), *Parliaments, Nations and Identities in Britain and Ireland* (Manchester, 2003); E. Longley, E. Hughes and D. O'Rawe (eds), *Ireland (Ulster) Scotland: Concepts, Contexts, Comparisons* (Belfast, 2003); W. Kelley and J. Young (eds), *Ulster and Scotland, 1600–2000: History, Language and Identity* (Dublin, 2004).

68. K. Brown, 'Seducing the Scottish Clio: Has Scottish History Anything to Fear from the New British History?', in Burgess, *The New British History*, pp. 238–65; T. Claydon, 'Problems with the British Problem', *Parliamentary History*, xvi (1997), pp. 221–7; P. O'Leary, 'Historians and the "New" British History', in P. Lambert and P. Schofield (eds), *Making History: An Introduction to the History and Practices of a Discipline* (London, 2004), pp. 215–26.

69. S. Collini, *English Pasts* (Oxford, 1999), pp. 3–4; J.C.D. Clark, *Our Shadowed Present: Modernism, Postmodernism and History* (London, 2003), pp. 59–109; P. Mandler, *The English National Character: The History of an Idea from Edmund Burke to Tony Blair* (London, 2006), p. 4; J.P. Parry, *The Politics of Patriotism: English Liberalism, National Identity and Europe, 1830–1886* (Cambridge, 2006).

70. Pocock, *Discovery of Islands*, esp. pp. 269–88.

71. J. Black, *Convergence or Divergence? Britain and the Continent* (London, 1994); T. Claydon, *Europe and the Making of England, 1660–1760* (Cambridge, 2007), esp. pp. 1–12; M. Peters, 'Early Hanoverian Consciousness: Empire or Europe?', *English Historical Review*, cxxii (2007), pp. 632–68; N. Harding, *Hanover and the British Empire, 1700–1837* (Woodbridge, 2007); D. Howarth, *The Invention of Spain: Cultural Relations between Britain and Spain, 1770–1870*

(Manchester, 2007); B. Simms, *Three Victories and a Defeat: The Rise and Fall of the First British Empire, 1714–1783* (London, 2007).

72. R. Connors and J.R.D. Falconer, 'Cornering the Cheshire Cat: Reflections on the "New British History" and Studies in Early Modern British Identities', *Canadian Journal of History*, xxxvi (2001), pp. 85–108; J. Ohlmeyer, 'The "Old" British Histories?', *Historical Journal*, l (2007), pp. 499–512.

CHAPTER 8, DOMINION, pp. 196–213

1. I am grateful to Professor Ged Martin for kindly inviting me to deliver the lecture on which this chapter is based, and also for his subsequent comments and suggestions. The original lecture was entitled 'Imperial Canada', but I am embarrassed to admit that I agreed to the invitation having misheard these words on the telephone as 'Imperial Cannadine'. I should also express my thanks to the late Professor Robin Winks of Yale University for his help, advice and encouragement and, more recently, to Roy and Lee MacLaren and Dr Andrew Smith.

2. Walter Bagehot, *Physics and Politics* (London, 1887), chs 3 and 4 on 'Nation-Making'; E. Weber, *Peasants into Frenchmen: The Modernization of Rural France, 1870–1914* (Stanford, 1976); E.J. Hobsbawm, *The Age of Empire, 1875–1914* (London, 1987), pp. 142–64. See also above, Chapter 7, pp. 173–4.

3. J.H. Elliott, 'A Europe of Composite Monarchies', *Past & Present*, no. 137 (1992), pp. 48–71; C. Russell, *The Causes of the English Civil War* (Oxford, 1990), pp. 26–57.

4. R. Hyam, *Britain's Imperial Century, 1815–1914* (London, 1976), p. 15.

5. C. Bridge, *Holding India to the Empire: The British Conservative Party and the 1935 Constitution* (Delhi, 1986); R.L. Watts, *New Federations: Experiments in the Commonwealth* (Oxford, 1966).

6. For a witty discussion of the general problem of boundaries in North America, see J. Garreau, *The Nine Nations of North America* (New York, 1981). The most suggestive historical treatment of the relationship between national identity and national borders is P. Sahlins, *Boundaries: The Making of France and Spain in the Pyrenees* (Berkeley, 1989).

7. K. McNaught, *The Pelican History of Canada* (Harmondsworth, 1982 edn), pp. 7–20; cf. Goldwin Smith, *Canada and the Canadian Question*, ed. C. Berger (Toronto, 1971), for a similar analysis made in 1891.

8. R. Fisher, *Contact and Conflict: Indian–European Relations in British Columbia, 1774–1890* (Vancouver, 1977); A. Perry, *On the Edge of Empire: Gender, Race and the Making of British Columbia, 1849–1871* (Toronto, 2001); R. Rudin, *Making History in Twentieth-Century Quebec* (Toronto, 1997).

9. J.L. Granatstein, *Who Killed Canadian History?* (Toronto, 1998).

10. N. Mansergh, *The Commonwealth Experience* (2nd edn, 2 vols, London, 1982), vol. i, p. 59.

11. M. Chamberlain, 'Canada's International Status', in C.C. Eldridge (ed.), *From Rebellion to Patriation: Canada and Britain in the Nineteenth and Twentieth Centuries* (Cardiff, 1989), pp. 82–90.

12. J.L. Granatstein, *How Britain's Weakness Forced Canada into the Arms of the United States* (Toronto, 1989); J.L. Granatstein and N. Hillmer, *For Better or For Worse: Canada and the United States to the 1990s* (Toronto, 1991).

13. J. Smith, N. Nevitte and A. Kornberg, 'National Images of Canada and the United States: Their Structure, Coherence and Meaning', *American Review of Canadian Studies*, xx (1990), pp. 327–56. For a recent re-statement of Americans' generally hostile bewilderment about Canada see M.T. Kaufman, 'O Canada, Oh, Canada. Oh...', *New York Times*, 16 April 1995.

14. For two studies which emphatically revise the importance of these episodes downwards, see G. Martin, *The Durham Report and British Policy: A Critical Essay* (Cambridge, 1973); idem, *Britain and the Origins of Canadian Confederation, 1837–67* (London, 1995).

15. R. Davies, *One Half of Robertson Davies* (Toronto, 1977), pp. 272–3.

16. B. Anderson, *Imagined Communities: Reflections on the Origin and Spread of Nationalism* (rev. edn, London, 1991), p. 6; H. Seton-Watson, *Nations and States: An Enquiry into the Origins of Nations and the Politics of Nationalism* (Boulder, 1977), pp. 227–32; G. Paquet and J-P. Wallot, 'Nouvelle-France/Quebec/Canada: A World of Limited Identities', in N. Canny and A. Pagden (eds), *Colonial Identity in the Atlantic World, 1500–1800* (Princeton, 1987), pp. 95–114; P.W. Bennett and C.J. Jaenen (eds), *Emerging Identities: Selected Problems and Interpretations in Canadian History* (Scarborough, Ontario, 1986). See also E.J. Hobsbawm, *Nations and Nationalism since 1780: Programme, Myth, Reality* (2nd edn, Cambridge, 1992), p. 78: 'the mere setting up of a state is not sufficient in itself to create a nation'.

17. R. MacNeil, 'Looking For My Country', *American Review of Canadian Studies*, xxi (1991), p. 410.

18. This is well demonstrated by both the titles and the contents of two special issues of *Daedalus*: vol. 114 (1985), 'Australia: Terra Incognita?', and vol. 117 (1988), 'In Search of Canada'. It is also worth noting that in this context, New Zealand has always played Canada to Australia's United States.

19. A.R.M. Lower, *Colony to Nation: A History of Canada* (Toronto, 1946); D.G. Creighton, *Dominion of the North: A History of Canada* (Boston, 1944); idem, *John A. Macdonald* (2 vols, Toronto, 1952–55).

20. C. Berger, *The Writing of Canadian History: Aspects of English-Canadian Historical Writing since 1900* (2nd edn, Toronto, 1986), pp. 112–36, 208–37.

21. Ibid., pp. 259–320.

22. J.M. Bumsted, *The Peoples of Canada: A Pre-Confederation History* (Toronto, 1992), pp. xi–xii; idem, *The Peoples of Canada: A Post-Confederation History* (Toronto, 1992), pp. xiii.

23. Mansergh, *Commonwealth Experience*, vol. i, pp. 63–6.

24. See below, Chapter 9, pp. 215–20.

25. For the fullest recent discussion of the British financing of post-Confederation Canada, see P.J. Cain and A.G. Hopkins, *British Imperialism*, vol. i, *Innovation and Expansion, 1688–1914* (London, 1993), pp. 258–73.

26. For two early biographies, which discuss and debate Strathcona's life and work in the context of imperial Canada, see: W.T.R. Preston, *Strathcona and the Making of Canada* (New York, 1915); B. Willson, *The Life of Lord Strathcona and Mount Royal, GCMG, GCVO* (2 vols, New York, 1915). See also the review

by G.M. Wrong in *American Historical Review*, xxi (1915–16), pp. 804–6. For the most recent study, see D. McDonald, *Lord Strathcona: A Biography of Donald Alexander Smith* (Toronto, 1996).

27. G.P. Marchildon, *Profits and Politics: Beaverbrook and the Gilded Age of Canadian Finance* (Toronto, 1996); D. Cannadine, *History in Our Time* (London, 1998), pp. 243–9.

28. Sir R. Syme, *The Roman Revolution* (Oxford, 1939), pp. 10–27, 78–96, 350–68, 500–8; idem, *Rome, Spain and the Americas* (London, 1958), pp. 4, 13; D. Cannadine, *Aspects of Aristocracy: Grandeur and Decline in Modern Britain* (London, 1994), pp. 109–10.

29. D. Cannadine, *The Decline and Fall of the British Aristocracy* (London, 1990), pp. 588–601; A.H.M. Kirk-Greene, 'The Governors-General of Canada, 1867–1952: A Collective Profile', *Journal of Canadian Studies*, xii (1977), pp. 35–57.

30. R.H. Hubbard, *Rideau Hall: An Illustrated History of Government House, Ottawa* (Montreal, 1977), pp. 19–147; B.J. Messamore, 'The Social and Cultural Role of the Governors-General, 1888–1911: British Imperialists and Canadian "Nationalists"', in C.M. Coates (ed.), *Imperial Canada, 1867–1917* (Edinburgh, 1997), pp. 78–108; D.W. Thomson, 'The Fate of Titles in Canada', *Canadian Historical Review*, x (1929), pp. 236–46.

31. W.A. Henry, 'Royal Representation, Ceremony and Cultural Identity in the Building of the Canadian Nation, 1860–1912' (unpublished Ph.D. dissertation, University of British Columbia, 2001).

32. N. Frankland, *Witness of a Century: The Life and Times of Prince Arthur, Duke of Connaught, 1850–1942* (London, 1993), pp. 269–353.

33. I. Radforth, *Royal Spectacle: The 1860 Visit of the Prince of Wales to Canada and the United States* (Toronto, 2004); P. Buckner, 'Casting Daylight Upon Magic: Deconstructing the Royal Tour of 1901 to Canada', in C. Bridge and K. Fedorowich (eds), *The British World: Diaspora, Culture and Identity* (London, 2003), pp. 158–89.

34. K. Munro, 'The Crown and French Canada: The Role of the Governors-General in Making the Crown Relevant, 1867–1917', in Coates, *Imperial Canada*, pp. 109–17; W.A. Henry, 'Imagining the Great White Mother and the Great King: Aboriginal Tradition and Royal Representation at the "Great Pow-wow" of 1901', *Journal of the Canadian Historical Association*, new ser., ix (2000), pp. 87–108.

35. J. Morris, *Pax Britannica: The Climax of an Empire* (New York, 1968), p. 391.

36. D. Cole, 'The Problem of "Nationalism" and "Imperialism" in British Settlement Colonies', *Journal of British Studies*, x (1971), p. 172.

37. Ibid., pp. 161–82; C. Berger (ed.), *Imperialism and Nationalism, 1884–1914: A Conflict in Canadian Thought* (Toronto, 1969).

38. Bumsted, *Post-Confederation History*, p. 151. This case was eloquently made by G.M. Wrong, 'The Growth of Nationalism Within the British Empire', *American Historical Review*, xxii (1916–17), pp. 45–57.

39. Berger, *Writing of Canadian History*, p. 276; J. English, *The Decline of Politics: The Conservatives and the Party System, 1901–1920* (Toronto, 1977), esp. pp. 52–88.

40. P.J. Cain and A.G. Hopkins, *British Imperialism*, vol. ii, *Crisis and Deconstruction, 1914–1990* (1993), pp. 138–45.

41. P.G. Wigley, *Canada and the Transition to Commonwealth: British–Canadian Relations, 1917–1926* (Cambridge, 1977); N. Hillmer, *Britain and Canada in the Age of Mackenzie King*, part i, 'The Outstanding Imperialist': Mackenzie King and the British (London, 1979), pp. 8–9; D.N. Dilks, *Britain and Canada in the Age of Mackenzie King*, part ii, *Britain, Canada and the Wider World* (London, 1979), pp. 17–19; J.L. Granatstein, *Canada's War: The Politics of the Mackenzie King Government, 1939–1945* (Toronto, 1975).

42. F. Donaldson, *Edward VIII* (London, 1974), pp. 69–72, 135; P. Ziegler, *King Edward VIII: The Official Biography* (London, 1990), pp. 114–24, 148–54, 186–8; J.W. Wheeler-Bennett, *King George VI: His Life and Reign* (London, 1958), pp. 371–94; S. Bradford, *King George VI* (London, 1989), pp. 281–90.

43. Hubbard, *Rideau Hall*, pp. 181–208; J. Adam Smith, *John Buchan: A Biography* (Oxford, 1985), pp. 401–3; T. MacDonnell, *Daylight Upon Magic: The Royal Tour of Canada – 1939* (Toronto, 1989).

44. A. Buchan, 'A Memoir', in P. Lyon (ed.), *Britain and Canada: Survey of a Changing Relationship* (London, 1976), p. 32.

45. Berger, *Writing of Canadian History*, p. 131; Adam Smith, *John Buchan*, pp. 422–4.

46. G. Ignatieff, 'Vincent Massey', in *Dictionary of National Biography, 1961–1970*, pp. 739–41; Hubbard, *Rideau Hall*, pp. 219–26; V. Massey, *What's Past is Prologue: The Memoirs of Vincent Massey* (Toronto, 1963), pp. 456–507; idem, *Canadians and their Commonwealth* (Oxford, 1992); C. Bissell, *The Imperial Canadian: Vincent Massey in Office* (Toronto, 1986).

47. M. Peterman, *Robertson Davies* (Boston, 1986), pp. 82, 122; J. Skelton Grant (ed.), *Robertson Davies: The Well-Tempered Critic* (Toronto, 1981), p. 124; J. Madison Davis (ed.), *Conversations with Robertson Davies* (Jackson, Miss., 1989), p. xv.

48. R. Davies, *The Cunning Man* (New York, 1994), p. 468; Madison Davis, *Conversations with Robertson Davies*, pp. 74–5, 190, 195.

49. J.M. Bumsted, review of the second volume of Bissell's biography in *Canadian Historical Review*, lxviii (1987), pp. 297–9; Peterman, *Robertson Davies*, p. 127; Madison Davis, *Conversations with Robertson Davies*, pp. xi–xii, 100, 117, 169; J. Carol Oates, 'One Half of Robertson Davies by Robertson Davies', in E. Cameron (ed.), *Robertson Davies: An Appreciation* (Peterborough, Ontario, 1991), p. 181; see also the entry on Davies by R. MacLaren in the *Oxford Dictionary of National Biography*, vol. xv, pp. 400–2.

50. D.K. Adams (ed.), *Britain and Canada in the 1990s* (Aldershot, 1992); J.E. Igartua, *The Other Quiet Revolution: National Identities in English Canada, 1945–71* (Vancouver, 2006).

51. C. Coates (ed.), *Majesty in Canada* (Dundurn, 2006).

52. For some recent studies, see J.L. Granatstein and K. McNaught (eds), *'English Canada' Speaks Out* (Toronto, 1991); R.A. Young, *The Secession of Quebec and the Future of Canada* (Montreal, 1995); D. Johnston, *If Quebec Goes* (Montreal, 1995).

53. MacNeil, 'Looking For My Country', pp. 412–13.

54. See, in particular, the essays in P. Buckner (ed.), *Canada and the End of Empire* (Vancouver, 2005); P. Buckner and R.D. Francis (eds), *Canada and the British World: Culture, Migration and Identity* (Vancouver, 2006).

55. For similar arguments from, respectively, a South Asian and Australian standpoint, see C.A. Bayly, 'Returning the British to South Asian History: The Limits of Colonial Hegemony', *South Asia*, xvii (1994), pp. 1–25; L. Trainor, *British Imperialism and Australian Nationalism: Manipulation, Conflict and Compromise in the Late Nineteenth Century* (Cambridge, 1995); N. Meaney, 'Britishness and Australian Identity: The Problem of Nationalism in Australian History and Historiography', *Australian Historical Studies*, xxxii (2001), pp. 76–90; idem, Britishness and Australia: Some Reflections', *Journal of Imperial and Commonwealth History*, xxxi (2003), pp. 121–35. For a general argument, see P. Buckner, 'Whatever Happened to the British Empire?', *Journal of the Canadian Historical Association*, new ser., iv (1993), pp. 3–32.

56. R. MacLaren, *Commissions High: Canada in London, 1870–1971* (Montreal, 2006), pp. 232–4.

57. D. Dilks, *The Great Dominion: Winston Churchill in Canada, 1900–1954* (Toronto, 2005), opens up some suggestive perspectives.

58. P.T. Marsh, *Joseph Chamberlain: Entrepreneur in Politics* (London, 1994), pp. 226, 293, 448; Dilks, *The Great Dominion*, pp. 1, 427.

59. B. Porter, *The Absent-Minded Imperialists: What the British Really Thought About Empire* (Oxford, 2004).

60. Many of these issues have now been explicitly addressed in P. Buckner (ed.), *Canada and the British Empire* (Oxford, 2008). For a comparative study of another former dominion, see D.M. Schreuder and S. Ward (eds), *Australia's Empire* (Oxford, 2008). Both of these volumes form part of the companion series to W.R. Louis (ed.), *The Oxford History of the British Empire* (5 vols, Oxford, 1998–99).

CHAPTER 9, EMPIRE, pp. 214–34

1. This chapter began life as an essay for a special issue of *Common Knowledge*, and I am grateful to the editors for their initial invitation and subsequent comments. Earlier versions have also been given at symposia held at the Australian National University in Canberra, and the University of Chapel Hill in North Carolina. I am also indebted to Professor J.G.A. Pocock for his advice and encouragement.

2. Calculated and extrapolated from G. Barraclough (ed.), *The Times Atlas of World History* (London, 1984). For the continuing challenges of the subject, see also L.J. Colley, 'What Is Imperial History Now?', in D. Cannadine (ed.), *What Is History Now?* (Basingstoke, 2002), pp. 132–47.

3. For two conspicuous, honourable and recent exceptions to this, which seek to de-parochialize the British and American empires, see C.S. Maier, *Among Empires: American Ascendancy and its Predecessors* (Cambridge, Mass., 2006); J. Darwin, *After Tamerlane: The Global History of Empire* (London, 2007).

4. J. Holland Rose, A.P. Newton and E.A. Benians (eds), *The Cambridge History of the British Empire* (8 vols, Cambridge, 1929–59).

5. P.N.S. Mansergh, *The Commonwealth Experience* (London, 1969); D.K. Fieldhouse, 'Can Humpty-Dumpty be Put Together Again?', *Journal of Imperial and Commonwealth History*, xii (1984), pp. 9–23; B.R. Tomlinson, '"The Contraction of England": National Decline and the Loss of Empire', *Journal of Imperial and Commonwealth History*, xi (1982), pp. 58–72; D.A. Low, *'The Contraction of England'* (Cambridge, 1984); R. Oliver, 'The Battle for African History', in W.R. Louis (ed.), *Still More Adventures with Britannia: Personalities, Politics and Culture in Britain* (London, 2003), pp. 285–98.

6. D. Cannadine, 'The Empire Strikes Back', *Past & Present*, no. 147 (1995), esp. pp. 190–1.

7. A. Briggs, *Victorian Cities* (Harmondsworth, 1968), pp. 277–301; E.J. Hobsbawm, *Industry and Empire: An Economic History of Britain since 1750* (London, 1968); idem, *The Age of Empire, 1875–1914* (London, 1987).

8. D. Cannadine, 'British History: Past, Present – and Future?', *Past & Present*, no. 116 (1987), pp. 170–5; see also above, Chapter 4, pp. 97–103, below Chapter 10, pp. 237–42.

9. See above, Chapter 7, pp. 178–82.

10. B. Bailyn, 'Preface', in D. Armitage and M.J. Braddick (eds), *The British Atlantic World, 1500–1800* (Basingstoke, 2002), pp. xvii–xix, gives figures for scholars migrating from the United Kingdom to the United States, and also discusses the intellectual consequences.

11. See above, Chapter 7, pp. 183–4, and especially the references cited at note 30. See also D. Armitage, 'Greater Britain: A Useful Category for Historical Analysis?', *American Historical Review*, civ (1999), pp. 427–43.

12. NACBS Report on the State and Future of British Studies in North America (1999), at http://www.nacbs.org/NACB/report.html, esp. pp. 6–13.

13. A. Burton, *After the Imperial Turn: Thinking With and Through the Nation* (Durham, NC, 2003).

14. L. Stone (ed.), *An Imperial State at War: Britain from 1689 to 1875* (London, 1994).

15. J. Black, *The British Seaborne Empire* (London, 2004); L.J. Colley, *Captives: Britain, Empire and the World, 1600–1850* (London, 2002); N. Ferguson, *Empire: How Britain Made the Modern World* (London, 2002); C. Hall, *Civilising Subjects: Metropole and Colony in the English Imagination, 1830–1867* (Chicago, 2002); K. Wilson, *The Island Race: Englishness, Gender and Empire in the Eighteenth Century* (London, 2003).

16. W.R. Louis (ed.), *The Oxford History of the British Empire* (5 vols, Oxford, 1998–99); D. Kennedy, 'Imperial History and Postcolonial Theory', *Journal of Imperial and Commonwealth History*, xiv (1996), pp. 345–63; idem, 'The Boundaries of Oxford's Empire', *International History Review*, xxiii (2001), pp. 604–22; S. Howe, 'The Slow Death and Strange Rebirths of Imperial History', *Journal of Imperial and Commonwealth History*, xix (2001), pp. 131–41.

17. E. Said, *Orientalism* (New York, 1978); idem, *Culture and Imperialism* (New York, 1993).

18. For recent compilations, see: C. Hall (ed.), *Cultures of Empire* (Manchester, 2000); N. Lazarus (ed.), *The Cambridge Companion to Postcolonial Literary Studies* (Cambridge, 2004); K. Wilson (ed.), *A New Imperial History: Culture,*

Identity and Modernity in Britain and the Empire, 1660–1840 (Cambridge, 2004).

19. See above, Chapter 7, p. 194, and the references cited at note 70.

20. D. Cameron Watt, *Succeeding John Bull: America in Britain's Place, 1900–1975* (Cambridge, 1984).

21. W.R. Louis, *Imperialism at Bay: The United States and the Decolonization of the British Empire, 1941–1945* (New York, 1978).

22. H. Pelling, *America and the British Left: From Bright to Bevan* (New York, 1957); J. Charmley, *Churchill's Grand Alliance: The Anglo-American Special Relationship, 1940–57* (London, 1995).

23. See above, Prologue, pp. 9–12.

24. N. Pyke, 'Schools ignore it – but is it time for the empire to strike back?', *The Guardian*, 5 July 2003. See also the comments by the then Chancellor of the Exchequer, Gordon Brown, calling for an 'end to Empire guilt': *The Times*, 15 March 2005.

25. Quoted in N. Ferguson, *Colossus: The Price of America's Empire* (New York, 2004), p. 7.

26. Despite a lack of political or popular recognition of this fact, the literature on the American Empire, in both its guises, is substantial, and growing: for recent works, in addition to Ferguson, see M. Hudson, *Super Imperialism: The Origin and Fundamentals of US World Dominance* (New York, 2003); A.J. Bacevich, *American Empire: The Realities and Consequences of US Diplomacy* (Cambridge, 2002); C.A. Johnson, *Blowback: The Costs and Consequences of American Empire* (New York, 2000).

27. R.A. Billington, *Westward Expansion: A History of the American Frontier* (New York, 5th edition, 1967); C.A. Milner et al. (eds), *The Oxford History of the American West* (Oxford, 1994).

28. D. Cannadine, *In Churchill's Shadow: Confronting the Past in Modern Britain* (London, 2002), pp. 29–30.

29. P.M. Kennedy, 'Mahan versus Mackinder: Two Interpretations of British Sea Power', in his *Strategy and Diplomacy, 1870–1945: Eight Studies* (London, 1983), pp. 43–86; V. de Grazia, 'Mass Culture and Sovereignty: The American Challenge to European Cinemas, 1920–1960', *Journal of Modern History*, lxi (1989), pp. 53–87; idem, *Irresistible Empire: America's Advance through Twentieth-Century Europe* (Cambridge, Mass., 2005).

30. E.A. Cohen, 'History and the Hyperpower', *Foreign Affairs*, lxxxiv (July/August 2004), pp. 49–63.

31. R. Robinson and J. Gallagher with A. Denny, *Africa and the Victorians: The Climax of Imperialism* (New York, 1968), pp. 1, 2, 4.

32. The best recent comparison of the British and American empires, which does full justice to their similarities – and also to their dissimilarities – is B. Porter, *Empire and Super-empire: Britain, America and the World* (London, 2006).

33. For three recent discussions of these issues, from varying perspectives, see: P.M. Kennedy, 'Mission Impossible?', *New York Review of Books*, 10 June 2004, pp. 16–19; A.M. Schlesinger, jr, 'The Making of a Mess', ibid., 23 September 2004, pp. 40–3; J. Chance, 'Empire, Anyone?', ibid., 7 October 2004, pp. 15–18.

34. J.S. Gordon, *An Empire of Wealth: The Heroic History of American Economic Power* (New York, 2004), is a rare introduction to this subject.

35. W.D. Bowen, M.A. Kurzweil and E.M. Tobin, *Equity and Excellence in American Higher Education* (Charlottesville, 2005).

36. R. Sennett and J. Cobb, *The Hidden Injuries of Class* (New York, 1972); P. Fussell, *Class: A Guide Through the American Status System* (New York, 1983); M.J. Burke, *The Conundrum of Class: Public Discourse on the Social Order in America* (Chicago, 1995); J. Epstein, *Snobbery: The American Version* (Boston, 2002). Significantly, none of the authors of these fascinating books is a professional historian.

37. For a rare exception, see D.K. Shipler, *The Working Poor: Invisible in America* (New York, 2004).

38. D.G. Hart, 'Conservatism, the Protestant Right, and the Failure of Religious History', *Journal of the Historical Society*, iv (2004), pp. 447–93; G. Wills, *Under God: Religion and American Politics* (New York, 1990).

39. G. Himmelfarb, *The New History and the Old* (Cambridge, Mass., 1987); idem, *On Looking into the Abyss: Untimely Thoughts on Culture and Society* (New York, 1994).

40. For recent examples of non-academic presidential biographies, see: E. Morris, *The Rise of Theodore Roosevelt* (New York, 1979); idem, *Theodore Rex* (New York, 2001); R.A. Caro, *The Years of Lyndon Johnson* (3 vols so far, 1982–2002). For an outstanding (and all-too-rare) example of a presidential biography by a professional historian, see R. Dallek, *An Unfinished Life: John F. Kennedy, 1917–1963* (Boston, 2003).

41. N. Dirks, *Castes of Mind: Colonialism and the Making of Modern India* (Princeton, 2001), p. 312. For recent discussions of the claims (and limitations) of cultural history more generally, see M. Rubin, 'What is Cultural History Now?', in Cannadine, *What Is History Now?*, pp. 80–94; P. Mandler, 'The Problem with Cultural History', *Cultural and Social History*, i (2004), pp. 94–117, and the ensuing debate in ibid., pp. 209–15, 326–32.

42. T. Bender, *A Nation Among Nations: America's Place in World History* (New York, 2006), is a powerful antidote to many of these views.

43. The prime ministers of the United Kingdom and of Canada, and the president of India, have all recently made this point. As one historian has recently exhorted us, we should not 'wish to engage in a post 9/11 stocktaking of the virtues and vices of the British Empire, for as earlier efforts at creating a ledger of imperial credits and debits have shown, such attempts invariably falter over what is measureable and what is not, not to mention deeper ethical and ideological debates over what is actually beneficial'. See D.M. Peers, 'Reading Empire, Chasing Tikka Masala: The Contested State of Imperial History', *Canadian Journal of History*, xxxix (2004), p. 92.

44. See above, Chapter 1, pp. 27–32.

45. L.J. Colley, '"This Small Island": Britain, Size and Empire', *Proceedings of the British Academy*, cxxi (2003), pp. 171–90.

46. D.R. Headrick, *The Tools of Empire: Technology and European Imperialism in the Nineteenth Century* (Oxford, 1981); D. Cannadine, 'Engineering History, or the History of Engineering? Re-writing the Technological Past', *Transactions of the Newcomen Society*, (2004), pp. 163–80.

47. S.M. Walt, 'Defying History and Theory', in G.J. Ikenberry (ed.), *America Unrivaled: The Future of the Balance of Power* (Ithaca, 2002), p. 137.

48. C. Newbury, *Patrons, Clients and Empire: Chieftancy and Over-Rule in Asia, Africa and the Pacific* (Oxford, 2003); T. Dodge, *Inventing Iraq: The Failure of Nation Building and a History Denied* (New York, 2003); R. Watson, 'Civil Disorder is the Disease of Ibadan': Chieftancy and Civic Culture in a Yoruba City* (Ohio, 2003).

49. D. Cannadine, *Ornamentalism: How the British Saw their Empire* (London, 2001); idem, 'Second Thoughts on *Ornamentalism*', *History Australia*, i (2004), pp. 169–78. For signs of a lack of interest in class vis-à-vis gender and race, see the index entries in Wilson, *A New Imperial History*, pp. 376, 378, 382; and note the title of R.R. Pierson and N. Chaudhuri (eds), *Nation, Empire, Colony: Historicizing Gender and Race* (Bloomington, 1998). Whatever happened to class?

50. D.K. Fieldhouse (ed.), *The Economics of Empire* (London, 1967), remains a useful introduction.

51. The economic history of the British Empire has received little attention in Britain between the publication of P.J. Cain and A.G. Hopkins, *British Imperialism* (2 vols, London, 1993) and of Ferguson, *Empire*, and scarcely none in the United States since L.E. Davis and R.A. Huttenback, *Mammon and the Pursuit of Empire: The Political Economy of British Imperialism, 1860–1912* (Cambridge, 1986), a book written, incidentally, by members of economics, not history, departments. For the subsequent, inconclusive discussion of Davis and Huttenback's findings, see P.K. O'Brien, 'The Costs and Benefits of British Imperialism, 1846–1914', *Past & Present*, no. 120 (1988), pp. 163–200; A. Offer, 'The British Empire, 1870–1914: A Waste of Money', *Economic History Review*, 2nd ser., xlvi (1993), pp. 215–38; J.R. Ward, 'The Industrial Revolution and British Imperialism, 1750–1850', *Economic History Review*, 2nd ser., xlvii (1994), pp. 44–65.

52. A. Porter, *Religion Versus Empire? British Protestant Missionaries and Overseas Expansion, 1700–1914* (Manchester, 2004).

53. For two recent books which suggestively address some of these issues in a South Asian contxt, see J. Cox, *Imperial Fault Lines: Christianity and Colonial Power in India, 1818–1940* (Stanford, 2002); J.M. Brown and R.E. Frykenberg (eds), *Christians, Cultural Interactions and India's Religious Traditions* (London, 2002).

54. D. Armitage, *Ideological Origins of the British Empire* (Cambridge, 2000); D. Bell, *The Idea of Greater Britain: Empire and the Future of World Order, 1860–1900* (Princeton, 2007). For British royalty and the British Empire, see above, Chapter 2, pp. 54–6, Chapter 8, pp. 205–8.

55. For one recent example, see K. McKenzie, *Scandal in the Colonies: Sydney and Cape Town, 1820–1850* (Melbourne, 2004).

56. For which see in particular the pioneering work of C.A. Bayly: 'The First Age of Global Imperialism, 1760–1830', *Journal of Imperial and Commonwealth History*, xxvi (1998), pp. 24–48; idem, *Imperial Meridian: The British Empire and the World, 1780–1830* (Harlow, 1989); idem, *The Birth of the Modern World, 1780–1914* (Oxford, 2004).

57. G. Hosking, *Russia: People and Empire, 1552–1917* (London, 1997); idem, *Rulers and Victims: The Russians in the Soviet Union* (London, 2006); D. Lieven, *Empire: The Russian Empire and Its Rivals* (London, 2000)

58. Darwin, *After Tamerlane*, p. 23; Peers, 'Reading Empire, Chasing Tikka Masala', p. 101.

CHAPTER 10, RECESSIONAL, pp. 235–73

1. R. Jenkins, *A Life at the Centre* (London, 1991), p. 210. This chapter first came into focus during a train journey from Madras to Bangalore. It has been given as a seminar paper at the University of Glasgow, at the annual conference of the Institute for Contemporary British History, and at the Institute of Historical Research in London. I am especially grateful to David Armitage, Pene Corfield, Sir John Elliott, Julian Hoppit, John Morrill, David Reynolds, Quentin Skinner, Alan Smith, Sir Keith Thomas and Max Travers for their comments and suggestions.
2. J. Burckhardt, *Judgements on History and Historians* (London, 1959, ed. H. Trevor-Roper), p. 158; see also above, Chapter 7, pp. 177–8, Chapter 9, pp. 216–17.
3. C. Hill, *The Century of Revolution, 1603–1714* (London, 1961); idem, *Intellectual Origins of the English Revolution* (Oxford, 1965); E.P. Thompson, *The Making of the English Working Class* (London, 1963); A. Briggs, *The Age of Improvement, 1783–1867* (London, 1959); idem, *Victorian Cities* (London, 1963); E.J. Hobsbawm, *The Age of Revolution: Europe, 1789–1848* (London, 1962); idem, *Industry and Empire* (London, 1968); R. Robinson and J.A. Gallagher, *Africa and the Victorians: The Official Mind of Imperialism* (London, 1961); A.J.P. Taylor, *English History, 1914–1945* (Oxford, 1965).
4. A. Marwick, *The Sixties: Cultural Revolution in Britain, France, Italy and the United States, c1958–1974* (Oxford, 1998), pp. 3–22.
5. A. Hughes, *The Causes of the English Civil War* (London, 1991), pp. 3, 62, 65; T. Harris, *Politics Under the Later Stuarts: Party Conflict in a Divided Society, 1660–1715* (London, 1993), pp. 2, 4, 53, 176; J. Hoppit, *A Land of Liberty? England, 1689–1727* (Oxford, 2000), pp. 515, 541.
6. See above, Chapter 4, pp. 97–9.
7. Jenkins, *Life at the Centre*, p. 210.
8. D. Halberstam, *The Best and the Brightest* (New York, 1972.)
9. L. Stone, 'Epilogue: Lawrence Stone – As Seen by Himself', in A.L. Beier, D. Cannadine and J.M. Rosenheim (eds), *The First Modern Society: Essays in English History in Honour of Lawrence Stone* (Cambridge, 1989), p. 594.
10. J. Turner and S.P. Turner, *The Impossible Science* (London, 1990), pp. 133–41; B. Moore, *Social Origins of Dictatorship and Democracy: Lord and Peasant in the Making of the Modern World* (Harmondsworth, 1969 edn), pp. v–vii.
11. D. Cannadine, 'British History: Past, Present – and Future?', *Past & Present*, no. 116 (1987), pp. 170–5.
12. E.J. Hobsbawm, 'From Social History to the History of Society', *Daedalus*, Winter 1971, pp. 20–45.
13. H.R. Trevor-Roper, 'Fernand Braudel, the *Annales*, and the Mediterranean', *Journal of Modern History*, xliv (1972), pp. 468–79; F. Braudel, *On History* (London, 1980), esp. pp. 25–55; J.H. Hexter, *On Historians* (Cambridge, Mass., 1979), pp. 61–145; C. Hill, 'Past and Present: Origins and Early Years', *Past & Present*, no. 100 (1983), pp. 3–14; J. Le Goff, 'Past and Present: Later History', ibid., pp. 14–28.
14. W.W. Rostow, *The Stages of Economic Growth: A Non-Communist Manifesto* (Cambridge, 1960); Thompson, *Making of the English Working Class*; H.J.

Perkin, *The Origins of Modern English Society, 1780–1880* (London, 1969); Briggs, *Victorian Cities*; see also above, Chapter 4, pp. 99–100.

15. L. Stone, *The Crisis of the Aristocracy, 1558–1641* (Oxford, 1965), pp. 3–4; J.H. Plumb, *The Collected Essays of J.H. Plumb*, vol. i, *The Making of an Historian* (London, 1988) [hereafter *Essays* i], p. 171.

16. W.W. Rostow, *The United States in the World Arena: An Essay in Recent History* (New York, 1960); idem, *View from the Seventh Floor* (New York, 1964); E.P. Thompson (ed.), *Warwick University Limited: Industry, Management and the Universities* (Harmondsworth, 1970); H.J. Perkin, 'Social History', in H.P.R. Finberg (ed.), *Approaches to History: A Symposium* (London, 1962), pp. 51–82; D. Cannadine, *The Pleasures of the Past* (London, 1989), pp. 172–83.

17. E.H. Carr, *What is History?* (Harmondsworth, 1964), p. 55.

18. G.R. Elton, *The Practice of History* (Sydney, 1967); idem, *The Future of the Past* (Cambridge, 1968); idem, *Political History: Principles and Practice* (London, 1970); idem, *F.W. Maitland* (London, 1986); J.P. Kenyon, *The History Men: The Historical Profession in England since the Renaissance* (London, 1983), pp. 278–80; N. Annan, *The Dons: Mentors, Eccentrics and Geniuses* (London, 1999), pp. 92–7. For a cogent critique of Elton's conservative preoccupation with political history, see R.J. Evans, *In Defense of History* (New York, 1999 edn), pp. 140–1, 165–7, 197–8.

19. D. Reynolds, *One World Divisible: A Global History Since 1945* (New York, 2000), pp. 289–321, outlines these developments well.

20. For some contemporary responses, see H. Kidd, *The Trouble at LSE, 1966–67* (London, 1969); E. Ashby, *Masters and Scholars: Reflections on the Rights and Responsibilities of Students* (London, 1970); J.A. Michener, *Kent State: What Happened and Why* (London, 1971); J.R. Searle, *The Campus War: A Sympathetic Look at the University in Agony* (Harmondsworth, 1972).

21. J.M. Blum, *The Years of Discord: American Politics and Society, 1961–1974* (New York, 1991), deals with this period admirably. See also M. Flamm and D. Steigerwald, *Debating the 1960s: Liberal, Conservative* Perspectives (New York, 2007).

22. For biographies of Stone and Plumb, see C.S.L. Davis, *Oxford Dictionary of National Biography*, vol. lii, pp. 900–2; D. Cannadine, *Proceedings of the British Academy*, cxxiv, *Biographies of Fellows*, iii (2004), pp. 269–309.

23. *Essays* i, p. 290; L. Stone, 'R.H. Tawney', *Past & Present*, no. 21 (1962), pp. 73–7; idem, 'Introduction' to R.H. Tawney, *The Agrarian Problem in the Sixteenth Century* (New York, 1967), pp. vii–xviii; idem, 'R.H. Tawney', in *International Encyclopaedia of the Social Sciences*, vol. xv (New York, 1968), pp. 518–20; idem, 'As Seen by Himself', pp. 575–80.

24. L. Stone, 'The Anatomy of the Elizabethan Aristocracy', *Economic History Review*, xviii (1948), pp. 1–53; H.R. Trevor-Roper, 'The Elizabethan Aristocracy: An Anatomy Anatomised', *Economic History Review*, 2nd ser., iii (1951), pp. 279–98; L. Stone, 'The Elizabethan Aristocracy: A Restatement', *Economic History Review*, 2nd ser., iv (1951–52), pp. 302–21; H.R. Trevor-Roper, *The Gentry, 1540–1640* (London, 1953); J.H. Hexter, *Reappraisals in History* (London, 1961), pp. 117–62; L. Stone, *Social Change and Revolution in England, 1558–1641* (London, 1965); idem, 'As Seen by Himself', pp. 582–4;

R. Davenport-Hines (ed.), *Letters from Oxford: Hugh Trevor-Roper to Bernard Berenson* (London, 2006), pp. 130–2.

25. Stone, 'As Seen by Himself', pp. 584–5, 588; J.H. Elliott, 'Lawrence Stone', *Past & Present*, no. 164 (1999), pp. 3–5.

26. N. Mckendrick, 'J.H. Plumb: A Valedictory Tribute', in idem (ed.), *Historical Perspectives: Studies in English Thought and Society in Honour of J.H. Plumb* (London, 1974), pp. 2–3; J.H. Plumb, 'Elections to the House of Commons in the Reign of William III' (unpublished Ph.D. dissertation, University of Cambridge, 1936); idem (ed.), *Studies in Social History: A Tribute to G.M. Trevelyan* (London, 1955); *Essays* i, pp. 180–204.

27. *Essays* i, pp. 97–9; see also above, Chapter 3, pp. 65–8.

28. J.H. Plumb, *The Growth of Political Stability in England, 1625–1725* (London, 1967) [hereafter *Stability*], p. 25; *Essays* i, pp. 289, 370–1; D. Cannadine, *G.M. Trevelyan: A Life in History* (London, 1992) [hereafter *Trevelyan*], p. 218; Elton, *Practice of History*, pp. 41–7.

29. *Essays* i, p. 165; ii, pp. 171–263; J.H. Plumb, *England in the Eighteenth Century* (Harmondsworth, 1950); idem, *Chatham* (London, 1953); idem, *The First Four Georges* (London, 1956); idem, *The Death of the Past* (London, 1969), p. 145.

30. Elliott, 'Stone', p. 3.

31. Many of his essays are reprinted in L. Stone, *The Past and the Present* (London, 1981); idem, *The Past and the Present Re-Visited* (London, 1987).

32. L. Stone, *The Causes of the English Revolution, 1529–1642* (London, 1972) [hereafter *Revolution*], p. ix; D. Cannadine, 'The Era of Todd, Plumb and Snow', in D. Reynolds (ed.), *Christ's: A Cambridge College Over Five Centuries* (London, 2004), pp. 192–8; idem, 'C.P. Snow, "The Two Cultures", and the "Corridors of Power" Revisited', in W.R. Louis (ed.), *Yet More Adventures with Britannia: Personalities, Politics and Culture in Britain* (London, 2005), pp. 109–10.

33. Hexter, *On Historians*, pp. 149–226; G.E. Aylmer, 'Crisis of the Aristocracy, 1558–1691', *Past & Present*, no. 32 (1965), pp. 113–25; D.C. Coleman, 'The "Gentry" Controversy and the Aristocracy in Crisis, 1558–1641', *History*, li (1966), pp. 165–74.

34. Stone, *Crisis of the Aristocracy*, pp. xviii, 1–17.

35. J.H. Plumb, *Sir Robert Walpole*, vol. i, *The Making of a Statesman* (London, 1956), pp. 30–78; vol. ii, *The King's Minister* (London, 1960), pp. 7–39; Kenyon, *History Men*, p. 232.

36. G.R. Elton, *Reform and Renewal: Thomas Cromwell and the Common Weal* (Cambridge, 1973), pp. 9–37, 158–66; Plumb, *Walpole*, vol. i, pp. xi–xvii; vol. ii, pp. 325–33; idem, 'The Walpoles: Father and Son', in *Studies in Social History*, pp. 179–207.

37. *Revolution*, p. ii; L. Stone, 'Theories of Revolution', *World Politics*, xviii (1966), pp. 159–76; idem, *Social Change and Revolution in England*, pp. i–xxvi; idem, 'The English Revolution', in R. Foster and J.P. Greene (eds), *Preconditions of Revolution in Early Modern Europe* (Baltimore, 1970), pp. 55–108.

38. *Revolution*, pp. xii–iii.

39. *Trevelyan*, pp. 114–19; *Essays* i, pp. 194–8.

40. J.H. Plumb, 'The Elections to the Convention Parliament of 1689', *Cambridge Historical Journal*, v (1937), pp. 235–54; idem, 'Political History, 1530–1885', in *VCH Leicestershire*, vol. ii (London, 1954), pp 102–34; idem, 'The Organisation of the Cabinet in the Reign of Queen Anne', *Transactions of the Royal Historical Society*, 5th ser., vii (1957), pp. 137–57. See also: H.J. Habakkuk, 'Marriage Settlements in the Eighteenth Century', *Transactions of the Royal Historical Society*, 4th ser., xxxii (1950), pp. 15–30; idem, 'The English Land Market in the Eighteenth Century', in J.S. Bromley and E.H. Kossmann (eds), *Britain and the Netherlands* (London, 1960), pp. 154–73; J.P. Kenyon (former research student), *Robert Spencer, Earl of Sunderland, 1641–1702* (London, 1958); J.R. Jones (former research student), *The First Whigs: The Politics of the Exclusion Crisis, 1678–1683* (Oxford, 1961); J. Beattie (former research student), 'The English Court in the Reign of George I (Ph.D. Dissertation, University of Cambridge, 1963); G.V. Bennett (former research student), 'King William III and the Episcopate', in G.V. Bennett and J.D. Walsh (eds), *Essays in Modern Church History* (London, 1965), pp. 104–31.

41. *Essays* i, pp. 157–63; J.H. Plumb (ed.), *The Horizon Book of the Renaissance* (London, 1961); L. Stone, *Sculpture in Britain: The Middle Ages* (Harmondsworth, 1955); idem, 'The Educational Revolution in England, 1540–1640', *Past & Present*, no. 28 (1964), pp. 41–80; idem, 'Social Mobility in England, 1500–1700', *Past & Present*, no. 33 (1966), pp. 16–55; idem, 'Literacy and Education in England, 1640–1900', *Past & Present*, no. 42 (1969), pp. 69–139; idem, 'History and the Social Sciences in the Twentieth Century', in C.F. Delzell (ed.), *The Future of History: Essays in the Vanderbilt Centennial Symposium* (Nashville, 1977), pp. 3–30; idem, 'As Seen by Himself', p. 577.

42. *Revolution*, p. 147; *Stability*, p. 13.

43. See above, Chapter 4, pp. 97–103.

44. *Revolution*, pp. xii, 10, 14, 16, 22.

45. *Revolution*, pp. 31, 36.

46. *Revolution*, pp. 58–117, esp. pp. 67, 112–17.

47. *Revolution*, pp. 10, 116–18.

48. *Revolution*, pp. 117–34.

49. *Revolution*, pp. 135–7.

50. *Revolution*, pp. 49, 71.

51. *Stability*, pp. 9–14.

52. *Stability*, pp. 13, 16.

53. *Stability*, pp. 16–27, 118–19.

54. *Stability*, pp. 73, 131, 133–60.

55. *Stability*, pp. 31, 42–57.

56. *Stability*, pp. 31, 75, 110–11, 160.

57. *Stability*, pp. 78, 161–88.

58. *Revolution*, p. 34; see above, Chapter 9, pp. 216–17.

59. But note, for instance, his admiration for Moore, *Social Origins of Dictatorship and Democracy*, comments on back cover of paperback edition.

60. J.G.A. Pocock, 'Introduction', in idem (ed.), *Three British Revolutions: 1641, 1688, 1776* (Princeton, 1980), pp. 3–20; L. Stone, 'The Results of the English Revolutions of the Seventeenth Century', in ibid., pp. 23–108; *Revolution*, p. 147.

61. *Stability*, pp. 14–15, 41.

62. *Revolution*, pp. 57, 117; *Essays* i, pp. 289, 300–8; H. Koenigsberger and L. Stone, 'Early Modern Revolutions: An Exchange', *Journal of Modern History*, xliv (1974), pp. 101. 106; P. Burke, 'History of Events and the Revival of Narrative', in idem (ed.), *New Perspectives on Historical Writing* (Oxford, 1991), pp. 234–6.

63. *Revolution*, pp. 26, 47, 92, 148–50; R.C. Richardson, *The Debate on the English Revolution* (3rd edn, London, 1998), pp. 91–6, 207–8; J. Adamson, 'Eminent Victorian: S.R. Gardiner and the Liberal as Hero', *Historical Journal*, xxxiii (1990), pp. 641–57; T.K. Rabb, 'Parliament and Society in Early Stuart England: The Legacy of Wallace Notestein', *American Historical Review*, lxxvii (1972), pp. 705–14.

64. R.H. Tawney, 'Harrington's Interpretation of His Age' (1941), reprinted in J.M. Winter (ed.), *History and Society: Essays by R.H. Tawney* (London, 1978), p. 75.

65. Tawney, 'Harrington', pp. 66–84. Subsequent accounts of Harrington have suggested that his work should be seen as conveying rather different messages. See J. Shklar, 'Ideology Hunting: The Case of James Harrington', *American Political Science Review*, liii (1959), pp. 662–92; C. Blitzer, *An Immortal Commonwealth: The Political Thought of James Harrington* (New Haven, 1960); C.B. Macpherson, 'Harrington's Opportunity State', *Past & Present*, no. 17 (1960), pp. 45–71 ; J.G.A. Pocock, 'James Harrington and the Good Old Cause', *Journal of British Studies*, x (1970–71), pp. 30–48; idem (ed.), *The Political Works of James Harrington* (Cambridge, 1977).

66. *Revolution*, pp. xi, 38–9; J.H. Plumb, *Chatham* (London, 1965 edn), p. 106; J.A. Cannon, *Parliamentary Reform, 1640–1832* (Cambridge, 1973), pp. 20–1, 47–52, 184–9, 245–53.

67. *Revolution*, p. ix.

68. *Revolution*, pp. 9, 12, 135.

69. *Revolution*, pp. 49, 146.

70. *Revolution*, pp. 53, 146–7.

71. *Stability*, p. 173.

72. *Stability*, p. 13; *Essays* i, pp. 24–8.

73. *Essays* i, pp. 12–19.

74. R. Walcott, *English Politics in the Early Eighteenth Century* (Oxford, 1956); *Essays* i, pp. 100–4; *Stability*, pp. 10, 55–7, 139–41.

75. *Stability*, pp. 186–8.

76. See the following reviews of *Revolution*: Anon, *Times Literary Supplement* (*TLS*), 29 June 1972, p. 1137; J.P. Kenyon, *The Observer*, 2 July 1972; R. Schlatter, *American Historical Review*, lxxviii (1973), pp. 1052–3; G. Aylmer, *History*, lviii (1973), pp. 288–9.

77. See the following reviews of *Stability*: R. Blake, *The Spectator*, 24 February 1967, p. 229; K.G. Davies, *New Statesman*, 12 May 1967, p. 656; J.B. Owen, *History*, liv (1969), pp. 105–7.

78. For Elton on Gardiner, Notestein and Tawney, see G.R. Elton, *Studies in Tudor and Stuart Politics and Government* (4 vols, Cambridge, 1974–92), ii, pp. 6–8, 164–89; iii, pp. 156–82; iv, pp. 286–92; idem, *Future of the Past*, pp. 15–16; idem, 'Europe and the Reformation', in D. Beales and G. Best (eds), *History,*

Society and the Churches: Essays in Honour of Owen Chadwick (Cambridge, 1985), pp. 89–104. For a more balanced view, see W. Lamont, 'R.H. Tawney: "Who did not write a single work which can be trusted"?', in idem (ed.), *Historical Controversies and Historians* (London, 1998), pp. 109–19. For Elton versus Stone, see: Elton, *Practice of History*, pp. 29–33; idem, *Studies in Tudor and Stuart Politics*, iv, pp. 303–8; idem, *Return to Essentials: Some Reflections on the Present State of Historical Study* (Cambridge, 1991), pp. 20–1; Stone, *Past and the Present Re-Visited*, pp. 107–14, 143–7.

79. B. Worden, 'Classical Republicanism and the Puritan Revolution', in H. Lloyd-Jones, V. Pearl and B. Worden (eds), *History and Imagination: Essays in Honour of Hugh Trevor-Roper* (London, 1981), pp. 182–201.

80. B. Worden, review of *Revolution*, *New Statesman*, 4 August 1972, pp. 167–8; G.R. Elton, review of ibid., *Historical Journal*, xvi (1973), pp. 205–8.

81. See the following reviews of *Stability*: Anon, *TLS*, 8 June 1967, p. 513; B. Kemp, *English Historical Review*, lxxxiii (1968), pp. 570–3; R. Beddard, *Historical Journal*, xii (1969), pp. 175–8; Owen, *History*, pp. 105–7.

82. Many of these questions were raised in C. Russell, review of *Revolution*, *English Historical Review*, lxxxviii (1973), pp. 856–61; P. Christianson, 'The Causes of the English Revolution: A Reappraisal', *Journal of British Studies*, xv (1975), pp. 40–75; Koenigsberger and Stone, 'Early Modern Revolutions', pp. 99–110.

83. Anon, *TLS*, 8 June 1967, p. 513.

84. J.S. Morrill, *Revolt in the Provinces: The People of England and the Tragedies of War, 1630–1648* (London, 1999), pp. 6–7.

85. Elton, *Studies in Tudor and Stuart Politics*, vol. iii, p. 483; vol. iv, p. 304; Evans, *In Defense of History*, pp. 165–7.

86. I I. Tomlinson, 'The Causes of War: An Historiographical Survey', in idem (ed.), *Before the English Civil War: Essays on Early Stuart Politics and Government* (London, 1983), pp. 7–11; H. Butterfield, *The Whig Interpretation of History* (London, 1931), p. 95.

87. This is a vast literature. For guidance, see Richardson, *Debate on the English Revolution*, pp. 162–83, 203–38. Among especially noteworthy revisionist works are: C. Russell, *Parliament and English Politics, 1621–1649* (Oxford, 1979); idem, *The Fall of the British Monarchies, 1637–1642* (Oxford, 1991); A. Everitt, *The Local Community and the Great Rebellion* (London, 1969); J.S. Morrill, *The Revolt of the Provinces: Conservatives and Radicals in the English Civil War, 1630–1650* (London, 1976); idem, *The Nature of the English Revolution* (London, 1993), esp. pp. 31–175; A. Fletcher, *The Outbreak of the English Civil War* (London, 1981). See also above, Chapter 7, p. 186.

88. C. Russell, *Unrevolutionary England, 1603–1642* (Hambledon, 1990). See also above, Chapter 7, pp. 184–6.

89. P.G.M. Dickson, *The Commercial Revolution in England: A Study in the Development of Public Credit, 1688–1756* (London, 1967); C. Brooks, 'Public Finance and Political Stability: The Administration of the Land Tax, 1688–1720', *Historical Journal*, xvii (1974), pp. 281–300; J. Brewer, *The Sinews of Power: War, Money and the English State, 1688–1783* (New York, 1989); G.S. Holmes, *British Politics in the Reign of Queen Anne* (London, 1967); idem, *The Electorate and the National Will in the First Age of Party* (Kendal, 1976); W.A. Speck,

Tory and Whig: The Struggle for the Constituencies, 1701–1715 (London, 1971); B.W. Hill, *The Growth of Parliamentary Parties, 1689–1742* (London, 1976); L.J.K. Glassey, *Politics and the Appointments of Justices of the Peace, 1675–1720* (Oxford, 1979); J.P. Kenyon, *Revolution Principles: The Politics of Party, 1689–1720* (Cambridge, 1977); G.S. De Krey, *A Fractured Society: London in the First Age of Party, 1688–1715* (Oxford, 1985).

90. G. Holmes (ed.), *Britain After the Glorious Revolution, 1689–1714* (London, 1969); G. Holmes and W.A. Speck, *The Divided Society, 1694–1716* (London, 1967); D. Baugh (ed.), *Aristocratic Government and Society in Eighteenth-Century England* (New York, 1975); S. Baxter (ed.), *England's Rise to Greatness, 1660–1763* (Berkeley, 1983); J. Cannon (ed.), *The Whig Ascendancy: Colloquies on Hanoverian England* (London, 1981), p. 26; C. Jones (ed.), *Britain in the First Age of Party, 1680–1750: Essays Presented to Geoffrey Holmes* (London, 1987); C. Roberts, N. Landau and S. Baxter, 'Political Stability: A Symposium', *Albion*, xxv (1993), pp. 237–78.

91. D. Hirst, *The Representative of the People? Voters and Voting in England under the Early Stuarts* (Cambridge, 1975), pp. 1, 105, 113; J.R. Jones, *Country and Court: England, 1658–1714* (London, 1978), pp. 1–7, 363; W.A. Speck, *Stability and Strife: England, 1714–1760* (London, 1977), pp. 1–7, 293; R. Porter, *English Society in the Eighteenth Century* (London, 1982), pp. 125, 136–9, 397; J. Brewer, *Party Ideology and Popular Politics at the Accession of George III* (Cambridge, 1976), pp. 3–8; B. Bailyn, *The Origins of American Politics* (New York, 1968), pp. 31–6.

92. C. Clay, 'Marriage, Inheritance and the Rise of Large Estates in England, 1660–1815', *Economic History Review*, 2nd ser., xxi (1968), pp. 503–18; idem, 'The Price of Freehold Land in the Later Seventeenth and Eighteenth Centuries', *Economic History Review*, 2nd ser., xxvii (1974), pp. 173–89; J.V. Beckett, 'English Landownership in the Later Seventeenth and Eighteenth Centuries: The Debate and the Problems', *Economic History Review*, 2nd ser., xxx (1977), pp. 567–81.

93. P. Langford, *The Excise Crisis: Society and Politics in the Age of Walpole* (Oxford, 1975); P. Fritz, *The English Ministers and Jacobitism between the Rebellions of 1715 and 1745* (Toronto, 1975); E. Cruickshanks, *Political Untouchables: The Tories and the '45* (London, 1979); B. Lenman, *The Jacobite Risings in Britain, 1689–1746* (London, 1980); E. Cruickshanks and J. Black (eds), *The Jacobite Challenge* (Edinburgh, 1988); P. Monod, *Jacobitism and the English People, 1688–1788* (Cambridge, 1989), esp. pp. 343–50; L.J. Colley, *In Defiance of Oligarchy: The Tory Party, 1714–1760* (Cambridge, 1982), esp. pp. 3–24; J. Black, 'Introduction: An Age of Political Stability?', in idem (ed.), *Britain in the Age of Walpole* (London, 1984), pp. 23–44.

94. J.C.D. Clark, *English Society, 1688–1832: Ideology, Social Structure and Political Practice During the Ancien Regime* (Cambridge, 1985), p. 73.

95. J.C.D. Clark, *Revolution and Rebellion: State and Society in England in the Seventeenth and Eighteenth Centuries* (Cambridge, 1986), pp. 105–6, 112–16, 159–60.

96. Reynolds, *One World Divisible*, p. 289; R. Kimball, *Tenured Radicals: How Politics has Corrupted Higher Education* (Chicago, 1991); A. Brinkley, 'Victoria Revived', *TLS*, 21 January 2000, p. 6.

97. N. Annan, *Our Age: Portrait of a Generation* (London, 1990), pp. 424–5; Clark, *Revolution and Rebellion*, p. 170.

98. I. Horowitz, *The Decomposition of Sociology* (New York, 1995); Richardson, *Debate on the English Revolution*, pp. 248–9.

99. L. Stone, 'The Revival of Narrative: Reflections on a New Old History', *Past & Present*, no. 85 (1979), pp. 20–1.

100. K. Wrightson, 'Interview with Lawrence Stone' (transcript of videotape, Institute of Historical Research, London, 1988), pp. 19–21; Stone, 'As Seen by Himself', p. 592.

101. Wrightson, 'Interview', pp. 23, 31–2; Stone, 'As Seen by Himself', pp. 589–92; idem, 'History and the Social Sciences', pp. 30–42; idem, 'Second Thoughts in 1985', in idem, *The Causes of the English Revolution, 1529–1642* (2nd edn, London, 1986), pp. 165–81; idem, 'Revival of Narrative', pp. 3–24.

102. M. Gould, *Revolutions in the Development of Capitalism: The Coming of the English Revolution* (Berkeley, 1987); J. Goldstone, *Revolution and Rebellion in the Early Modern World* (Berkeley, 1991); R. Brenner, 'Bourgeois Revolution and Transition to Capitalism', in Beier et al., *First Modern Society*, pp. 271–304; idem, *Merchants and Revolution: Commercial Change, Political Conflict and London's Overseas Traders, 1550–1653* (Cambridge, 1993).

103. L. Stone, *The Family, Sex and Marriage in England, 1500–1800* (London, 1977); L. Stone and J.C. Fawtier Stone, *An Open Elite? England, 1540–1880* (Oxford, 1986); L. Stone, *Road to Divorce: England, 1530–1987* (Oxford, 1990); idem, *Uncertain Unions: Marriage in England, 1600–1753* (Oxford, 1992); idem, *Broken Lives: Separation and Divorce in England, 1660–1857* (Oxford, 1993); idem (ed.), *An Imperial State at War: Britain from 1689 to 1815* (London, 1994); see also above, Chapter 9, p. 218.

104. L. Stone, 'History and Post-Modernism', *Past & Present*, no. 131 (1991), pp. 217–18; idem, 'History and Post-Modernism', *Past & Present*, no. 135 (1992), pp. 189–94; idem, 'As Seen by Himself', p. 580.

105. J.H. Plumb, 'The Growth of the Electorate in England from 1600–1715', *Past & Present*, no. 45 (1969), pp. 90–116; idem, 'Political Man', in J.L. Clifford (ed.), *Man Versus Society in Eighteenth-Century Britain* (Cambridge, 1968), pp. 1–21; idem, *Death of the Past*, p. 106.

106. J.H. Plumb and H. Wheldon, *Royal Heritage: The Story of Britain's Royal Builders and Collectors* (London, 1977); N. McKendrick, J. Brewer and J.H. Plumb, *The Birth of a Consumer Society: The Commercialization of Eighteenth-Century England* (Bloomington, 1982); *Essays* i, pp. 156, 372.

107. B. Pimlott, *Harold Wilson* (London, 1992), pp. 686–90; P. Ziegler, *Wilson: The Authorized Life of Lord Wilson of Rievaulx* (London, 1993), pp. 494–8, 504, 509.

108. M. Cowling, *Religion and Public Doctrine in Modern England* (Cambridge, 1980), pp. 389, 394–9; idem, 'The Sources of the New Right', *Encounter*, lxxiii (November, 1989), p. 8; J.C.D. Clark, review of *Essays* i–ii, *English Historical Review*, cv (1990), pp. 989–91; J.P. Kenyon, *TLS*, 23–29 June 1989, pp. 685–6.

109. G.R. Elton, *The History of England* (Cambridge, 1984), p. 18; Stone, *Revolution* (2nd edn), p. 165; T.K. Rabb, 'Revisionism Revised: The Role of the Commons'; D. Hirst, 'Revisionism Revised: The Place of Principle'; C. Hill, 'Parliament

and People in Early Seventeenth-Century England', all in *Past & Present*, no. 92 (1981), pp. 55–78, 79–99, 100–24. See also J.H. Hexter, 'Power Struggle, Parliament and Liberty in Early Stuart England', *Journal of Modern History*, 1 (1978), pp. 1–50; idem, 'The Early Stuarts and Parliament: Old Hat and Nouvelle Vague', *Parliamentary History* i (1982), pp. 181–215; T. Cogswell, 'Coping with Revisionism in Early Stuart History', *Journal of Modern History*, lxii (1990), p. 551; F. O'Gorman, 'Recent Historiography of the Hanoverian Regime', *Historical Journal*, xxix (1986), pp. 1005–20; J. Innes, 'Jonathan Clark, Social History and England's Ancien Regime', *Past & Present*, no. 115 (1987), pp. 165–200; J.C.D. Clark, 'On Hitting the Buffers: The Historiography of England's Ancien Regime', *Past & Present*, no. 117 (1987), pp. 195–207; R. Porter, 'English Society in the Eighteenth Century Re-Visited', in J. Black (ed.), *British Politics and Society from Walpole to Pitt, 1742–1789* (London, 1990), pp. 29–52; R. Brent, 'Butterfield's Tories: "High Politics" and the Writing of Modern British Political History', *Historical Journal*, xxx (1987), pp. 943–54.

110. M. Kishlansky, review of Clark, *Revolution and Rebellion*, *Parliamentary History*, vii (1988), pp. 330–2.

111. Richardson, *Debate on the English Revolution*, pp. 218–19; Cogswell, 'Revisionism in Early Stuart History', p. 540. For two efforts, see C. Russell, *The Causes of the English Civil War* (Oxford, 1990); Hughes, *Causes of the English Civil War*. But see the reservations entered by J.P. Kenyon, 'Revisionism and Post-Revisionism in Early Stuart History', *Journal of Modern History*, lxiv (1992), pp. 686–99.

112. Richardson, *Debate on the English Revolution*, p. 219; Hughes, *Causes of the English Civil War*, pp. 125–30, 158; R. Cust and A. Hughes (eds), *Conflict in Early Stuart England: Studies in Religion and Politics, 1603–1642* (London, 1989); G. Burgess, 'On Revisionism: An Analysis of Early Stuart Historiography in the 1970s and 1980s', *Historical Journal*, xxxiii (1990), pp. 609–27. For a very different approach, see J. Adamson, *The Noble Revolt: The Overthrow of Charles I* (London, 2007).

113. N. Rogers, *Whigs and Cities: Popular Politics in the Age of Walpole and Pitt* (Oxford, 1989); K. Wilson, *The Sense of the People: Politics, Culture and Imperialism 1715–1785* (Cambridge, 1995).

114. J. Brewer, *The Pleasures of the Imagination: English Culture in the Eighteenth Century* (London, 1997); L.J. Colley, *Britons: Forging the Nation, 1707–1837* (London, 1992); R. Porter, *Enlightenment: Britain and the Making of the Modern World* (London, 2000).

115. Elton, *Studies in Tudor and Stuart Politics*, iv, p. 303; P. Langford, *A Polite and Commercial People: England, 1727–1783* (Oxford, 1989), p. 742; Hoppit, *Land of Liberty?*, p. 52; J.C.D. Clark, 'The Strange Death of British History? Reflections on Anglo-American Scholarship', *Historical Journal*, xl (1997), pp. 787–809; idem, 'Protestantism, Nationalism and National Identity, 1660–1832', *Historical Journal*, xliii (2000), pp. 249–76; idem, *English Society, 1660–1832: Religion, Ideology and Politics During the Ancien Regime* (2nd edn, Cambridge, 2000).

116. C. Russell, 'Introduction', in idem (ed.), *The Origins of the English Civil War* (London, 1973), p. 7.

117. See above, Chapter 4, pp. 102–7.
118. Hexter, *On Historians*, p. 8.
119. Burgess, 'On Revisionism', p. 614; Morrill, *Revolt in the Provinces*, p. 7, note 24. I have substituted the name of J.H. Plumb for Christopher Hill: the argument remains the same.
120. Stone, 'R.H. Tawney', p. 77.
121. Tomlinson, 'The Causes of War', p. 26; A. Knight, 'Revisionism and Revolution: Mexico Compared to England and France', *Past & Present*, no. 134 (1992), pp. 159–99; A. Hughes, 'Introduction to the Second Edition', in idem, *The Causes of the English Civil War* (2nd edn, London, 1998), pp. 1–9.
122. Elton's 'non-ideological' and 'empirical' historical method looks distinctly less value-free and robust these days: see Q. Skinner, 'Sir Geoffrey Elton and the Practice of History', *Transactions of the Royal Historical Society*, 6th ser., vii (1997), pp. 301–16.
123. N. Canny, 'The British Atlantic World: Working Towards a Definition', *Historical Journal*, xxxiii (1990), pp. 479–97; D. Armitage, J. Ohlmeyer, N.C. Landsman, E.H. Gould and J.G.A. Pocock, 'The New British History in Atlantic Perspective', *American Historical Review*, civ (1999), pp. 426–500.
124. J.G.A. Pocock, 'The New British History in Atlantic Perspective: An Antipodean Commentary', *American Historical Review*, civ (1999), p. 499. See also above, Chapter 7, p. 185.
125. Hexter, *On Historians*, pp. 241–2; C. Hill, *TLS*, 7 November 1975; see above, Chapter 1, pp. 27–32.
126. But note J.P. Kenyon's lifelong equivocation between Plumb and Elton, for which see Kenyon, *History Men*, pp. 209–13, 267, 278–83; J.S. Morrill, 'John Philipps Kenyon, 1927–1996', *Proceedings of the British Academy*, ci (1999), pp. 441–65.
127. Tomlinson, 'The Causes of War', p. 24; Hughes, 'Introduction to the Second Edition', p. 6; see also above, Chapter 7, pp. 171–2.
128. Adamson, 'Eminent Victorians', pp. 642, 656; Lord Dacre of Glanton [H.R. Trevor-Roper], 'The Continuity of the English Revolution', *Transactions of the Royal Historical Society*, 6th ser., i (1991), p. 122.

EPILOGUE, pp. 274–97

1. In preparing this lecture, I have been grateful (once again) for the help of Helen McCarthy, Elaine Walters and Jane Winters.
2. H.R. Trevor-Roper, *History and Imagination* (Oxford, 1980); R. Harris, *Selling Hitler: The Story of the Hitler Diaries* (London, 1986).
3. M. Howard, *The Lessons of History* (Oxford, 1991), p. 188; idem, *Captain Professor* (London, 2006), pp. 206–10.
4. See above, Prologue, p. 18.
5. Strictly speaking, I was the ninth Director of the IHR, but Cyril Flower had only been Acting Director between 1939 and 1944.
6. D. Birch and J. Horn, *The History Laboratory: The Institute of Historical Research, 1921–96* (London, 1996).

7. Shortly after I joined the IHR, I was the subject of a very generous profile: see D. Snowman, 'David Cannadine', *History Today*, October 1998, and later reprinted and updated in D. Snowman, *Historians* (London, 2007), pp. 19–30.

8. Tony Benn, Lord Carrington, Lord Deedes and Lady Soames, 'Epilogue: Churchill Remembered', in D. Cannadine and R. Quinault (eds), *Churchill in the Twenty-First Century* (Cambridge, 2004), pp. 219–40.

9. D. Cannadine (ed.), *What Is History Now?* (Basingstoke, 2002); idem (ed.), *History and the Media* (Basingstoke, 2004).

10. See above, Prologue, p. 15.

11. The British History Online site can be accessed at: http://www.british-history. ac.uk. For the proceedings of a conference associated with this project, held at the IHR on 7 July 2003, see: http://www.history.ac.uk/conferences/digitisation2003/ index.html.

12. A. Fletcher, '"Englandpast.net": A Framework for the Social History of England', *Historical Research*, lxxv (2002), pp. 296–315; P. Thane, 'What Difference Did the Vote Make? Women in Public and Private Life in Britain since 1918', *Historical Research*, lxxvi (2003), pp. 268–85; D. Keene, 'Metropolitan Comparisons: London as a City-State', *Historical Research*, lxxvii (2004), pp. 459–80.

13. A. Richard, *Public and Private: Universities, Government and Society* (Cambridge, 2005); C. Ondaatje, 'Giving it all away', *New Statesman*, 15 January 2007, pp. 38–9; J. Dalley, 'World-class collection to support: please give generously', *Financial Times*, 3/4 November 2007.

14. A. Sampson, *Anatomy of Britain* (London, 1962), pp. 20–1, 504–7.

15. D. Rockefeller, *Memoirs* (New York, 2003 edn), p. 439.

16. J. Kirk, *Her Majesty's Historiographer: Gordon Donaldson, 1913–1993* (Edinburgh, 1996), pp. 202–17.

17. Cannadine, *What Is History Now?*; idem, *History and the Media*; idem (ed.), *Admiral Lord Nelson: Context and Legacy* (Basingstoke, 2005); idem (ed.), *Trafalgar: A Battle and its Afterlife* (Basingstoke, 2006); idem, *Empire, the Sea and Global History: Britain's Maritime World, c1763–1840* (Basingstoke, 2007).

18. Titles so far (or soon to be) published are: D. Mattingly, *An Imperial Possession: Britain and the Roman Empire, 54BC–409AD* (London, 2006); D. Carpenter, *The Struggle for Mastery: Britain, 1066–1314* (London, 2003); M. Rubin, *The Hollow Crown: Britain, 1272–1485* (London, 2005); S. Brigden, *New Worlds, Lost Worlds: Britain, 1485–1603* (London, 2000); M. Kishlansky, *A Monarchy Transformed: Britain, 1603–1714* (London, 1996); P. Clarke, *Hope and Glory: Britain, 1900–1990* (London, 1996); C. Dyer, *Making a Living in the Middle Ages: The People of Britain, 850–1520* (London, 2002); K. Wrightson, *Earthly Necessities: Economic Lives in Early Modern Britain, 1470–1750* (London, 2000); J. Mokyr, *The Enlightened Economy: An Economic History of Britain, 1700–1850* (London, 2009); C. Wickham, *The Inheritance of Rome* (London, 2009); W.C. Jordan, *Europe in the High Middle Ages* (London, 2001); T.C.W. Blanning, *The Pursuit of Glory: Europe 1648–1815* (London, 2007).

19. Though it clearly took me all of 1998, and on into 1999, to disengage, during which time I reviewed P. Ziegler, *Osbert Sitwell* (London, 1998), *The Observer*,

24 May 1998; R. Jenkins, *The Chancellors* (London, 1998), *The Observer*, 23 August, 1998; H. Young, *This Blessed Plot: Britain and Europe from Churchill to Blair* (London, 1998), *The Observer*, 8 November 1998; R.T. Shannon, *Gladstone: Heroic Minister, 1865–1898* (London, 1999), *The Observer*, 2 May 1999; J. Dalley, *Diana Mosley: A Biography* (London, 1999), *The Observer*, 19 September 1999. Thereafter, I did give up reviewing almost entirely, although I lapsed occasionally: see my reviews of J. Mordaunt Crook, *The Rise of the Nouveaux Riches: Style and Status in Victorian and Edwardian Architecture* (London, 1999), *The New York Times*, 6 February 2000; P. Brendon, *The Dark Valley: A Panorama of the 1930s* (London, 2000), *The Observer*, 10 April 2000; B. Porter, *The Absent-Minded Imperialists: Empire, Society and Culture in Britain* (Oxford, 2004), *The Sunday Times*, 14 November 2004; and L. Olson, *Troublesome Young Men: The Rebels Who Brought Churchill to Power and Helped Save England* (New York, 2007), *The Washington Post, Book World*, 22–28 April 2007.

20. D. Cannadine, *History in Our Time* (London, 1998). For an earlier collection, see idem, *The Pleasures of the Past* (London, 1989).

21. J. Sutherland, 'Of course I haven't read the whole of it', *The Times*, 12 January 2008, *Books*, p. 11; P. Bayard, *How To Talk About Books You Haven't Read* (London, 2007). For the text of my speech, see above, Appendix, pp. 298–306.

22. D. Cannadine, 'Noel Gilroy, Baron Annan (1916–2000)', in *Oxford Dictionary of National Biography*, vol. ii (Oxford, 2004), pp. 171–5; idem, 'Writer and Biographer', in A. Adonis and K. Thomas (eds), *Roy Jenkins: A Retrospective* (Oxford, 2004), pp. 271–305; idem, 'Harold Perkin', *The Guardian*, 23 October 2004; idem, 'Sir John Harold Plumb (1911–2001)', *Proceedings of the British Academy*, cxxiv, *Biographies of Fellows*, iii (2004), pp. 269–309; idem, 'Lawrence Stone', *The Independent*, 26 June 1999; idem, 'Giles Worsley', *The Guardian*, 26 January 2006.

23. D. Cannadine, 'The Age of Todd, Plumb and Snow: Christ's, the "Two Cultures" and the "Corridors of Power"', in D. Reynolds (ed.), *Christ's College: A Cambridge College Over Five Centuries* (London, 2004), pp. 181–226; idem, 'Introduction: The Fifth of November Remembered and Forgotten', in B. Buchanan et al., *Gunpowder Plots* (London, 2005), pp. 1–8; idem, *Nelson*; idem, *Trafalgar*; idem, *National Portrait Gallery: A Brief History* (London, 2007); idem, 'Orchestrating his Own Life: Sir Edward Elgar as an Historical Personality', in N. Kenyon et al. (eds), *Elgar: An Anniversary Portrait* (London, 2007), pp. 1–35; idem, 'What Is History Now?', in J. Morrill (ed.), *The Promotion of Knowledge: Lectures to Mark the Centenary of the British Academy, 1902–2002* (Oxford, 2004), pp. 29–51, revised and reprinted above as Chapter 1, pp. 19–38. For the background history of national commemorations, see R. Quinault, 'The Cult of the Centenary, c1784–1914', *Historical Research*, lxxi (1998), pp. 303–23.

24. In addition to the lectures collected here, see also the following: D. Cannadine, *Empire and Hierarchy in Modern Britain* (Lancaster, 1999); idem, 'The Embarrassment of Riches: Historians and Wealth in Modern Britain', *The Rothschild Archive* (2001–02), pp. 12–23; idem, *Kenneth Clark: From National Gallery to National Icon* (London, 2002); idem, *A Century of Civic Grandeur: History all around us in Colchester Town Hall* (Colchester, 2002); idem,

'Engineering History or the History of Engineering? Re-Writing the Technological Past', *Transactions of the Newcomen Society*, lxxiv (2004), pp. 163–80; idem, 'C.P. Snow, "The Two Cultures" and the "Corridors of Power" Revisited', in W.R. Louis (ed.), *Yet More Adventures with Britannia* (London, 2005), pp. 101–18.

25. D. Cannadine, *In Churchill's Shadow: Confronting the Past in Modern Britain* (London, 2002).

26. Cannadine, *In Churchill's Shadow*, p. ix; idem, *G.M. Trevelyan: A Life in History* (London, 1992), p. 211.

27. D. Cannadine, *Class in Britain* (London, 1998), p. 188.

28. D. Cannadine, *Ornamentalism: How the British Saw Their Empire* (London, 2001).

29. See above, Chapter 2, pp. 54–6, and the references cited there.

30. D. Cannadine, *Mellon: An American Life* (London, 2006), pp. 625–7.

31. V. Gregorian, 'They Gave Much: Top Biographies of American Philanthropists', *Wall Street Journal*, 4 August 2007

32. 'Britain's top one hundred public intellectuals', *Prospect*, no. 100, July 2004, p. 23.

33. *Listening to the Past, Speaking to the Future: Report of the Archives Task Force* (London, 2004).

34. 'Copyright and Research in the Humanities and Social Sciences: A British Academy Review' (September 2006) published online and available at http://www.britac.ac.uk/reports/copyright/report.pdf.

35. House of Commons, Public Administration Select Committee, The Honours System, Minutes of Evidence, Thursday 11 March 2004, QQ. 431–512. For highly frivolous press coverage, see A. Anthony, 'A laughing matter honoured in the breach', *The Guardian*, 12 March 2004; A. Gimson, 'History men take honours as double act', *The Daily Telegraph*, 12 March 2004; Q. Letts, 'Some twitchy teasing by the jabber-happy monster', *Daily Mail*, 12 March 2004. For more serious treatment, see: Sir H. Phillips, *Review of the Honours System* (London, 2004); House of Commons, Public Administration Select Committee, *A Matter of Honour: Reforming the Honours System*, Fifth Report of Session 2003–04 (2 vols, 2004), esp. ii, pp. 42–4; D. Cannadine, 'Re-Ordering Honours: Perspectives and Possibilities', *Political Quarterly*, lxxvi (2005), pp. 124–7.

36. P. Riddell, 'When you are in a hole, history can show you the exit', *The Times*, 7 December 2007; P. Toynbee, 'Posturing and peddling myths, these prison enthusiasts are blind to history', *The Guardian*, 7 December 2007.

37. Cannadine, *In Churchill's Shadow*, pp. 224–43.

38. I have discussed the history of the historic environment above in Chapter 5, pp. 112–34.

39. In 2007, the Royal Mint issued a £2 coin commemorating the Act of Union between England and Scotland, for which see: *United into one Kingdom: 300th Anniversary of the Treaty of Union* (London, 2007).

40. M. Fisher, *Britain's Best Museums and Galleries* (London, 2004), p. 655.

41. Cannadine, *National Portrait Gallery*, pp. 8–9, 22–30; J. Conlin, 'Poor Relations: The National Portrait Gallery and how the English see themselves', *Times Literary Supplement*, 11 January 2008, pp. 14–15.

42. D. Cannadine, *The Decline and Fall of the British Aristocracy* (London, 1990), esp. pp. 572–80; E. Kehoe, 'The British Museum: The Cultural Politics of a National Institution, 1906–1939' (unpublished Ph.D. dissertation, University of London, 2001); A. Geddes Poole, 'Conspicuous Presumption: The Treasury and the Trustees of the National Gallery, 1890–1939', *Twentieth-Century British History*, xvi (2005), pp. 1–28.

43. *Hansard* (Commons), 27 June 2007, col. 334; J.K. Rowling, *Harry Potter and the Deathly Hallows* (London, 2007), p. 607.

44. R.P. Basler (ed.), *The Collected Works of Abraham Lincoln* (8 vols, New Brunswick, NJ), viii, p. 333.

45. Ibid, pp. 332–3.

Index

Compiled by Sue Carlton

9/11 terrorist attacks 21, 112, 167, 232
1066 and All That (Sellar and Yeatman) 175, 176
1960s *see* sixties
Abercrombie, Sir Patrick 121
Access to Mountains Act (1939) 120
Access to Mountains Bill 118
Act for the Preservation of Ancient Monuments (1882) 117
Acton, John Dalberg-Acton, Baron 22
Addison, Christopher, Viscount 80
Adie, Kate 280
Agriculture Act (1947) 126
Aitken, William Maxwell *see* Beaverbrook
Albert, Prince Consort 42, 46, 48, 53
Alden, Sir Percy 80
Alexandra, Queen 44
American Empire 214
    see also United States, and understanding of imperial past
American Friends of the IHR 277, 281
American historians, approaches to British Empire 217–18, 228–32, 233
Amery, Colin 125
Amery, Leopold 231
ancient monuments
    protection of 117, 118
    see also historic buildings
Anderson, Benedict 179, 200
Andrew, Christopher 21
Andrew W. Mellon Foundation 281, 288, 291
Anglo-American Conferences of Historians 14, 279
Annales school 30, 239, 247, 259, 266
Annan, Noel, Baron 12, 24, 264, 285
Annual Bibliographies of British History 3
Appleby, Joyce 33, 36, 37
Areas of Outstanding National Beauty 124
Arne, Thomas 137, 142
Arnold, Matthew 161
Ashley, Sir William 89
Ashton, T.S. 95, 96, 97, 101
Astor, Waldorf, Viscount Astor 78
Athlone, Alexander Cambridge, Earl of 208
Australia 173, 197, 198, 201, 202, 222, 232

Bagehot, Walter 46, 58
Bailey, John 121
Bailyn, Bernard 262
Baldwin Brown, Gerald 116, 118
Baldwin, Stanley, Earl 78, 119–20, 212
Barlow Commission (1940) 123
Barnes, George 79
Barrow, Geoffrey 181
Barzun, Jacques 32
Battiscombe, Georgina 44
Bayly, Sir C.A. 185, 218
BBC
    and Promenade Concerts 136–7, 140, 144–5, 148, 152, 155–7, 160, 169
    televising of ceremonies 150, 155
BBC Symphony Orchestra 146, 151, 156, 158, 162, 169, 170
Beard, Charles 89
Beaton, Sir Cecil 159
Beaverbrook, Maxwell Aitken, Baron 80, 204–5, 213
Beckett, J.C. 181
Bellairs, Carlyon 79
Benn, Tony 279
Betjeman, Sir John 122
Beveridge, William, Baron 93–4
Bin Wong, Roy 109
Bingley, George Lane-Fox, Baron Bingley 78, 81
Binney, Marcus 125, 128–9
Birt, John, Baron 166
Birtwistle, Sir Harrison 164
Bissell, Claude 209
Black, Conrad, Baron of Crossharbour 213
Black, Jeremy 218, 219
Blair, Tony 172, 189, 191, 192, 274, 276, 295–6
Bloch, Marc 28, 37, 239
Blue Plaques panel 292–3
Boer War 85
book reviewing 285, 298–306
    for general reader 301
    responding and replying 303–5
    rules for 300–2
    value of 306

Boosey, William 140
Booth, Charles 85, 87
Borden, Sir Robert 207
Boulez, Pierre 162
Boult, Sir Adrian 146, 148, 152, 153–4
Bowes-Lyon, Lady Elizabeth 53
    see also Elizabeth, Queen (wife of
        George VI)
Bowles, Sir Henry 80
Brace, William 80
Bradford, Sarah 44, 45
Bragg, Melvyn, Baron 280
Braudel, Fernand 29, 179, 239, 254
Brenner, Robert 266
Brett, Oliver 121
Brewer, John 262, 269
Briggs, Asa, Baron 216, 235, 239, 240
Britain
    decline as world power 180
    devolution 172, 180–1, 190–2, 217
    entry into EEC 180, 183, 194, 205
    immigration 180
British Academy 19, 28
British Empire 212–13, 214–15
    American historical approaches to 217–18,
        228–32
        see also United States, and
            understanding of imperial past
    complexity and ambiguity 229–30
    decline of 215–16
    dominions of settlement 197–8, 199
        see also Canada
    functioning of 231
    historical approaches to 215–20
    and imperial project 229–31
    and nation-building 198, 199
    and politics of empire 232
    and religion 232
British Empire and Commonwealth Museum
        221, 294
British historians
    alliances and antipathies 272
    in higher education 3–4, 5–6, 9, 24–5
    in international context 8–13
    published works 3, 4, 6–7, 24, 25
    as university administrators 10–11
        see also sixties, English history/historians
British history 171–95
    Atlanticist scholars 184–5
    and English history 171–2, 175–8, 182,
        188–9, 193–4, 217, 235
    and exceptionalism 173, 176, 180, 182,
        188, 223

'four nations' approach 186–7
importance of Canada 211–12, 213
and international developments 178–84
and Irish, Welsh and Scottish history
    181–2, 186–7, 188, 189, 194, 217
multi-authored works 175, 181
single-authored works 174–5
Whig interpretation 171, 172, 173–8, 182,
    261
British North America Act (1867) 199, 206
British universities 9–13, 17
    bureaucracy 10, 12
    underfunding 9–10
Britishness 165, 172, 185, 186, 188, 189,
    192, 194
Brooke, John 65, 66, 67–8, 69
Brown, Gordon 4, 172, 189, 192
Bryce, James , Viscount 19–20, 23, 25, 118,
    120
Buchan, Alistair 209
Buchan, John, Baron Tweedsmuir 26, 120,
    208, 209
Buckle, H.T. 174
Buildings of England 59, 71
Bumsted, J.M. 202
Bundy, McGeorge 238
Burckhardt, Jacob 235
Burgess, Glenn 270
Burke, Edmund 116, 257, 258
Burke, Peter 29
Burns, A.F. 92
Bury, J.B. 28
Bush, George W. 134, 223, 224
business cycle 92–4, 97, 98, 99
Butler, R.A., Baron 97
Butterfield, Sir Herbert 261
Byron, Robert 122

Cain, Peter 185
Callaghan, James, Baron 181, 190
Cambridge History of the British Empire 215
Cambridge, Prince George, Duke of 47
Cameron, Basil 148, 152, 153
Cameron, David 192
Canada 197–213, 222
    boundaries 198
    and British investment 203–4
    and British monarchy 205–6, 208
    decline of British connection 210–12
    as Dominion 199
    and First World War 207
    Governor-Generalship 205
    and Imperial Canadian identity 203–10,
        211

Canada *continued*
  importance in British history 211–12, 213
  and nationhood 199–203, 207, 211
  racial and ethnic diversity 198–9, 202, 211
  relationship with US 199–200
  royal visits 206, 208
  and Second World War 209, 212
  as strong unitary state 202–3
  trends in historiography 201–2
Canada House, London 211–12
Canadian High Commissioners 212
capitalism
  in decay 91–2
  rise of western capitalism 97
Cardus, Sir Neville 159
Carey, John 37
Carlyle, Thomas 22
Carr, E.H. 25, 241, 279
Carrington, Peter, Baron 279
cars 114, 121, 134
Cecil, Hugh, Baron 80
Centre for Contemporary British History
    (formally Institute) 14, 278
Centre for Metropolitan History 14, 278
Chadwick, Owen 293
Chamberlain, Joseph 204, 212, 231
Chamberlain, Neville 1, 3, 212
change, pace of 36, 112
Channel Tunnel 180, 194
Chappell & Company 140
Charles I 40, 250, 256
Charles, Prince of Wales 50, 128, 129
China 134
  and empire 222, 233
Christie, Ian R. 67
Churchill, Sir Winston 26, 43, 45, 150, 177,
    279
  funeral 149, 151
  and *History of Parliament* project 75, 78
  visits to Canada 212
  and worth of history 1, 3, 5, 6, 18
cities and towns
  expansion 113–14, 130
  redevelopment 124–5
  renewal 128
Civic Amenities Act (1967) 124
Civic Trust 124
Clapham, Sir John 89–90, 95, 103, 106
Clarendon, Edward Hyde, Earl of 261
Clark, Alan 4
Clark, Christopher 29
Clark, Sir George 175, 177
Clark, J.C.D. 263, 265, 268, 269

Clark, Kenneth, Baron 26, 112, 115, 122,
    292
class, United States and 226
Class in Britain (Cannadine) 287, 288
classical music, popular interest in 139–40,
    141, 156
Clean Air Act (1956) 124
Cliometricians 28, 110
Clore, Sir Charles 125
Club of Rome 103
Clynes, John 80
collective scholarly works 14, 59–60, 175,
    177, 181
  see also History of Parliament
Colley, Linda 29, 186, 193, 218, 219, 269
Collini, Stefan 32, 34
commemorative enterprises 285–6
Commonwealth 51, 56, 150, 180, 192, 209,
    215
Communism, collapse of 178
Connaught, Prince Arthur, Duke of 47, 205,
    208
conservation 115–34
  and democracy 132–3
  impact of Second World War 123
  and planning 117–18, 120, 122–6, 128–30
    see also Town and Country Planning
    Acts
  and popular opinion 127–9
  voluntary organizations 118–19, 128
    see also ancient monuments; cities and
    towns; countryside; historic buildings
Conservation of Wild Creatures and Wild
    Plants Act (1975) 124, 126
Continuity and Change 29
Cooke, Alistair 26
Cossens, Sir Neil 292
Costa, Sir Michael 139
Cotton, Jack 125
Council for the Preservation of Rural
    England 26, 121, 122
country houses 125–6, 128, 292
countryside
  access to 118, 122, 124
  conservation 119–20, 126
  ruination of 121
  threat from farming 126–7, 130–1, 133
  and urban development 129–30, 133
Countryside Act (1969) 124
Cox, David 163
Crafts, N.F.R. 107
Crawford and Balcarres, David Lindsay, Earl
    of 294

credit cycle 92, 93, 95
Creighton, Donald 201
Crosland, Anthony 127, 238
Crosse, Gordon 162
Crossman, Richard 238
Cruickshank, Dan 125
Cruickshanks, E. 69
Cunningham, Rev. William 89
Curzon, George, Marquess Curzon of
	Kedleston 231
Czechoslovakia 178

Dalton, Hugh 123–4
Damazer, Mark 285
Darnton, Robert 30
Darwin, Leonard 77
Davies, Norman 193
Davies, Ralph 193
Davies, Sir Rees 183, 184, 186, 193
Davies, Robertson 210
Davis, Sir Andrew 162, 163, 164, 170
Davis, Sir Colin 158, 161, 162
Davis, H.W.C. 175
Davis, Natalie 30
de-industrialization 84, 105–6, 107, 108, 111
Deane, Phyllis 100, 101, 102
Death of the Past (Plumb) 267
Decline and Fall of the British Aristocracy
	(Cannadine) 288, 294
Deedes, Bill, Baron 279
Del Mar, Norman 162
Department of Culture, Media and Sport
	294–5
Derrida, Jacques 20
devolution 172, 180–1, 190–2, 217
Diana, Princess of Wales 50, 167
Dictionary of National Biography 2, 59
Dimbleby, Richard 150–1, 155, 156, 157, 160
Donaldson, Frances 44, 45
Donaldson, Gordon 181
Douglas, Keith 140, 146, 147
Douglas-Home, Alec, Baron 257
Dower Committee (1945) 123
Drummond, Sir John 163–4, 165, 166
Duncan-Smith, Iain 192
Durham, John Lambton, Earl of 198
Durham Report 200

Eagleton, Terry 303
economy 83–111
	and cycles 91–6, 97–8
	economic growth 97–103, 113
	limits to growth 103–9

Education Act (1870) 22, 174
Education Act (1944) 24
Edward VII, King 42, 44, 47, 53
Edward VIII, King 43, 44
	as Prince of Wales 206, 208
Elder, Mark 162, 163
Elgar, Sir Edward 137, 139–40, 142–3
Elizabeth II, Queen 43, 45, 56–7, 150, 151
Elizabeth, Queen (wife of George VI formerly
	Lady Elizabeth Bowes-Lyon) 44, 45,
	208
Elliott, Sir John 279, 290
Elton, Sir G.R. 25, 31, 182, 188, 216, 241,
	261, 263, 268, 269
	relations with Plumb 244
	relations with Stone 259–60, 302
	response to review 304–5
empire 214–34, 287–8
	see also British Empire
energy crisis (1973–74) 103
English Civil War 186, 243, 246, 255, 259,
	262, 269
English Heritage 26, 128, 131, 292
English Historical Review 22, 239
English history 171–2, 175–8, 182, 188–9,
	193–4, 217, 235, 243
English Revolution 248–51, 254, 256–7, 266
environment
	attitudes to 115–16
	see also conservation
Esher, Reginald Brett, Viscount 42
European Union 9, 178–9
Evans, Richard 35
Everage, Dame Edna 170

Falkender, Marcia, Baroness 267
Falklands War (1982) 180
'Fantasia on British Sea Songs' (Wood) 137,
	142, 143–4, 145, 152, 155, 165
	attempts to dispense with 153, 154, 161–2,
	167–8
farming 113, 114
	organic 128
	as threat to countryside 126–7, 130–1, 133
Feiling, Sir Keith 177
Feinstein, C.H. 107
Ferguson, Niall 4, 218, 219
Ferguson, William 68
Fernando-Armesto, Felipe 30
fertilizers and pesticides 126–7
Figes, Orlando 4
Firth, C.H. 22, 24
Fisher, H.A.L. 75–6, 175

Fletcher, Anthony 261
Flinn, Michael 100–1
Foch, Marshal 13
Forestry Commission 120
Forster, E.M. 121, 174
Forster, W.E. 22
Foucault, Michel 20, 219
France
    student demonstrations (1968) 242, 245
    universities 9
Freeman, Edward A. 22, 174
Friends of the Earth 128
Friends of the IHR 14, 277, 281
Froude, J.A. 22, 174
Fukuyama, Francis 21, 176
Fylingdales, early warning system 126

Gaitskell, Hugh 64, 65
Galbraith, J.K. 92, 97, 104, 105, 237, 238
Galbraith, V.H. 2, 17
Gallagher, John 223–4, 235
Gardiner, S.R. 22, 174, 255, 259, 260
Gaulle, Charles de 242
Gayer, A.D. 94–5
Geddes, Sir Eric 80
George, Henry 77, 85
George V, King 43, 44, 45, 47, 54, 145,
    211–12
    as Duke of York 206
George VI, King 43, 44, 45, 56, 57, 208
Georgian Group 26, 121–2
German Empire 222
Gibbins, Henry de Bettgens 89
Gilmour, Ian, Baron 4
Ginsburg, Carlo 30
Girouard, Mark 26
Gladstone, William 46, 53
Glendinning, Victoria 303
global warming 128, 133–4
globalization 35, 179
Glock, Sir William 148, 157, 159–60, 161,
    162, 163
Gold Standard 91, 93
Goldring, Douglas 122
Goldstone, Jack 109
Gooch, Henry 79
Gowers Committee (1948–50) 123
Great Exhibition (1851) 85
Great Reform Act (1832) 255–6
green belts 122
Green, J.R. 22, 174–5
green-field sites, building on 129–30
Greene, Sir Hugh 157, 165

Greenpeace 128
Gregorian, Vartan 289
Gregory, Theodor Emanuel 93
Grey, Edward, Viscount 120
Grey Seals Protection Act (1914) 117
Groves, Sir Charles 162
Guest, Frederick 80–1
Gulf War (1990) 163, 180

Hague, William 192
Hailsham, Quintin Hogg, Viscount 127
Halifax, E.F.L. Wood, Earl of 120
Hall, Catherine 218, 219
Halle, Sir Charles 139
Halsey, A.H. 5–6
Hammond, J.L. and Barbara 86–8, 89, 90, 95
Handley, Vernon 162
Hansard 74
Harrington, James 255
Harris, John 125
Harris, Sir Percy 78, 80
Harrod, Sir Roy 98
Hartwell, Max 101, 102
Hawtrey, Ralph G. 92
Healey, Denis, Baron 238
Heath, Sir Edward 242
Heaton, Herbert 89
Hechter, Michael 182–3
hedgerows 126–7, 130
heritage see ancient monuments;
    conservation; countryside; historic
    buildings
Heritage Lottery Fund 60, 281, 295
Heroic Materialism 112–13, 115, 131
Heseltine, Michael, Baron 128
Hexter, J.H. 270, 306
higher education, expansion of 24–5
Hill, Christopher 216, 235, 264
Hill, Octavia 118
Hilton, Rodney 264
Himmelfarb, Gertrude 20
Hirst, Derek 262
l'histoire événementielle 29, 187, 259, 265,
    2554
historic buildings
    conservation 116–19, 123, 124, 131
    demolition of 121–2, 125
    listing of 128
    see also ancient monuments
Historic Buildings and Ancient Monuments
    Act (1953) 124
Historic Buildings Council 124
Historical Association 2, 23

Historical Journal 239
Historical Research 284
history
  continuity and change 27, 29, 240
  controversies 27–32, 193–4
  elite versus popular 30–1, 34, 244, 253
  end of 20–1, 176
  evolution of 22–7
  and human nature 34–5
  and imagination 18, 28, 32
  institutionalization of 22
  micro versus global 30
  narrative versus analysis 28–9, 248, 266
  new approaches 19–20, 25–6, 37, 172–3,
    182–95
    see also new British history
  and popular interest 22–3, 26
  in schools and universities 22, 23, 24–5, 27
  as science or art 28–9
  and state funding 27, 32
  and truth 32, 36–7, 271
    see also American historians; British
    historians; British history
History Compass 284
History in Our Time 285
History Panel 5–6
History of Parliament 59–82, 244
  and biographies 62, 63, 65, 66, 68, 69, 70,
    72, 73, 75
    questionnaires 76–81
  bringing up to date 73–6
  criticism of 66–9
  funding for 60, 64, 68
  history of the Commons 69, 70, 72, 76
  and House of Lords 71–2
  and IT revolution 71
  and pre-1836 period 73
  re-launch 65
  surveys of constituencies 65, 66, 69
  Trust 63–4, 70
History of Wales 188
Hoare, Sam 78
Hobhouse Committee (1947) 123
Hobsbawm, Eric 14, 101, 216, 235, 264, 279
Hong Kong 215
honours system 52
Hopkins, A.G. 185
Hopkinson, Austin 79, 80
Hoppit, Julian 269
Hoskins, W.G. 127
Howard, Michael 192
Howard, Sir Michael 275, 279
Howard, Philip 68, 82

Hughes, Merion 168
Hunt, L. 37
Hunt, Tristram 280
Hunt, William 175
Hunter, Sir Robert 118

In Churchill's Shadow (Cannadine) 286
India 56, 134, 185
  independence 149, 150, 205, 215
Industrial Revolution 83–111, 239, 248, 262
  benefits of 96
  consequences for working classes 86–91,
    110
  cyclical nature of 91–6, 110
  down-sized interpretation of 106–9, 110
  and economic development 99–103, 110
  global history approach 109
  gradualist interpretation 107–8
information technology (IT) revolution 35–6,
  179
Institute of Historical Research 2, 3, 13–16,
  17, 24, 65, 244
  Advisory Council 278
  buildings refurbishment 14, 277, 281
  Directorship role 283–5, 289–95
  fund-raising 14, 276, 277, 280–3
  HEFCE grant 279, 281
  January conferences 279–80
  re-structuring 277–9
  Trust 280
International Monetary Fund (IMF) 223
Iraq Wars 163, 180
Ireland 53, 177, 180–1, 183, 185, 187, 191,
  250, 262
  see also Northern Ireland
Isaacs, Sir Jeremy 280

Jacob, M. 37
Jay, Douglas 238
Jenkins, Roy, Baron 4, 238, 279, 285, 290
'Jerusalem' (Parry) 137, 142, 143, 154, 155,
  165
Joad, C.E.M. 122
Johnson, Lyndon 226, 237, 242
Johnstone, Maurice 154
Jones, J.R. 262
Journal of Maritime History 284

Kearney, Hugh 186–7, 192
Keegan, John 4
Kennedy, John F. 16, 98, 156, 224, 237, 238
Kennedy, Michael 159
Kennedy, Robert F. 16, 242

Kennet, Edward Young, Baron 78
Kenyon, Sir Nicholas 166
Kershaw, Sir Ian 45, 280
Keynes, John Maynard, Baron 92, 98, 121
Keynesian economics 94, 95, 103
King, Martin Luther 242
Kipling, Rudyard 220, 223
Kishlansky, Mark 261

Lambert, Constance 148
Lamont, Sir Norman 78–9
'Land of Hope and Glory' *see* 'Pomp and
    Circumstance'
Landes, David 102, 109
Langford, Paul 269
Lansbury, George 79
Lascelles, Sir Alan 43
Laud, Archbishop 250
Law, Andrew Bonar 204, 212
Leacock, Stephen 207
Lecky, W.E.H. 174, 177
Lee, Arthur, Viscount Lee of Fareham 78
Lee, Sir Sydney 42
Lees-Milne, James 122
Leppard, Raymond 162
LeRoi Ladurie, E. 30
Leverhulme Trust 281
Lincoln, Abraham 296, 297
Lipson, Ephraim 90, 96
Lloyd George, David, Earl 81, 86, 120, 207
Lodge, Sir Richard 175
London Philharmonic Orchestra 148
London Symphony Orchestra 148
Longford, Elizabeth, Countess of 44
Longmans-*History Today* book awards 285
Lorne, John Campbell, Marquess of 205
Loughran, James 162
Lower, Arthur 201
Lubbock, Sir John 117, 118
Lyons, F.S.L. 181
Lyttelton, Oliver, Viscount Chandos 283

Macaulay, Thomas Babington, Baron 22, 28,
    31, 77, 174, 177, 246, 298–9
McCord Museum 199
Macdonald, John A. 201
MacDonald, Malcolm 212
MacDonald, Ramsay 78, 212
Mackenzie, Alexander 142, 143
Mackenzie King, William Lyon 201, 208
Macmillan, Harold, Earl of Stockton 67, 98,
    125, 237, 243, 257
McNeil, Robert 211

McNeill, William 30
Magnus, Sir Philip 44
Mahan, Admiral A.T. 222
Maitland, F.W. 23, 31, 241, 302
Major, Sir John 171, 172, 176, 180, 190
Mandler, Peter 116
Mansergh, Nicholas 199
Marsden, Gordon 4
Marshall, Peter 185, 278
Marshall Plan 98
Martin, Theodore 42
Marwick, Arthur 235
Marx, Karl 20, 32
Mary, Queen (wife of George V) 43, 145,
    211–12
  as Duchess of York 206
Mass Observation techniques 76
Massey, Vincent 209, 210
Masterman, C.F.G. 85
Mathias, Peter 101, 102
Matthew, Colin 293
Matthews, R.C.O. 95
Mattingly, Garrett 29
Mearns, Andrew 85
Mellon, Andrew W. 288–9, 296
Mellon, Paul 288
Mellor, David 167
Mentmore Towers 125–6
Military Service Act (1917) (Canada) 207
Milner, Alfred, Viscount 86, 231
Mitchell, Wesley C. 92
Mitchison, Rosalind 181, 188
Mokyr, Joël 108
monarchy 39–58
  and biography 41–6, 55
  and continental connections 53–4
  democratic 52
  downsizing 57
  as elite institution 46–51
  gender roles 49–50
  as imperial institution 54–6
  and marriage 49, 54
  and matriarchy 50
  and media 52
  new roles/functions 46–8, 51, 56–8
  recent developments 56–8
  relations with church 47
  relations with parts of United Kingdom
    52–3
  royal court and bureaucracy 48–9
  traditional functions of 41
  and warfare 47
  and wealth 47–8

Monsell, Bolton Eyres-Monsell, Viscount 78
Moody, T.W. 181
Moore, Barrington 238
Morrill, John 261
Morris, Jan 206
Morris, William 118
Morrison, Arthur 85
Moser, Claus, Baron 280
Mountbatten, Edwina, Countess 151, 153
Mountbatten, Louis, Earl 44, 47, 204–5
Murdoch, Rupert 179
Murray, Gilbert 86

Nairne, Sandy 293
Namier, Sir Lewis 14
    and *History of Parliament* 60–3, 65–8, 69,
        70, 72, 81
    influence on Plumb 244, 247, 257–8
    relations with Taylor 28–9, 67
    and Trevelyan's book review 301
narrative, and analysis 28–9, 248, 266
nation-state 35, 173, 179, 196–7
National Archives (Kew) 27
National Bureau of Economic Research (US)
    92, 94
National Heritage Act (1983) 128
National Heritage Memorial Fund 126, 128
national identities
    and, imagined communities 179, 200, 203,
        209
    erosion of 178–9, 180
National Land Fund 123–4, 125, 126
national parks 123, 124, 126
National Parks and Access to the Countryside
    Act (1949) 124
National Portrait Gallery 293
National Trust 23, 26, 105, 118, 119, 121,
        122, 128, 131
    Country House Scheme 125, 292
nationhood 200–1
NATO (North Atlantic Treaty Organisation)
    223
Nature Conservancy Council 124, 127
Nature Reserves 124
Neale, Sir John 14, 65, 69
Nelson, Jinty 278
new British history 172–3, 182–95
    and new British politics 189–94, 195
New History of Ireland 188
New Labour 274, 276
    and devolution 191
New Zealand 222
Newman, Robert 135, 138, 140

Nicolson, Sir Harold 43–4
Nixon, Richard 226, 242
Norman, R.C. 121
North American Conference on British
    Studies 279
Northern Ireland 180, 181, 191, 217
    see also devolution
Notestein, Wallace 255, 259, 260
Novick, Peter 21

obituaries and memoirs 285
O'Brien, Patrick 107
Oman, Sir Charles 175
Open University 238
Ornamentalism (Cannadine) 287–8
Ottawa 202
Overy, Richard 4
Oxford Dictionary of National Biography 71
Oxford History of the British Empire 219
Oxford History of England 175, 177

Palavicino, Sir Horatio 243
Pares, Richard 67
parliament *see History of Parliament*
Parry, Sir Charles Hubert Hastings 137, 142,
    143
Partridge, Frances 290
Past & Present 28, 239, 244, 279, 290
Pax Americana 230
Pax Britannica 230
Pembrokeshire, oil terminal 126
Perkin, Harold 239, 240, 285
Ph.D.s 24
Philip, Prince, Duke of Edinburgh 56, 293
Phillips, Tom 279
Pimlott, Ben 45
Plumb, Sir J.H. 28, 216, 240, 244–8, 251–5,
    267–8, 272
    attack by Clark 268, 269
    Growth of Political Stability 235–6, 246,
        247–8, 251–3, 254, 257–63, 267, 269,
        270
    influence of Trevelyan 244, 246, 247, 255,
        258, 260
    and National Portrait Gallery 293
    as supporter of IHR 285
Pocock, J.G.A. 183, 185, 187, 192, 194,
    217–18
political history, United States and 227
Pollard, A.F. 2, 13, 15, 16, 17, 23, 175, 276
Pomeranz, Kenneth 109

'Pomp and Circumstance' March No.1
    (Elgar) 137, 142–4, 146, 152, 154, 161,
    164, 165
Ponsonby, Robert 163, 164
Poole, Reginald Lane 175
Pope-Hennessy, James 43
population explosion 113
Porter, Roy 262, 269
post-colonial scholars 219, 220, 229, 231–2
post-modernism 4, 20, 36–7, 108, 267
Postan, Sir M.M. 91, 98
Powell, Colin 222
Pritchard, Sir John 162
Profumo, John 257
Profumo Scandal 156
Promenade Concerts 135–70
    and BBC 136–7, 140, 144–5, 148, 152,
        155–7, 160, 169
    during Second World War 146–8
    early concerts 138–44
    'Last Night' 136–8, 140–9, 152–6, 157–9,
        160–8
        and 9/11 167–8
        and audience behaviour 153, 154, 164,
            166
        and controversy 164–5
        and death of Princess Diana 167
        future of 168–70
        global audience 169–70
    as national institution 145
    and patriotism 142, 144, 145, 149–50,
        161, 166, 168, 169
    post-war period 149–56
    Prom in the Park 166–7
    and television 154–5
    ticket sales 165
    and tradition 135, 136, 137, 139, 155,
        160, 168–70
public history 23, 26–7, 31
    see also history, elite versus popular
Putin, Vladimir 233

Quebec 202, 206
Quebec Party 210
Queen's Hall Orchestra 139, 140, 146

Rackham, Oliver 131, 132
railways 106, 113, 114
Ranke, Leopold von 30, 31
Rawnsley, Canon Charles Hardwicke 118
Reagan, Ronald 264, 268
Redford, Arthur 90
Reith, John, Baron 144, 145

religion, United States and 227
republicanism 40, 57
Research Assessment Exercise 3, 6, 11–12,
    299
Restriction of Ribbon Development Act
    (1935) 120
reviewing see book reviewing
Reviews in History 284
revisionism 260, 261–5, 271, 272
revolution 253–4, 260–3
    see also English Revolution
Richardson, H.G. 67
Ridley, Nicholas, Baron 129
Rivers (Prevention of Pollution) Act (1951)
    124
Robbins, Keith 185, 186, 193
Robbins Report 238
Roberts, John 30
Robinson, J.H. 20
Robinson, Ronald 223–4, 235
Robinson, Stanford 152, 153
Rockefeller, David 283
Rodger, Richard 130
Roosevelt, Franklin D. 221
Rose, Kenneth 44, 45
Roskell, J.S. 69
Rostow, W.W. 94–5, 99–100, 102, 103–4,
    105, 239, 240
Rothschild, Jacob, Baron 280, 290
Rowling, J.K. 274, 296
Rowntree, Seebohm 85
Royal Academy of Music 139–40
Royal Commission on Historical Monuments
    23, 26, 117, 119
Royal Commission on the Housing of the
    Working Class 85
Royal Festival Hall, dedication concert 153–4
Royal Historical Society 3, 22, 279, 290
Royal Mint, commemorative coins 293
'Rule Britannia!' (Arne) 137, 142, 143, 144,
    146, 151, 154, 155, 165
Ruskin, John 116
Russell, Conrad, Earl 184, 186, 193, 261,
    262, 270, 272
Russian Empire 222, 233

Said, Edward 98
Sandys, Duncan, Baron 124
Sargent, Sir Malcolm 137, 145, 148–9,
    150–9, 161, 163
    professional reputation 159–60
Saumarez Smith, Charles 293
SAVE Britain's Heritage 125

Sayles, G.O. 67
Schama, Simon 4, 26, 28, 132, 280
Schlesinger, Arthur, jr. 238
Schonfield, Andrew 98
School of Advanced Study 15–16, 17, 276, 290
Schumacher, E.E. 103
Schumpeter, Joseph 91, 92
Scotland 53, 126, 172, 177, 190–2, 262
  see also devolution
Scott Committee (1942) 123
Scott, Sir George Gilbert 118
Scottish Parliament 191
Seabirds Protection Act (1869) 117
Sedgwick, Romney 69
Seeley, Sir John 22, 222
Sen, Amartya 290
Septennial Act 260
Shakespeare, William 40
Sharpe, Kevin 261
Shaw, George Bernard 16
Shawcross, William 44
Shoard, Marion 124
Simpson, Robert 155
single currency 179
Sites of Special Scientific Interest 124, 126
Sitwell, Sir Osbert 122
sixties
  disillusion 241–2
  English history/historians 235–6, 238–40, 247, 255, 264–5, 269–70
    see also Plumb, J.H.; Stone, Lawrence
  and progressive agenda 237–8, 240
  student unrest 242, 259
Slatkin, Leonard 167
slum clearance 125
Smith, Donald Alexander, Baron Strathcona and Mount Royal 204
Smith, Goldwin 207
Smith, John 189
Snow, C.P., Baron 245
Snowden, Philip, Viscount 78
Snowdonia, copper mining 126
Soames, Mary, Baroness 279
social conditions, surveys 84, 85–6
Society for the Preservation of the Commons of London 118
Society for the Protection of Ancient Buildings 118, 119
Society for the Protection of Birds 118, 128
South Africa 197, 198, 201, 222
Soviet Union, break-up of 178
species, decline 126, 127, 131

Speck, W.A. 262
Speyer, Sir Edgar 140
stability 253–5, 257, 259, 260–1, 263, 270
Stansky, Peter 218
Starkey, David 26
Stenton, Sir Frank 64
Stevenson, Frances 81
Stone, Lawrence 29, 216, 218, 238, 240, 242–4, 268, 272
  Causes of the English Revolution 235–6, 246–51, 253–6, 259–62, 265–7, 269, 270
  Crisis of the Aristocracy 245–6, 247
  relations with Elton 259–60, 302
  as supporter of IHR 285
Stormont Parliament 191
Strachey, Lytton 26, 42, 235
Stradling, Robert 168
Stubbs, William 22, 23, 174
Suez crisis 180
Sullivan, Sir Arthur 139
supermarkets, on green-field sites 129–30
Survey of London 23, 59, 71, 118–19

Tawney, R.H. 86–7, 243, 245, 255, 259
Taylor, A.J.P. 28–9, 67, 175, 177, 183, 216, 235
Thatcher, Margaret, Baroness 264, 265, 267, 268
  and devolution 190, 192
  and English history 171–2, 176, 180, 182
  and environment 128, 129
Thatcherism 84, 189, 265, 268, 272, 287
Third Reform Act (1885) 85
Third World, and economic development 98–100, 101, 102–3, 104–5, 240
Thomas, Sir Keith 29, 290
Thompson, E.P. 30, 216, 219, 235, 239, 240, 264
Thomson, Kenneth, Baron Thomson of Fleet 213
Thorne, R.G. 69
Thorold Rogers, J.E. 89
Thurley, Simon 292
Times Atlas of World History 214
Tout, T.F. 23, 24, 175
Town and Country Planning Act (1932) 120, 122
Town and Country Planning Act (1944) 123
Town and Country Planning Act (1947) 124
Town and Country Planning Act (1968) 124
Town Planning Act (1909) 117, 118

Townsend Warner, G. 89
Toynbee, Arnold 14, 84, 86, 87, 88, 89, 90, 95
trade cycle 93, 94, 95, 98, 101
trade unions
  membership explosion 85
  suppression of 89, 105
Trevelyan, George Macaulay 10–11, 26, 31, 175, 188, 259, 287, 293
  book reviewing 301
  and controversies 27–8
  and countryside 120, 121
  history and imagination 18, 32
  influence on Plumb 244, 246, 247, 255, 258, 260
  response to reviews 306
Trevor-Roper, Hugh, Baron Dacre of Glanton 7, 31, 243, 259, 275
Tucker, Rev. Canon Norman 206
Tusa, Sir John 279

United Nations 223
United States
  absences in academic study 224–8, 229
    class 226
    politics 227
    religion 227
    wealth 225–6
  exceptionalism 223, 224
  as imperial power 222–3
  and inequality 225–6
  Social Security 225
  and understanding of imperial past 220–4, 228–9
  universities 9–10, 12
universities 9–13, 17, 24–5
Unwin, Raymond 117–18
Urban Task Force 130
Uthwatt Report (1942) 123

Vaughan Williams, Ralph 140
Victoria County History 2, 14, 23, 59, 71, 278, 281
Victoria, Queen 42, 44, 46, 47, 48, 52, 53
Victorian Society 26, 125
Vietnam War 103, 242, 245
Vimy Ridge, Battle of 207

Vincent, John 6
visions and dreams 16

Walcott, Robert 258
Wales 53, 126, 172, 177, 187
  see also devolution
Walker, Peter, Baron 127
Walpole, Robert, Earl of Orford 246, 247, 252–3, 267
Walton, Susanna 159
wealth, United States and 225–6
Webb, Mary 120
Webb, Sidney and Beatrice 86, 87–8, 89, 90, 91, 95
Wedgwood, Josiah, Baron 2, 60–5, 72, 73, 75–8, 80–2
Weighill, Sir Archibald 80
Weineer, Martin J. 106
Welsh Assembly 191
Wheeler-Bennett, Sir John 43–4
Wheldon, Sir Huw 267
Whig history 171, 172, 173–8, 182, 261
Whitelaw, William, Viscount 80
wildlife, conservation 115, 117, 126
Williams, Glanmor 181
Williams, Glyn A. 181
Williams-Ellis, Sir Clough 121, 129
Williamson, Malcolm 161
Wilson, Harold, Baron 68, 156, 237, 238, 242, 245, 257, 258, 267
Wilson, Kathleen 218, 219
Wilson, Woodrow 220
Wolfson Foundation 277, 281
Wolfson, Leonard, Baron 283
Wood, Sir Henry J. 135, 137, 138–9, 140–9, 151, 159, 162, 168, 169
Wood, Lady Jessie 153
Worden, Blair 33, 259–60
working classes 122, 225, 226, 237, 270
  social conditions 84, 85–91
World Bank 223
Worsley, Giles 285
Wrigley, Sir Tony 108–9

Yugoslavia 178

Ziegler, Philip 44

GPSR Compliance
The European Union's (EU) General Product Safety Regulation (GPSR) is a set
of rules that requires consumer products to be safe and our obligations to
ensure this.

If you have any concerns about our products, you can contact us on

ProductSafety@springernature.com

In case Publisher is established outside the EU, the EU authorized
representative is:

Springer Nature Customer Service Center GmbH
Europaplatz 3
69115 Heidelberg, Germany